HUNTING ETHICS
A Personal Journey

Nick Fox

First published 2025
© 2025 Nick Fox

All rights reserved. No part of this publication may be reproduced, stored in a retrieval system, or transmitted by any means, electronic, mechanical, photocopying, recording or otherwise, without the prior written permission of the copyright holder and publishers.

ISBN 978 1 84674 435 8

All materials used in the manufacture of this book come from sustainable sources.

Published by Countryside Books, Newbury
Produced by The Letterworks Ltd., Reading
Designed and Typeset by KT Designs, St Helens
Printed in India

Contents

	Dedication	8
1	Introduction	9
2	The roots of behaviour	13
	2.1 Introduction	13
	2.2 Genetics	13
	2.3 Instincts and ethotypes	14
	2.3.1 Individual temperaments	15
	2.4 Imprinted behaviour	18
	2.4.1 The mother figure (filial imprinting)	20
	2.4.2 Siblings	24
	2.4.3 The fear response	25
	2.4.4 Nest	25
	2.4.5 Habitat	25
	2.4.6 Food	25
	2.4.7 Cultural values	27
	2.4.8 Future sexual partner	28
	2.5 Learned behaviour	30
	2.6 The component roots	31
	2.7 Intelligence	34
	2.8 Emotional intelligence	35
	2.9 Linguistics	38
	2.10 Learning and culture	41
	2.11 Emotions, Personhood and Sentience	41
	2.12 Fear, or wildness	43
	2.13 Addictive behaviour	44
	2.14 Understanding time and space	45
	2.15 Understanding 'persons'	51
3	What is 'Hunting'?	53
	3.1 Introduction	53
	3.2 Hunting, hope and motivation	55
	3.3 Types of hunting	59

    3.4 The demographics of human attitudes to wildlife. 59
    3.5 A definition of terms. 61
    3.6 Hunting as a continuum 63
    3.7 Humans as hunters. 64
    3.8 Hunting tools and assistants. 69
    3.9 Natural and artificial hunting. 74
    3.10 What animals are hunted?. 80
    3.11 Weeds and pests 82
    3.12 Hunting for food. 89
    3.13 Recreational hunting 95

4 Predation and aggression. 97
    4.1 Introduction. 97
    4.2 The psyche of the predator 99
    4.3 What prompts an animal to start hunting?. 102
    4.4 What does the prey think?. 105

5 Animal welfare issues. 106
    5.1 What is 'suffering'?. 106
    5.2 Welfare in recreational hunting 113
    5.3 Hunting by cats and dogs 116
    5.4 Wounding rates in shooting 117
    5.5 Assessing suffering. 127
    5.6 Welfare benchmarks. 131
    5.7 Is suffering 'acceptable'? 132
    5.8 What is cruelty?. 137
    5.9 Wild and Free 140
    5.10 Human welfare 142

6 The Morality of Hunting 144
    6.1 Introduction. 144
    6.2 An intellect-based morality. 144
    6.3 A natural morality. 145
    6.4 The genetic components of morality 146
    6.5 Ethotypic morality and learned morality 149
    6.6 Morality and sin 152

7 The mechanism of morality **154**
7.1 Introduction 154
7.2 Types of social group 154
7.2.1 The individual 154
7.2.2 The Pair 154
7.2.3 The Family 155
7.2.4 The Kinship Group 155
7.2.5 The Tribe 156
7.2.6 Crowds 157
7.2.7 Patriotism and international struggles 158
7.3 Meme or cultural groups 158
7.4 Territorial groups 162
7.5 Moral community 163
7.5.1 Companion animals 169
7.6 Bonny's world 170
7.7 Out-groups 173
7.8 Internet Groups 174
7.9 Morality outside the social group 177
7.10 Ethotype or Culture? 180

8 Shared ethical values **185**
8.1 Priorities 185
8.2 Values that change with time 186
8.3 Values are not 'truths' 187
8.4 Corruption 190
8.5 Does human ethotypic morality vary? 191
8.6 Legal values 192
8.7 Intent and recklessness 197

9 Morality: the judges **201**
9.1 Introduction 201
9.2 Your conscience 201
9.3 Other people in your group 204
9.4 Other people outside your group 204
9.5 Anti-hunting groups 204

	9.6 Religion	207
	9.7 CyberGod	207
10	**Morality: enforcement systems**	**209**
	10.1 Enforcement mechanisms	209
	10.2 Hunting Ethics	211
	10.3 'Animal Rights'	212
11	**The Evolutionary Trap**	**216**
	11.1 Individual welfare	219
	11.2 Welfare at species level	220
	11.2.1 The morality of re-introducing species	222
	11.2.2 Bats	223
	11.2.3 Northern Goshawks	224
	11.2.4 New Zealand Falcons – a gene bank	225
	11.2.5 Big falcons - offset conservation	226
	11.2.6 Red Kites	226
	11.2.7 Red Squirrels	229
	11.2.8 Brown Hairstreak Butterflies	230
	11.2.9 Water Voles	230
	11.2.10 Houbara	233
	11.3 Habitats and a land ethic	237
	11.3.1 Deciding a baseline	237
	11.3.2 Shared resources	237
	11.3.3 Managing resources	239
	11.3.4 Managing a habitat	245
	11.3.5 Designing habitats	248
	11.3.6 Creating habitat	252
	11.3.7 Habitats and farming	259
	11.4 International habitat projects	267
	11.4.1 Saker Falcons in Mongolia	267
	11.4.2 Falcons in vineyards	270
	11.5 Ecosystems at level two	271
	11.5.1 Arctic peregrines	271

  11.6 A global 'eco-ethic' **272**
    11.6.1 What can we do? **275**
    11.6.2 Genes and brains. **279**
12 Epilogue. **283**
  12.1 Conclusions **285**
  A Horse in the City. **288**
  Acknowledgements **289**
Further Reading. **290**
  Chapter 2 The roots of behaviour. **290**
  Chapter 3 What is 'Hunting'? **293**
  Chapter 4 Predation and aggression **299**
  Chapter 5 Animal welfare issues **300**
  Chapter 6 The Morality of Hunting **309**
  Chapter 7 The mechanism of morality **312**
  Chapter 8 Shared ethical values **313**
  Chapter 9 Morality: the judges **314**
  Chapter 10 Morality: enforcement systems **315**
  Chapter 11 The Evolutionary Trap **317**
Index **321**

Dedication

This book is dedicated to many of the 'persons' in my life: Bobby, Sooty, Smokey, Mayfly, Jenny, Sarah, Rocket, Midnight, Pudding, Nipper, Seamus, Susan, Colin, Red, Otter, Tessie, Gail, Peter, Jamie, Ratty, Jaws, Bramble, Barbro, Rebel, Buckskin, Morgan, Spitty, Fury, Danceaway, Maggie, Megan, Jo, Sisal, Pipit, Holly, Tamsin, Vanity, Joy, Stingray, Fancy, Flamenco, Herself, Salsa, Pushkin, Helen, Gem, Bonny, Cinders and others, too many to mention. Seven are humans, most are dead now, but I remember them.

1 Introduction

I believe I am an evolving animal.

If you think you are something special, not an animal, or if you don't believe in evolution, this book is not for you. But if you do believe that you are a mammal, evolved from a long successful line of hunter/foragers, this may help you understand more about yourself and some of the strange impulses you get.

I am a zoologist, a farmer and a hunter and I'm trying to understand more about myself. So I have to start from first principles to get a full perspective. Only then can I narrow down to my particular circumstances. The starting point is the sun; that's what allows Life on our planet. Some life forms, the plants, can photosynthesise and grab this solar energy. The next trophic layer, the herbivores, get energy from the plants, and the next layer, the predators, eat the herbivores. That's the trophic layer I'm in. I can't photosynthesise and I can't easily digest raw plants.

I've hunted in some shape or form all my life. Over the years I've tried, and rejected, some forms of hunting, but focussed more on others; I've become an 'anti' for some forms, and a 'pro' for others. Why? This book is the culmination of a lifetime journey looking for an ethical approach to my activities, to become at peace with myself and what I do. You may drink oat milk and consider yourself on unassailable moral high ground. But are you wearing wool or leather, derived from animals? Or cotton, derived from a monoculture? Or polyester, derived from petroleum-based polymers, unsustainable and polluting? Do you take pills and excrete chemicals or hormones into the ecosystem, feminising fish? Your moral journey will be different to mine, and end differently. My journey has been uncomfortable at times; yours may be too.

One of my earliest jobs was hunting for duck eggs when I was five or six. We lived

I've paid someone to catch these wild prawns.

then at Ashmore, a little village built around an old Saxon dew pond, a watering hole up on the chalk downs in Dorset. I would crawl under the old wooden barns to find the Aylesbury duck nests, and up into the hollows in the old elms for the Muscovies. By taking the eggs as they were laid, they could be washed and sold for eating. Some ducks would keep laying for weeks. The geese laid in wooden arks by the pond and I was terrified of them. Whenever I crept to the entrance I would be greeted by a savage hissing, like a snake. An old gaffer said to me: "Boy, get yerself a big stick and 'it 'im on the 'ead!" I tried, but the gander chased me up the lane on my tricycle…

My Game Books start when I was twelve, and record almost all my hunting experiences over the next 62 years. I did my PhD on New Zealand falcons and as a zoologist, my approach has always been science-led, based on observations, note-taking and statistics.

I have been a livestock farmer all my adult life. I started proper hunting by snaring rabbits, then went on to shooting, hunting with dogs, and falconry. Over the years, in the course of farming and wildlife

Age 11.

management, I have used spring traps, cage traps, poisons, gas, shotguns, rifles, ferrets, cats, pointers, setters, spaniels, lurchers and gazehounds, sheepdogs and pig dogs. In falconry I have flown shikras, sparrowhawks, goshawks, Harris hawks, Red-tails, Hawk-eagles, merlins, kestrels, New Zealand falcons, Aplomados, luggers, lanners, peregrines, sakers, gyrs and hybrids. I've hunted with packs of fox hounds, harriers, stag hounds, otter hounds, mink hounds, coyote hounds and beagles. I've used my horses for hunting, hawking, in shafts and for packing. I've farmed sheep, cattle, horses, pigs, ducks, geese, chickens, quail, pigeons, pheasants, rats, mice, beavers and over 5,000 birds of prey. I have worked alongside local peoples during my fieldwork on conservation and on hunting in many countries including the Siberian Arctic, Mongolia, China, Kyrghyzstan, Pakistan, the Gulf States, Morocco, Zimbabwe, South Africa, Australia, New Zealand, Czech Republic, Hungary, Germany, France, Netherlands, Denmark, Sweden, Finland, UK, Ireland, USA, Mexico and Canada. During my PhD fieldwork in New Zealand I didn't have a sleeping bag or tent and often didn't see a human for a week or two at a time. But I could always find a rabbit or an eel and put tussock up my homespun jersey and sometimes find a hut with a delicious name such as The Tinpot, The Wild Pup, The Seldom Inn or Flynn's Whare. I apologise for mentioning all this, but hunting is complex and if you haven't done it, it is hard to understand hunters. As you can imagine, during all these years, there have been situations I have been uncomfortable with, and others which I have found inspiring. Is there any logical or ethical consistency or biological root to the 'feelings' I have had in these situations?

I still carry on my hunting traditions, with my dogs, horses and falcons. I don't need to do so, not now there is cheap food in shops, and freezers to cache spare food in, but my instinct to hunt is still strong. Surprisingly, I have come across people who tell me it is 'wrong' to hunt, even though it is to hunting that I owe my very existence. I've ended up, not as a red-necked hunter, nor as a bunny-hugger, but something in between. In recent decades I've been looking into hunting, and predation, into welfare, morality and ethics, trying to make sense of it all. It meant going right back to basics, and often having to research an aspect for a few years. I've been my own study animal. Being a zoologist, my approach has been science-led, but from there it has wandered down the highways and bye-ways of anthropology and philosophy. It's been an interesting journey. Has my hunting become just an anachronism, an ox-bow lake on the winding river of modern life?

My ancestors were hunters. They hunted animals, large and small. Mammals, birds, fish - anything they could catch. When times were hard they foraged the shorelines for shellfish, and the woods for nuts and fungi.

They survived and bred me.

Long before our species differentiated as *Homo sapiens* 200,000 or more years ago, we've been hunters. That's about 10,000 generations of us. My ancestors didn't leave me any messages or time capsules, but I know they were here on this planet, living where I too now walk. Sometimes on the steppes of Mongolia or in the deserts of the Middle East and Africa, I've come across broken arrow heads, or middens of shells. Sea levels have risen and fallen, Ice Ages have come and gone. Land bridges have formed and been lost. Times have been hard and many people didn't make it to breed.

But my ancestors did.

Recently, maybe 23,000 years ago, dogs joined us in our hunting and we got used to working together, a mutual domestication. Hunting is hard and uncertain. With primitive gear and game often sparse, we couldn't easily settle or live in large groups. A few tribes living in more favoured areas managed to grow crops and domesticate goats, sheep and cattle, but most of us relied on hunting, and a few tribes still do to this day. My own immediate ancestors started farming about a thousand years ago but we still hunt when we can. By the time my father was born, in 1895, many people were living in towns and cities, relying on role partitioning and industrialisation, removed from contact with the natural world. I still see traces of those who came before me on our farm: a carefully laid stone land-drain, a bit of clay smoking pipe, or an old mis-shapen tree once laid as a sapling to form a stock-proof hedge before wire netting was invented.

The subject of this book – my search for ethics within hunting – is in an overlap of the sciences and the humanities. While for many human 'hunters' there is some element of spirituality, I will not involve the prescribed religions. Until there is evidence that one of the putative Gods really exists, it is a fruitless exercise, reduced to human practices and beliefs. Neurotheology is still a young science feeling its way through some tricky inter-disciplinary waters. Within zoological taxonomy, humans are included within the Kingdom Animalia, but the humanities tend to take a more anthropocentric approach, emphasising a division between humans and other species. This has created a 'them and us' attitude which is both misleading and unhelpful. Even the term 'non-human animal' takes humans as its starting point whereas there are 78,533 other species of vertebrates, not to mention the arthropods, cephalopods and so on.

Hunting is a huge, even nebulous, subject which ramifies through all our daily lives, even if you are a vegan. Think of it like this leaf.

Look at the very tip of the leaf. You could say that trying to understand it is all about reaching this tip. If you were a PhD student, the tip may be where your thesis lies. Artificial intelligence could take you straight up the spine of the leaf and produce your entire thesis in a day. But the thesis, the book, the 'end-product', is not really what it is all about. It is about exploring all the side branches wherever they lead. Some connect to other branches, some are dead-ends. But even these dead-ends are not really dead-ends; they help to define the whole. Gradually, through following these leads, seeing where they go, you come to decipher through the fog of your own ignorance, the shape of the leaf. Similarly, when I am teaching students, most want straight answers. They want me to steer them up the spine of the leaf to the tip in the quickest and easiest way possible. They don't want to know about the ramifications, the dead-ends which somehow are irrelevant to their journey, a waste of time. I can take them there quickly but with such narrow knowledge, as soon as circumstances change, they have no width to adapt. And of course your own journey may not have started at the stalk of the leaf at all. You may already be out on one of the side branches, a skilled fisherman perhaps but with no experience of ferreting, or of trapping mice. Can you fully appreciate your fishing when you have little understanding of the whole leaf? Or you may be in a little bubble of your own – a cat-owner perhaps – with a limited perspective of your position on the leaf; you may be prejudiced about other parts of the leaf and reluctant to see how you are connected.

In this book, as a personal journey, I'm not necessarily trying to get to the tip of the leaf (how do I know the leaf hasn't got several tips, like a maple leaf?), I'm exploring the leaf, looking at connections, relationships, dependencies. It's a fascinating journey and my thoughts have ended up in some unexpected situations. Writing this as a book is an indulgence because I don't have to stick to the rigours and strictures imposed on me when I write as a scientist. Also, I am totally independent of commercial interests, politics, academic institutions, or NGOs; I am free to tell it as it is. But as a zoologist, or as an anthropologist, I would have always been on the outside looking in; not a participant. Being a participant is important, not only for first-hand authenticity, but because ethics, morality, in its most intense form, is expressed as your conscience, an internalised code of behaviour. What is written on the whiteboard of your conscience is personal, and as you go through life, you will make some changes. Your journey may take you to a different place from mine. To help you on your own journey there are references for each chapter at the end of the book.

Hunting is a keystone element of our behaviour and as such it derives from the same roots as all our behaviour. So first I look at those formative roots before examining hunting itself in its various forms, its demographics and motivations. I look at predation as distinct from aggression, and at issues often raised about hunting, such as animal welfare, cruelty and suffering. Our attitudes to hunting depend on our moral values, so next I examine how morality works as a mechanism, not just in our own species, but for all of us animals; how values are reached, who judges them and who enforces them. How do we use morality in our territorial behaviour, which links to hunting, to our diet and our other relationships with animals? Hunting can only take place in relation to land and land use, so I look at land ethics, our priorities and the evolutionary trap we now find ourselves in. Our veneer of 'civilisation' is a thin and fragile one, a group pretence that we are somehow raised above our animal nature, that we are separate from other species, and independent of Nature herself. We can maintain this charade for a little while, over-spending on our bank balance of finite global resources. But now Nature is beginning to call in our over-draft and pull the rug out from under our inflated egos, reminding us that we are animals, subject to Nature's laws just like all other species.

2 The roots of behaviour

Every human being has a 2 million-year old man within himself; if he loses contact with that 2 million-year old self, he loses his real roots.

Laurens van der Post

2.1 Introduction

The behaviour of human hunters, politicians, anti-hunters, hunting companions such as dogs, horses and falcons, and prey, ranging from deer to pheasants to rats, in fact all vertebrates, all share the same roots. So we need to be clear on these roots of behaviour – 'eth-ology' – before we can examine the more complicated subject of 'eth-ics'.

Our behaviour stems from three fundamental roots: genetic, imprinted and learned.

2.2 Genetics

All organisms receive an individual set of genes which, for most practical purposes, are immutable. Together they form a code which dictates what each individual will become. We call this set of genes the genotype and it will dictate what the individual looks like, its physical form or phenotype. It also dictates the suite of instincts it will have, a core set of behaviours, and this package of instincts is called the ethotype.

Even before the discovery of genes, biologists concentrated on phenotypes. The whole of taxonomy was based on what species look like. It's much easier to study things that you can see and measure than something nebulous like behaviour. To this day most health care is based on physical ailments. Behavioural problems are not so straightforward.

The first vertebrates evolved over 500 million years ago. Traces of their bodies – their phenotypes – appear as fossils. Their backbones and four limbs meant that they could move, and anything that can move, behaves. Early behaviour was simple, such as a response to a stimulus: light or dark, hot or cold, that kind of thing. Other evolutionary lines, such as the insects and the cephalopods, also faced the same problem – how to behave. So we know that the roots of our human behaviour, and of all moving creatures, go back not just a few hundred thousand years, but many millions of years.

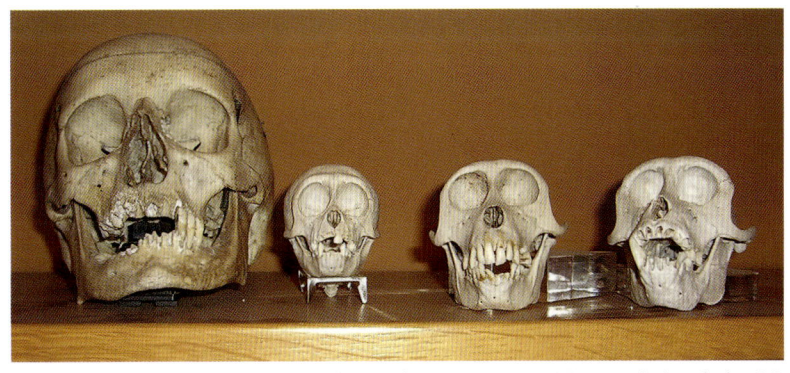

My mother gave me this old woman's skull when I was ten. Next to it is a baby Macaque and a female and male adult Macaque from Mauritius. I keep them above my desk to remind me of our shared ancestry.

2.3 Instincts and ethotypes

Collectively our suite of instincts make up our ethotypes, and these have evolved in parallel with our phenotypes. Imagine if your genotype only held genes for your phenotype, your physical body, but didn't include any genes for your ethotype, your instinctive behaviour. Splat-gurgle… you'd arrive from your mother's uterus in a slimy heap and just lie there. Instead of crying because you are cold, you'd just lie there, inert. You'd make no attempt to seek your mother's nipple and suck. You'd just lie there. And then you'd die, a genetic dead end.

There's not much point in having a body if you haven't got any behaviour to go with it. Learning is all very well but it takes time, and by then it is too late. You need a starter pack at least to get you going. Some species have such short life spans that they don't have much opportunity for learning; they've got to survive and breed first time, no rehearsals. Most of their lives are instinct-based.

'Instinct' refers specifically to behaviour rooted in genetics. This is its sole criterion: *'an observable pattern of behaviour derived from the genotype'*. I don't accept all the bells and whistles that people like Abraham Maslow have applied to the definition. It does not include learned or habituated behaviour. For example, when you learn to ride a bicycle, with practice you no longer have to 'think' about it. You have become habituated, and you may even have some muscle memory. But none of this is instinctive. You have no genes for riding a bicycle. On the other hand, your ancestors were all successful hunters, with an instinct to chase things. This instinct easily transfers to chasing a ball or one another. While some instincts provide a quick fix solution, their roles are usually more proactive and dynamic than that. Instincts create feelings, impulses and drives. Of course, as Maslow says, one may be able to over-ride these drives, but that doesn't mean they don't exist.

Although you can't see an ethotype, you can follow behaviour and see patterns. These patterns or templates are most easily studied in short-lived specialist species, such as a Wren (*Troglodytes troglodytes*). With such a short life span, the wren has to build its nest and breed first time, without any teaching, and with minimal learning. Its young, once they fledge, have to forage for themselves quickly and become independent within days so that the parents can start another brood. So its behaviour, which is complex and targeted, is governed by a series of ethotypic templates. These templates may be complex and sequential, such as the whole repertoire of the breeding cycle. They may be simple and stereotyped, such as the search and attack sequence of a predator. Or they may be some kind of image, such as in the mate preferences of a female Lyrebird (*Menura novaehollandiae*), watching displaying males. Together, these templates make up the ethotype which can be thought of as the 'genetic character' of the species.

A wren's nest in our forge.

These genes seldom act alone; usually they are acting in combinations with other genes, in groups. Some can also be switched on and off epigenetically by chemicals or hormones, so they are by no means simple cause and effect.

Genes form codes that trigger certain behaviours without requiring any learning. The stimulus may be the cheeping of chicks to a mother hen or the appearance of a predator which triggers them to freeze. The ethotype includes the formation of social groups; for example, horses instinctively form herds with a certain structure, whereas lions form groups with a different social structure. Most reproductive behaviours are ethotypic, as are territorial behaviours and defence of resources. Some of these instinctive behaviours do not need a stimulus but are pre-programmed to appear at certain stages in the life cycle. The genes work together; some kick in early in life; others wait quietly and then activate later, perhaps to do with the breeding cycle. For example sub-adult males instinctively explore new opportunities. When all goes well they thrive in new places and careers, opening fresh opportunities for the social group as a whole. When things don't go so well, many of these adventurous sub-adult males will die, or in the case of humans, end up in prison.

Some, such as Yuval Harari, treat instincts as if they were biochemical algorithms. Algorithms are formulaic; they are a sequence of decisions or programmes that give a consistent result each time. Some instincts can appear algorithmic, but most function as drivers or motivators of behaviours which may or may not have structured sequences. While instincts derive from the genotype and do not entail conscious thought, they usually require some situational or learned input to be carried out.

I had a female goshawk once. It was towards the end of the hunting season, late winter. After hawking she used to sit on the back of a chair in an alcove. She appeared quite contented but now and then she kept glancing at an electric cable dangling nearby. I went outside and collected an armful of sticks. Straight away she was down on the seat of the chair, arranging them into a nest. She had an instinct to build a nest released by the increasing spring day length triggering her hormones to change. The stimulus was a twig-like cable, and once given the ingredients, she instinctively went straight into nest building for the first time in her life. The nest wasn't brilliant to start with, but as she got more practice, she learned to improve her twig handling skills. For my part, mine was learned behaviour; this was the second time I had seen it in a goshawk. When I was a boy at school I had left the goshawk I had then on the back of a chair in my room over lunchtime. When I came back she had shredded a brown shirt and was lying down in her new nest in the chair. The seat of the chair is like a nest platform and the back of the chair is like the adjacent tree trunk, not such a big jump from the natural situation.

2.3.1 Individual temperaments

The root of temperament is also genetic. Just as there are individual variations in phenotype – we all appear slightly different – so there are individual variations in ethotype of which temperament is one. Although ultimate personality is the result of both nature (genetic) and nurture (imprinting and learning), when nurture is standardised, there is still genetic variation in temperament. Unless there is a perturbation such as an endocrine disorder or brain damage, temperament remains unchanged throughout life insofar that its roots are in the ethotype. The friends you knew as a child still have the same traits now as they did decades ago.

We flatter ourselves that we humans are free-thinkers, masters of our own destiny. To a large extent we are, and our lives are by no means pre-determined. We have some free will. But it is shocking to discover just how much of our behaviour is influenced by our genes. There are many studies of identical twins that have been reared apart and yet, because they have virtually identical genes, share all sorts of personality traits. Steven Pinker in *Enlightenment Now* records how twins may show similar talents in spelling and mathematics, share opinions on subjects such as apartheid, the death penalty, religion and tastes in dating. They may even share strange little foibles such as always entering the water backwards and only up to the knees, sitting out elections because they feel insufficiently informed, obsessively counting everything in sight, becoming captain of the volunteer Fire Brigade, and leaving little love notes around the house for their wives.

While some of these instinctive behaviours or ethotypic templates seem to appear spontaneously, or to follow an external trigger, others show up through indirect mechanisms such as the endocrine system. When an individual reaches certain stages in its life cycle, or in the season of the year, a menu of hormones is released into the blood stream and these in turn trigger behaviour. It is thus possible to create the same behaviour by dosing with appropriate hormones.

This interplay of instinct, hormones and stimuli can lead to some bizarre situations as an animal switches abruptly from one 'mode' to another according to circumstances. Many years ago in New Zealand we had a cat called Moses. Moses had some kittens, and, as feral cats are a major ecological menace in New Zealand, I killed them all. The next day I was out on the horse checking sheep when one of the dogs caught a milky doe rabbit. I knew that the baby rabbits would now starve to death so I fossicked around until I found the 'stop', the covered-over entrance to the short nest tunnel. I reached in and pulled out the blind baby rabbits and carried them home in my jersey. Then I put them in the box that Moses had had her kittens in. She started to lick them and clean them and was soon settled in comfortably with her adopted brood. Rabbits grow quickly and it was not long before they started to venture out onto the kitchen floor, with the dogs looking very uncomfortable about the whole thing. (I'd told them that their new ethic is that, although they are encouraged to hunt rabbits out on the farm, at home these rabbits are part of the 'family', our moral community.) Soon I built a mesh run and put the youngsters outside on the lawn. Moses would lie on top to guard them and every so often we would let her in to suckle them. As the rabbits got bigger we had to keep moving the run every few hours onto a fresh patch of lawn as they mowed it. Instinctively, as they weaned off milk, Moses started to catch solid food for them. This meant she went off hunting and caught rabbits the same size as her own rabbits and brought them back to feed them. Of course our rabbits had no intention of eating the dead rabbits; their ethotypes told them that they eat grass. Moses's ethotype told her that at that stage in the breeding cycle she should hunt fresh prey for her young.

Genes must pass on to the next generation with as high a fidelity as possible. Mutations occur from time to time and these are the building blocks that evolution applies selection to. While we can easily see mutations in the phenotype, the ethotype is also subject to both genetic mutations and developmental changes, so we can draw parallels. There is also the complication that several genes may be implicated in a 'mutation', and some may be recessive and produce no observable result. Autism, for example, is partly heritable through the genes, but not always actually inherited. The ethotype is so much harder to study, but the genetic mechanism controlling the phenotype gives us some inkling as to how the ethotype could also become altered.

The ethotype is very powerful in animals which have a very short lifespan. They may have only one or two seasons in which to breed. They might need to select and collect nest material, make an intricate and species-characteristic nest, find a mate with an ability to support the family, hold a territory to defend much-needed resources, court and copulate, lay eggs or give birth, rear the young, defend them against perils and even as the young approach independence, start the cycle again to try to raise maybe three broods in one season. All this is extremely complex behaviour which has to be performed very appropriately to each circumstance or it all goes wrong. The young breeder cannot be taught all this by its parents. It wasn't alive to see how its parents built the nest that it was reared in. In a way you could say this is evolution's finest hour. The hiding of nuts by squirrels and jays in the autumn might look like wise provision for the vicissitudes of winter, but it is all instinctive, all genetically determined. It is a supremely fine-tuned mechanism.

A longer-lived animal, such as an elephant or a human, has a different life strategy, based on fewer young but a bigger investment in a longer developmental period. This gives more opportunity and more requirement for learning but even so, all the genetic templating is still there, providing a solid base for the life strategy of the individual, the group, and of the species.

Looking at human behaviour around the world, behaviours and traits that are universal are probably ethotypic (genetic) in origin while those that vary locally might be more cultural or learned behaviour. Globally: most nurses are female, most politicians are older males (unfortunately!), most prisoners are younger men, most hunters are male, most people who prepare the meals and run the household are female, most soldiers are male, most self-adorners are female, most explorers are younger men, and so on. But art, music, food preferences, religion, and so on are learned, and vary. And of course, this being biology, the divisions tend not to be totally black and white. Instinctive behaviour merges gently into learned behaviour; in some cultures women are becoming politicians and business executives, and perhaps the world is better for it.

Our **core ethotype** is our spectrum of instincts that make us human as a species: our groupishness, territoriality, diet type, breeding strategy, hunting and foraging.

Gender differences make males and females behave slightly differently. Many of these differences are at least partly cultural or learned, but the underlying differences are ethotypic. These gender differences occur in many other species too and of course are strongly linked with breeding strategies.

Temperament is ethotypic whereas personality is a socio-cultural concept. You are born with a certain temperament but your personality can be modified during your upbringing. Our temperaments include aspects such as introversion/extroversion, emotional levels, empathy, humour, sociality, parenting, self-control, caring, fairness, spirituality, liberalism, optimism/pessimism, loyalty, tribalism, adventurousness and so on. Although we are born with them, some may become apparent only later in life, when we become sexually mature. And we can modify some of them by our own free will, to mould them into our personality. It's not easy; if you were born tone deaf, or without a sense of humour, there's not a lot you can do about it.

These elements of our ethotype go back a long way into our ancestry. Chimpanzees share many gestures with humans, so it is likely that our common ancestor shared them too, four or more million years ago in the late Miocene or early Pliocene. Our common ancestors with a backbone, the first vertebrates, appeared about 525 million years ago, in the Cambrian. Just as their genotype created a phenotype with a backbone, it is certain that that genotype also shaped their ethotype and that there were elements of their primitive behaviour that we would recognise today. Throughout most of our evolution, we existed in small numbers on the planet, and in groups of fewer than 200 individuals. Our whole suite of ethotypic behaviour was geared to this small group size. Being hunter-foragers prevented us living in large groups until the last few thousand years when we started farming. We do not have an ethotypic mechanism for existing in larger groups. This is why our larger groups simply don't work properly.

Politics don't work, monarchies don't work, nor do dictatorships. They all crumble in a short time. They are all examples of learned rather than ethotypic behaviour, and learned behaviour can vary immensely, and be argued and fought over.

2.4 Imprinted behaviour

Imprinting is a fast type of learning that takes place early in life and equips the youngster for survival both in the short term and in the long term. It is more or less irreversible. It can be thought of as a halfway house between ethotypic behaviour and learned behaviour; it requires a degree of sentience and yet is also to some extent mechanistic. It is an uncritical exposure to stimuli in early life while the brain is still developing resulting in fixed patterns of behaviour that almost mimic instincts. Studies of human early socialisation and attachment all emanate from the imprinting process. The Jesuits claimed: 'Give me the child for the first seven years and I will give you the man'. In my case, we had a collie x springer puppy called Bobby, when I was a week old. We grew up together; he was my mentor. Although I never identified as a dog, I grew up thinking like a dog, so I never suffered from the illusion, common to so many, that humans are superior. Bobby's sense of smell, hearing and eyesight, and his thinking and physical speed and agility were far better than mine. Only slowly did I outclass him in intellect.

The classic filial imprinting is seen in precocial species whose young are active and on their feet within hours of birth or hatch. They have a sensitive period of less than a day in which they imprint on their mothers. Many of these are social prey animals such as waterfowl, gamebirds, deer, sheep and horses. During this time the young lamb or chicken first identifies its mother. In mammals, the mother usually also identifies the young by smell and also has a brief acceptance period which is followed by rejection once the youngster has been identified and 'mothered'. This bonding period is critical. At the same time the precocial youngster is developing muscle tone and within minutes is able to stand up and walk about. When things go wrong, the results are spectacular and remain with the individual for the rest of its life. A lamb might imprint on a sheepdog, or a chick might imprint on a boot (with a human inside it).

When we are mothering a lamb onto a foster ewe, it needs to be done as soon as possible, within hours of the mother having given birth and lost her baby, and while the new baby is just hours old. We often skin the dead lamb or foal and put it on the new youngster because in those species, at that time, smell is the dominant sensory link.

Altricial species, which include humans, have a longer early developmental period than precocial species and the young are helpless and often blind at birth or hatch. This means that the imprinting process, although just as strong, is much more protracted. Instead of lasting hours during a limited sensitive period, it may take several weeks, and about seven years or more in humans. Imagine if humans were precocial. You could give birth in the morning and walk out of the hospital with the baby trotting along behind you in the afternoon! After a couple of days the baby would follow you while you go shopping.

This is the classic filial imprinting described by Oskar Heinroth, Konrad Lorenz and Eckhard Hess, but farmers and pastoralists have worked with it for centuries. This is how Anatolian sheep dogs are taught to identify with their flocks and guard them. Imprinting is not just for precocial species; it occurs in species with prolonged development periods too - like us. And it occurs in widely unrelated taxa of vertebrates that care for their young, including mammals and birds. It is not just a quick fix evolutionary add-on for a few species; this is behaviour that is deeply embedded in the wider vertebrate ethotype. Birds and mammals diverged from each other about 310 million years ago.

The exact neural mechanism for imprinting is unclear. In mammals it seems that imprinted changes are stored in the intermediate and medial parts of the ventral hyperstriatum. In birds and reptiles it appears to be slightly different. When the dorsal ventricular ridge was removed from the brains of newly hatched chickens they were unable to imprint.

Some claim that imprinting is irreversible, but like everything in real life there are exceptions and continuums. Nor is a closely defined critical period a prerequisite criterion, nor does the animal have to be precocial. But just because you cannot give it a ring-fenced definition doesn't mean to say it doesn't exist. The work that early researchers did was mainly on filial imprinting in precocial species, because this is where it is most obvious and clear-cut. To be precocial you need to get these bonds fixed rapidly. But imprinting covers many more elements than this, and they come into play at slightly different phases of development. Although precocial species imprint the filial bonds very early in a narrow critical period, as far as I can tell the other elements of their imprinting are more protracted, just as they are in altricial species.

Imprinting fixes a lot of behaviours that an animal carries with it for the rest of its life. These include:

- The parent figure (filial imprinting)
- Siblings
- The fear response
- The nest
- The habitat
- Food
- Cultural elements

Bonding with the mother, or 'filial' imprinting, is not the only element of the imprinting process. Bonding with the father, the siblings and the social group is also imprinted. The fear response is partly genetic and partly imprinted, and then refined by learning. The recognition of the nest type, home and habitat is imprinted. The urge to return home later in life (philopatry) is instinctive, but the recognition of where home is, and what it looks like (oikophilia), is imprinted. In farming we say sheep are 'hefted'. The mechanisms by which navigation and homing are achieved have a genetic root.

Studying imprinting is not easy; ethology generally is a tricky subject for statistical science. The chart below is not based on controlled studies. Such a study would be hard to design and I do not have the resources. So it is based on anecdotes, observations and records, trial and error. But we have imprinted several hundred falcons over 40 years on the farm, not to mention other species - and even some humans.

The observations show a general consistency with a degree of individual plasticity. The main difficulty is teasing out what is ethotypic behaviour on the one hand, and learned behaviour on the other. The genetic core ethotype provides an initial suite of instincts, a starter pack to see the individual through the critical early hours and days of life. But it also kicks in during later phases of the life cycle, for example at sexual maturity. These instincts have, as it were, lain dormant or buried before being roused to action by a biological time clock and hormonal triggers. They can be confused with imprinted behaviour. At the other end of the spectrum is learned behaviour (of which obviously imprinting is a form, albeit a specialised one). Conventional learning, such as conditioning and habituation, seamlessly takes over from imprinting and is reversible, except perhaps where memory is concerned. If a goshawk discovers a chicken house, you cannot get her to 'unlearn' that bit of information; she is not safe to be flown in that area ever again.

2.4.1 The mother figure (filial imprinting)

Falcons are altricial and their imprinting extends over a period of about 70 days, so it gives us a chance to see the progression of the different stages and look at the different permutations of malimprinting. The process is more drawn out than in precocial species, but not so extended as in humans, so we can notice the changes and influences almost day by day and week by week. For example, we can look at dual imprinting in which a chick is reared by two different parents, perhaps a falcon and a human. If the falcon chick develops for the first week or two being reared by a falcon mother, and then is taken and reared by a human foster mother, we call this asynchronous dual imprinting because the two parents came one after the other, separately. Similarly it can work the other way round with the chick reared by a human and then later, by a falcon. On the other hand, sometimes we use a tame mother falcon for rearing. She is herself a human-imprinted bird so is totally tame around humans and does not give alarm calls when her human 'mate' enters the pen. If we foster an egg or new chick onto her, it will grow up imprinted both on the falcon and on the human 'parent'. It will be a synchronous dual imprint. While the chick imprints on its parents, it also imprints on its nest type and site and on things which are familiar and not to be frightened of. Later in life, if given a choice, it will tend to choose a similar nest type to that on which it imprinted. If it was exposed to a potentially scary object, such as a dog, or a tractor, and neither parent showed signs of fear, it will tend not to show a fear response to that object or situation.

Developmental Stages

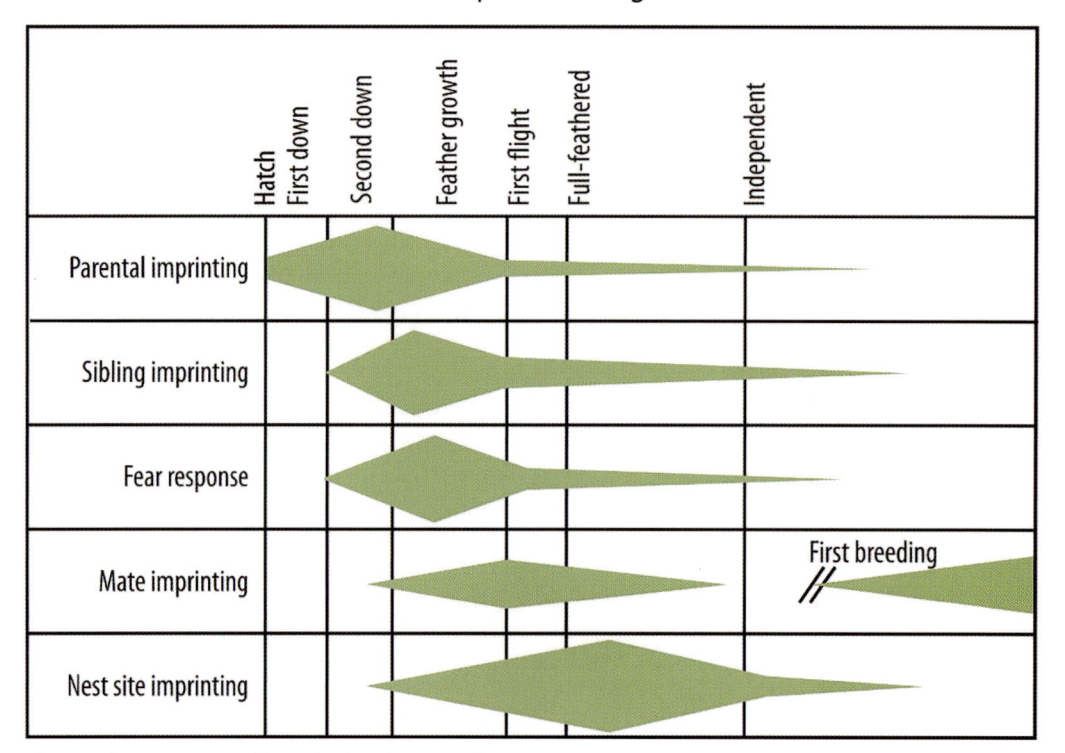

Approximate stages of imprinting in peregrines.

Parents themselves have different rearing systems. A primate mother with only one single young can afford to carry the baby with her wherever she goes and this requires a strong attachment bond, the kind investigated by Harry Harlow with his dummy mothers experiment. The baby has a strong instinct to cling on. It allows the mother some freedom of movement to forage and it shelters the young from predators or from mistreatment by members of the group.

In other species the imprinted bonding is just as strong but the rearing system is different. For example, the mother rabbit leaves her blind young in her fur-lined nest burrow while she goes out to feed. Many species with dens or lairs do this. Unlike other anthropoids who don't have permanent nests, humans have incompletely evolved to use dens and will leave their young physically separated from the mother for short periods, especially at night. During this dis-attached period the baby is normally asleep and if he wakes and finds his mother missing, will be distressed. Surrogate mothers, such as cuddly dolls or comfort blankets are used as a substitute but in evolutionary terms this is a work in progress. For her own convenience the mother would like time to herself, but the baby's ethotype has not yet caught up to this evolved change.

In other non-primates such as cows, deer and hares, the young are ethotypically adapted to lying quietly, even surreptitiously, while the mother is absent, whereas with sheep the lambs tend to stay close to their own mothers. Our human ability to construct dens, a type of tool use, is both ethotypic and learned. Children and adults often seem to want to construct primitive dens and log cabins in the woods. People want modern conveniences, electricity, heating, concrete boxes, steel and glass, but then find they want to 'get away from it all', back to nature. We have this conflict because culturally we have moved away from our ethotype.

Of course human attachment and bonding have been intensively studied. John Bowlby in *The nature of the child's tie to his mother* outlines attachment theory and subsequent researchers such as Mary Ainsworth, Rudolf Schaffer and Peggy Emerson have elaborated on it. Imprinting is a process but is also a product of the ethotype. So, for example, they documented the stage of attachment in human babies. These behaviours, such as sucking and clinging, and the sequences in which they appear, are innate. They arise from the core ethotype, but the object that the baby attaches to (usually the mother) has to be learned and this is a very powerful, long-term bonding which we describe as imprinting. Their research showed:

Birth - 6 weeks, no particular attachment.

6 weeks to 7 months, indiscriminate preferences towards primary and secondary care givers.

7 – 10 months, discriminates and forms strong attachment to the primary carer.

Over 10 months, develops bonds with multiple care givers.

A longer imprinting period means that when things go wrong, they can get complicated. For example, if a human baby is removed from his mother at birth and reared by a surrogate mother, he will go through his imprinting and bonding stages with that new mother. If, seven years later, he is returned to his birth mother, he may not establish the same relationship with her as he would have done. Similar problems may arise with imprinting on the father figure.

Because imprinting involves a variety of inputs, not just parents, there is scope for some aspects to be 'normal', for example two natural parents of its own species, but for other elements, such as the nest or home, to be asynchronous dual or even triple imprinted. In these early formative stages of life the chick, or baby human, is only aware of his immediate surroundings and stimuli, especially the face of his mother. But as he gets older he starts to identify his siblings, then his nest or home. If the human toddler is moved from one home to another during childhood, and the two homes differ markedly, for example a town flat and a rural farm, there will be a disruption of the home imprinting or oikophilia, a confusion or weakening of the imprinting effect. He may grow up feeling he doesn't 'belong' anywhere.

In some societies the family situation for the developing child may vary from the 'norm', namely two natural bonded parents, reared all through the formative years in the same home. The child might have only one functional parent, and might change homes several times, maybe in a hospital, orphanage or boarding school. With this kind of upbringing the child may later be dysfunctional at breeding time and we see the same effect in other species. Similarly, if the child is reared together with another species in the house, such as a cat or dog, this will influence the child's attitude later in life.

Without early experience of them, these other animals may induce a fear response.

Although inter-generational learning is highly developed in primates, the role of imprinting of social moral values is underestimated. What we know as 'conscience' originates in inherited, imprinted and learned values. The risk of studying the minutiae of learning in a single species (humans) as done by Jean Piaget, Lawrence Kohlberg and many others, is that there is little evolutionary perspective.

When a lamb imprints on its mother in the space of a few minutes or hours, the mother also bonds with her lamb. Her bond is a strong and accurate one, but it is both genetic and learned. The ewe is too old for imprinting in the conventional sense but, who knows – maybe the imprinting mechanism can function later in life? The bonding has a narrow time band (about 48 hours from birthing) and once this is passed it is very hard to persuade her to bond with a

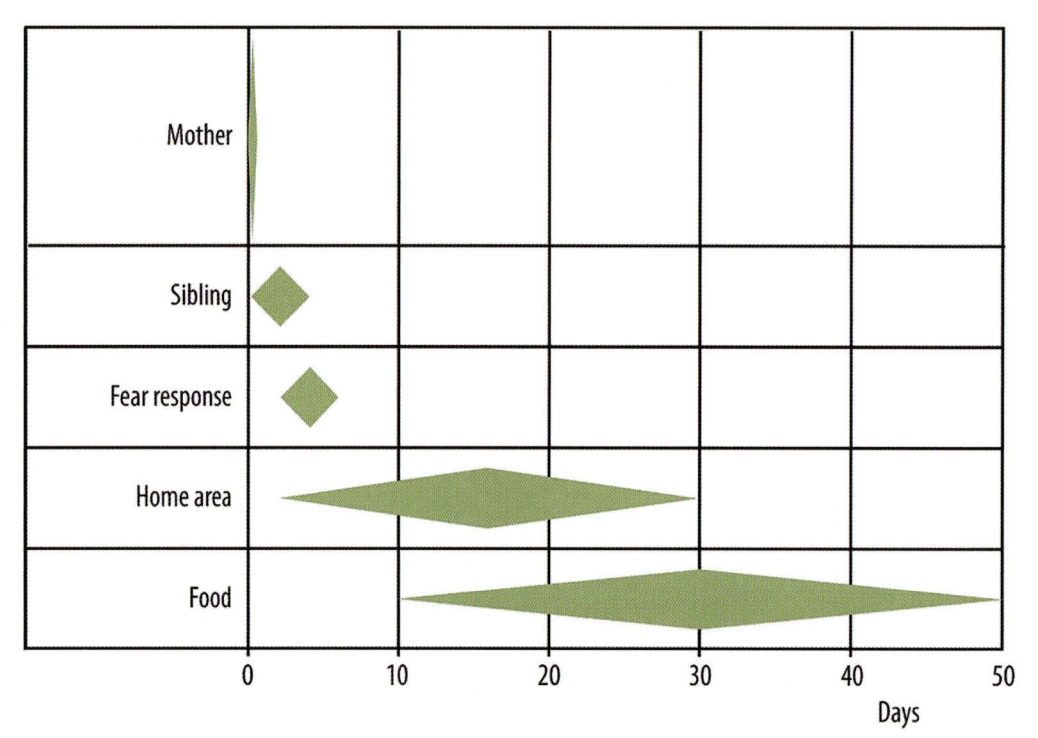

Approximate stages of imprinting in sheep.

strange lamb. Her instinct leads her to reject and butt away all other lambs and to mother only her own. This sensitive period is linked to the changing hormonal levels in the new mother as well as to the age of the strange lamb. I've spent many a long hour trying to get ewes to take on strange lambs, and the longer it takes, the less the chance of success. The two-tooths are the worst; the first timers. Some are astonished at this wet squirmy thing that has just come out of them and, given a chance, may just walk away. Older ewes have learned from previous lambings and are more reliable.

Discriminating towards one's own offspring is common in mammals with a good sense of smell. Birds of prey have little sense of smell and will adopt chicks of other species. For example peregrines have adopted and reared a Common Gull (*Larus canus*) together with their own chicks. This does not mean that they cannot tell them apart; birds of prey have a very good sense of recognition and recognise siblings and other individuals even after years of separation. It just means that they have a strong instinct to adopt and rear when the hormone levels call for it. Sometimes we have hatched goose eggs under bantams. The mother bantam tries to brood and cover the goslings. As they grow older the goslings walk around the yard with the bantam surrogate mothers riding on them like jockeys!

Humans too, having a poor sense of smell, can easily be induced to adopt and rear a baby that is not their own, and childless couples or 'empty nest' females often adopt interspecific 'babies' such as lap dogs and cats, that have features resembling human babies.

There is another type of powerful late learning that is hard to reverse, which I call trauma learning and which has now been given the name 'post-traumatic stress disorder' or PTSD. This can, but does not always, occur in a matter of seconds during a traumatic experience, such as a car accident. Often the 'flicker fusion frequency' increases at the same time so that the incident is experienced in slow motion. Conventional learning and conditioning techniques may gradually reverse trauma learning but it is an unusually hard job, which makes me think a mechanism akin to imprinting is going on.

Mother birds have an additional problem in that they 'give birth' twice; the first step is to lay the egg and incubate (this is heavily controlled by hormones) and then, when the egg hatches, to switch to a massive change in behaviour triggered by stimuli external to her own body. Inert eggs suddenly become wriggly chicks. Both behaviours are instinctive and dependent on the hormones of the female. They are triggered by stimuli – first, the eggs, and then the chicks. Usually this change of behaviour works well, but in artificial circumstances where we take the real eggs into an incubator and leave the female sitting on dummy eggs, there comes a point where we have to remove the dummies and replace them with tiny vulnerable chicks. It is possible to do that with experienced falcons who have bred before, but for the first timers such a change is massive and they may kill the chicks as if they were rats or some kind of predator in their nest. To provide the biological trigger of the chicks hatching we use a 'Born Again' egg. This is a fibreglass egg the size of a goose egg, painted mottled brown like a falcon egg. It is a super-stimulus. The bottom of the egg is missing, so we can gently squeeze a falcon chick into the egg. Then we remove the dummy eggs and put the Born Again egg into the nest. The mother comes in and continues incubation. Then she feels and hears the chick struggling in the egg. Instinctively she crouches over the egg and sooner or later it rolls over and 'hatches'. This triggers her to shift into brooding and rearing mode. Once she has accepted and fed one chick, we can easily add more; she is already in rearing mode.

The male on the other hand has a bit of a problem. His instincts and hormones too have led him to copulate, hunt to provision the female and take a share of the incubation.

A Born Again egg.

But he has to stay flexible and adapt his behaviour appropriately to circumstances. The female has been on a sequential cycle of hormones to do with ovulating, egg laying and incubation, but the male takes a more generalised role and fits in with whatever is going on.

2.4.2 Siblings

Altricial species are usually born almost blind and helpless. Initial interactions with the mother are instinct driven and often a matter of trial and error until some muscle tone and vision allow more co-ordinated efforts. Gradually the youngster becomes aware that there are others in the nest and that these siblings are a source of warmth. As the brood or litter develops further then these siblings also become competitors for food from the mother. Sibling rivalry may be fatal when food is scarce and this is a mechanism for matching brood size with food supply.

Notwithstanding the conundrum of Adam and Eve's children and the concept of incest being a sin or taboo, imprinting between siblings is an interesting biological mechanism that discourages incest. An imprinted sibling relationship is a strong one and not easily altered through life, so when sexual maturity is reached, any sibling still around will usually be ignored as a potential mate. This is the Westermarck effect and it works both horizontally (between siblings) and vertically (between parents and their children). In humans the sensitive period is the first six years or so. This has the effect of preventing or minimising incestuous matings and thus, through an imprinted route, prevents inbreeding and maximises genetic diversity. In morality-speak we call this the 'incest taboo'.

Although the ethotype may be the driver behind this mechanism, the upfront mechanism depends on recognising specific individuals, which can only be done through learning, and as the process starts at a young age, and persists throughout life, we can assume that imprinting is the main operating factor. This assumption is reinforced by the fact that siblings reared apart tend not to show incest inhibition whereas unrelated young, reared together, do. When we are breeding the falcons, we have to be careful to record who they were reared by (real or adoptive parents) and who they were reared with (real or adoptive siblings). If you inadvertently try to pair up two birds that were originally reared as siblings, you can have a very long wait without anything happening.

2.4.3 The fear response

Imprinting usually builds on and reinforces the core ethotype and temperament. But it can also go against them. For example, the fear response includes instinctive, imprinted and learned channels. If you take a young animal before its fear response has developed and expose it to whatever you don't want it to be afraid of – humans, for example, or tractors – the habituation at that age will imprint and over-ride the instinctive fear. Being imprinted, this trait then continues for life without a need for learned reinforcement. Normally though, the three channels build one upon another in an indiscernible continuum.

2.4.4 Nest

Most of nest building is ethotypic, but there are elements of it that are imprinted. Falcons, (who don't build nests), have to find pre-existing sites and scrape a little nest hollow for the eggs. They could nest on the ground, as merlins (*Falco columbarius*) do, but this exposes them to ground predators. Or they could nest up on a cliff ledge, but these may be in short supply, or they could commandeer a stick nest built by a crow or maybe a heron. And if none of those are available, a hollow tree or a clump of epiphytes on an old tree might suit. If several of these options are available, what makes a falcon choose one rather than another? The short answer is that most of the time they select the kind of nest site that they were reared in, and this is imprinted rather than ethotypic. You can answer that question by swapping young chicks around into different nest types.

2.4.5 Habitat

When the youngsters are able to look out from the nest and perhaps make short forays from it, they gain an impression of the surrounding area and habitat. They imprint on it both as a type, and as a specific natal area. Once they are mature they still 'know' what home should look like and choose a similar place for their own new homes, and migratory species may return from thousands of miles to their natal area. Our juvenile Siberian peregrines travel independently from their parents to their wintering grounds, so this must be ethotypic, but young birds learn from this and are able to create a 'navigational map' guiding their future migrations more effectively.

2.4.6 Food

Young animals develop imprinted food preferences, and in predators, later we see this following through in their search images. With falcons, if you want them to relish eating crow meat, then feed it to them as chicks. If you introduce this meat later in life they often find it unpalatable and reject it. Similarly in humans, rearing on a variety of foods will result in being more adaptable in diet preferences later in life.

We had a bay mare in New Zealand called Bumblebee. Foaled and reared at St James, and backed at Molesworth, she had spent her life entirely in the hills, never knowing anything other than natural food. She wouldn't touch carrots or apples. The only things that would attract her were sprigs of green willow that she had been used to eating in the shade of the creek beds with her mum. Her delight was to go swimming in the river, towing me on a line, and then afterwards, clean and gleaming, roll in the fine silt drifts luxuriously until totally plastered.

Teaching Bumblebee to go in shafts.

After work a swim to cool off…

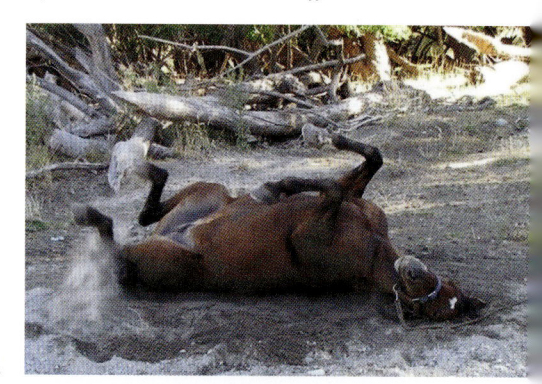

and a good roll.

Bumblebee holds a steady trot.

2.4.7 Cultural values

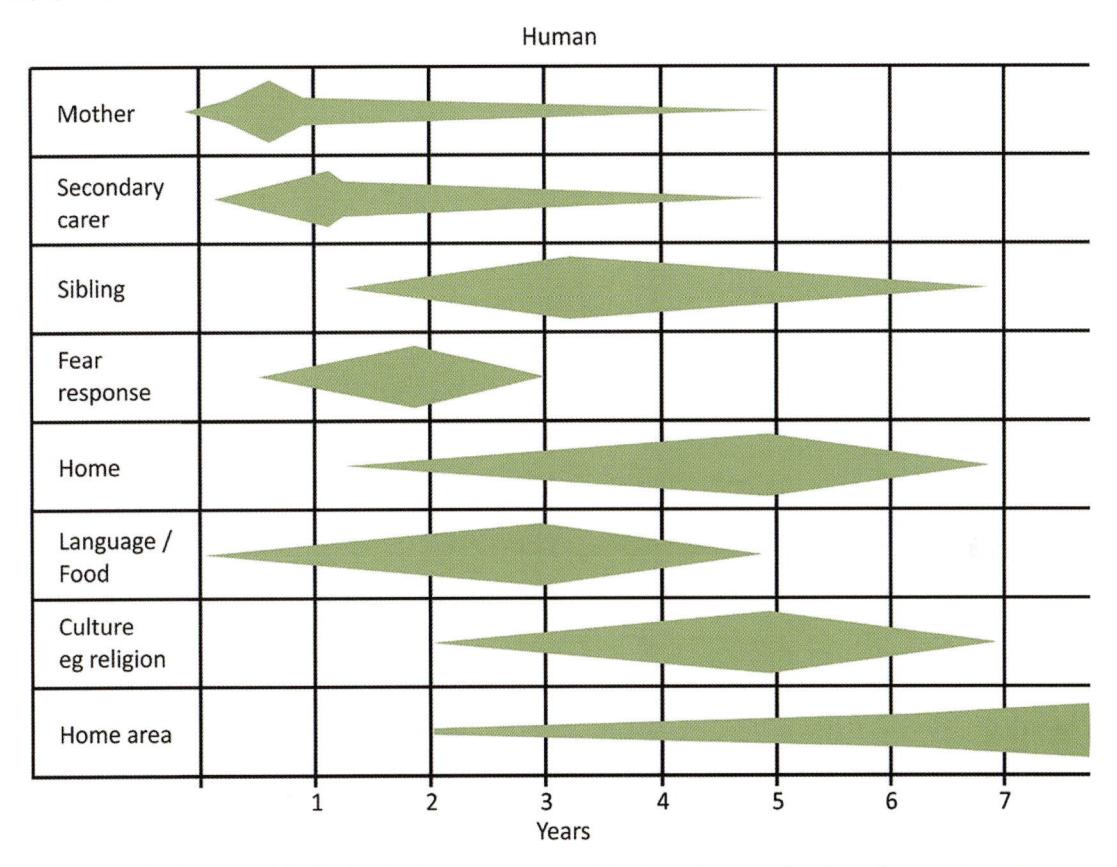

Human

Category	Timeline (Years)
Mother	peak around 0–1, tapering to ~5
Secondary carer	peak around 0–1, tapering to ~4
Sibling	~1.5 to ~5, peak ~3
Fear response	~0.5 to ~2, peak ~1
Home	~2 to ~6, peak ~4
Language / Food	~0.5 to ~4, peak ~2
Culture eg religion	~2 to ~6, peak ~4
Home area	~2.5 to 7+, increasing

Imprinting in humans. My family had great fun with this chart. Invite a few friends around and argue about it!

Many values, including some of the moral ones, are established at the imprinting stage. This can be seen most clearly in precocial species with a very short imprinting period. In altricial species such as humans, the imprinting process is extended and intertwined with learning, although humans still show many imprinted values, such as philopatry, and imprinted fear responses. Religions and many social attitudes and values are taught to children during their imprinting period, up to about seven years old, before the child is fully capable of rational thought. Languages too are easily assimilated at this stage. Imprinted values in young humans cannot easily be changed by subsequent learning. They have become internalised and, if challenged, re-emerge later as a 'conscience'.

The conscience (whatever it may be) is formed from the ethotype, through imprinting and from learning. Basically it is internal guidelines telling you what you should do, and what you shouldn't do. A lot of modern dog-training and child training is based on positive reinforcement and conditioned reinforcers. These can be used to shape new behaviour and work for both social and non-social species. They are about what you <u>should</u> do. They don't work so well for shaping boundaries, things you <u>shouldn't</u> do. Dogs trained in modern dog classes using treats and pats can look impressive in a ring, but they can be real devils at chasing sheep and thousands of sheep are killed every year. Children too, trained this way, have poorly developed 'boundaries'. Social animals understand dominance hierarchies and negative reinforcement ethotypically. These can be used painlessly to discourage unwanted behaviour until it has been internalised into the conscience.

Subsequent logic or intellectual arguments struggle to overcome imprinted convictions from childhood. There are attempts to break down some of these barriers, by mixing children while they are still young. The *Hand in Hand* schools work hard to mix Hebrew-speaking Jews and Arabic-speaking Muslim children, although in some ways the battle has already been lost in so far as the children, even at primary school age, self-identify in their parents' religion.

Imprinted beliefs persist in modern human societies despite advances in knowledge because it is a biological mechanism. Religious ideologies will not die out quickly just because intellectual argument or science might dissuade them. People reared with Creationism will stalwartly defend it against all evidences from Evolutionists; nothing will convince them to change their minds. People with an imprinted belief are likely to continue with it all their lives, and may well imprint their children with it. The result is that the demographics of religions reflect imprinted values rather than any ultimate logic or truth. Most people share the same religion as their parents and society. Your religion is an accident of birth, but it is imprinted onto you. There may be a slight genetic basis for spirituality, as there seems to be for political attitudes, but not for a specific religion. It is interesting, talking to people of different religions around the world, what diverse explanations they come up with for the origin of the universe and of humans. Because so few have any real knowledge of biology there tends to be little engagement with the evidences of modern scientific discoveries. While on the one hand people readily put their faith in devices such as mobile phones which are based on modern science, or seek medical aid based on pharmacology or genetics, when it comes to their own origins people tend to fall back on the stories or conspiracy theories fed to them as children.

Hunting is considered a cultural 'Belief'. A child taken out hunting may grow up to accept hunting, or farming animals, as 'normal'. Conversely a child reared with no experience of animals or hunting may grow up to consider them strange, abnormal, maybe 'bad' or to be feared. With cultural beliefs imprinted at this deep level, intellectual approaches later in life do little to change attitudes and it is no wonder that the debates about hunting are so vehement and intransigent.

2.4.8 Future sexual partner

There is another element to imprinting which I don't properly understand yet: the identification of the future sexual partner. We have worked on this for many years in falcons but it is hard to untangle. Will a falcon reared by a black-morph falcon choose only a black morph partner? How do cuckoos know to mate with a cuckoo when they have been reared by another species in isolation from other cuckoos? Some of these life decisions must be rooted back in ethotypic behaviour. Cuckoos don't attempt to mate with just any species; they know to target cuckoos of the opposite sex, so they must genetically recognise the signals given by that bird. They have no chance to imprint, or to learn this, on the contrary, they have been reared by a very different foster species. Not only that, but cuckoos have to lay eggs matching that of the host species, and this must be genetic, which implies that there are strains of cuckoos each specialising on different hosts.

The various ways of learning have been well-studied nowadays and things have moved on from the rather simplistic determinism of Skinner. Many years ago I

Chapter 2 – THE ROOTS OF BEHAVIOUR   29

This female peregrine displays to me as her imprinted sexual partner.

wrote a paper titled *'Latex sex aids and how to persuade females to copulate voluntarily with you'*. It was presented at a conference of the Avian Incubation and Fertility Research Group and attracted good attendance! We have been working on the domestic breeding of birds of prey since the late 1960s. Many people said these solitary predators would be impossible to breed; they would require large chunks of sky for their courtship flights and anyway, would kill each other in confinement. We use two main methods: natural breeding with pairs of birds in aviaries, and breeding using artificial insemination using birds that are imprinted on humans. I discussed this with a colleague, Karen Pryor, who had just published a book called *Don't shoot the Dog*. She was giving demonstrations of developing conditioned reflexes using clicker training. All sorts of strange behaviours can be created by using clicker training or similar methods and it is widely used in the film industry. But there are some behaviours that don't work by this method and copulation is one of them. For a male to copulate, the underlying drive is instinct, not learning. On top of this his hormonal levels need to be right in order to bring him into breeding condition. And then you need a stimulus, a sexy object that triggers copulation. Some aspects of this trigger seem to be instinctive, ie genetic. For example, what a Japanese man finds sexy in a Japanese woman is slightly different from what an African man finds sexy in an African woman, and over the years this has been selected for, so that the females of these two ethnic groups have different body shapes. Perhaps the ethotype has shaped the phenotype? But other aspects of this sexual stimulus are imprinted, and if we imprint a young animal on a rubber boot, later in life it will attempt to copulate with a rubber boot. Literally it has a foot fetish. (So when imprinting baby falcons we have to raise them up on tables so that they are seeing our upper bodies rather than our feet.)

The observations of René Spitz and John Bowlby on humans and Harry Harlow on monkeys demonstrated aspects of the role of imprinting and attachment in the young and their roles in mate selection once mature. It is easy to show how inappropriate imprinting of a young animal screws up its mate selection later, but it is not so easy to do it predictably so that it will mate with an artificial dummy reliably. We are still working on this in falcons. Once a falcon has started to copulate with a specific dummy it will continue to use that dummy for the rest of its life. The difficulty is in getting all the young falcons to copulate with dummies. Some do and some don't. Some are wallflowers.

A Gyrfalcon (Falco rusticolus) copulates on a hat.

When it comes to hunting, some predators imprint on certain prey species or groups of species and ignore other potential prey. In falconry we say a falcon is 'wedded' to certain prey. Different groups of orcas similarly wed to certain prey species, such as seals, or penguins. When we design artificial prey, the closer it is to real prey, the easier it is to fixate the falcon onto it.

2.5 Learned behaviour

The various types of learning are well documented. Group knowledge can be shared between living individuals and, in some cases, between generations. So while the ethotype, being gene-based, can only be transmitted vertically, through the generations, taught or imitation-based learning can also be transmitted horizontally. For example, we use imitation when training falcons. Rather than teaching each falcon one at a time, we can use one falcon to provide an example that the rest of the group can copy. Using our robotic prey bird we can teach a falcon to chase it around the sky; the rest of the trainees can sit and watch and understand what is going on. Of course then they want to join in. So we pre-empt this by feeding the rest of the falcons beforehand. This means that they can mentally learn the action without being motivated to actually do it. The next day, when they are hungry, we give them their opportunity to chase the prey themselves, one by one. Parent falcons use the same method. They fly up into the sky carrying prey and drop it for one of their youngsters. The other youngsters in the brood may not participate, but they watch, and learn. Susan Blackmore claims that memes are the preserve of the human species but learning from one another is one of the commonest types of learning in vertebrates, if only because it side-steps the need for insight learning, which is intellectually more demanding. (By the way, the most spectacular failure of imitation and insight learning I have ever seen was in Zimbabwe. Someone had parked a lorry on a hill and put a stone under the wheel – on the uphill side! He'd managed the imitation bit, but not the insight bit.)

As the young animal grows it is actively learning things. This tends to occur in developmental stages documented in humans by Jean Piaget and many others since. Some of this learning is experiential (which tends to cover both questions and answers) and some is taught (which tends to cover mainly answers).

So much has been written about learning and education that there is no point in me re-hashing it here. But most of what has been written is about learning in social animals, such as humans, dogs or horses. These understand social mores, dominance hierarchies and punishment systems. Less social animals, such as cats, have a very different mind-set.

People often claim that cats are untrainable, therefore owners cannot be responsible for what they do. But cats are not stupid; they are perfectly capable of learning. They just don't fit into the hierarchies and moral communities that we social humans are used to. Raptors are even more solitary, and capable of flying away rapidly. Yet we can train them, building on their ethotypes with imprinting and conditioning without using punishment. I do smile sometimes though when I see a young falconer trying to call his hawk to come to him for a piece of meat and the hawk ignores him. So the falconer moves a little closer to try again. Who, I wonder, is training who? We have to teach him the simple maxim: *Never call in vain*.

Taught behaviour is the most efficient way of reaching an end goal in learning, being spoon fed the answers by some sort of mentor. But it is also the most limiting; you end up using words like 'correct' and 'wrong' and being worried about making mistakes. Experiential learning is much better quality, leaving the learner in a much stronger position to adapt when situations change. Armies and some religions teach prescriptively; they don't want to be questioned. Blind adherence is key. Some human societies are held back because of this.

2.6 The component roots

So first we have our core ethotype, common to every human and characteristic of our species, 'universal traits'. It includes things such as living in sociable groups up to 200 or so, with dominance hierarchies usually headed by an alpha male. Competitive displays for mates by both sexes. Broadly speaking a monogamous pairing strategy during breeding. Active parenting of young until adolescence. Hunting and foraging for food. Broadly omnivorous diet with meat being a preferred option. Attachment to a permanent or semi-permanent home base. Defence of territory with a wider foraging range. Hostility towards alien groups. It also includes aspects that make us sentient, sometimes defined as the capacity to have pleasant or unpleasant experiences, and thus a 'quality of life', which in turn demands moral consideration.

To summarise the roots of behaviour:
Core ethotype
Species specific instincts
Breeding behaviours
Curiosity
Diet
Dominance hierarchies
Empathy
Experience feelings/sensations
Groupishness, co-operation, leadership

Hunting/foraging
Intuition
Memory
Nocturnal/diurnal
Potential motor skills
Self-preservation
Subjective awareness
Territoriality

Gender roles
Males
Defence and support of family
Dominance hierarchies
Exploration/risk taking
Tribe and territory

Females
Care of the home
Competition for social hierarchy
Foraging and distribution of food
Primary carers of dependants

Individual temperament
Addictive tendencies
Adventurous/adaptable
Artistic ability
Benevolence
Bold/fearful
Competitive/cooperative
Creativity
Credulous/gullible
Curiosity
Emotional level/neuroticism
Mathematical ability
Musical ability
Optimist/pessimist

Empathetic/sympathetic
Hunting/foraging
Imagination
Intelligence
Introvert/extrovert
Intuition
Jealousy
Leadership
Liberalism/conservatism
Linguistic ability
Sense of humour
Sensuousness
Shyness/boldness

32 HUNTING ETHICS

    Patience
    Phobias
    Selfish/unselfish

    Spiritual
    Territorial
    Tribalism

Learned behaviour
  Imprinting
    Mother/parents (filial)
    Siblings
    Fear response
    Concept of home

    Native language
    Food preferences
    Religion

  Personality
    Angry/kind
    Bold/fearful
    Caring/sharing
    Competitive/cooperative
    Creative
    Honest/dishonest
    Leadership
    Linguistic skills

    Loyal
    Parenting abilities
    Religious
    Self-control
    Selfish/selfless
    Sense of fairness
    Social skills
    Trustworthy

  Rational thought
    Concepts
    Empathy
    Factual knowledge
    Ideas/abstraction

    Motor skills
    Objectivity
    Problem solving
    Reasoning skills
    Relationships

These attributes pile one on top of another, resulting in how an animal behaves. In the case of the European Sparrowhawk (*Accipiter nisus*), it has a massive infant mortality (70% in the first year) and a short life expectancy of about four years.

SPARROWHAWK

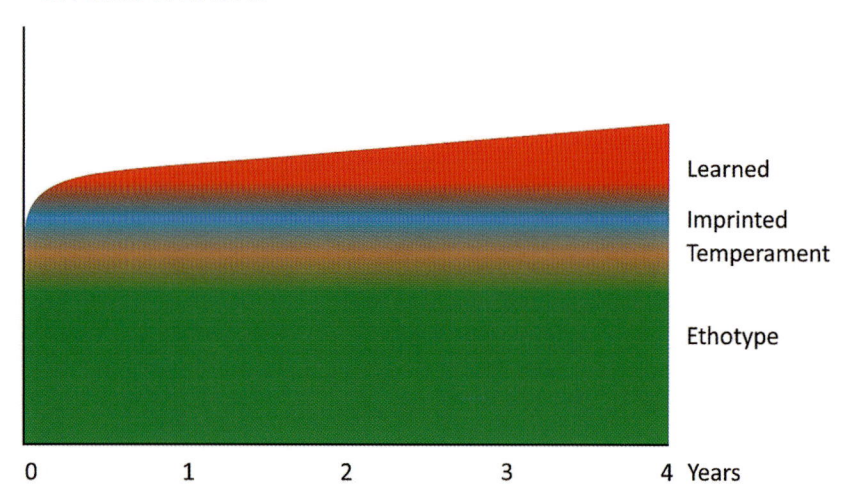

Chart showing layers from bottom to top: Ethotype (green), Temperament (orange), Imprinted (blue), Learned (red), plotted over 0 to 4 Years.

It has severe gender role partitioning both at breeding and in hunting. Imprinting is short – about two months – after which it becomes an independent solitary obligate hunter. All of its breeding behaviour and initial hunting behaviour is ethotypic; it is not taught, or learned from experience. There is little time. Hunting skills, home ranges and territories are developed through learning.

Humans have a longer imprinting and developmental period. They are also social and omnivorous, both of which have a high learning requirement. While the core ethotype is pan-specific, imprinting and learning are experiential and thus malleable, which means that different cultures can diverge.

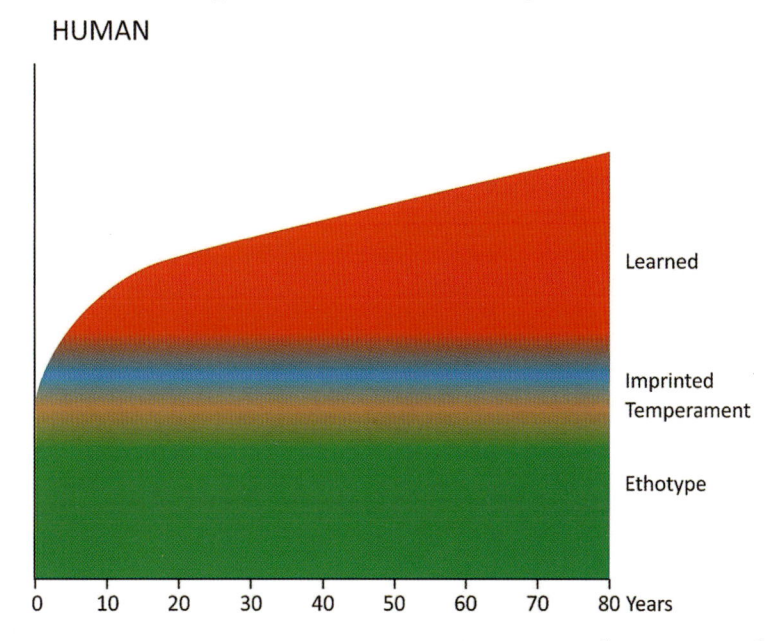

HUMAN

[Chart showing Learned, Imprinted Temperament, and Ethotype layers over 0–80 Years]

DIVERGING LEARNED CULTURES

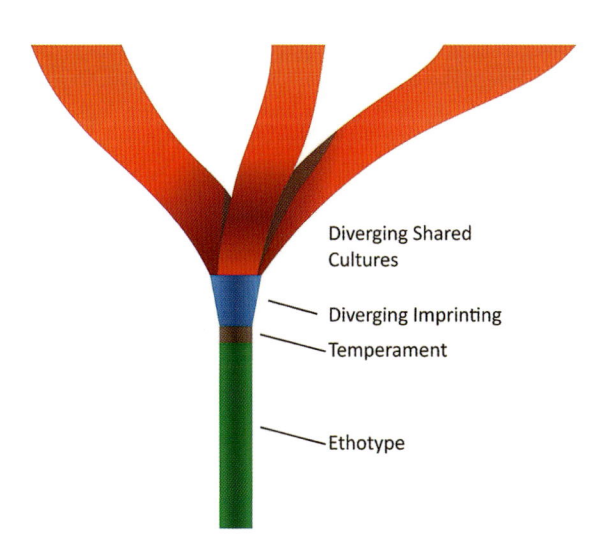

[Diagram showing Diverging Shared Cultures, Diverging Imprinting, Temperament, and Ethotype]

If we look at the previous chart from the side, each individual has a slightly different imprinting experience and learning, gradually creating diverged cultures yet sharing a common ethotypic core.

None of this has come about overnight. It is the product of many millions of years of evolution. To look at it from the perspective of our own species, our history and where we are going next, look at our population growth.

The earliest recognisable anthropoid apes, the Eosimiidae, evolved about 45 million years ago, with early humans differentiating about 7 million years ago. If, instead of going back only 12,000 years, as on this chart, I included all of our pre-history, the chart would extend to the left about 375 metres. Much of our ethotype and our phenotype

Population, 10,000 BCE to 2021 CE

Population by country, available from 10,000 BCE to 2100, based on data and estimates from different sources.

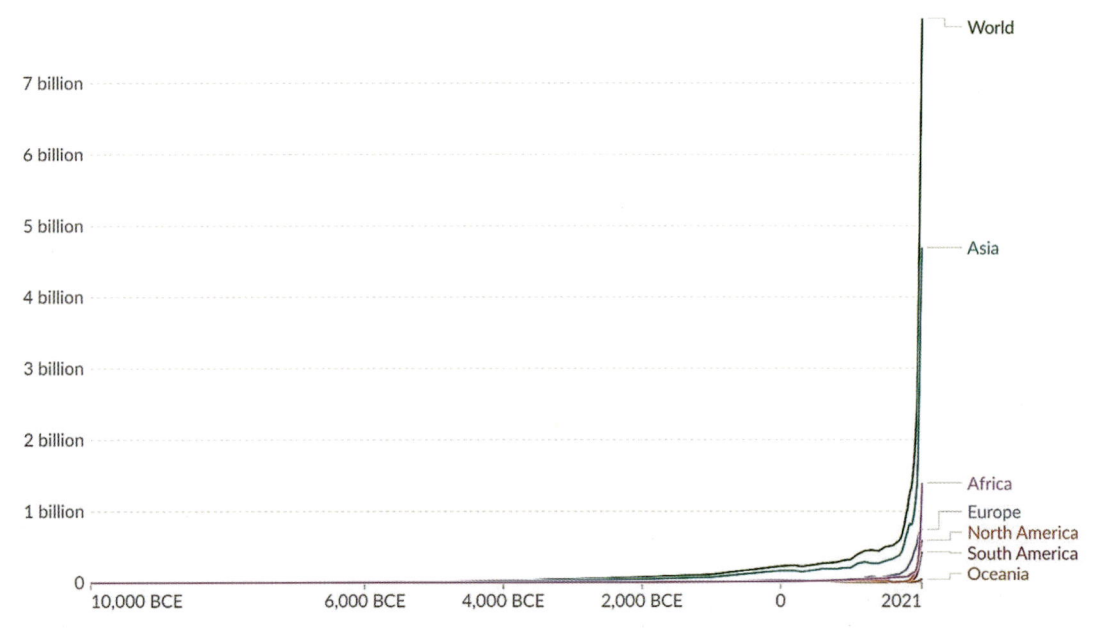

Our World in Data

[Chart showing world population growth from 10,000 BCE to 2021, with lines for World, Asia, Africa, Europe, North America, South America, and Oceania. Y-axis ranges from 0 to over 7 billion. X-axis shows years from 10,000 BCE through 2021.]

Data source: HYDE (2017); Gapminder (2022); UN (2022)
Note: Historical country data is shown based on today's geographical borders.
OurWorldInData.org/population-growth | CC BY

extends even further back than this, as part of the 518 million year evolutionary journey of the vertebrates. Our population was limited by breeding success and by hunting/foraging success. Even in 1765 infant mortality (up to five years) was 40% and life expectancy was 39 years. Now infant mortality is 0.4% and life expectancy is 82 years, resulting in a spike, or maybe a new, higher, plateau. But given that we are outstripping the Earth's resources by 2.5 times, most likely it will be a spike.

For millions of years the pinch points limiting our populations have been breeding success (to do with child birth, rearing and the home base, a largely female role) and food supply (a largely male role). We have powerful ethotypic drives for those two elements, both of which are gender-based role partitioning and not to be subsumed by a few generations of urban living disconnected from our roots in nature. Also, during all those generations, we lived in small groups, little tribes and clans, many of whom died out along the way. That is our core human nature, our ethotype. Later we will see how this affects our various attitudes to hunting.

2.7 Intelligence

While imprinting is a form of learned behaviour, it is an uncritical approach. It accepts whatever is there. Experiential learning takes place from day one, in parallel with imprinting. As the imprinting period reaches completion, learning continues throughout the creature's life. The ability to make correlations, recognise causality and develop concepts, and the capacity to process them into new creative approaches, are all part of intelligence. The intelligence of each species and each individual varies according to its own sensory inputs and the needs of its own lifestyle. This is hailed nowadays as 'new knowledge' but it has been common knowledge for a long time; just look at Richard Jefferies for example, writing in *The Gamekeeper at Home* (1880, p96). To claim that humans are the most intelligent species, while true in some respects, is misleading. Intelligence is not easy to measure, especially in non-humans, and the measurement systems we apply tend to be anthropocentric. But in some aspects that we can measure, for example, memory, humans are by no means top of the class. The feats of memory of some food-caching birds and mammals outclass humans probably by two or three factors of ten.

If intelligence is so good, why aren't all animals super-intelligent? Any attribute has both a potential benefit and a cost in the evolutionary stakes. Wings offer great benefits, but if you don't really need to fly then it is better not to have them. Learned behaviour is wasteful. It takes time to learn, and often a lot of trial and error. It is handy in a fast-changing environment, but when things are more stable, instinct is quicker and better. It is plug in and go. So all species have a balance between the two, depending on their lifestyles. Short-lived specialists rely more on instinct than long-lived generalists who have to learn a lot of strategies for survival and need a long dependency period. Highly social species with omnivorous foraging strategies have the most need for intelligence.

2.8 Emotional intelligence

There was a horse in Berlin called Clever Hans. Clever Hans was claimed to be able to do basic arithmetic, tell the time and understand German, amongst other things. A panel of 13 specialists, the Hans Commission, was set up in 1904 and verified this. Only later did another researcher, Oskar Pfungst, de-bunk the claim. It turned out that Clever

Clever Hans 1904.

Hans was not capable of doing these things, he was just picking up cues from his owner to tap his foot when the right answer came up. Even his owner did not believe that this was happening. So poor old Hans was de-claimed as stupid after all, and his case was held up for ever after as an example of how not to design an experiment.

But the de-bunkers threw the baby out with the bath water. Apart from the obvious question: 'What human could have done these tests without any previous tuition in arithmetic?', there was the matter that Clever Hans could give the right answers and fool his owners, a panel of experts and thousands of the public. He got there, but by a different route too subtle for mere humans to detect. So, as humans, we beat our chests about how intelligent we are, and how stupid the horse is, but conveniently sweep under the carpet how unobservant we are and how observant and subtle the horse is. It is a different kind of intelligence. Some call it emotional intelligence, or empathy.

What if the experiment had been re-designed so that, instead of doing arithmetic, Clever Hans and a test human had both been asked to predict a playing card being held by Hans' owner? Hans would have picked up on the subliminal signals produced by his owner whereas the human would have floundered. The horse would have won hands down.

When you see what a 'horse whisperer' like Monty Roberts can do, you start to realise that, if we really are as intelligent as we like to think we are, we would adjust ourselves to the attributes of the study animal, not expect the animal to adjust to us. When I am out hawking on a horse, the last thing on my mind is the horse. We go together as one. The cues I give to the horse are mostly invisible even to my conscious brain. When I think of going right, we go right, just as if I was on foot. Even without being able to see me, he is picking up on tiny changes of motion from me on his back. Bear in mind that even without mental steering going on, there is a lot of normal movement between horse and rider. The horse can pick out, through a saddle on its back, the slight changes that give it instructions, out of a white noise of other movements. Similarly, I might give instructions to him via the reins and the bit in his mouth. But often I don't bother, I might be using my hands for something else. Horses are brilliant; I could never manage to do this.

Buckskin and I made our shared centenary last year. Verity Johnson

'Empathy' and 'sympathy' are often used inter-changeably, but they are different. Empathy is the ability to assess the feelings or thoughts of another individual. That's as far as empathy itself goes, it's mind reading. If the individual is distressed, the empathetic person may feel sympathy ie shared feelings, feeling the same, matching moods. 'I feel your pain', but this is beyond empathy itself. Sympathy and compassion tend to be used in reference to misfortune or sadness of some kind. But sympathy can also be about sharing the good stuff. When you laugh, I feel like laughing. This is emotional contagion which can be very powerful, especially in crowds.

Carl Safina equates empathy to mood-matching but I think of it as 'mind-reading', possibly leading on to divining intentions. To detect the signals another person is giving out is done through normal sensory channels, such as sight, hearing, touch and smell. Humans tend to use sight and hearing but other species are stronger with other senses. These sensory cues may be very small and, as animal trainers, one of the first things one does after training a response is to diminish the cues so that they become virtually imperceptible to other observers. Humans are easily hood-winked, not least because many rely heavily on verbal language and overlook body language. Poker, a game of predation, pits empathy against a poker face. The real experts in empathy in my own experience are dogs and horses, both social species, one a predator and one a prey.

Although a lot has been written about empathy in the context of social cohesion, empathy is also vital in predation, both for the predator and the prey. Both must divine the intentions of each other, while at the same time concealing their own intentions. While sympathy tends to be applied mainly between 'persons' in a shared moral community, predators need empathy to connect with their prey which are from completely different species and communities.

Most farm children of my generation knew the trick of catching a rabbit or hare in the open. First you spot your hare out in the field, a little distance from cover. From then on, you never look at it directly, only from the corner of your eye. You wander in a direct line out into the field at a tangent to the hare, maybe looking into the distance, but definitely not looking at the ground as if you were searching, nor deviating from your line. The hare or rabbit will press itself down. Presumably it is hoping you have not seen it. If you were to walk directly towards the hare it would realise that you are on a collision course and that its discovery would be inevitable. It would get more and more uncomfortable until a point is reached when its nerve breaks and it dashes away while you are still too far away to chase it. So instead, you walk past the hare at a tangent, looking unconcerned. You keep walking at a tangent so that you are gradually spiralling in on the hare. Now the hare is committed to clamping tight. You never give it an escape point or direction. Soon you are just a metre away – still not looking at it – and suddenly you jump on it and grab it.

This spiral mind game approach has probably been used by humans since ancestral times. Frederick II (1250, p288) described its use in hawking cranes but it is the sort of hunting lore that is passed down during practical hunting rather than in texts. Another is the 'stickle' or human fence. Probably derived from the Swedish staket or stängsel, it was used by otter hunters and we use a form of it in crow hawking. You line up like the spines on a stickleback to stop the prey getting through. Footballers use it at penalties.

When working with predators all the time, and with their prey, this empathy business is stock in trade. Predator mobbing by small birds and mammals is all about blowing the mind-reading game out of the water. When we watch our falcons chasing the crows it is as much a mind game as it is a physical thing. Both are constantly evaluating the wind, the landscape, the available cover, one another's strengths and abilities, and then trying to predict the intentions of each other, constantly re-calibrating decisions.

I remember a flight on Dartmoor, years ago. A pair of crows were feeding in the open 600 metres away. I unhooded my experienced New Zealand Falcon. She looked at the crows for a moment or two. She knew that if she flew straight at them (a Direct Flying Attack), they would immediately take wing and, with such a long start, would outfly her. So she left my fist at 90° to the crows, and steadily climbed away. She gave no indication that she was attacking the crows and my three companions took their eyes off her and started chatting. Soon she was at about 120 metres high, a position of dominance. The crows stopped feeding and watched her uneasily. Then, lazily, she drifted over towards the crows until she had them within her 'killing cone', an area below her in which she could stoop. Now the crows hunched their shoulders and squinted up at her. They realised that there was nothing they could do other than hope that my falcon, being a falcon, would not attack prey on the ground. But New Zealand Falcons are not typical; they will hunt in forests as well as the open, it's in their ethotype. Once she was directly above them she 'canceleered' – the deadly spiral stoop. With the spiral there was no direction for the crows to try to escape. Down she came and took one on the ground, where it stood. A masterful battle of minds and an example of energy-saving predation. I couldn't have planned it better myself.

The template for this type of deception flight is ethotypic – I had a Changeable Hawk-Eagle (*Nizaetus cirrhatus*) who used it to catch hares this way, but the hawk-eagles are only very distant relatives to the falcons and thus the template must be convergent. From what I have seen in naïve young raptors, they start with Direct Flying Attacks, only to find that the prey flees. So they become aware of the effect they are having on the prey, in other words, they develop self-awareness. Only once they have become self-aware do they try deception flights. Then it is a question of: 'If I do this, you'll do that. So I will pretend to do this, so you will think that's what I'm going to do, and do that, then I will be in an attack position.' To an ethologist this is quite a sophisticated interaction of minds; perhaps a form of Machiavellian intelligence.

Predation is probably more significant as a selection pressure than social cohesion. An awkward social moment is one thing, but a mis-judged predation moment can be terminal.

For us humans, in developing artificial intelligence which can supplement or even exceed our own individual intelligence, we can make more and more powerful computers able to handle big data. What we have not yet done is to create artificial consciousness, because of course intelligence and consciousness are two completely different entities. Clever Hans was initially postulated to be intelligent, in answering various questions. But he didn't have that kind of intelligence. Instead, he succeeded by using his emotional intelligence, which is an advanced form of consciousness. There are many, many examples of emotional intelligence and empathy in non-human animals; many probably outstrip humans in this regard. While appreciating this, we should at the same time be a little bit cautious, in that the understanding of time in non-human animals is more limited than ours. In many cases their memories seem to be on a par with ours, but their comprehension of the future is more limited, and this can affect their empathetic responses.

Emotional intelligence and empathy are also important at the group level. An individual in a social group can assess hierarchies and relationships by observation, without needing to test each one. This is standard in social species, including our own.

2.9 Linguistics

Many claim that linguistics has been the making of humans, and is the driver for 'civilisation'. They are probably right. Some, such as Michael Dummett, even went so far as to claim that human thought is impossible without language. But thinking in words is just a tiny part of our thinking, even if you define 'thinking' as conscious mental processes and ignore all the unconscious ones. I'm sure that if I had thrown a bowl of soup at Dummett's head, he would have dodged as quickly as he could, long before he had verbalised the thought of action. His ethotype would have stepped in before his intellect.

When I am in countries such as Manchuria or deep Arabia, where nobody speaks English and I cannot read the writing, non-verbal language is important, and I have hawked pheasants all day with falconers in Yunnan quite happily and perfectly co-ordinated, without using language.

In Mongolia I can still converse with my horse. Gombobaatar.

Nowadays about 85% of people live in cities, which are virtually single-species environments, human monocultures. Few people have intimate contact with other species, animals or plants. Ethics Committees make it harder and harder to undertake Koko the gorilla-type linguistic experiments. Few people train animals or are trained by animals and the level of other-species awareness in graduates now is desperately low.

Language has two main uses: communicating between two individuals in real time (speech, a form of meme) and in delayed time (writing, a form of treme). In the electronic age we can record speech and film and play it later so that it serves as writing. Crude language is probably quite old, but writing and digital is spanking new in evolutionary terms and has no presence in our ethotype. It will be interesting to see if the Baldwin Effect starts to favour some evolutionary advantages for digitally specialised societies, or whether the rapidly growing dependency on digital support systems peaks and then backfires. Languages, whether oral or digital, are one of the greatest barriers separating social groups. Voice recognition and translation software are improving rapidly, although they are still unreliable. If we could reach the point where one could hold a fluent telephone conversation between different language speakers, this would be a great step forward towards world peace and harmony.

With limited verbal or written communication, non-human animals have little opportunity to pass on cultural knowledge to each other or inter-generationally. Of course there are plenty of examples of this happening, of groups developing habits that are passed on, and of the use of tools and so on, but this is handicapped by limited communication.

When you are on your own you don't need language because you have nobody to communicate with. You can get along very well with non-verbal thinking; it is quicker and you can travel light, especially in fast moving action situations. Very little of our thinking is conscious anyway. Most of our thought processes do not bubble up into our consciousness and most of our body language is non-conscious.

While instinct provides an adequate template for living for short-lived species, increasing intelligence allows a species to adapt and diversify in a short time frame, much more rapidly than genetic mutations allow. But whereas some genetic adaptations, such as a differently shaped beak, allow for a quite specialised change in lifestyle, increased intelligence can be used for many things that are not to do with its original 'objective'. In other words it opens the door to adaptations not directly in line with the Darwinian evolutionary process.

We get philosophers pondering on the meaning of art for example, and people trying to figure out how this fits into the evolutionary template. What selective advantage does it confer to the species, they ask? But because intelligence is a multi-functional tool many aspects of its use are outside the constraints of evolutionary pressures, and art is one of them. Take a very simple analogy: a pencil evolved through an iterative process as an implement for making graphite marks on a surface, usually for drawing or writing. Having evolved this item, it turns out that pencils can be used for other things outside this original design objective. For example, a nice sharp pencil could be just the tool for stabbing another kid in the eye. In evolutionary biology this kind of consequential secondary use is called a 'spandrel'. Moving onto a more complex example, think of the internet. Designed by an iterative process with certain functions in mind, it took only a few years for people to start using this tool for all sorts of other functions, many of them nefarious. As an omnivore, curiosity is one of our human ethotypic traits. Combine that as a driver, with a general purpose intelligence, and there are all sorts of outcomes far beyond the genetically controlled processes, and far faster moving, leading to exponential changes. This is where humans are now at. Art and music are very recent in our evolutionary history, but they are peanuts compared to the digital age that we have now entered. Daubing pigments onto canvas is giving way to the moving image and to digitally generated sci-fi technologies such as Virtual Reality. Children brought up in the digital era have little patience with the old technologies. Never mind Lamarck, the Baldwin Effect is sending us on a helter-skelter path which is bound to end in tears.

Before I go on to the next section, I want to flag up how important a tool linguistics is in human learning and culture. Before we had proper languages we could not discuss the nuances of learned morality and ethics. Language has enabled them to become much more sophisticated. At the same time, over-reliance on language has diminished our awareness of non-verbal communication.

Species without language are more reliant on ethotypic morality than humans. Reciprocity (keeping tabs on who owes who a favour) has an ethotypic root but a learned application. Position in a social hierarchy also has an ethotypic root but a learned application, as do many aspects of moral behaviour such as territoriality and family life. Do not fall into the trap of thinking that without language there can be no morality.

Similarly we need to be very careful about how behaviour operates through different sensory systems. Christopher Boehm in *Moral Origins*, for example: *"When a territorial Norway rat instinctively attacks a non-group member, this rat is programmed to react aggressively to any member of the same species that does not carry the odour of its own social community. It's that simple. Even though Chimpanzees also attack their neighbours on contact, they have far more 'sophisticated' means of identifying them psychologically, because they know where their territories are, and they know by sight that their neighbours are strangers. What we have here is merely a case of analogy: a pair of similar-seeming behaviors, both making for strong group territoriality, are based on very different underlying mechanisms and hence on disparate genes. This is a matter of convergent evolution."* I don't see that these two examples are based on different underlying mechanisms, or that one is more sophisticated than another. Territorial behaviour is a core ethotypic behaviour across a very wide range of species. Methods of detecting intruders, whether by sight, smell or sound are incidental to the basic behaviour. Both the rat and the chimpanzee, and also us humans, are subject to ethotypic programming for territoriality. Also bear in mind that species which do not defend territorial areas still have their own personal territory or space. I'm making this point quite firmly because, while human behaviour is indeed more 'sophisticated' than that of most other species, there are no essential *'very different underlying mechanisms'*. We all of us share the same roots of our behaviour and the differences are ones of degree only. This point is core to everything I am writing about in this book and to the behaviours I have experienced in my lifetime. There are no doubt examples of convergence to be found in the phylogeny of ethotypes, but territoriality goes back into our deep vertebrate ancestry or beyond.

The major edifice of morality is ethotypic; learned morality is just the icing on the cake, albeit a very thick icing, despite the amount of time we humans spend agonising over this aspect of it. Morality needs neither language nor religion, all of the core of it is native, and that is its major handicap. If morality was purely learned, intellectual, we might not be in the evolutionary trap that we now find ourselves in.

2.10 Learning and culture

Vertebrates, including humans, learn through several routes. Perhaps the commonest is through *imitation*, copying what others do. Building on this, they may use *trial and error*, which becomes a form of *experiential learning*. This may entail various types of reinforcement or habituation. They may be lucky enough to have a *teacher* or mentor, maybe a parent who provides short cuts and saves the learner from having to go down a lot of blind alleys. And more intelligent creatures are capable of assessing a situation and coming up with a solution using insight. This solution may then become established as a meme and spread throughout the whole group. The varying abilities to learn are ethotypic but the learning process itself is not. Learning may also entail physical skills; you cannot learn to ride a horse without getting on one.

Music and singing are learned behaviours. Many people are tone deaf, and many cannot hold a rhythm or dance properly in time. Practice may help, but even so, these people are just not genetically prepared for it. Despite modern digital homogenisation, different cultures still have their own musical styles. To another culture, some of these styles may seem monotonous, tedious, jarring or even distinctly unpleasant. We all have our likes and dislikes and there is no universal truth in music. Because culture is learned, this opens the door for rapid change, otherwise known as fashion. Fashions in music and clothes are constantly changing, and as digital communication brings the world into more rapid contact, so fashions change even more rapidly. While this can be a boon to producers and marketers, it increases the stress and costs to those attempting to follow trends.

2.11 Emotions, Personhood and Sentience

We have been stupidly warned not to project human emotions onto other animals, the implication being that other species do not have the same emotions as us. For sure animals vary immensely, from primitive chordates, to vertebrates, and also invertebrates such as octopuses, but all have varying degrees of sentience and consciousness. Their social world, their life cycles, intelligence and so on differ from humans, often in ways we struggle to decipher and imagine. They interact with one another and with their environment, both external and their own internal environment of hormones and drives. They express various emotions in so doing, and most of these have direct parallels with our own. If you do not have much direct contact with animals, try looking at some of the examples portrayed by Marc Bekoff or Carl Safina and similar writers.

We could make up some specialist terms for emotions in non-humans, but then few people would understand them. So we tend to use our own words, such as angry, jealous, greedy or bad-tempered. There is nothing wrong with this, in fact it is probably pretty accurate. Of course our understanding has been filtered through our non-verbal observation, which has its limitations, but we are constantly finding ways to probe through this. The big danger is not so much in being anthropomorphic but in the converse, mechanistic. Our own emotions and instincts, and interactions, are nothing special; they are just extensions of our evolutionary inheritance that we share with other vertebrates. It's not that other animals are like us, it's us who are like them. Emotions such as guilt, shame, anger, possessiveness, dutifulness, territoriality and so on are all manifestations of our underlying instincts derived from our ethotypes. And behaviours, just like physical traits, are also capable of convergent evolution as well as divergent or progressive evolution. The defence of territory by an octopus may have a very different genetic route, but the end result looks very similar to vertebrate behaviour. Our human emotions have the same source as emotions in other species, and this primary source is our instincts. Emotions or feelings are the 'heart' that Blaise Pascal was writing about. The ultimate well-spring of emotions is the ethotype, bubbling up through a mixture of hormones to sway the intellect. Beyond overt emotions is intuition, listening to our feelings to help us make decisions.

How do we know when we are acting instinctively? What is the mechanism by which an instinct lets itself be known and filters up to our consciousness, or even makes us act without conscious thought, by short circuiting that longer route? Instincts make us 'feel' things, they drive us, they urge us. It comes from 'deep down'. It may be a straight head thing, thoughts that come into our minds, or hormones may be involved too. We are not determinist machines; our behaviour has some degree of predictability ("He's not going to like it if you say that…") but it is not stereotyped; there is individual variation that arises from our ethotypes, imprinting and learning through life. These interplay and create variation.

These instincts that give us these feelings and urges are powerful things. We really want to satisfy them and do what they are telling us to do. If we satisfy them it makes us happy, the drug of requitement; that is the premise that Utilitarianism is based on. But what if we can't? What if we are frustrated? Maybe we can manage to stifle it, to internalise it. That can work. But there comes a point when if you bottle things up too much, it will come out one way or another, perhaps in mental breakdown, or in stress-induced illness. Or it can explode in verbal or physical violence. A lot of domestic violence stems from this, a conflict of emotions within and between individuals. Therapists nowadays make a business from listening to the out-pourings of these emotions, acting as safety conduits and helping to seek resolution to these conflicts.

Instincts are very powerful motivators indeed and we frustrate them at our peril. We can do our best to understand them, but we cannot always just rationalise them away, like using a Photoshop eraser key. And many of them arise from our hunter-forager past and are no longer appropriate to modern urban living.

Animals too, especially social species, display emotions, even quite complex ones such as shame, embarrassment and regret. I remember one occasion when my dog Smokey got very excited when he saw I was going out. In between bouncing in front of me, he turned and charged for the door, which he must have thought was open. But it was closed, and he ran straight into it. He wasn't hurt, but he was very embarrassed and I struggled not to laugh at him. Animals hate being laughed at or ridiculed; they know what you are doing. Yet many humans enjoy laughing at animals, or dressing them up in silly clothes and so on. This is deeply insensitive.

You can't argue with emotions; they're real and they are irrational. We are influenced by our emotions, even totally steered by them, and then we tend to try to rationalise and justify what we have already subconsciously emotionally decided. We convince even ourselves that we are acting rationally, but our human intellectual veneer is often perilously thin. Jonathan Haidt has documented some of this in *The Righteous Mind*. Ethotype trumps culture.

2.12 Fear, or wildness

Love looks forwards, hate looks backwards, fear has eyes all over its head.

On islands where humans have only recently arrived, other species are more trusting. Fear of humans does not feature highly in their ethotype. What we know as 'wildness' has evolved as a survival strategy in the face of human predation. It is a reflection of our own species, not of theirs.

Fear has genetic, imprinted and learned roots. In young falcons it develops about the same time as the second down coat. This is when the chick has sufficient visual acuity to look around, and it can start to identify what is a harmless cloud and what is a potential predator. It may make these distinctions unaided, but equally it can be told them by its parents. If the parent makes alarm calls, the young not only react instinctively, perhaps by crouching, but also they learn and at this age the learning imprints on the brain.

The part of the brain responsible for the fear response is the amygdala, a very primitive part of the brain that is able to short cut the conscious part of the brain and produce a rapid response from the adrenal glands, preparing for fight or flight. I'm not sure whether this early 'programming' of the amygdala is a form of imprinting or not. At any event it takes place during a specific growth phase and is irreversible except by significant habituation techniques. In Elizabethan times falconers were admonished not to fly their wild-taken goshawks until they had roused their feathers three times. Every day the taming habituation process has to be gone through all over again because even overnight, wildness sets back in.

By the same token, if we take a mother falcon who is herself imprinted on humans and is tame, and approach her and her chicks, she will make an approving reaction that is noted by the chicks. The human is then entered under the mental category 'not to be feared'. Thus the youngsters grow up with little fear of humans, although they could still be fearful of something else, like dogs or tractors. Somehow there is a mechanism so that the amygdala produces the rapid fear response, but only does so for certain stimuli, and these stimuli can be varied according to the exposure and signals relating to it in early life.

Other fears or phobias, such as the fear of spiders or snakes, appear as part of the instinctive repertoire of a percentage of humans, but not all, and don't seem to have any connection to early exposure. Perhaps they have genes all of their own, and perhaps those fears are targeted at primeval threats that had survival significance for our ancestors, even if they are not really relevant to us in a modern world. Joel Berger has studied the diminution of the fear response in prey species in the absence of their natural predators and this research parallels what we have found with our falcons: that imprinting and learning can overcome ethotypic fear responses, but equally, are reversible in one generation because the ethotype remains unchanged.

In precocial species such as sheep, the fear response develops over a few days after the initial parental imprinting. Hand-reared sheep ('molly' lambs or 'cade' lambs), brought up on the bottle, are exposed to humans and dogs etc during this sensitive period and thus have little fear of them. If you introduce a molly lamb into a flock of sheep, it may 'make friends' with the others, but will always identify itself with humans and come running up to the gate when one appears. Trying to work a flock of sheep with a dog is hopeless if there is a molly lamb in the flock. The molly lamb has no fear of the dog (they used to try to suckle our old Huntaway dog's penis, which made him most embarrassed!). Instead, you can call the molly lamb with a bucket of food, and when it follows, the rest of the flock will follow.

In humans, fear also has genetic, imprinted and learned roots. Some people are naturally (genetically) shy, some are shy through imprinting. Having been raised in the country, I am uncomfortable in cities, and having broken a number of bones, I have learned to be less reckless out riding horses than I used to be.

There is another type of fear learning – trauma learning – that emulates imprinted learning, it is fast, and is equally hard to alter and is not always rational. It can take place at any stage in life in vertebrates and is not to do with natal imprinting.

Fear is nothing to be afraid of. Lots of people who lead dull lives pay money to get frightened by watching violent films. People who have to wear all the health and safety gear at work fling it all off to do adventure sports for fun. A life without fear would be dull indeed and it is something which is part of every vertebrate's behavioural repertoire.

So much for 'wildness' at the individual or species level. Animals have minds, they are conscious, and that means that they can be fearful in respect to certain things. Some people interpret wildness as 'self-willed', doing your own thing. This way of looking at it enables it to be applied to non-sentient things such as habitats and landscapes and even as a management tool: 're-wilding'. Self-willed still implies the potential presence of humans who might influence a landscape.

2.13 Addictive behaviour

Mental addiction is natural and stems from our hunter-forager past. All predators fail most of the time. If they fail and give up, they die. So they try again, and again, until eventually they succeed. Our ethotype is programmed for hunting failure. We all come from long lines of successful hunters who have had to overcome failure on a daily basis in order to succeed. In fact the most powerful rewards system is not a reward every time, but at a lower frequency, maybe every fifth or seventh time. When we are reinforcing behaviour in training our falcons, we reward every fifth time or so, but not on a regular basis, on a random basis. Sometimes we reward at the first attempt, then maybe the tenth, then maybe the third. This elicits the strongest response. It is a variable ratio reward system. Slot machines in gambling arcades use similar reward frequencies for maximum addiction. If you reward every single time, the addiction is weaker. People use coffee machines but they don't get addicted to the machines because the reward is guaranteed.

There was a fisherman who died and went to Heaven. There was a superb trout river there and, lying on the bank, a beautiful fishing rod and a box of flies. He tried casting on a pool and the very first cast he caught a lovely shimmering trout. He cast again and in moments he'd landed another fish on the bank. He cast a third time and immediately a trout rose and took the fly. Then he started to understand. He'd been sent to Hell! Things hoped for have a higher value than things assured.

The uncertainty that had made fishing a challenge for him had been taken away. The pleasure was destroyed. Fishermen struggle with this balance. They buy all the latest gizmos, the carbon rod, the latest floating line, and yet they eschew easy methods such as the worm or spinner and confine themselves to fly-fishing. This makes it harder, so there is more of a challenge, a balance between man and fish. This is what recreational fishing is all about, it is not simply a matter of catching fish. If he had wanted to do that, maybe for research purposes, he could have electro-fished and stunned the lot. This balance is how recreational hunting works and it taps straight into our natural psyche as predators. Too easy or too hard, and it doesn't work.

The more desperate we are, the longer the odds we are prepared to take. We invest more effort for less reward. So lotteries target poorer sectors of society, creating a virtual voluntary tax for the poor who have no other hope of ever making big money. A rich person doesn't need to gamble on the lottery, she can invest in something with a smaller reward, but guaranteed. Even casinos give better odds. But players can't or don't want to understand the statistical odds against them. They live in hope of the lucky strike. Are lotteries for poor people really a 'good' thing, morally? Clearly the players think so, or they wouldn't want to play. But that is their ethotypic hunter addiction talking. For myself, should I accept a grant of money from a Lottery Fund? Am I just exploiting others who clearly need the money more than I do?

I will look more closely at hunting and gender later on but, briefly, a 'hunt' consists of two parts: searching for an attack opportunity, and carrying out an attack. This can be a spectrum, some species or individuals tend more towards the searching, and some to the attacking. In birds of prey we see differences between 'searchers' and 'attackers'. Searchers, such as kites, vultures, harriers and owls tend to have low wing-loadings so that they can fly more slowly, to search better. Their attacks are simple and straightforward, on small or dead prey. Their hunting success is high and their sexual dimorphism is small – males and females are similar in size. Attacking raptors, such as peregrines and accipiters, have bigger sexual size differences, higher wing-loadings; they are faster flying and focus on the attacking phase of the hunt, with a lower success rate but a larger size of prey – a bigger reward.

We describe humans as 'hunter-foragers' because humans cover both ends of this spectrum on a gender basis. Women, as foragers, spend more time searching, and have a higher success rate on berries, nuts or shellfish, which do not try to escape. Foragers face a different challenge: how to collect the most berries quickly when they are scattered around an area? Can one detect a pattern anywhere? Is one place a better bet than another? Is it better to collect all the berries in one area before moving on, or to keep moving and just choose the areas with the biggest bunches? Will a competitor get the berries first?

Men are physically stronger and more athletic, they tend to actively hunt live animals capable of escape, and the hunt may be risky, with a low success rate but a good reward. In our modern societies all this may seem irrelevant, but our ethotype is still there, just expressed in new ways. Diaz records 73% of men in USA choose sports betting, compared to 40% of women. Men tend to be more sensation-seeking and risk-taking than women. Wong found that 2.9% of women were problem gamblers compared to 4.2% of men. About 85-90% of violent crime and robberies (a form of predation) are by men, and there are many gender differences in shopping behaviour (a form of foraging).

2.14 Understanding time and space

Time consists of the past, the present and the future. None of them really exist because the past has gone, the future hasn't happened yet and the present is only the moving interface between the two, like the tideline between land and sea. So you could say that time itself does not exist, it is merely a progression of events. And if those events don't exist then maybe time doesn't either. It's all very confusing!

But time is a useful concept which we can at some level understand and work with. Try doing a little exercise. Every ten minutes, while you are awake, for a whole week, jot down what period of time you were thinking about. Were you thinking about today's events? Or yesterday's? Or tomorrow's? You should have about 6 x 18 x 7 = 756 sampling points. OK, don't actually do it, but from your own experience of your thoughts, draw the following histogram. I've plotted it on a schematic log scale to try to get it all in, with the present day in the centre.

Most of our thoughts probably relate to the current day. Some thoughts relate to the week just gone, and some (probably slightly fewer) relate to the week ahead. Beyond this, the graph tails off dramatically. Very few thoughts relate to more than a month or so either side of the current day. We seldom think of events ten years or more in the past or in the future. There is a bias towards the past because there is more material to think of there, whereas the future is mainly so far uneventful. We have far more historians than futurians, and we have no memories of the future. The human lifetime is around 80 years or so. This is the timescale covered by at least 99% of our thoughts. Beyond fifty years either into the past or into the future, we struggle. The human brain has not evolved to cope with longer periods of time and in fact we find it almost impossible to imagine it. Go further, a hundred years, five hundred, five thousand, fifty million… These are just a blur, they are just numbers. The exercise is so tough that 40% of British adults

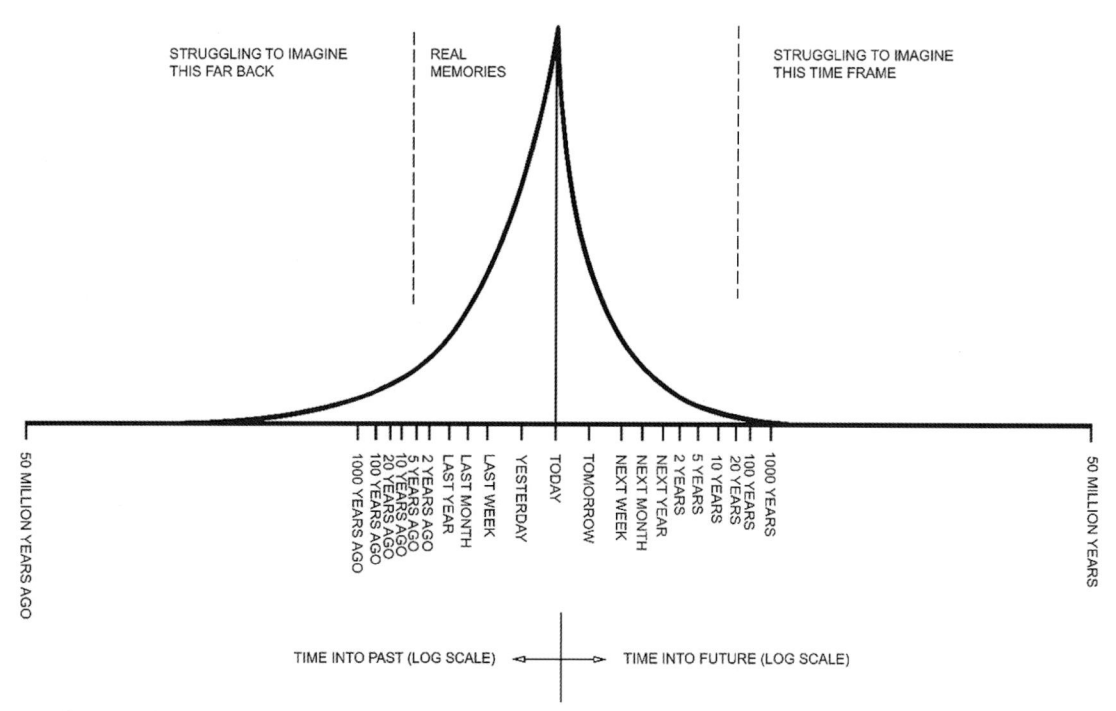

A schematic histogram of human thought periods.

fail to take out a pension or make provision for their old age. They simply cannot imagine it happening. They are too busy living in the here and now. While Piaget worked on cognitive development in children, his presumption was that there is some kind of end-point: the 'formal operational' adult thinker. How we preen ourselves! The reality is that even as adults our thinking is severely constrained by our ethotype, which only caters for life's immediate needs.

Now *pretend* you are an elephant. Similar life span. We know that elephants have excellent memories, they have proved this many times. So potentially they could also have a similar graph on the historic left-hand side. As to the future? Well, we know that matriarchs will lead the herd for long journeys to reach water. They not only remember but also, in setting off on a journey lasting days or weeks, presumably they have some ability to project into the future. We don't know if an elephant can or does think about events beyond its own life-time scale, but without language or the written word, it is unable to communicate in abstract detail with its compatriots or with past or future generations. So its capacity is probably quite limited.

Some people claim that animals have no imagination. But we know they can think. And if they are thinking about events not in the immediate present (bearing in mind that the present is an interface between the past and the future, rather than a set period) then clearly they must be imagining things. This ability to project into the future is a form of temporal intelligence and I will return to it later with the marshmallow test, and crime and punishment. So for the elephant we could expect that the histogram of thoughts would cluster much more around the central spike of the present day than the human graph, and for most animals, especially the short-lived ones, the graph would basically consist of a single narrow central spike, with no tails back far into the past or forward into the future.

So pretend you are a mouse. You have a fast metabolic rate and a lifespan of two years if you are lucky. You don't have much time to learn from experience. Your life is governed more by instincts that provide you with sufficient templates to deal with your short life experiences. We know you are a conscious being and that you can learn and think. But most likely the majority of your thoughts focus on the few minutes surrounding the present; a time spike.

Of course all this is conjecture. It would be hard to measure any of this scientifically.

It seems that many animals understand death. Some look after their dead for a while and appear to 'mourn' them. Elephants will return even years later to old bones. Can they understand this well enough to consider their own eventual mortality? Probably not. If you cannot imagine your own eventual demise, then the question need not worry you, and even less so the follow-on question – what happens to 'you' after you have died?

Within a time span of about a hundred years, we can conceive of a time before our birth and after our death. We ask ourselves – where did we come from, and where are we going? We cannot know the answers to these questions and we find them unsettling. It is a two-edged sword. Most animals do not have such a good appreciation of time as we do, they live very much 'in the moment'. A dog can be happy because he doesn't have a burden of worrying about tomorrow, he can enjoy today. For us, we have bills to pay, illnesses to face and many other unpleasant prospects lying ahead. Human appreciation of the future allows us to experience a new, exquisite kind of suffering: anticipation of pain to come, a suffering which may outclass the eventual painful experience itself. Religions provide a comfort blanket for us, and the best ones were invented earlier than our own conceivable time frame, thus providing them with an authority beyond our own experience. Our growing appreciation of Time and of the future was probably the original *raison d'être* of all religions.

For us humans, although we don't spend much time thinking about it on a daily basis, we can conceive of our own deaths, our own mortality. And it is not a very nice thought to contemplate. Once you start thinking about it, your thoughts invent all sorts of scenarios. Clearly the physical body decomposes, but is there some element of it that can somehow continue? And if so, where does it go, and for how long? Unconstrained by hard evidence, because people do not come back from the dead to tell us, the mind is free to fantasise all sorts of eventualities, and before long, religion has been dreamt up to fill the gaps. Maybe religion is a panacea for our sense of existential dread.

If, instead of projecting forward into the future, you project backwards into the past, the first question that springs to mind is 'where did I come from?' And of course, leading on from this – where did the world come from? The universe? We are thus caught in the joint conundrum of events before human experience, and after it. We have sufficient intelligence to recognise the two problems, but we are unable to resolve them with any degree of proof.

Cross checking now with Man's evolutionary development, we can conjecture that when humans developed sufficient brain power to expand their thoughts beyond the time frame of their own life spans, then they were able to contemplate their post-mortem future and invent possibilities. This might have been around the time of Australopithecus, 4-5 million years ago. We don't know what early beliefs our ancestors had, but by about 5000 years ago humans were showing respect for their dead and placing items in tombs that might indicate that people had the notion of some kind of after-life. They also started using pictograms in some cultures by then, and by 4,500 years ago the earliest forms of writing started to appear. The written language enabled stories and beliefs to be passed down from one generation to the next with more accuracy than oral history. Culture became more sophisticated. Gradually a variety of religious cultures developed in different human populations. The formalised religions that we see today were all invented within the last 2,500 years or so and vary from region to region. What you believe in depends on which population you were raised in; it is an accident of birth.

Predators and prey that rely on high speed activity may perceive events at 120 Hz or more. In other words, they live their lives in what we would think of as slow motion. Their brains must be capable of processing the information at this speed too. Thus, paradoxically, while we dismissively talk about 'bird brains', for this paradigm at least, the bird brain is far superior to the human brain. Even a fly's brain is able to outsmart ours in perception and reaction time.

Humans have a flicker fusion threshold of around 50-60 Hz which gives us limited ability to perceive movement and thus react. So we cannot form flocks like starlings and waders can, or shoals like some fishes. Relatively crude formation flying by seven Red Arrows is about our limit. Otherwise we crush together and smother like sheep.

We are trapped by our biology. We can only perceive events happening within a certain time frame, and our minds struggle to conceive events occurring outside our perception. Modern time lapse photography can give us an inkling of living in a different time frame, but not enough for us to visualise a longer view of the world. Conversely, slow-mo photography at maybe 2,400 fps allows us to see events that are 150 times faster than real life. When we film our falcons catching robotic prey, the slow-mo reveals the incredible positions the falcons get into, positions we did not know were possible.

The morphology, behaviour and sensory systems of different species have all evolved together to produce individuals fit for their ecological niches. The differences in visual acuity, hearing, scenting and to a lesser

Upside down and inside out!

extent taste and touch are well-documented. Temporal resolution, the ability to perceive and to understand events at different frequencies, are less well documented. But time itself has no such boundaries. It extends into infinitely small units and infinitely large ones. Our own meagre understanding of it is but a paltry subjective one. We set our baselines to suit our own comprehension. But other species live in different time frames. The swallows hawking insects in our farmyard have reactions that far exceed our poor human ones. Others, such as some plants, base their life cycles in centuries, stagnating gene flow to a low level. We struggle to imagine the vast evolutionary time frame that has shaped the world today.

For short-lived animals, an intellectual understanding of time is unnecessary, depending as it does on the ability to project from past experiences. But still they need to prepare for future hard times, for the onset of a winter that they have never experienced before. Here the ethotype steps in, powerful instincts urge squirrels and jays to cache food and build up hoards for the winter. We have a steep north-facing field of five acres or so and one day in spring I went out and marked all the young oak seedlings that had sprouted. I put in over 600 canes. Had the jay that had hidden the acorns died and been unable to make use of its own handiwork? It had literally, by its own death, created a new oak wood. So then I thought: "If a jay can do it, then I can too", and I collected bags of acorns and planted them out, tucking each one deep in the vegetation and marking it with a cane. But none came up that I could find, they all just disappeared, probably eaten by mice and voles. I felt a little inadequate somehow. Had the jay in reality planted thousands of acorns, for a 600 germination rate?

Our understanding of sound is equally limited. Human ears, and our brains that process the incoming signals, are geared to a certain sound range. Above and below this sound range we are unable to comprehend the sounds. If we record a human conversation and then speed it up, we first reach a point where we cannot understand the words, and then a point where it starts to sound like the twittering of bird song. Similarly, if we slow the human voice down, first we lose comprehension and then the notes go very extended, like whale song. So our own musical attainments are designed for the human ear and brain, that narrow band that we tune into. Other animals who see and hear at much faster rates than us process the signals much faster than we do. We are unable to decipher much of their visual and aural communication. They in turn do not always appreciate the noises we make. Our fluorescent lights that appear steady to us, must really annoy birds with their flickering, and our underwater sound pollution with boat engines must upset aquatic animals.

One thing that all human languages share in common is that they are all spoken at the same speed and as long as we are within our own bandwidth we can be pretty conceited about our abilities. But it doesn't take much to reveal our inadequacies. When we are designing robotic prey birds that can be caught by falcons, the human pilot can manage large crow-sized models pursued by the falcons. But if you down-scale to the size of a merlin chasing a pipit, the human eye cannot see and follow all the twists and turns and the reaction time of the human brain cannot keep up with the bird brain. Our arrogance rests on shallow foundations.

Similarly our understanding of space is equally limited. Most of our comprehension is restricted to distances between the width of a hair and the furthest the eye can see, Even with the aid of microscopes and telescopes, we struggle to comprehend distances outside this band width.

Some belief systems declare human dominion over other species. Others decry our exploitation of other species and exhort us to minimise it, perhaps with a vegetarian lifestyle. But in nature, of which we are a part, all species constantly try to exploit each other. There is tension in the forest, a silent struggle for light and nutrients. Animals have survived by being the best at exploiting others, not by being polite and saying 'after you'. Climax ecosystems are the result of ecological battles, not some mystical creation. And we humans living today are the genetic outcome of thousands of generations of successful hunters and foragers. That genetic make-up equipped us physically and behaviourally to survive and a few generations of urban industrial living cannot magically erase that genetic heritage, our ethotype. For better or for worse, we are what we are.

Paradoxically, our ancestry of hunting and foraging kept our own population low and our resource use sustainable. It has been our agrarian, then industrial, and now digital lifestyles that have allowed our population to creep up and outstrip our resources, putting us on a road to global ecological crisis. From the ecological point of view, there is no moral superiority in these new lifestyle changes.

2.15 Understanding 'persons'

We humans, who see the world largely through sight and sound, and in limited scales of time and space, tend to assume that other species perceive the world in the same way as we do. But each species experiences the world slightly differently. Dogs have good sight and hearing, but they have an even better sense of smell. They see you, they hear you, but more importantly, they <u>smell</u> you. They can smell if you are ill, cancer maybe, even when you don't know it yourself. Unless they are trained to signal it, they have no way to tell you, nor any particular need to do so, but they know. When I was younger and my senses less dulled with age, I could smell someone smoking a cigarette from 500 metres. I could probably not detect a grouse smell from more than five centimetres yet with reasonable air-scenting conditions a pointer can often draw onto a grouse from 150 metres. Silly humans: when we train dogs, we tend to do it on our own terms, using <u>our</u> sensory cues – visual signals and whistles or calls – not scent cues. We really have no idea how we could tackle it on dogs' terms.

When a horse 'sees' another horse, I think it takes in the whole horse. The senses of horses are similar to dogs'. They seem to place little relevance on the colour of the horse, more on form, movement, scent and sound. One can read a horse partly through its ears and Steve North tried making robotic ears to mimic the signals. But horses signal and perceive signals through their entire bodies. When I am shoeing a horse, I am concentrating on say, one back leg. I cannot see what is going on at the head end. The head end of the horse is usually also concentrating on what is going on at its back leg. I can feel, through the pressure of the leg on my knees how the horse is responding to me. I am very close to the horse in one way, but two metres away from its head. Where is the 'person'?

When Helen goes into the pen of her female New Zealand falcon 'Manuka', the falcon responds mainly to Helen's head. If Helen wears a hat, Manuka still recognises it as an object that is not 'Helen' and may remove it, but not be frightened of it. She still understands that Helen's head is there, just partly obscured. If Helen goes in wearing a different coat, as long as Manuka can see Helen's head, she recognises her as Helen. But if Helen changes her shoes, Manuka attacks them as if they are two new strange 'persons' entering the room. So if Helen presents herself 'normally', Manuka keys in on Helen's head and the rest of her body is accepted as part of the package. Maybe Manuka sees Helen's normal shoes as two

Manuka and part of Helen.

little harmless 'persons' who always hang around with Helen. Hands too can be perceived as separate entities. A falcon could be happy with Helen's head but be upset if her hand approaches.

So are falcons ethotypically programmed to experience 'persons' as about the same size as they are themselves, maybe 40 cms or so tall? And another part of Helen, of similar size, is construed as a separate 'person'? Does the horse perceive a 'person' as horse-size, rather than falcon size? Does the dog primarily perceive the human 'person' as a complex QR code of scents? We humans recognise our clothes as separate from our 'persons', but clothes are not a natural concept for most other species, so they often integrate them into their image of 'us'. While humans too, at one level, understand that clothes are separate from 'us', many use clothes for social signalling and this extends to more intimate changes to our appearance, from masks, to make-up, to plastic surgery. But if I put on a fox mask, the dogs get very upset and confused – is it Nick or is it a fox? Similarly, if I want to get close to a deer, the easiest way is just to ride close on a horse; the deer doesn't comprehend me as a person then, unless it winds me.

I can't find much on this in the scientific literature, but we need to understand it better if we are to understand how other species experience us, and each other, and thus social interactions, predatory interactions and stress. This lack of understanding leads us into assuming that other species share our experiences in the same way as we do. We say things like 'How would you like to be chased by a pack of hounds?' The fox may not 'like' to be chased, but equally, half an hour later, once the danger has passed, it will have resumed normal behaviour and will not be suffering PTSD, as a human might. Similarly, a human might be happy to be alone in a small flat all day, but a dog might not be. The dog may prefer a five mile run, not a short walk on a lead. Or a lion, shut up in a zoo and given all the food it wants, may be stressed at not being able to hunt because hunting is a different ethotypic drive to feeding. It paces up and down, fed but frustrated, and our human ethics dictate that the keeper must not give it live prey to assuage this hunting drive. But our human ethic also says it is unkind <u>not</u> to let our domestic cats out to hunt live prey. We have very mixed-up attitudes to other species, to predation and hunting, because we don't understand ourselves very well, and our understanding of other species and our comprehension of how they experience us, is rudimentary.

3 What is 'Hunting'?

3.1 Introduction

Hunting by humans is multi-faceted. And the definition can be far-ranging. Just think of all its varied strands: factory fishing, catch and release fishing, fly sprays, driven game shooting, neonicotinoids, mist-netting birds for research, trapping rats and mice, eradicating badgers with bovine Tb, Ivermectin used as cattle wormers killing insects in the pastures, cats, pricking seagull eggs, whaling, deer stalking, sheep dogs, treating woodworm, the list goes on and on. Few of us do not either hunt, or pay someone else to hunt. Don't imagine that a vegetarian diet does not involve killing animals or at very least, depriving them of their habitats that they need for their survival.

Hunting is a fascinating subject, and it is multi-disciplinary. Not many people are able to provide a balanced approach. Seldom in the various debates, national legislations, in the literature of all shades, or on the internet, have I seen well-informed, balanced material. Platitudes, plagiarism and heated emotions abound, most studies are too narrowly focussed to reveal the broad perspective, even among the hunters themselves. Douglas Higbee and David Bruzina in *Hunting and the Ivory Tower* and Nathan Kowalsky (Ed) *Hunting – Philosophy for Everyone: In search of the Wild Life* have made brave attempts to tackle hunting from the philosophical point of view but they suffer from lack of breadth and first-hand experience.

In its simplest form, hunting is a kind of predation. It involves two participants, like this:

Hunter ⟷ Hunted

Think of a cat and a mouse, or a falcon and a pigeon. Two minds are at work, both show various forms of behaviour. Empathising with one another, trying to predict what the other will do.

If the prey has no mind, no sentience, whatever that may mean exactly, then the relationship is one way. Our attempts to control infectious diseases of plants and animals or invertebrates such as house flies, clothes moths or woodworm, fall into this category. The relationship looks like this:

Hunter ⟶ Hunted

With us humans, hunting can become more complicated. We could have several humans hunting one animal:

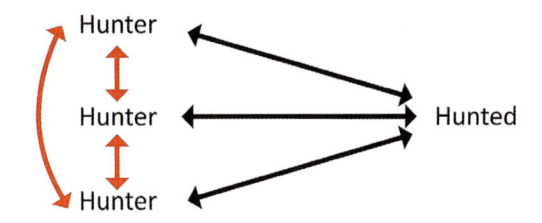

Hunter
⇅
Hunter ⟷ Hunted
⇅
Hunter

Or perhaps a human hunting several animals:

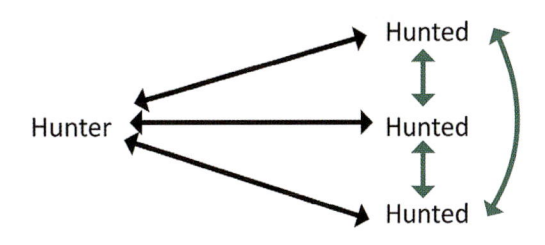

Hunted
⇅
Hunter ⟷ Hunted
⇅
Hunted

All those minds are interacting with one another (and of course I have left a lot of the interactions out).

What if the human hunter has a dog?:

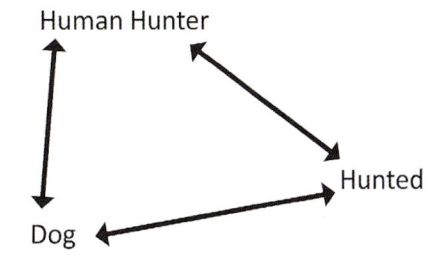

Human Hunter
↕   ↘
Dog ⟷   Hunted

Now we see one human mind and two non-human minds all interacting. A similar relationship occurs if the animal on the human team is a trained bird of prey. And we could increase the numbers on each side, more humans, more dogs, more prey.

If the hunter is on a horse with a pack of hounds, it gets complicated and fascinating, even when we leave out a lot of the arrows:

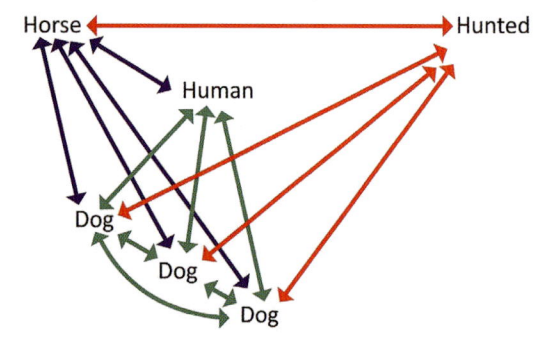

Horse ⟷ Hunted
Human
Dog
Dog
Dog

In this particular scenario, for the time being, the human hunter and the hunted may not be aware of each other. The hunted may hear the hounds, but the hounds may only be connected to the hunted via scent rather than sight. The horse and hounds will be aware of each other most of the time and the horse and the human are physically together. The hounds are constantly communicating with each other by sight, sound and scent.

What if the human uses a tool, such as a spear, arrow or gun? The prey has not evolved to escape from bullets, which travel faster than sound. It has no comprehension of what is happening. So the diagram, simplistically, looks something like this:

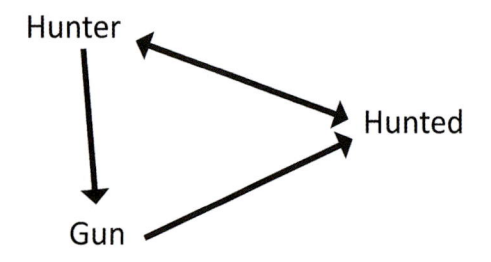

Hunter ⟷ Hunted
Gun

In this hunting/predation scenario, there is a constant interaction of minds, some fast interactions honed by millennia of evolution, but also, in the case of artificial aids, a lack of comprehension.

Take angling, fishing with a hook. The fisherman is the predator but the fish is not a prey. The fish in this scenario is a predator too. The bait on the hook is tricking the fish into a predatory sequence in which, unknown to the fish, the fish will end up as prey to the fisherman. So the fish is not acting as prey. It is not using escape strategies as it would towards its natural predators. The challenge to the fisherman is to create artificial prey in such a convincing fashion that the fish 'takes the bait'. The thought map looks something like this:

Fisherman ⟶ Bait ⟵ Fish

Throughout this procedure the fisherman is not in mental contact with the fish. He may not even know if there is one there at all, or what species it is, let alone what individual it is. One of his most powerful motivations is simple addiction. It is his failures that spur him on. This trend to addiction is a legacy of our hunting ethotype.

Nor is this sequence simple. First the hunter needs a motivation to hunt. Then he has to search for and find the prey. But not just find the prey, find a prey that is potentially catchable, in other words, an attack opportunity. Having found the attack opportunity the hunter may somehow have to get within attack range of the prey. He might need surprise, and he must gauge the ability of the prey. The prey in turn may have detected the hunter and gauge his ability, threat level and intentions. If the hunter attacks, there may be a chase, and a catch and he may need to subdue the prey before killing it, without sustaining injury himself.

These interactions go on millions of times per day and have done so for many millions of years. They are the very stuff of life and death. They have many permutations, and in the case of us humans, lots of cultural baggage. Let's unpick some of these interactions.

3.2 Hunting, hope and motivation

The fisherman who catches a fish at every cast finds he has gone to hell. Hope had been taken away from him. Equally if you say to a fisherman "You may fish in this lake as often as you like" but then say "Oh, by the way, there are no fish in it" you have equally destroyed that essential component, hope, anticipation. Outwardly he could go through the motions, haunting the bank side, casting and casting, but why bother? It is not the physical action of casting that brings him enjoyment, it is the driver of hope.

What if you took an intermediate position and told him that there was just one single fish in that lake? There is hope now, but the odds are long. Tell him it is just an average fish. If the situation was a commercial venture, maybe the cost of trying to catch the fish would not be worth the reward of catching it for food. Is it just a fish, equivalent to one you could easily buy in a supermarket? Or is it about a challenge, the achievement of catching the fish against all odds, an Old Man and the Sea scenario? What if the fish was the last remaining individual of an entire species; would he still want to catch it and destroy it? What if it was the biggest trophy fish ever recorded for its species; pride, status, prestige come into play. What if you told him that the fish was a massive Pike, a cannibal, a monster predator which made it futile to re-stock the lake with trout until it had been removed, a pest? Then the fisherman would have both a challenge and also feel pleased for removing a 'pest', a little bit of wildlife management.

What if you tell him, there are plenty of fish in the lake, but the moment he hooks one he must cut his line, quickly knot a hook onto it, hook it into his own lip (or swallow it) and 'play' the fish until he has either got it ashore, or it has pulled him into the water and drowned him. For many fishermen, a fish that 'fights' is an important part of the experience, despite the fish being sentient, and it being a one-sided contest.

For others, fishing provides intangible benefits. Perhaps an escape from the pressures of home, or a chance to connect with nature. Maybe a space in which the brain can unscramble itself; mental health benefits for young and old. Some enjoy the camaraderie of competition events. As in so many activities, especially in hunting, our real motives are obscured by a façade of more palpable ones. Many people never truly understand why they do things.

These are all different motives and scenarios, but with one common denominator: the presence of a fish. Take the fish out of the equation and there is no equation. Even the rumour of a fish is enough for hope to flourish. Thousands of people have searched for the legendary Loch Ness Monster. This is how the God illusion works.

Just as fishing requires the presence of a fish, so do other types of hunting require the presence of the prey, even when the primary motive is something other than killing it. To sit on the bank of an empty lake is as pointless as a football match with no goal posts.

It is very hard to explain the atavistic motivation of hunting to people who don't have the hunting 'gene' or who have never experienced the chase. The excitement of being on a horse, risking one's neck and following who knows whither, needs to be experienced to be understood. Don't look back! Devil take the hindmost! During the chase the pursuer – human, dog or hawk, is blind to all around him.

Trail hunting, which might to the uninitiated look like real hunting, is no substitute. Some (invoking the Westermark effect) liken it to kissing your sister. If you take out the unpredictability, the uncertainty, and tame the activity into channelled courses, with no prey, no target, you gut hunting of its very being. Would you go

We have fun rides for the Hunt in summer, but it is not the same as real hunting.

to watch a football match if you knew for certain, the outcome, the score? The whole point is the hope, the shattering of hope, the disappointments, the emotional roller coaster. Other aspects are just icing on the cake.

For me, to go hunting is to become wild again, to take my place as a participant in the drama that is Nature. I shudder at the thought of being tamed, of being beaten down by petty laws, artificiality and urban thought, the routine of domesticity, the very stuff of 'civilisation'. I want to be free again, if only for a few hours; to shrug off pretence and artifice and be me, the ancestral me.

This is the core of what hunting is about, not just for humans, but for other predators too.

Some anti-hunters struggle to understand the motives of hunters. Catherine Deering for example:

…it may never be known precisely why people hunt for pleasure, given the complexity of the subject. But it may be that a fox hunter has something deep in his or her psyche which is so troubling to them, so painful, so terrifying to confront, so abominable, that they seek to sublimate it in the total subjugation and destruction of a helpless and terrified creature. It may be, out in those beautiful fields, hills and coverts, in galloping after his need for power and control, the fox hunter is, fundamentally, hunting himself. https://www.actionagainstfoxhunting.org/the-hunted-animal-by-catherine-deering/ . Deering is totally off-target. The instinct to hunt is built into the human ethotype through all the successful generations of the evolution of our species, and those of other predator species. It is not some kind of mental illness or troubled psyche. But to misunderstand it so fundamentally must mean that she has never experienced it herself. She could as well equate love, romance and courtship with rape and pornography.

Fox-hunting is often portrayed as a class-riddled sport originated by Hugo Meynall jumping hedges at speed and popular in the home counties and southern England. Victorians would train out to their Hunting Seats around Melton Mowbray where their horses would be groomed and waiting for them for a Saturday Meet. This was all true and for Londoners, this was likely all they would see. But fox-hunting is not all about class and privilege in southern England, far from it. Surtees has Jorrocks say: *"Rot ye, sir! hangin's too good for ye! you should be condemned to hunt in Berwickshire the rest of your life!"* As you head out into the unfashionable provinces, into livestock country – Devon and Cornwall, Wales, the Black Country, the Lakes, Cumbria, Northumberland and the Scottish Borders – most of the packs are still farmers' packs, followed on horses, quad bikes, foot and SUVs by all classes and ages of people from the local communities. Many of these are 'registered' packs, subscribing to the British Hound Sports Association, but there are also Gun Packs, as well as harriers, beagles for hares, staghounds, mink hounds and then all manner of hunting dogs such as lurchers, whippets and terriers. Few of these can be accused of being privileged. When I first hunted with the Pembrokeshire in 1968, hacking out from the farm, we had sack cloths under our saddles and no hard hats. Gypsies and Travellers are also keen hunters, often too keen for some land-owners. This egalitarian side of fox-hunting does not reach academia, the written word, the urban gaze, or the Christmas cards. The fell packs, the farmers' packs, gun packs, trencher-fed packs and bobbery packs receive little attention, yet in the provinces they are the back-bone of hunting. Even when the woods are drawn with spaniels and pointers, there may be No 6 in the open barrel for woodcock, but BB in the choke barrel in case a fox emerges.

In *The Analysis of the Hunting Field* Surtees wrote: *'People hunt from various motives, some for love of the thing, some for show, some for fashion, some for health, some for appetites, some for coffee-housing, some to say they have hunted, some because others hunt.'*

What Surtees wrote in 1846 is equally true today. A few ride to hunt, but most hunt to ride. What nobody does is hunt to see foxes torn to shreds by hounds. Having hunted foxes sporadically for over five decades I can recall seeing foxes killed in the open within 100 metres of me on only three occasions. Often hounds will kill a fox in covert without it running far at all and few people, apart from the Huntsman, realise it has happened. From what I have seen, and from film footage, the fox is killed within 3-5 seconds of the first hound catching it. If seeing animals being killed is your thing I recommend some of the wildlife programmes such as *Planet Earth*. There you can watch seals being tossed by killer whales and water buffalo dragged down by crocs to your heart's content.

While different authors have defended fox-hunting variously as a tradition, a communal activity, a control of a pest, a reminiscence of English pastoral and so on, few seem to understand that it is possibly the only activity that unites people of all classes, ages and genders in a communal activity without pre-ordained boundaries and usually covering more than one private property. Since the Enclosures Acts, most of the farmed land has become essentially private, miniature fiefdoms of a few dozen to a few thousand acres, inaccessible to the public, or even to neighbours. The average family farm in England is 215 acres (87 ha) and in Wales 111 acres (45 ha). These are far too small to host a day's fox-hunting which may take an unplanned route of 10-30 miles (16-48 km). Just a single day's hunting in southern England may entail 'carding' or seeking permission, from 150 land-owners. The followers get to visit places they would never otherwise see and, just for the day, property boundaries seem to have dissolved. The whole landscape has temporarily reverted to a communal hunting area as it used to be hundreds of years ago. The mounted Field, foot and car followers all help each other with advice on the progress of the hunt, where the hounds are working, and how best to get to them. A ten year-old girl can go out on her pony, although exposed to the vicissitudes of cross-country riding, knowing that she could turn to any one of those followers who would immediately help her and her pony out of any difficulty. That is extraordinary in today's times.

The other aspect of fox-hunting which is seldom heralded but which is a primary motivation for most mounted followers is that it is the only organised, non-competitive off-road horse riding available. Public roads are now dangerous for horses because there are so many cars driven by people uneducated in the ways of animals. In 2022 in Britain, 68 horse were killed, 125 injured and 139 riders injured were in a total of 3,552 road accidents. Many bridleways too are now flooded by mountain bikers which scare or collide with the horses. Options for riders are very limited. I say this as someone who has just been notified that our kitchen, yard and adjacent fields will be declared a 60 feet wide Restricted Byeway, based on a paper road survey from 1840. Paths and bridleways used 200 years ago to link isolated farms are being being resuscitated for users being encouraged to come to the countryside.

Most horse riders now are female, and this is reflected in the hunting Field in which most followers are female, although the hunt staff, who manage the hounds – the Huntsman and Whippers-in – are predominantly male. These followers go out, not to see hounds catch a fox, but to enjoy riding in one another's company. It is a complaint of many a Field Master that the mounted followers often spend too much time talking and not paying attention to the hounds, which for them are just subsidiaries to the day's activities.

Some farmers are delighted to host a Meet as a social occasion. Some have to be cajoled into allowing the Hunt on their land, livestock farmers are sweetened by the Hunt collecting their fallen stock, others because the Hunt kills foxes and provides a call out service for problem foxes. Damage is reported to the Field Master who organises for it to be fixed or repaired, possibly providing a bottle of tipple to leave a good taste in the mouth.

My descriptions of hunting may seem prosaic. Others have taken a more theoretical approach. Kheel for example categorises hunters as *Happy*, hunting to fulfil a psychological need, (which I might describe as an ethotypic urge), *Holist*, hunting as part of an ecological/conservation process, and *Holy*, fulfilling a spiritual need. Her *Holy* category equates to Kellert's *Naturalistic*, an approach broadly followed by Scruton, a desire to participate in nature. These categories are mostly based on individuals. Some hunting is to do with rites of passage for young men and some of it is to do with competition and group approval. Coarse fishing competitions are very popular and the fish are returned at the end of the day. In driven bird shooting there is often a

Young Arthur has made himself a spear and has gone rat hunting with his mum and Gem, the one-eyed lurcher. (Gem did most of the work!) Hunting with dogs is not all about top hats and pink coats.

camaraderie, but also an element of 'fitting in', of group etiquette, of what clothes to wear, and of conspicuous consumption; all things which are of little importance to the solitary hunter. Many solitary hunters are on their own for that very reason, to escape from the human herd (which can be a constant reminder of the artificiality of modern life) and have a more one-to-one elemental experience of raw nature, to clear the mind of the fog of extraneous superficiality.

3.3 Types of hunting

Most animals hunt or forage for their food using only their own physical bodies. They may combine efforts by hunting in groups or symbiotically. There is a limit to what can be done using only our own bodies and we humans are armed only with our hands and our brains. But these enable us to make tools of ever-increasing degrees of sophistication, totally out-gunning the natural defences of our quarry. They even enable us to side-step the whole process of predation by farming plants and animals and hence commodifying them. By no longer hunting wild animals we have no need to allow them living space. Instead we can grow plants and, because it is not feasible to forage for wild plants on any scale, it entails farming plants in monocultures. Fields are dedicated to just one plant species. Plant monocultures require all animals to be excluded because they compete in some way for the resource. So we remove from them their supporting ecosystems, in other words we destroy nature. Instead of destroying sentient animals by acts of commission, we destroy them by acts of omission; we simply deny them anywhere to live. The only alternative for them then is compartmentalisation; they are tolerated if they can live on the fringes of habitats that humans currently don't need to exploit. These fringes shrink each year as human numbers increase. But we can kid ourselves, we haven't actually killed them; we just want palm nut oil more than orang utans, veganism rather than eating animals.

So the types of hunting we humans use depend on the tools and systems we employ. These are a spectrum from the natural or primitive to systemic, landscape scale, toxins. To talk about hunting as if it is one single activity is naive. It's not all about shooting elephants – have you today just used a chemical that 'kills 99% of all household germs' or sprayed the aphids on your roses?

Humans kill wild animals for four main reasons:

Food. Although there are still some subsistence hunting societies, most wild animals eaten for food are killed in the course of recreational hunting or management.

Management. Pest control and wildlife management is a major reason for killing wild animals, in all societies.

Recreation. Hunting as a sport is widespread and is the reason for most opposition to hunting.

Incidental. This is mainly when we prioritise something we want and don't care as much about animals that are killed incidentally. When my father was born in 1895 there were no cars, now there are 41.3 million on British roads causing millions of deaths. Hedgehogs have declined from 35 million fifty years ago to just one million now. We have about 12 million cats killing wildlife. Millions of animals are killed in the course of agriculture to produce food for humans or livestock, a lively source of debate for vegans and meat-eaters.

3.4 The demographics of human attitudes to wildlife

Let's look at the demographics of killing wildlife to see who does what:

97% of rifle certificates and 94% of shotgun certificates in England and Wales are held by men. (Govt statistics 2021)

Of 155 cat-owners on Cat-owners UK Facebook, 96% are female.

Of 76 commentors on Wildlife Rescue UK Facebook 87% are female.

Of 125 owners on Land Rover Series 1 Facebook 100% are male.

Of all the pilots falcon racing at Vowley in the first five years 100% were male.

Activities in which an animal is killed directly or indirectly by a person, such as shooting and fishing, tend to be done by men. There is an obvious historical precedent for this but other factors may also be at work. In organised driven shoots, the majority of the shooters are male but a high proportion of the people picking up using dogs, are female.

Indirect methods of hunting in which the prey is killed by another animal, such as by a dog, cat or falcon are followed by a wider spectrum of society including a higher ratio of women and a wider range of ages. This may indicate that killing the prey oneself is repulsive to the squeamish and that hunting with dogs and cat-keeping are recreations which are followed not for the killing, but because of other benefits.

Non-recreational killing, e.g. for population management or for food, tends to be done on the most cost-effective basis, usually by men. The suffering involved for example in poisoning, can be immense, but is kept out of the public eye and the public is prepared to justify it because plagues of rats and mice are intolerable. A colleague of mine was engaged to kill the pigeons inside one of Britain's famous cathedrals. He had to wait until 11 pm when all the public had gone. Other pest control operators have to use rifles to snipe the eggs of herring gulls nesting on roofs. The British public have a fine ability for being in denial about all aspects of these uncomfortable deaths.

Research killing is done by both men and women, usually with some training and following a code of ethics. These experiments are trending to reduce in number and severity, but no doubt cause suffering to the victims, whereas the derived benefits usually go to another species and other individuals, mainly human.

Looking at the demographics gives a clue as to what is going on. For example, for people hunting with hounds, many packs hunt on foot all or some of the time, and many riders undertake other riding activities such as point-to-pointing, racing, eventing and showing. The Value of Shooting Report 2024 reveals that many shooters participate in more than one discipline and that about the same numbers shoot targets as shoot live quarry.

	DISCIPLINE	PARTICIPANTS	%
Target Disciplines	Clay target	366,000	66%
	Air rifle and pistol	106,000	19%
	Small bore rifle	104,000	19%
	Full bore rifle	97,000	18%
	Other	90,000	16%
	Sub total	**763,000**	
Live Disciplines	Game shooting	293,000	53%
	Pest and predator control	255,000	46%
	Deer management/stalking	120,000	22%
	Wildfowling/inland duck and goose shooting	95,000	17%
	Sub total	**763,000**	
	Total	**553,000**	

Note: some participants are active in more than one discipline.

CAPTURE METHOD	APPROX UK ANNUAL VOLUME (1000s)	%
Cats	261,547	79.4
Poisons	24,697	7.5
Shotgun	24,697	7.5
Dead traps	12,447	3.78
Rifle	3,622	1.1
Gazehounds	593	0.18
Gassing	593	0.18
Snares	247	0.075
Live traps	49	0.015
Scenthounds	33	0.01
Terriers	16	0.005
Ferrets	10	0.003
Birds of Prey	7	0.002
Total	**328,468**	**99.75**

Percentage volumes of animals killed by some of the different methods. (Fox and Macdonald 1995).

3.5 A definition of terms

Now let's try and get some broad-brush figures on the situation. Although we cannot measure suffering or happiness, we can at least see where the main areas of concern are, and the orders of magnitude. I'm doing this exercise for the British situation because it is the region I know best, but similar analyses can be done for other countries and activities. The data are from a study I did in 1995, since when some of the poisons, and some types of hunting with hounds, have been banned. The figures are not exact, obviously, because these data are not collected by any central body, and apart from a very few studies, such as our study of wounding rates, most of these activities are not generally understood nor have they been studied. Some of the traps have been tested to comply with international humane trapping criteria, but some of those tests are either comparative, or the sample sizes are small. We consulted the main governmental, hunting, and wildlife management organisations with the data and came to a consensus on percentages and volumes, but as better data become available, they should be substituted. Let us look more closely at the ways humans catch or kill wild animals deliberately. We need first to define our terms.

Natural selectivity: Natural selectivity indicates that weak or infirm individuals are more likely to be caught than healthy strong ones. No selectivity indicates that prey animals are captured in about the same proportions as existing in the local wild population which may include 20-30% weak or sick individuals.

Legal selectivity: 100% selectivity indicates that only certain legally unprotected target species are captured (but not necessarily killed). 0% selectivity indicates that species are caught in about the same ratio as available in the locality. Bycatches of non-target fish species can exceed 5.7 bycatch fish for each targeted legal catch fish.

Human supervision of control method: Whether or not the activity is supervised by a human, or, in the case of traps, the time interval between checking.

Pre-capture pursuit interval: The length of time from the start of evasive action by the prey to its capture or escape. In the case of scenting hounds it is important to distinguish between the period in which the hounds are following the scent line, rather than the quarry, and the period when the hounds start to directly pursue the quarry by sight.

Catch-to-kill interval: The length of time between initial physical contact between the predator (or weapon) and prey, and the death of the prey. The time span shown indicates approximately 90% of the distribution curve but excludes prey which survive the attack.

Abandonment of maimed prey: Prey which have been significantly injured (i.e. more than losing a few feathers) and which are not killed by the predator. These animals may or may not survive.

Approximate annual volume: The figures given are for England, Wales and Scotland and, except for scenthounds, cats and birds of prey (for which supportive data exist) are very much estimates based on expert opinion, factual information at present being unavailable. The figures therefore indicate only the order of magnitude.

Gazehounds: Dogs such as greyhounds, salukis, lurchers and whippets which hunt by sight and kill in a sprint. They are usually used singly or in pairs, sometimes at night, catching hares and rabbits.

Scenting hounds: Dogs such as foxhounds, staghounds, harriers and beagles which hunt by scent, usually in a pack. Scenting hounds used to catch foxes, red deer, brown hares and mink. The deer were not normally killed by the hounds but brought to bay and shot by the huntsman. Many of the foxes ascribed to foxhounds were not killed above ground by hounds but were run to ground, located by terriers, and shot.

Terriers: Dogs used to find foxes underground (excluding their use above ground for rats, etc.) Once the fox is located, the terriermen dig down to it and shoot it.

Cats: *Felis catus*, the domestic cat. Used to control small mammals on farms and industrial sites, kept widely as pets with a major impact on small vertebrates near areas of housing.

Ferrets: A domestic form of the Polecat *Mustela putorius*. Normally used to bolt rabbits or rats into nets or to guns or hawks, but occasionally killing prey underground.

Birds of Prey: Raptors commonly of the genera *Falco*, *Accipiter*, *Buteo*, *Parabuteo* and *Aquila*.

Gassing: Government approved gases, such as aluminium phosphide used to kill mammals such as moles, in their tunnels.

Anticoagulant poisons: Government approved substances (e.g. 'Warfarin,' 'Klerat' [brodifacoum], 'Ratak' [difenacoum], 'Storm' [flocoumafen]) used to kill mammals such as rats, mice, squirrels and moles. Warfarin based baits have recently been discontinued in the UK.

Dead Traps: Government approved spring-traps, such as break-back mouse and rat traps, pliers-type mole traps and 'Fenn' type tunnel traps, intended to kill any creature triggering them.

Snares: Wire loop traps or humane cable restraints of government-approved specification and method of use, designed to hold the prey alive until released.

Glue traps: A card, board or twig covered in glue to catch anything that contacts it.

Live traps: Government approved traps, usually a wire cage, box, or pitfall, designed to capture animals alive and physically uninjured.

Bird ringing: The practice of catching birds, usually in mist nets, then releasing them alive. Of course, up until the point of release, the bird does not understand that it will survive the ordeal.

Shotgun: A smooth-bore gun firing many small pellets in a spread pattern, used to kill birds and medium-sized mammals, usually while moving.

Rifle: A rifled-barrel gun firing a single

Chapter 3 – WHAT IS 'HUNTING'?   63

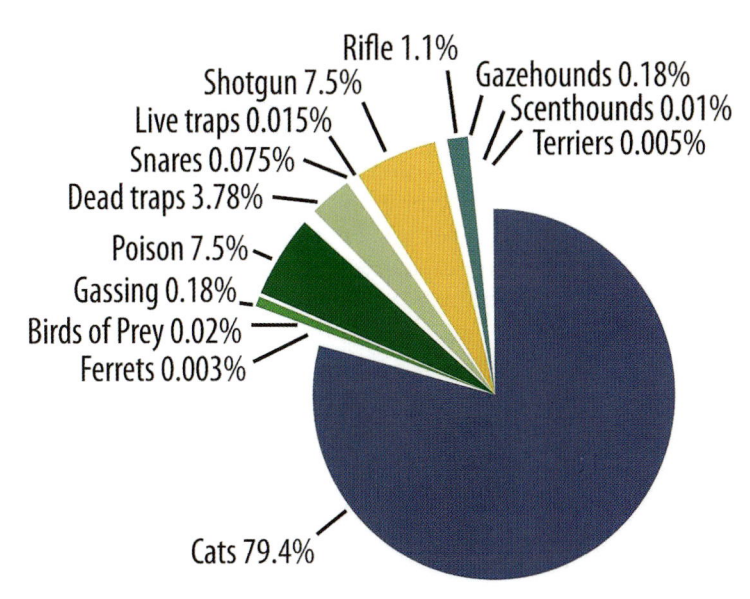

Percentage volumes of animals killed by the different methods prior to the Hunting with Dogs Act 2004. (Fox and Macdonald 1995).

Pie chart data:
- Rifle 1.1%
- Shotgun 7.5%
- Live traps 0.015%
- Snares 0.075%
- Dead traps 3.78%
- Poison 7.5%
- Gassing 0.18%
- Birds of Prey 0.02%
- Ferrets 0.003%
- Cats 79.4%
- Gazehounds 0.18%
- Scenthounds 0.01%
- Terriers 0.005%

bullet, used mainly to kill static, medium-sized to large mammals.

Angling: Fishing using hooks for fresh or salt-water fish.

Net-fishing: Fishing using nets for fresh or salt-water fish.

Game: a mammal, bird or fish usually hunted for sport and food.

3.6 Hunting as a continuum

Let's take it step by step. Every vertebrate hunts. You hunt. I hunt. Gorillas hunt. Sheep hunt. Even mice hunt. The only vertebrates which don't hunt are individuals, such as dependent young, who rely on others to provide food for them. Hunting is simply obtaining food. That sounds straightforward, but if we examine the statement more closely we find it is both complex and a continuum.

All vertebrates eat food. Each has a mouth and puts food in it. This is in contrast to some invertebrates, such as tunicates, or the shellfish, which stay put and filter water. But vertebrates have backbones, limbs and mouths. And one of the main functions of their limbs is to enable them to move around and put food into their mouths. Food seldom pops into their mouths of its own accord, so the vertebrates have to go and find it. And this first phase of hunting is the search. Every vertebrate, one way or another, has to search for its food.

If you watch a sheep, she doesn't just eat any grass, munching away across a field non-selectively like a lawn-mower. She is a forensic feeder; she picks and chooses. She prefers certain grasses and herbs over others. Some are more palatable than others. Some are more sour, bitter or tainted. Some contain chemicals that her body craves. So she wanders gently here and there, searching and rejecting. For herbivores without an attendant shepherd, such as wildebeest on the African savannas, the search may not be so simple. It may entail days of arduous trekking to find edible vegetation in a parched landscape. We call this foraging. Most then eat it on the spot, but some species may forage it and take it elsewhere to eat later and possibly share with others.

Plants tend to stay put, so for herbivores, once they have found their food, eating it is a relatively simple matter. I call them 'searchers' because for them the searching phase is their main element of the hunt. For plant-eaters reliant on farmed plants, monocultures of crops, there is also a bycatch of vertebrates and invertebrates killed or eliminated in order for the crop to flourish.

Carnivores also have to search for their food. If their food is relatively static, such as a plague of insects, it may just be a matter of eating them as easily as eating berries on a bush. They too are 'searchers'. But most prey are not so obliging. They may be cryptically coloured and hard to detect. Or they may notice the predator and move out of the way, becoming harder to catch. So although the hunter may have found the prey, it is a question then of assessing how good a chance it has of catching it. Thus its search extends not just to locating the prey, but to finding a feasible opportunity to catch it. All sorts of factors then come into play: the agility of the prey, the attack distance, the escape distance, and so on. Although guided by instinctive templates, the hunter will need experience to learn and evaluate these things, and it might die before succeeding.

Once it has found what it judges to be a feasible attack opportunity. The predator then launches an attack and, if it can succeed in around one out of five attempts, it may live long enough to breed.

Thus hunting is a continuum. It is not bimodal, a question of diet, of whether the hunter eats plants or whether it eats animals. Plenty of hunters eat both; they are omnivores. Many seed-eating birds switch to insect diets when rearing their young. We thus cannot say (as many do) that humans are hunters but gorillas are not. Gorillas emphasise the searching phase of the hunt, humans (and chimpanzees) both search and attack, and lions mainly attack. Vultures are carnivores which wait until their prey is already dead, so all they have to do is search for it, just like a herbivore. On the other hand the Wren (*Troglodytes troglodytes*) is more of a predator than the Golden Eagle (*Aquila chrysaetos*) because eagles supplement their live prey with scavenging carrion. Humans who forage the shore line for shellfish are searchers for meat. Although many herbivores can, to some extent, digest meat, most obligate carnivores cannot digest plants.

Therefore whether or not you are a 'hunter' is not so much about the type of food you eat, but about the way your food behaves and where it is distributed. And because you and your ancestors have hunted like this for many generations then selection pressures will have got to work on you and specialised your phenotype and your ethotype to make you more successful.

3.7 Humans as hunters

Hunting goes deep in the human psyche but we have never been obligate carnivores, we are omnivores, hunter-foragers. This means we are adapted to exploit a wide variety of food sources, depending on availability and season, from nuts and berries in the autumn, to shellfish and whatever can be gleaned along shore-lines, to carcasses killed by other predators, and to hunting meat for ourselves. To achieve this, our ethotype has created a species that is innately curious, with instincts to work together in teams, to persist in the face of failure, to divide foraging behaviour between the genders and ages, and with a high quotient of learned behaviour requiring a long developmental period and imitative cultural learning. Some of these diets have low calorific values and take a lot of time to forage. Digging up wild tubers and roots is slow work and the food is not very nutritious or appetising. Meat on the other hand is high in energy and we find it tasty, so we value it more than plant diets. Plant foods, such as nuts, can be stored and our ethotype includes a strong hoarding instinct.

Our ancestors have probably been omnivorous for at least eight million years, certainly beyond our common ancestor with our relatives, the chimpanzees, bonobos and gorillas. Gorillas have adapted to a herbivorous existence but the remaining bloodlines, including humans, are omnivores and have powerful instincts to search for, hunt and eat live prey.

In our pre-pastoral period, which lasted millions of years, we literally lived a hand to mouth existence and evolutionary pressure was severe. Having radiated from the more equitable climate of Africa, we could breed all the year round, but this strategy proved limiting in climates and latitudes with severe seasons.

From the age of about 15 to 30, females were either pregnant or nursing young children. This tied them to the home base and restricted their physical activity. They could make short foraging outings for nuts, berries or shellfish but not arduous or violent hunting trips. Males did the hunting of vertebrates and protected the family. Large groups were not feasible. We could not digest cellulose or store meat. Meat had to be distributed and consumed promptly and, without money, we depended on so-called 'reciprocal altruism'. One good turn deserves another. Our population was kept in check in a rather brutal boom or bust demographic. The evolutionary pressure finely tuned our ethotype, including our gender roles. Our pre-pastoral profile looked like this, and it still does to this day:

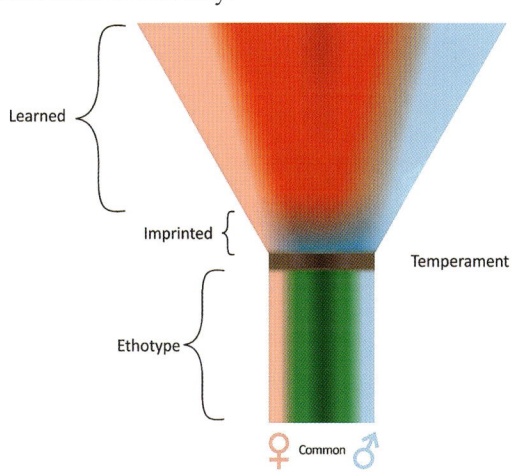

This is the same figure as in 2.6, but this time showing gender variations. Females have some differences in their ethotype, and probably in imprinting and cultural learning, from males who also have differences. But both share a common species-specific core and both can show traits more common in the opposite gender,

When we developed fire and cooking about 400,000 years ago, this was equivalent to having an artificial caecum. We could join the herbivores in digesting cellulose suddenly giving much greater scope to our diet and social demographics. Fire also took us from the Stone Age to the Bronze and Iron Ages, with more sophisticated tools. Pastoralism enabled us to store fresh meat in live flocks so that we could access it as and when we needed it, and it enabled us, indirectly, to skip a trophic layer and access a lot of plant material which we could not utilise ourselves. All this enabled an increase in our population numbers, densities and distribution, and larger social groups, leading to job role partitioning and ultimately the Industrial and Technological eras. Contraception allowed females to control when they became pregnant, or to never become pregnant. All this has hugely diminished the pre-pastoral gender roles and imprinting and learning have blended the genders. But the ethotype has scarcely changed and so gender roles persist, often resulting in tension and conflict between ethotypic behaviour and learned behaviour. Hunting and pseudo-hunting such as ball games and gangs, and foraging and pseudo-foraging, such as 'retail therapy' are still to a large extent, sex-linked.

The 'hunting genes' are deep in the ethotype of some humans and play a large

When hawking with goshawks in Pakistan the Muslim falconers were all male.

part in the make-up of their characters. Some people maintain that hunting by humans is learned, cultural behaviour with no basis in our ethotype (see Garry Marvin in *Killing Animals*, 2006 for a useful summary) but none of the evidence I have seen supports this view. Of course hunting techniques can be learned but hunting itself arises spontaneously in some individuals. People often ask me how I came to take up falconry. None of my family or anyone I knew were interested in it and I did not meet another living falconer until I had already been one for two years. It was as if I had been a falconer in a previous life, yet I don't believe in re-incarnation, at least not in the literal sense. But if one is born with a particular talent or trait, then presumably it is in your genes. The particular genes may lie dormant or unexpressed for several generations before re-emerging through the right recombinations or genetic triggers.

Behavioural traits in the ethotype are inheritable just as phenotypic traits are. And of course the process is not totally predictable because of the constant recombinations of alleles. Am I a 'throw-back'?

Paradoxically, I don't have the 'killer' gene if there is such a thing. I do really struggle to understand canned hunting, driven pheasant shooting or trophy hunting for big game. I would shoot an elephant if I had a compelling reason to do so, for example if it was in some situation of terminal injury or disease, or even in super-abundance and destroying the habitat on which the population depended. But I would hate doing it. I even dislike burdening birds with satellite tags unless the tag is well-fitted and the research benefits outweigh the costs to the individual. And for me, the research benefit is not just a scientific paper, it must lead to an applied benefit.

My own experience parallels almost

Our team in Mongolia radio-tracking saker falcons in the 1990s. Field research can be a form of hunting.

exactly the detailed description given by Vladimir Dinets (*Spontaneous development of hunting-like behaviour in a juvenile human: a case study.*) Neither my parents nor my siblings had any real interest in hunting. Just as Dinets did, I rambled on my own from the age of five onwards, keeping diaries of my activities from the age of five to 22. Certainly in my own case I was hunting long before meeting anyone who later taught me hunting rituals. From searching for birds' eggs to scrumping apples, I was always hunting something and as I got older, my hunting became more sophisticated, leading to me becoming a falconer and raptor biologist.

Interestingly, Dinets raises two points which I have also noted independently many times and in many species. One is that the instinct to hunt is separate both from the instinct to kill and from the motivation of hunger. I do not enjoy killing things and nowadays need a pest control or food motive to kill an animal. My recreational hunting has been by proxy (I don't catch the prey, my falcons do) or is subsumed into my biology fieldwork activities. Much of it merges seamlessly into aspects of wildlife management that create habitats and species benefits, balancing populations and pressures on resources. Other people subsume it into ball games and sports, or even retail shopping, but these do nothing for me. If you don't have these hunting genes in your ethotype, I can well understand that you find it hard to imagine it in other people, that you find the concept weird, that you might scorn it. One can probably make a very similar example of religion, which I personally find hard to understand. Is religion entirely learned, or do some people have one or more genes for religion? And if you are one of those people who don't have these particular genes, and struggle to understand those who do, should your moral values lead you to judge others and impose your beliefs onto them? Isn't this discrimination?

Can the tone-deaf understand the mind of the musician, do people who cannot draw understand the mind of the artist? I'm not a hugely talented artist but I get very frustrated sometimes when someone is trying to explain something to me in words and I say "Just sketch it for me", and they can't. It's not just a physical inability to hold a pencil, it is something going on (or not going on) in their minds. They simply are not able to visualise it in their 'mind's eye'. Many of us have talents or traits of some sort which are not shared by others. We are born with them, so they must be in our ethotype. Some, like the fear of spiders or snakes, have some potential survival benefit. Some people go on to progress these traits further by learning, while others never use them; they lie dormant, neglected, perhaps a source of quiet frustration or life-long regret.

Another feature that Dinets raises is the tendency to check out places where a successful hunt has taken place. This is a well-known phenomenon in predators. It can be quite annoying in Harris hawks that insist on going to previous kill-spots on subsequent visits. For myself, I am hopeless at remembering names, but as I go around the countryside I can recognise previous spots where my falcons have caught a crow. I may not remember the name of the falcon, or the people who were with me, but I can point almost to the exact rock two or three decades later. I notice this in myself, the landscape is haunted by my memories. Sometimes I imagine that if my falcons left a skein of silk behind them, like spiders do, the sky of my memories would be full of cobwebs.

Most of my own hunting is by sight and sound. For my dogs it is mainly by scent, then sound and sight. For the hawks, it is mainly by sight. Humans have an ability, which may be exceptional, to interpret a trail of footprints visually and track that way. Can any other species do that? Dogs track by scent and sometimes go in the wrong direction, the heel line. So these tracking stages of a hunt are part of the search phase, but raptors cannot do this. Their search phase

We track the hares at dawn, while the story in the sand is still fresh.

is by eye, and their pursuit is by eye contact. If they become unsighted, they flounder until they spot the prey again. Sometimes when a falcon is chasing a clever old crow, the crow will hide on the blind spot of the falcon, behind it and a little below. It looks as if the crow is chasing the falcon. It may earn itself several precious seconds; enough to reach the safety of cover. An experienced falcon learns, the moment she is unsighted, to cast her gaze wider, to reconnect.

We are hunter-foragers. It's not that we were; we still are. Our hunter-foraging instincts are alive and well and bubbling up all the time out of our ethotype. Although in the last few thousand years we have developed livestock and arable farming, and in the last few hundred years, more of us have clustered into cities that depend on external land for food, we are still hunters and foragers. For modern urbanites the need or the opportunities to hunt and forage wild food have gone, but the powerful instincts remain and are sublimated in a whole host of directions.

When you hunt for food for survival, you cannot have too many scruples. You might drive mammoths or bison over a cliff. But on bad days you wish you could find prey and be successful. Rituals were developed, intending to promote success in the hunt. The concept of the Noble Savage is mainly a modern construct. In reality savagery was more the order of the day, combined with pragmatism, and one sees this still in many modern societies.

As agriculture took hold, wild lands and game animals became scarcer and hunting reserves were created, allowing some privileged people to continue to hunt as a social activity. Gradually various customs and ethics came to surround venery and it became more ritualised.

In any activity, especially group activities,

in order to co-operate effectively, we have moral obligations to one another. It may be a trading format – you give me your saucepans for my beaver skins, or a hunting format – you wait there in ambush while I beat out this cover towards you. Or it could be reciprocity, such as sharing of food.

3.8 Hunting tools and assistants

Across the whole spectrum of hunting behaviour in humans and in other predators the picture is similar. The only difference is in the use of tools. Whereas natural predators hunt their prey using only their phenotypes and their ethotypes, humans now have tools, such as guns, that enable them to kill more efficiently. Critically the prey animals, which also use only their phenotypes and ethotypes to evade capture, are not adapted to evade these tools and the balance is swung against them. When we go hunting with our dogs or falcons, following on foot or on horses, we are not using these lethal unnatural tools, we are using only our own collective natural abilities and the quarry is fully able to use its own natural abilities to evade us. This creates an element of natural selection against weak individuals and it enables us to experience the myriad natural escape responses the prey species use, responses that are not seen by gun-hunters.

You could claim that hunting with dogs or falcons is not hunting at all per se but rather the witnessing of, or abetting, a natural predation sequence, voyeurism even. It is not the human that makes the attack, it is the animal predator. This is the argument that cat-owners use to absolve themselves from culpability. "I know my cat catches little birds when I let him out but it is part of his natural behaviour. My role extends only to letting him out to hunt; I don't take any pleasure from it and I absolve myself from any responsibility for this aspect of his behaviour." The owner of the predator may even feed her animal on a vegetarian meat-substitute diet, forcing the carnivore to go against his ethotype and adopt the human's individual moral values on diet.

A few people have floated the notion that somehow the human should obtain 'consent' from animals. Your horse should give 'permission' for you to ride him. Your sheep should give 'consent' to being 'farmed'. The rabbit should 'consent' to you hunting it. This is a fruitless approach to our relationship with other species or, indeed to our own. You cannot go up to a rat and say "Excuse me Mr Rat, would you mind awfully if I set a trap for you because I don't want you in my kitchen cupboard?". The rat might reply: "Your cupboard? This is my home, where I have my nest of babies!". So instead of the rat consenting to walk voluntarily into your trap and be killed, offering its life to you, you are reduced to baiting the trap with peanut butter to tempt him in, or, as you don't have the rat's consent to be in his house, you have to vacate. The horse and the sheep cannot 'consent' to being confined in a field with fences around it. We are all of us fenced, constrained or influenced in some way without the luxury of 'consenting'. The moral mechanism itself, as we shall see later, is predicated on balancing our desires as individuals with the constraints of the various communities in which we live. The converse of 'consent' of course is 'dissent'. If my dog chases my sheep, who will do the consenting, and who will dissent? The concept is a non-starter.

There is a gradation in the efficacy of hunting methods. Hunting by natural predators such as raptors or dogs does not cause wounding and often selects out the weak or diseased. For example, in 1958-60, Eutermoser caught 100 Hooded Crows *Corvus cornix* using seven falcons around Rosenheim in Germany. The crows were in flocks so the falcons had a choice of which to attack. He also shot a random sample of a hundred with a shotgun. He sorted them for age and health status, and weighed them. Although the samples were small, the trend is clear: 40% of the hawked crows were ailing in some way compared to 23% of the shot crows, and even the healthy ones were not as heavy. He did not record how many of the crows that were shot at escaped wounded.

Crows	Hawk	Gun
First year	31	39
Adult	69	61
Healthy	60	77
Ill	40	23
Mean Weight		
Healthy	524g	549g
Ill	466g	469g

Hunting with arrows or spears requires knowledge of the prey and skill in approaching it. Ailing animals are likely to be selected preferentially. Shotguns and rifles require far less skill and can kill at a distance. Beyond these are methods used for pest control including traps, poisons and ecosystemic poisons such as pesticides. Similarly with fishing: fly-fishing, then worms or spinners, then nets and factory fishing ships. Most of these methods are relatively unselective.

Primitive tool-use in hunting has probably reached our ethotype. Our human hands are not well adapted for killing, nor are our teeth, so we instinctively cast about to grab a stone or a stick to use to defend ourselves or to kill an animal. But guns are a very recent invention and we definitely don't have genes for them. How hard would it be to change our hunting ethotype, I wonder? Apart from genetic engineering to re-jig our whole ethotype, the speed of natural evolution depends on the extent of genetic variation, the selection forces on the variation, and the rate of turnover or generation interval. Species with a very rapid generation turnover, such as some influenza viruses, adapt very quickly, but for species with a long generation interval, the pace of change is much slower. Our human ethotype is probably substantially identical now to what it was 5,000, 40,000 or even 8 million years ago, and hunting is a very complex suite of behaviours. It is not an on-off switch. Yet there are people who believe that we could and should turn predators into vegetarians. They think this would reduce suffering in this world.

A falconer with his bird and a drum for flushing ducks, in Peniarth MS 28, f.9r, the Law of Hywel Dda. Mid 13th Century, Wales.

What about our companion species, another social omnivore that has evolved alongside us, the dog? The phylogeny of the dog is shrouded in the mists of time. Humans and dogs may have lived together for 100,000 years or more. If you gave me a choice between lugging around a stone axe or having a dog, I would opt for the dog any time. Dogs can find all manner of prey far better than humans can. They have an extra sense – scenting – that we don't have. They can flush prey from cover. They can act as a team and overwhelm bigger animals than themselves. They can guard the camp. They can self-replicate and move themselves around at high speeds. They can survive on all manner of foods. And if, with a primitive bow and arrow or spear, a human succeeds in wounding an animal, the chances are it will escape unless a dog tracks it down and kills it or bays it, especially in landscapes where foot tracking is not feasible. Dogs die and their remains disappear, whereas stone tools bear silent testimony. Maybe we underestimate the role dogs have played in our shared ancestry.

Since their initial domestication, dogs have been selectively bred for more specialist roles by a controlled type of evolution. By about 2,000 years ago, some of these roles were becoming more recognisable: guard dogs, dogs that hunt by scent or by sight, and with the domestication of sheep and cattle, various types of livestock dogs were bred. By about 1,500 years ago in Europe the dogs were bred for very specialised roles in hunting, such as brachets, alaunts, lymers or bloodhounds that hunt low scent, often in packs, to spaniels that flush game for falconers or netters, to greyhounds, galgos, tarzis, salukis and borzois that hunt singly or in pairs using speed, high scenting pointers, and terriers that hunt prey underground. All of these breeds show a huge variety of phenotypes and ethotypes which had to go hand in hand. A sheep dog that has no herding instinct is no use. The speed with which these breeds were developed has been a much faster process than natural evolution normally takes.

We cannot trace the way our own ethotype evolved, but we can look at parallels in our ethotype with those of chimpanzees and bonobos. They too are social omnivores like us. Our modern phenotype has not altered hugely over the past eight million years. For sure there have been developments, but nothing like the differences between modern dogs and ancestral wolves. So probably our ethotype has not changed massively either.

But that's all in the past. What of the future? Humans in urban or even agrarian societies no longer need to spend time foraging for food. Many don't even need to go shopping, they just have to sit down and eat meals that almost magically appear in front of them. One effect of this is that the phenotype struggles with this sudden abundance, obesity and diabetes have become common, along with all the additional complications of too much food. And the ethotype struggles too; all those instincts to hunt are now redundant, frustrated. They have to seek outlets in substitute activities such as sports or computer games. But for those in a more rural setting, a game of football or a workout in the gym are no real substitute for real foraging, for nuts, berries, fungi or catching real prey. Even though abundant food is available, many humans have a strong instinct to hunt, as do dogs and cats.

Anthropological studies of hunting in humans have focussed on remnant primitive societies now ably catalogued by Christopher Boehm. He claims these hunting groups are egalitarian, which may well be the case in regards to the distribution of the food once caught, but all the hunting groups I have experienced have had a leader and a loose structure. Anthropologists such as Tim Ingold, John Knight and Paul Nadasdy describe concepts of animal spirits and prey 'giving' themselves to hunters and so on. Perhaps these are characteristics of primitive superstitious groups, akin to early religions, but I have never noticed this kind of thing in the hunting groups I have hunted with.

The Enclosures Acts in the 18th and 19th centuries in Britain led to the sequestration of much Common and some tenanted land which became subsumed into field systems bounded by hedges and walls. This in turn made access difficult, there were both legal and physical barriers to crossing the countryside for whatever purpose. Activities such as hunting on horses, which relied on accessing open country, became difficult and with the advent of shotguns, the 'art of shooting flying' became popular. The breech-loading gun enabled rapid firing rates and heralded the battue or driven

Hawking with this little group in Turkey. Their leader wears a tie and is just visiting. They have wild-caught sparrowhawks for hunting migratory quail. Their hawking traditions go back hundreds of years.

The hawk is held in the hand ready to throw like a spear when the quail flushes.

Hawking crows in Northumberland. Verity Johnson

game shooting, still practised to this day. Hugo Meynell developed a faster form of fox-hunting with hounds by jumping the various hedges and this became popular in lowland farmed areas. Now it is the only organised wide-scale equestrian access to the farmed countryside in the UK. The roads have been increasingly monopolised by cars, with drivers often unsympathetic towards horses, with the result that many public access routes are unsafe to ride on. Similar changes have occurred throughout western Europe. Horse riders have had to restrict their activities to controlled areas such as manèges and courses, and to various competitive events in equestrian disciplines. We find many riders who visit us have never ridden freely across open terrain before and it can come as quite a shock, especially when they thought they could ride.

While hunting in some shape or form continues, it is an increasingly difficult task to keep the countryside 'open' for access on horses on private land. Despite this, land has been kept open for hunting in Britain continuously since pre-historic times. With ongoing urbanisation and partitioning of land this has become an increasingly onerous task for Hunt Masters. Permission has to be sought and maintained from all the land-owners over a considerable area. This aspect of hunting has been well-documented by the naturalist Frances Pitt in 1948 in *Hounds, Horses and Hunting*; it is an element under-appreciated by anthropologists and by legislators. It is an ancient social contract which includes all levels of land-based communities and has no parallel elsewhere in legislation. Because it is an intangible social contract it has proved impervious to legislation. Legislators, who naively thought that hunting was solely about killing animals, found that efforts to ban it were ineffectual and that they had no way of preventing activities so ingrained in social history and mores. Although hunting in the Home Counties still has an element of class pomp, the strongholds of hunting are in the provinces. Wales is so full of hunting packs that it is by no means uncommon for one hunt to bump into another while hunting on a Saturday, even now 20 years after a theoretical ban. For myself, I prefer to hunt in places that are still unenclosed, such as the hill lands of Wales and the wilder parts of England. Here hounds can run naturally as they have always done since they were wolves.

3.9 Natural and artificial hunting

The dog (which emulates its ancestor, the wolf) and birds of prey, are natural predators. The way they prey is natural. They are in an evolutionary arms race with their prey but it is one they can never win. They are constantly in an uneasy balance. Prey availability dictates the survival and numbers of the predators. The weak and sickly prey are naturally selected first as victims and thus the health of the prey populations is maintained and welfare is enhanced. Instead of a long lingering death from old age or infirmity, prey animals are found and killed by predators. Top predators themselves cannot expect such treatment. A hawk with an injured wing has no choice but to carry on as best it can, most likely to a lingering death.

Years ago when I was working on Australasian harriers, I trapped, measured, ringed and released about 70 around our farm in New Zealand. One day a neighbour brought in a harrier with just a healed stump for a wing. It was one I had ringed a year earlier and it had survived by eating frogs at a waterhole. It was very lucky. On another occasion a New Zealand falcon I had ringed and released, later attacked a Muscovy Duck on a farm pond. The falcon was in a state of collapse and died the next day. A thorn had penetrated the front of her head from some previous hunt, and the wound had become infected. In extreme pain and barely able to see, she had attacked the duck as a last resort.

Hunting is a process as old as life on earth. It is one of the key evolutionary selection

This patrolling harrier didn't understand wire fences. She caught both wings on the barbed wire, flipped over and suffered a lingering death.

Chapter 3 – WHAT IS 'HUNTING'?   75

Many of the crows our falcons catch have something wrong with them. This one had a foot tangled up.

This grey squirrel had an ulcerated foot so couldn't run away fast enough to escape from Bonny.

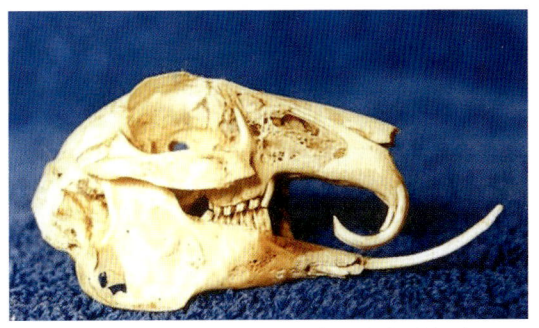

This rabbit, caught by my goshawk, had broken a tooth, so the remaining teeth kept growing, with nothing to wear against.

pressures. Predators and their prey have evolved together. Just as predators have evolved bodies and senses, and search and attack strategies, so prey species have evolved ways of concealment, escape strategies and compensatory breeding strategies. Some more intelligent species, especially humans, developed the use of tools which enabled them to forage more efficiently. Humans developed these tools from primitive spears, to traps, to bows and arrows, to guns, vehicles, radios, night vision scopes and GPS tracking devices. On the evolutionary time scale this has been a sudden development, too quick for the prey species to evolve strategies in response. Cryptic plumage is no defence against infra-red detection devices. By winning the predation arms race, humans have destroyed the balance between predators and prey and now have the capacity to destroy other species at will. The result is that, both intentionally and unintentionally, wildlife populations are plummeting, both in numbers and in ranges.

Paradoxically, in recent years, the arms race of hunting technology has been pushed into reverse with the enthusiasm for 'bush-craft'. But people from western 'civilisation' trying to 'live off the land' with subsistence hunting find themselves in a moral dilemma: coming face to face with the prospect of killing an animal. One bush-crafter, writing about hunting squirrels with a catapult, received death threats from other bush-crafters. And the constraints of private property, legislation and animal welfare curtail their hunting efforts. The desire to somehow re-visit their roots is there, but the practicalities are confining. Often 'life in the wild' just means camping in some farmer's wood overnight.

Some other hunting tools and activities, such as shooting, are not at all 'natural'. Increasingly sophisticated weaponry swings the balance heavily in favour of the shooter and denies the prey any chance to use its natural escape behaviours. In privately managed areas the shooter may select the weak and the infirm, but these confer no bragging rights. Most shooters prefer to go for the prime animals, the trophies. Technology has a place in pest control and warfare, but not in sport hunting.

I was invited partridge hawking in Lincolnshire recently. My hosts cruised the stubbles in SUVs, stopping intermittently to scan the fields with thermal imaging scopes to spot the partridges' body heat. When you are trying to hawk partridges with a falcon waiting on overhead, it is important to be certain that the game is there before you unhood the falcon. But I felt using thermal imaging was a travesty. Of course we use these scopes when monitoring our beavers, and of course we use binoculars to scope for prey. But we had two pointing dogs with us which remained unused, and I felt the whole thing was weighted too much on the side of artificiality to be a genuine hunting experience.

Additional technologies, such as vehicles, swing the balance still further in favour of the hunter. The hunter may try to compensate by breeding and releasing game animals for hunting, but this further

Pheasant rearing for shooting.

unbalances wild populations and only a small percentage of released game survive until the next spring.

The ultimate artificiality is driven shooting in which beaters drive the game birds over a line of shooters who simply stand there shooting away at these living targets. The Guns may have a Loader re-loading a second gun for faster shooting, and Pickers-up with retrievers to collect fallen birds. Birds that are 'pricked' and fly on wounded are not found. Big bag driven shoots can be big business, but as a hunting experience they are nothing to be proud of.

The reason that Plato, Aldo Leopold and I support hunting with dogs and with raptors is that these are the only forms of hunting which humans participate in that are still natural. Plato thought: *"Accordingly, the only kind left for all, and the best kind, is the hunting of quadrupeds with horses and dogs and the hunter's own limbs, when men hunt in person…"*

Leopold wrote:

"The most glamorous hobby I know of today is the revival of falconry. It has a few addicts in America and perhaps a dozen in England – a minority indeed. For two and a half cents one can buy and shoot a cartridge that will kill the heron whose capture by hawking required months or years of laborious training of both the hawk and the hawker. The cartridge, as a lethal agent, is a perfect product of industrial chemistry. One can write a formula for its lethal reaction.

The hawk, as a lethal agent, is the perfect flower of that still utterly mysterious alchemy – evolution. No living man can, or possibly ever will, understand the instinct of predation that we share with our raptorial servant. No man-made machine can, or ever will, synthesize that perfect coordination of eye, muscle, and pinion as he stoops to his kill. The heron, if bagged, is inedible and hence useless (although the old falconers seem to have eaten him, just as a Boy Scout smokes and eats a flea-bitten summer cottontail that has fallen victim to his sling, club, or bow). Moreover the hawk, at the slightest error in technique of handling, may either 'go tame' like Homo sapiens or fly away into the blue. All in all, falconry is the perfect hobby." A Man's Leisure Time in *A Sand County Almanac*.

The prey species have evolved to deal with their natural predators such as canids and raptors and by watching them one gains fascinating insights into the predator-prey interactions and into one's own psychology as a predator.

Human hunters who hunt recreationally find themselves in a quandary. Killing or catching prey is not their primary motive, although a necessary one. Yet pride necessitates some kind of return on invested effort. So on the one hand, the trout fisherman restricts himself to fly-fishing to prevent the fishing being too easy, yet at the same time equips himself with the best rod and reel he can obtain, to maximise his chances of catching a fish. All this makes suppliers of fishing and hunting gear very happy.

When I was young in Cranbourne Chase in Dorset I used to watch people practising with the long bow. Hunting animals with a bow is now illegal in the UK but it has a strong following in North America. The ethos behind this is that it takes a lot more skill to hunt with a bow than with a gun. For sure, some bow-hunters then back-pedal and use every possible gizmo and aid they can, but bow-hunting is still not easy. That swings the balance more in favour of the prey. The problem is though, that arrows are not very humane compared to a gun. It is very hard to kill an animal stone dead on the spot with an arrow. It was this welfare issue that led to a bow-hunting ban in the UK.

For myself, as a hunter, I think we must be careful to retain the natural balance of the hunt, and we can do this by using natural predators, such as raptors or dogs. Yes, take care over the breeding and conditioning of our animals for hunting. Yes, use tracking devices and phones to reduce the risk of animals being lost or straying into the wrong places. Yes, use vehicles to reach the hunting grounds. Seek out prey who are living in their natural environment, who know all the escape features of the landscape, and who have a sustainable surplus. But when you get there, as far as possible, strip yourself of the trappings of human modernity and return to the elemental, natural predator and prey relationship, recognising that we ourselves are participating predators but that ours is a secondary role to the main players. We are watching an age-old life and death struggle. These are some of the ethical values which I put on hunting and will discuss later.

If your hawk kills on about every fourth or fifth attempt, this is a natural balance. Less than this, or more than this, and you need to examine what you are doing. Any bragging rights are not yours to claim.

There have been questions raised in Scribehound about the ethics of driven game shooting, perhaps most eloquently expressed by Jonny Carter. Many feel unease, some even despair, but what is to be done about it if fieldsports generally are to continue?

We need to dig deeper into motivation. Shooting game birds is a recreational activity which people usually pay to do, whereas pest control is a service which people usually get paid to provide. Pest control entails killing as many pests as possible with minimal effort and cost. Recreational hunting involves maximising the pleasure element, the challenge, the man-days of enjoyment, per head of game taken.

This is the theory at least, but sometimes things go astray, and I think driven shooting is losing its way at the moment. It is all a question of balance. Let's look at the crudest of indicators: man-days per head of game taken. If you are a shooter, try going through your Game Books and tot up your figures.

Are you a salmon fisherman? How many fish did you catch last season, for how many days of fishing? Is your figure 0.1 fish per man-day? Or 1.0? If you caught only one fish in ten days, do you feel you had a good season? Would one per day make you feel content? Maybe one every second day a happy medium? In 2023 in Scotland, 32,477 salmon were caught but 96% were released. Maybe if you release your fish alive, it doesn't 'count', as a 'kill', certainly from the conservation of the population perspective, but it does from the welfare perspective.

What about fox-hunting, a communal sport as it used to be practised before the ban? Maybe 30 people on horses, 20 in cars or on foot, catching a fox perhaps every second outing. That's 100 man-days per fox or 0.01 foxes per man-day. Modest Hunts would be content with that scenario. For the Huntsman, thinking of his hounds and their enthusiasm to hunt, maybe they find two foxes a day, and catch one in four, a good ratio for a natural predator.

For the past 32 years my chosen sport has been flying falcons at crows from horseback. Crows are a pest in our livestock district, pecking out the eyes of the sheep and predating ground-nesting birds, and falconry is the most humane way to catch them. Our hawks, horses and humans all suffer injuries from time to time. We have had two people with broken backs, and plenty of bust ribs and collar bones. So the humans are not passive spectators; they are active participants each with a role to play. Last season in 267 man-days we had 91 flights, killing 38 crows and wounding none. That's one crow in 2.4 flights which is fine for a hunting falcon. That's 7 man-days per crow or 0.14 crows per man-day. We used to hawk more days and kill five times this many, but I was younger then, and more active. We are very fortunate to be able to do this. Others go out without human companions, maybe with just a goshawk and a spaniel. This is the way to get to know the dynamics of the countryside. The writings and observations of Richard Jefferies, Aldo Leopold and probably Beatrix Potter were fed by their solitary wanderings. You stop thinking in human words and start thinking naturally again.

What about driven pheasant shooting? I asked the Game Conservancy in 1995 and they estimated that on average each Gun shot 10.3 pheasants. Looking at the figures for 2023, this is now about 27 pheasants per man-day, going up to 44 pheasants per man-day in big shoots. You could add in a few pickers-up operating free of charge, but the figure is still pretty steep. Shooting quite well at one bird retrieved for four cartridges, that means 81 shots either missed or wounded per shooter, per day. About 864 shots fired that day mean about 218,600 No 6 pellets scattered on the site, hopefully not lead.

So in my index of 'sport', we have fox hunting at 0.01 foxes per man-day, crow hawking at 0.14 crows per man-day, salmon fishing at say 0.5 fish per man-day and driven pheasant shooting at 27 birds per man-day. Although these are rough calculations and the variables are quite large, driven pheasants have a direct kill per man-day 2,700 times that of fox hunting. Where should the balance be? And for your chosen sport, where is your balance?

Perhaps you like to watch predators hunting so you watch wildlife films on TV. These seem to revel in the killing, with the action slowed down for better effect. It is hunting by surrogacy. By circulating a film, one death can be 'enjoyed' by many thousands of people.

If your hunting substitute is football, this also depends on triumph and disaster. The stats are of similar magnitude: the average total number of goals per game is around 3.3 with about 10% of shots scoring a goal. These are very addictive ratios for a game design.

But this is such a crude approach; surely 'sport' is much more subtle than that? It is not just about killing things. OK, let's take killing out of the equation. What about simulated driven days using clays, or trail-hunting? With those activities you know you are not going to have blank days; every day will provide shots, or runs. But a real hunting experience is defined not just by the successes, but by the disappointments.

For the fisherman who died and went to heaven, catching a fish at every cast, the uncertainty that had made fishing a challenge for him had been taken away. The pleasure was destroyed; he'd gone to hell. Fishermen struggle with this balance. They buy all the latest gizmos, the carbon rod, the latest floating line, and yet they eschew easy methods such as the worm or spinner and confine themselves to fly-fishing. This makes it harder, so there is more of a challenge, a balance between man and fish. This is what recreational fishing is all about, it is not simply a matter of catching fish. If he had wanted to do that, maybe for research purposes, he could have electro-fished and stunned the lot. This balance is how recreational hunting works and it taps straight into our natural psyche as predators. Too easy or too hard, and it doesn't work.

We evolved as hunter-foragers. We have predator psyches. All predators fail most of the time. If they fail and give up, they die. So they try again, and again, until eventually they succeed. We are programmed for hunting failure. We all come from long lines of successful hunters who have had to overcome failure on a daily basis in order to survive. For us predators the most powerful rewards system is not a reward every time, but at a lower frequency, maybe every fifth or seventh time.

But balance is important too. The fisherman who went to hell had plenty of success, but no disappointment. We need to chase both. Shooting more and more pheasants in a day is chasing success, but neglecting disappointment, hardship. Rough shooting over spaniels or pointers emphasises the 'search' phase of hunting and minimises the 'attack' phase, the shot. This is the most fascinating part of hunting: getting oneself into a situation where you can make an 'attack'. The shot, when it comes, is almost an anti-climax. The pheasant doesn't understand the shot, pellets whizzing towards it at the speed of sound. It dies and the hunt is over.

But whereas the shooter slips his safety catch and pulls the trigger, the falconer slips his goshawk. Far from being over, his hunt is just beginning. The pheasant, both from instinct and from experience, knows what a goshawk is and how to escape from her. She in turn quickly assesses the strength of the pheasant in comparison to her own. The pheasant may outfly the hawk, or it may seek cover. If the hawk is young and needs encouragement, the falconer will put his dog in and flush it at the 'retrove' (the second flush). But if the hawk is a good one, he will leave the pheasant with its glycogen-depleted white muscles and look for another point elsewhere. He wants his hawk to take pheasants in the air, not to get into the habit of tail-chasing them until they put in.

So we maximise the sport per head of game taken. The 27 pheasants for one day's driven shooting would last the falconer a whole season, and then some. I gave up driven shooting 50 years ago, without even properly starting. To me it is such a waste. Nowadays, watching a neighbour's driven shoot and seeing all the pheasants flushed out of the woods by the beaters, and hearing the crackle of gunfire and seeing the pheasants faltering and tumbling, the vision that comes to my mind is of villagers fleeing their burning houses and being gunned down by the Khmer Rouge.

But how to make shooting entail less killing, more enjoyment and more disappointment? Guns are so efficient nowadays. The ban on repeating shotguns is overcome by using pairs of guns. The result is carnage. How to make game shooting less 'efficient'? Muzzle-loaders? Clouds of black powder? Walking up with pointers? Grouse moors and all the wildlife habitat they provide are a huge asset. How can we sweat the asset rather than lose it, making the shooting less efficient and thus providing ten times the man-days per head and per season? How can we make the most of the peripherals, the dog work, the socialising, the fun and yes, more of the tough stuff, the days when you get soaked to the skin, when you walked all day and only shot a squirrel... Many of the shooters on driven game have never plucked a bird. Perhaps they could limit their bag to what they can eat and then go home, pluck or skin the game, cook it and eat it with companions and family as part of the celebration of the day. Dumping a pile of unwanted shot pheasants to rot is obscene.

When I get a pheasant I prefer to pluck it while it is still warm.

So our 'balance' has two criteria: the proportion of successful to unsuccessful 'attacks', and whether or not the hunt is one-sided: a human with an artificial device, or both sided, in which the prey can use its own natural escape strategies.

3.10 What animals are hunted?

Humans usually hunt animals for population management, or for food, or as a recreational resource or combinations of these. The rabbit, for example, is all three. Some, such as foxes, can be a recreational resource in one locality and a pest in another. It can be difficult to agree on what is, and what is not 'a pest'. At present in the UK it seems to be more socially acceptable to kill some pests (such as rats and rabbits) with dogs than to kill other pests (such as foxes) with dogs. Rabbits and foxes have equally developed nervous systems, and presumably experience similar levels of pain. The movement against hunting foxes therefore hinges, not on biological grounds, but on the perception that the hunters enjoy hunting, which they obviously do. But their enjoyment is based on the activity rather than in killing foxes or in seeing foxes being killed.

Let's get down to brass tacks and examine the main species of wild animals hunted in the UK, the methods used to hunt them, the reasons for hunting them, and the approximate numbers involved. Similar tables could be made for other parts of the world.

	Gaze hounds	Scenthounds	Terriers	Cats	Ferrets	Raptors	Poisons	Dead traps	Snares	Live traps	Shotgun
Red deer											
Red Fox						R1		P3	P2		P4
Brown Hare				R3		R2			F2	F2	PFR3
Rabbit	PFR4	PFR3	PFR3	R4	PFR5	PFR5		PF4	PF4	PF4	PFR6
Mink			P2					P3		P3	P2
Badger									P2	P4	
Brown Rat			PR3	PR6	P3		P7	P4		P4	P3
Mice/small mammals				PR7			P7	P7		P2	
Pheasant				R3		RF3				P4	RF6
Red Grouse				R3		RF3					RF4
Grey Partridge				R3		RF2					RF4
Mallard				R2		RF2					RF4
Carrion Crow						RP3				P4	PR4
Woodpigeon											PRF7
Small birds				R7		R2					

Reasons for killing
P = Population Management
F = Food
R = Recreation

Numbers killed
1 = 10 - 100
2 = 100 - 1,000
3 = 1000 - 10,000
4 = 10,000 - 100,000
5 = 100,000 - 1 million
6 = 1 million - 10 million
7 = 10 million - 100 million
8 = 100 million - 500 million

Reasons for killing, methods and numbers of some wild animals killed annually in the UK (Fox and Macdonald 1995).

'Game' is a cultural construct, encoded in law in some countries but without any taxonomic basis. Its common denominator is that it is hunted recreationally for sport and is good to eat.

Fish are the commonest wild animals hunted today. http://fishcount.org.uk/uk-strategy#2wild . Recent research shows that fish are at least as sentient as mammals and birds, yet they are treated as if they are incapable of feeling. There is very little public concern to improve welfare in the various forms of fishing and fish farming. Fish are mainly just treated as a commodity. This is likely to continue for a long time, partly because most of us don't see fish suffering, and partly because it is an inconvenient truth. There is almost no research into welfare friendly fishing techniques. Sports fishing in some places has developed catch and release strategies to help preserve fish stock, but neither sports fishing nor commercial fisheries have developed alternatives to nets and hooks. Sports fishing is almost entirely centred on using hooks and could not continue if hooks were banned. Fish farming entails a number of issues – infectious diseases, genetic contamination, environmental pollution and so on – but there has been little improvement in the handling and slaughter of farmed fish.

3.11 Weeds and pests

The Preservation of Grain Act was passed in 1532 by Henry VIII and strengthened by Elizabeth I in 1566. This Act demanded that every man, woman and child should kill as many creatures as possible that appeared on an official list of 'vermin'. This Act's purpose was to conserve grain stores and prevent the spread of disease in a time of expanding population and bad harvests. In 1958, Chairman Mao Zedong's edict to kill all sparrows resulted in uncontrolled insect plagues on crops in China. About 45 million people starved to death. Weeds and pests can be tricky.

'A weed is simply a plant in the wrong place.' In reality it is a lot more complicated than that. I try not to use the word 'wrong'? Who decides the 'right' and 'wrong' of what plant should live where? If it is your garden, then you do. You are the Garden God. You have a vision for your garden, and in your vision, grass should grow on the lawn and not between the flagstones or on the gravel. You want the lawn for walking on, so you don't want thistles on it. The lawn has a function, not just an aesthetic. The flower bed's function, as far as it goes, is to be aesthetic, and it may have a theme. Many self-seeded plants there are dug out or poisoned because the Garden God considers them to be weeds; not coherent with the vision.

Weeds do at least have the merit of staying put. Animal pests on the other hand move around. They can be a pest in one place but not in another. In England it is illegal to set a Larsen cage trap for Magpies (*Pica pica*) in a garden because a garden is not agricultural. You must set it on the other side of the hedge in the field, because magpies can be killed

The Larsen trap works by enticing a magpie into a cage, using a decoy magpie.

for 'agricultural purposes'. There is also the question of density. Woodpigeons (*Columba palumbus*), Quelea (*Quelea quelea*) or locusts (*Locusta migratoria*) in low numbers do not do significant damage, but in hordes they can devastate a crop, so people kill them.

Knowing that a woodpigeon can devastate crops, isn't it better to kill them before they damage the crop? Isn't a pre-emptive strike the best strategy? The whole point of the exercise after all is to grow a good crop, rather than to kill pigeons. Or should one wait until the crop is ruined, and then kill the pigeons? That seems a bit futile. Or maybe scare them away so that they raid someone else's field? But not all the pigeons are feeding on your own field; should one only kill the pigeons that you catch in the act right there, on the field? What if the pigeon is not a pigeon, but a human? Would it be better to kill off the naughty humans before they murder someone? What if they hadn't then gone on and murdered someone after all, you would have killed them off for nothing? So <u>you</u> are the murderer! Or should you wait until after the murder and then kill them or lock them up? That's too late to help the victim. Hmm. Pest control isn't all that simple…

And anyway, who promoted you to Garden God or Farmer God? The pigeon is just doing what pigeons do, eating corn. Why kill them for just being pigeons? Wouldn't it be better if humans didn't set themselves up as Gods at all? We're just control freaks…

What if you go to town and build a massive 'pigeon cliff,' a block of high-rise apartments. And when the pigeons come and make a mess, first you decide to deter them so that they go to someone else's pigeon cliff, but then when there are too many to deter, you decide to kill them. But you are too squeamish to do it yourself and you don't want the tenants to see either, so you employ a professional pest controller to do it for you. So, morally, did <u>you</u> kill the pigeons, or did he? After all, like the prison guard at Auschwitz, he was simply doing what he was paid to do. (As a school boy in Surrey, my 12 bore cartridges for shooting woodpigeons were paid for by a Ministry of Agriculture subsidy. Being Captain of Shooting I also had the keys to the Armoury: 300 Lee-Enfield .303 rifles and two Bren guns. Nowadays the kids aren't even allowed a knife. Times change.)

And then, when you look at the pile of dead pigeons, some have got rings on; they were owned by someone, private property. And some are clearly phenotypically rare, protected rock doves. Same species - *Columba livia* - but killing them is illegal. Who has broken the law? If we shift the time baseline back a hundred years, maybe the site where you built the block of flats was a field, producing food, or an area of woodland hosting wildlife. If you go back further, maybe it was a wetland, alive with wildlife. Britain has lost about 85% of its wetlands now, so that humans could use the land. If we shift the baseline forward fifty years instead, will the block of flats still be there? Few high rise buildings, however 'sustainable' survive that long. Who, really, is the pest: the pigeons, or you?

In the examples above, the pigeon is the pest and the human is the 'manager' or predator. If we take the scenario up another trophic level, the ethics get even more complicated. The numbers of curlews in Britain are plummeting. In Wales they are expected to become extinct as breeding birds by 2030. One problem is constant disturbance by humans and their dogs, resulting in eggs or chicks chilling or being exposed to predators. Fox and crow numbers have increased. Now the Game and Wildlife Conservation Trust estimates that there are 375,000 foxes and a million pairs of carrion crows in the UK. These are obligate predators. Hunting is what they have to do. You cannot catch one, fine it or put it in prison then let it out and tell it not to do it again, as with a human criminal, such as a murderer.

With increasing human populations in the UK, many wanting to access the countryside and 'connect' with nature, or just let their dogs off leads, many species face ever-increasing disturbance. Most of the time the walkers do not understand the damage they are doing to ground-nesting animals, the lapwings wheeling pathetically overhead. Predation on top of this can tip the balance and the bird numbers enter a downward spiral. So we are faced with the dilemma of killing or controlling some species in order to favour or help others. In 2023 the Royal Society for the Protection of Birds used contractors to shoot 598 foxes at ranges of up to 200 metres. As our fox shooting study (see section 5.4) showed, this can lead to significant wounding so the RSPB authorised the use of dogs to hunt down wounded animals. Similarly the RSPB each year catches an unknown number - about 700 – of carrion crows, often using Larsen traps. The Larsen trap uses a live wild crow as a decoy, huddled in the trap day and night. The freshly caught crow may be extracted and killed within 24 hours, but the decoy remains there, sometimes for weeks, until it too is eventually killed. A lot of the public don't like this (they want wonderful wildlife but none of the unpleasantness) so the RSPB instructs the shooters to 'keep out of view of the public and appropriately dispose' of the dead animals. In this scenario, a value judgement has been made. A curlew is given a higher value than a fox or crow. I wonder, if you made a list of British species in order of their 'values', which would come out on top? The highly endangered Red List ones, or humans?

What if you think the place is yours, but another animal thinks it is theirs? Maybe a pair of crows are nesting in a tree in your lambing field. It's no good shooing them away; they live here. You could shoot them, but their young would starve to death. Or you could leave them to peck a lamb's eyes out.

The crows and ravens (*Corvus corax*) here have learned to jump up and peck out a lamb's tongue as soon as it appears. It is a cultural meme, like blue tits pecking shiny milk bottle tops. They attacked this ewe's udder too and I had to shoot her. I left her body (illegally) in the field 200 metres across the valley from the house where I could see her. First a fox came hobbling. It had a

Crows have pecked out the eyes and tongue of this unborn lamb and started on the udder of the ewe.

broken front leg and couldn't put it down. The next fox was fairly average, with a wispy tail. The next fox had a very black tail. After that I got muddled up. A pair of ravens were in close attendance, a black-backed gull, two buzzards and a kite came and went. Diversionary feeding will keep these predator/scavengers off the live sheep for a week or so, a method of pest control which is only temporary.

But if you decide that you have a weed or a pest on your hands, how do you go about controlling it? In pest control, as in predation for food, the efficiency strategy is one of minimum effort for maximum gain. The difference being that in hunting for food, retrieving the prey is essential, whereas in pest control it isn't. The aim of pest control is to eliminate the pest, as quickly and cheaply as possible. It is critical to understand this, because it affects the 'morality' of the hunter. When hunting for food, he will minimise risk and only shoot where he has a good chance of retrieving the body. But in pest control, people will shoot at long ranges, in the forlorn hope that a stray pellet may cause the prey to die later. Obviously this can create a lot more suffering. I have seen people shoot at foxes with No. 5 shot in shotguns at 80 metres. There is no way this will kill outright; there is insufficient penetration. The pellets will lodge under the skin and may get infected because each pellet pulls a little tuft of fur in with it.

For me, as we will see in section 5.6, killing foxes with dogs alone is the most humane, but not as efficient as shooting; but foxes should not be shot without dogs present to hunt the wounded. A pack of hounds can aways kill a fox more quickly than just two dogs. For crows, hunting them with falcons is the only truly humane option and one can target the solitary pairs out on the moors where they predate on ground-nesting birds and sheep. In other places, shooting is the most effective and quick option.

What if, despite our best efforts to control the pest, their numbers do not go down or their 'pesty' activity does not decrease? Maybe instead of reducing the total population, we are just creaming off a harvestable surplus on a sustainable basis? Or maybe our efforts are too localised and as fast as we kill off the pest on our patch more flood in from elsewhere. Maybe we should focus our efforts on late winter when the population is at its lowest and our impact will be maximal. For example, Tom Porteus, Jonathan Reynolds and Murdoch McAllister undertook a study in which foxes were culled on monitored estates and the numbers reduced to about half of estimated carrying

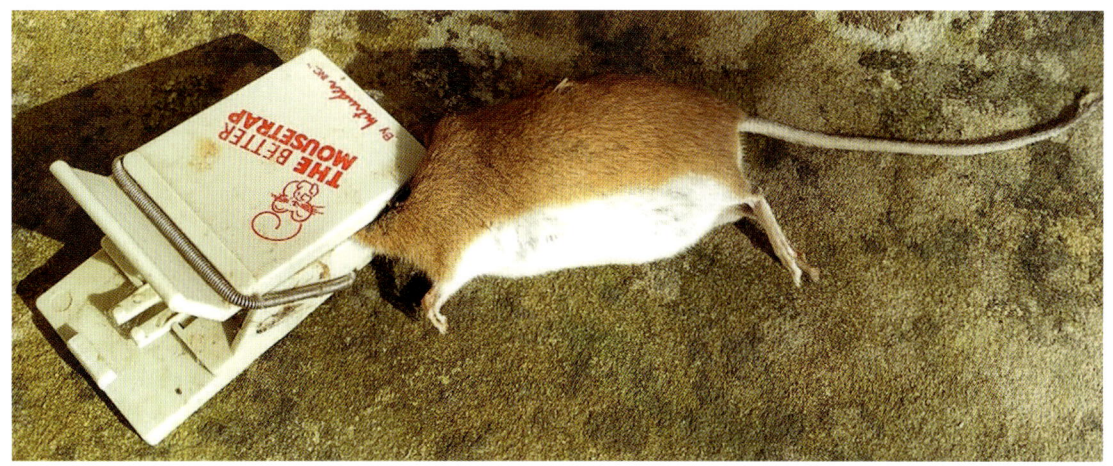

This House Mouse was pregnant. Two more days and she would have had baby mice which would have died of cold. Mice breed all the year round, so who cares?

A fine young oak completely ring-barked by a grey squirrel. I simply don't have time to shoot or trap the squirrels.

capacity, but foxes came in from surrounding areas. So the estates were sink spots. At the same time, the movement of foxes out of the surrounding areas was effectively a 'cull' for those areas. The reduced densities could only be achieved over a short critical period to reduce seasonal predation on nesting birds in those sensitive areas. In some situations pest control might be a waste of time and effort. But in others, such as mice and rats in the house, it is a question of keeping our fingers in the dam and not caring if they are breeding or not.

Wild boar were re-introduced into the Forest of Dean on the Welsh border a few years ago. Their numbers increased year on year until local people started complaining about them. But others wanted them left alone. The Forestry Commission carries out a low-profile culling operation but it is failing to meet its targets for a balanced population and is having to up its game. So gradually the pigs are destroying the forest ecosystem because the wildlife management regime is not robust enough. Pigs are great at low densities, but you can have too much of a good thing. It is our human planet problem in microcosm. Meanwhile others object to keeping pigs in farrowing crates, while others want cheap meat regardless of humaneness.

Controlling cockroaches, mice and rats are probably familiar activities to many people. Even the most ardent bunny huggers are not keen on rats in the house. An article in the *Guardian* (12 December 2023) 'There are rats in my attic, should I live and let live?' attracted over 303 comments. Of these, 299 (98.7%) supported getting rid of the rats. Only four respondents suggested leaving them there. Of the 'get ridders' identifiable to gender, 33 (35%) were female and 60 (65%) were male. A few of the comments, tongue in cheek, suggested 'nuking' the rats. Actually, when other humans themselves are seen as pests, because they trespass on our territory or steal our resources, we are far more drastic than we would be with non-human pests. Carpet bombing cities, gassing, poisoning, biological weapons, blowing the legs off young children and pregnant mothers; this goes on all over the world. Yet none of these methods would come close to passing the International Humane Trapping Standards that we apply to fur-bearing animals. Why then do Western cultures show such an inconsistency in attitudes between animal and human welfare? If an animal is in terminal suffering we feel ethically obliged to kill it, but if it is a human we feel obliged to keep it alive to continue suffering.

People are prepared to use quite nasty methods to clear household pests. The UK's Pesticide Safety Directive describes anticoagulant rat and mouse poison as 'markedly inhumane' yet they are still in common use, primarily because the home owner can put the poison out and not have to face dealing with an animal in a trap. Rats

Chapter 3 – WHAT IS 'HUNTING'? 87

A weka checks out two possums I have just trapped in order to protect habitat for native species. I am a Patron of Picton Dawn Chorus, a community group set up to conserve native species by trapping introduced predators.

are becoming immune to more and more poisons, just as bacteria are no longer being killed by antibiotics.

I cannot say anything; we used poisons to clear rats from 600 acre Caldey Island off the Welsh coast and poisons such as 1080 are still used extensively in New Zealand. At the moment they are the only realistic method suitable for habitat management level applications.

Although the Agreement on International Humane Trapping Standards was finally signed in 2008, it applies only to fur-bearing species, of which only one, the stoat, can be legally hunted in the UK and there is no actual market for UK stoat furs. It is a saga of blithering incompetence. The reality is that trapping of mammals in the UK is because they are pests, not because they bear fur, and therefore they are not covered by the AIHTS. So there is no moral consistency at all. The break-back traps in common use in homes do not pass international humane trapping standards and yet are still licensed for sale and use for mice and rats. Nowadays there are even traps that enable squeamish householders to remove the mouse without having to touch it. Squeamishness is more of a selling point than humaneness! While there is a big furore about the trapping of fur-bearing animals, rats attract little welfare concern and yet they are very intelligent, sentient animals. Various welfare standards or criteria have been proposed for different pest control scenarios, such as >80% of trapped animals should lose consciousness within three minutes, but even the best options could leave 20% of victims still suffering indefinitely. Time and time again in wildlife management we see politics over-ruling consistency and common sense so that in the end some people become disillusioned by silly legislation and just ignore it.

Bycatch is also an issue for trapping, especially in net fishing, but how to come up with an alternative that ticks all the right boxes? I will examine this in 5.7.

Some people regard raptors as pests because they conflict with their activities, such as game-rearing. I had a falcon shot by a gamekeeper while she was chasing a crow over his head. I had 20 people with me, including a Justice of the Peace, and we recorded the actual flight and shooting on film. But still the Public Prosecutor would not press charges, and of course I had pressure from the National Gamekeepers' Organisation not to publicise the shooting. On the other hand, if you ask some protectionists how many peregrines they want, they place no limit on them, even though the population has been saturated for two decades. One person's pest is another's icon.

When you hunt an animal to eat it, obviously you want to retrieve the body and therefore you need to kill it or catch it where you can reach it. When you are hunting an animal for sport, killing the animal may not be a priority; you may release it afterwards

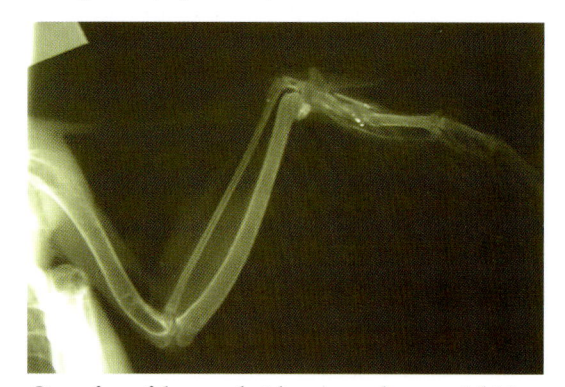

One of my falcons, shot by a gamekeeper right in front of us, when she was chasing a crow.

or even be hunting using a camera. But when you are hunting an animal because it is a pest, you just want it killed. Retrieving the body (unless it is going to smell under the floorboards) is often not a priority and, sad to say, suffering is often not a priority either. So the ethics of hunting and wildlife management are a tangled web. People are quick to come up with opinions often based on limited experience or sample sizes and this can result in legislation that may be counter-productive.

An interesting ethical twist came up the other day. I was in a zoom meeting with officials from the government Animal Plant and Health Agency. It was about reducing the risk of avian flu, which although now global, has peaked and subsided. The officials were concerned about poultry farms being infected. Tens of thousands of chickens are kept in each shed. If disease gets in there it kills the lot in days, or the vets kill them. What is the morality, and what are the economics, of farming chickens intensively like this? Highly dubious - but the public want cheap food. Meanwhile on our farm we have falcons, but they all have their own separate pens. The officials have created a new regulation in which anyone in Britain who keeps any bird must register on a national database. If any birds from two holdings 'gather' the APHA must be notified seven days ahead. So if two falconers go hawking together with their birds, even though they may be 100 metres or more apart, they are considered to have 'gathered'. But if one of their hawk catches a wild bird, that is not a 'gathering'. So I asked about the swallows and house martins and sparrows and wrens and wagtails and jackdaws and barn pigeons who nest in our various sheds. Should I notify the APHA about them? Or kill them? The lady hesitated and told me I could keep the swallows but should get rid of the jackdaws. But it is illegal for me to do that, so I have a choice of which law to break. And in this case, it is not the birds themselves who are being a pest; it is simply that they could potentially be vectors for disease which could impact the commercial poultry farms. So where are the ethics? It gets worse! Avian flu is also being found in cats, foxes and dairy cows. Should I get rid of those too? And it is also found in humans… Hang on a minute, how far are we going with this charade? And avian flu can remain active in dead birds, infecting scavengers. So if I kill a pheasant, and then give it to a falconer friend, will I have 'gathered'?

I told you pests can be tricky!

3.12 Hunting for food

Humans are phenotypically and ethotypically omnivores. It is possible to survive on a full vegan diet or on a purely animal diet, but this requires great care to balance nutrients. Extreme diets can have sub-lethal effects, such as shortened lifespan, reduced fecundity, or proneness to some diseases or deficiencies, but all this is far from fully understood at the moment. So, suffice to say, our choice of diets, both physically and mentally, is open to a full spectrum of options. Paradoxically, as more meat-eating people in Western cultures switch to vegetarian diets, vegetarian populations in Asia are beginning to eat more meat.

Hunter forager!

Foraging for fungi and shellfish, together with marine fishing, are probably the only direct hunting for food we do in Britain. Venison and game birds are mainly by-products of wildlife management or recreational hunting, as are salmon and trout. Even these are mainly the products of game farms and fish farms. A lot of Brits are quite squeamish about eating any food that is a little strange to them, or even offal such as liver and kidneys. So as far as food is concerned, for most of us our diet is based on farming rather than hunting.

For most animals, their choice of diet, if it is available, is ethotypic. Herbivores, omnivores, carnivores and so on are what they are. They can learn refinements in their diets, that certain items are, for example, more palatable than others, and they can vary their diets, for example when granivorous birds increase their protein levels by feeding insect diets to their young, but essentially they have to eat what they are capable of digesting. Birds of prey eat raw meat, end of story; don't expect them to become herbivorous. As humans, being omnivores, we can make choices in our diets. These are learned, cultural choices; 79% of American vegans are women and 59% of American vegetarians are women. Why the gender difference?

Why do people chose different diets? Often the first reason people develop food preferences is because of taste and palatability, starting at weaning. These learned preferences are also imprinted at this young age and tend to remain favourites throughout life. After the age of seven, cultural influences are strong and there is peer pressure to conform on diet. Other than maintaining the social group, there is no further special underlying morality in these diet decisions.

When the food preferences come to be more considered, then the decisions have some underlying motivation. For example a certain diet might be thought more healthy for you in some way. There is a massive industry built around this, so I need say no more about it.

There may also be some moral reasoning going on. One of the reasons for a vegan diet is because the person is against killing animals. Killing an animal can involve pain and generally we seek to make death as swift and painless as possible. Somehow, our religious rituals take precedence over this in halal and kosher slaughter. But killing can be instantaneous and painless and if I shoot a sheep in the field at home it drops with grass still in its mouth. However, if I have to transport the live sheep to a slaughterhouse, this entails some suffering, and with increasingly tight veterinary regulations, all the small local slaughterhouses have closed down, which means the sheep have to travel considerable distances to be killed. So the method of killing can range from totally humane to really rather horrid.

I was chatting to Erian, the other day; he's a neighbour who kills and butchers our sheep for us. "Strange thing" he said, "I'm allowed to kill and barbecue our pigs for my own family consumption but it's illegal for me to kill the same pigs for sale at a public Hog Roast. I have to take them to the slaughterhouse in Llanybydder to be killed, then bring them home and cook them. But the ones killed in Llanybydder take an hour longer to cook than the ones I kill at home. It's the stress you see. Makes the meat tough."

Often the concern is not just about the manner of death, but the living conditions during life, for example, beef cattle kept in feedlots in America without access to grass. Rearing systems vary, some are very natural and humane, others decidedly less so. Therefore I am happy to eat my own sheep, but not keen to support some other farming practices, such as farrowing pens for pigs. These are all moral value judgements, none necessarily more valid than others, and we have to find our own opinions. But the only ultimate way to avoid death is to avoid life. Most of our domesticated food species would be extinct if we did not kill them, and there would be no farm animals in the landscape. So an animal-welfare decision can result in their eradication.

We haven't kept any pigs lately. Usually we buy a few weaners in the spring, fatten them up over the summer and kill them in the autumn. We have a pig field where succeeding generations have rootled and dug craters and wallows. But the field is empty now. When I top the grass in the summer I bounce up and down on the tractor when I hit each hole, a legacy from our happy pigs. Since foot and mouth in 2001, it has been made illegal to feed human food slops to pigs so it is no longer practical to keep a couple of pigs at home. Profit margins are so tight that the only way to make a success of pig-farming is a commercial large-scale operation, the sort detested by vegans, and often rightly so. We live in a crazy world. Perhaps a pre-condition for a restaurant licence should be to keep a pig to eat all the slops. Strange that restaurant food is considered fit for humans but not for pigs…

Attempts have been made in recent years to improve the lives of chickens by enriching their environment and giving them a little more room. But the fact remains that in the UK, whereas it is illegal to keep any bird in a cage too small for it to fully extend its wings, an exception is made for poultry, which is by far the largest group of birds kept in captivity. Laying hens are allowed a battery cage floor area about the size of the cover of this book. Farmers operate on tiny profit margins because, although chicken is an increasingly popular food, people want it cheap and if they cannot get British chicken at a competitive price they will eat chicken from other countries, such as Brazil, and not ask too many questions. Currently, you can buy a plucked, oven-ready chicken for £2 which represents about 15 minutes worth of paid labour at minimum wage rates. Have you ever tried hatching, rearing, killing, plucking, packing and taking a chicken to market? For £2? It is absurd! I wonder what

Really?

quality of brief life that chicken had, and what pitiful pay the workers received, and what environmental pollution it entailed?

We seem to have one set of welfare standards for pet animals that we deem inside our own moral community and another set for food animals kept away from human gaze, or for wild animals, although of course they all have similar levels of sentience. We use euphemisms; on the one hand people refer to 'culling' (which is normally for removing unwanted animals towards some kind of management target) or 'harvesting', as if the animals were a plant crop being garnered in. Both these terms tend to exclude the animal from our own moral community and thus tacitly assume it is OK to kill them. Other people try to include all animals in our moral community and refer to any killing of them as 'murder', which again has its own connotations. The problem with including all sentient beings in one's moral community are several; the first is, why then exclude the non-sentient ones, such as plants, or brain-dead people? The second is, how do you then do any form of livestock farming or wildlife management? And the third is, what is the logical argument for never killing an organism just because it is sentient? No religions ban killing sentient animals and all the trophic ecosystems of the natural world are predicated on sentient animals killing one another. If they didn't the whole living world would collapse in days. How can you explain to a falcon that it shouldn't kill animals and eat them? Is being a herbivore in some way more virtuous than being a carnivore? I don't think so, and I don't think sentience is a useful criterion. Nor is killing necessarily

Livestock never liked this north-facing bank. I've planted it into deciduous woodland. Don't try to take a tractor on it, even in summer.

relative or proportional to suffering. One can suffer a lot while alive yet have a quick death that halts suffering. It irks me that at the one extreme vegans are advocating plant-only diets and somehow claiming the moral high ground, while in other large areas of the planet the cultures treat animals as commodities without any consideration at all for their suffering. Shifting attitudes towards more humane systems is a Sisyphean task which may take several human generations to change, if ever. Where people are locked in some of the medieval beliefs and practices there seems little hope of progressing moral responsibilities towards non-human animals.

Perhaps it would be a good thing to ban livestock farming altogether? Instead of having sheep and cattle (which in a feedlot have a poor conversion ratio for corn), we could just grow arable crops instead? Cut out the middle man! An excellent theory, but it doesn't take land quality into account. For example, 95% of land in Wales is Agricultural Grade 4 or 5 or worse; it is too wet, too steep, or its soil quality is too poor for growing arable crops. The choice of land use is limited to either grazing animals or woodland, so this moral decision is based on a concern for habitats. The theory behind virtuous vegetarianism has rather a big gap from reality. Livestock farming is uneconomic without subsidies, yet the public want food cheaper than production costs, so what do we do?

Planting the trees in woodland enables me to claim Carbon Credits. So I paid £3,000 (plus 20% VAT for it to be validated, then £4,450 plus VAT for verification, and consultants, then 6p per unit to be registered, followed by an additional 3p per unit once marketable. I'm told I could get the equivalent of £58,890 - £98,150 at today's prices in a hundred years' time. So I pay all these consultants and registries etc cash now against the prospect of making some money once I'm well dead, in order that some company somewhere can carry on polluting, but declaring themselves virtuously 'carbon neutral'. Meanwhile all the other woods I have planted are not eligible because they were not registered at planting because the scheme wasn't running then. Are we all mad?

So should the human population of Wales (somehow, magically) be reduced to the carrying capacity of the land? Should it be a moral global policy that human populations should be limited to the carrying capacity of each area? Since 1984, Britain's self-

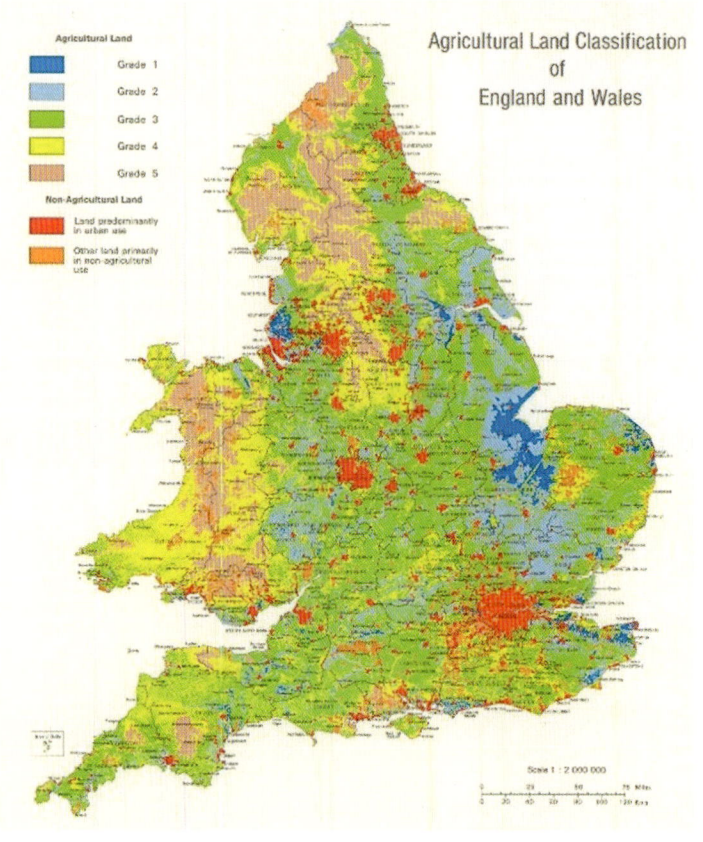

Agricultural land classification for England and Wales. What grade land do you live on?

The same view a few years later. This plantation has been accredited for carbon credits.

sufficiency for food has dropped from 78% to 56%. Should each country be self-sufficient for food and natural resources? If they aren't, then some will be net consumers and some must therefore be net producers, and there must be a trade between them.

What if we take part of an animal to eat it or wear it? Skins with the fur still on (or off), feathers for duvets, bones for Chinese medicines? Is it so bad to kill an animal for its fur? Is it worse to kill an animal and then not use its fur at all? Wouldn't the use of the fur somehow, in some small way, compensate for the animal's death? Rats have lovely smooth fur. I'm sure some creative fashion designer could make them into G-strings. It seems a pity to waste them! Is it worse to kill an animal for its fur than for its meat? If you've killed an animal for whatever reason, don't you have an obligation to make the most use of it that you can?

Is it the killing bit that is the ethical problem? Why not just shear the fur off the live animal? Is being shorn better or worse than a quick bullet in the head? It takes a few minutes to shear a sheep and they bleat a bit, depending on the way you hold them. Of course the sheep doesn't realise that it is not in the process of being killed.

Is it the method of killing that is the problem? Is shearing better than halal killing?

What if the animal was not killed deliberately but by accident on the road, or of old age? Is it OK to use it then; is it better to use it than to squander it? What if I make my wife a nice pair of mitts from a road-killed fox (as I have done). Or would it be better for her to wear gloves made from man-made fibres, petroleum derived plastics that will shed microfibers polluting the environment? These issues are explored by Melissa Kwasny in *Putting on the Dog*.

Is it the killing of a sentient animal that is the problem? Does it matter if you kill a plant for food, such as wheat, rather than keep it alive and crop it sustainably, such as orchard fruit? As long as the plant isn't sentient, does that mean that killing it doesn't matter? Killing plants may not entail a welfare issue; the plant probably doesn't feel pain. But destroying it denies the next trophic layer the use of the resource and growing monocultures of food crops destroys entire natural ecosystems full of plants and animals. Is it better to kill and eat a sheep living in a semi-natural ecosystem than to destroy the whole ecosystem to grow a monoculture so that you can be a vegetarian or vegan?

Trade in food stuffs means that most countries are cash-cropping. They are growing crops not just to sustain themselves, but for cash from exports. This puts more pressure on the last remnants of wild habitat, such as rainforests, and on the species that depend on them. Is it morally better to eat imported nuts and soya from these cash-cropping countries, or should one aim to be self-sufficient in one's own country? Today I ate a banana shipped into the UK from Costa Rica. Is this really sustainable for our climate?

The food supply chain creates 26% of the greenhouse gas emissions, and 61% of this is from farming, so overall farming is responsible for 16% of the GHGs. The ecological impacts of farming are complex and hotly contested and of course GHG emissions and animal welfare are not the only criteria. Whereas I can grow sheep and cattle on our farm in Wales, feeding them on grass pastures with no grains or concentrates, we cannot easily grow vegan foods outdoors. Having *flygskam* and reducing one's personal air travel is somewhat offset if all your food is flown in. Long supply chains cannot be sensible. Vegan diets include pomegranates and mangos from India, lentils from Canada, beans from Brazil, blueberries from the US and goji berries from China. About 16% of land in the UK is suitable for arable cropping and could be used for growing plant proteins for direct human consumption, such as fava beans, peas, hemp seed and sweet lupins. These could contribute to food self-sufficiency and reduce the need for imports. Another alternative is lab-grown foods, either general food compounds that can be flavoured to make them palatable, or replica plant-based or cell-grown meats. These have their own pros and cons. Personally I find beef burgers a travesty enough, let alone substitute 'meats' and 'cheeses'. When we kill an animal at home we only mince the cuts that cannot be eaten whole: the flaps and the bits and pieces after boning. A good steak or roast joint from grass-kept beef cattle or sheep is something to be savoured as a treat. Substitutes have yet to compare and, personally, I like to sit down and enjoy meat from an animal we have grown on the farm, or hunted, moving the cycle of nutrients from one trophic level to the next. Although Compassion in World Farming claims that 70% of farm animals in the UK are 'factory' farmed, they do not so much as mention sheep, our staple animal in Wales. Given the foul weather we have in winter here, cattle enjoy much better conditions in the sheds during winter and the land benefits too.

Buying and importing food from overseas impacts the economies of the source countries. Some products such as avocados and quinoa are now too expensive for locals to buy in their own countries. And, in the rush for cash cropping, wildlife habitats are destroyed to grow palm nut plantations or for beef ranching. Reliance on other countries for staple commodities, such as food or oil, is a dangerous strategy and the Coronavirus is already making people think again about self-sufficiency for staples.

There are large parts of the world where vegetarianism is not an option. Many arid and steppe landscapes do not have sufficient rainfall or soil to grow crops and people sustain themselves mainly by herding. They do not have the option or cash to go down to a local organic shop and buy exotic plant-based foods. In Mongolia the increasing bad weather events or *dzuds* are causing the Gobi to expand northwards with encroaching desertification. Often 30% or more of the horses, sheep and yaks die over winter and herders are having to leave ancestral grazing lands and crowd into the *ger* districts on the outskirts of Ulaanbaatar to scratch a living. I remember an American lady there had got together a women's group and they had cultivated a small patch of green vegetables in a garden. The women were tasting things like lettuce and radishes for the first time and looked apprehensive, while a few men looked on incredulously. An interesting social experiment, but not one that can be rolled out on a wider scale. The Russians tried cropping in Mongolia and large areas of steppe testified to their efforts to grow wheat. There are huge abandoned fields and ruined grassland ecology. It was part of their great agricultural disaster.

This leads one on to the old saying: *'The only good conservationist is a dead conservationist!'* As long as you are alive, you are making demands on the Earth's resources, which are finite. At least once you die your nutrients can return to the soil. At the end of the day, it is not just what you eat that is the problem. You, yourself are the problem. I am the problem. Collectively, we humans are the problem. With the human population rapidly climbing out of control, we have already outstripped the Earth's renewable resources. Soon it will not be a question of a moral decision on diet fads, soon we will be grateful just to eat at all. Efforts have been made in the last two decades to increase food production and access, but in the end, this is a blip. We cannot continue increasing food supply, wrecking the environment and increasing the human population indefinitely – what is the point?

As we put more and more pressure on farming (I cannot remember a time when we farmers have not been exhorted to be more 'efficient'), something has to give. While getting exercised about the morality of eating animals, spare a thought for the soil. We are losing soil quality and quantity and spreading more and more chemicals. Our invertebrates are crashing, insect biomass has fallen by 75%. We are making a silent, insidious ecological Insect Holocaust which we barely understand and scarcely care a damn about. Furry animals with pleading eyes tear our heart strings, but screw the whole planet for cheap junk food, who cares?

George Monbiot maintains that by 2050 farming will be redundant and our diets will be satisfied by lab-grown food; a somewhat depressing prognosis. While there are changes ahead for sure, it takes more than thirty years to change the food habits of millions of years. With a diet of processed proteins we won't need teeth. Somehow a romantic candle-lit dinner just won't be the same…

3.13 Recreational hunting

I have a friend who manages a golf course. I was telling him how before the ban, fox-hunts would kill 50 or so foxes a year. "Oh," he said, "we kill much more animals than that maintaining the golf course. Rabbits mostly, some moles and rats and a few foxes. We poison the moles and rats and shoot the rabbits and foxes at night." So in this scenario, the golf was the 'fun' and the killing was 'pest control'.

Recreational hunting is the main objection of anti-hunters. It is the hardest aspect to explain and it is a thread all through this book. Trophy hunting has even more detractors but when you go into the detail, the financial and ecological benefits often outweigh other criteria. The actual killing part does not entail much of an animal welfare problem. Other animals, from bush meat to chickens carried in bunches upside down, on bicycles heading for market, probably suffer a lot more. There is considerable literature on trophy hunting which is outside my area of expertise. Britain also exports animal trophies, especially red stags' heads, but these don't seem to impinge on the moral consciousness the way Big Game animals do. Funnily enough, when we are taking blood or DNA samples from falcons overseas to send back to the UK labs for analysis, we still have to have CITES permits, just as you would a lion trophy.

Looking at all these types of hunting in the round, it is possible to sum up with a simple matrix relating to purposes rather than to methods.

Purpose Criterion	Food	Pest control	Recreation	Trophy	Cat-keeping	Livestock farming
Requires huntable surplus	Usually	No	Yes	Yes	No	Yes
May require re-stocking	Yes	No	Yes	Yes	No	Yes
Depresses below carrying capacity	Sometimes	Yes	No	No	Sometimes	No
Culls poor animals	Sometimes	Neutral	Yes	No	Yes	Yes
Culls prime animals	Sometimes	Neutral	Yes	Yes	Yes	Yes
Legally selective	Mainly	Mainly	Yes	Yes	No	Yes
Takes non-target animals	Sometimes	Sometimes	No	No	Yes	Sometimes
Minimises cost/hours per animal	Sometimes	Yes	No	No	Yes	Yes
Maximises cost/hours per animal	No	No	Yes	Yes	No	No
Minimises suffering	Neutral	No	Yes	Yes	No	Yes
Can cause local extinctions	Yes	Yes	No	No	Yes	No
'Suffering index'	Low	High	Low	Low	High	Low
Carcass retrieved	Yes	No	Yes	Yes	No	Yes
Operator paid	No	Yes	No	No	No	Yes

I will go into some of these aspects in much more detail in the next chapters.

Roger skins a stag. An enjoyable hunt for a meaty pest.

4 Predation and aggression

4.1 Introduction

This may be a good point to expand a little on the biology of predation. Humans are hunters, predators, as are some of our relatives, such as the chimpanzees. We often use words, such as 'fierce' rather loosely but it is important to understand the roots of our fierce or aggressive behaviour. In social groups, including our own, there are three types of behaviour that could be described as 'aggressive'. One is internal to the group and is to do with maintaining dominance hierarchies and enforcing the group's moral values. Another is external to the group and is to do with fighting for territory or resources. The third is predation or hunting.

Predation is not aggression. Predation is when one trophic level feeds on another. When a deer browses on a bush, we do not normally think of that as predation because the bush is insentient and immobile. This does not mean that the bush cannot react. Its reaction may not be on an individual basis, nor on a short time scale, but on an evolutionary scale. The bush may develop thorns, or toxins or the ability to coppice. Lack of adaptation to browsing animals can be seen in some of the New Zealand vegetation, or in the devastating effects of alien beavers introduced to Patagonian wetland ecosystems. But normally we think of predators and prey as being at least sentient and mobile. Even insects can be aware of one another and make avoidance reactions. Predation is natural and indeed unavoidable for the predators. The lion does not have the option of eating grass. The whole ecosystem is predicated on predation and carnivory. The killing of prey is not immoral, it is natural. Thus the wolf is morally inhibited from killing a member of its own group, but not from killing a prey animal.

There are people who maintain that killing is 'wrong'. It makes an easy sound bite but blandly ignores all the trophic levels above plants. The whole of the natural world consists of webs of organisms who kill one another. To ignore that, or to condemn it as 'wrong' is simplistic beyond serious consideration. Try to imagine a world with no deaths. What would animals feed on – they cannot photosynthesise energy from the sun; they have to eat the plants that do. Birth condemns you to death. Without birth there can be no deaths, and without deaths there can be no births. Ecosystems would go haywire. And deaths, whether by predation or some other means, may entail various levels of suffering or release from suffering, just as births do.

It is important to maintain connections with nature, with births and deaths, with the elements, the tides, the hills. We have a deep ethotypic attraction to shorelines, a source

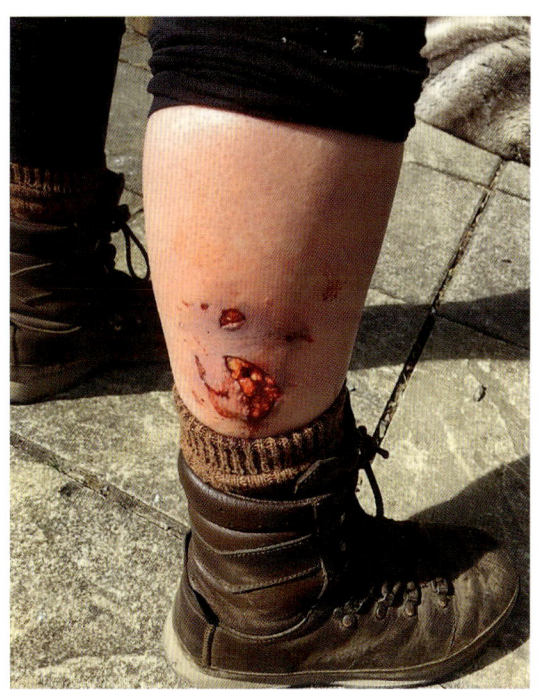

When a dog bites you it is usually to do with defence of a group, or dominance.

of our food and opportunities for thousands of generations. To have to wait for a tide is elemental; never mind watches, and phones, and puny politicians with their laws, the tide is remorseless. And death is too. Why object to a dead rabbit hanging up outside a butcher's? We are all of us in this cycle and it is well to remember that, and not fight it but to make the most of life while we live. Farming and hunting are front line when it comes to births, deaths and the cycle of the seasons.

The other position is to postulate that it is wrong for humans to kill things because we are not natural; we are not part of the natural world, that we sit in some privileged position of supremacy. But again, it is simplistic beyond serious consideration to suggest that we are not natural organisms, subject to the same resource needs and constraints as other species. We are not avatars. Basically the moral premise 'killing is wrong' is dreamed up out of thin air, an anthropocentric approach that denies our real nature and substance. It can be amusing to follow the moralistic contortions people go through attempting to reconcile this idealistic position with real life situations in predation. The caring and nurturing aspect of the nature of some humans is, I think, noble; but taken to extremes it can become ridiculous. Imposing a vegan diet on your pet cat and then letting it out to hunt animals is a rather mixed-up interpretation of morality.

Predatory behaviour is complex. The predator that waits until it is hungry, or worse still, lean, before it starts to hunt, is doomed. While hunger is linked to the drive to hunt, hunting itself must start before then, while the predator is strong and with fat reserves. Predators must also be able to exploit temporary abundances or vulnerabilities of prey. Some will kill more than for their immediate needs, like a fox in a chicken run. Surplus food may be cached, but not always. Humans do similarly and many marketing strategies rely on this behaviour. Buy one, get one free. Buy it now before the offer closes…

As well as the behaviour of the predators themselves, predation has direct effects and feed-back effects on their prey species and the trophic levels below them, so that their impact goes right up to the habitat level. The classic example touted around is the cascade effect of wolves in the Yellowstone. But the evidence is all around. Too often there is public concern for the individual prey animal, while completely failing to see the bigger picture.

Mammalian and avian predators have intense drives to hunt, and we see that in their search and attack behaviours that are expressed in play. They love to pounce on substitute prey and there is a big market in prey toys for cats and dogs. Our falcons play with scraps of fur, tennis balls, squeaky toys and pine-cones. Wild New Zealand falcons have been known to fly down and play-attack a ball that children are playing with. They will also catch a small bird, fly up into the sky, then release it and catch it again, like a cat with a mouse. Predators also play with one another, without harming each other, and social predators play-enact social hunting. Many human games are a form of social hunting. If an animal is too full of energy or bored, play can be continued well into adulthood, but if it is physically or mentally depressed it may not play at all. Being unable to carry out these drives can result in stereotypical frustrated pacing behaviour as seen in bored mammalian predators in zoos. These are powerful drives, and it is not surprising that humans, being social omnivores, exhibit both play hunting and play food foraging, as well as real hunting and foraging.

Most predation is about food. It is not a simple cause and effect relationship: 'I am hungry therefore I will hunt', but in the main, predation is a food thing. Predation can also include pest control, for example we hunt rats, and a lion may swat a troublesome fly. This, at root, is not predation but protection of a resource or defence of territory. Non-human predators hunt for food or recreation, but not specifically for population management, although their hunting often has that outcome.

Where defence of resources is involved, a whole different suite of moral values kicks in. Killing an enemy soldier is not considered 'murder'. Almost anything goes to achieve the end. Morality-based inhibitions that apply to members of one's own moral community do not apply to members of another group. Time and time again in human history there have been groups of humans in positions of power who have regarded other groups as sub-humans and treated them as slaves or even killed them. Critics of hunting often describe it as 'murder' but this is an emotive misuse of the word, nor can non-human animals 'murder' humans. I know of no evidence supporting a causal link between hunting and aggressive or abusive behaviour in humans. Some studies of American gun hunters have shown correlations, but not causality.

4.2 The psyche of the predator

There are various aspects of predation that could be thought of as impinging on 'moral' behaviour. Some people hold very strong views about the morality of hunting, perhaps without appreciating that they themselves owe their very existence to their own pedigree of successful hunting ancestors. In many urban human societies, hunting, in its natural sense, is redundant. The food supply has been subsumed by agriculture, and the instincts to hunt have been channelled into competitive games and into retail therapy shopping. One could therefore claim that, if we no longer need to hunt, then we should not do so; it is not 'necessary'. That then moves the debate on as to the moral consequential aspects of agriculture and vegetarianism, and ultimately of exceeding the carrying capacity of our planet both for our own species and for other species that we out-compete.

Solitary specialist obligate predators, such as the peregrine, show hunting behaviour that is very ethotypic, with a limited repertoire of strategies, not a huge learning component and a relatively short dependency period. Their main strategy is the high search followed by a stoop or tail-chase at avian prey, in the air. Other falcons, such as the New Zealand falcon, have a much wider spectrum of hunting behaviours at a variety of species, both in the air and on the ground, in a variety of habitats. This requires more learning, and a longer dependency period.

Closer to home, the domestic cat is a solitary predator specialising in watch and pounce or stalk and pounce techniques which are ruined if another cat joins in. So it has nothing in its ethotype to do with cooperative hunting unlike social semi-obligate predators such as the pack-hunting canids, which hunt in groups and require an additional layer of learning because they have to cooperate with one another. Some canids also have the ability to digest some plant foods in time of meat scarcity and are thus potentially omnivorous. Being forced to live and cooperate together fosters empathy and signalling of intentions as well as maximising the abilities of each individual.

Humans share many similarities with the canids, except that we are more omnivorous than obligate predators. We also maximise our foraging success by role-partitioning, if you like: 'sexual di-ethotypy'. Just as our phenotypes are sexually dimorphic, so our ethotypes are differentiated by gender. Males are larger, stronger and form hunting parties for active predation for meat. Females are smaller and weaker, foraging for static foods while at the same time caring for the young. So while we are 'hunter-foragers' it tends to be the males who hunt and the females who forage. These two approaches require different foraging strategies and are reflected in gender differences in our ethotypes, our attitudes and our diet choices. Fitzgerald (The Emergence of the Figure of "Woman-The-Hunter:" Equality or Complicity in

Oppression?) portrays these differences as feminism, but role partitioning is not the same as inequality.

Even within the gender roles, age brings changes. The fire in the belly of the hunter burns down to embers in old age. Hunting is for the fit and active. In Western societies these gender role differences, now consigned to urban obsolescence, still rear their heads in public opinion polls. Males are more likely to support various types of hunting whereas females are more likely to object to them, and to eat plant diets.

Bear in mind the concept of kinship groups and meme groups. Hunting parties tend to be both; that is to say, the individuals are often genetically close, and they learn from each other. On their success may hinge the future of their immediate hunting group and also of the women and children left behind, and through all of them, the precious genes that they are carrying. To be a successful hunting group, the individuals have to be equipped with a whole suite of instincts that, together, make for quite a complicated ethotype. They have to want to band together, to 'pull their weight' and have a good reputation in each other's eyes, they have to trust each other and be loyal to each other. This is not just about reciprocal benevolence, this goes beyond that to a deep-rooted instinct to work together, often in fast-moving crisis situations, without counting the cost or posting it on an imaginary 'reciprocating tally sheet'. It requires leadership both in terms of physical bravery and in terms of wisdom and strategy. It requires the ability to understand the intentions of others, to signal one's own intentions, and to work together towards a common goal. Leadership is not the same as a dominance hierarchy; the leader of a hunting group has to show the necessary skills and operates through the voluntary compliance of the other members of the group. A hunting trip is not the time for dominance squabbles. It requires the urge to leave home, to explore the unknown and to take risks. Where the ethotype fades out, learning steps in, strategies, customs and rituals develop, creating a meme group. And if real hunting is taken out of the equation, the instinct to form these groups is still strong, so we have inner-city gangs.

The first phase of the hunt for all predators is the searching phase. This may first entail defending a hunting area against encroachments by competing groups. This is ethotypic. Then you need to know your area well, and when and where the best opportunities are to find prey. Most of this is learned behaviour transmitted both vertically between generations and horizontally across age cohorts. To search for the prey requires a search image. The ability to develop a search image is ethotypic and is more apparent in some species than in others, but the identity of the prey species being searched for is largely learned behaviour; either learned directly or mimetically by copying more experienced members of the group. The more of a specialist you are, the narrower the range of species in your search image and, conversely, the more omnivorous you are, the wider the range of species that you are prepared to contemplate, until you are more or less opportunistic. Of course 'image' implies sight. For dogs it can equally be a scent image. They are in a different sensory realm. Because scent lingers, a hunt with a dog has an intermediate stage. First he searches for a scent, then having found it, he follows the scent gradient until he sees the prey.

But it is all very well locating a prey animal, the real question is: is it catchable? That question is complicated. To answer it, first you have to be aware both of your own abilities and those of your companions. You have to know where they are, their attack distances, and the escape distances of the prey. You have to be able to judge the escape abilities of the prey, is it weak and on its own? Is it young but defended by adults? Is it a long way away from cover? Has it got an explosive white-muscle-fuelled start, but no endurance, or is it liable to go on and on, without giving up? The urge to judge these things is instinctive but the judgements themselves stem from learning from experience. So the search phase is not just about finding prey, it is about finding a realistic attack opportunity.

The second phase is the attack itself. Its success hinges first on how good the initial attack opportunity is. The next element is the attack strategy. Most of the core strategies are recognisable and ethotypic, refined by a learning element. But they can also be opportunistic and require an instinct for curiosity. For example, if you learn to read the behaviour of vultures, you can see that they have pin-pointed a lion kill. If you reach the spot quickly enough you may be able to drive off the lions and steal the meat. This ability to look out for and discover opportunities developed intelligence and has probably been pivotal to the success of our human ancestors.

The attack itself may require courage, a fine line between bravery and stupidity, and physical co-ordination. Most attacks will fail. There needs to be an instinct to persist, to try again and again. And, if successful, the prey may require dismembering, sharing, transporting home and later, waiting patiently for food to be prepared, possibly cooked, and apportioned fairly, as well as dried or stored for later use. These are all elements of our human psyche evolved through hunting. They have shaped our ethotype and made us what we are today.

The foraging side of activities poses different problems. The emphasis this time is on the search element and not the attack element. With dependent young, the foraging area may have to be close to home. Searching for berries, tubers, grubs and shellfish requires an opportunistic curiosity. It also needs an instinct for optimum foraging strategy. Is it best to strip all the berries off one bush before moving on to the next? Or is it better to go for the low-hanging fruit, grab them and move on to another bush? These kinds of decisions are being made by many foraging species, from bees, to humming birds, to monkeys, all the time. These foraging instincts are best developed in women; often men cannot understand why women enjoy browsing the shops and men's clothes shops target women rather than men because they are often the ones choosing their men's clothes. Foraging for plant foods requires a basic instinct to go and search but then, rather than the attributes that men need for hunting, it requires patience and ability to assess ripeness or suitability. On top of this it requires learning: what foods are suitable and where to find them. Most of the foods require taking home, preparing and sharing out; all this entails instincts for empathy, cooperation and delayed rewards.

When you look at human foraging behaviour as we have inherited it from our ancestors, you appreciate how thin is the veneer of what we consider to be modern life and civilisation. Modern living is just a small extension of our hunter-forager instincts, and, because there are gender differences, women often struggle to understand what drives men to hunt in various real or artificial formats. They cannot understand why men would want to go out and chase an animal and bring it home, or why they want to spend hours glued to the sports channels, cheering on teams of people who they have never met and pretending that they are part of those teams. Men on the other hand cannot understand why women spend hours cruising the shopping malls, picking things up, looking them over, then putting them down again.

Sadly, only our ancestors were successful at hunter-foraging. We know they were successful because we are alive and here. Many others died before they could pass on their genes. Of all the aspects of our human life cycle, obtaining food has been, and still is, one of the main pinch points, a major selection pressure. Groups who perform poorly may die or they may have a reduced reproductive rate, or an increased infant mortality. Their genes will feature less and less in the genome. The instincts to hunt and forage are amongst the most powerful ones permeating our ethotype, possibly rivalled only by the instincts for personal survival and for reproduction. They have shaped our human character, both now and for the foreseeable future. Any moral values we may care to put on our hunting behaviour need to be looked at in this light.

4.3 What prompts an animal to start hunting?

The under-lying drive to hunt is instinctive; it is deeply embedded in our ethotype. Our basic ethotypic drives are very powerful, so powerful that they go way beyond their initial evolutionary 'purpose'. Our sex drive is so strong that we copulate all the year round throughout most of our adult lives, yet most of these copulations are recreational sex; very few result in pregnancies. The drive to rear young is also powerful, starting off in playing with dolls when we are young to adopting children or even animal surrogates to care for if we have no children of our own. Even subsistence hunting usually has an element of ritual and recreation. And just as with sex, there are always critics who maintain that recreational expression is wrong and that we should confine our instincts solely to the immediate purposes for which they evolved.

The lamb weans itself by starting to nibble plants here and there, finding some palatable and some not. But its initial hunting behaviour is instinctive. Because the plants cannot run away, the lamb is able to complete the full sequence of hunting rewarded by eating food. In contrast, the young of 'attacking' species, such as dogs, cats and falcons, cannot go out and complete a whole hunting sequence all at once. First they show some curiosity, and this then begins to focus on prey-like objects, items that are the size and shape of potential prey and especially ones that move. This may be a sibling, or an old bone or bird wing. They make mock attacks, 'playing' with the object. They may also include other parts of the hunting repertoire such as creeping up on the object before pouncing, or chasing after it if it makes a move to 'escape'. These behaviours are part of their ethotypic templates, complete instinctive patterns that are gradually improved by learning and practice. Their parents will start bringing in solid food and the youngster imprints on the taste and form of the food. Gradually the parent may bring in whole prey, or even prey that is still alive. Under parental guidance the youngster learns to complete the hunting sequence and catch the handicapped prey, to kill it and eat it. It is on its way to independence. From there the youngster makes its first attempts to capture wild prey, and we see entire search and attack sequences being used as instinctive templates. The lamb does not have this hunting template; it does not play at creeping up and pouncing on grass. Instead its play is more a social interaction, gambolling, stotting and head butting with companions.

Some species specialise in only one or two search or attack strategies, and maybe only one or two types of prey food. In falconry we call this becoming 'wedded' to a prey species. Having imprinted onto chosen prey they may ignore certain other prey although they could have easily caught it. Orcas do the same. Other predators are more opportunistic and generalist. If they happen to come across something they will try and get it. We humans fall into this category. For generalists, the best ethotypes and phenotypes are versatile all-purpose ones. Standing on hind legs to free up the fore-limbs, an opposable thumb for gripping things and an intelligent curious brain, sets us up for developing tools and radiating into so many directions that we are now falling victims of our own success. But even amongst humans, some are more entrepreneurial and opportunistic, while others stick to what they know, a nice steady job. Some favour a low interest, low risk investment strategy; others like high stakes.

Young, newly independent hunters are inexperienced and have poorer motor skills. Ask a car insurer who are the high risk groups! Birds of prey in their first year are still developing their skills in the attacking phase of hunting and of necessity often rely on the searching end of the hunting continuum. Flying fast is hazardous; they need to fly more slowly to start with and seek out simple prey to catch, before attempting more difficult attack opportunities. This is mirrored in their phenotypes, with longer feathers providing lower wing-loadings and slower flight.

We see this spectrum of hunting behaviour develop in all vertebrates (and many other taxa too). Some are at the searching end of the spectrum, others at the attacking end. It stems from the ethotypes and is aided by adaptive phenotypes. But what triggers the hunting behaviour?

To be in peak condition for hunting, you need to be fit and not too fat. Your base weight which includes your skeleton, skin and internal organs remains relatively static, but muscle mass and fat can vary enormously. We weigh our falcons every day during training and hunting, seeking to maximise muscle while reducing fat. If there is surplus fat the body has less need for food intake because it can metabolise fat, albeit not as quickly as glycogen in the blood stream. If there is no fat, and no food coming in, then the body starts to metabolise muscle tissue, resulting in wasting and weakness.

If you are not in peak condition you will be less motivated to undertake the more strenuous kinds of hunting, such as active attack methods. You may fall back towards searching types of hunting that can be done at a more leisurely pace. If you are very young, or pregnant, or ill, or frail, you may have to rely on someone else to provide food for you.

If you are a searcher, you are likely to eat little and often, with bouts of eating throughout the day punctuated by periods of digesting the food. As you go along the species spectrum towards the attacking end, you are likely to catch your food in one large package and gorge on it. So you may only eat once a day, or if a large predator, only once every two or three days. If you are maintaining body condition, then you are not going hungry or starving in the sense that you are having to metabolise fat or muscle to compensate for lack of food. But, once you have digested your last meal you will slowly develop an appetite, anticipating your next meal.

Thus, for a falcon, during the period immediately after feeding, we say the falcon is 'fed up'. She will not want to do anything except sit around digesting her meal. As her meal is digested she perks up a little and takes more interest in the world around her. She won't initiate searching but if an easy prey such as a mouse happens to show itself nearby she may be unable to resist the opportunity and drop onto it.

As the hours tick by, her appetite increases. She may start to fly from perch to perch scanning the area for an attack opportunity. Gradually her flights become more frequent until she may start searching quite purposefully. She might attempt an attack or two and fail, but if she is lucky she will catch something and start the whole feeding cycle all over again. If she is unlucky - perhaps it has been raining all day - she may go to sleep hungry, with only her fat reserves to keep her going. Her weight will trend further down. Although some species, such as seals and penguins, can live off their fat for long periods, many species cannot metabolise their fat fast enough to meet all their immediate energy demands, so they have to metabolise muscle too. That makes them weaker. If you are weaker, you are less able to catch food; you are on a downward spiral that may end in death. A small raptor in winter can starve to death in hours, even though fat.

Obligate carnivores, species that can only eat meat, are in a tricky position. Maybe two thirds of their young will starve to death in their first year because they fail to catch food and go into a death spiral. An alternative is to turn to food that is easier to obtain, such as worms or berries. In other words go down the spectrum and become more of a searching hunter than an attacking one. This is the position that us humans are in, together with many other omnivorous species. We can be attackers, but if this fails, we can fall back on foraging.

In temperate zones, such as Britain, when you try real foraging, you quickly discover that foods that stay still, such as nuts, fungi and berries, are scarce and seasonal. Until we started to use fire we could not eat uncooked grains because we cannot digest cellulose. And without deep freezes we could not store meat. So we had to share what we had and amass credit points with our colleagues so that later, when they succeeded but we failed, we could lay claim to some of their food. These pressures are at the root of some of our social behaviours, such as reciprocity, and also dictated our original geographical distribution favouring reliable hunting grounds such as shore-lines.

Specialist attacking species use a limited number of search and attack techniques and this can be provided by templates from the ethotype - characteristic instinctive behaviours. Of course some learning is involved, but the ethotype provides the behavioural framework. The same applies to the searchers. But the ones in the middle, the omnivores, have to be jacks of all trades; they have to turn their hands to anything. This requires more learning and longer developmental periods. Imitative learning is more effective than solitary trial and error learning, so social mimetic groups improve hunting success.

For the 'attackers', it is essential that they start to hunt based on appetite rather than hunger. Their instinct to hunt kicks in before and separately from their need to eat. It is too easy to slip into the death spiral. Although the outcome of a successful hunt is food and a meal, the hunt itself is primarily motivated by instinct, not starvation. While increasing hunger increases the motivation to hunt, beyond a certain point, low blood sugar lethargy sets in and the animal stops attempting to obtain food. For us humans living in an urban society with food delivered to our doors, it is hard to appreciate the knife edge that all hunters - including our own ancestors - live on. A few days of failing to obtain food means death. Perhaps the nearest analogy one can make is that a considerable portion of humans have very little savings in the bank. If they lose their job, without wages coming in, they may only have sufficient funds to pay their bills for a few days before becoming destitute.

When 'attacking' hunters, including humans, are in this happy zone of good body condition, then they hunt strongly without needing a food reward. We see this with our falcons chasing robotic prey. Their fastest, highest hunts are in this condition, and although we put a piece of meat on the prey as a reward, usually they don't even bother to eat it. We see the same with dogs and humans; throw a ball into a group and some are guaranteed to chase it. Do the same with sheep and they will ignore it.

It is important to understand this separation of hunting instinct from food reward because it is key to understanding hunting behaviour and the morality of hunting. Many people can accept hunting for food, or at least subsistence hunting, but not recreational hunting or 'hunting for fun'. Recreational hunting is satisfying this instinct to hunt, and is not necessarily about the desire to eat. Perhaps the best example of this is the domestic cat, an attacking species with a strong ethotypic instinct to hunt regardless of how well it is fed. And, as in many other predators, the hunting instinct is strongest in young adults.

Some people oppose recreational hunting of sentient vertebrates but enjoy recreational hunting of fruit, berries, fungi and even inedible cut flowers. It is fortunate that we are all different.

4.4 What does the prey think?

Prey vary immensely. Berries probably don't think at all! Mussels *Mytilus edulis* on the other hand, although they don't have a brain as such, can respond to basic stimuli. They can 'clam' up. Further up the brain scale lobsters have significant capacity to suffer and as Peter Godfrey-Smith points out, the brain of octopuses is sophisticated. Although a totally different evolutionary strand from the vertebrates, octopuses are sentient as are reptiles, amphibians, birds and mammals. But sentience can mean many things and the one thing that is indisputable is that sentience varies between species and of course between humans and non-humans. It is clear that all of us experience life somewhat differently. Our sensory systems differ and our understanding of the future and the past differs too. Often humans have attributed their own thoughts and feelings to other species, simply because that is all they know. Most people, philosophers and anthropologists included, have only very superficial experiences with other animals and this leads to deep misunderstandings. Higher vertebrates can anticipate, think into the future, although not as well as humans can (not that we are very good either). So when approached by a predator they can anticipate what might happen and make moves to stymie the attack before it happens. Provided that the predator is a species within their evolutionary cognizance, the prey has ethotypic templates it can use to escape. It might instinctively freeze to avoid detection. It might fly up into the sky to avoid a ground predator, or seek cover on the ground to avoid an aerial one. Its responses are tuned to the type of predator and attack. If the prey survives the attack, it will have learned something from the experience and will be even better at avoiding a subsequent attack. This is how the balance between predator and prey works.

Obviously we cannot know what goes on in another's mind, we can only conjecture, and suffering can take many forms. Some suffer more, some less, all differently. Can you imagine the suffering of whales and dolphins when bombs fall into the sea, when ships hammer radar noise into the ocean? Or of animals that swallow plastic bags and beads in mistake for food? How does the frog feel when, returning to its pond to spawn, it finds the area concreted over because you have built your house there?

Having been a falconer all my life, when I go hawking, my mind identifies with my falcon. When the chase is on I am mentally urging her on. We are predators together. But a few years ago when I developed robotic birds for the falcons to catch, who was the operational 'mind' for that robird? Me! Suddenly I became the prey. I had to think like the prey, anticipate what the falcon would do next, judge the wind, the height, my own speed, my staying power. Things happen so fast, my brain could hardly keep up. Panic and you're dead…

I designed the first models to finely balance the prey with the predator, so that a good pilot could escape but only if he was good. Then we started exporting the models to the Middle East falconers. Immediately we got calls for more powerful engines. The pilots wanted us to swing the balance more in their favour because they didn't like getting caught unintentionally. They didn't mind getting caught on their own terms to encourage the falcon, but if they felt unable to escape by just hitting the throttle, they didn't like it. Interesting stuff, not conclusive, but insightful. Of course many human-simulated hunting or warfare games entail both offence and defence. If one side has over-whelming dominance, there is no contest. Collecting mussels off a jetty at low tide hardly gets the adrenaline flowing.

5 Animal welfare issues

Some of this section is supported by our film *The Hunting Act 2004: Animal Welfare Implications* published by the All Party Parliamentary Middle Way Group on Hunting with Dogs.

5.1 What is 'suffering'?

We need to be clear about two terms: 'suffering' and 'cruelty'. They are often used interchangeably, but they are fundamentally different. To *suffer* is to experience some form of pain. To be *cruel* is to delight in the suffering of others. Suffering is something experienced by the 'victim'. Cruelty is something experienced by the 'persecutor'. As Emma Griffin (p.150) points out, in the history of debates about human-animal relations, these two terms have frequently been conflated, sometimes deliberately. Thus attacks on hunting often masquerade as concern for the suffering of the prey, but are in reality more about the perceived cruelty of the hunters.

I know what it is like to be an animal trapped in a leg-hold trap. When I was six we were living on the edge of Cranbourne Chase in Dorset, a medieval hunting forest. I put my hand down a hole under a tree and was caught in a badger trap. It was like a miniature version of a man-trap, a gin trap with serrated teeth and double springs, now illegal. In this type of trap there is a risk that the animal will twist and turn trying to escape and that the teeth will cut the leg off, so the gamekeeper had put a stop on it so that the jaws did not totally clamp shut. I was caught by the wrist. My own weight was insufficient to bend the springs but fortunately my brother was with me, and with one of us on each spring we managed to ease the jaws sufficiently for me to get my hand out. I was badly bruised but fortunately had no broken bones. If he hadn't been there I would have had to wait there all night until the gamekeeper showed up, and that would have meant losing my hand through lack of blood supply.

The table opposite is based on data gleaned where possible from published information but primarily from a consensus of expert opinion. More detailed research into these parameters is needed. In examining this table you could apply additional criteria, and you could apply different weighting to the seven criteria used here. It is not easy to quantify such things: it is only possible to assess them comparatively as best we can. The values given are obviously indicative rather than absolute. Some of these methods are now illegal in the UK.

Trapping a possum outside my bedroom window in New Zealand.

	Natural selectivity	Legal selectivity	Human supervision	Pre-capture pursuit interval	Catch-to-kill interval	Maiming	Approx UK annual kills
Gazehounds	Yes	99%	Yes	<2 mins	0-5 secs	0	500,000
Scenthounds	Yes	99%	Yes	>2 mins	0-5 secs	0	20,000
Terriers	No	99%	Yes	<2 mins	0-5 secs	?	15,000
Cats	Yes	0%	No	<30 secs	0-30 mins	20%	275,000,000
Ferrets	No	99%	Yes	<5 mins	0-30 mins	2%	10,000
Raptors	Yes	97%	Yes	<2 mins	0-3 mins	0	6000
Gassing	No	70%?	Yes	N/A	0-30 mins	1%	500,000
Anti-coagulant poisons	No	80%	No	N/A	0-30 mins	?	20,000,000
Dead traps	No	80%	Yes	N/A	0-24 hours	10-53%	10,000,000
Snares	No	80%	Yes	N/A	0-24 hours	10%	200,000
Live traps	No	80%	Yes	N/A	0-24 hours	0	40,000
Bird ringing	Yes	100%	Yes	N/A	1-30 mins*	0	660,000
Shotgun	No	100%	Yes	<2 mins	0-15 mins	30%	20,000,000
Rifle	Yes	100%	Yes	0	0-15 mins	5%	3,000,000
Angling	No		Yes	1-60 mins	1-180 mins		?
Net fishing	No		Yes		?		?

*A comparison of the hunting methods and the welfare criteria. *Bird ringing shows the catch-to-release interval.*

It would be nice to have some firmer figures for these parameters, but meanwhile it is possible to make some simple, broad-brush analyses. For example, cats are responsible for about 83% of all kills in our UK analysis. If you look at the parameter that you are interested in, such as the catch-to-kill interval, or maiming, and multiply it by the volume, you can see quite clearly where the major sources of suffering really exist. Not shown here are other human-induced tolls on wildlife which don't have even approximate estimates, such as those killed on roads, electrocuted or colliding with glass windows or wires.

Terriers are small dogs bred to work in tunnels. Used for foxes, and following the guidelines of the National Working Terrier Federation, they carry radio collars so that once the terrier has found the fox it can be quickly dug directly down to and shot or removed. Above ground terriers are extremely effective at killing rats, usually in one quick bite. Terriers, lurchers and hounds have the huge advantage in that they kill quickly and leave no wounded.

In attempting to reduce animal suffering as represented above, one must take into account the consequences of eliminating these methods. What would happen if rats and mice were allowed to proliferate unchecked? What would happen if deer and rabbits could not be controlled on farmland? What efforts would landowners make to

This lactating vixen was hit by a car and crawled into our field. We took the dogs and searched for the den but couldn't find it. The cubs will have died.

maintain and improve habitat benefiting all wildlife if they obtained no sporting return? Tourism, such as at Knepp or Alladale, is an option, but a limited one. Would the alternative deaths awaiting the prey animals be preferable to the ones they have now? How many more deaths would some of the predators cause if left to live longer?

I have excluded fish from this study because it has proved impossible to get quality data. The fishing problem is huge, it suffers from the 'tragedy of the commons', by heavy over-fishing, by destruction of the seabed, by massive bycatches, plastic pollution, not to mention the effects on seabirds such as albatrosses caught on tuna long-lines, and now the increasing exploitation of krill which is a major cornerstone of higher trophic levels. It is a whole book in itself, waiting to be written, especially as fish are now recognised to be sentient. The film *Seaspiracy* by Ali and Lucy Tabrisi illuminates the sea fishing issues, but independent research is still thin on the ground and solutions further away still.

Given that an animal is born, then it must also live and die. While we think of death as being somehow a bad thing, death itself marks the end of suffering. What kicks the whole thing off is birth, the beginning of life. To prevent all suffering, simply prevent births; by the time death is reached it is already too late. One must also remember the antonym of suffering, which is pleasure. We tend to focus on the unpleasant aspects, but if you go through the points below you will notice that pleasure can be experienced in mostly the same ways as suffering. One defines the other, just as black defines white. Could you invent a pleasure/suffering meter with a needle on a dial, and maybe several dials running simultaneously to encompass the pleasure of eating chocolate while suffering from toothache? What would life be like if one experienced neither pleasure nor suffering, a sort of suspension of all feelings?

It has become fashionable in the Western world to be obsessed with death. It is a recent trend not found in most other cultures. Apparently, death and dying must be avoided or postponed at all costs, even by eschewing birth and life itself. But birth, as any female will tell you, can entail a lot of pain, and a considerable risk of death. Life is only bought at the cost of pain and suffering. Death is part of life cycle strategies: once you have passed on your genes to the next generation and secured their survival, your job is done. Don't hog the stage; it's time for others to have their day. You are using up resources that they need. Deaths must balance births if the population is to remain stable and not exceed its resource capacity. This is how nature works, how evolution works. The only priority that comes into it is the continuation of the genes.

An animal can meet its death in a variety of different ways, some of which are more painful than others. It might also suffer and survive. Therefore any assessment of this suffering should consider:

- The ability of each species and individual to feel conscious mental suffering.
- The ability of each species and individual to feel physical suffering.
- The link, if any, between physical suffering and mental suffering, for example, a horse with a broken leg may continue grazing without apparently feeling undue pain, or it may limp badly.
- Short-term mental suffering during an actual pursuit or attack, e.g. panic or terror.
- Anticipatory suffering: the ability to anticipate a real or imagined bad experience that may or may not come. Worry, foreboding, dread. This may require a more advanced or 'intelligent' comprehension of time as discussed in 2.14. Lower animals which live more in the moment may not experience this kind of suffering. Fear is a type of suffering and the fear response is modifiable by changes in imprinting (2.4.3) although it also stems from temperament in the core ethotype, and from life experiences.
- Long-term mental suffering or distress: for example, an unharmed animal caught in a trap or a cage for some hours, or a sow in a farrowing crate unable to escape. Just living in a different environment to that in which it was imprinted and raised can cause sufficient low level stress to inhibit breeding behaviour. When feelings or natural drives are thwarted or frustrated, some level of suffering is experienced, which turns to pleasure when they are satiated. We suffer hunger and enjoy feeding.
- Short-term physical pain, for example, during being attacked and killed. Data from many sources, such as soldiers and athletes, indicate that the ability to feel pain is much reduced at this time.
- Long-term physical pain, for example, being caught by a limb in a trap, suffering a prolonged death through poisoning or being injured and killed only later. This pain includes shock and its aftermath.
- Escaping wounded, to survive or die later.
- Natural selectivity: whether the method tends to cull animals which are already old, sick, diseased or injured from another cause, and therefore tends to curtail other suffering.
- The life quality and suffering which the animal might have experienced if it had not been killed.

All the above aspects consider suffering in relation to an individual animal. We also need to consider:

- Welfare of dependent young, orphaned by the death of the parent.
- Welfare of the total population e.g. by becoming extinct, by becoming too common and outstripping its resources of food, space etc; by becoming genetically unbalanced; by becoming unbalanced in age or sex structure; by destabilising populations by removing natural population control mechanisms (e.g. by removing predators).
- Welfare of non-target species such as in systems of agriculture, industry, water, energy, communications and transport, which incidentally and sometimes avoidably, cause suffering to animals, for example, by the misuse of sprays and poisons, fishnets which catch marine mammals and diving birds, marine sound and radar noise, lack of provision for animal

movements in the design of roads and fences, ingestion of lead shot by waterfowl and so on. The very inadequate data available indicate that about 220 million vertebrates are killed or maimed by British drivers every year, a toll on wildlife which is new. In Germany, more game is killed by drivers than by shooters. Many studies have quantified animals killed in the course of agricultural activities, collateral damage caused by mowing, ploughing and rolling. Steven Davis and Gaverick Matheny argued the merits and de-merits of vegetarian diets on the basis of 'Least Harm'. Despite disagreeing with one another, both agreed that the numbers of small wild mammals killed incidentally in farming by far outnumbered the domestic animals killed, even for vegetarian diets. Despite increasing evidence of sentience in invertebrates, such as slugs, snails and insects, we really have little concept of the suffering involved in pesticide usage, direct or indirect.

- Benefits to non-target species by maintaining habitat for game species.
- Socio-economic benefits to humans, e.g. control of rats, mice, rabbits.
- Recreational enjoyment, e.g. through fieldsports, or cat-keeping.
- Food benefit, e.g. fish, game meats.
- Whether the entity receiving the benefit is the same as the one suffering.

When we are catching or hunting animals, for whatever motive, sometimes we apply legal close seasons to allow them to breed. This may be because they are a valuable food or recreational resource and we want to maximise their breeding and our sustainable harvest. On the other hand, if they are a pest, we may decide to kill them at any time of year, and many pests, such as mice and rats, breed all the year round. So we know perfectly well that by killing parents with dependants, that their young will starve to death. We probably won't see them getting colder and colder, crawling out of their nests in desperation looking for the lost parent, so we don't concern ourselves too much about it. What the eye doesn't see, the heart doesn't grieve over, but we are prepared to do this because our convenience over-rides their suffering.

Another approach to benchmark suffering is to compare it with what happens in nature. For example, could you compare the quality of life and death of a domestic sheep with that of a wild sheep? Or a farmed chicken with a wild junglefowl? Should we aim to do better than wild nature, or are we saying "No, even this is not good enough. No animal should ever suffer. Period."?

We tend to think that everything in

This mouse was caught by one leg and struggled all night until I found him. I have never seen such levels of suffering caused by hawks or hounds.

Sparrowhawk

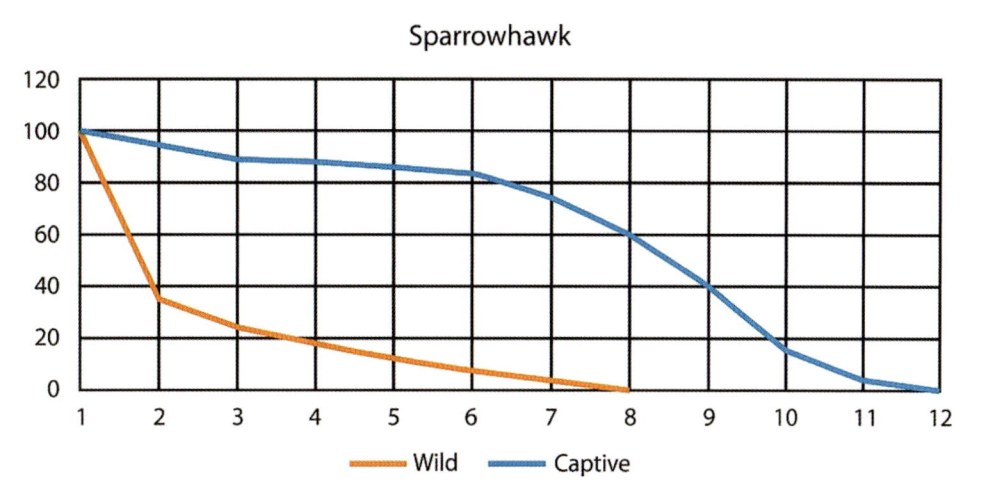

A cohort of 100 young Sparrowhawks (Accipiter nisus) dies off year on year. The red line shows a wild cohort and the blue line shows birds in captivity. (From Fox 2022).

Mother Nature's garden is rosy, but of course, it isn't. We talk of 'saving' things, and setting them 'free'. Nature isn't like that and in reality humans have just added more and more hazards for wildlife. For many species that breed once a year, such as European Sparrowhawks (below), their population looks like saw teeth. Big numbers are produced each spring, and they are killed or starve off over the autumn and winter until by the following spring, in a stable population, the population is reduced to the same level as before. About 70% of youngsters die each year, with most of these deaths in the six winter months. So in making moral judgements about our human activities in relation to wildlife, we always have to take into account the prospects faced by animals in the absence of humans.

You have to consider each case on its merits. A broiler chicken killed at 42 days old, or a battery chicken, with a 50:50 chance of being gassed at a day old if male, or, if female, living perhaps 18 months in close confinement, doesn't sound like a high quality of life compared to a junglefowl. But then, of say twelve junglefowl eggs that hatch, probably only one will survive long enough to breed. As for 'free range', this can range from idyllic on a summer's day with fresh pasture and no foxes, to pretty miserable on a wet winter's day poking around in filthy, slimy mud with nowhere to hide from a hungry goshawk. Alternatively one could say, let's just kill the whole lot off and we'll become vegans. No animals, no suffering, what a simple solution… Maybe we should apply the same advice to ourselves?

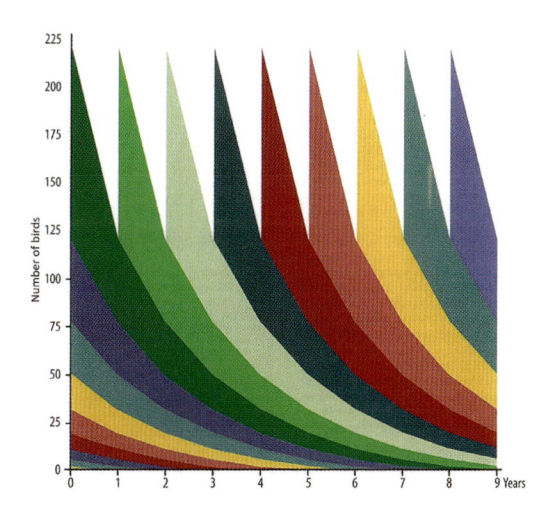

In any one year, the wild Sparrowhawk population consists of about eight year groups. How large the population is depends on the time of year. (Data from Newton, 2010.)

Even between individuals, the perception of pain can vary immensely. Humans with genetic mutations that reduce their ability to break down the neurotransmitter anandamide, (which affects the sensation of pain, mood and memory), suffer less pain and feel happier than normal people and technically it would be possible to edit for these genes and thus reduce global suffering.

These are all things that need to be taken into consideration and the reality is that however hard we try to be objective about suffering, we end up making personal judgements about something that is subjective.

Nature does not seem to take suffering into account. Perhaps in this context, pain confers no significant survival advantage or disadvantage. Given that an animal is sentient for other reasons, and capable of emotions, then the ability to suffer is just a consequence, a by-product. Sentience itself does not seem to be an inhibiting criterion; humans kill enemy soldiers with little consideration for their sentience. A prey animal will attempt to minimise its own pain and suffering, and of course pain has a function in helping to avoid injury, but the predator that is inflicting it will probably be indifferent, yet react strongly to distress calls of its own young.

Physical pain is part of nature's warning system to protect ourselves from serious injury. If you could not feel pain, you might not suffer, but you might easily burn your fingers off. The only way to avoid pain is to be dead, and the only way to avoid dying is not to be born. I don't think any of us would prefer a lifeless planet. So we are not talking about avoiding pain, but about minimizing it. But time after time experiments which have set out to reduce pain on the 'spare the rod' principle, have ended up 'spoiling the child'. Pain is part of nature's reward and punishment system, and by eliminating pain in one incident, we do not necessarily reduce the total pain on this planet. For example, if my falcon catches a crow, she might cause the crow pain but save countless other small birds and lambs the pain which the crow would have inflicted. Of course this is simplistic; the logical sequel to this would be to eliminate (painlessly) all animals on the planet which kill other animals. This would then totally destabilize the herbivore populations which would be controlled solely by food supply and thus suffer periodic mass starvation. Pain is a fact of life, and we are part of life.

Nor can one judge quality of life solely by absence of pain. Some people become vegetarians because they disapprove of killing animals. They would like a utopia in which animals are born each year and live a carefree existence, but somehow never get killed. This can't be done. From the farming point of view, if we don't eat meat then we don't have farm animals. So the vegetarian, in wishing to prevent the death of existing animals, would preclude the lives of future generations of animals. These are not the actions of real animal-lovers, but does it really matter? We don't really need farm animals. On the other hand, eating plants is much more resource efficient than feeding plants to animals and then eating the animals. This may be true for feedlot-beef, but many areas of the world are not fit for arable farming, only for grazing. For example, 95% of land here in Wales is Agricultural Grade 5 or worse; it is too wet,

A rat in a (theoretically) humane cage trap. It has popped its left eye out trying to escape.

too steep, or too poor quality soils to grow arable crops on it. Livestock or woodland are the only management options. We need that trophic layer.

For all our high opinions of ourselves, we humans are inextricably bound up in the web of life systems on this planet. We cannot exist without these life systems. The system depends on energy from the sun, combined with nutrients from the Earth, being constantly recycled and recombined. Some of the life forms, such as plants, can harness the sun's energy directly and can therefore exist without eating any other life forms. Others, such as all the animals, cannot use energy from the sun and are totally dependent on eating those which can. Some, such as herbivores, are directly dependent, while others, such as carnivores, cannot even eat plants and must eat other animals.

From the human species' point of view, in our current evolutionary state, we are hunter/foragers. Although we can subsist for extensive periods on either an exclusive meat diet or an exclusive plant diet, we are essentially omnivorous.

There is no particular merit or demerit in your diet type. Humans are capable of adapting, but many other species aren't. Cows cannot eat meat. Hawks cannot eat grass. It is not a question of morality, these are the facts of life. The only option for a hawk is to eat meat, and the only way it can obtain meat is by using the combination of physical and mental attributes which we have already examined in this book. Killing by a hawk cannot therefore be said to be cruel. It is natural, and it is a condition of existence on this planet.

5.2 Welfare in recreational hunting

As discussed in the last chapter, humans and other predators hunt because we want to. We may not be hungry, but we feel a strong urge to hunt. Hunting is an instinct deep in our core ethotype; our enjoyment comes in satisfying the urge to hunt. The end reasons why we hunt are not mutually exclusive. For example, rabbits and wood pigeons are hunted for food, as pests and for recreation.

Whilst acknowledging that religions have both positive and negative impacts on animal welfare and management, they are not substitutes for sound science. Also, the dogma that animals have 'rights' is not a fruitful one in real life wildlife management. The concept of the 'Five Freedoms' advocated by some welfare groups is fine as far as it goes, but the issues are a lot more complicated than that. Rather than 'rights', we should consider our responsibilities towards animals and to do that we have to be clear on defining our terms.

Given that one of the legally acceptable reasons for killing wild animals is as a recreational resource, and that the enjoyment is derived from the total hunting experience rather than from the kill itself, it seems logical to maximise the experience benefit and minimise the amount of suffering or kills. This is a cost-benefit, utilitarian approach as I have outlined in 3.9, the sort of thing beloved by Jeremy Bentham. From the point of view of biological impact, this turns the concept of 'efficiency' on its head. When hunting for food or as pest control, the most efficient strategy is maximum numbers of prey taken per minimum time and effort spent. When hunting for enjoyment the reverse is true. We wish to maximise the time and effort spent (because they are enjoyable) while minimising the impact on the resource (to maintain sustainability and minimise suffering).

You may say: " So much for cost-benefit analysis! The prey bears the cost and the hunter gets the benefit!". Pet cat keeping is the most cost-expensive recreational activity. In the UK, around 275 million deaths a year bring no benefit whatsoever to cat-owners other than farmers etc.

Recreational hunting includes trophy hunting. This is pursued to a minor extent in the UK where deer are the only trophies. In countries where there are still some big game species, this remains a major activity, as is poaching for ivory and rhino horn. While it is hard to explain the economic and management benefits of trophy hunting, it does ultimately provide a reason for maintaining populations and habitats for these species. For myself, I struggle to understand what big game hunters enjoy in slaughtering these animals, especially as the technology and modern logistics are so much in their favour. We get people helicoptering in to New Zealand and led up to trophy stags in enclosures. All they have to do is pull the trigger. The stags are from deer farms, animals now past their prime. There are similar canned shooting set-ups in many countries, including Arabia where you can pay to shoot penned Oryx (*Oryx leucoryx*). Certainly managed animals need killing for various reasons, and I have shot many sheep myself, but what kind of person enjoys doing it? Modern high-powered rifles and sights swing the balance totally in favour of the shooter. From the game management point of view the culling strategy is best based on removing the old, weak or poor animals and leaving the prime trophy animals for breeding.

Trophy hunting is a subject of hot debate at the moment, with some African host countries accusing the UK of neocolonialism. Amy Dickman and colleagues at WildCRU have contributed useful material to this debate and I have little original to add. I don't think a ban on importing derivatives from CITES 1 species will contribute to the conservation of these species, or their habitats, or their local communities and economies. It is just virtue signalling from people who are not on the sharp end and who don't want to engage with the nuances of the situation.

In the UK we still have driven gamebird shooting. About 57 million pheasants and partridges are reared for shooting each year. Without parents to teach them survival skills, many do not even make it to the shooting season, being slaughtered on the roads, but of those which are shot at, wounding rates are around 40%. Great pride is taken in shooting high birds, often 50-60 metres high, even though this is known to increase wounding rates. The shooting of driven game, made possible by the invention of the breech-loading shotgun, essentially entails shooting at large numbers of gamebirds flying over a line of shooters, as living targets. If you watch carefully you can see the 'pricked' birds flying on. They may die in a few minutes, or topple off their perches when at roost that night after bleeding internally, or they may struggle on and die later, or perhaps recover in time to be shot again another day.

I remember hawking a moor at Kinlochewe years ago, running my pointers on the days after shoots. We constantly got points on injured grouse, and picked up others that had died some time after being shot.

Few released pheasants survive beyond the end of the season at the end of January, and if they do, few of them breed because they have been hatched from incubators and have had no parenting or awareness of predators. The shooters themselves do nothing other than shoot, and pay others to rear and drive the game. It is thus not a complete hunting experience and could be replaced by clay pigeons, which happens in some places now with 'simulated game days'. But this does not have quite the same social cachet. Rough shooting on the other hand, in which one or two people go out with their dogs to find various game and bring food home for dinner, are more genuine hunting experiences and require both effort and field-craft on the part of the hunters. Rough shooters stop all proceedings if game is down but not found. They keep searching with the dogs until they have recovered it and made sure it is dead. They take pride in eating what they have shot.

It is possible, and much cheaper, to set up simulated gamebird shooting days using clay pigeons. If all you need is targets to hit, then this is a humane alternative. I'm not against killing or hunting, but if you are going to do it, do it humanely and as naturally as possible. My falcons catch carrion crows which are pests that have to be managed. In all the thousands that the falcons have caught, not one has escaped wounded or injured in any way. The crows are either killed promptly or escape clean away, and that is important to me.

Recreational hunting can also include an element of competition, such as in 'coarse' fishing in which anglers win prizes for catching the most or the biggest fish. When each fish is caught, the hook is removed (which may injure the fish) and it is held in a keep net until the end of the competition when it is released and may be caught again another day. Fishermen struggle in retaining the balance between predator and prey. On the one hand, some may limit themselves to more difficult methods, such as fly fishing, but then they succumb to the temptation of buying the best rod, reel and lines to maximise their chances of catching a fish. This balance is important and activities that entail catching or killing large numbers of prey, especially if whole habitats and trophic levels have to be modified in order to produce a harvestable surplus of prey animals, go beyond the natural hunting experience into exploitation. There may well be ancillary conservation benefits to habitat management, and economic arguments, but there are other ways to achieve these benefits that do not entail emphasising the exclusive management of one or two game species. It is easy in competitions or in a desire to be seen by others as a good performer, to supersede the original objectives of hunting, and technological developments that add an advantage are a mixed blessing. Modern athletic shoes enable runners to beat old records and some golf courses are now too short for the modern drivers and aerodynamic balls which enable golfers to drive further than the fairways were designed for.

Recreational hunting, unlike hunting for food or as pest control, often has a 'sporting ethic'. While each activity has its own etiquette and health and safety procedures, there is also the unwritten concept in Western forms of hunting, of giving the prey a 'sporting chance'. This is in itself a tacit recognition that the activity is not primarily about killing things, but of the hunting experience itself. Legal enforcement cannot extend out into rural situations and, instead, the sporting ethic is a type of regulating mechanism enforced by peer pressure and internalised as a conscience. Despite this, driven shooting is still big business inspired by social prestige rather than a genuine hunting experience. The balance has been lost. Brian Luke has codified a sporting ethic for shooters in the USA but it is not at all universally followed and for many forms of shooting, such as winged game, there is no possibility of avoiding wounding.

Paradoxically, some opponents to hunting with hounds object on the basis that it is not sporting to have so many hounds chasing one single fox. Of course there are reasons why a whole pack is needed, because most of the hunting is of a scent line, rather than by eye, and scent is tricky to follow, needing many noses casting about. But when hounds catch up with the fox, it is killed immediately by over-whelming force. In a one-to-one situation, such as with a raptor and its prey, most soon learn not to attempt to catch prey that they cannot quickly subdue, because of the risk of personal injury. If a hawk breaks a feather, soon the adjacent feather, being unsupported, will break, and eventually flight performance will deteriorate. The hawk will die.

A mammalian predator, such as a domestic cat, will often fail to kill its prey, even though it could do so in one quick bite, because it has satisfied its instinct to hunt and catch, and if not hungry, the next step, killing the prey, is not followed through. It is like the coarse fisherman letting his fish go again.

Few people who hunt or shoot or fish have any desire to be cruel. They do not enjoy seeing animals suffer. So is it possible somehow to analyse their hunting experience and distil out of it what really provided their enjoyment? Is it the thrill of the chase, the social cachet, competition, a 'one-ness' and involvement with natural processes? Might it be possible to re-design the hunting experience to minimise or eliminate suffering or harvest rates and maximise the positives?

Take driven grouse shooting for example. Could the resource – a moorland habitat for grouse – be utilised more efficiently by shooting fewer grouse per day and thus increasing the number of shooter days or decreasing the size of the shootable surplus and the need for so much predator control? Bag limits won't work because they are unenforceable. Banning double guns or reducing fire-power in some way might make life more challenging for the shooters. The modern breech-loading gun is too efficient now. Banning driving the game and encouraging shooting over pointers would improve the kills to shooter day ratio. In other words, looking at being more 'efficient' by being less 'efficient'.

Apart from wounding, shooting causes unintentional lead poisoning in scavengers who find and eat the dead and dying. Waterfowl also ingest lead pellets when sifting mud in wetlands. The density of lead shot lying on the ground is sufficient in some places to kill partridge chicks who ingest it in mistake for grit. Lead has a number of well-documented effects and is being phased out in favour of non-lead ammunition. Some shooters have embraced this willingly whereas others have resisted it for various reasons.

If hunters really were to enjoy seeing a prey torn to pieces, as many anti-hunters claim, perhaps the best approach would be to simply sit and watch films of animals being killed. Many wildlife documentaries show orcas catching seals on ice flows, sharks tossing penguins in the air, cheetahs pulling down impala and so on, often in high definition slow-mo. Some film-makers follow wildlife film-making codes of ethics, but not all do. Some take short cuts and set up scenes. If you zoom out from some of the footage of crocs taking water buffalo you can see groups of tourist vehicles. The internet is full of gory shots of lion kills and so on. Clearly these are fascinating to some people. One step beyond this are computer games which essentially are non-stop shooting sprees, killing humans or aliens. Most of the people watching this kind of death porn would be upset at having to deal with a live rat in their kitchen. There is no doubt that violence and death porn sells film yet the hunting people I know, including myself, are not keen on it. It certainly has nothing to do with the hunting I experience. Anti-hunters claim that hunting makes hunters more likely to become violent criminals, but I have not seen any evidence supporting this.

5.3 Hunting by cats and dogs

There is increasing concern about the impacts of domestic cats on wildlife. In Britain about 11 million cats are catching about 275 million prey per year, but recent studies show that about 82% of their prey are not brought home. They show that each cat probably kills about 59-123 prey a year. Of prey that are brought home, about 7.2-21.6 million are still alive and it is likely that, overall, 38-66 million prey are not killed on capture, but played with or abandoned. Of 3,597 live prey taken to four RSPCA wildlife centres, Baker et al found that 78% died, on average three days later. It is likely therefore that about

30-50 million prey animals, caught by cats each year, suffer for about three days before dying. This is a rough ball-park order of magnitude. As a perspective, 2.76 million licensed scientific procedures on live animals were carried out in 2022. So the cats are hurting 11-18 times the number of licensed vivisections, and for longer periods. Macdonald and others found that cat owners are in denial and unwilling to take steps to reduce this suffering. As well as welfare issues, the impact of cats on wildlife populations is of huge concern, and there is increasing information on diseases spread by cats.

Joy catches a grey squirrel. She will either kill it or bring it to me to kill. It won't escape wounded.

Before the hunting ban, packs of hounds caught about 20,000-25,000 foxes each year. Of these, the hounds will have killed all of them within about 15 seconds of capture. I have never heard of a case of a fox freeing itself and escaping from a pack of hounds. Yet the foxhounds are vilified and the cat-owners claim the moral high ground. Extraordinary!

Bonny doesn't know what to make of a hedgehog.

5.4 Wounding rates in shooting

To understand this section you need to be familiar with the basic technicalities of shooting, subjects such as shot sizes, chokes, shot patterns, stringing, penetration, non-lead shot options, rifling, calibres and so on. There is a huge amount of information available but not enough space to go into it all here. Some of it is explained in our film *The Hunting Act 2004: Animal Welfare Implications*.

One can attempt to measure physical or mental suffering scientifically by quantifying some aspect such as blood chemistry or behavioural patterns. In Australia, the Humaneness Assessment Panel (Pestsmart.org.au) have created a matrix to assess suffering in various pest control scenarios. This is a useful, systematic approach, giving a good overview. Unfortunately it can also lull one into believing this is a scientific reflection of what actually happens. It pre-supposes ideal conditions. For example, shooting a fox with a high-powered rifle through the head will kill it instantly – if the bullet hits the brain. What if the shot is two centimetres forward? The fox escapes with its jaws shattered. And the welfare implications go from zero to massive. The British Deer Society recommend against head shots for this reason. A shot in the chest is a bigger target area and even if the heart itself is missed, there will be extensive damage to the internal organs that will soon be fatal.

If the shooter wants to retrieve the carcass, for example venison from a deer, it is in his interest to kill the animal stone dead without need for a follow up. If the carcass is not needed, there is little incentive for the shooter to be certain of the shot being fatal. On the contrary, even risky shots are worth taking.

In the UK, foxes are shot or snared because they are considered pests and I wanted to know what suffering was entailed. So in 2005 we did a study *Wounding Rates in Shooting Foxes*, published in the Journal of Animal Welfare. A film of this study is also available. I wanted to investigate what happens to foxes when people shoot at them. How many are missed completely and escape unharmed? How many die instantly? How many die slowly? How many are injured and linger, but survive? What about the skills of the shooters, the types of gun, the calibres, the ammunition, the range; are some combinations more or less humane than others? I sawed a frozen fox in half and created life size paper targets on which all bones and organs were accurately traced so that, later, the pathologists could estimate the potential injuries each type of ammunition would have caused had the fox been alive. We also did shot penetration tests, and shot dead foxes to see what damage shots caused in different parts of the body.

Exactly how you define, detect and report wounding rates in shooting wild animals is difficult. Different types of wounds can have very different consequences in terms of short and long-term suffering. We tested different regimes of gun types, ammunition, range and shooter skill. The full details of the study are available online, so I will just provide an overview.

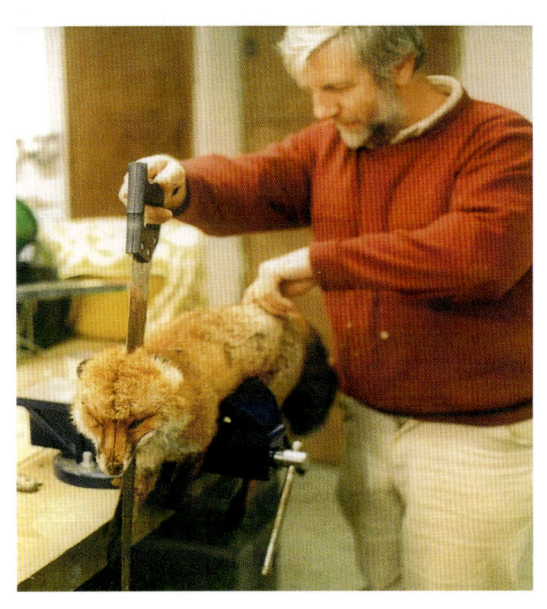

Sawing a frozen fox longitudinally to map the internal organs.

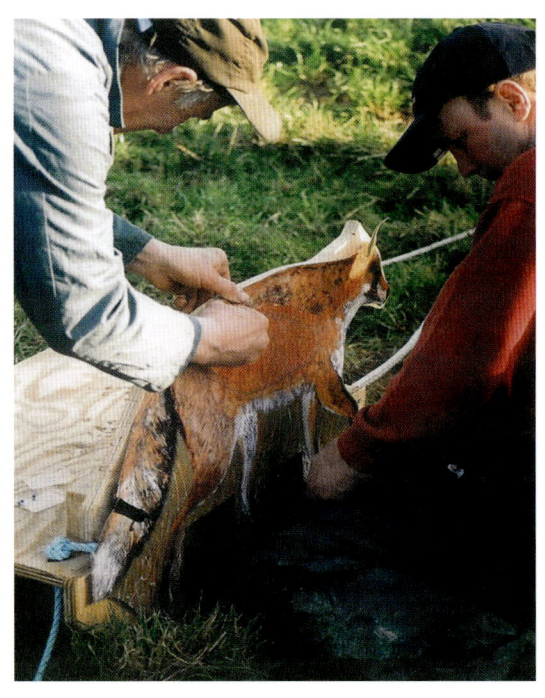

Preparing a fresh target for the next shot.

The target fox 'runs' across a gap and the shooter fires.

Both shotguns and rifles are used to shoot foxes and we observed and filmed foxes shot at by all the main methods. We obtained data from the Scottish gunpacks for the 2002-2003 season documenting the outcomes of 574 shots fired at 386 live foxes. This revealed an average kill rate of 55% (with a wide range of 20-79%) for all shots fired, but did not permit exact calculations of wounding rates because some foxes escaped.

We undertook target fox shooting and examined 51 shooting regimes: 35 shotgun regimes including .410 and 12 bore shotguns using No 6, BB or AAA shot sizes at 25, 40 and 60 yards, using open choke and full choke barrels, and shooters that were skilled, semi-skilled or unskilled. We undertook 16 rifle regimes using both rimfire and centrefire rifles at 50, 100 and 150 yards from both supported and unsupported positions and by day and by night. Shoots took place in England, Wales and Scotland and involved 199 shooters, of which those in the skilled categories frequently shoot real foxes and used their usual fox guns for the tests.

The targets were life-size colour paper sheets, cut to the silhouette of a trotting fox, traced from a frozen longitudinal section of a real fox and mapped with the internal anatomy. For shotgun trials the targets moved both right and left across an 8 or 10 yard gap taking 3 or 3.5 seconds to cross. For rifle trials the targets were static and exposed for 4 seconds.

Fifteen dead foxes shot with the same ammunition, range and angle were supplied to independent pathologists for them to assess internal injuries caused by each shooting regime. Penetration of ammunition was also tested in comparative card penetration tests.

1,283 shotgun shots and 885 rifle shots were fired during the trials and the outcome of these shots was scored by two independent pathologists as killed, two or three grades of wounding, or missed. The shotgun results showed a trend; as shooter skill increased the kill rate increased, missing decreased but wounding stayed much the same at around 60%. No 6 shot was a major source of wounding, even at 25 yards because of poor penetration, at 40 yards wounding reached 97%. AAA suffered from poor pattern density beyond 40 yards, even well-centred shots having insufficient pellets to ensure that a vital organ is hit. Up to 40 yards both AAA and BB performed well, BB being the shot size of choice tested. We did not trial No 3 or No 4 shot. .410 shotguns with No 6 shot are totally unsuitable for

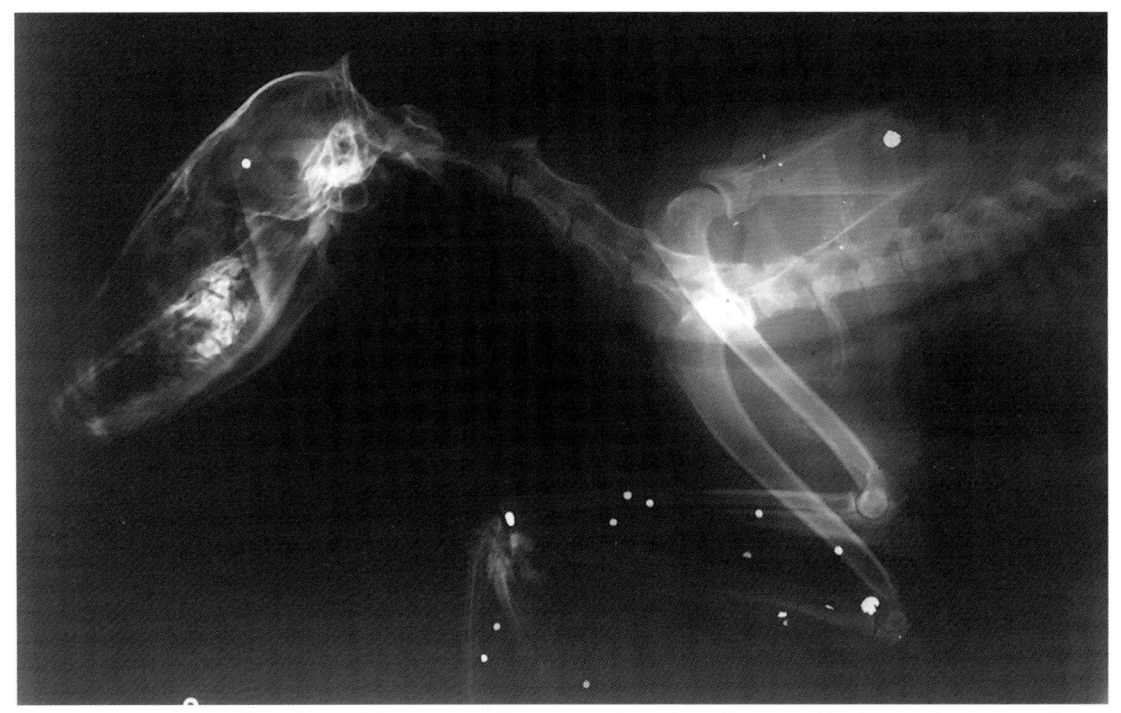

The dead carcase of this fox was shot with a 12 bore cartridge of BB (larger pellets) and also a cartridge of No 6 shot (small pellets) and then examined by the pathologists to investigate internal injuries and penetration.

foxes, wounding but seldom killing.

The best 25 regimes scored 0.1-1.0 foxes wounded per fox killed. The remaining 25 regimes wounded 1-13 foxes per fox killed. Briefly, what it boils down to is that the shotgun is a messy tool that wounds as much as it kills outright. Paradoxically, we found that the more skilled the shooter, the higher the wounding rates. Rifles wound less because they are normally used only on static targets.

Rifles killed considerably more than shotguns and wounded less. High-powered rifles in skilled hands were accurate, even at 150 yards (the furthest we trialled) both by night as well as by day. Poor marksmanship due to inexperience or lack of a gun support lowered this standard. A bullet from a high-powered rifle causes death or fatal injury quickly when hitting almost anywhere on the thorax, skilled shooters under good conditions scoring about 97%.

When foxes are shot at, some are killed stone dead (group 'k') and some are completely missed (group 'm'). There is no major welfare problem with these two groups. The third group ('w') is the foxes that are wounded but not killed stone dead and either die or recover later, suffering pain and stress in the process. This is the group of concern.

Some of these wounded foxes may be recovered by means of a second shot, or by dogs, and dispatched. Others will escape, and there is no reliable way to differentiate between them and the foxes that have been missed completely.

Thus number of shots fired $S = k + (m + w)$. In the pie charts which summarise our results, the sector we are concerned about are the lightly wounded animals, shown in ochre.

Many hours, even days, are expended in getting a shot at a fox. We could not

Chapter 5 – ANIMAL WELFARE ISSUES 121

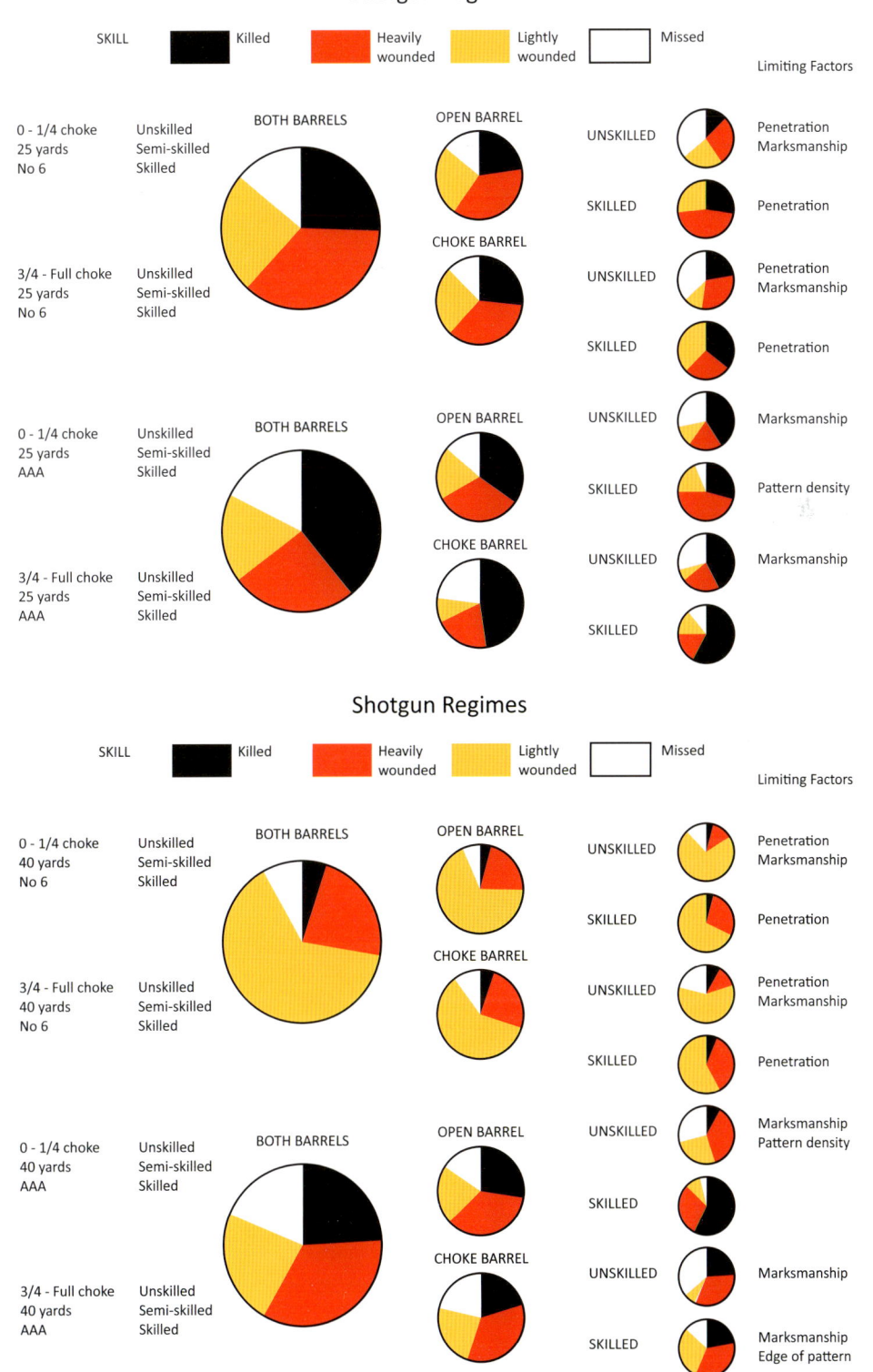

Shotgun Regimes

| SKILL | ■ Killed | ■ Heavily wounded | ■ Lightly wounded | □ Missed | Limiting Factors |

Conditions	Skill	BOTH BARRELS	OPEN BARREL / CHOKE BARREL	Skill	Limiting Factors
0 - 1/4 choke, 25 yards, No 6	Unskilled / Semi-skilled / Skilled		OPEN BARREL / CHOKE BARREL	UNSKILLED	Penetration, Marksmanship
				SKILLED	Penetration
3/4 - Full choke, 25 yards, No 6	Unskilled / Semi-skilled / Skilled			UNSKILLED	Penetration, Marksmanship
				SKILLED	Penetration
0 - 1/4 choke, 25 yards, AAA	Unskilled / Semi-skilled / Skilled		OPEN BARREL / CHOKE BARREL	UNSKILLED	Marksmanship
				SKILLED	Pattern density
3/4 - Full choke, 25 yards, AAA	Unskilled / Semi-skilled / Skilled			UNSKILLED	Marksmanship
				SKILLED	

Shotgun Regimes

| SKILL | ■ Killed | ■ Heavily wounded | ■ Lightly wounded | □ Missed | Limiting Factors |

Conditions	Skill	BOTH BARRELS	OPEN BARREL / CHOKE BARREL	Skill	Limiting Factors
0 - 1/4 choke, 40 yards, No 6	Unskilled / Semi-skilled / Skilled			UNSKILLED	Penetration, Marksmanship
				SKILLED	Penetration
3/4 - Full choke, 40 yards, No 6	Unskilled / Semi-skilled / Skilled			UNSKILLED	Penetration, Marksmanship
				SKILLED	Penetration
0 - 1/4 choke, 40 yards, AAA	Unskilled / Semi-skilled / Skilled			UNSKILLED	Marksmanship, Pattern density
				SKILLED	
3/4 - Full choke, 40 yards, AAA	Unskilled / Semi-skilled / Skilled			UNSKILLED	Marksmanship
				SKILLED	Marksmanship, Edge of pattern

122 HUNTING ETHICS

Shotgun Regimes

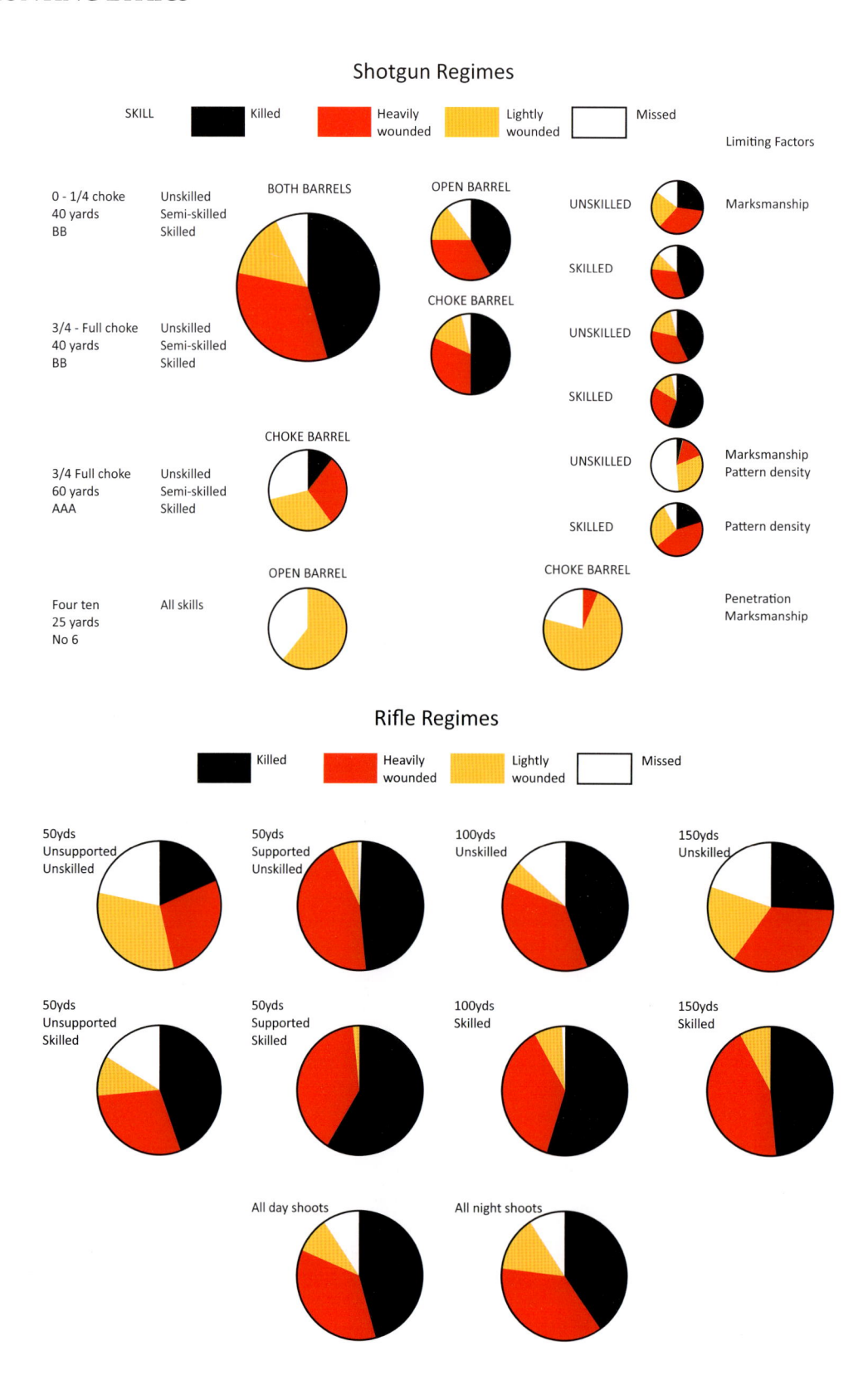

SKILL — ■ Killed ■ Heavily wounded ■ Lightly wounded □ Missed **Limiting Factors**

0 – 1/4 choke, 40 yards, BB	Unskilled / Semi-skilled / Skilled	BOTH BARRELS	OPEN BARREL	UNSKILLED — Marksmanship
			CHOKE BARREL	SKILLED
3/4 – Full choke, 40 yards, BB	Unskilled / Semi-skilled / Skilled			UNSKILLED
				SKILLED
3/4 Full choke, 60 yards, AAA	Unskilled / Semi-skilled / Skilled	CHOKE BARREL		UNSKILLED — Marksmanship, Pattern density
				SKILLED — Pattern density
Four ten, 25 yards, No 6	All skills	OPEN BARREL	CHOKE BARREL	Penetration, Marksmanship

Rifle Regimes

■ Killed ■ Heavily wounded ■ Lightly wounded □ Missed

- 50yds Unsupported Unskilled
- 50yds Supported Unskilled
- 100yds Unskilled
- 150yds Unskilled
- 50yds Unsupported Skilled
- 50yds Supported Skilled
- 100yds Skilled
- 150yds Skilled
- All day shoots
- All night shoots

provide enough observers to document sufficient fox shooting to determine the kill rate ourselves. We observed foxes shot both by shotguns and by rifles, by day and by night, and we saw foxes killed and foxes wounded by all these methods. However in the Hunt Returns for the Scottish Gunpacks 2002-2003 their average kill rate was 54.9% (range 20% - 79.3%). The Welsh Gunpacks estimated their kill rates at around 33% (Aled Jones pers comm.). The kill rate is clearly a very variable figure, depending on circumstances. In general, from what we saw, and from questioning the shooters who participated in the trials, we estimate that the kill rate of real foxes with shotguns with BB or AAA is around 35% and with high powered rifles, 80-95%.

As we could not use captive live foxes for this research, we used artificial targets to simulate as closely as possible the same conditions as found in real life situations. The advantage is that by shooting at a lot of dummy targets one can easily see which ones are hit ($k + w$) and which ones are missed (m).

The theory is simple. In practice there are many variables and confounding factors. These need to be assessed, both so that we can assess the accuracy of our estimates and so that we can understand the variation. Cadavers from fox shoots were examined to assess injuries caused by the different shooting regimes. This information was then applied to score the target fox sheets. We can thus estimate what percentage of target foxes are 'wounded' (w) and assess what shooting parameters cause more or less wounding. There is no standard way to quantify suffering, and probably never will be, and therefore we have not attempted to assess the welfare implications of these wounds.

Shooting foxes is not a single, standard activity; rather it is a multi-faceted activity with a host of variables. The only common denominator is that all shooting of free-living foxes inevitably entails some wounding. Variables include type of weapon (rifle or shotgun), calibre, choke, size and number of shot and load, range, ability of the shooter, movement and direction of the fox, and exposure time. These are the most obvious variables. When looking at welfare it is not just the welfare of the target that needs to be considered. The fox may be a vixen with dependent cubs that will starve. The fox may be misidentified and be a non-target species such as a dog or small deer. A human may be injured accidentally during the attempt to shoot the fox. By failing to kill the fox, it may inflict suffering on further prey animals, or if injured, it may be unable to forage normally and may become a rogue 'killer' fox specialising on easily-caught domestic animals, and thus cause further economic loss. The list is elastic and we will confine the study to the most immediate variables. It is possible that by studying some of these we may be able to identify shooting regimes that cause less suffering than other regimes and this could lead to regulations or codes of practice that might confer some practical welfare benefit, as is already done for deer.

The wounding rate is based on the outcome of a single shot. It either kills, wounds or misses. An individual fox can be missed or wounded by multiple shots before finally escaping or being killed by a last shot. Thus while a <u>fox</u> can be scored as more than one outcome, a <u>shot</u> can be scored as only one outcome. This is well illustrated by the data from the Scottish Gunpacks 2002-2003 season, compiled by the Master of Foxhounds Association from the Hunt Returns from the Masters of eight Scottish packs.

In their Hunt Returns, Foxes shot at (T), Foxes shot dead (K), Foxes escaping (E), Shots fired (S) and Escaped wounded foxes killed by dogs (WD) are all knowns. What is impossible to establish is the exact ratio of wounds to misses. When a fox is shot at and runs off it is often possible to see if it is wounded, but it is impossible to see if it is clean missed. The highest-killing packs were under instructions not to shoot at more than 30 metres. Most of the packs used AAA shot. It was believed that most, if not all, the foxes that escaped had been hit. Thus there is a degree of uncertainty in the minimum wounding figure. They found:

Foxes seen escaping probably wounded (E) = 71.

The probable minimum wounding rate = E/S = $71/574$ = 12.4%.

If there were no misses, $M = 0$, the maximum possible wounded = 259.

The maximum possible wounding rate = $259/574$ = 45.1%.

Therefore the wounding rate was in the range 12.4% - 45.1%.

The missed rate was 0% - 32.7%.

The kill rate was 54.9% (range 20% - 79.3%).

Overall, the shooting trials showed that:
- Unskilled shooters missed more often than semi-skilled or skilled shooters.
- There were significantly more 'kills' using BB shot than AAA or No. 6 shot.
- AAA shot regimes had significantly more 'kills' than the No. 6 shot regimes.
- AAA shots missed significantly more than BB and No. 6 shot regimes.
- There were significantly more 'misses' at 60 yards.
- There were significantly more 'kills' at 25 yards.
- There were no 'kills' or 'serious wounds' in either .410 regime.
- There are significantly more kills with a supported rifle.

Reports on wounding rates have been based on different aspects that are not directly comparable. For example, Ericsson and von Essen (1998) recorded the fates of 1746 elk that were shot at in Sweden. Of these, 1,312 (75%) died on the spot. A further 11% fell after 100 metres, another 9.3% were tracked, found and killed, mostly the same day, a further 1.1% were hit but never found, there was no information on the fate of a further 1.7%, and another 1.6% were presumed to be missed. They concluded that 2.8% were shot at and not retrieved. But from their data, only 95.3% of the elk that were shot at were in fact retrieved, the remaining 4.7% being unaccounted for. From the wounding point of view, 75% died on the spot, 20.3% were heavily wounded, ran some distance but were found and killed within hours, and 4.7% were unaccounted for and could have been lightly wounded. Therefore the wounding rate was between 20.3% and 25%. Thus *retrieval* rates and *wounding* rates are not comparable and even these calculations are uncertain because they are animal-based, rather than shot-based.

Others, such as Bertsden *et al.* (1999) examined 143 foxes from rural Denmark and found that 25% carried shotgun pellets from previous injuries. That they had survived indicates that they had been only 'lightly wounded'. Further shot animals may have survived with no pellets present in their bodies. If such a high percentage had been lightly wounded, how many others had been heavily wounded and died? In contrast, in the same study, they found that only 4% of 48 foxes from urban areas of Denmark carried shotgun pellets, which could indicate that urban foxes are less likely to be shot at than rural ones.

Although this type of information may be interesting, it is impossible to draw many conclusions from it. How many foxes had originally been shot at? How many had recovered from their injuries? How old were they when they were shot? How long could they have expected to live even if healthy?

Records from Wildlife Hospital admissions face similar problems. Between 1993 to 2004, 2020 foxes were admitted to three RSPCA Wildlife Hospitals (Dr A. Lindley pers comm.). Of these only three foxes were admitted because they had been shot. Some of these admissions data have been used by Harris (1997) and Swann (2000) to indicate that shot wounding is not a problem for foxes. The examination on admission to the hospitals is undertaken to diagnose the immediate problem and does not normally include the whole body X-rays and so on required to determine old shot wounds, as was undertaken by Bertsden on the Danish foxes. There are many imponderables, such as what proportion of the original sample had ever been shot, and how many of those had survived. How long and how likely is a wounded fox to be badly enough incapacitated to be able to be caught alive by humans but yet be alive at all, or be only lightly wounded and thus able to elude humans? Brash (in Mullineaux *et al*. 2003) considered that 'most adult foxes presented to the surgery have traumatic injuries, usually from gunshot wounds, road traffic injuries or snare injuries', and 'many foxes will tolerate minor gunshot injuries, particularly 'scatter' from shotgun pellets, without any clinical signs'.

Other studies, such as Bradshaw and Bateson (2000) and Urquhart and McKendrick (2003) relied on reports from shooters or studies of butchered carcasses at game dealers, rather than making direct observations, methods that are inherently flawed because lightly wounded animals may never be retrieved. The starting point of any wounding study should be the <u>shot fired</u>. Percentages should be based on this, not the number of animals fired at, nor the animals retrieved, nor the animals surviving old wounds, nor the carcasses of dead animals. These observations, while being of interest, can be misleading indices of total wounding. Similarly, comparisons between species, or between circumstances, can be misleading. Large ungulates are slower, more predictable and have a larger vulnerable area than a fox. They are normally shot with a rifle while static (Gladfelter 1985, Green 1992, and Morrison 1979). Smaller mammals and birds, being shot mainly with shotguns while moving, usually require 3-4 shots per retrieved animal (Bertsden *et al*. 1999), some of these being still alive, and some of those escaping being lightly wounded. The fox, being intermediate in size, is shot at with both rifles and shotguns and tends to meet the limitations of each method. It can be rather quick and unpredictable to allow a measured rifle shot, and yet is rather large to kill cleanly with a shotgun unless a balanced load, pattern and range is used.

Baker and Harris (1997) assessed the different known causes of mortality of British foxes, such as road deaths, shooting, terriers, snares, lurchers and hounds. They concluded that 80,000 foxes were shot and retrieved each year and that a theoretical further 115,000 fox deaths remained unaccounted for. Some of these may be foxes that have been shot and died later without being retrieved.

It should not be assumed that the wounding rates seen in our study would all result in continued suffering in the field. What we have shown are the baseline figures, and it is essential to emphasise that in the real world many of these wounded foxes will not suffer long. If a fox is shot at but not killed, especially with a shotgun, it may be possible to take a second shot or even more. Unless the fox is physically impaired, the chances of a kill with subsequent shots is the same or less than the first because the fox will be alarmed and moving faster, probably away from the shooter and at a longer range. The data from the Scottish Gunpacks showed that 32.7% of their shots were repeat shots. Assuming that their kill rates were about the same as for first shots (55%), the second shots will kill a quarter of the wounded foxes within seconds.

The strategy of using second shots depends on the priorities of the shooter. The fox has no meat or fur value and it is not important if the carcass is retrieved. Fox control aims to remove and reduce foxes and their effects on livestock, game and wildlife (Reynolds 2000). Fox welfare is not a first priority. Bertsden *et al*. (1999) examined the use of the second shot in shooting flying mallard. They concluded that if the shooter reserved the second shot for use only on ducks wounded by the first shot, ie a 'damage repair' strategy, then overall crippling was reduced. On the other hand, if the shooter used the second shot on an apparently uninjured duck, then injury rates increased. They found that of 341 shots fired at an average range of 23 metres, 29% were killed, 16% wounded and 55% missed. The shooters averaged 3.44 cartridges per bagged mallard. But the skilled shooters, who averaged less than 3 shots per retrieved duck, wounded only 0.32 additional ducks for each duck killed whereas poorer shots, averaging over 3 shots per duck, wounded 0.86 further ducks for each duck killed.

In fox shooting, shooters tend to keep firing for as long as they have shots available and the fox in range. Although a 'damage repair strategy' might reduce wounding, it is not the primary priority in fox shooting, and the obvious way to minimise suffering is not to fire the first shot either, if welfare was the priority.

When an animal is a pest the priority is to put it out of action. Shooters in our study claimed to have shot at foxes with shotguns at up to 120 yards. Several shots (up to 11) were fired at one fox. When the priority is to put the fox out of action, and the carcass is not required, it is logical to fire at extreme ranges on the off chance that a lucky pellet might hit a vital spot. In this logic, a long shot has at least a slim chance, whereas a withheld shot has no chance at all.

The rifle shooters who shot foxes as a sport took pride in their accuracy and kill rate. With time no object they could afford to pick their shots. In pest control situations cost effectiveness becomes a priority over welfare. When the immediate task is to shoot the fox, riskier chances are taken. Reynolds (2000) found that 0.2-0.6 foxes per hour could be killed by lamping in autumn and winter but that this figure dwindles as fox density decreases. If one searches for several hours at night and just gets a glimpse of one fox, there is a temptation to take a chance and shoot. Thus, by spring many foxes are 'lamp-shy' having survived previous attempts to shoot them. Additionally, in pest control the aim is to kill the most for least effort, and cubbing time in February to May is the main season for fox lamping. This is when the population is at its lowest ebb and when pregnant or lactating vixens can be shot, thus negating their whole breeding effort. In these circumstance dogs are indispensable for finding and disposing of the cubs.

Keepers in mixed or arable country lamp foxes or use thermal imaging with rifles because they pose a threat to ground-nesting game birds that nest in April or so. They have another peak of fox shooting in August and September, between harvest and the pheasant poults being released. In sheep-rearing districts there is less game-rearing and foxes are controlled more because they are a pest to sheep that tend to lamb earlier – from January to March. The gun-packs in Wales concentrate their efforts on this period, using hounds and shotguns in daylight. The terrain they cover is often steep and densely wooded, with high densities of foxes. Thus different methods suit different situations and fox welfare is not always the prime criterion.

When shotguns are used it is common to use dogs to flush the foxes so that they come within shooting range of waiting people with guns. If the shooter shoots but fails to kill the fox, the fox may return to cover or get beyond shooting range. The dogs can be used to pick up the scent line quickly and have a chance to catch the fox, especially if it is wounded. In the Scottish Gunpack returns, 54.9% of the escaping foxes were killed by the hounds. In the film which accompanied our study we show a fox shot at five times and running off wounded, to be eventually overtaken and killed by the hounds.

Dogs are less commonly used in conjunction with rifles. To use a rifle the fox must be stationary and is usually not fully aware of the shooter's presence. A dog is liable to make a noise or movement at the critical moment and scare the fox. Dogs are often used with the lamp without a rifle. These are large lurchers, capable of coursing and killing a fox within the length of the field.

All this begs the question – why wound the fox in the first place? Why not just use hounds and thus ensure that wounding is zero? The IFAW submission to the Burns Inquiry quoted the work of Kreeger *et al.* (1989, 90) as indicating that being chased by a dog was as stressful for a fox as being in a leghold trap. But this was carried out in a confined 10 acre enclosure and Kreeger himself has since commented that such a comparison is not a valid one. Most of the 'chase' phase of a 'hunt' is not pursuit of the fox but the following of the fox's scent trail. It is only in the final phase that the hounds actually see the fox and give chase. Further research is needed to assess physical or mental distress during the hunt, or as a result of it. Most fox hunts are of relatively short duration; foxes are seldom exhausted to the point that they are unable to run away. When hounds catch a fox their relative strength is overwhelming and death occurs in seconds (Thomas and Allen 2002).

5.5 Assessing suffering

We have not attempted to say how long an animal will be wounded for before it dies or recovers. A second shot may kill it almost immediately, a dog may find it and kill it, or it may linger on for weeks. What we do know is that wounding is inevitable in shooting and some individuals are liable to be in pain for a long time. What this pain is like in terms of physical or mental suffering we do not know.

There are three ways of looking at welfare standards in this context:

Species specific. The fox, as a species, can be killed by several legal methods, such as a variety of shooting methods, snares, cage traps, dogs and (theoretically at least) gassing. If sufficient scientific evidence is forthcoming, one can rank these in order according to the welfare criteria chosen.

Method specific. Each individual method can be used to kill several species. Rifles or dogs can be used on many species from rats to red deer. The welfare performance of each method may vary from species to species (Sainsbury *et al.* 1995).

Against agreed standards. The alternative that combines the benefits of both the above methods is to assess against agreed standards. This is already used for some of the methods, such as traps, poisons and gasses. Specific welfare criteria (such as the catch-to-kill interval) are used to assess the method against internationally recognised standards, such as the ISO standards or the AIHTS standards. DEFRA then issues appropriate licences for their use, or does not permit their use. For example DEFRA tests on the poison bait T3327 MRM showed that the caged foxes convulsed, retched and showed obvious signs of distress before death occurred (Health and Safety Executive 2003). The foxes responded to stimuli during these seizures. T3327 was considered more humane than strychnine which causes bone-breaking convulsions, haematomas and (in humans) an 'overwhelming fear or hysteria' and has now been banned in the UK but is still used elsewhere. Some of these poisons easily affect non-target organisms, T3327 for example being classed as 'potentially extremely dangerous to fish or other aquatic life' and also to children, birds and pets.

From the scientific point of view, standardised criteria are the only supportable route to follow. The first two ad hoc methods inevitably lead to inconsistency and controversy. One wonders why DEFRA is prepared to assess certain methods scientifically and yet leave others, such as hunting with dogs, cats and shooting, to the ravages of public opinion.

DEFRA's licensing system is by no means comprehensive or all-embracing. The common break-back mouse trap does not meet the EU protocol on ISO trapping standards and DEFRA, in its Assessment of Humaneness of Fully Approved Vertebrate Control Agents (DEFRA 1997), noted 'As severe discomfort, which can last for several days, occurs in a large proportion of all the

Spring traps like this may only be set in boxes or tunnels where non-target animals cannot reach them. Some models are being phased out because they do not meet AIHTS. This grey squirrel was killed humanely but a scavenger, probably a rat, has been at it before the trapper has arrived.

reported studies, anticoagulant rodenticides must be regarded as being markedly inhumane'. Welfare standards are at present context-dependent. In pest control, welfare is treated as a secondary priority over efficiency in many cases, and the application of standards and controls is clearly unbalanced.

Having done the fox shooting study, presented it to Parliament and published it in a peer-reviewed journal, we had some interesting reactions. Neither antis nor shooters wanted this study done. The antis did not want it to be shown that the Hunting Bill they were supporting would increase suffering, not decrease it. The shooters on

This Fenn trap for stoats and weasels is properly covered and set on a pole bridge across a ditch on a grouse moor. But most of the traps are not checked every 24 hours. The tunnel traps had rotted bait at least a month old.

Chapter 5 – ANIMAL WELFARE ISSUES   129

We present our findings in Westminster.

the other hand did not want an image that shooting entailed wounding.

The antis were in a state of denial. Jackie Ballard, Chief Executive of the RSPCA, commented on our study: 'There is not absolute proof that wounded foxes suffer, yet it is a basic assumption of the Middle Way Group's position that they do'. Professor Stephen Harris said 'There are no wounded foxes from shooting in the countryside as far as I am concerned'. But his study of fox X-rays, which he used to back his claim in a presentation to the Labour Party Conference, which was referred to by David Rendel MP in the House of Commons, and by the RSPCA, was rejected by a scientific journal and indeed, despite repeated requests, is not available and was never published.

Dr Harradine, then Head of Research at the British Association for Shooting and Conservation also tried to rubbish it. He claimed that his uncompleted and unpublished research 'shows that, in following the BASC Code's advice, using the most appropriate cartridges and ranges, more than one shot if required, and effective dogs, the wounding loss rate of foxes is under 10 per cent – a very different figure from our study'. He claimed to use our same targets to repeat our study, but his results were never published. Both sides tried to challenge the statistical treatment of our data, without success. We kept the raw data available online for ten years but nobody produced a different result.

None of the ways of shooting foxes killed them as quickly and as certainly as a pack of hounds. Some of the regimes were more humane than others. One would have thought therefore that the anti-hunters, who claimed their opposition to hunting was all about welfare, would have called for restrictions on types of shooting for foxes, as we already have for deer. But no, they wanted to create an illusion of the 'skilled marksman' humanely shooting the foxes. To this day it is still legal to shoot at a fox with an air rifle in Britain, at any time of year.

In an effort to reduce wounding rates in geese, Denmark reduced the legal range to shoot with a shotgun to 25 metres. This was effective and cut the number of live geese carrying old shot from about 30% to less than 10%. The number of foxes carrying embedded shot fell from 24.9% to 8.5% between the late 1990s and the late 2000s. Remember, these are live animals surviving with old wounds. The initial wounding rates are much higher because many animals die from their wounds.

In driven pheasant shooting five shots per bird killed is considered good shooting, but with pigeons or doves the kill rate is lower. However, the reality is more likely that for five shots, one falls to the ground dead or unable to fly, two escape uninjured, and two are 'pricked' with pellets that do not immediately disable the bird. I can find no definitive data on this for pheasants, but there are many studies on waterfowl.

At 25 metres, with small size shot such as #5 or #6, even using an unchoked barrel, the shot pattern is dense and consistent. A bird inside a 100 cm diameter circle will most likely be brought down by at least one pellet that strikes a wing bone. But at 40 metres, the pellet density and striking energy are both reduced, and even when the bird is centred in the circle, although it

This shot duck came down on our land. She survived for a while until a buzzard finished her off.

will be hit, there is a chance that none of the pellets will bring it down. Increasing the shot size reduces pattern density and decreasing the shot size reduces the strike energy. Increasing the choke focusses the pattern but does not increase the strike energy. But in practical terms, reducing the legal range for shotguns in the UK would impact most shooting sports and would meet stiff resistance from shooters.

Shotguns thus intrinsically create a much higher wounding rate than rifles. Most people do not realise this, so there is not much public resistance. The RSPCA in Australia have come out against shotguns and I am inclined to agree with them. I shot quite a lot as a young man and my real life experiences tally quite closely with published studies. By contrast, natural hunting using dogs or raptors has a wounding rate of virtually zero. Although wounding rates are not the only parameter to consider in the ethics of hunting, they are probably the most significant by far. A chased animal may get a fright and be tired, but if it is not killed outright by the predator it will be back to normal in a few minutes or hours, whereas a shot-wounded one may suffer for days or months. And as for the ones recorded as 'missed', only if you have the animal in your hand afterwards, as we did with our fox shooting study, can you be sure that the animal was missed entirely. Often, on close inspection of the target, we could find a single pellet hole, pulling a tuft of fur into the body cavity, an injury causing a slow death from peritonitis.

In their studies of Red Deer *Cervus elaphus* hunted by staghounds, Patrick Bateson and Elizabeth Bradshaw stepped outside the limits of objective science by stating subjectively that the suffering they measured was 'unacceptable.' Others use the phrase 'not acceptable in a civilised society.' By ranking the measured suffering (individual suffering x volume) in a variety of activities one can see a spectrum of comparative levels of suffering. Logically, at some point in this list comes the limit of social acceptability, and this varies between national cultures and moral communities. Currently the fashionable term is 'social licence'.

Another route is to compare these levels of suffering with those seen in natural predation For example, Bateson and Bradshaw compared hound predation of red deer with wolf predation; while hounds and wolves hunt and kill in virtually identical ways, some people find wolves acceptable but hounds unacceptable. Another route is to compare with welfare in killing farm animals. Another route is to compare these levels with other common life experiences. For example, is a particular level of suffering at death better or worse than the suffering experienced during birth, or during other experiences throughout life? How does the level of suffering in the animals' deaths compare with the suffering involved in human deaths? Paradoxically we keep terminally ill human patients alive far longer than we would a pet animal. Is there more suffering going on in a ward for terminally ill people than in a maternity ward? The one has death at the end of suffering, the other has hope.

Should our target be zero suffering, aiming to eliminate it altogether for all people and all species? This of course is completely unrealistic, a mirage slipping away before us. So we all have to accept that some level of suffering is inevitable. Suffering is a sensation and sensations, like coins, have two sides: pleasure and pain. One cannot have the one without the other. Many would say suffering is necessary; it is a continuum at one end of perception and consciousness and a safety valve against increasing physical injury. Somewhere along this continuum our desire to do something to reduce suffering kicks in.

5.6 Welfare benchmarks

After looking at what humans do to other animals, and, in warfare, to other humans, and after looking at the various forms of suffering, what benchmarks can we use to be consistent in our attitudes? The Golden Rule – do unto others as you would have them do to you – obviously doesn't work. Taking nature as a benchmark only works for natural scenarios such as hunting with dogs or cats. Shooting or trapping are not natural so the analogy doesn't work for artificial methods. For these, artificial standards have been used, such as the ISO standards, the Five Domains model, the Sharp and Saunders Humaneness Assessment model and the Agreement on International Humane Trapping Standards (AIHTS). Some are more nuanced than others. The bar on these has been raised over the years to create improved welfare. Although the AIHTS was primarily developed to regulate welfare in trapping fur-bearing species, we can do our best to use its criteria and standards and apply them across the board.

I'm going to be controversial, and I'm going to make some fairly sweeping generalisations and guestimates. Different readers will contest some of these figures. That's OK, they are not set in tablets of stone. I'm doing it to put animal welfare into a broad perspective, rather than tackle it piecemeal as almost all studies do. Using the definitions in 3.5 and taking the six criteria in the table in 5.1 I have allocated a benchmark figure to each, based broadly on the AIHTS standards, like this:

Natural selectivity	20%
Legal selectivity	95%
Human supervision	Yes or <24 hours
Pre-capture pursuit interval	10 minutes
Catch-to-kill interval	3 minutes
Maiming	5%

Benchmark welfare criteria aligned with AIHTS standards.

These are my benchmarks. They mean that at least 20% of the animals caught were old, sick or young, not in their prime, roughly in the proportion to those found in balanced natural populations. At least 95% of the animals were of the intended species, conforming to any legal constraints and seasons, not protected animals. Human supervision indicates that a human was present or attended within 24 hours. The pre-capture pursuit interval is the period not exceeding ten minutes, during which the predator is chasing the prey by sight. This varies from species to species but aims to prevent exhaustion, acidosis and myopathy. In reality a white-muscled rabbit could not sustain a ten minute chase whereas a red deer could manage a lot more than ten minutes. This interval does not include the period when, for example, dogs are hunting by scent and cannot actually see the prey to chase it. The catch to kill interval is roughly based on the AIHTS standard of 70% of the caught animals being rendered permanently unconscious within 3 minutes. Other standards set this bar at 80%. The maiming is of animals that escape to freedom and survive for more than a day, possibly recovering. I'm thinking of average or best case scenarios. One must recognise that there are also worse case scenarios, such as deer being poached at night, foxes shot with air rifles, and traps left unchecked for weeks at a time. There are also many different degrees of suffering varying from a trapped animal biting its own leg off, to one of our beavers which would enter a box trap night after night, eat the bait apples, have a good snooze and wander off again on being released. Rifles have the potential to be humane, but used casually they can equally cause a lot of suffering, even if only in lead fragments from bullets poisoning scavengers at carcasses. Secondary lead poisoning can have major impacts on dabbling ducks and on scavengers such as Californian Condors *Gymnogyps californianus*.

The catch to kill interval and the % maiming are probably the most significant of these criteria. You could look at any activities that you are personally involved in, refine your figures and see how they would fare in this table. There is huge variation even within certain activities, for example in catch and release competition angling, holding the caught fish in keep nets, and so on. For me, natural hunting with dogs and raptors come out tops, but you must remember that welfare is not the sole criterion. Especially in pest control, methods with minimum human work time are at a premium. Live and dead traps are subject to trapping standards, but there are plenty of now-illegal traps still in circulation. Snares and humane cable restraints are also now being banned in the UK. Yet without adequate predator control, and with increasing human disturbance, many ground-nesting species are declining at an alarming rate in the UK.

5.7 Is suffering 'acceptable'?

Imagine you're married to a nice man and you like nothing better than to sit together on the sofa watching television. But then sometimes he goes out at night and disappears for a while, coming back later with blood stains on him. He cleans himself up and comes back and sits on the sofa again with you. Then one night he goes out and returns dragging a four year old girl. He hits her around and she crawls under the table, whimpering and frightened. Whenever she makes a move he jumps on her and hits her again until eventually she lies silent. You go into the kitchen and look at him with the poor little girl dead or dying under the table. What would you do? Would you see if the little girl was alive and call an ambulance? Would you call for the police to have your husband arrested? Or would you just wait until he had cleaned himself up and get back together on the sofa, in the morning picking up the body of the girl and dumping it in the garbage?

To re-visit the table in 5.1:

	Natural selectivity	Legal selectivity	Human supervision	Pre-capture pursuit interval	Catch-to-kill interval	Maiming	Approx UK annual kills
Welfare benchmarks	>20%	>95%	<24 hours	10 mins	3 mins	<5%	
Gazehounds	Yes	99%	Yes	<2 mins	0-5 secs	0	500,000
Scenthounds	Yes	99%	Yes	>2 mins	0-5 secs	0	20,000
Terriers	No	99%	Yes	<2 mins	0-5 secs	?	15,000
Cats	Yes	0%	No	<30 secs	0-30 mins	20%	275,000,000
Ferrets	No	99%	Yes	<5 mins	0-30 mins	2%	10,000
Raptors	Yes	97%	Yes	<2 mins	0-3 mins	0	6000
Gassing	No	70%?	Yes	N/A	0-30 mins	1%	500,000
Anti-coagulant poisons	No	80%	No	N/A	0-30 mins	?	20,000,000
Dead traps	No	80%	Yes	N/A	0-24 hours	10-53%	10,000,000
Snares	No	80%	Yes	N/A	0-24 hours	10%	200,000
Live traps	No	80%	Yes	N/A	0-24 hours	0	40,000
Bird ringing	Yes	100%	Yes	N/A	1-30 mins*	0	660,000
Shotgun	No	100%	Yes	<2 mins	0-15 mins		20,000,000
Rifle	Yes	100%	Yes	0	0-15 mins	5%	3,000,000
Angling	No		Yes	1-60 mins	1-180 mins		?
Net fishing	No		Yes		?		?

*The elements in green meet benchmarks based on the Agreement on International Humane Trapping Standards but the elements in red fail them. *During bird-ringing most birds are released unharmed, rather than being killed after capture.*

What if he was not your husband, but your cat? Do you feel any sense of responsibility for your cat's action? Do you think it is something outside of your control and therefore it's not your responsibility? Was your loyalty to your husband greater than any feeling of responsibility you might have towards the toddler? Do you think that because it was not you who killed the girl that therefore no responsibility lies with you? Do you think that because everyone's husband in your street is doing it then it doesn't matter? Do you think, as long as he goes away from home and grabs a strange little girl, it is OK? Do you think you should keep him locked in the house at night to prevent his nightly forays, like a were-wolf? Do you think you should share your house with such a man? Do you think it is obviously wrong for your husband to molest a four year old girl but not for a cat to torture a mouse or small bird because the mouse and bird are either not sentient beings, or not as sentient as the toddler, or of different species? Or do you think your husband is doing wrong because he knows he is doing wrong and has a choice, but that the cat doesn't know it is doing wrong; it is just following its natural instincts? And if the cat is just following its instincts and doesn't think it is doing wrong, then it's OK and not your problem? Or is it something to do with a little girl being in your husband's 'moral community' (which makes his act 'murder') but the mouse is not in the cat's moral community; it is a straightforward predator/prey relationship? What if your dog did the same thing, would you feel the same? Plenty of people deny responsibility for stock-worrying on the grounds that their 'dog couldn't help itself'. Do you think that the dog is under your control and therefore you bear responsibility for its actions whereas the cat is uncontrollable? Do you think you have no responsibility for your cat? In which case why do you feed it? If you have some responsibility, why could you just not keep the cat in? If you open the door and let the cat out, knowing it is likely to catch a small animal, have you not deliberately relinquished control of the cat? Couldn't you have just controlled the cat by keeping your door shut? If a politician proposed a law to ban you from letting your cat out, would you still vote for her? If you personally did to the mouse or bird the same treatment as your cat did, would the victim's suffering be the same, or different? Would your responsibility

The British Prime Minister, Keir Starmer, sees nothing immoral in keeping two cats at No 10 Downing Street. They are allowed to kill any protected species, at any time, on anyone's property. Meanwhile he votes to prevent trail-hunting with dogs on the off chance that they might catch a fox, an unprotected pest species which can be killed at any time, by trapping or shooting with any kind of gun, but only with land-owner's permission.

be the same or different? How could the law punish you for something a cat did, while you were fast asleep in bed?

Wow, that's quite a lot to mull over, isn't it? Take a little time to consider what you think. How could you decide what suffering is 'acceptable' to you or not? Should others have to share your levels of 'acceptability'?

Rochlitz, Broom and Bradshaw having reviewed the hunting of deer, foxes, mink and hares by hounds declared: *"Hunting with dogs is not analogous to the predator-prey interaction that occurs naturally in the wild. Even if it were, what happens in the wild between predator and prey, following the rules of natural selection, should not be a blueprint for the way humans behave towards wild animals. The way animals kill and are killed in the wild is not an acceptable way for humans to kill animals."* This is where a lot of studies fail. They make a number of straightforward observations and then jump from facts to opinions, slipping in words like 'acceptable'. The weakness of the opinion becomes visible in that they excluded cats from the same treatment that they give dogs. Do they really believe that it is better to allow cats to hunt unsupervised, taking protected species and maiming millions, compared to properly controlling dogs and the prey they hunt? The other weakness is in assuming that individual animal welfare is the sole, or even main, criterion. The reality is that welfare is just one of the criteria to be considered and certainly, in the case of cat owners, it is tertiary to their own convenience and to the welfare of their cats. This is the fallacy often touted by vets, for whom animal welfare is their business. Of course welfare is a consideration, but it is not the only criterion by any means. Never ask a barber if you need a haircut.

In reality our 'civilised society' is anything but logical. Despite our much-vaunted intelligence, we tend to consider things that are under our eyes and neglect things which we may know about but which don't impinge on us. We have a huge capacity for kidding ourselves. So while we protest against trapping fur-bearing mammals for clothing we neglect the even greater numbers of trapped mammals that are not used for fur, such as rats and mice. We are also highly anthropocentric and judge things in relation to ourselves. So, for example, it is now considered unethical or even illegal to do experiments on primates, because taxonomically they are closely related to us and by implication have similar sensory systems. We extend the Golden Rule to them: treat them as we would wish to be treated. But taxonomic proximity is not the only indicator; other species, not closely related to us, have similar characteristics and potentially suffer in similar ways. For example, Kristin Andrews and Susana Monsó writing in Aeon, have summarised studies showing how rats are capable of laughter and of empathy, that they will help a trapped or drowning rat, that they can suffer from anxiety and depression, and live in familial and social groups with a normative moral structure as humans do. Yet they enjoy no protection from experimentation and of course, that is just the tip of the iceberg: there are almost no limits on the methods humans use to kill wild rats. We are not just deluding ourselves; we know perfectly well we are being downright hypocritical.

The keeping of pet cats involves high levels of wildlife suffering and yet is acceptable to many in our society, whereas the same people stigmatise the catching of mammals by dogs. Often we weigh the suffering of others against our own inconvenience. Huge numbers of people and other species are killed or injured on the roads each year. We could end this suffering at a stroke by not using cars, but we don't want to do that; it would inconvenience us too much. When the Welsh government introduced a 20 mph speed limit they were forced to partly rescind it. If we are to make genuine progress in wildlife welfare these inconsistencies need to be faced.

A majority vote based on claimed opinion

The last slow-worm I've seen on the farm I retrieved from a cat in the lane. But it died of its injuries.

rather than logic is no measure of social acceptability. One must look not at how people vote, but at what they do. The reality is that the British have a soft spot for animals and, especially around death, we often treat non-humans more humanely than humans. But in other human cultures, including most of Asia, the Middle East and Indian sub-continent, Africa and South America, the attitude towards animal welfare is very different, often almost non-existent. Even in Buddhist Mongolia I have seen a horse allowed to limp around with a shattered leg for five days before finally being garrotted with a cord. Some of the anthropocentric religions consider animals to have been created solely for humans to use them as they wish. Christians teach that Man was created to have dominion over the animals, essentially a *carte blanche* to do what we like with them.

If I want to do something for animal welfare, would I achieve more by chiselling away at activities in the West, or by going to some other cultures where welfare issues are more acute? My step-daughter worked with the Brooke Hospital on body condition scoring in equines in Egypt and found poor scores that you would almost never find in the UK. To change those cultures, you first have to be certain that your views are intrinsically more valid than theirs, then you can try education (which works a bit but is very slow), economics (which can work quite well except in Third World countries where manual labour is cheaper than machines), legal enforcement and politics (gets you nowhere) or, as we have sometimes done, come up with a substitute that makes economic sense and improves welfare while gradually moving towards cultural changes.

People in the Western world have become very afraid of death. Although they love to watch people killing each other on the media as a form of entertainment, they have a taboo now against seeing humans killing animals. Death as a fantasy is some kind of titillation, yet as a reality it is socially unacceptable. We are in a state of denial of our own impending deaths, and of any deaths that occur to provide us with our own food so that we can live. Life is sacrosanct; death must be evaded for as long as possible.

People often fail to distinguish between suffering, and death. Death can be instantaneous, without suffering. Death can end suffering. Suffering can be prolonged, without entailing death. Suffering can be minimised, but the only way to minimise death itself is to minimise life. By obsessing over death it is easy to ignore the whole point, which is: life and its quality. Feedlot cattle or factory farmed pigs may have a poor quality of life, but our sheep have a very good time of it by any standards. They live as permanent members of their own flocks, naturally outdoors on fresh grass. They have medical attention if they need it and a certain and quick death. What more could one ask for? Would you deny them their lives because you don't want them to ever die? Birth, life and death all go together, just as a piece of string has two ends.

The activities to change the status quo have largely been confrontational rather than research. Most attempts at 'education' by both anti-fieldsports and pro-fieldsports are very short on facts and rely heavily on emotion. The major thrust by the anti-fieldsports lobby has been to push for legislation against fieldsports, and to do this it has of necessity concentrated on numerically small fieldsports which it might have some prospect of banning. Paradoxically therefore, the legal efforts have insignificant benefit to wildlife. Considering that, of all mammals killed by cats and dogs in Britain, dogs only kill 0.4 %, to exclude cats (99.6%) from the issue seems somewhat one-sided. Arie Trouwborst's study on domestic cats reveals the devastating effects they have on wildlife and animal welfare and yet, despite the plethora of international treaties and so on, governments are reluctant to legislate and control cats. In Britain 80% of cat-owners are female, there are about 10.8 million cats, and 26% of households keep a cat. This represents a lot of voting power and leads to a depressing amount of hypocrisy.

Animals are usually killed because they are pests, food, or a recreational resource, or combinations of these. The rabbit, for example, is all three. Some, such as foxes, can be a recreational resource in one locality and a pest in another. It can be difficult to agree on what is and what is not a 'pest.' At present it is more socially acceptable (and legal) to kill some pests (such as rats) with dogs than to kill other pests (such as foxes) with dogs. Rats and foxes have equally developed nervous systems and presumably experience similar levels of pain. The movement against fox hunting therefore hinges, not on biological grounds, but on a perception that the hunters enjoy hunting. Many of the anti-hunting organizations are supported by cat keepers who believe that because they do not enjoy watching their cats mauling little birds, they are therefore eliminated from the charge of cruelty. This is not a source of consolation to the cats' victims. The question of human enjoyment is not relevant to the suffering animal. Their position quite literally is: the suffering doesn't matter because, by not enjoying it, they are not being cruel.

As a young man, I used to shoot with both shotguns and rifles, for a variety of game, but I stopped some years ago. I didn't like the wounding rates, and when we undertook the fox study the data were all there in black and white. If we had done a study of bird shooting with shotguns, I know from experience that the wounding rates would have been similar or worse. My shooting was always pottering round the farm with a dog, getting a pheasant or two for supper or killing a grey squirrel that was damaging the trees. Occasionally a quiet stalk on a summer's evening with a .22 would bring home a few rabbits, but even then I recorded 25% of the rabbits hit were not retrieved. Many quickly crawled down nearby holes before dying.

So, I am against unnecessary suffering, particularly the prolonged kind that you see in some kinds of 'factory' farming, such as pig farrowing crates, which deprive animals both of physical comforts and the ability to engage with their natural instincts. But I am by no means against quick painless deaths, in fact I support them, for all species, including our own. I hope I have one.

5.8 What is cruelty?

(of persons) *Disposed to inflict suffering; indifferent to or taking pleasure in another's pain or distress; destitute of kindness or compassion; merciless, pitiless, hard-hearted.* Of actions etc: *Proceeding from or showing indifference or pleasure in another's distress.* OED.

We have looked at the different types, amounts and extents of suffering involved in the various ways of hunting animals. This is what is experienced by the 'victims'. Now, what is going on in the minds of the 'predators'? Are they enjoying the suffering, are they being cruel? Or does their enjoyment or motivation lie elsewhere? For those who oppose hunting, are they objecting to the suffering, or are they in reality more concerned with the 'predators' causing it?

I have witnessed some appalling suffering in some human cultures, both of animals and of human workers. Most of this has not been wilful cruelty but simply indifference to another's pain. There just seems to be a lack of empathy. I believe that this means that human indifference to another's pain is deep in our ethotype, and it appears to be so in other species too. Predators can munch away at a prey animal while it is still alive, without making any attempt to put it out of its misery. For the predator, the prey animal is simply food. The predator doesn't 'hate' the prey, they are not 'enemies', it is not being cruel. The predator may have an ability to sympathise with members of its own group, without it extending to prey relationships. We need to differentiate between *indifference* to suffering, and taking *pleasure* in it. The cat that plays with a live mouse is indifferent to its suffering but the pleasure that it is taking (such as we can judge) is not derived from the mouse's pain, ie from cruelty, but simply from satisfying its own urge to play. Victor Nell maintains that one needs a 'theory of mind' to be cruel; by this I think he means that one needs to be able to appreciate the suffering that the victim is going through. This is much more developed in humans than in other species.

In terms of distance, it is hard to ignore what is under your nose compared to something far away. Shooting a distant figure is emotionally easier than looking him in the eye and bayonetting him. Shooting an animal at a distance is easier than breaking its neck with your bare hands.

The buzz word nowadays is 'neurodiversity'. People are self-diagnosing with all sorts of mental health issues such as ADHD or PTSD. There are people, a tiny minority, who are cruel and enjoy causing pain or watching others suffering. This cruelty may be to a human or another species, an individual or a group, usually weaker than they are. This might be one of our uniquely human characteristics and certainly not one for our species to be proud of. Wilful cruelty to other humans, as social workers know, is fairly common, consisting of physical, mental or economic abuse; controlling behaviour. It is probably only less common towards animals because most of our dealings are with humans, rather than with other species. But it still occurs, for example with some terrier men with their 'hard' dogs. Usually the victim is trapped in a confined space. There is a streak in human nature that enjoys the suffering of others, from schadenfreude to boxing. I don't like watching boxing, yet it is an Olympic sport. Many computer games are based on killing scenarios, and I don't like those either. But in my experience hunters are not any more cruel than other sectors of society; this is not why they hunt.

There is a kind of paranoia amongst some Animal Rights groups that death is somehow a taboo and that wilfully killing an animal is 'wrong', almost obscene. They feel that hunters are de-sensitised to death. As a farmer and hunter, the natural cycles of life are integrated into each day, each month, each season of my years. In the spring I wonder at the new life around me. I hold a falcon egg in my hand – how can it possibly be that this egg, in two months' time, will become a feathered falcon carving her way across the sky?

As I go into the log shed, some loose moss on the floor tells me that a wagtail has

A ten day old falcon egg with the chorioallantois half formed.

built her nest in an old swallow's nest in the rafters above. I must not look up at the nest. The owner may be watching me, and seeing my glance, as a predator, realise that her nest has been detected, and abandon it. Outside in the lambing field everyone is quiet, except for a single voice. A twin has lost its mum who is busy with the other twin. She looks up, says one 'Baaa' and the lamb scampers back to her, butting her udder. I wander past quietly, not using the whistling alarm call which I use when I want to move them. Another ewe is licking her new lamb but nearby, at the end of a trail of slimy afterbirth, another one, still unlicked and yellow, lies cold and dead. A raven has already pecked out its upper eye. Looking more closely I can see that the socket is relatively clean, so it looks as though the lamb was born dead and did not suffer when the raven came. All around me are the triumphs and disasters of Spring. It is like the Grand National horse race; lots of eager starters, but some fall at each fence. Not all will make it to the finish, to breed.

As the Summer turns to Autumn and Winter starts to bite, one by one youngsters die from starvation, accidents, illness or if lucky, predation. For the predators themselves, with no predators to finish them off, starvation is a slow death. A young buzzard wails and wails in a tree across the valley. By October his parents get fed up of bringing him food; they have enough problems of their own. One day I don't hear him any more, and in February, when the cover has died back, I find his half-rotted remains. This is how the cycle works. I am not de-sensitised to it. Actually, I am probably more aware of it than most. I cannot judge it – birth 'good', death 'bad'. But for people whose lives are isolated from nature, it is easy to become over-sensitised, even appalled. I have had many a student gulping and lost for words seeing a lamb born, and then later being told to remove the remaining half of the lamb after a fatal visit from a vixen with cubs down in the wood. I think to myself 'Girl, you'll be in for a shock when you have to push something wet and squirmy out from between your legs, in a puddle of blood and fluid. You'll be amazed when the oxytocin let's your milk down, and astonished at how powerful your maternal instincts become'. All logic and reason will fall like corn before the combine harvester of your ethotype.

The opposite of cruelty could be called 'compassion' in which one experiences pain, rather than enjoyment, in witnessing another's suffering. Our compassion I think is rooted in our instinct to care, our ability to empathise and thus sympathise, and that instinct is better developed in women than in men. Women tend to care strongly for any individual, human or non-human, that is suffering right here, right now. Perhaps they have more mirror neurons than I do? They seem to be better at extending sympathy beyond their own meme groups than many men are. I think that it is one of the more splendid aspects of the human race and I wish I was better at it. There is a danger though, and we see it in some of the Animal Rights groups, that the focus is heavily on alleviating suffering of *individual animals*. This is fine in itself. The problems arise when we move up to the species level and to the habitat level. If you introduce restrictions on killing individual animals then you virtually slam the door on all species and habitat management. That is a disastrous situation, and one that comes back to bite in the end as individual animals start to starve and suffer.

Cruelty refers to the experience of the 'persecutor'. For example a driver may hit a badger on the road and cause the badger to suffer greatly. The driver's act may have varied from unwittingness (he did not know the badger was there), to negligence (he knew the badger was there but did not take evasive action), to risk assessed (swerving to avoid the badger could have endangered other road users), to wilful cruelty (he deliberately intended to hit the badger and cause it to suffer) to wilful pest control (he deliberately intended to hit the badger and kill it either cleanly or at least prevent it surviving long term).

Similarly, a cat-owner, in pursuing the hobby of keeping a pet cat, is likely to cause <u>suffering</u> for many small animals. In this instance the owner's action is <u>witting</u> (because the event is repetitive), probably not <u>wilfully cruel</u> (because most cat owners do not derive enjoyment from watching their cat toy with a captured live prey), but <u>negligent</u> in that the owner failed to prevent it happening. The lack of human enjoyment is not relevant to the suffering animal, whereas the negligence of the owner, in preventing it, is.

The Royal Society for the Prevention of Cruelty to Animals' 1996 report showed 235 convictions for cruelty to cats and 892 convictions for cruelty to dogs in Britain. None of the cases were of cruelty in the sense of 'taking pleasure in another's pain or distress'. The legal charges were mostly of 'causing unnecessary suffering', i.e. the owners were 'indifferent to another's distress'. In Wales in 2017, there was an increase of prosecutions for neglect, linked to an economic downturn when people could not afford to care for their animals properly. It is unfortunate that most animal welfare societies don't analyse their data in this way, because in order to alleviate animal suffering we need to understand why people mistreat animals the way they do. Current data from animal and child welfare societies list their prosecutions, but you have to examine each one in more detail to find the sad back-story. Negligence and sheer inability to cope are far more common than deliberate cruelty.

This is a critical distinction. Some societies and cultures are institutionally 'indifferent to another's distress' either because they do not understand biology, or their religion's ethics teach them so, or because it suits them. For example, both dogs and cats are kept for pest control and recreation. But whereas cats are allowed to kill whatever they want, dogs are supervised and used to catch selected, legally unprotected individuals and the dog owners ensure that the prey is killed quickly and is not played with or tortured unnecessarily. In other words, dog owners are not indifferent to suffering and ensure that it is minimal. However, 18,000 sheep are killed each year by dogs that are out of the control of their owners, and in Britain we have laws and penalties for this, primarily to protect the farming resource (sheep). But we don't provide protection for the 275 million wild animals captured by free-roaming domestic cats.

I am no bunny hugger. New Zealand has a robust attitude to wildlife and disease management because introduced species such as rats, cats, mustelids and possums are having a devastating effect on vulnerable endemic species. I am a member of Picton Dawn Chorus which sets traps for introduced animals to reduce the pressure around a core fenced protected bush area at Kaipupu, in Queen Charlotte Sound. We aim for a trap in every fifth garden in a block. Pest control in New Zealand is an over-whelming issue with no real prospect of winning the battle.

5.9 Wild and Free

We keep animals ourselves and so we have to ask them if they are happy. Social animals need to live in social groups and we keep the horses in a little herd, not in stables. But sometimes they bully one another and we have to arrange things so that any underdogs can safely find food and shelter and not be pushed out. On the other hand solitary predators need sufficient space and some need segregating in the non-breeding season. We try to ensure that they get to fly free and develop hunting skills while they are in their formative stages. That all the animals breed is one way of them telling us that they have a reasonable quality of life. Many live to be well beyond breeding age.

But chimpanzees in solitary cages, rabbits having chemicals put in their eyes... is this really something our species can be proud of or justify?

Perhaps we should never keep animals in captivity? Maybe we should keep only domestic ones, not wild ones? How will you ever domesticate a wild animal if you never keep it in captivity? Falconers have domesticated over 40 species of birds of prey in the last few decades. People argue over the definition of 'domesticate' (especially people who have never domesticated anything, or, perhaps harder still, tried to avoid domesticating a species, to maintain a genetic wild-type while breeding in captivity). This is because domestication is a continuum, not a black and white situation, a bit like the 'species' concept. Nowadays with genome editing one can produce an animal that is definitely not wild type in just one generation. And what is captivity? Are our sheep captive because we keep them in the same fields, ones they are familiar with, where they have been born and raised, fields that they don't like to leave? Would they be less captive if we hefted them onto an open hill, to seek their fortunes, but suffer the vicissitudes of the weather without us there to care for them? Maybe eating each other's wool when trapped for days in a snow drift?

But pigs in farrowing crates, chickens in laying cages, cows in sheds their whole lives, this is the other extreme. So again, not a black and white decision.

Perhaps we should set the captives free? American mink from the mink farms were set free in Britain by Animal Rights groups and almost exterminated the water voles. I remember the chaos on the Avon. Now we struggle to keep on top of them by trapping and the Labour government banned hunting them with dogs on political grounds. (But we can still use the dogs to hunt rabbits and rats.) And what is 'free'? Should we let them go back to the wild? But where is 'wild'? Our farm is not 'the wild', and if you go over the boundary, our neighbour's farm is not 'wild' either. In fact, apart from a few cliff ledges, every single square metre of Britain is managed in some way. There is no 'wild' left. But maybe wildness is not a place, maybe it is just a state of mind? An animal out of the control of humans perhaps? Like a cat let out at night? Tame by day, wild by night. I discuss the mental state of wildness in 2.4.3. Some wild animals are naturally tame, some can be reared to be tame, and some domestic animals can be extremely wild and need a good dog to round them up. And when one of my falcons disappears into a cloudless sky, can she really get any freer? Free as a bird?

We have a strange paradox on the farm at the moment. Having built a lake, we put some beavers on it. They breed there and have a massive lodge. Beavers are a native British species but were exterminated here in the 1600s and deleted from the British list. So we are not allowed to release our beavers to the 'wild' and we have a long fence all around the downhill side of the lake so that they cannot go further down the catchment. Recently a pair of Black Swans arrived. They are native to Australia but a few have escaped from collections and are breeding in the UK. They have flown to our lake under their own steam and now it looks like they may nest. So for our native Eurasian Beavers the lake is classed as 'captivity' but for the non-native Black Swans the same place is 'wild'. And if the swans breed, would I be culpable for introducing non-native animals into the wild? Should I go and shoot them right now? Are they protected? Are they in season? (They resolved it for me – one died and the other flew away...)

Freedom is a tricky concept. We are all tethered by our minds.

When we keep animals in association with us, for whatever reason, in as much a state of freedom as we all can be, then we have a chance to connect with one another, to relate and interact, and gradually, at some level, to understand each other's perspectives and predicaments. I think we need more connectivity, not less. Some ways in which we humans keep animals, and one another, are horrid, for sure, but we should not throw the baby out with the bathwater.

Sometimes people say "Why can't you just leave it alone and stop killing these poor animals?". Let's unpack that for a moment; it sounds an ideal, but what would it entail? Let's start off by taking it literally. To leave it alone means that it is you that has to leave, not the natural world. So, OK, here's your suicide pill… Oh! Not so keen on that eh? But look at what demands you are placing on the planet, the food you need, your house, transport, electricity, water, waste products. Try totting it up. Spend some time calculating your resource audit. Now multiply it by 7.6 billion people. Try checking out what the human population is doing: https://ourworldindata.org/world-population-growth .

So if you don't want to physically leave, perhaps you could live in one place, and wildlife in another? Maybe segregation is the key? Why don't we move the 5.5 million people out of Scotland, and the 3 million people out of Wales and designate Scotland and Wales as wilderness areas for wildlife? Meanwhile everyone would pack into England and grow all the food we need on farms in England. No nuts or soya imported from other countries, but a vegetarian diet of cabbage, carrots and turnips in the winter might keep us going. What about the rare metals needed for mobile phones, and electronic devices, all imported from China or mined in Africa using child labour? That doesn't sound a very attractive option either. Could you persuade voters to support such a downturn in their standard of living? And what would the Scots and Welsh be feeling about a modern Highland Clearance?

What if we take a less drastic approach and instead of clearing out Scotland and Wales, we just empty the humans out of the National Parks? How much would it cost the government to buy all these farmers out and pay for the land? Would people pay for the tax increase, especially considering that humans would no longer be allowed into the National Parks? Would the National Parks be big enough to maintain minimum viable populations of all the representative species? Would most of them revert just to woodland and lose all the open landscapes needed by open country species such as waders? Would the wildlife populations in the National Parks be able to reach one another or would they become genetically isolated?

Leaving wildlife alone makes a nice sound bite, but it is the mantra of the naive. We are the biggest pest species on this planet and we don't want to control ourselves. Our only feasible approach is to look for compromise and do our best to maintain room for wildlife to live alongside us in some sort of man-maintained balance. We need to manage our own impact, and we need to manage and support other species. Sometimes that means dedicating an area of habitat to one group of species. Other times it means killing animals or plants to benefit more needy species. To do that we need to expand our concept of 'moral community' to include whole habitats and species, in fact the whole planet, Spaceship Earth.

5.10 Human welfare

You may have noticed that until this chapter I have maintained we are all animals, yet in this chapter I have left out humans. In this section I will redress that imbalance.

My mother suffered from morning sickness when she was pregnant with my two older siblings, so when it was my turn, she took some medicine. Fortunately this was before the days of thalidomide or it could have been a lot worse. But as a result I was born with a distorted skull and no right ear. Plastic surgery was still fairly basic in the early fifties and the surgeons had got their experience treating burnt airmen. So, from the age of three until twelve I would be in hospital for three week sessions during the school holidays while they skinned parts of my arms or legs to graft skin onto my ear. The result looks like a cauliflower on a bad day. I remember being woken at night by screaming children running up and down trying to tear the bandages off their burn or scald injuries. Or finding the curtains drawn around one of the beds because the occupant hadn't made it. The Ward Sisters ruled like Sergeant Majors and visiting times were twice a week.

I would go back to school a week late, with a bandage around my head and had to be treated three times a day for nine years. When I reached twelve I asked the doctors when I would be able to hear in my right ear. "Oh no!" they said, "You'll never be able to hear from that side; you have no inner ear at all."

So I refused to have any more operations or have a prosthetic ear. In my late teens I perforated my left eardrum by coaching shooting (no ear muffs in those days), so I had to have the eardrum patched up. It has meant that I cannot tell the direction of sounds, so fieldwork in woodland is no good. If someone in an audience asks a question I have no idea who spoke and often answer someone on the other side of the hall, which is mildly amusing.

So the God concept did not get off to a good start with me. Not only do I think the whole idea is highly implausible and unsupported by evidence, I resent people, whether they be Popes, Archbishops, Imams or anyone else, foisting their beliefs onto me and expecting me to follow their prescriptions on morality. Democracy may be the best of a bad political job but often has little logic under-pinning it. Opinion makers start the herd moving in a certain direction and the whole lot follow, for good or bad. As any sheep farmer will tell you, this works a lot of the time, but equally can end up with sheep in a blind corner, with unfortunate individuals trampled by those following, and smothered, and dying. Or the herd can self-perpetuate, the blind leading the blind. I remember one day bringing a flock of sheep into the yard. They were quite strung out and I was at the back seeing to the tail-enders.

The leaders swung around the back of the barn, came round the blind side and re-appeared just in time to see the tail-enders disappearing. Seeing that they were getting left behind, they hurried on to follow. Now the whole lot were running round and round the barn, following each other. I almost died laughing but had to stop them before they exhausted themselves.

Why do we have this huge hypocrisy between our treatment of humans and our treatment of other species? Why would I be prosecuted if I failed to put a terminally sick and suffering sheep out of her misery, yet my wife would be prosecuted if she did the same for me? Why is some human life sacrosanct, whereas others, such as enemy soldiers, are not? Some religions and societies are to this day into stoning to death, beheadings, honour killings and so on. Other societies permit euthanasia and assisted dying. Why is our Western society so terrified of death, even more so than of someone's suffering? We don't want to play God by assisting a suicide, yet, in preventing others doing so, that is exactly what we are doing. Are we in some sort of group denial, running round and round the barn, never questioning why?

I will go into this in more detail in Chapter 7, looking at moral relationships.

6 The Morality of Hunting

6.1 Introduction

So far I have looked at hunting as one of our core behaviours and the root components that shape this behaviour. Then I've examined hunting itself and some of the issues that might flag up ethical concern. But morality itself is a behavioural mechanism influencing our behaviour, so I need to look at this mechanism before applying it to hunting.

6.2 An intellect-based morality

Morality is one of those things that is often quoted but not clearly defined. The dictionary is not very helpful either:

'Principles concerning the distinction between right and wrong or good and bad behaviour'.

'A particular system of values and principles of conduct'.

'The extent to which an action is right or wrong'.

'Conformity to ideals of right human conduct'.

'A responsible relationship towards the laws of the natural world'.

Larry Churchill, amongst most others, restricts morality to humans and confines it to the intellect: *'Ethics, understood as the capacity to think critically about moral values and direct our actions in terms of such values, is a generic human capacity.'*

Christopher Boehm in *Moral Origins* also restricts morality to humans, but structures it both on the intellect and the genes on the basis that only humans can feel shame. But animals can show guilt and contrition too. Others, ranging from Kant and Bentham, to the Godlovitches, Ryder, Regan, Korsgaard, Gruen, Scruton, Singer and many more, have pondered on concepts such as the ability to feel pain, moral personhood, moral consideration, contractarianism, speciesism and so on, all from an anthropocentric position, which is weak. Why should there be an assumption of the primacy of humans, and, in particular, individual humans?

Donald Broom narrows the morality field down: *'Actions which would never affect another individual are not moral or immoral'*. This would exclude any moral responsibility towards ecological aspects, such as polluting the sea or climate change.

Others look for universals such as the 'Golden Rule': do unto others as you would have them do unto you, a somewhat facile approach.

These various philosophical theories and principles of morality have been debated for centuries, but they haven't made it into mainstream society. Nor have they forged proper links with religious moral codes. Most 'ordinary' people know nothing about them, yet somehow they muddle through their lives. So rather than starting with theories, I would rather look at the world as it actually functions, and from there try to decipher any underlying principles.

If morality is confined to humans and to no other species, then somewhere along the line of human evolutionary history a pair of non-moral parents must have given birth to a child that was suddenly moral. This seems unlikely because morality, like all behaviour, is complex, and relies not on just one gene, but thousands. These would not all mutate at the same time. So morals must have evolved step by step in humans, along a progressive continuum of mutations. This seems much more realistic; so when did it begin? Was it perhaps eight million years ago when humans differentiated from a common ancestor shared with the other anthropoid apes? Studies of those closely related species also reveal elements of moral behaviour, so maybe the process started earlier? But when you look at other vertebrate taxa you also find recognisable elements of moral behaviour, in birds as well as in mammals. Therefore the early forms of morality must have a long and venerable history way back into vertebrate evolution or beyond. How far beyond awaits investigation.

Marc Bekoff and Jessica Pierce in *Wild Justice: the Moral Lives of Animals* credit non-human animals with morality and define it as:

'A suite of interrelated other-regarding behaviours that cultivate and regulate complex interactions within social groups. These behaviors relate to well-being and harm, and norms of right and wrong attach to many of them. Morality is an essentially social phenomenon, arising in the interactions between and among individual animals, and it exists as a tangle of threads that hold together a complicated and shifting tapestry of social relationships. Morality in this way acts as a social glue.'

This is fine as far as it goes, but later they assert: *'we've limited our moral suite to behaviors in which there is a certain level of cognitive complexity and emotional nuance'*. Others talk about the need for 'rationality' and 'control'. They are in effect saying: 'This is what we call morality and therefore anything within this is morality and anything outside this, isn't.' But their arbitrary construct has come from human minds rather than from real life, which is my starting point. Mark Rowlands in *Can Animals be Moral?* says *'What makes a proposition a moral one is something that I shall not discuss. I shall assume we have a reasonable grasp on which propositions are moral ones and which are not'*. And so he fell at the first fence.

The concepts of 'right' or 'wrong' describing particular values are not absolutes. Much as we may flatter ourselves with these 'higher' thoughts, in real life, politicians, priests and philosophers are just as likely to follow base instincts as anyone else, because at root, morality is itself the realisation of base instincts, our ethotype. Of course one could postulate that, on the contrary, morality is all about somehow rising above these base instincts on to some kind of higher moral plane. But such artificial intellectual moral ideas and values soon break down in cultural dissonance and arguments. They are the life blood of philosophers and academics who debate them endlessly and fruitlessly. The disparity between their ideas and real life is a chasm many are reluctant to cross, and other disciplines – neuroscience, social sciences and ecology – are stepping in now to decipher them by taking real life as their starting point and trying to untangle how things work together at different levels, from the genes to the universe. Right now, an intellect-based morality, like the concept of souls, is struggling to have any definition or existence. They are conceptual mirages.

6.3 A natural morality

To me, morality is a mechanism extending beyond our own species and pre-dating it. In a nutshell, just to get us started, I will venture my own definition:

'Morality is behaviour that promotes genetic survival through social cohesion. It requires four elements:
- *A social group.*
- *Shared ethical values.*
- *A judge.*
- *A system of enforcement.*

Morality is biological in origin and has evolved in higher vertebrates. Its roots lie in genetic, imprinted and in learned behaviour.'

There is no need to believe in a God to have morals. Morals pre-date both religion and our human species. The elements required for morality, namely a social group, a shared value system of ethics, a judge and a system of enforcement, are all there without a need for religion, or even humanity.

We humans are the gold standard against which we measure all the other 1.26 million or so species of animals. We call ourselves the Primates. The rest are the 'Secondrates'! We put paint brushes into their paws or trunks and marvel when they make crude marks. But we down-play all the attributes at which they excel but we fare poorly. Our brains are too primitive to process the scents that are commonplace to a dog. Our spatial memory has no hope of competing with a jay's or a squirrel's. Our thought processing speed is archaic compared to a swallow's, and if we have the temerity to try to compete physically, we are often doomed to failure. Our ignorance of other species leads us into an artificial separation between humans and other species. This is a profound error. Non-human animals have their own systems of morality, as well as being within our human moral sphere.

The concept of dualism, as proposed by people like Descartes, is a false trail. We are all of us slightly different from one another, but fundamentally we all come from the same root-stock. Rather than, slightly desperately, trying to prove that humans are separate from other animals, we should examine our commonalities, celebrate them and use them to help us understand ourselves. It is about relationships, not isolating things in boxes.

Morality is not just about 'right' and 'wrong', it is a continuum, a spectrum. It disperses into the nebulous. While at one end there is the big stuff: 'Thou shalt not kill', this grades right through to wider aspects such as complying with social expectations. You wear one set of clothes to work and another for a social event. If you turn up in the wrong clothes, you will receive social disapproval, enough to prevent you doing it again; this is etiquette, a soft kind of morality supporting social cohesion. The new social media also exert social pressure to comply with established norms.

Most philosophers consider morality as solely emanating from the rational mind, a product of reasoning, of justice and fairness. I believe that morality goes much, much deeper than this; its roots are in evolution and it spans at least the vertebrates. It's not just the civilised icing on the human cake, it is about our very survival. If morality is a mechanism promoting the ongoing survival of the genes, then there is no ultimate 'right' or 'wrong'. Anything goes, as long as those precious genes get through to the next generation. Words like 'immoral' mean nothing. That doesn't mean that it is an ethical free-for-all out there, far from it. Morality is a highly sophisticated mechanism. It is as much about cooperation as competition, possibly more so.

6.4 The genetic components of morality

Perhaps when Richard Dawkins published *The Selfish Gene* in 1976, he later regretted using the word 'selfish' because of the way that people have misinterpreted it. Maybe he also regretted using the singular word 'gene'. The thing is, no organisms have only one gene; evolution depends on organisms having a whole assortment that gets re-shuffled at each generation. It needs new combinations to create variations that can then prove their worth in the battlefield of survival. Genes have another problem; not only can they not hang out singly, they cannot exist without a body to live in. They are like endoparasites that design their own host. Genes have to have a body, or phenotype, to live in. If the phenotype is static, such as a plant, this is as far as the genes need to go. But if the genes create a design that is capable of movement, then they have to design the movements too; we call it behaviour.

While a lot has been written in science about the genotype, which is the replicatory unit consisting of the full complement of genes, and the phenotype, which is the physical body that manifests it and is derived from it, I use the word '*ethotype*' for the behaviour emanating from the genes. It is the behavioural analogue of the phenotype and is equally the vehicle for the genes as is the phenotype, being subject to similar selection mechanisms. Whereas an 'instinct' refers to a specific behaviour or drive that is genetic in origin, 'ethotype' refers to an individual's entire suite or complement of instinct templates. Just as incremental changes in the phenotype can be traced back through evolutionary history, so we can also decipher phylogenetic changes in the ethotype. We just have to be careful to differentiate between ethotypic behaviour and learned behaviour. Learned behaviour obviously does not feature in the genotype, although the capacity to learn does.

At the group or taxon level, the genome represents the genetic complement shared by all the individuals in the group. But because of individual variation, the individuals, in their own genotypes, will vary slightly, one from another. The physical expression of the genes is the phenotype. So at the species level, we can recognise the human phenotype for example, but as well as this we can recognise individuals. Maybe one person has brown eyes and another has green eyes. This is all to do with genetics and is fixed. But beyond this are variations caused by living. Twins may be born genetically and phenotypically identical, but through life style, one may grow fat and another grow thin. This is 'nature' (genes) and 'nurture' (lifestyle), examined by Steven Pinker in *The Blank Slate*.

The same applies to your behaviour; there is the genetic component, the ethotype, and there is a learned component that has been picked up through living. In so far as there could be any 'ultimate truth' for any particular species, the ethotypic component of morality is it. These are 'core' values. This is what Thomas Aquinas was grappling with in his 'Natural Law'. The learned, cultural elements of morality are more adaptable and prone to variation, and thus to perpetual debate.

Within a group of organisms with the same genotype, morality stemming from the ethotype should be consistent across all individuals in the group, just as the genes are. Although this seems to be more or less true, ethotypic morality is not entirely consistent because the mechanisms that translate from the genes to the end-behaviour are not simple. They operate via the brain, and through hormonal influences. These are complex mechanisms. Robert Sapolsky provides a useful primer on them in his book *Behave*. An animal under the influence of hormones, such as in courtship mode, or in child-rearing mode, is likely to behave and react differently compared with when those hormones were not flooding its system. A timid ewe, who normally would move away from me, will stamp her foot, stand her ground and glare at me when I approach her with her new lamb. Because the system is not directly mechanistic, the behaviour cannot be totally predictable, or pre-determined, and thus we can say that the moral values it portrays are not absolutes but rather they are adapted to maximise genetic survival in the prevailing circumstances.

Then there are *learned* morals. For example, as pack leader, I can teach my dogs that sitting on the sofa is not allowed. I counter any approach to the sofa using operant conditioning and negative reinforcement. When I am not there some dogs will still keep off the sofa; they have internalised the learned 'moral' into a 'conscience'. They have passed their own 'Marshmallow Test'. Others are naughty. As soon as the coast is clear they sneak up onto the sofa. When they hear me coming, they sneak off again as if butter would not melt in their mouths. But I go across to the sofa. I can feel it is warm. There are some tell-tale hairs. I look at the dog. He realises he has been sussed. He starts to look guilty. He looks guilty because he has not only broken our shared and learned moral value about the sofa; he has also been found out. (He could equally look guilty just because I look at him in a certain way, regardless of his conduct.) But a clever dog, if you don't find him out, may act all innocent and not look guilty. Think about that for a moment; this is more complicated than appears at first sight.

Of course this is all most unscientific. But that does not make my interpretations wrong. It just means scientists haven't figured out a way of testing them. Some scientists have become so zealous in their

Her hormones give this ewe the courage to stand her ground as I approach.

application of scientific rigour to studies of non-human behaviour that they have become, to all intents and purposes, autistic towards non-humans. Sadly, philosophers and psychologists often brush non-anthropoid behaviour aside as almost irrelevant.

Behaviour has no corporeal existence of its own; it relies on a physical body to perform the behaviour, and in most cases a brain to instruct the body (not all behaviour goes through the brain). In a way the ethotype potentially has even more impact on the fortunes of the genes than does the phenotype, because the ethotype can function at the group level both vertically (ie through the generations) and horizontally (through siblings), as well as at the individual level, and even beyond the kinship group to unrelated meme groups. The phenotype tends to evolve mainly through a competitive Darwinian selection pressure, whereas the ethotype can also function co-operatively, at the group level, and, not being totally reliant on gene transmission, can evolve in a Lamarkian way. If a learned cultural attribute gives a particular meme group a survival advantage, the genes of that group will trend towards dominating the population genotype, religions being a prime example.

As a semantic aside, people often use the verb 'designed', which, to me, implies the presence of a 'designer'. When we are talking about examples of evolutionary changes, there was no 'designer'. The changes came about through natural selection pressures over many iterations, most of which were genetic dead-ends. 'Intelligent design' implies the input of an intelligent designer. We suffer a little here with the inadequacy of the English language. We use the noun 'design' to denote a specific configuration without necessarily implying the existence of a 'designer'. Perhaps someone can come up with a noun meaning a design, pattern or configuration that specifically has <u>not</u> arisen from the actions of a designer as an entity, but from evolution, which is a process of self-selection by attrition?

At whatever trophic level you may be, as a species, there are some benefits to be had from living in groups. Indeed, even the solitary predators, such as the falcons that I work on, have to spend some of their life cycle interacting with one another in order to breed. The smallest 'group' is the breeding pair, then the family with progeny, then the multi-generational family, followed by a herd or group in which the individuals know one another, and then larger communities. Once a group is formed, there will be a conflict between the needs of the group as a whole, and the needs of each individual within it. To resolve this conflict and to maintain the cohesion of the group, there is a mechanism, and this is what we call 'morality'.

Morality, as a form of behaviour, has the same roots as all behaviour, namely genetic, imprinted and learned, and the sum of these three moral roots may be described as our 'conscience'. Our genetically inherited moral behaviour, which is part of our ethotype, is internal to each one of us and could loosely be described as 'intuition'. Ethotypic morality is genetically fixed inside us and this means that we can be our own judges. We don't need an external person or group to tell us right from wrong when it comes to this deepest personal ethotypic morality. Of course this still doesn't mean any of the values are ultimately right or wrong, an ultimate truth, it just means that in evolutionary terms, they have conferred on our ancestors, both as individuals and as groups, sufficient survival skills to be selected for breeding successive generations, of which we are the most recent. Extended ethotypic behaviour can result in kin-altruism (preferential benevolence towards relatives) because usually the group an animal is in is genetically inter-related. By influencing the genetic social group, an individual's ethotypic behaviour has the potential not only to create kin-altruistic behaviour right then, but also it can carry over after the individual is dead.

6.5 Ethotypic morality and learned morality

Fundamental or ethotypic morality, the part that is genetic in origin, has been honed by evolution. Ethotypic morality can be hypocritical; it struggles to resolve conflicts between the needs of the individual and the needs of the group. The learned moral values show a great deal of variation at all sorts of levels, and this means that some learned values can conflict with other learned values or even with ethotypic values. If an individual employs both these values that are in conflict, the individual himself is in conflict, there is a moral dissonance. At best we may describe this as hypocrisy, at worse it may lead to mental breakdown, or in a group situation, war.

Let me flesh this out with some examples. Think of an ethotypic behaviour which is expressed in a physical format that we can see: a bird's nest. When a bird builds its nest, most of its behaviour is instinctive. For sure there is a small learning component, particularly in repeat nestings, but by and large the nest building is instinctive and is consistent across the ethotype. Thus the wren has a phenotype that we can all recognise, and a nest that is consistently similar so that we can also recognise it as a wren's nest. All wrens look pretty much the same and all wren nests look pretty much the same. The phenotype and the ethotype work hand in hand, both expressing instructions from the genotype. The blackbird (*Turdus merula*) on the other hand looks different, and so does its nest. But all blackbirds look the same and all blackbird nests look the same. Again, their phenotype and ethotype are consistent. Other aspects of nest building have much more of a learned component. For example the selection of nest materials has a basic instinctive component restricting the selection to a limited range of items. Wrens don't try to select twigs the size of broom handles. Within their limited size range they learn, by trial and error or by insight, to select fibres suited to nest building and their choice will be limited by availability.

They have some flexibility to adapt to circumstances. For example, on the steppes of Mongolia there are virtually no trees, so many stick-nesting raptors build their

This Upland Buzzard (**Buteo hemilasius**) *has built a nest of wire, string and a magazine on one of our artificial nests in Mongolia.*

nests with wire and rags. I even have a couple of very nicely carved horse sweat scrapers retrieved from eagle nests there. Without trees, they are unable to bring in sprays of green leaves to maintain nest hygiene, but they still manage, if at a reduced productivity.

You may think collecting twigs to make a nest is a simple, almost trivial thing. Not at all. Try building a nest yourself and you will quickly discover that it is not simple, and you have to have just the right materials. Branched sticks are no use, nor are brittle dead ones. The best are broken off by splitting at the 'Y' junction to provide a single stick. When we are supplying sticks for nest-building raptors in captivity their whole breeding success depends on getting it right. And it is no good just building the whole thing for them. The act of nest-building is often part of the courtship process. The ethotype programmes the birds to look for exactly the right materials and in many species, the act of home-building reinforces the pair-bond.

Moving on now to learned behaviour. Whereas nest construction is mainly instinctive, a consecutive series of ethotypic templates, nest site selection can be learned from imprinting and one can see multi-generational familial and group traits in nest site selection. For example, peregrines reared on cliff nests tend to select cliff sites for their own nests. Peregrines reared on stick nests in German forests tend to choose similar sites when they are old enough to breed. This trait can be so marked that two populations of peregrines that are sympatric, sharing the

Chapter 6 – THE MORALITY OF HUNTING   151

Collecting sticks for storks' nests.

same area, can be genetically isolated by their differences in nest site selection, just as Orcas (*Orcinus orca*) are genetically segregated by learned cultures in prey selection. On the other hand, the steppes of Mongolia offer few nest site options for saker falcons (which don't construct their own nests). So we found some nesting straight on the ground, some on bridges or old water tanks, and some on the 30 cm wide top of concrete tubular pylons. They are forced to learn to be innovative.

How do genes express themselves? In the case of the phenotype, we can see cells dividing and differentiating into specific organs and bodies. I'm not clear exactly how this mechanism works; I'm not sure if anyone really knows. But how do the gene sequences go from bits of DNA to turn into some behaviour? Again, I don't know. But somehow, either directly through the brain, or indirectly through hormones and even feed-back loops, the brain gets a 'feeling'. I don't mean a feeling as in 'you've hurt my feelings'. I mean a feeling like 'I feel hungry', an urge, a drive, something that motivates you into a behavioural action to comply with or assuage that feeling. Some of these feelings may be quite emotional, high arousal, others may be less well defined: 'I feel lonely' or 'I want to go home'. This is your ethotype talking, but it is not so deterministic that you have a single gene for loneliness.

Similarly, for example, the 'fight or flight' response resulting from fear. These are two options, apparently in conflict, but are just one instinct. First there is a trigger (not an instinct, an experienced event). This creates fear (an instinctive response). This floods the body with hormones that raise the heart rate, increase blood flow to the muscles and heighten awareness ready for action. All of this is involuntary and fast. The conscious mind then has to make a decision for action, either to fight or flee depending on the circumstances. The instinct has prepared the body for the conscious decision. So instinct and intellect work hand in hand, the instincts prepare the set up and the intellect makes the conscious decisions based on the local information at the time. If we struggle to make a decision, it's called panicking or even freezing; tonic immobility.

Now let's look at humans. Humans also are phenotypically consistent. We have variations in skin and hair colour, but almost all of us have the same number of fingers and thumbs and many shared behaviours, what Donald Brown calls 'Human Universals'. We can infer that the human ethotype parallels our phenotype. They are broadly the same, with only minor or superficial variations which may be heritable at the group level or the family level. At the individual level, we describe the variations in ethotype as our 'temperament' as discussed in Chapter 2. Temperaments and personality traits stay with us all our lives, as Jerome Kagan has demonstrated.

In humans, especially with our long developmental period, we have a lot of learned behaviour that entails developing 'moral' values. These moral values can easily conflict and when they do there is internal conflict, hypocrisy or corruption. Most other animals are relatively straightforward. They are straight up kind of folk. What you see is what you get. But for humans, life is more complicated and probably all of us have learned value systems that conflict at some point. Most of our debates on morality centre on these areas of conflicting values and when you look at them closely, it is mainly the learned moral values. The ethotypic morality has an underlying principle of genetic survival, but learned and cultural values lead down all sorts of highways and bye-ways. I will be expanding on this later, but I just want to flag up that all moral values, both ethotypic and learned, for all species, are dependent on Darwinian evolution which is leading us into an evolutionary trap.

For some philosophers morality is only about learned behaviour; it is solely an intellectual exercise. It leads on to postulating about post-human situations and the development of ethical positions within artificial intelligence (artilect). Many, such as Dan Faggella, have speculated on post-human morality and the doom and gloom situation of when we are over-taken by our own technology. Be that as it may, morality extends far further into vertebrate biology than a merely intellectual approach and it may surprise some philosophers that humans and many other species use moral mechanisms entirely unaided by the intellect or by philosophy. How did we all manage before Thales of Miletus, a mere 2,600 years ago? Morality isn't just some kind of intellectual add-on; it's about survival. While humans have a better intellectual capacity for evaluating morality than any other species, this does not necessarily translate into us acting more morally than them. Other species have more rudimentary moral systems but their 'immoral' behaviour is more basic too. Few have the capacity for genocide, corruption, destruction of habitats or failure to limit population size and density that we indulge in.

6.6 Morality and sin

Various aspects follow on from my definition of morality. Ethotypic morality is to do with balancing the needs of the individual against the needs of the social group. While the survival of the individual is all about 'selfish genes' as expounded by Dawkins, this is only part of the story. The survival of social animals (in contrast to solitary predators) hinges on the survival of the group, as explained by Peter Kropotkin and Edward Wilson. Individuals cast out from the group have a reduced chance of survival, and small, fragmented groups have worse prospects than strong coherent groups. So for social animals, ethotypic morality is about maintaining group cohesion at the expense of the individual. There is a conflict here. Darwin postulated 'survival of the fittest' (individual). Parts of the genomes of individuals must reflect this. But if the unit of survival is also the social group (based on co-operation), then some elements must reflect this too. Two potentially conflicting routes to survival are present in the one individual genotype. The most survivable individuals are the ones living in and maintaining the most survivable groups. It's all about surviving, and breeding, passing on those successful genes. Selection at the individual level and at the group level are not mutually exclusive. Both are subject to forms of selection and mutation, prerequisites for evolution.

So for individuals to survive, their group has to survive, and morality is the mechanism for resolving conflicting issues between the two. Let's try out a few examples of sins, and see how this works.

You are a teenage girl, your hormones are rushing, your instincts are pushing you to go and find a mate. You want to go out for an evening with your boyfriend. Your mother is worried about you. She thinks you are still young; you might get into trouble. You want to go, but you don't want to upset her. So you tell her a little lie. You say you are going to spend the evening with a couple of girl friends. You tell her the lie to spare her feelings. You know that if she knew, there would be a row, that it would rock the boat of your family equanimity. In a small way it threatens your family group cohesion. So, in an effort to follow your instinct to find a mate, and in an effort to maintain group cohesion, you resolve the conflict by lying. You commit a 'sin'. Both drives were ethotypic in origin, and you resolved the conflict at an intellectual level. You weren't happy with that way of resolving it, the moral dissonance made you feel uncomfortable, 'guilty'. You think it was your 'conscience' talking to you.

What about bullying? Social groups have hierarchies in order to function. The mechanisms for establishing and maintaining the social hierarchies are many and varied. Males may try to look bigger and stronger than they really are. Females try to look prettier and more nubile than they really are. Climbing the ladder entails treading on the shoulders of others. One way to appear 'better' than someone else is to make the other person look worse than you are. Everything is relative. So we get the bullied, the down trodden, the outcasts. At an intellectual level this seems not nice, as sinful, but from the moral mechanism point of view, this makes for a more survivable social group. The quickest way to improve a group without making changes is to cull out the bottom 25%. It doesn't matter if you are selecting paintings for an art exhibition or breeding a flock of sheep. Get rid of the bottom 25% and the overall group quality automatically improves.

So we can go right on to ethnic cleansing. Here, one social group wipes out another. From an exterior perspective, we deem this 'sinful', but clearly the group doing the killing is the group that survives and breeds. For them, it was a good strategy. Similarly, when fighters kill all opposing men in a battle and then rape the women, this has the effect of reducing the genetic contribution of the defeated side and multiplying the genes of the victors. From the outside we may consider this morally 'bad', but the winning genes obviously benefit, so the behaviour doesn't extinguish.

This behaviour is deep in our genes, it is ethotypic. However much we try to cover it with an intellectual veneer of 'civilisation', it stays there, lurking, deep down. It isn't the Devil's work; it is our moral mechanism resolving conflicts between the individual and the group levels of survival. Many of the examples propounded by philosophers, examine many aspects of our behaviour, such as 'sin', using only intellectual explanations. Sometimes you need to dig below learned and cultural behaviour, and get down to the ethotype. We can be judgemental at an intellectual level, but it is a sticking plaster.

Some of this stuff isn't very nice. But morality isn't about being nice; it's about survival. It's about how you – you in particular – got to be the one who is alive today, reading this book, and it is about what lurks within you, behaviours that may surface if circumstances arise.

7 The mechanism of morality

7.1 Introduction

In 6.2 I listed four components of morality: a social group, shared ethical values, a judge, and a system of enforcement. These work together with the overall aim of maintaining the cohesion of the social group and, as a consequence, the genetic bloodlines.
Let's look at these components in more detail.

7.2 Types of social group

This element is complicated, so I am going to build it up in layers. Only later can we see how this is relevant to hunting. Let's look first at physical social groupings:

7.2.1 The individual

The smallest social group is one individual. He consists of a complement of his own genes (his genotype) carried in a physical body (his phenotype) and with an inherited suite of behaviours (his ethotype). If he is not a male, but a female, then her genotype will have two X chromosomes but no Y chromosome (this is in mammals; it is the opposite in birds). This means her phenotype and ethotype will be slightly different. These gender-based differences are all separately subject to evolutionary selection pressures. Both genders also carry inside them a biome of bacteria, fungi and viruses, each with their own genetic complements, influencing the survival of the individual. Some, such as mitochondria and chloroplasts, have integrated themselves so thoroughly that the organisms could not function without them. But for the subject of this discussion we don't need to worry about them right now.

We all claim a small space around us as our own. It varies slightly between cultures, but it is always there and it is ethotypic. We feel uncomfortable if someone gets too close, and the word 'feel' usually indicates the presence of an instinct. If we have some type of bond with someone, such as a mother-child relationship or a pair of lovers, then we allow that person inside our personal space. This extends not just to distance apart, but to touching as well. In a packed train or bus, everyone goes to a lot of trouble to preserve their personal space as much as possible. And of course some parts of the body are public and some parts are private.

Although a greeting ceremony is instinctive, even if only reduced to a faint smile to show lack of hostility, it can be elaborated into all sorts of cultural rituals from hand-shaking, kissing, hugging to presenting one's business card. There is even a social etiquette being promoted at the moment dictating how many seconds one can hug for, before it is considered to be sexual harassment. Most animals also have instinctive greeting ceremonies too, with a fine mixture of assuaging hostility and judging the newcomer.

A lot of philosophical debate centres on the level of the individual, or multiples of individuals. Is it better to sacrifice one, to 'save' three, that kind of thing, often without consideration of their relative positions within a moral community. War sits uncomfortably in these debates.

7.2.2. The Pair

The next level of social group is the pre-breeding pair. This consists of a male and a female bonded and interacting together. Homosexual pairings also come under this category. In some western societies, human relationships are stagnating at this stage; many couples do not go on to breed. In many vertebrates breeding does not entail pair-bonding, instead there may be a lek system, or a harem system.

7.2.3 The Family

The next social group is the breeding pair with a family of one or more offspring. The Western human 'nuclear family' is increasingly failing at this stage, with a lower reproductive rate than that of some Asian and African cultures whose families are structured at the extended level.

Families consist of a group of bonded individuals, normally of shared genetic kinship. The family occupy a home, nest, den, cave, burrow, sett, or lodge, depending on species. In some species the male lives separately, perhaps independently, or visiting intermittently to provision food. The female tends to line the nest, burrow or home and defend the young, while the male may be involved in constructing the nest or home, and defending both the home and the female with young. I'm putting it in this generalised way in order to flag up the commonality we humans share with other species, and to notice that the instincts to behave this way are broadly common across many species.

7.2.4 The Kinship Group

The next level is the extended multi-generational (vertical) and pan-generational (horizontal) family or kinship group with grand-parents, uncles and nieces, all blood relatives sharing a diminishing percentage of one another's genes. Contrary to some common misconceptions, Darwinian 'survival of the fittest' is not necessarily about competition between individuals. Precedence in passing on genes is not necessarily through a single individual outcompeting others, physically or mentally.

We go pheasant hawking in Yunnan.

Co-operation is as powerful a selector as competition, possibly more so in social ethotypes, especially as ethotypic co-operation can extend to many individuals, not just at this level but up to the tribal one too. For example, although a phenotype evolving strong arms may provide some advantage to an individual, an ethotype evolving co-operation means that together, a group can achieve much more than one stronger individual. They could co-operate to build a house or kill a bison.

Another example at this level is the hunting group or fighting group, typically a band or gang of young men who know one another well. There is a strong bond in such a group, resulting in teamwork, group co-operation to face a shared goal or adversity. Ties of loyalty at this level usually exceed ties of loyalty at a large group level, such as 'patriotism'. It is harder to fight for a vague future ideal than for your mate right beside you, right now. These ties of loyalty strongly influence moral decision-making and, because the group share a common goal or benefit, individual actions cannot always be classed as altruistic or reciprocal.

7.2.5 The Tribe

This is ethotypic morality's finest hour! The tribe consists of up to about 150 individuals who can identify one another and who mostly have a degree of genetic relatedness. They may also share memes, elements of culture that could promote or detract from their genetic survivability. In the majority of species, this is as far as it goes. This is the limit where evolutionary kinship selection pressures operate on individual ethotypes and on the genes they carry. Evolution operates at several group levels, from the individual up to about the tribe; at the individual level it is about competition, but at the group levels the individuals need to co-operate within their group and the group competes with rival groups. The tribe is the natural unit for the human species. It entails a single leader known to all the members of the tribe and a dominance hierarchy that leads to a class system. Most tribes tend to be 'lick up, kick down' social systems.

The group may be based on a settlement or village, or it may be nomadic. Even nowadays it may be an ethnic minority community or diaspora sprinkled in a city full of other people and yet retaining its tribal identity. As well as sharing genes, the tribe shares its cultural habits and rituals and that reinforces its sense of group identity and cohesion.

Apart from establishing and defending the tribal homes and the families in them, the tribe defends the resources around it, such as the water supply and plant or animal food. In humans we may also defend cultural spaces that are sacred or have some significance for us. We band together to do this, young and old, male and female. Unlike a hunting party, which usually consists of young males, tribal defence involves everyone, acting in different roles according to their capabilities, because defence is played out on the home turf.

A successful tribe will flourish and breed up. Then one of two things can happen. As numbers increase, the tribe gets so big that not everyone knows each other, so factions start to form and the tribe becomes harder and harder to govern, until in the end it divides and part of the tribe goes off to live somewhere else. Alternatively, before numbers reach this level, the tribe may outstrip its resources of food or water. It then either has to up sticks and move on, or take steps to limit its numbers, maybe by killing female babies, as has happened in India, or by a government limiting family size, as in China.

Perhaps because of dwindling resources, a tribe might decide to attack and over-run a neighbouring tribe. To do this it will partition roles; young males will be sent out as soldiers to do the fighting while the old, and the women and children, stay back at home. These young males show immense loyalty to one another, and take pride in their prowess in battle. The best performers are rewarded with the best rewards, including the pick of any available females.

These ethotypic behaviours are common across all human groups and indeed we see parallels in many other social species too. When an entire social group behaves in a certain way it is itself acting as an individual entity, a tribe. Thus the ethotype is capable of extending beyond individuals and acting collectively at the group level.

As you go up the scale beyond the groupings that may share genetic kinship into larger groups, morality starts to fade out. Some residual behaviour – concern for others – may continue and we call this altruism, but it may be transmitted by learning from the example of others rather than from a residual ethotype. Motivation dissipates as group size gets larger. A point is reached where no moral obligation is felt. By this point, strangers may walk past a person lying injured in the street, without stopping.

Unlike humans, few other vertebrates attempt social groupings above the tribal level. For sure, wildebeests form vast herds, but they are aggregations without a social structure. We humans have various sub-sets of social groups within larger group sizes, extending up to nationhood. Nationhood is centred on an area of land, and is subject to group territorial behaviour, that has an ethotypic root. But at this level the tribal hierarchical system breaks down and for the nation to function at all, artificial laws need to be established. These may reflect and incorporate ethotypic moral values but essentially they are agreed and learned values that can therefore vary from nation to nation, and be argued over. To be effective, nationhood requires a single, shared culture. A multicultural society often has a diversity of moral values; it is more syncretic than accultural.

Some cultures still do not recognise Western notions of land ownership and many indigenous peoples have been exploited because of this. Is 'multi-cultural society' a contradiction in terms? Small groups, up to 150 or so, are to some extent genetically related, but they are also socially cohesive; they share the same culture. When two or more groups of different cultures come together, they do not usually form a 'society'. They may interact together, but until they are fully integrated and sharing the same cultural norms, they are not a single social group. When I worked with UNESCO on Intangible Cultural Heritage, it was quite obvious that the small nations were the ones with the clearest sense of cultural identity and cohesiveness. Some of the larger nations, who pride themselves on their 'multi-culturalism' have not signed the UNESCO ICH Convention. It is because they have lost their clear sense of cultural identity in a miasma of cultural exchange, and to this extent they can no longer describe themselves as a single nation, even though their citizens share the same land area. Depressingly, I've come to think that 'multicultural society' is a contradiction in terms.

7.2.6 Crowds

As groups get bigger, there comes a point where individuals have never met one another. They are no longer in a shared moral community and morality starts to erode. Our vocabulary is weak at recognising this distinction. In New Zealand we tend to call a group of sheep who know each other a 'flock'. They may be partly a kin group – genetically related – and partly a meme group, hefted together on the same patches of ground. A flock will usually behave cohesively. A mixed group of sheep, maybe fresh from the market, tend to be called a 'mob'. They have no coherent structure, no leaders, no hierarchies.

Similarly in humans we have lynch mobs which, as morality erodes, may do things that they would be inhibited from doing as individuals. The mob doesn't need to be physically together; people can be anonymous online and this is where, without the inhibitions of the tribe, some of the nastier side of human nature reveals itself. Online, you can hide behind anonymity. Equally misleading can be online surveys. Carefully crafted questions can evoke uninhibited responses leading to conclusions which may be misleading or even downright dangerous. Clever journalism can sway 'public opinion' off the moral piste.

7.2.7 Patriotism and international struggles

Beyond the tribal level the ethotypic component of our behaviour starts to fade. In our evolutionary history, few groups extended much beyond this level. Native American tribes had their own identities and competed or fought against one another for resources, but when faced with a larger scale threat from a European invasion, they were unable to act cohesively. Partly this was due to communication and distance, and partly it was because they did not identify themselves as a larger, continent-wide group. Similar situations pertained in other regions, such as what is now Europe. As communications improved, this had the effect of overcoming the drawbacks of distance, so people could identify themselves as a group, even though they had never met one another. Broadcasts to the 'nation' created a sense of shared identity and patriotism.

Currently there are 195 'nations' on the planet, split up by geography and ideology. These nations all have a footprint on the ground. Could we ever progress to the stage where the whole planet became just one nation? This would greatly enhance the chances of tackling global challenges such as climate change. Some of these nations have tried clumping together in federations or unions, often based on shared trade agreements but such efforts have tended to hit the buffers because of cultural barriers such as language, and because of difficulties in organising leadership.

On top of these nations with footprints on the ground, there are other international groups based on ideologies, especially religions and political ideologies such as communism. These factions compound the problems of nations functioning co-operatively. When co-operation fails, the usual method of conflict resolution is warfare. We can draw an analogy between warfare for territory and warfare for ideology, and the phenotype and ethotype. Territorial warfare is about land (which you can see), and the phenotype is about form (which you can also see). Early warfare and taxonomy both concentrated on these tangible approaches. Ideologies and ethotypes on the other hand are invisible, intangible. They are much harder to grasp, to understand, or to change.

Finally, beyond nations, is the concept of planet Earth as a group enterprise. Most human cultures have not yet taken this concept fully on board. It is too big for our imaginations, our understanding of space and time. We thus struggle with those two major issues – human demographics and climate change. Sadly, because the sphere of influence of politicians extends only to their own national boundaries and until their next election, our species is poorly equipped to deal with global issues. We humans are probably the only species able to think about the future of the entire planet, not just our immediate needs, but then, we are probably the only ones that need to, because we are the only ones screwing it up.

7.3 Meme or cultural groups

As well as physical social groups, we have cultural groups such a religious groups, a generation group, an army platoon, a professional group; these are meme groups, each of which has its own specific shared moral and cultural values. An individual may have to hop from one moral value set to another because he or she is in more than one society. A teenager out on the town with his buddies may get up to things which his buddies approve of, but his parents wouldn't. Many human societies have class systems, caste systems or even slave systems, which are part cultural and part physical separations. Golf has always been elitist and sexist. The Royal and Ancient only started to admit women in 2014. While fox hunting has been charged with historical elitism it has in fact been extremely egalitarian for a century or more. Similarly, while golf is most popular in the south east of Britain and less so in the provinces, hunting is also more elitist in the south east but popular and non-elitist elsewhere.

From the hunting point of view, your meme group may be your local Hunt, or you may be a member of an angling club or shooting syndicate. You will have some loyalty to your group and may volunteer to help out. On the other hand, if you pay for your fishing or shooting by the day, your relationship may just be a commercial one.

All these types of social groups are not mutually exclusive, on the contrary, most overlap. A traditional Hunt in the UK (which includes, huntsmen, riders, foot followers, 'countrymen' and supporters) make up a tribal group of perhaps 100-1000 people. They are of all ages and classes but linked to a 'Hunt Country', a solely held area of land, a traditional hunting territory. Most of Britain is covered by these Hunt Countries, which are mapped with defined boundaries, and the boundaries by no means coincide with county or other municipal designations, but may follow natural features. A Hunt may not draw for a scent in an adjacent Hunt's country without its prior permission, but if a chase goes into another's country, it is permissible to follow in hot pursuit. These areas and etiquettes go back into the mists of time.

Foxes as well as deer, boar and hares were hunted *par force* since before the Normans conquered Britain in 1066, and the hunting laws and etiquette have been documented by many authors since, such as Gaston Fébus writing in 1389. But since 1888 any disputes have been arbitrated by the various Hunt associations, such as the Master of Foxhounds Association, and now the British Hounds Sports Association. Within this local Hunt 'tribe' the members will probably have some kinship relationships, but otherwise they are a meme group tied to a territory. When fox hunting was banned in the UK in 2005 by invoking the Parliament Act, it was clear to all (and openly admitted by some Labour MPs) that although it was ostensibly about animal welfare, in reality it was about party politics. So a law was passed which did not meet with the mores of the Hunting Tribes or the owners of the land (the farmers) on which they operate. Claims were made that 70% supported a ban on hunting. But these various polls were mainly from people outside hunting. Most had little knowledge of hunting and hunting did not impact their lives in any way. But neither the politicians, nor the police, nor these voters, had any means to enforce the Act, so 20 years on, fox hunting still enjoys local support all over British land-based communities.

We see similar scenarios put upon other indigenous hunting communities such as Innuit seal-hunters or Icelandic whalers. What we are looking at here is the failure of artificial structures, such as 'democracy', online surveys and so on, to impact a meme group at tribal level.

In 2003 UNESCO created a new Convention for Intangible Cultural Heritage. It had realised that heritage is not just about ancient ruins like the pyramids, but is also about cultural elements or memes that were intangible but passed down from one generation to the next. Falconers realised that falconry was a form of ICH and wanted falconry inscribed by UNESCO. The government of Abu Dhabi asked me to prepare a submission. There followed six years of organising meetings and attending conferences all over the world. My team got falconers from many countries together, and there were a lot of governmental hoops to jump through. One by one, countries fell by the wayside because their countries had not completed UNESCO's requirements. But in 2010 falconry was inscribed by UNESCO on the Representative List of Mankind's Intangible Cultural Heritage on behalf of 11 countries. Since then we have added 13 more countries. It is the most international meme group UNESCO has to date.

When I wrote the initial submission I had to bear in mind that potentially it needed to cater for up to 80 countries that practise falconry. Although they shared a common core, many cultural details were local. And some countries were more 'advanced' than others. In the UK we put GPS tags on our falcons, whereas in Yunnan in China they still used long trailing white cockerel feathers attached to their hawks, to follow them by. They call them 'Flying Dragons'. Of course, once the Chinese saw GPS tags, they wanted them too. So unwittingly, by cultural pollution, we were destroying the very cultures we had set out to protect.

A Huang ying (goshawk) equipped with a cockerel feather or 'Yemal'. Alan Gates.

UNESCO recognises that cultures must be allowed to continue to evolve; nothing is static. While history is about the past, heritage is about passing the cultural baton on to future generations. But with increased communications around the world, local cultures disappear and we all become the same. Grey people in grey suits. I have even tried wearing a baseball cap myself (only for a few minutes, and not back to front...).

Mr Xu fits a 'Yemal' to a Huang ying (goshawk). Alan Gates.

The latest technology from Marshall Radio.

Hunting has been integral to our evolution, but with increasing urbanisation, human evolution is heading into an unsustainable future. When we signed contracts and MOUs with central Asian countries in the 1990s, Ministers always wanted a clause 'Technology Transfer'. So we showed the professors and students how to use telemetry and modern survey techniques. Gradually we would notice the occasional satellite disc on the roofs of gers, with horses and motorbikes outside. Peering inside to see what was going on, everyone was crowded in watching a TV set, and the programme? – *Dallas*! A series about a Texan oil dynasty living in high style. For the Mongolians, this was America, flash cars and the Big Apple. And of course they wanted a slice too. They contracted the Chinese to put powerlines across the steppe to bring electricity to the settlements, wasting away since the Soviet withdrawal. Our Western influence just made them aware of the toughness of their existence and introduced envy and dis-satisfaction.

In western Mongolia, in Bayan Ölgii, the ethnic Kazak eagle hunters quickly learned that they could make more money from tourists and film-crews than from fox pelts. Soon everyone was getting themselves an eagle and posing, and the local eagle nests were getting hammered. Similarly, in Kyrghyzstan, when I first went there with their Minister, our evening amusements were vodka drinking competitions and lamping wolves. The saddles were rough as guts, with the stirrup leathers made of old industrial belting. A few years further on and they were zooming around in SUVs.

There can hardly be a tribe left which has not been studied by anthropologists and film crews. They all know to take off their tee shirts, put on their loin clothes, ready to creep about after wildlife or paint up and do a bit of dancing. But, like the Bedouins of the Arabian Peninsula, as the older ones die off, their cultural knowledge seeps away too.

Culture is a form of learning that gives you a point of view. This might vary from a slight opinion to a full blown hard-core, non-negotiable prejudice. When you see life through a certain perspective although you may be seeing exactly the same situation, your interpretation may be very different to someone else's. In Britain, while in recent decades there has been a lot of noise about 'discrimination' and 'multi-cultural societies' these movements have mainly focussed on diasporas, especially urban ones, while indigenous cultural groups, most of which are land-based activities such as hunting and farming, have been vilified rather than valued.

We have various bits of legislation on this, such as The Scotland Act 1998: *"the prevention, elimination or regulation of discrimination between persons on grounds of sex or marital status, on racial grounds, or on grounds of disability, age, sexual orientation, language or social origin, or of other personal attributes, including beliefs or opinions, such as religious beliefs or political opinions."*

The Equality Act 2010 requires 'due regard' to :
- eliminate unlawful discrimination
- advance equality of opportunity
- foster good relations

And the United Nations Human Rights

https://www.ohchr.org/sites/default/files/Documents/Publications/MinorityRights_en.pd gives clear guidance on the rights of cultural minorities such as Falconers.

The cultural heritage of Falconry equipment making is on the Red List of Endangered Crafts https://heritagecrafts.org.uk/Falconry-furniture-making/ . Falconry is a legitimate activity, a Protected Belief, and while both it and fishing enjoy good public support, shooting and hunting are subject to silent discrimination. Most TV channels refuse to cover them, and if they do, it is mainly to be both hostile and facile. On the other hand, as a land-owner, why should I be forced to allow people to introduce alien invasive predators - cats - onto my land to hunt and kill protected wildlife?

7.4 Territorial groups

Territory: a defended space.

We own a farm in Wales. We have lots of papers written by expensive lawyers to prove it. The farm doesn't make much money, in fact as a return on investment it is terrible. It is more of a liability than an asset! As such, it is something that we are responsible for, and this can be a burden. In a way, rather than us owning it, it owns us. Potentially we could sell it in exchange for money, but we cannot remove it; it just stays where it is. It was there during the last Ice Age, and will probably be there for a few million years. But our so-called ownership is just some kind of quasi-imaginary thing lasting a few decades. It's just something in our heads.

Lots of others also own the farm, or think they do. The wrens nesting in the log shed get very irate if other wrens come near. And the family of beavers on the lake will try to kill any strange beavers trespassing on their lake. Even the trees silently struggle against one another in a competition for sunlight, and, below ground, their roots chase the water and nutrients. Clearly this ownership thing can be complicated.

Most territorial behaviour is against conspecifics. I could radio-track some of the resident animals on the farm and plot their home ranges, and their defended areas. I could come up with ownership GIS maps covering the same ground as that drawn up by my lawyers and surveyors. The farm plan would show one mosaic of territories for robins, another for blackbirds, and another for buzzards, like layers of jigsaw puzzles. Lots of us think we own it, and our ownerships lasts only as long as we are able to defend it in some way against the incursions of conspecifics.

Our territorial behaviour has a genetic root. As hunter-foragers, or as agrarians, we have to stop others exploiting the resources that we have won for ourselves. If we are lucky, these will be sufficient for us to raise a family, or even for a larger social group. The ethotypic precursor for territorial behaviour is jealousy and envy. Both usually arise only in response to some form of external threat or a desire to take over resources.

Territorial defence does not have to be overt. The dawn chorus of birds is mostly males advertising their territories, enticing potential mates but warning off rivals. Scent-marking by mammals serves the same purpose. Human tourists have the classic leaving a towel on a sun lounger to signal at least temporary 'ownership'. And if we come down to the sea, to a quiet beach or cove, and find someone there already, we may turn away and go somewhere else.

Around our 'territory' (the defended space) we have a 'home range'. This is usually a much bigger area where we go from time to time and share with other conspecifics. Our ancestors would have had a camp, small village or cave, where the family group lived and where the dependent young were kept safe. Then groups would go out hunting, either foraging for shell fish, nuts or berries, or as hunting parties searching for game. The size of the home range was governed by the mobility of the people and how long they could afford to be away from

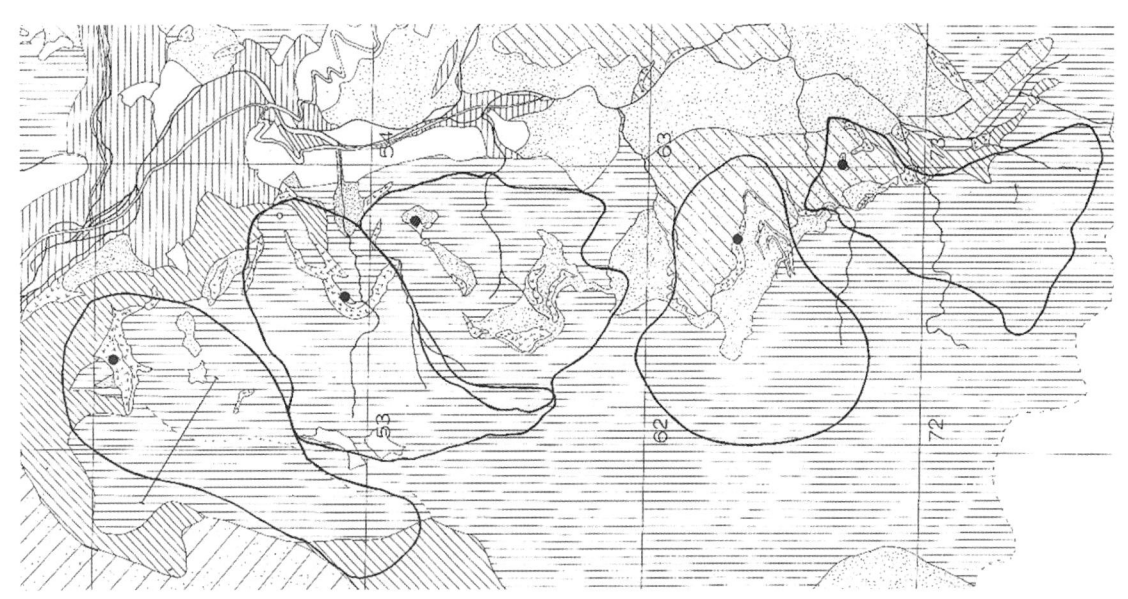

Home ranges of five radio-tracked pairs of wild Mauritius kestrels, Fox et al. 1985.

home. If the resources in the area became too depleted, either from over-hunting or because of seasonal changes, then the group might move to a new place. Often there were seasonal movements from inland to coast and back again, exploiting known resources of food, water and shelter. This pattern is seen across many species, from African Wild Dogs *Lycaon pictus*, to eagles, to humans. Our ethotype still inspires us to build dens and hideaways, and attracts us to shorelines.

Defending a territory is energy expensive. So it is normally reserved just for perceived threats. A falcon will chase off a neighbouring falcon, but it doesn't worry about a harmless deer wandering by. Similarly, if a strange male wanders into a human camp, he will be challenged by the owners, but if a nubile female wanders into the camp, she will be assessed as less of a threat and much more readily accepted in. This is useful in marketing cars.

Nomadic groups may carry their territories around with them in terms of personal space or group space. A group of elephants, led by a matriarch, may be on the move looking for water or fresh feed. Elephants require a lot of feed and can only survive by constant moving. So they don't have homes or lairs to go to; they just keep moving along. But they will still defend their group and the young ones. Their territory is about the living animals, rather than a particular patch of ground on the map. Many indigenous peoples have a similar approach, and have a large hunting range. They don't have the Western concept of land ownership, and this has caused a clash wherever the cultures have met.

7.5 Moral community

We can also look at social groups, not just as kinship, meme or territorial groups, but as moral communities. These are relationships in which there is some sort of moral bond, or (just as importantly) no moral bond. These can be multi-species relationships or even relationships with inanimate objects, such as an ocean. What we might do about climate change depends on motivation from our moral perspective of 'community'. Philosophers call these things 'worthy of moral consideration', but more to the point, we need to think of how <u>much</u> consideration, relatively speaking?

164 HUNTING ETHICS

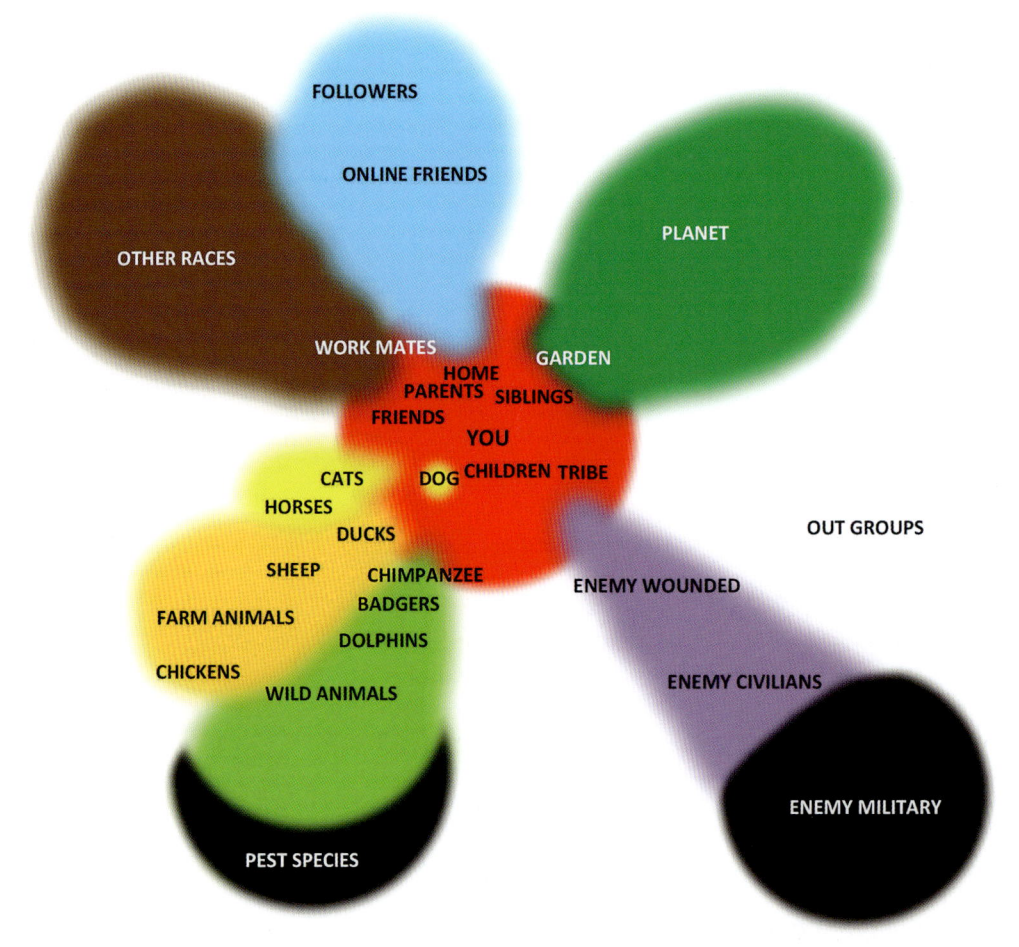

A Moral Map for a typical British person showing relationships with physical entities. I have not shown conceptual entities such as patriotism, religion or climate change.

If you sit back for a moment and reflect on your life, how many moral social groups or communities are you in? Are you in a drama club, or a basketball team? A book club, an ante-natal class? Are you in the police or the armed services? As you mentally go through your day, think of all the groups, large and small, that you interact with. Some of these groups may be physically close on a daily basis; some you may know only online. With some you feel extreme loyalty, but with others, you feel distant, remote, perhaps just because you all just happened to be crushed into the same rush-hour train. How close do you feel to the driver who just pushed in on you in a traffic jam?

This is a moral map for a typical white male adult Brit like me. We all have our own, different, individual maps which change as we go through life. One person might include <u>all</u> animals within her morally closer red zone. She would eschew any form of hunting. Another might cut non-humans off entirely. Another might give preference to iconic species such as lions, dolphins or badgers. One might give chimpanzees 'personhood', treating them as an honorary human being (would that include trialling them in court for 'crimes'?). The same can be said for races, online friends or the planet. Murder is usually thought of as killing a human in any of the zones except the black zone. Some claim that killing non-human animals is 'murder', which it isn't. Most

Chapter 7 – THE MECHANISM OF MORALITY

are happy to kill bacteria, viruses, rats and cockroaches, species in 'out groups'.

The area I have shown in red is your core moral community. As the distance out from this increases, you feel less and less moral responsibility. Some of this distancing is deliberate. Despite watching horrendously gory and violent films in which people are killed, the British have a horror of recognisable dead animals. They want their meat in small bits with non-animal names like 'beef' and 'pork'. They don't want to see rabbits and pheasants hanging up outside a butcher's shop. They want to be detached from the notion that they are eating parts of animals and detached from consequential moral responsibility. This is a conflict situation for the farmer who has reared an animal and then has to face slaughtering it. It is easier killing TG38654 than to kill 'Primrose'. People in the black zone and animals such as wolves and squirrels ('tree rats') in the pest zones will be given a bad press and vilified to maintain moral distance.

The obverse of this is the soldier who tries to kill an enemy, only wounds him, and then takes him into his moral community and helps him. Shooters too may wound an animal and, instead of continuing the hunting process, take it home and look after it.

I have sometimes held one of our old horses, friends for 20 or more years, while someone shot it. They are buried in the field and I pass them every day. Last year, my old horse Buckskin, was 34. Most of his teeth had gone, but although he was fine in himself, he couldn't hold condition even on summer grass and I knew he wouldn't make the winter. It was his time to go. But I knew that if I held him while he was shot, I would be left with a painful memory, a mental scar. So I said a last goodbye to him and asked two friends to do it while I was away, so

Saying farewell to Buckskin.

that when I came back he was buried. After thirty years of hawking together, so many shared adventures, we shared our moral communities. I've had to wipe my eyes after writing this paragraph.

Try drawing your own personal moral map. You might flag up some inconsistencies. Which elements of your map are ethotypic in origin, and which are cultural? Bearing in mind that we all have individual ethotypic differences – none of us are exactly the same – some positionings on your map can be embedded in your own ethotype and hence be more or less unchangeable, and other people will differ from you and have positions that are equally unchangeable.

In the map I have shown, I have only drawn in real entities; I've left out conceptual entities such as patriotism, religions and climate change. They muddy the water considerably. Patriotism, an extension of tribalism, has a strong ethotypic root. Religions and regimes tend to be morally prescriptive. Some of these virtually dictate your moral map for you. Other concepts, such as climate change, are so nebulous that it is hard to evaluate your moral position. Climate change does not feature in your ethotype, so there is no guidance there. Would you stop travelling by air if your carbon footprint was above some threshold level? If your family dog incurred a similar carbon footprint, would you prefer to kill the dog rather than stop flying? Hmm. Moral relativism…

People who follow a religion are often divided into sub-groups according to region or belief. Apart from factions such as Roman Catholics and Protestants, there are regional Christian groups that are divided over issues such as homosexuality. How long before these factions divide and give themselves different labels? Another ostensibly religious group, such as Jews, may also include a very powerful ethnic element of cultural practices not immediately relevant to their core beliefs. This may go so far as to prevent out-breeding and genetic exchange with other groups, but the genetic differentiation has not continued long enough for the group to become a genetic 'race'. Similarly, lumping someone as 'black African' is not very helpful. Genetically the person may have black skin and have ancestors that came from Africa, but we all came from Africa. And Africa contains thousands of separate moral groups, divided on tribal lines and on many other lines. Only by looking more carefully at these underlying roots can we hope to understand relationships and move towards harmony and peace, accepting and enjoying our differences rather than bullying and victimising one another.

Is a political party a moral group? Party politics, like established religions, tend to have set menus. You either vote for the whole menu or go for another menu. Of course you have no way of knowing if a party will carry out its manifesto or whether it will abandon it once elected. Others pledge things in the full knowledge that they are unlikely to be elected and therefore never called upon to implement them. However, if you vote purely on the basis of what an electorate wants, and of course there are many instantaneous online voting systems around nowadays, you will get decisions that suit the immediate wishes of the voters but which may well conflict with the long-term needs of human society and the planet. You need some sort of vision and sufficient leadership courage and power to carry it out. However if too much power falls into the hands of one person, a dictator or monarch, or just a few people, a politburo, then they too suffer from the same syndrome, focussing more on what suits them rather than the greater 'good'. Corruption is not far away. A benign dictatorship does at least have a certain amount of stability and long-term vision. Democracy on the other hand seldom ventures much further along the timescale than the next election. This can lead to a wild see-sawing of policies. Sadly, humans do not have any good systems of self-governance at much above the tribal level. Other species do not have systems of social governance beyond the herd or group level at all. Now that humans have recently increased in numbers beyond the tribe level, this is a new problem we face, and evolution is unable to help us out. Our morality systems have never evolved to operate at this level. It would be nice if a benign God stepped in and steered us all in the right direction, but as of today, we are still waiting for a divine intervention.

If we go back to the genotype/phenotype/ethotype concept, at physical death, the phenotype dies, taking with it your genes. The ethotype also goes because it has no body left to do its behaving for it. But during its lifetime, your ethotypic personality interacted with other members of your social group. It had effects on them, it influenced them, it made memories. Those effects, those memories, those memes, live on amongst the members of your group. Nowadays they can be extended to further generations through photos, video and the internet (what Susan Blackmore calls 'tremes'), although they had never met you in life. In a way, perhaps this is your 'soul'. And once those memories have gone from your group, that finally is when your soul fades away. It is not immortality, but it is post-mortality. Maybe it is not what we'd been hoping for, but perhaps it is some consolation to the bereaved. There are businesses now set up to run your Facebook page for you after you are dead. Long live your online soul!

Some animals don't live in social groups. For example, the falcons I live with are solitary predators. But even these, for a period of their lives, form pair bonds and rear families. During periods when they are on their own, morality becomes largely irrelevant; their map is just one individual red dot. Predation, of course, has nothing to do with morality.

Sociality can vary even amongst close relatives. For example, a domestic dog (a Canid) is a social animal which understands social hierarchies, including human ones. The Red Fox (*Vulpes vulpes*) on the other hand, although tame enough as a hand-reared cub, as it matures, tends to become wary and will not heed human social mores. Dmitry Belyaev, in his classic experiment in Russia, managed, through severe selection, to create domestic dog-like social traits in his farmed foxes in about 40 generations. Interestingly, their phenotypes changed as well as their ethotypes.

Outside your social group are other individuals of your own species who are not in your social group. If you come into contact with them, they may be friendly and co-operative, or they may be hostile. Whatever they are, they are potential competitors for resources such as land, food and water, or even for the last remaining seat on the bus. Their ethotypic morality will be the same, but their imprinted and learned morality may vary from yours to a greater or lesser extent. Ethotypic morality dictates that murdering a member of your own social group is 'wrong', but killing a conspecific not in your own social group, if the need arises, is 'acceptable'. You may even pay members of your group to do it, and call them soldiers and give them medals.

Similarly, if you are of a species that lives in one place, you may defend it as your territory. Within that territory will be your 'home', which may be a sett if you are a badger, or a house if you are a human. For humans, our cars are extensions of our home, which is our family personal space. So we find people keeping their cars clean by throwing their litter out of the window, just as a badger cleans out its old bedding material from its sett. For those litterers, the sense of social responsibility extends little further than their own personal space. What hope then for any caring for a larger space, a street, a town, a country, a planet? These people are operating just at the lowest level of the priority scale, putting individuals first before consideration for any wider group.

Words such as caring, sharing, bonding, emotional investment and commitment apply to moral communities. Your family is

Fruits of the public road through the farm.

at the core of your moral community: your parents, your siblings, your children and your spouse (who is not a genetic relative). Genetic kinship does not automatically entitle someone to be inside your moral community. You may not be able to stand your Auntie Flo and perhaps neither of you are on speaking terms. Maybe your family is not a nuclear one, perhaps you have foster parents or same-sex parents, or are divorced. Your family pet dog is also in your inner moral community. Radiating from these, your uncles and aunts, nephews and nieces are in, but more distant, and you may have special personal friends who are in your close moral community. These are all 'persons' with whom you have some invested moral commitment arising either from kinship or from close friendship.

Non-animate organisms, such as your cherished house plants, may also be treated with some moral commitment and you may find yourself texting a friend to ask her to pop in and water them while you are away. Inanimate objects such as jewellery may also hold sentimental value above market value. Places and areas also are part of your moral community, and this melds into territoriality. You take pride in caring for your garden, but neglect the rubbish on the other side of the fence.

What is not in your moral community? While we may respect other people and their property, the further we go from home the less affinity we share with them. A person, or group, or nation who has declared hostility towards us will be outside our moral community and any taboo we feel against hurting them will be weak or non-existent. We accept killing an enemy soldier although we may find it repugnant to kill a civilian from an enemy nation.

Similarly, we may accept killing a non-pet animal such as a sheep or a wild rabbit and relish a nice juicy beef steak. Reared specifically for food on a farm, the meat animal or field of wheat will be processed for the table without a qualm. People have moral difficulties in deciphering their line between moral groups. Are all dogs, even non-pet ones, taboo? Are all horses taboo? Are sheep and cattle taboo? Do we define our moral communities along species lines, or on an individual basis? These are the moral quandaries we all share and the only feature in common is that we tend to put ourselves unquestionably at the centre of our own moral universe. All our moral judgements are in relation to ourselves and these judgements are based on learned cultural norms which vary from group to group. Only the moral mechanism itself is ethotypic.

Moving outside immediate physical objects we struggle to find moral commitment to the big stuff – the well-being of our planet. Yet with space travel, long-haul flights and films we are more and more realising that we are trapped on Planet Earth and that we need to look after it. We are slowly becoming more and more concerned about climate change. But our global moral concerns are still weak in comparison to the pull of our closer moral communities. We are very reluctant to let ourselves or our immediate communities suffer even though we know that in the long run they will do so if we fail with our global efforts.

We can even include ideas in our moral community. We may have a strong view on politics, religion, wars, sexuality or food habits. We may have intellectual property rights. We tell people our views and to some extent our opinions become 'part of us'. They become integrated into our moral values, into our culture, into our identities. None of this has anything to do with absolute 'right' or 'wrong', although we may be eager to declare it as such.

The bonds, the obligations, the responsibilities, that we feel towards members of our moral community are ethotypic 'feelings'. They well up from our core ethotype. Like most of our behaviour, they can be refined by learning concepts such as 'duty' and 'honour', but the primary motivator is ethotypic. Some people extend it further into concepts and arguments concerning 'rights'. The concept of 'rights' includes at least two persons: the recipient (the one holding the 'right') and the doer (the one obligated to the recipient). While I am happy to use the words 'obligation' or 'responsibility' which puts the onus on the doer, I think that claiming that a recipient has some kind of 'right' to that obligation is taking it too far. One can have expectations, reciprocal altruism even, but it is a false hope to rely on a moral 'right', even when it is translated into a legal 'right'. Legal rights are an expression of local culture, both in time and space. They change from country to country and from time to time. They are not absolute and are often unenforceable. One can have expectations that other members of your moral community will display at least these core ethotypic moral obligations towards you. One can hope so. But don't bank on it.

Some raise the concept of 'natural rights'. By 'natural' they mean ethotypic, which I'm fine with. If you remove the 'right' from the recipient and translate it into 'obligations' of the doer, then I'm happy with that too. But the whole 'rights' thing is also too confining; it is restricted to a transaction between two moral 'persons'. In the case of humans, the recipient might be brain-dead and therefore not qualify as a 'person'. What if the recipient is not a 'person' at all, but for example, a habitat? Habitats cannot have 'rights', but persons can have moral obligations towards their welfare. You might think that by denying the concept of 'rights' I am somehow diminishing morality in some way, but it is the opposite; I am expanding it both in scope and in applicability.

All this is my personal approach to the concept of 'moral community', based on what I see in real life. Philosophers have a slightly different approach and debate whether an animal is sentient or not and thus qualifying to be in our moral community: do we have responsibilities towards it as a living being? The problem with this is that it is not a consistent model – we do not treat enemy soldiers as within our moral community for example, and also it shrugs off inanimate elements, such as our moral connection with habitats and our entire planet. It is more of an academic one-way categorisation, rather than an emotional commitment. I don't accept the argument of Michael Allen Fox (Ethics in Practice, 10) that only humans are moral 'persons' and therefore that no non-humans can have moral communities. To me, this is an arbitrary anthropocentrism, a little bit of species self-flattery perhaps. Biologists have their own, narrower, concept of 'social group' which is more concerned with kinship and gene flow. Social groups, kin groups and moral communities are not interchangeable categories, but over-lapping ones.

7.5.1 Companion animals

For most people, a companion animal is their most likely point of contact with other animal species. To varying extents we accept them into our 'family' and they become part of our moral community. Some people even celebrate their birthdays or funerals, or dress them up in clothes. We keep them, often because we have a personal need for contact in some way; we may have an urge to stroke, cuddle, care or 'parent'.

Providing that they have had early socialising during the imprinting periods, companion animals mainly rub along with humans quite well. The social system of the dog probably matches ours the best; cats, rabbits and cage birds less so, although even fish can recognise the person who cares for them. We, in our turn, do best with these animals if we have socialised with them during our own childhoods. Nowadays it is quite common to come across people with little first-hand experience of dogs and they can be quite scared of them and unable to read their body language. And if you have little experience with companion animals you will certainly have difficulty in understanding other species and their issues.

Humans have managed to screw up some of the species that have been domesticated for a long time. Show dogs, cats and rabbits have been bred with the most ridiculous phenotypes, some of which create joint problems, eye and ear defects and, in an effort to make the face more flattened and human-looking, jaw and teeth problems. While perhaps not intending to be cruel, doing this certainly entails a great deal of unnecessary suffering. James Serpell covers this well and of course, humans are not the only species to have companion animals. Many other species do too, on a social or a commensal basis.

Animals that are used for work, such as some types of dogs and horses, tend to be selected for on the basis of their performance and genetic defects are less common, being weeded out fairly ruthlessly. On the other hand, in some cases, once they are unable to function in their working roles, many of these animals will be euthanized before they reach old age.

Companion animals probably keep more people sane than all of the psychiatrists and pills put together. They teach us to look after another 'person' instead of just putting ourselves first. Dogs especially tend to be very accepting and always cheerful. For sick people, old people and lonely people a pet animal can raise their quality of life hugely and often give them something to live for. Animal Assisted Interventions have become popular in the West and anthrozoology has adopted it enthusiastically as a research topic. Companion animals provide therapy for autistic or mentally impaired people and some of the results have been impressive. Sometimes they open up lines of communication which we, in our language-bound world, have lost the ability to use. For me, a household that consists only of humans seems incomplete somehow, and when I am in countries where I cannot understand the human language, I can always rely on a dog, cat, horse or falcon to have a little tête-à-tête with, a simple meeting of minds.

Perversely, 'Positive Lists' are now being touted. This would mean that nobody would be allowed to keep any animal apart from a handful of domestic species. Ostensibly this is for the welfare of animals, but the effect is that people are becoming less and less connected to real animals. The kids know more about pandas and bamboo than about the local wildlife around them. Magpies have recently been protected – I have no idea why – so it is illegal to have a pet one. While on the one hand the philosophical concept of human/animal dualism is being undermined, a practical dualism is being reinforced more than ever.

7.6 Bonny's world

Bonny is a Munsterlander, a German HPR breed of hunting dog. She is bred to Hunt, Point and Retrieve. Phenotypically she has a dense coat to protect her from brambles, yet with silky hair that sheds mud as she dries out. She is long in the leg and back so that she can gallop for long periods and cover a lot of ground. Ethotypically she has been bred to hunt, so she will go into thick cover following ground scent and flush out a rabbit or pheasant, creeping under brambles and if necessary biting away roots or branches to get to the prey. She will point, that is, on scenting the prey using air-borne scent she will freeze in her advance and mark the hidden prey somewhere upwind. If it is a bird, such as a pheasant or woodcock, she will usually lift a front leg, if a mammal, such as a rabbit, she will usually keep both front legs down.

These instinct templates have been bred into her, but also I have taught her, by associative learning, the meaning of the words 'Pheasant' and 'Rabbit'. If I shoot something she will go and find it and retrieve it to me. But if the falcon has caught something, her learned role is to stay by the falcon and protect her until I come. This role of a falconer's dog has been described as far back as 1250 by Frederick the Second (p. 267). If Bonny catches a rabbit when I am not around, she will eat some of it and cache or bury the rest. This is instinctive. If she is allowed out on the farm and there is a sheep carcase lying around, being eaten by foxes, she can't resist a bit of carrion, even if it is quite 'ripe'.

We got Bonny as an 8 week old pup and our 8 year old one-eyed lurcher called Gem became her surrogate 'aunt'. Pup Bonny would lie on top of her and to this day defers to her in all things. So for her, Gem is a pack 'elder'. This relationship is ethotypic. Helen and I are her pack leaders and we all live together in a house on the farm. Bonny sleeps in the stable across the yard at night. Above the yard are the farm offices with staff and interns coming and going in their cars and on foot. Bonny is friendly with them and will take direct orders from them, and she knows the sounds of all their cars. She doesn't make an alarm for them, but they are not fully in her 'pack'. Their relationship is learned. If a strange car or person arrives the two dogs will immediately bark and race out to see what is going on. This is ethotypic. The farm yard is 'home', their territory, their defended space. The farm itself is their 'home range'.

Bonny pointing a grouse.

Bonny as a pup establishes her moral community.

Nearby are the horses. The dogs largely ignore them, until one of us appears with some tack which they associate with us going riding. So they stick around while we saddle up and come out with us wherever we go. For them it is a bit of a hunting foray. The horses, for their part, have their own little moral world which I won't go into now.

In another field is a flock of ewes and lambs. They are all born and bred here and have their own moral community and home range. As I go round them I will either keep Bonny at heel or she can wander where she wants but she will not look at them or go near them. This is learned behaviour; I have taught her our sheep are taboo. Even with some hard dogs we will use an electric shock collar and zap the dog at the moment it lunges towards a sheep. Usually one zap is enough if applied pre-emptively and the dog is trained for life. A sheep-killing dog is a liability and thousands of sheep are killed by dogs that have not been taught to avoid them. In a case like this, where the lesson is swimming against the strong tide of the ethotype, negative (aversive) conditioning is the best tool. This is pre-emptive – it happens immediately before the act and prevents it, rather than punishment, which comes after the act and may not even be associated with it. Positive conditioning, including food rewards, are of limited use in extinguishing ethotypic behaviour. They are best in encouraging new behaviour.

When we are up in Northumberland, up on the open fells, sheep are tucked into all sorts of hollows and will jump up in front of the dog like a deer or hare. Her instinct then is to chase it, and while in pursuit, predators such as dogs and raptors become heedless of all else, as do we humans. So we have to keep an eye on Bonny and if a sheep jumps, immediately drop her with the whistle. One long blast is her learned signal from a distance. Close up her signal is a raised hand or the spoken word 'Sit'. When we are stalking and cannot make a sound, her signal is a click of the fingers, a diminished visible cue without the 'click' sound. So there is constant interplay between ethotypic and learned behaviour, including generalisations to create a moral community or world.

Currently we have a molly lamb, being hand-reared on the bottle. 'It' (we have castrated him) is imprinted on us, the dogs and the farmyard. It will follow Bonny or me around and sleeps with Bonny in the stable at night. Bonny is not imprinted on the lamb. She has been 'told', mainly by example, that the lamb is a new member of our little pack. Ethotypically she can accept a new pack member. But a sheep is also potentially a prey animal. So there is a conflict for Bonny. But she has internalised it, in some shape or form, into her 'conscience'. She doesn't mother the lamb, apart from occasionally licking its bum because lamb shit is quite tasty and nutritious. But to her, this is not any random lamb, it is this particular individual lamb; this 'person'.

When early summer comes round and we have baby falcons running around on the lawn, Bonny knows also that these are 'taboo'. They may not be exactly members of her 'pack' but her pack leaders have told her that she must not touch them.

A lot of things are going on here, between Bonny's ethotypic templates, her learned behaviour, her taught behaviour, her social group, her home territory and home range, her prey, intruders, taboos. We are straying from ethology to the philosophy of morality. While Bonny defends her home and pack, she doesn't seem to have any concept of wider things, such as habitats or the planet. She has a good memory and the past means something to her, but she doesn't seem able to anticipate far into the future, and her food-

Gem, the lurcher, the lamb, and the house are all on Bonny's moral map.

caching is ethotypic. So perhaps her moral world looks something like this:

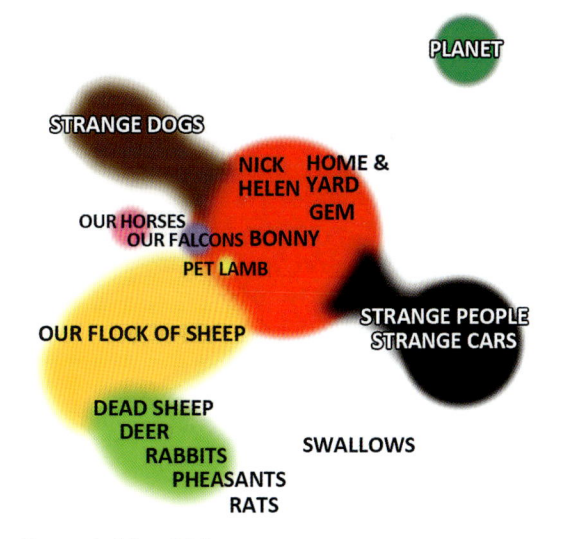

Bonny's Moral Map.

7.7 Out-groups

Beyond the moral communities are the out-groups. They could be other humans, other animals or even places. They could be in an out-group because they are irrelevant – a stick or a cloud perhaps, or a passing swallow – or they could be in an out-group as a positive designation, usually because they pose a potential threat to our in-group. Ethotypic morality has something to say about this.

Humans in an out-group, such as opposing forces in a war, are not treated as sacred; far from it. Huge amounts of military budgets are spent on developing ever more efficient weapons to kill humans from outside our group. Pious politicians talk about unintentional collateral damage when women and children non-combatants are killed, the opposing side calls it mass-murder. And for a Western soldier who is threatened by lawyers back home, he now faces a moral dilemma. At some point in the fighting he is paid to kill an enemy, but then, if he only wounds him, suddenly the soldier is supposed to stop killing him, switch behaviour and start treating him as sacrosanct and give him first aid, as if, being injured, he suddenly enters him into the in-group. Failure to make this moral switch on the battlefield can lead a soldier to languishing in prison on return to the UK. Is this a case of the soldier being morally weak or confused, or frightened of the enemy who may not be fighting by the same rules and have a 'take no prisoners' policy, or of the lawyer, (who may have never experienced battle) being immoral and seeking to capitalise on the situation at no risk to himself, or the state being immoral for starting the fight in the first place, or the judicial system being immoral for trying to apply civilian moral codes of conduct to a war zone situation?

While many organisations make noble efforts to stop war and make peace, the reality is that both sides will not be motivated to stop fighting until both conclude that one out-group or the other has won and the situation has been resolved. War is brutal, horrid, destructive and unfair. We might like to think of it as some kind of game, with rules such as the Geneva Convention. But it isn't; war is war. Why follow 'rules' set by your opponents that could mean you lose? There is really only one universal code in war, and that is to win it.

Modern military ethics, as propounded by people such as George Lucas, hinge on assessing the various scenarios for warfare that could arise from the emerging technologies. Just as we have become heavily dependent on multiple aspects of digital technologies, which have made so many new things possible, at the same time this has made us vulnerable to new forms of warfare and attack. A lot of this would affect civilian populations at home, outside conventional war zones. It would blur the line between military action and civilian activities. A failure of the internet for a few days could now have more far-reaching consequences than a nuclear bomb, and of course in the event of civil unrest, one of the first reactions of authorities is to close down or restrict the communications systems.

7.8 Internet Groups

A massive social experiment is underway and nobody knows what the outcome will be. Just in the last few years, the internet has gone mainstream. Everyone has smart phones and people become addicted to them. Children report traumatic stress if separated from their phones for an hour. Some are taking 50 photos a day of themselves, editing them and posting them on Facebook. They hope to have 300 'Likes'. Face to face social intercourse falls silent as more and more people turn to their screens.

Let's refer back to my four criteria for morality:
- A social group.
- Shared ethical values.
- A judge.
- A system of enforcement.

For the teenager, glued to her phone, her social group may not be her immediate friends. Instead they will be a wider group, her Facebook 'Friends'. She judges her own social approval rating by how many 'Friends' she has, and how many 'Likes'. So this is not a normal social group; it is a group of peers, but she may not have met them all, and some of them may be fraudulent. Some may be adults 'grooming' her, or seeking to steal her identity and any money she may have. The values she is sharing may be equally unreal. The photos are heavily edited to make her appear glamorous, successful, popular and exciting. They don't show the real her. She creates an image which she hopes will make her 'Friends' envious and want to associate with her. Her dream is that one of her images will go 'viral' and she will become a minor celebrity. Her 'Friends' also post their own pictures, so that there is an image arms race. Inevitably, not everyone can match up to the expectations, so then there is depression, anorexia, even suicidal thoughts and self-harming.

She judges herself and edits her projected image. And the 'Likes' provide a very immediate and measurable assessment of the group judgement. There is no escape. Tomorrow there will be more, and more. She is on a treadmill of imaginary social approval.

The enforcement system is immediate and harsh. The 'Likes' are so quantifiable; there may even be 'Dislikes'. And the comments can be disparaging and cruel, driving her to despair. In vain she labours with make-up, hair-dos, even cosmetic surgery. Image is everything. Intellect or substance is not required by these instant media.

The sad thing is that the internet has tapped into her psyche. It has taken normal human behaviour and turned the girl into a captive, unable to tear herself free of the digital bonds.

When people are not from the same social group, the whole situation gets seriously horrible. Not sharing the same values, people feel free to pass unfavourable judgements in the crudest and harshest comments, trying to destroy the person's sense of self-worth. This modern method of communication suddenly allows the worst side of human nature free rein. Instead of the 'morality' being used to reinforce social norms and bonds, it does the opposite. There is no way to make these people conform to societal norms. They know it and are completely uninhibited in destroying people in another social group. It is psychological warfare.

And boys lose themselves in imaginary worlds of computer games. They can adopt whole new identities, contrasting strongly with their real life situation. Some become so addicted that they spend perhaps 18 hours a day on the computer, neglecting their real lives and the people around them.

All this is just the beginning. What will it be like in another ten years? In another 50 years? Our moral systems are becoming dysfunctional. Our grasp on real people and our social groups is weakened and we stop identifying with those around us and lose ourselves in cyber groups. At the moment, most people were brought up in the 'real' world and do still have some sense of normality to return to. But now children of five years old are being given phones and i-pads and becoming addicted, just as previously children had been indoctrinated into religions before they were old enough for critical thinking. These children may not be able to escape from their digital bonds. Their whole lives will malfunction. They will struggle to hold down a job or raise a family. What have we done to them?

More sinister even than the effects on our children are the potential effects in territorial behaviour and warfare. For the first time, our species now has a system of communication over the entire globe, that is virtually free and in real time. But we have not evolved a moral mechanism to go with it, and any attempt to impose moral values on it fail because the group using it is not a single coherent social group, it is just a bunch of people with no allegiances to one another and no shared ethical values. And even if they did have, there is no workable enforcement mechanism. So the internet is a free for all, with no morality at all, open to any tricks and scams that anyone cares to throw at it. Libel, infringement of copyright and IPRs, fraud, leaks, impersonations; it's all there, a tribute to the darker side of human nature unfettered by morality. It is an example of what the human species would have been like if we had not had a moral mechanism evolving alongside us to maintain the cohesion of our social groups. The people who are designing the system did not install a moral mechanism and it is hard to see how they could have managed to.

And now we've got it. At the same time we are developing more and more sophisticated artificial intelligence systems. Put the two together and what do we get? Algorithms embedded in the internet monitor our every move. At the moment they are relatively primitive, they track our browsing histories and our shopping histories. But they are getting more and more sophisticated, as outlined by Harari. Our computers can now handle big data which enables statistical trends to be immediately evident. We have voice and face recognition. We have GPS tracking of our phones and machinery. We have entire manufacturing and economic industries predicated on the internet controlling them through 5G. We have created a CyberGod who is able to monitor our every move and decision and maintain an indelible record indefinitely of each one. Whereas we used to believe in an all-seeing God, now we've just made one.

Harari envisages a future in which our species combines our genome with artificial intelligence to create a super-species that starts a new era in the evolutionary progress of the planet. This in itself is a gloomy picture, leaving all other species in at best a precarious position. But before it can even reach this stage it will be undermined by individuals and groups who feel either hostile, threatened or under-privileged, who can corrupt the systems. Any society that has based itself on the internet will have become so vulnerable that the effects could be catastrophic. In theory the internet cannot fail because it is a network. If one route goes down, signals will simply take other routes. In practice, with entire cities dependent on last-minute logistics, whole economies dependent on real time data flow, to mention just a couple of examples, we have not only created systems that are vulnerable, but we have also binned our old systems. Our new generations of children do not have the cultural learning to operate systems that became obsolete just a few years ago. We have 20 year old interns here who cannot even light a fire. In Britain, a few inches of snow can bring everything to a standstill, let alone a power failure.

All this is ripe for cyber warfare and the major nations are developing this rapidly and covertly. How long will it be before primitive jihadist warfare in the Middle East is over-shadowed by warfare between the developed nations? Will we even know if we are being attacked? Will the aim be not to collapse a system, but to steer it and take control of it? Swinging an election is just toy town stuff, what is round the corner?

Ray Kurzweil believes that artificial intelligence will pass the Turing Test very soon. We will no longer be able to distinguish between a human and an artificial intelligence. By 2030 he thinks we will have computers capable of reading thousands of books per second. The whole repository of written knowledge will be gulped up by these machines in a day or two. None of us humans have a hope of reading so many books. If I had spent my lifetime reading books to 'support' this book you are now reading, I wouldn't have had time to do the real life stuff which is the basis of the book. Incomprehensively powerful as these machines will be (and no doubt they will change our lives beyond recognition), they suffer from two vulnerabilities: input and output. Books have already been transcribed into various forms of code such as a human language, and text formats.

These can relatively easily be 'read' by the artificial intelligence and entered as digitised data in its memory and processing systems. But, despite our huge libraries, the written, photographed and filmed store that we currently have is but a miniscule pathetic snippet of real world data. The twinkling of light on water, the silent doings of microbes in the soil, the permutations of radio waves, everywhere things are going on and interacting. Certainly machines can scan, measure and record some of these things, as 'parameters', but just the process of doing that in itself would destroy or alter them. Artificial intelligence will struggle to digest unprocessed intellectual 'food'. And then, at the other end, what is the outcome? The data may be in the machines but they are useless there unless they can be expressed in some way. If I wanted to access a million books stored in the artificial intelligence, how can I transfer this information to my own neocortex? I suppose I can enter some search words and tortuously investigate it from there, but I couldn't just magically download the whole lot in one go. My neocortex does not have the capacity to handle this amount of incoming data. For every zettabyte of data coming in I would probably have to sleep for a few weeks while my brain processes it. Maybe I would wake up with the equivalent of a thousand university degrees, but would I be able to make a cup of tea? And of course factual knowledge, data, is just stuff. Only when I process some of that 'stuff' creatively into new formats is it going to benefit me.

Having all that information to hand at the click of a button turns me into an internettual, but I still need to have my own native intelligence to make use of it. Smart phones enable many things, such as international trade and business, to expand and flourish, but then I take a peek at the passenger next to me. What can he possibly be doing looking at his phone all this time? He's playing a game where a little man leaps through an endless succession of obstacles! Next to him she is scanning picture after picture of people gawping out of the frame making 'Wow' expressions. My high hopes for the human race are dashed…

No doubt in the next few years artificial intelligence is going to totally change our lives, and even our concept of being dead. With the rise of internettualism, what need will there be for undergraduate degrees with their emphasis on the assimilation of knowledge, knowledge which in this fast-moving world will already be out-dated even before Graduation Day? The artificial intelligence will not just be a data store, it will also be a data processor, a generator of new ideas, a fast-track invention machine. It will far outstrip human creativity and take naive, simple activities such as 'Art' far away from pigments into virtual realities we cannot even dream about. Will people seriously pay millions of dollars for old-style hang on the wall paintings in a few years' time? Music? Will people seriously use those funny old wooden things called violins? With artificial intelligence and communications systems this powerful, where will this leave us poor inadequate humble human beings? We were once so arrogant, so anthropocentric, so proud of our superiority over other species, and now we've given birth to a child that leaves us, with our hopes and dreams, our aspirations, everything that gave our lives meaning, looking desperately shallow and even silly. Religions, cultures, tourism, fashion… what's the point?

7.9 Morality outside the social group

We tend to think of morality as a 'good' thing. We say: 'She is a very moral person'. We think of morality as promoting good in the community, fairness, justice, and so on. But it has a dark side.

Morality is a biological mechanism that promotes cohesion within a social group in the face of conflicting interests of the individuals of that group. It is just a mechanism; there is nothing 'good' or 'bad' about it in absolute terms, all it is trying to do is to keep the social group together because that has survival benefits. But to keep that group together, morality also has to include a mechanism to exclude individuals who are not in the social group, and exclude all other social groups. This is expressed through discrimination and intolerance.

The exclusion process has several layers. Within the social group itself there may be individuals that for one reason or another 'don't fit in'. They may be malformed or ill physically, or they may have strange behaviour. There is bullying of weaker members of the group, which reinforces the hierarchical positions of the bullies in the group. Males tend to bully females. The strong use their power to control the weak. This, sad to say, is how morality as a mechanism retains the 'health' of the social group and the hierarchical structure of the group, which is necessary for its functioning. We may think it is not nice, not fair, and so on. But biology is not about being nice; it's about surviving, and it is operating at the group level rather than at the individual level.

Looking outside the primary social group, there are other individuals or groups, and they could be more powerful and threaten the existence of the primary group in some way. They could compete for shared resources, or they might attack and try to steal the primary group's resources, such as food, or breeding females. We thus have forms of territorial behaviour.

How do individuals recognise what group each one is in? In some mammals, each group smells different. In most non-human animals, individuals belong to only one group, and this makes things more straightforward. It was the same for early humans too. But as our numbers increased and we formed 'aggregations', people from different social groups started mixing together and, further than this, individuals started to identify themselves with more than one group. Things started to get complicated. We thus had to create little labels for ourselves to show which groups we were in. Soldiers have uniforms to stop them killing their own men. Sports teams have uniforms and supporters have their colours and scarves. Religious people wear religious symbols or distinctive clothing. Companies have logos; the list is endless. Some of these labels are quite subtle, perhaps just a slight twang of an accent that gives away a person's origin. And of course some of the labels are phenotypic: skin colour and physical features. Whereas a boy can wear a school uniform during the day time and then change clothes in the evening for a night out with friends, phenotypic labels cannot easily be changed. So we carry these labels around with us wherever we go. In Manchuria I am stared at because I am white. In a school football team I am ostracised because I am too old. In a women's refuge I would be rejected because I am male. These are all phenotypic badges that I can't avoid. As soon as people see these badges I am wearing, they make assumptions, they discriminate, for better or for worse. In Manchuria they immediately assumed that I didn't speak Chinese. In the football team they assumed I am no longer fast enough. In the women's refuge they assumed I was a threat.

This is all morality in action. It's doing its job. The football team will be better without me in it. The women's refuge will feel more secure without me in it. Their discrimination preserves their group identity and function. And this moral tendency we have is buried deep in our ethotype, really deep. In evolutionary terms it goes right back to the formation of social groups, possibly before even the evolution of vertebrates, over half a billion years ago. It's deep and it's indelible.

For the rejected individuals or groups it is not very nice. But it is important to understand and recognise that all this is a moral mechanism supporting the survival of the primary social group. What to do about it in a modern society is a whole other issue. All of us experience some sort of discrimination, whenever we rub up against an outside group that we don't belong to. And we can't stop that happening, it goes on all the time. We have our family groups, our work groups, our student groups, our sports groups, our religious groups; the list is endless. All of us, one way or another experience discrimination, bullying, the 'cold-shoulder', whatever you like to call it. And we don't like it. We can tackle it intellectually by passing laws to prevent the worst excesses, and we can campaign and educate, but deep down our primeval ethotype is telling us to protect our own group, that's how we've survived this long.

Despite our differences, we all share some things in common. By studying the behaviour of relatively 'primitive', usually tribal, groups, unadulterated by the artificialities of 'civilisation', anthropologists can establish various traits in common, others that are similar, and others that are different. Donald Brown's *Human Universals* describes our core ethotype and theoretically this could be sub-divided taxonomically, mirroring the phenotypic taxonomy.

We can assume that most of the traits that are universal across our whole species, and to a lesser extent the traits that are very similar, are probably ethotypic in origin. They are as permanently connected to our genotype as our phenotypic features are. We can no more change them than we can change the colour of our skin. But we have to be careful how much detail we ascribe to instinct. Daniel Dennett argued that all tribes that use spears throw them pointy end first but that this is learned, not instinctive; this may well be true, but on the other hand it seems that all humans, and some of our ancestors too, have an instinct to pick up objects and throw them at things. We learned the refinement of spears, and bows and arrows, later.

Western anthropologists are just as prone

I discuss wolf and fox hunting with an eagle hunter near Bayan-Enger in western Mongolia.

to outgroups as anyone else. For them and their Ethics Committees the cultures of Western hunting may be disapproved of and considered unsuitable for academic study. Some anthrozoologists carry a load of psychological baggage on this. There is very little coverage of hunting on public television in the UK. But far away 'primitive' societies are considered as outgroups and their cultures are treated non-judgementally because they are not expected to conform to British urban cultural values.

Is a multi-cultural society, that mythical group propounded by sociologists and politicians, really possible? Certainly in some places and at some times, two or more cultures have lived alongside one another in apparent harmony. But they do this by compartmentalising their lives. We all do this. We are one person when we are at home, another when at work and another when playing a sport or other activity. Unlike most other animals who live pretty much in a fixed group and in real time, humans can have many personas in parallel compartments of their lives. With the internet you can even pretend to be someone else entirely. This compartmentalising allows different cultural groups to rub along together in apparent harmony. But they manage this by only interfacing in certain neutral compartments, such as the workplace. They stay apart for compartments with deeper cultural identity such as home life or in mate selection. A Muslim and a Jew may succeed in working together but equally might recoil in horror at the prospect of their daughter marrying the other's son. So we struggle to decide what we really want. Do we want immigrants to blend in, for all the cultures to meld together? Or should we spend time and energy supporting local cultures, indigenous peoples and languages, emphasising our differences, as UNESCO is doing?

Once we start compartmentalising and identifying ourselves in more than one social group, there is a very real risk that the mores of one group will conflict with those of another. You end up behaving one way in one group and another way in another. If you try to fit in with a group and cannot be true to yourself, this causes an internal conflict and mental dissonance. On the other hand being true to yourself may in some cases result in you being punished or ostracised from the group, and for some people this is even worse. Cult groups exert pressure to conform on their members this way. The whole fashion industry plays on this element of our ethotype.

Anthropologists also view hunting very differently in different cultures. Often hunting practices which they accept in primitive cultures are deemed unacceptable in their own culture. Sometimes we see the phrase 'unacceptable in a civilised society', perhaps an intentional distancing from the natural world. Do I want to be 'civilised'? It is almost a synonym for urban living in a town disconnected from the natural world. Cities which are monocultures of humans, with air pollution, light pollution, sound pollution, dysfunctional social groups? Hunting enables me to connect with nature and elemental situations.

7.10 Ethotype or Culture?

While we are on moral mapping, let's see if we can untangle things a little. You may be thinking "This is not my understanding of morality or ethics. This isn't what they taught me in Philosophy. Morality is about things like Contractarianism, Utilitarianism, Deontology and so on; much more intellectual stuff than whether or not I love my cat!". How can we decipher which bits are simply ethotypic and which bits are learned cultural values? One way is to eliminate the social element, and eliminate the learned element, and see what we have left.

Let's map the morality of the New Zealand Falcon, a species I know well. I studied them for four years in the Southern Alps for my PhD, have trained fifteen in falconry and have kept a closed breeding colony in the UK from six founder birds for 40 years. The first thing we notice is that they have two moral maps: the breeding season and the non-breeding season.

In the winter the falcons are mainly solitary although some pairs stay in loose contact on the same home range. They don't defend a territory. So a falcon has little need for morality and her map looks something like this:

FALCON

BLACKBIRD

CHAFFINCH

PREY   **RABBIT**

The falcon's winter moral map.

She has a small personal space into which nobody is allowed to enter. She hunts various prey without compunction; as a predator, her prey are not on her moral radar. That's about it, and it is all ethotypic.

When the breeding season comes round, the ethotype's buddies – hormones – come into play, triggered by daylength and so on. She pairs up with a mate, lays eggs and rears chicks. So her moral circle now includes her mate and family. She also defends a territory around her home, her nest. The territory is three dimensional, stretching up into the sky. She 'hates' any enemy that threatens her chicks. Australasian Harriers will be stooped at violently and driven away, as will mustelids and cats in the daytime. (At night she is defenceless and they may kill her and the chicks at the nest.) As long as they are not about to blunder onto the nest, she ignores deer and sheep. Interestingly, her ancestors have probably not seen any of these mammals for 10 million years, but her ethotype, being genetic, has a long 'memory'. So now her moral map looks like this:

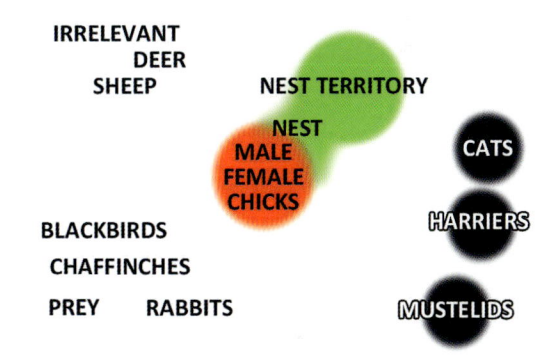

IRRELEVANT
DEER
SHEEP   **NEST TERRITORY**
NEST
MALE
FEMALE   **CATS**
CHICKS
BLACKBIRDS
CHAFFINCHES   **HARRIERS**
PREY   **RABBITS**   **MUSTELIDS**

The falcon's summer moral map.

Of course these diagrams are schematic; her actual physical territory looks like this:

The nest is on a rocky bluff.

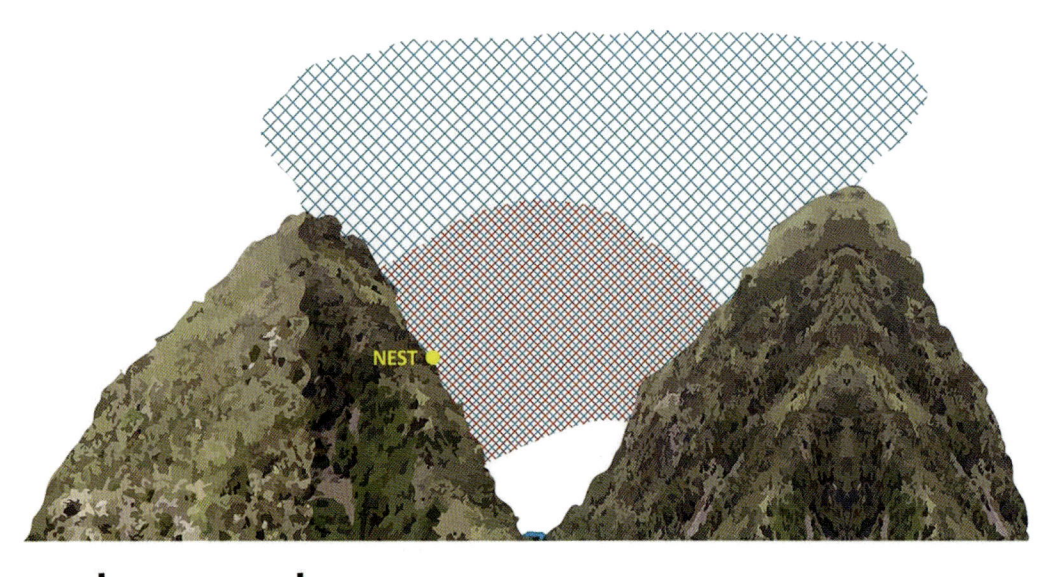

ABOUT 100 METRES

From the side view, the female (red) defends most intensively near the nest and on the same contour. You may be able to walk up the creek without her flying. The male defends a larger area within line of sight of the nest and to a considerable height above it. In plan view their nest defence looks like this:

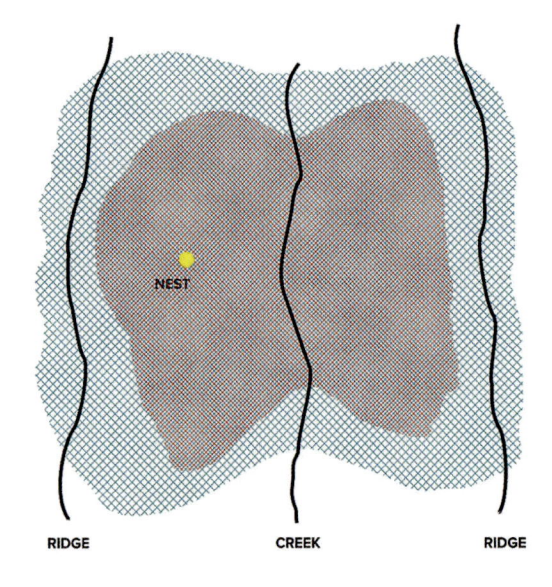

RIDGE   CREEK   RIDGE

I used to catch the falcons in nooses on my hat when they stooped at me in nest defence. The distances they defended were quite clearly delineated. The male defended a bigger space and their defence was most fierce when there were chicks on the ground unable to fly. So I could see quite clearly, to within about 20 metres, for 31 pairs, how far away from the nest they would defend, and against whom, bearing in mind that, like a goal keeper, the further they strayed away from the nest, the more they were leaving it undefended, so females stay close.

Although New Zealand Falcons are quite intelligent, most of this behaviour is ethotypic rather than learned. First time breeders show it without practice. Now, comparing her map which is almost totally ethotypic, with <u>your</u> map, can you see commonalities? Quite a lot of your map must be ethotypic. Hunters and livestock farmers also have seasonal moral relationships with their prey or livestock. Spring and summer is time for cherishing. Autumn is the time for creaming off the harvestable surplus before winter's self-levelling attrition.

Hunting itself, in its natural form without artificial aids, is not a single activity. At the very least it consists of the *search*, the *pursuit* and the *kill*. There must be several genes for these distinct ethotypic templates. Searching, or foraging, was universal in both genders of our ancestors and still is today. Pursuing, the desire to chase something, is not so universal and is more common in men. Killing is almost always a male instinct and is not universal. For myself, I have strong instincts to search and chase, but little desire to kill, although I like to see my falcons successfully catching their prey, because for them, as obligate predators, the killing gene is mandatory.

Without wishing to ignore the important role of imprinting, maybe religion too has an ethotypic root. Some people just are religious, and others just aren't. My father was a vicar, a Christian minister. Of four siblings, reared in Christianity, two continued as Christians and two of us never believed. Some people, imprinted and living in a religious culture, go through all the motions but clearly have not internalised 'God'. To escape from the strictures of their professed religion they have 'Allah's blind spots'. Despite their imprinting and rearing, their ethotype is in conflict, and in the end, it wins out. So when they want to do something 'wrong' they create the concept that their all-seeing God has blind spots where they become morally invisible. Some of the Catholics we have had here have done it differently: sin all week, confess on Sunday, start again with a clean slate on Monday!

Similarly, my parents and siblings were not hunters, but I am. Your individual ethotype, right down to some specific genes, is so powerful, that no amount of logic, debate, argument or legislation can shake it. Not only are you convinced of your own viewpoint, you are equally convinced that other viewpoints are invalid. You may feel the need to cut off the head of a heretic, or burn him at the stake.

You could explain that these things are your 'moral principles'. One of your moral principles is that you will defend your family against anything or anyone who threatens it. What is NOT ethotypic is the identity of the invader. If you were Ukrainian in 1939 you might have been fighting alongside Russian troops against the Germans but, 85 years later you might be asking Germans for weapons so that you could fend off Russian invaders. The moral map has altered to deal with changed threats. but the ethotype hasn't; the ethotype defends against threats from any direction.

The falcon is mainly a solitary animal. With no society, she has nobody to teach her refinements such as dominance hierarchies, or etiquette, such as table manners. But then, she doesn't need them. Sociality brings learned moral relationships into the equation. Although the underlying ethotypic templates remain, the cultural overlay is learned. It has validity in the existing circumstances, but may not have any ultimate validity, no 'Ultimate Truth'. One can philosophically debate these cultural elements of morality, but in the end they owe any validity they may have to the circumstances. If you can understand the mechanism of how you are reaching your solution to the Trolley Problem (regardless of what your solution may be), then you are getting a grasp on how ethics works in practice and hence perhaps get a handle on the motives for war, and for peace. If you think morality is purely an intellectual problem then you have not considered your ethotype, your human nature, and that is what leads us into the Evolutionary Trap, which I will examine in Chapter 11. For the ethotype, its ultimate validity is simple: the survival of the genes.

If hunting, and perhaps spirituality, have genetic components, each depending on some gene clusters, we will probably find out in the next decade or two as the human genome is researched for personality traits. This would explain the individual variation that we see. But it also means that these genes, or clusters of genes, will probably appear in different frequencies in different populations, just as we see variations in phenotypes. These variations would have arisen through evolutionary pressure and those pressures, in some populations, may have gone. I have friends whose parents or grand-parents were Bedouin, but the true nomadic Bedouin is now almost extinct on most of the Arabian Peninsula. Yet these friends have more of a hunting instinct than me. They want to carry on tracking and hunting long after I've said 'Let's stop now and have a little uffwah (a siesta)'. Other populations, especially in the West, have more generations since their ancestors were hunters, so the selection pressure has eased and the gene frequency could be diminishing too. Dmitry Belyaev's foxes changed their ethotypes from wild type to domestic dog type in 40 generations. So our hunting drive reduces as we become more estranged from the natural world, with a dependency on systems rather than self-reliance. Our 'civilisation' is a self-imposed helplessness.

The selection pressure for spirituality is hardship and uncertainty of the future. Religions offer an insurance policy for the after life, but as concepts such as 'souls' become less and less plausible, and faith reduces, hardship remains. For the new secular, there is always the National Lottery to provide hope for a way out of the daily grind.

8 Shared ethical values

8.1 Priorities

Ethotypic morality is saying: 'Stay alive. Breed. Feed the family, guard their resources and keep them safe from any threats.' This is what it boils down to, survival of your genes. This is our core human ethotype and it is the same for most vertebrates. We can prioritise them like this:
1. The genes.
2. The individual.
3. The breeding family unit.
4. The wider family, sharing relatedness.
5. The tribe.

Beyond the tribe level we have little instinct for any moral obligation. We may develop concerns for people or events at international level, but this is <u>learned</u> behaviour.

The ethotype is the bedrock of most behaviour, including ours. Evolving behaviour, being genetic in origin, is subject to the same pressures and constraints as the evolution of the phenotype, including constraints of time scale. Behaviour that confers a survival advantage for the genes is more likely to continue. But genetic-based evolution is slow. A few thousands generations may be neither here nor there. The instincts that we have inherited now, are probably virtually identical to those of our ancestors forty thousand years ago before the last Ice Age, most even date back to our common ancestors with birds and reptiles. And we are stuck with them for a few more thousand years whether we like it or not. We cannot change this root component of our behaviour. The hormone systems and emotions are also genetically based and slow to change. Hunting and foraging are fundamental to our core priorities.

Overlying instinctive behaviour are imprinted behaviour and learned behaviour. Language, the written word, and now the advent of the internet and mobile phones, has brought forward our knowledge, connectivity and learning extremely rapidly. So we have a widening gap between our inherited roots of behaviour (our instincts), and the veneer of 'civilisation' (our intellect). And this gap is not evenly spread around the peoples of the globe. While there are some societies that are knowledge-based and heavily connected, there are still very many primitive peoples. And because the digital age has been so fast in development, there is even an inter-generational gap in behaviour. Non-human species, which do not have good learned language skills, are still in balance between their inherited behaviour and their learned behaviour. But humans are walking into an evolutionary trap with increasing conflict between their inherited behaviour and their learned behaviour.

When you look at the two value systems I have listed above, the ethotypic one and the 'intellectual' one, and then compare them with the various moral value systems espoused by philosophers, such as deontological ethics, consequentialism, virtue ethics, pragmatic ethics, 'rights' and so on, it is hard to find a foundation for the philosophical approaches. Some of these hinge on virtue, some on happiness for oneself or for all, some on the consequences, or intended consequences of one's actions. Some propose a 'duty of care', perhaps in a specific role as a member of a family or group, with duties and 'rights'. Some value always telling the truth, or protecting others from the truth, some value equality for all, some reject the idea of any universal guiding moral principles; that we should just muddle through. Others are more concerned with ethics guiding specific areas of life, such as social etiquette, medicine, business, warfare, animal welfare, religion, politics, intellectual property rights or artificial intelligence.

Also, these approaches tend not to distinguish between ethotypic values, and learned ones. The learned values can vary, that's why people agonise over them. And of course our ethotypic values can be dictated by our ethotypic drives, such as defence of our family, tribe or territory, which some simply class as 'emotional' responses. Moral values depend on the perspective of your starting point and the objective of your finishing point. In other words they are subjective, not absolutes.

In 1985 I was studying the predation ecology of the last remaining Mauritius Kestrels, then down to a handful of individuals. They clung on in the last forest remnants in the Black River Gorges. Even as I radio-tracked them and mapped the forest cover and related their hunting time budgets to habitat types, women were walking down the tracks carrying bundles of firewood on their heads, inexorably stripping the forest. I started to ponder: what is more valuable, a single human life or the loss of a species? What do you think?

Did you fall into the trap and start to address the immediate question? Or did you zoom in on the word 'valuable' and ask yourself: valuable to whom? Humans or kestrels? Time after time in reading philosophical debates about human/non-human relationships the wording is phrased strictly from the human viewpoint, and taken from that perspective the answer (surprise, surprise) comes out in favour of humans. Anthropocentrism combined with a profound ignorance of other species slants the dialogue in an inevitable direction and closes minds off to other viewpoints. Multispecies ethnography is only belatedly starting to catch up.

While human ethotypic values share the same spectrum although varying slightly between meme groups, other species have different spectrums according to their lifestyles. Often the debate compares humans and 'animals' with blatant disregard to there being about eight million non-human animal species. We can expect social omnivores to have ethotypic values similar to our own human ones, even though not taxonomically close, whereas social herbivores, such as sheep, have different, perhaps simpler, priorities, and solitary predators, such as falcons, will differ too.

These values are not all black and white, or 'right' and 'wrong'. They often depend on the circumstances, and trying to do the best one can. Some humans are very uncomfortable coping with uncertainty. They want black and white answers. They want moral rules or guidelines; Utilitarianism maybe, or perhaps Contractarianism. But biology, real life, is not like that and you just have to get used to continuums and spectrums. Different things pull you in different directions. It's messy. Some people hate that; others revel in it.

8.2 Values that change with time

Learned ethical values change all the time and their primary role is to promote the cohesion of the group. As the situation of a group changes, the moral values adapt to those changes. These learned moral values are not absolutes, they are moral relativity. For example, the current dilemmas faced by the Christian groups in Britain lie between either evolving their moral values on homosexuality or risking the cohesion and fragmentation of the group. The Christian moral values are based on teachings from 2,000 years ago in a very different society to modern Western ones. Can modern theologians somehow 're-interpret' these scriptures to reconcile their teachings with the new mores of Western society?

We also now have modern societies trying to do the opposite, to post-date their current values onto people or events that happened a few decades ago. Once respectable people, now dead, have their reputations blackened by people still living, who are applying their new values to past events. This is a kind of time-sensitive cultural relativism.

Hunting has its own ethical values which evolve over time. Primitive societies which hunt have a wide variety of belief systems going back into pre-history before the prescribed religions. They were the precursors of early religious systems such as shamanism, invoking various deities or simply good fortune to influence the outcome of hunts.

Overlying these mystic beliefs, hunters in different cultures developed their own ethics of how to behave while out hunting. The main breeds of hunting dogs, such as the scenting hounds and the sight hounds were recognisable 5,000 years ago and so probably were developed in the last 10,000 years or so. There are about 30 breeds of sight hounds from all around the world still extant.

Dogs are used in widely separated cultures and these indicate different roles for the dogs in the hunt, and for their handlers. This required co-operation and a shared system of ethics. Originally the hunting dogs would have been bred to obtain food effectively, but gradually a sporting element came in, with roles becoming more stylised. By medieval times in Europe, the breeds of hounds, and how they were employed in hunting, and the roles of their handlers, were highly refined and there were many rules of the chase, complete with ceremony and pageantry.

Class came into the picture, with the best hunting areas and quarry reserved for royalty and upper classes, and the more lowly prey, such as rabbits, consigned to peasant classes. The more spectacular hunting, such as falconry, were practised by the upper classes, whereas the lower classes often resorted to poaching or more nefarious techniques of trapping or hunting by night.

"Even though he lived by hunting, primitive man worshipped animals. In modern man also, the desire to hunt is paradoxically compatible with love of wild life. Hunting is a highly satisfying occupation for many persons because it calls into play a multiplicity of physical and mental attributes that appear to be woven into the human fabric…Certain aspects of a hunter's life are probably more in keeping with man's basic temperament and biological nature than urban life as presently practiced." René Dubos, writing in his *So Human an Animal: How We Are Shaped by Surroundings and Events*, Scribners Sons, New York,1968.

8.3 Values are not 'truths'

Moral values are not about 'truth'; they are simply values. Something is either eligible to be true, such as two plus two equals four, or it isn't. This mathematical truth is of course 'absolute' but the implication is that there can therefore be 'truths' which are not 'absolute'. Truth needs no qualification. Truth is black and white. If something is not absolute then it is a 'value'. Concepts such as 'cultural relativism' are about values, not truths. Truth cannot be subjective. To say 'my truth' is different to 'your truth' is nonsense.

The American Declaration of Independence written in 1776 is a statement of values:

A shaman blesses our fieldwork in the Mongolian Altai.

We hold these truths to be self-evident, that all men are created equal, that they are endowed by their Creator with certain unalienable Rights, that among these are Life, Liberty and the pursuit of Happiness.

What is 'self-evident' about Creationism? It implies that it is absolved from needing any evidence at all. Somehow by skipping out from any evidential basis, the statement converts what is only a belief into a 'truth'. Yet the Americans didn't abolish slavery until over a century later, in 1865, and they maintained racial segregation well into the twentieth century. Clearly this Declaration was intended not for '*all men*' in America, just for a select few. Slaves apparently were not considered to be '*men*' (ie humans); they were deemed to be property and therefore not eligible to enjoy those '*unalienable Rights*'. Many, including Thoreau, were jailed for contesting slavery. Women weren't included as 'men' until 1920 when the Nineteenth Amendment finally gave them the vote. Over 40% of Americans still believe in Creationism and this Declaration is still taught to American school children to this day. I wonder how many stop and consider its implications?

Moral values, being a form of behaviour, have their roots in genetic, imprinted and learned behaviours. These values were listed as 'Natural Laws' by Thomas Aquinas:
1. Self-preservation.
2. Reproduction.
3. Educating one's offspring.
4. Seeking God.
5. Living in a social group.
6. Avoiding offence.
7. Seeking knowledge.

Not a bad crack at it considering he died almost 750 years ago, although he didn't cover the full spectrum of instincts, such as territorial behaviour. If you omit #4 they equally apply to other social vertebrates, not just humans.

Our ethotypic moral values have evolved in line with our social groups. But as human populations build up beyond the tribal level and reach the exponential growth track that we are now on, this genetic model falls disastrously apart. The current system operates on the basis that Earth's resources are functionally infinite. But humans have plundered Earth's resources, such as whales, seals, bison and forests for years.

So, to date our moral priorities have mirrored those of our social groups. We put ourselves and our families first, then the wider family, then the tribe. We start to waver at the national level. It has always worked for us like this, always. All our instincts point us that way. But it is leading us inexorably into a demographic and ecological crisis within the next hundred years or so, an evolutionary trap.

Our instincts, our ethotype, cannot be changed in this time frame. They are leading us like sheep into crisis. Our only hope is to alter the only other two drivers of our behaviour – imprinted behaviour and learned behaviour. We can alter those within a generation if we change the way we educate ourselves to re-align our moral priorities to survive. This means turning our current priorities upside down into the exact opposite list of our social group listing. Our new, intellect-based, priorities need to look like this:
1. Planet Earth and sustainable global systems.
2. Shared regional resources, such as water, and fisheries, the 'commons'.
3. Habitats for full biodiversity for at least minimal viable populations of all species.
4. Single species management programmes.
5. Individual animal welfare.

Mankind is failing abysmally in the first two categories. Many of the issues that are being debated at the moment arise because of people taking these priorities in the wrong order.

Philosophers, too, form a social group based on their intellectual interests. Individuals may be geographically or temporally isolated but they share the same areas of thoughts, even when they disagree with one another. Philosophers pride themselves in free thought, but even they have surrendered to preconceived values handed down from the ancient philosophers and beyond. One of these is the sanctity of human life at the individual level. This promotes #4, a single species management programme for only one species – humans – to the detriment of others, and it promotes #5 by operating at the individual level. The root cause, of course, is embedded in our ethotype, reinforced by learned behaviour. But whatever its root, it is nonetheless a value, not a blank sheet. Free thought was surrendered to an inherited value which we are reluctant to discard or even challenge.

How can one break free of these assumed values when they emanate from our genes and are even integrated into the thoughts and writings of philosophers? Because, like it or not, our species has reached a critical point in its evolution in which adhering to these values, values that have worked for us since our beginnings, will lead us to a demographic and resource collision.

Philosophy has the Golden Rule. '*Do unto others as you would have them do unto you.*' It is normally applied to moral communities only, members of your own tribe or immediate social group. Not to strangers. Thus indigenous tribes in the Americas, Africa, Australia and New Zealand could be treated as non-human (even though they clearly were human) and killed off or treated as slaves. So 'others' is narrowed down so tightly that it refers just to your close group, in other words it lines up with your ethotypic morality that you have anyway. If it was expanded in any useful way, it could mean all humans, or all sentient beings, or all beings. But this would be learned behaviour, not ethotypic.

Most of what people know about wildlife comes not from real life, but from films. Otters, orcas, cheetahs – how many of us have seen them in real life? Even so-called wildlife encounters are heavily engineered safari operations getting paying public close to an animal for a photoshoot. Very few people in Western countries live cheek by jowl with nature, day in day out.

Western film makers have a voluntary code of ethics for filming wildlife, to reduce disturbance or unnecessary suffering. I had a film company for several years, making 14 films about bird of prey management and wildlife management. Much of this footage was shot in Asia, the Middle East and Africa. Ethics towards animals in some of these regions are very different to those in the West, and in some cultures there is very little cognisance that animals can suffer. Changing attitudes to improve animal welfare is very challenging and I give an example on Houbara Bustards. The management of wildlife and film-making in those countries falls far short of what we would hope for in the West.

It is not just wildlife documentaries any more. Now there are thousands of clips on YouTube of some remarkable wildlife interactions, but even more of set-up situations vying to attract viewing figures. Beyond this are clips of people doing stupid things with their pets, ranging from tricks to dressing them up in party clothes. Young people watch these and their attitudes are shaped accordingly.

But film making can stray away from real life altogether. In the 1940s the Disney cartoon film *Bambi* shaped a generation's view on deer and other wildlife species. But with the advances in model-making and computer graphics, it is possible to stray completely from real life into fantasy. From *The Lord of the Rings* to Sci-Fi, it is not possible to separate fact from fiction any more. So viewers are in the hands of the film-makers who can portray any message they wish without need for ethics. In the West this has created strange ethical bed fellows. Night after night films portray humans being killed in as many possible ways as the imagination can conjure up. The baddies get killed in droves. The heroes get wounded but carry on heroically, recovering from their injuries remarkably quickly. Yet if a dog or cat is shown being killed or injured there is public objection. Showing animals being hunted is a big no-no, unless it is done by a natural predator in which case it attracts big viewing figures, or is done by an indigenous hunter in some far off land in a culture totally different from our own.

The causes of these attitudes seem to be two-fold. First, companion animals are included within our moral circle in our Western culture, and by familiarity from films other species, especially cuddly ones, have also become included. Second, most people simply do not have any significant interaction with the natural world, the closest perhaps being mowing the lawn, if they have one. Their food appears in the shops, water comes from taps, power from a switch and waste products are discreetly taken care of. Any kind of physical disfigurement, while ostensibly the subject of compassion, is covered up as much as possible to avoid embarrassment. So it is easy to pontificate about eating meat, or the merits of veganism. The realities of growing your own food, whether meat or plants, is one which almost nobody in the urban West faces any more. Our capacity for self-delusion is unlimited.

The advent of social media on the internet now allows rapid dissemination of information, much of it false or misleading. There is no verification or quality control. Opinions can ripple out in hours and there is little inhibition or good manners on line. Surveys are concocted to prove or disprove just about anything. Self-styled experts abound. Influencers, addicted narcissists, come up with an incontinent stream of rubbish to desperately boost their viewing figures.

In such a scenario it is impossible for those people who are actively engaged in some aspect of wildlife or land management to function. Ethical issues are far too nuanced for the sound-bites of the media and the shortening attention spans of the public. The democratic process means that if the majority votes that black is white, then the law will follow accordingly. Factual evidence and science, inconvenient truths, are ignored.

8.4 Corruption

Humans can cheat. They can be corrupt. Corruption is rife in most human societies and there is even a corruption score ranking for the nations of the world. Corruption works through Game Theory. If a limited number of people cheat, they can get away with it, but beyond a certain threshold level, the whole system collapses. Similar cheating, or 'free-riding' can be seen in some other higher vertebrate social groups. But there still has to be an overall 'social contract' for the system to continue to work. The bank robber, having managed to escape with his ill-gotten gains, still must have faith that his banknotes will be honoured by someone and translated into tangible assets.

Even corruption has an ethotypic basis. It is inversely related to genetic relatedness. You tend not to cheat with yourself or your family, but non-familial individuals outside your moral community are fair game and the stranger the individual is, the more distant he is from your group, the more liable he is to being cheated. The ultimate stranger is not even a person at all, but a faceless institution, a shop, insurance company or government. This is the 'victimless crime': shop-lifting, insurance or benefits fraud.

The same can be seen in social responsibility such as littering. In an effort to keep their house or car clean, many people are prepared to throw their litter into public spaces, outside the responsibility of their social group. We collect about two Land Rovers full of litter from the public road through our farm every year. Mainly canned energy drinks, fast food and cigarette packets. And on a bigger scale, nations pollute land and sea. Game Theory can still apply; it just takes longer and is more catastrophic.

Over the years I have been libelled, slandered, had my copyrights infringed, been fraudulently scammed, been divorced, been an expert witness undertaking valuations for court cases, been foreman of a jury, trained Customs officers and inspectors, taken part in raids for wildlife infringements, been fined for speeding, bought and sold properties, established and run charities, claimed compensation against individuals and corporates that have damaged my property, and so on. My experience has been that the British legal system, although perhaps better than most, is a far from perfect system for dispensing justice. It is a gravy train for lawyers who naturally wish it to continue unchanged and delight in creating legal texts that normal people cannot understand. The adversarial system is about winning the case, not seeking the truth, as science does. There is little attempt to make the offender compensate or even apologize to the wronged party and the punishments and enforcement systems are ineffectual, with huge re-offending rates. There is little comprehension of the psychology or biology of behaviour-shaping mechanisms. In our rural areas, unless there has been physical injury, we cannot hope for any significant police intervention. Fortunately in Britain, corruption is not as widespread in the legal system as it is in some countries. So in this situation there can be a dissonance between what ordinary citizens perceive as morally 'right' or 'wrong' and the treatment they receive through the legal system. This is when disillusioned people decide to take the law into their own hands.

8.5 Does human ethotypic morality vary?

I am British, brought up in a Western society, absorbing many of its values. But I have worked in many other countries: Russia, Mongolia, China, Japan, Pakistan, Arabia and in Africa. Some of these people are not phenotypically the same as me, not massively different, but recognisably so. Although I have worked with them, and negotiated with them, shared many trips and projects with them, I cannot say I understand any of them. Apart from the language barrier, it is very hard to really know what they are thinking. I find it hard enough to guess what people in my own culture are thinking. Of course many of their imprinted or learned cultural ethics are different to mine. But I wonder, given that we all show phenotypic variations, how much do our ethotypes vary too? Does our human species follow a single, universal ethotype? Obviously not, because the alternative hypothesis is that we are all ethotypically identical, which clearly we aren't; we are not all clones. My own experiences tend to make me think that the human ethotype does vary slightly along phenotypically racial lines. But before anyone jumps to conclusions, ethics is about social cohesion, not about any ultimate 'right' or 'wrong'. From the evolutionary point of view, the only criterion of interest is: does it work? Do those genes survive through the generations?

Morality in early human cultures, on which our ethotype is still based, hinged on small groups. It is about ensuring the survival of the genes in that small group, up to tribal level. Many modern human societies are still based on a tribal ethos and even modern 'democratic' societies retain strong undercurrents of tribalism. This is not a 'good' thing, or a 'bad' thing. It is just how things are as human populations expand beyond the small group stage to increasing conglomerations in which individuals no longer know one another. Some societies, such as those I work with in the Arabian Gulf, still have a strong sense of tribal identity and resist attempts by Western politicians to 'democratise' them. Kuwait has one of the most democratised political systems in the region, but, as a friend there told me, the Members of Parliament tend to 'arrive in slippers and leave in Bentleys'. Often too there is a more primitive approach to organised competitions (which are, in themselves, a dim mirror of Mankind's primeval struggle for survival). For many cultures, competitions are all about winning. It doesn't matter too much how this is achieved, but winning is everything. Cheat, bend the rules, nobble opponents; these are all a means to an end. They are not necessarily seen as 'corruption' in the Western sense. Newbolt's *'Play up! Play up and play the game'* which portrays our Western ethos of fairness is not shared by some of these cultures. So from these ethical differences one can conclude that either this attitude to competition and survival is ethotypic and genetically varied between human groups, or it is not ethotypic at all, but learned, cultural, and therefore without ethotypic moral authority, in as much as there might be such a thing.

How does this pan out in practical terms? I have designed various falconry events involving up to 80 nations of very disparate cultures. All goes well until you get to competitions. You have to design competitions that are as rigidly quantifiable as possible, with minimal scope for judgement. Thus a falcon race needs electronic starting and finishing gates accurate to 1/1000ths of a second (and costing the thick end of £100k). And you need severe drug-testing regimes. Competitions that require a judge, whose decisions can be argued with, end up with blood on the floor.

What happens when people of these opposing moral approaches contend in the same competition? Will the corrupt competitor win first prize and thus feel he is the winner, while the Newboltian one comes second but feels he is the moral winner? And, looking into our planet's uncertain future, which ethical approach offers the best prospect for our ultimate survival?

Once you realise that morals are all about ensuring the survival of genes through the generations, rather than about some abstract human construct labelled 'right' and 'wrong', then you can see how morals permeate throughout the behaviour of higher vertebrates. When it is about the survival of both the individuals and the groups, you can see how it achieves this end in a variety of ways. For example, jumping off a cliff is likely to kill you and extinguish those precious genes. Your ethotype, your instincts, scream at you not to do it. You are inhibited from doing it. Whether or not it is morally 'right' or 'wrong' doesn't apply. Jumping off a cliff is no more about being 'wrong' than it is about being 'pink'. But you can lose that inhibition under the influence of drugs. When I was young, doing Army training on Malta, several of us got drunk one night and jumped over a small cliff in the dark, landing in a heap at the bottom. The next day, aching but sober, we recoiled from that drop with horror and were once more inhibited from going near it. That instinctive inhibition clearly has survival value.

8.6 Legal values

A lot of what goes on in the home is governed by parental values. At the tribal or primary social group level there are further values that may superimpose on family values. Beyond this level moral mechanisms start to fail and with increasing group sizes humans have had to prop up natural morality with artificial laws. Some of these were first propounded by religious leaders but this has been expanded upon by an increasingly complex system of codified laws. We have layers and layers of them, from club rules and constitutions, to local Council regulations, national laws, European Union directives, international laws, you name it, they go on and on. Governments make laws faster than they repeal them. None of them are ultimate truths. They are all lists of values that have been agreed on for the time being. They are in a constant state of change, of flux. Some go out of date, some are tweaked, new ones are proposed. They are written down in massive tomes far too big for any one person to read, and yet everyone is supposed to adhere to them. The EU regulation 'Markets in Financial Instruments Directive II' has 7,000 pages! Some of these laws are fair, some are markedly unfair or inconsistent, the result of political manoeuvring, even blatant attempts by one sector of society to impose their values on another sector. And when you travel from one country to another, you will be faced with laws which in some cases are diametrically opposed to those that you'd previously supposed were inviolable.

Daniel Greenberg, who drafted the Hunting Act 2004 under the premiership of Tony Blair said: *"As a lawyer, I have often been struck with how little politicians and policymakers recognise the fact that a new law dealing with a particular matter is a sign of failure and not a sign of success. Take the case of racial discrimination, one of the earliest forms of discrimination to be made unlawful, back in the 1960s. Nobody would argue that as a society we have succeeded in conquering or even taming racial discrimination; it is as powerful a poison today as it was in 1965 if not more so, despite the law having had more than half a century to counter it. And that of course is the whole point: law does not and cannot change attitudes, and if anything it entrenches unpleasant attitudes by setting their parameters in the stone of law which by aiming to coerce both creates the temptation, and sets the curriculum, for circumvention and avoidance. Attitudes and ethics can be changed by discussion and by informative education; but they cannot in general be changed by law; and having recourse to legal enforcement by way of declaring certain attitudes unlawful is in general no more than a recognition of failure to change those attitudes by other and more effective methods.*

So a society that has an increasing number of laws protecting different aspects of diversity, is by definition a society in which those diversities are causing tensions of a kind that politicians and policymakers have failed to resolve through effective means; and they resort to the compulsion of the law to change attitudes, despite the lack of any evidence that there is any positive correlation between legal compulsion and change of attitude. Law can work well when it reflects consensual morality: the offence of bear baiting is never updated, and rarely if ever prosecuted, because it remains a successful monument to a moral development that was won by argument and the victory cemented through the emergence of consensual moral abhorrence. Modern slavery legislation is an example of law which has not yet succeeded, but which ought to be able to succeed being again based on a solid foundation of generally shared moral perceptions.

The law of hunting is in my opinion a significant example of an issue where an ephemeral majority in the House of Commons sought to enforce and perpetuate its own opinion on a moral issue without caring whether or not the balance struck by the legislation corresponded to the consensual morality of the country as a whole. It was an attempt by one side of a moral argument to coerce the other into submission. On that basis it was unlikely to be a success on any level, and it has not proved so. Sadly, it leaves unresolved some genuinely important practical issues of animal welfare, and it has widened the gulf between opposing views rather than creating a mechanism for them to explore and refine common ground." Speech to the R.S. Surtees Society 3rd November 2020.

All adult humans within a jurisdiction are supposed to follow these laws. Children and the mentally incapacitated may be excused. Some humans such as Jane Nosworthy, in *The Koko Dilemma: A Challenge to Legal Personality*, claim that animals are legal entities with their own 'rights'. For example PETA, People for the Ethical Treatment of Animals, tried to claim that a Celebes Crested Macaque *Macaca nigra* should own the copyright of some selfie photos it had taken using a camera owned by David Slater. Despite various appeals, PETA was unable to show that non-humans have rights or duties under human laws. Should I offer my camera trap pictures to the animals who have triggered them? Should I prosecute a bee for stinging me? Conversely, no hot-shot lawyer can turn a human into an honorary animal. He can explain his tortuous legal argument as much as he likes to a tiger or shark that is about to eat him and regards him as legitimate prey. Having their own rights implies some kind of responsibility for their actions according to our human moral codes, not just their own. So we have the old medieval courts sitting in judgement on an animal and hanging it. Or we give medals to dogs, horses and pigeons for bravery in warfare or crisis situations. We are ascribing to them our own moral values while ignoring theirs.

Jen Girgen's *The Historical and Contemporary Prosecution and Punishment of Animals* is a fascinating catalogue of these misinterpretations of moral codes. The medieval courts often dealt with pigs that roamed free in the streets and occasionally killed small children. Although these domestic pigs mingled with humans, they were for the most part not in the same moral community and have had no training in the required human moral values. Further, pigs are intelligent opportunists which are less amenable to pack social codes than dogs. They are more maverick and more liable to get up to mischief if the chance arises. Most trials were of domesticated animals living with humans; as such there was some expectation that the animals should follow human moral codes. However, ecclesiastical courts also legislated against non-domesticated animals such as insect plagues.

Convicted wild animals which failed to obey the ecclesiastical courts were 'anethamized' or cursed, effectively excommunicated or damned. The church courts based their approach on the Bible, especially the Old Testament, Exodus 21:28: *If an ox gore a man or a woman, that they die: then the ox shall be surely stoned, and his flesh shall not be eaten; but the owner of the ox shall be quit.*

Girgen's thesis is a useful historical account but it doesn't consider whose moral or legal codes are being followed by whom. When can humans reasonably expect a non-human to follow a human moral code? Why this anthropocentric perspective? Why not the reverse? Why shouldn't humans follow the non-human's moral code? Is prescribing a punishment to a non-human for violation of a human moral code any different from prescribing a reward or medal to a non-human for bravery or an act favouring human welfare?

Only if two individuals of different species have similar ethotypes and moral codes and consider themselves in the same moral community can they commit a 'crime' or a 'good' deed towards one another. In practice, pet dogs are probably the main individuals capable of internalising human moral codes. No doubt other species, such as chimpanzees, can do so too, but very few are kept in human households.

In Britain the Dangerous Dogs Act 1991 is all about protecting people, not livestock, from dog attacks. And in their ignorance, the politicians and lawyers tried to differentiate on the basis of breeds (which are not taxonomically identifiable) rather than individuals. This is tantamount to claiming that one ethnic group of humans is more prone to commit a crime than another and therefore the whole ethnic group, insofar as individuals can be identified, should be eliminated.

Legal values reflect current attitudes, most of which are historical, with little scientific basis. For example, we now know that fish are not only sentient but have many

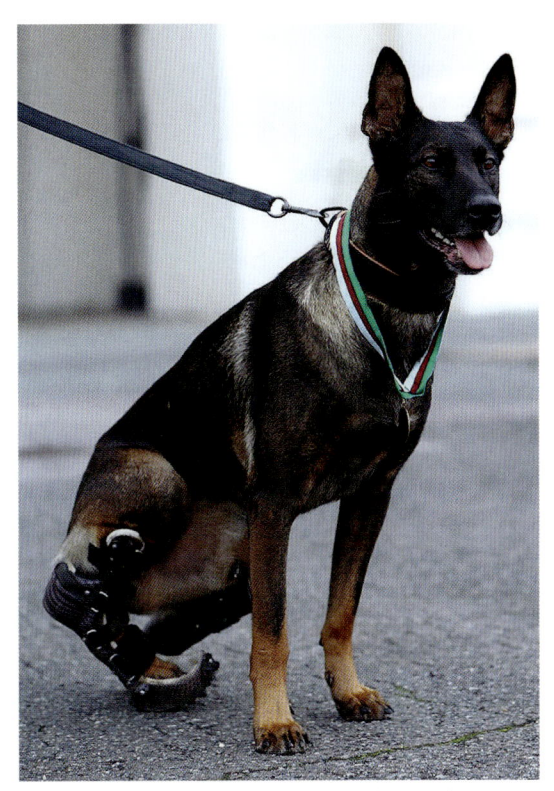

Kuno, a retired military working dog with a prosthetic limb replacing his shot leg. Kuno was awarded the Dickin Medal by the People's Dispensary for Sick Animals. The Dickin Medal is equivalent to the Victoria Cross, for gallantry in war. Crown copyright.

other attributes reflecting 'personhood'. But because they live in water where we cannot easily see or relate to them, we tend to dismiss their sentience and there is little public objection to hooking a fish in a mouth. There would be an outcry if I dangled a baited hook out of my bedroom window and hauled up my neighbour's cat. Or if I put the cat in a net bag and threw it in the river to drown, the equivalent of hauling out a fish to suffocate out of water.

The British legislation on animals and hunting is a tangled web, a miasma of contradictions. Working on the Hawk Board, which represents hawk-keepers to the government, I have spent four decades dealing with new rules, regulations and laws bubbling up out of the festering mass that is politics. You can shoot a pigeon on a Sunday, but not a pheasant. You can shoot a black grouse without a licence, but need one to shoot a starling, sparrow or crow. You can release 53 million non-native game birds a year, but not an indigenous beaver. You can shoot a fox at any time of year, with any kind of gun including an air rifle, but you mustn't let a dog catch one. You can catch a rat or a rabbit with a dog, but you mustn't let your dog catch a hare. You can kill stoats and weasels any time, but never a badger. The madness is endless and influenced more by *The Wind in the Willows* or *Bambi* than by science or even by common sense.

Trying to find out what the law is in any particular circumstance requires a specialist lawyer. Legal jargon has no foundation in science whatsoever. Laws still talk about 'birds and animals'. There is no comprehension that Linnean taxonomy was based on putative genetic relationships or that taxa such as sub-species were never intended to have legal definition. Currently birds of prey, badgers and otters are seen as icons, immune from any kind of hunting or harvesting for whatever reason, and with no set goals for their populations' ceiling. Legislation emanates from local Council regulations, from the Animal and Plant Health Agency, from the regional governments, from the UK government, from the European Union and from international agreements such as CITES and the Bern Convention. Some of it dates back to 1831 and even to medieval times. Parkes and Thornley, and more recently, Russ and Foster, have collated these myriad laws, statutes and lists of precedents (because many are interpreted by case law rather than by clear legislation in the first place). A Law Review by the Law Commission is long overdue. There will always be a need for detail – what are your rights if you shoot a pheasant and it lands on your neighbour's land, etc – but we first of all need a clear legislative framework linking species with purposes, methods, licences, close seasons and status in some kind of logical order. This lets everyone, including the police, know where they stand in any particular circumstance. This would highlight some of the glaring inconsistencies in our treatments of animals and their individual and ecological welfare. Too often someone will pronounce XYZ 'has no place in a civilised society' or something equally facile. We need to be able to compare all the species and treatments side by side, and justify the legal treatment of each. We also need to include all birds, mammals, amphibians, reptiles, and fish together.

To create a Huntable Species List, at least eight elements need to be included for each species:

1. **Common name.** The name most people know.
2. **Scientific name.** This gives genus and species. Sub-species are not normally taken into account because they are not clear cut entities. DNA research is showing that the species concept has significant flaws which do not translate easily into legal definitions. Some species, such as the Rock Pigeon (*Columba livia*) and the Common Quail (*Coturnix coturnix*) have huge domestic populations as well as wild ones.
3. **Conservation Status.** IUCN and other organisations have definitions for conservation status, such as *Favourable, Near Threatened, Threatened, Endangered, Extinct in the wild*. From the point of view of hunting, there are additional elements to consider, such as Alien and Invasive. Some of these species, including Grey Squirrels (*Sciurus carolinensis*) and Signal Crayfish (*Pacifastacus leniusculus*) have special restrictions on keeping them in captivity or releasing them to the wild.
4. **Purposes.** The reasons why animals are hunted include *Public Safety, Disease Control, Damage to Livestock or Fisheries, Wildlife Management, Recreational Use, Scientific Research, Hatching Eggs, Genetic Re-stocking* and so on. Some of these purposes can be quite wide-ranging.
5. **Methods.** The methods include both capturing and killing the animal. If the animal is caught alive, for example in a cage trap or net, there are still restrictions on humane ways of killing it. Putting the whole cage into water and drowning the animal is not humane. If you catch a fox in a cage trap how are you going to kill it if you don't have a gun? And how long will it be between the fox entering the cage and it being killed? The lifestyle of the animal limits the methods; for example a high powered rifle is not suitable for killing Moles (*Talpa europea*). Common methods include: *AIHTS approved live traps, AIHTS approved kill traps, Humane cable restraints, Rifle (specified calibre, load and range), Shotgun (specified calibre, load and range), Poisons (specified), Raptors, Dogs, Ferrets, Nets (specified), Hooks* and so on. There may be additional specifications, such as frequency of inspection of traps and whether a trap can be set in the open or only under cover. Poisons may require the prompt removal of dead animals to prevent scavengers eating them.
6. **Licensing.** At the moment in Britain we have an unintelligible system of General Licences, Individual Licences or no licences required. Hardly anyone understands them, or their raison d'etre, and fewer still follow them. Often the raison d'être has very little to do with science and everything to do with history or prejudice. Appendices and Annexes are seldom updated in line with current status. Individual Licences are a waste of admin time and reporting. A proper, up to date matrix of huntable species would obviate the use of licences and provide clarity for both users and enforcers. Too often, obsession with process

completely ignores status in the wild or effectiveness of results.

7. **Land-ownership.** The freehold of a property normally includes all rights to hunt. An agricultural tenancy normally confers rights to control certain pests, such as rabbits, foxes, pigeons or crows. There are cases now where landlords, such as the National Trust, try to subvert the rights of their tenant farmers to hunt these pests. There are examples in which legislation seeks to make land-owners responsible for any hunting on their land, with or without their permission. This 'Vicarious Liability' is used to try and implicate land-owners in hunting, but it is not currently applied to cats. If another person's cat catches a protected animal on my land, I am not vicariously liable, but I have no means to prevent it, nor is the owner liable. Yet if my employee shot the cat, both he and I would be liable.

8. **Season.** Some species, especially game animals, have close seasons and hunting seasons. The Red Grouse (*Lagopus lagopus*) season for example, opens on 12th August to enable Parliamentarians to go north for a shooting holiday during the summer recess. But there are many cheepers scarcely able to fly in August. Falconers on the other hand require longer seasons because the young raptors must learn to hunt while the prey itself is still young and naive. Nature's timing for natural predators is very tight and any late developers won't make it. In the USA some falconers benefit from a 'let lie' clause in which their falcons are allowed to hunt naturally and eat their prey, but nothing can be taken home. For most pest species, such as foxes and rats, there is no close season, parents with dependent young are killed willy-nilly.

An online table, including all the birds, mammals, reptiles, amphibians and fish on the British List would enable everyone to be clear exactly what can be hunted, for what reason, by what methods, where, and when. It would also highlight some of the current inconsistencies which we have become culturally and historically accustomed to, such as regulations surrounding foxes and cats.

8.7 Intent and recklessness

There is a dichotomy in attitudes between suffering that is caused during a deliberate act, such as hunting with a dog, and suffering that is caused as collateral damage such as allowing a cat to hunt. Many ardent anti-foxhunters keep cats. The Hunts used to kill about 20,000 foxes per year, the cats about 275 million animals. Estimates vary, but for every fox there are about 40 cats, a huge additional uncontrolled hunting pressure.

The 2002 debate on the Hunting Bill chaired by Alun Michael, at which both Andrew Linzey and I were expert witnesses, was reported by S. Morros in The *Guardian* 11 September 2002:

Andrew Linzey was asked to explain why hunting with dogs was morally wrong while it was acceptable for him to have pets which hunted. Professor Linzey's evidence began in conventional style with an attack on the Burns report, the findings of Lord Burns and his committee of inquiry on hunting which concluded that the "experience seriously compromises the welfare of the fox". He said the report "fails to confront major moral issues" and "minimises the reality of suffering". He added: "There is ample evidence that mammals experience not just pain, but also stress, terror, shock, anxiety, fear, trauma, foreboding." Replying to the assertion that foxes, hares and mink killed by dogs die within seconds, Prof Linzey, a member of the faculty of theology at Oxford University, said: "Just one second of pain is morally objectionable."

Prof Linzey suggested that hunting could be "morally injurious" to society. He said: "We should not overlook the capacity of human beings to become desensitised through habitual exposure to practices which involve violence and suffering to animals."

But then came the cat issue. Questioned by the Liberal Democrat MP Lembit Opik, Prof Linzey admitted he had two cats, Harry and Pepper. How then could he justify having pets which hunted and which were sometimes attacked by animal welfare groups for killing many birds? Prof Linzey said he did not feel "morally responsible" for their actions. He said they were strays who found him rather than he them. "What do you do when a half-starved cat comes to you?" he asked.

After the hearing, Prof Linzey, a vegetarian, admitted he had faced a "moral dilemma" about what he should feed the cats but had put his doubts aside and cooked fish for them. More seriously, he also expanded his thoughts on the morality of hunting with dogs. He claimed that taking pleasure in "cruelty" was indicative of a "pathological state" and concluded: "Whether a creature has two legs or four legs, violence is violence."

He did not seem to understand that he had himself *'become desensitised through habitual exposure to practices which involve violence and suffering to animals'* namely, allowing his cats to hunt.

The crux of his argument is that he did not <u>intend</u> an animal to suffer, even though it is well established that domestic cats kill millions of animals a year. He absolved himself from the responsibility by claiming that his cats were, in some way, not 'his' cats. Cat-owners sometimes claim the defence of *Ferae naturae* for their cats which supposedly absolves them of any liability for their cats. However *Ferae naturae* applies only to non-domesticated animals and fowls that are no one's private property. Wild cats are *Ferae naturae*, but owned cats are *Domitae naturae*. Andrew Linzey was trying to claim that his two cats had originally been strays and that they were therefore *Ferae naturae*, rather than *Domitae naturae*. They were his, but not his... He wanted it both ways. The bottom line is that cat owners can prevent these millions of deaths simply by not letting their cats do it.

Later, Linzey published an online article in his www.oxfordanimalethics.com/:

Hunting foxes and catching mice
21st August 2008

Invariably behind with my reading, I have only just read Roger Scruton's memoirs Gentle Regrets (New York: Continuum, 2005). Scruton has the unusual distinction of being a right-wing intellectual, a professional philosopher, and an avid foxhunter. I was naturally interested to see what justification he could offer for his participation in this 'sport'.

At first it appears that Scruton has actually understood the moral argument: 'Those who hunt do so because they enjoy the sport. Enjoyment is not an evil in itself, but to enjoy an activity at the expense of an innocent animal, knowing full well that the animal is suffering, is immoral, so say the opponents of hunting. Even if it is true that hunt followers take no pleasure in the suffering of their quarry, their pleasure is bought at the expense of suffering, and this is wrong.'

So how does Scruton answer what he accepts as a 'serious and challenging' objection? He continues: 'However, a moral argument must be consistent if it is to be sincere. The pleasure taken by cat-lovers in their pets (who cause 200 million painful deaths each year in Britain alone) is also a pleasure bought 'at the expense of' animal suffering. The RSPCA, which moralizes volubly against hunting, shooting and fishing, keeps quiet about cat-keeping, for fear of offending its principal donors.'

But the analogy cannot withstand examination. I happen to keep cats, and I hope they derive pleasure from my company, as I do from theirs. But pleasure isn't principally why I keep them; I keep them because they do not give pleasure to others – specifically those who abuse, ill-treat, and abandon them. In fact, three I have not chosen to look after at all – they have chosen me, and arrived because they were hungry and had no other home. People in this situation have only three choices: hand them over to the local sanctuary (and thus pass on the responsibility), leave them to starve, or take care of them.

The analogy might have credibility if I had deliberately bred my cats so that they might hunt, and laboriously trained them for this purpose, actually preserving their prey for easy hunting (as foxhunters sometimes do with foxes), and if, moreover, I arranged regular meetings so that I could accompany and encourage them in hunting. But since I, like other cat keepers, do none of these things, the analogy is obviously false. As moral agents, humans are not responsible for what non-moral agents may do naturally without their direct help or encouragement. What the cat does is due to an innate behaviour that under different circumstances is necessary for the cat to survive, whereas foxhunters have no such excuse.'

Scruton continues that: *'To my mind this [not opposing cat keeping] is clear proof that the moral judgements so fervently expressed are not in fact sincerely held'*. Questioning the sincerity of one's opponents is always a low argument, and a sign of a weak case. Hunting with dogs in the UK was (thankfully) banned in 2005, but with the likely election of the Conservative Party in the near future, pledged to a free vote on hunting, we shall doubtless have to confront such obfuscations masquerading as argument all over again.

What he avoids is that, regardless of its origin, if you keep a cat, you are responsible for it, and you do not need to train a cat to hunt; the only 'direct help' you need to do is open the door and it will hunt, even when well fed and fat. Letting the cat out, knowing that there is a strong likelihood that it will catch an animal, betrays intent. The cat is not *'under different circumstances'*, needing to hunt to survive. You cannot switch your responsibility off and on like a light, to claim moral virtue. To claim that 'pleasure is not principally why' he keeps cats is not just feeble, it is moral contortionism. That is exactly why people keep cats, otherwise they wouldn't keep them.

Cat predation on wildlife is massive and well-documented world-wide. Loss *et al.* estimated that free-ranging domestic cats in the USA kill 1.4–3.7 billion birds and 6.9–20.7 billion mammals annually. Cats have caused 26 extinctions and in Scotland are the leading factor in the loss of the indigenous Wildcat through genetic introgression. In Britain we are in the extraordinary position with cats in that it is accepted to release an alien invasive predator, onto land without the land-owner's consent, to hunt protected species day or night, at any time of year, with no obligation to find and retrieve any maimed animals.

The debate over intent v recklessness is currently highlighted by the case of the Mountain Hare (*Lepus timidus*) in Scotland. In a coalition move with the Green Party, the hare has become protected on the basis of a putative 'threatened' status, yet could still be killed under licence as a 'pest'. So far, so ridiculous. Falconers who had traditionally hunted the hares with their Golden Eagles, were no longer allowed to do so.

Submissions were made to the examining Commission by NatureScot, Police Scotland and the Minister for the Environment and Land Reform. The Crown Office and Procurator Fiscal Service were also approached to seek their views on licensing

A cat raids one of our study nests at night and kills all the New Zealand falcon chicks.

and prosecution issues but did not respond. The key legal point is whether flying a bird of prey in an area with Mountain Hares constitutes the possibility that the Falconer might 'recklessly kill' a Schedule 5 protected species within the meaning of Section 9 of the Wildlife and Countryside Act 1981.

The Minister for the Environment and Land Reform submission was of the opinion that it depends on individual circumstances (thus speaks a true politician!).

NatureScot's opinion was that 1. The Falconer must have permission of the land-owner, 2. The Falconer must take reasonable precautions to ensure that there are only few if any mountain hares on the land, 3. The Falconer did not foresee, or could not reasonably foresee that the eagle might take a mountain hare, and 4. The Falconer took all practical steps to minimise the damage eg by recalling the eagle as soon as reasonably practicable. NatureScot then went on to specify where in Scotland Mountain Hares are at a 'high' density, and where they are at a 'low' density, and supplied a map.

Police Scotland were of a similar opinion to NatureScot with the added proviso that *'If the Falconers had carried out due diligence ... and thereafter a Mountain Hare was taken by a bird of prey, then this could be considered accidental. Police should be notified of the incident and thereafter the area should not be used for exercise again. If thereafter this area was used for exercise purposes again, and a further Mountain Hare was taken, then this could be considered reckless.'* They go on: *By choosing to exercise a bird of prey in an area with a known high population of Mountain Hare, then the act could be described as reckless.'*

These three submissions have tried to interpret the law narrowly without examining the precedents it would set for other related activities. These are not hard to find.

First of all, Mountain Hares are not the only protected species in Scotland. Most birds and mammals are protected and together they cover the entire area of Scotland. Based on the premise above, clearly it would be 'reckless' to fly a bird of prey anywhere in Scotland. Second, birds of prey are not the only animals being used. Dogs and cats are allowed to exercise in Scotland and both species not only kill Mountain Hares but also a wide range of protected species. If you put the word 'cat' into NatureScot's advice, instead of 'bird of prey', you will see that cats are 1. being allowed to roam without land-owners' permissions, 2. Cat-owners have not taken 'reasonable precautions to ensure that there are only few if any' protected species on the land, 3. The cat owners could 'foresee, or could reasonably foresee that' the cat might take a protected species (because it is happening thousands of times per day), 4. The cat owner did not take 'all practical steps to minimise the damage eg by recalling the cat as soon as reasonably practicable.'

Following Police Scotland's advice: '*Police should be notified of the incident and thereafter the area should not be used for exercise again. If thereafter this areas was used for exercise purposes again, and a further Mountain Hare* (protected animal) *was taken, then this could be considered reckless.'*

If *Ferae naturae* had been a defence for cats, it would apply even more so to birds of prey flying free in the sky, 'as wild as a hawk'.

Question: Given the thousands of protected animals being killed daily by the 685,000 owned domestic cats in Scotland, how many cat owners have the police prosecuted? Arie Trouwborst's meta-study gives a succinct overview of the cat problem.

The reality of the discrimination in favour of cat owners is simply their voting power. There are about 10.8 million domestic cats in the UK, with 26% of households owning one. No politician wants to poke that hornets' nest, but the few people who fly eagles can easily be rail-roaded. Of course there is legislation on discrimination against cultural minorities, and the Equality Act 2010, but in the UK there is a mind-set that somehow cats should be allowed to kill whatever they want, whenever they want, wherever they want regardless of all legislation.

9 Morality: the judges

9.1 Introduction

Your adherence to your moral values can be judged in two ways. One is by yourself, an internal judgement that we call 'conscience', and the other is by members of your social group. Members of other social groups may also judge you and try to impose their values on you, but that is another matter which I will come on to later. Or you can refer judgement to a God.

So there are four types of judges:
- Yourself – 'conscience'
- Other people in your group.
- Other people outside your group.
- A hypothetical 'God'.

One could perhaps add a fifth: pragmatism or the law of consequences. Drive on the wrong side of the road and even before you get prosecuted you might find yourself killed.

Our judges are all around us, from the cruel mirror, to our families, friends, colleagues, from employers to police, priests and taxmen. All of them may criticise you and judge you. Your car is too posh, or too much of a banger. You drive it too fast. You've shop-lifted, plagiarised an essay, wasted water, tattoo'd your arm, you've married the wrong person, been rude to your grandmother, caught a fish, killed an enemy soldier, over-spent your credit card or pinched someone else's parking space. The list is endless. These are the moral decisions, large and small, that we make every day of our lives. Often our decisions are made, not on the moral values, but on who is watching. *'When night-dogs run, all sorts of deer are chased.' (The Merry Wives of Windsor).* When nobody is watching, do you chase *'all sorts of deer'*?

9.2 Your conscience

In my experience the conscience has its behavioural roots the same as other behaviour, namely genetic, imprinted and learned. The core values are determined by your ethotype, they are expanded by imprinting and refined by learning. All this is internalised and becomes your 'conscience'. The same applies to other social species. For example, dogs are effective carnivores able to pull down prey bigger than themselves. And yet their moral codes enable them to live as a social group without killing one another. When they have arguments, as we all do, they have ways of expressing dominance or appeasement without much physical injury. They learn who is who in the dominance hierarchy of the pack and what they should and should not do. When they do something 'wrong' they show every sign of guilt. This is not as mechanistic as some suggest. In the example I gave earlier in which the dog was taught that sitting on the sofa was 'wrong', the dog showed signs of guilt and this means that he had to some extent, internalised this ethic, and this indicates that the dog has some kind of a conscience. Look on the internet for films of other guilty dogs. Ethologists will say you need to do a double blind test, and this is easily done. The hardened scientist will say there is no way you can tell what a dog is thinking, and this is perfectly true. None of us can tell for sure what anyone else is thinking, and yet somehow we have to muddle through life by reading the signs. If we are autistic and cannot read the signs, for our own species, or for another, life can be a struggle.

I was surprised to find that some anthropologists, such as Christopher Boehm, considered that the 'conscience' was something peculiar to humans, developed in the last few million years since we separated from our common ancestor with chimpanzees and gorillas. I have no experience of anthropoid apes but I would not be bold enough to state that other species do not have consciences of some sort.

There is so much we don't understand. For example, my old horse Buckskin was hot to handle all his life. He was quite bouncy and if you tried to fight him he would fight back and maybe dump you. He wasn't malicious, he was just an eager, high-energy horse. And yet, whenever I carried a falcon on him, he was noticeably kind to me. He would still go flat out in fifth gear if I let him, but even though I was riding one handed, he would come back in hand much more easily than if we were out hacking or exercising. Why this difference I wonder? Why did he seem to look after me?

Boehm postulates that humans evolved a conscience as a consequence of social pressures on alpha bullies and cheats during the portioning out of food from big game animals. He maintains that this evolved an egalitarian society whose members needed social awareness and thus a conscience. He cited examples of beta members of the group ousting or executing alpha bullies. There are several holes in this argument. First of all, effective hunting groups need effective leaders and their hunting success is the primary selective criterion in their evolution. A hunting party that is successful will have a surfeit of food and it doesn't matter how much each individual eats. A less successful group may have failed because there is less game about. In that case it is better for the young, old and weak to die rather than the stronger members of the group. This is the classic density-dependent predation model. Secondly, big game is not the only example of an over-abundant food resources; in late summer many nuts, berries and small game are available and the survival of the group will depend on its ability to store this surfeit for the lean months when the calorific demand is higher and the supply is lower. Safe-guarding and allocating this stored food may be critical to group survival; it is a group Marshmallow Test. Thirdly, what Boehm is describing is a 'lynch mob' mentality. I don't see this as a moral upgrade from a hierarchical society, let alone a trigger for a conscience. Fourthly, becoming egalitarian and less aggressive may make for a more harmonious group, but as soon as the group comes in contact with a more aggressive group, it will be wiped out. Fifthly, in my experience of alpha leaders, the magnanimous sharing of food, even the conspicuous over-provision of food has been the norm, as a display of power and resource wealth. Sixthly, if we cross the species divide to wolves and dogs which are another facultative social carnivore that hunts in packs and pulls down big game, we find that the hierarchical system holds sway, both in the hunting itself, and in the allocation of meat. Normally the size of the prey in comparison to the number of individuals in the pack is such that, while the alpha individuals eat first, the lower ranking individuals do not starve, they just have to wait their turn. This in itself requires a degree of social awareness, the fore-runner of manners and etiquette. I have eaten with top Arab sheikhs out hawking in the deserts of Baluchistan and once we had all had our fill and stood up, then the falconers and workers sat down to the same food; once they were done, the local Baluchis were offered the remnants and they took everything left back to the women and children who waited 200 metres away, not being allowed to join the men. It may well be that some of the relict hunter groups are egalitarian in their food distribution, but the contemporary groups that I have hunted with are certainly hierarchical.

Reciprocity is another feature that we share with many other species. It is a sense of doing each other favours and in a vague sort of way, keeping count. Many animals, not just us, know when they are being cheated, when interactions are unfair. For example, sometimes when we are calling the horses and they don't want to come, we put a few stones in a bucket and shake it so that it sounds like food. We are cheating them. In recompense maybe we grab some grass and offer it to them, even though they will probably refuse it. But it is a way of trying to maintain trust, to keep the faith, to fulfil our side of the bargain. Horses are not predators that are evolved for a variable ratio reward system.

So, other species also have moral codes with the same roots as our own. They too can internalise them into some sort of conscience, as well as impose them externally through group pressure. Just as surely as they have phenotypes with four limbs and a head, similar to ours, so their ethotypes have some similarities to ours. Any social group with no shared morals is doomed to disintegrate and be a genetic dead end. Thomas Hobbes was wrong.

For me, as an individual human, my conscience, like anyone else's, is shaped by my ethotype, my imprinted learning, my learning through life and by the various hormones that steer me through life's phases. For me, the whole point of this book is to examine, assess and understand as much as I can in relation to hunting and life, to reach conclusions and to modify my behaviour accordingly, internalising it into my learned conscience, my personal moral compass. If your own conscience fails, you may be judged by others:

Emory Wanger. 2024. A Very Uncomfortable Discussion About the Reality of Modern Hunt Culture. Online Blog:

There was another time when I bumped into a friend of mine from high school years after we had graduated. We were hunting the same spot and I was coming down off the mountain when I saw him dragging something up to the road. I didn't know it was him at the time but stopped anyway to give my congratulations and ask what he had shot. He told me he shot a small spike, which was legal in this unit, and as I drove away he yelled out "Emory?!"

I stopped and got out of my truck all excited to check out the harvest but as I rounded the pickup I found it was not actually a buck that he had shot. It was a doe and he was in a hurry to load it up and get out of there. Again…I was stunned. I didn't know what to do so I just stared at him like an idiot.

Maybe this isn't a big deal to you, but integrity is high on my list of character traits and I was immediately turned off by the whole situation. He gave me some stupid story about how time was limited for him and he wanted some meat for the freezer and I went along with it thinking the whole time how disgusting and selfish it was. Not to mention illegal.

While our conscience tells us what we <u>ought</u> to do, many times this conflicts with what we <u>want</u> to do. We fill in surveys declaring our stance on an issue – perhaps we disapprove of chickens in battery cages – but our action may be to look for the cheapest eggs on the shelf. Surveys are notoriously useless, not just from sampling bias but from conscience bias, yet they are often used by politicians pretending that this is democracy in action.

The British pride themselves on their love of animals, but in reality this is totally inconsistent. A current craze is 'puppy yoga' in which ladies cuddle 'cute, adorable' puppies. Then other ladies challenge them on the basis of the welfare of the puppies not getting enough sleep or water.

9.3 Other people in your group

For social groups at the family or tribal level, the values, judges and enforcement are local and may not be written down. In larger social groups, the laws are encoded and the judges may be unknown professionals from other families or tribes within the nation.

Families all have their own moral foibles. Some parents are very strict, others are more laid back. They are literally a 'law unto themselves' and often domestic violence is treated by police as something outside their jurisdiction. In Britain, to counteract domestic issues, such as physical violence, but also verbal or mental abuse or even financial abuse, legislation is now in place to intervene into what was previously seen as private affairs. While this potentially benefits many people who suffer silently behind closed doors, it is a delicate path to tread because at the same time it is an invasion of personal privacy and freedom.

Humans, as social animals, have a strong sense of ethotypic social hierarchy and need for social approval. It has obvious evolutionary benefits but takes precedence over rational thought. Despite protestations to the contrary, all humans care to a greater or lesser extent about how those around them judge them.

9.4 Other people outside your group

Which leads us on to external judging figures or groups. Because we usually belong to several social groups at the same time, each with their own moral codes and expectations, we can be judged differently by each group. Your parents may say do one thing, your boyfriend may say do another, your pastor another and a court judge another. Perhaps the worst difficulty in moral judgement is when the judges are in one social group but try to impose their values on others who are not in their own group. Wars start this way. Or indignant priests try to dictate to atheists on issues such as contraception or abortion when they have no more right to do so than the atheists have in dictating to the (celibate) priests. This is moral relativism at its worst. From there it is a slippery slope to religious fanatics beheading non-believers on YouTube.

The worst cases of compartmentalisation are when an individual subjugates his or her own conscience or set of internal values, to those of an authority figure such as a prison guard in the Holocaust. The willingness to do something that we 'know' is wrong because we are ordered to has been demonstrated time and time again in psychological tests.

9.5 Anti-hunting groups

Why do people hate hunting? First of all, who are they? Commenters on the Northumberland Hunt Watch Facebook were 81% female (n=157) and on the Hunt Saboteurs 75% female (n=159). Most of these were 'keyboard warriors' expressing approval on the postings of just a few contributors. Saboteurs active in the field obstructing hunting were mostly dressed in black with balaclavas, but of those identifiable to gender, 54% were female (n=50). As far as could be identified, almost 100% were white Caucasian and most appeared to be in the age groups 20-50. Of those active in the field as 'terrorists' there was a significant proportion of men in the 20-30 age group, and they appeared to regard the activism as a sport in itself. The comments on Facebook indicated that their main gripe was perceived cruelty to foxes ("These people have warped minds", "murdering thugs" etc) causing 'unnecessary suffering', and class – 'snobs', 'toffs on horses' etc. Some underlined that, in comparison, they themselves were from a lower class. There was also a strong cuddly animal theme.

The politicians who initiated the Hunting Bill were overwhelmingly from the Labour Party, championing the urban working classes. I was a Scientific Advisor to the All

Masked saboteurs paid £200 per day each to terrorise a grouse shoot. Wemmergill 12 August 2024.

Party Parliamentary Middle Way Group on Hunting with Dogs during the years of debates – 700 hours of British Parliamentary time. As such, I attended some of the Select Committee meetings and was called as an expert witness at the Public Hearing. As a scientist I was absolutely disgusted at the low intellectual level of the debates, the partisanships, the polarisation, the political manoeuvrings and the media sound bites. The Chairman of the Public Hearing which I contributed to was Alun Michael, Minister for Rural Affairs and a prominent Labour supporter of the ban. I found him totally partisan in his chairing. There was no science, no holistic approach to animal suffering. Instead, it was about 'acceptability' and 'social licence', posing under 'principles' of 'cruelty and 'utility'. Hansard recorded the proceedings. It became great copy for the press and media, who revelled in polarising issues, and a battle through social media for votes. It resulted in legislation that allowed dogs to hunt rabbits, but not hares, and was enacted by politicians who themselves could not tell the difference between the two species. It was all about party politics and class warfare, masquerading as concern for animal welfare. As one Labour MP openly admitted, it was 'payback time for Maggie Thatcher and the Miners'.

The way they approached this was first to ring-fence hunting with dogs from all other forms of hunting, by creating a separate Bill rather than including it within the Wildlife and Countryside Act 1981 where it belonged, and then, when the House of Lords objected, over-ruling them by invoking the Parliament Act. There was thus no perspective, no holistic wildlife management approach and no democratic process.

The result was an Act with no welfare benefit (it didn't protect foxes; it promoted shooting with wounding rates), it had no consistency (it applied to hares but not rabbits or rats) and it didn't apply to other forms of killing, such as by cats. It didn't understand that legislation made in Westminster is not enforceable without the goodwill of people in the countryside – the people who own the land and the hunters themselves. Daniel Greenberg, the lawyer who drafted the Bill was instructed to leave loop-holes, which enabled hunting to continue, despite surveys which were touted to support the ban. The result has been that in 2022/23 season there were about 15,180 public Meets of registered hound packs, (Protectthewild.org.uk data) as well as thousands of hunts by unregistered Hunts and individuals. In 2002, 407,000 people marched on London over this issue, with the slogan Listen to Us. Labour refused to listen, and now, twenty years later, 407,000 people are not listening to them. This brings the entire legal system into disrepute.

Another comment often made is that 'Hunting has no place in a Civilised Society'. Because anti-hunting groups have a high proportion of women, there is often a feminist slant and links are made to male dominance, aggression, abuse of women and so on. Women are often thought of as bringing a civilising influence to any proceedings, which can be a good thing. Perhaps their circles of moral community are wider than men's. But especially when it comes to home and family, women can be very intolerant of threats. The *Guardian* comments listed earlier showed 98.7% of commenters wanted rats in the attic killed or removed (preferably by someone else) and 35% of these comments were from women. Arguably the group most responsible for the majority of unnecessary killing of wildlife are cat-owners of whom around 96% appear to be female. So there is a dichotomy here and perhaps the process of 'civilising' is a process of disconnecting or denying our relationship with nature and a risk aversion to death. Hunting is the antithesis of this, which means not that hunters are murdering barbarians, but that they are kicking back against severance with nature.

From Facebook:

Hertfordshire Hunt Saboteurs
SEEK AND DESTROY
Nothing humane about it ignore the name
These things are lethal and should never have been invented.
Smashing an animals skull and then resetting to do again to the next animal. (Most don't get killed outright going by reading reviews online)
Now booted off the tree and humanely dispatched the goodnature trap is now not fit for purpose.
Fuel us with more Kofi to find more if you're able to:
https://ko-fi.com/hhsabs

For most online anti-hunters there is little nuance; it is more about a gut-feeling. The person who destroyed this trap will feel virtuous about 'saving' a squirrel or a rat and unrepentant about entering private land and destroying property. What would he or she do if the rat was in the kitchen? Of 39 comments, 27 were from women. Most didn't know what these traps are, how they work or why they are used. Typical responses included:

Jane Burke
Pity it can't be recommissioned to work on hunters.
Sue Drake
Robert Allan so it can also kill red squirrels, pine martens or any other hapless critter.
Linda Grigg
What is it please ? I know it's an instrument of torture but what's it called ? Disgusting that things like this are allowed
Jenny Uden
Please be careful. The enemy may just place cameras nearby.

Debbie Jane
Oh my god this is just disgusting who ever thinks of inventing these vile things needs some serious therapy

9.6 Religion

Religions are a human construct, having developed in the last few thousand years from spiritualism and superstition. Superstition, a non-causal association of events, is common to many species, but spiritualism probably arises from our human increased awareness of time. The big problem with religions is that most depend on the concept of one or more Gods, yet there is no evidence that any of these imagined Gods exist outside the human mind. The recent Covid outbreak was an excellent opportunity for one of the Gods to reveal itself as the 'one true God', but in reality none of the religious groups enjoyed any preferential survival from the disease. Without evidence for the existence of a God, the edifice of religion has no foundation or authority.

Moral codes vary from one religion to another, some elements derived from bye-gone ages where the subjugation of women and various nasty forms of death were deemed normal. A pernicious one invented by Christians was the concept of 'Original Sin', essentially blackmailing followers into obeying the priesthood.

The concept of a God is a world of make-believe yet religious groups try to impose their 'morality' on others, or as some authors do, re-interpret' the scriptures to align with their own viewpoints, claiming some kind of moral high ground. (For example Linzey, A. 1995. *Animal Theology*.) We have no God-given right to 'dominion over animals', for better or for worse, or to dominion over one another. The Koran allows for hunting, but when we are hawking in the desert we must slit the neck of the prey and utter the prayer *Bism'Allah, Allah Akbar* to make it halal to eat.

But to get back to the roots of religions, why do we 'need' them? Partly, as our species became more intelligent and widened its understanding of time, this brought with it an awareness of death, and the question of what, if anything, happens after death. Of greater concern for our ancestors was what happened before death – staying alive, getting food. Most of the early cave paintings portrayed prey animals and figures hunting them. This for them was their religion and to this day, hunting still has a religious basis, with its own rituals and superstitions. As a belief system, hunting pre-dates the prescribed religions by scores of millennia and to this day qualifies as a Protected Belief.

9.7 CyberGod

In the God Department there is a new kid on the block. Artificial intelligence, combined with the internet, is watching you. Your browsing history is being stored. All that Facebook stuff, all those selfies. Potential employers can scroll through them and make judgements about you. But CyberGod is onto you remorselessly with all the pernickety detail that the digital world can store, backed up by massive banks of big data. CyberGod knows you opened that porn site link three years, four months, two days, five hours and thirteen minutes ago. CyberGod knows you are contemplating a breast enlargement. CyberGod knows you are thinking of putting your Mum into a Care Home.

But hey, CyberGod wants to help you! He?/It will come up with lots of suggestions for you, links that you had never even thought of. He/It will not judge you… or will he? He has already got your measure. He knows you better than almost anyone. He is not trying to steer you along a path of righteousness. If you want to get into some kind of scam, he's with you all the way. By somehow being non-judgemental, he is both God and Devil rolled into one, constantly tempting you with those little sidebar links to YouTube sites, or free ads. Oh yes, he's only there to help! But he is a sneaky Devil too. Behind the scenes, without you knowing, he's selling your personal details to commercial companies who see you as market-fodder. He's showing you adverts that flag up how inadequate you are and how glamourous you could become if you only click on that link. He's working on your weak points, creating dissatisfaction with yourself without you realising it. Making you want to consume more and more resources…

You are just grist to CyberGod's mill. Even as he throws these temptations in your path, he is sucking the data out of you, pouring it into his coffers of Big Data. Every digit and pixel he gets out of you makes him more and more powerful. His medical knowledge already outstrips the combined total of a big hospital. His geopolitical knowledge outclasses the CIA and the KGB. Every millisecond that goes by a tide of data comes in. Even when you are dead, your digital trail will be left behind, a lifeless cybersoul, like glasses and false teeth in a pile at a Concentration Camp.

CyberGod shares one thing in common with all the other Gods: he is the product of human minds. What does this say about the humans who invented them all? But Cybergod has a weak link. He depends on digital data. That is the blood he needs, like a vampire. Deprive him of it and he loses power over you and you lose dependency on him. He already has many victims in his grasp, people who check their phones sixty times a day. Their brains have been taken over by him and his addictive seduction. They want more. They want Virtual Reality, freedom from the sad real world they are in. The Cyberworld is there, a constant prop. No need to store knowledge anymore; no need to be Intellectuals, not when they can be Internettuals, with all the knowledge of the world just a few clicks away. They want virtual friends, they crave virtual social approval.

The scenario would not be complete without CyberSatan. He will phish you, scam you, fraud you, blackmail you, steal your identity, drain your accounts, take you to the depths of depravity that only the human mind can reach.

CyberGod has huge potential benefits, but many unseen dangers too. Hmm. He can dance to my tune but I'm not going to dance to his. Don't call me, Mr CyberGod; I'll call you.

10 Morality: enforcement systems

10.1 Enforcement mechanisms

Enforcement can use a carrot or a stick, or both. Western societies use both rewards and punishments whereas some societies enforce their moral codes more through fear and punishment. This leads to increased conformity and decreased entrepreneurship. Paradoxically ISIS, which opposes western education, relies totally on imported Western technology to fight its battles.

Using fear of physical punishment or social ostracism is a powerful incentive. A social animal understands dominance hierarchies. It is behaviourally equipped to read social signals of approval and disapproval and to comply with social mores. A snarl from a senior member of the group keeps it in line and is interpreted as a social signal rather than a life-threatening attack. The social animal is afraid of being ostracised from the group. Survival chances are reduced on your own. We can thus train social animals such as humans, dogs and horses fairly easily by becoming a leader of the herd or pack and mimicking the natural rewards and punishments.

It gets trickier with solitary predators, such as falcons. They have no fear of ostracism; they can easily fly away. Any attempt at punishment is interpreted as a personal attack and will elicit a fight or flight. We cannot alter instinctive behaviour, so the only elements we can work with are imprinted and learned behaviour. If we wish, we can reduce or eliminate fear in the young falcon by a careful imprinting process whereby the falcon is exposed to all potentially scary things during the critical period when the fear response is developing. Beyond that we can mould learned behaviour using classic conditioning, positive reinforcement, operant conditioning and habituation. But we cannot use punishment, so this focusses the mind of the human trainer. Often punishment is the lazy way to coerce behaviour in an animal or person. Solitary animals can learn from negative reinforcement or from trauma learning, but not if it is linked in any way to the trainer. Can you imagine rearing your children without ever saying a harsh word? That's what it is like training a falcon. Try the same approach on a human child and he will soon walk all over you.

The most effective punishments are ones that mimic what happens in nature. The Marshmallow Test explores the willingness of people to put off rewards to gain more later. Some people are impulsive and cannot wait. There is a correlation between their ability to wait for the reward and their subsequent achievements in later life. The highest achievers are the ones that could defer the reward longest. But what about the effects of delayed punishment? If you flip the Marshmallow Test and instead of giving a delayed reward for a desired act, ie 'waiting', give a delayed punishment for an 'unwanted behaviour', will you find a similar spectrum of participants in extinguishing that behaviour, and will they be the same personalities, ie the impulsive ones tend towards the short delay whereas others can cope with a longer delay?

When trying to discourage or extinguish certain behaviour, we need to distinguish between *negative reinforcement* that can have an immediate effect of extinguishing the behaviour, such as touching a hot stove, and punishment which occurs after the behaviour has finished but could prevent future repetitions. The first says: 'Stop now', the second only says: 'Don't do it again'. The person being punished, who has already finished doing the 'act', cannot avoid the punishment by stopping what he is doing. Punishment therefore requires an element of intelligence to connect the two events together. The impulsive personality needs the punishment to be close to the act and cannot register punishment that is delayed. A court appearance weeks or months after the supposed crime does not have much impact on these impulsive personalities. Not only is the time distance between the 'crime' and the punishment subject to the marshmallow effect, the time distance between the punishment and potentially repeating the crime is subject to it too. Some young people have strings of court orders, knowing that nothing effective is really going to happen. There has been a move away from corporal punishment in Western societies; this has its good and its bad points. But the main point is that the punishment or the reward should be as close to the unwanted behaviour as possible. In animal training we prefer this to be no longer than three seconds. Most non-humans have only a short appreciation of time, so in training animals we always try to make the period between the action and the reward, or punishment, as short as possible, even using intermediary rewards, such as clickers, to bridge the gap when immediate response is not physically possible. This effect is based on differences in temporal intelligence. For the less intelligent, punishment needs to be so close to the action that it is, in effect, negative reinforcement.

There was something to be said for a clip round the ear from the village policeman, followed by the admonition: 'Do that again and I'll tell you parents!'. Quick, cheap to administer, and with no lasting paper trail of the follies of youth coming back to haunt the young person later in life. A lot of our legal system at this level is old-fashioned and obtains no benefit from modern knowledge of psychology; it could do with a good re-think. Why fine people who litter? Why not give them a 100 hours litter-picking? And I'm not just talking about the odd cigarette packet, chewing gum or even fly-tipping. How about the Board Members of some of the fast food and coffee chains being sent out onto the streets, rivers and beaches collecting litter with their logos on? Would this make them reconsider their throw away policy?

You can extrapolate this to many activities; it is a question of moving away from the simple concept of 'crime' towards a concept of responsibility.

Especially in the West we find politicians passing laws as a quick fix panacea for some social issue. It is 'wish-list' legislation; they have 'done something' about it. The legislation may have no chance of ever being enforceable. The police and courts have neither the capacity, priority or wherewithal to address the issue. So the legislation moulders on the statute books, rusting hulks bearing testimony to past political manoeuvrings. Without social acceptance there is no compliance.

Another natural element to enforcement is that the punishment must come from a more senior member of the <u>same</u> social group. We care more about approval and disapproval from our own group than from those outside it. A judge dressed in a wig and gown is almost on a different planet to a troubled teenage delinquent. The youth is far more concerned about not looking cool in front of his mates, or worse still, being chucked out of the gang.

Leading on from the concept of enforcing moral behaviour is the more positive aspect of promoting a sense of responsibility. This often falls foul of the law of unexpected consequences. For example, following the spate of witch hunts for paedophiles, fewer men put themselves forwards as primary school teachers or as Boy Scout leaders. Currently, because of a lack of leaders, there is a waiting list of 51,000 for the Scouts in the UK.

Somebody's student child had an accident. The parents employed no win no fee lawyers and sued the university. The court operated on the Western adversarial legal system and a culture of blame. The university insurers stipulated that students should not be allowed out on their own. So when we get students coming to do wildlife surveys of the beaver ponds on our farm, their health and safety requirements mean that they have to do a full risk assessment on paper and then work in pairs. Meanwhile I, as a 74 year old farmer, go by on a tractor or quad bike on my own doing seriously risky stuff with farm machinery in rough country. What kind of education and preparation for life is the university giving these students? As an employer, what use are these kids to me if they do not have the life skills that we had as five year olds? They have been through a programme of planned helplessness. One of the main difficulties of studying hunting in academia are the risk-averse university Ethics Committees.

When social groups are small, up to the tribal level, then ethotypic and learned morality are sufficient. Often the values are set by tradition and by the current tribal leader, and enforced by him or her. This natural morality is sufficient for most non-human vertebrate social groups. Once the population expands beyond this level then legal systems have to be instigated and formalised. Natural morality becomes more formalised in the 'social contract' and then into a legal system. Then there are two systems running in parallel – the natural morality and a legal system. This may be further compounded by religious codes of conduct such as Sharia Law. There are many examples of societies transitioning from the tribal level to the urban level, and I have followed some of these in the Middle East for thirty years. There, the biggest sheikh's authority is paramount and it is a lick up, kick down, hierarchy. The Sheikh's authority may be augmented by religious leaders, or even held in a social contract with the Imans, as it was in the Kingdom of Saudi Arabia. Despite these layers of control and harsh punishments, corruption is common and indeed I have been offered alcohol when dining with royal families in the Gulf, while other ex-pats have been jailed for possessing home brewing kits. These leaders have mainly been educated in the West and picked up Western cultural habits which, back home, clash with local mores, and for them, this creates a moral dissonance.

Once a group expands beyond the tribal level, legal systems are required as an enforcement mechanism. These have many failings, not least because they are set up by very fallible politicians. The first line of enforcement of laws is the police, and these are thin on the ground in rural areas where hunting takes place. The British government soon discovered that their bright and shiny new Hunting Act could not be enforced by the police in the face of civil disobedience.

10.2 Hunting Ethics

On the First of September, one Sunday morn
I shot a hen pheasant in standing corn
Without a licence
Contrive who can
Such a cluster of crimes against God and Man!

Since before the Laws of Hywel Dda, who died in AD 950, laws have gradually been developed and codified, many relating to the use of natural resources and hunting. The seasons for deer and other game were specified and some elements became laws, others remained as customs or traditions. While many hunting groups, especially subsistence and recreational hunters, have their own codes of ethics, pest control hunters have different motives and ethics. Hunting ethics are mostly concerned with sustainability and balance. We talk about 'a sporting chance' and giving an animal 'law'. In Britain these codes of ethics are seldom written down but in America the Boone and Crockett Club has established some principles for shooters of 'game' as distinct from 'pest' animals:

The Principles of Fair Chase

FAIR CHASE, as defined by the Boone and Crockett Club, is the ethical, sportsmanlike, and lawful pursuit and taking of any free-ranging wild game animal in a manner that does not give the hunter an improper or unfair advantage over the game animals.

The Fair Chase Hunter:
1. *Knows and obeys the law, and insists*

others do as well
2. *Understands that it is not only about just what is legal, but also what is honorable and ethical*
3. *Defines "unfair advantage" as when the game does not have reasonable chance of escape*
4. *Cares about and respects all wildlife and the ecosystems that support them, which includes making full use of game animals taken*
5. *Measures success not in the quantity of game taken, but by the quality of the chase*
6. *Embraces the "no guarantees" nature of hunting*
7. *Uses technology in a way that does not diminish the importance of developing skills as a hunter or reduces hunting to just shooting*
8. *Knows his or her limitations, and stretches the stalk not the shot*
9. *Takes pride in the decisions he or she makes in the field and takes full responsibility for his or her actions*

To unpack #3, one can look at the balance statistically, what percentage of hunts are successful? If all are successful for the hunter then there is no balance, nor is there a balance if in 100% of the hunts the prey escape. A success rate of about 20% ie one hunt in five, is a common natural balance. But this is still an anthropocentric judgement if an artificial method, such as a gun, is used for which the prey has not evolved escape strategies and has no comprehension. Surely an artificial device such as a gun is by definition an 'unfair advantage'? Shooters will deny this vehemently, but then – they are on the best end of the gun!

Islam too lays down rules for hunting, although they are not always followed:

'Falconry must be followed by a development of the human intellect, as a protection of the sport from the dangers it is exposed to, most notably 'unfair hunting' which exposes the environment and its contents of animals and birds to harm's way, which may threaten this prestigious Arab sport. Arabs who are the pioneers of this hunting sport are asked to take the initiative and lay down the rules, means and conditions regulating the hunting procedure and preserve the natural environment, such as:

Preserving the environment, animals and birds and refrain from hunting endangered species.

Study the types of birds and animals and their breeding periods and prepare hunting seasons accordingly.

Refrain from using highly advanced methods such as firearms and cars that can race with the birds.'

Al-Otaibi, 1996.

The thing about these ethics, whether they are written in law or unwritten, is that they need to be internalised if they are to work. They have to become part of your conscience so that you follow them regardless of who might be watching you. The police know how hard it is to enforce anything out in the countryside; ultimately it is up to each one of us to develop our own code of ethics and impose them on ourselves.

10.3 'Animal Rights'

Some people subscribe to the notion of 'rights': human rights, animal rights and so on. Some base them on 'personhood', rationality or even the possession of a 'soul'. Sentience has recently been proposed as a criterion. Laudable though these 'rights' may be, they cannot exist without enforcement. Power is the only right. Any law, or any 'right' without an enforcement mechanism, can exist only in name. The power may arise from a democratic decision, or it may stem from economics, or from force of arms, but without power to enforce, there are no 'rights'. This does not equate to 'Might is Right'; far from it. What it means is that without the power to enforce them, you have no 'rights' at all. Being powerful may enable you to do all sorts of nasty things, but that doesn't necessarily validate those things as ethically 'right' or as 'a right'.

We may feel that we have some kind of 'Right' to peace, but we haven't. To enforce our right to peace we have to be prepared to go to war.

The Declaration of Human Rights by the United Nations in 1948 was a step in the right direction and has been enshrined into a network of legislation in many countries. But it is fundamentally flawed; it is a statement of intent – note its word 'should'. It is not absolute and it does not apply to our entire human species. There are huge areas of the planet where corruption is rife and human rights mean nothing. The notion of 'rights' is a well-meaning one, but without power it cannot be enforced. Better I think to keep to the notion of our 'responsibilities', which in turn we base on our current moral values, in other words, Contractarianism.

Some differentiate between human rights and animal rights, in that while humans have both rights and responsibilities, non-human animals have rights conferred on them by humans, but have no responsibilities. This is an anthropocentric approach. Non-human animals have their own responsibilities according to their own moral codes: responsibilities to their families and group loyalties within their moral communities. It's just that we humans don't realise the moral pressures that other species are under; we simply can't help relating everything to ourselves.

Another problem with 'rights' is that they are limited to sentient beings. Singer, Bentham, Regan, Midgley and others rely on this. But if you refer back to my five priorities, this would encompass only the final one: individuals. Of course individuals are the building blocks of species, which are the building blocks of habitats, but starting at the individual level is an upside down approach. I believe our first priorities are to the planet as a whole and entire ecosystems consisting of a vast complex of animate and inanimate elements. These don't have 'rights', but in my morality we have responsibilities to them as our first priority over a few individuals. For me, 'eco-ethics' are our deontological duty, we cannot ignore them. We have to see the wood, before the trees. We may find this extremely hard to do. It is a step beyond the evolutionary criteria affecting the selfish gene, which I discuss in 8.1.

Some, such as Aarnio and Aaltola, accuse hunters of 'dementalising' animals, objectifying them to make killing them more acceptable. There is an element of truth in this. On the other hand, anti-hunters are equally guilty of anthropomorphising animals to give them 'rights'. This can lead to all sorts of ethical contortions in attitudes towards for example cute, cuddly kittens compared to nasty rats. Both approaches are linked to where people position animals within their moral communities.

'Rights' can promote a culture of dependency, the notion that someone – the Council, the Government, the World – owes me a living. We all of us need to take responsibility for our own actions, and that often follows a tortuous chain of events before reaching its final destination. For example, obesity is on the rise in Western nations. Many conditions, such as lower back pain, bad knees, cancer and so on, have a higher risk in obese people. If funds are short for state medical care, should they be prioritised towards people who are taking responsibility for their own obesity issues? We don't even dare label over-weight people as 'fat' any more. In America, fat is the new normal; they just make the seats wider. Between two people with lung cancer, should a non-smoker be prioritised over a smoker? Should you have a 'right' to expect the state to pay for your cosmetic surgery? In the private care sector, the attitude is increasingly commercial. If you take your dog to the vet, the first question asked is 'Are you insured?' If yes, they will propose every expensive solution, and gradually the insurance fees go up. It is a gravy train. Never ask a barber if you need a hair-cut!

Some animal rights campaigners, such as Andrew Linzey, claim that non-human animals, although they may be sentient, are unable to give us their consent to us exploiting them or killing them. This is true. Moreover, if they <u>were</u> capable of giving consent, they probably wouldn't. I wonder if they would give us their consent to destroy their habitats (level #3) so that we can grow soya, nuts or palm oil for our own vegetarian sustenance? I don't think they would. The conclusion to this animal rights argument is that we should leave non-human animals strictly alone. This would lead to the demise of farm animal species because obviously if we do not eat them or milk them, then there would be no point in us breeding them in the first place. I wonder if they would give their consents to having their entire species exterminated? I don't think they would. The logical end point of this animal rights approach is simple: In order to leave sentient animals alone and unexploited then it is us – humans – who must disappear, not them. In other words, the only real welfarist is a dead welfarist, and if we want to conserve their habitats rather than exploit them for crops then again, the only good conservationist is a dead conservationist. You cannot have your cake and eat it. As long as there is a single human left on Planet Earth, we will continue to exploit both sentient animals and the habitats they need for their survival. Even a laboratory farm that grows food using cell culture is exploiting resources taken from species other than our own.

There is nothing to be ashamed of about this. We all of us rely on, and compete for,

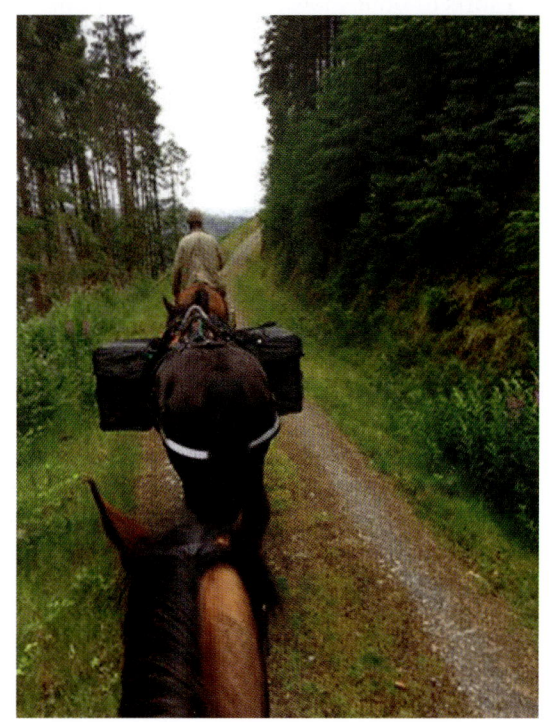

Training Cinders as a packhorse. She may not have consented, but she follows us without a lead.

the natural resources available on the planet. It is natural, and all species do it; it is how we have all got here. Some interactions could be predatory (or, in Andrew Linzey's terms, killing animals without their consent), some are parasitic, some are symbiotic. My relationship with my sheep is, I think, a symbiotic one. I provide everything they need to breed and live naturally in their flock. When they are too old, or ready for killing, I ensure they have a better quality of death than 90% of human deaths (ask

Thomas Fleischmann). Nor do I condone cruelty; I am an animal welfarist all the way on this. But the concept of animal 'rights' as a means of achieving it is a futile argument, as is claiming that Christianity promotes animal welfare. It doesn't. It follows tenets held 2,000 years ago. Of course, you can select out those tenets; bin them. But then you cannot call yourself a Christian. It is fashionable at the moment to go through all sorts of philosophical contortions to re-interpret biblical ethics so that they line up with recent changes in ethical values, such as homosexuality. But a point is surely reached where this is no longer Christianity, it is something else. Christ would assuredly have been dismayed if, on reaching the shore with a haul of fish, he had met Andrew Linzey telling him to put them all back.

The counter-argument to all this is, that because non-sentient animals, plants or whole habitats cannot feel pain, then we can justify doing whatever we please with them. I don't see it that way. Pain should be a consideration of course, but not the priority. We should treat habitats and all life forms responsibly. This doesn't preclude killing things, but it does entail managing sustainably.

In Britain we have introduced a new 'Right': the 'Right to Roam'. This already covers most of Scotland and now large areas of England, mainly moorland and common land. This is a conflict of needs between the increasing numbers of humans who want to 'escape' from the towns for a walk, often with a dog, and the decreasing wildlife, especially ground-nesting birds, who need these areas to nest but cannot do so because of disturbance. The humans often do not recognise or understand the distress calls of these nesting birds whose eggs or chicks are getting cold or exposed to predators. Human disturbance is a major factor in nest failure and some species such as curlews, lapwings, black grouse and skylarks are in serious decline. If we want to talk about Animal Rights, surely our responsibility is to allow them the 'right' to nest undisturbed? But they don't have the vote, so our disturbance will continue. A ban on access from April to July would go a long way to help these imperilled species. We have people coming on the farm wandering happily through the uncut mowing grass with their dogs without the faintest idea that they are doing any harm, either to the crop, or to the wildlife. This is not 'hunting' in the conventional sense, but it is impacting wildlife nonetheless.

11 The Evolutionary Trap

'Look after the Earth and the Earth will look after you.'

The evolutionary trap is because the evolutionary criterion has been for the selective survival of individuals, or, specifically, of certain 'selfish genes', as Dawkins puts it. Until now this has worked fine. But now we have learned skills and techniques that enable us to out-compete all evolutionary constraints and demographic balancing mechanisms. Our human population is thus able to burgeon uncontrollably, and yet the global resources are finite. Humans have sufficient intelligence to enable ourselves to breed up, but we do not have sufficient wherewithal to limit our own population growth. We are thus on a collision course between our resource demands and the finite resources available. How this collision course will resolve itself is not at all clear, but with most political systems reliant on short-termism it seems that a considered, globally-calibrated response to achieve a balance is unlikely. The alternative is to fall back on our instinctive strategies such as territoriality (warfare) and it is likely that the world's resources, including all other species, will be heavily depleted, destroyed or contaminated in the process. However, this may be no worse than the Earth being hit by a large asteroid. Earth has been there before and survived. Nuclear war may induce a dust cloud and winter causing an ice age for a few thousand years, and destroy most higher organisms, but it will just be a saw-tooth in evolutionary terms. The long-term result of evolution is not survival of any particular selfish genes, but of the Earth as a functioning ecosystem.

There is an inverse relationship between our ethotypic priorities (what our genes and instincts are telling us to do) and the intellectual priorities (what intellectually we know needs to be done). Whereas ethotypic values ripple out from the genes, to the individual, to the pair, to the family, and then to the tribe, the intellectual priorities are the reciprocal image. Call it 'hearts' (the ethotype) and 'minds' (the intellect). Intellectually we know that our first priority must be to take care of the planet because if that fails, all the lesser priorities also fail. Then it goes down the scale to the individual and genetic level:

Ethotypic priorities.
1. The genes.
2. The individual.
3. The breeding family unit.
4. The wider family, sharing relatedness.
5. The tribe.

There is no ethotypic concern for wider groups beyond the tribe level.

Intellectual priorities.
1. Planet Earth and sustainable global systems.
2. Shared regional resources, the 'commons'.
3. Habitats for full biodiversity.
4. Single species management programmes.
5. Individual animal welfare.

Our ethotypic values were fine while our impact on the planet was so small that the planet-scale systems were able to continue unaltered, with natural homeostatic mechanisms. Now our influence has extended but we are still only equipped with the suite of instincts we have inherited. In our heads we know we have to put the big stuff first but when it comes down to it, our instincts scream 'Me, me, me!'

These two approaches do not equate to anthropocentrism and geocentrism. The ethotypic strategy is used by <u>all</u> animals, not just humans. The second strategy, having an intellectual root, could be followed by humans, but meanwhile all other species will inevitably continue using the first strategy. One could claim that humans are superior to the 'brute creation' because of our intelligence. Many people feel this way. But when it comes down to it, when it comes to the crunch, the reality is that we don't use our intellect first; we use our ethotypic behaviour just the same as other species do. Look at the British parliamentary debates on hunting; scarcely anything from the intellect, science. It all emanated from 'feelings', emotion and tribal behaviour.

We listen to our feelings before our sober intellect. For sure one can see adverts aimed at 'saving' big vertebrates such as rhinos, elephants and lions, species whose habitats are day by day being reduced and eroded by increasing human populations. But the very next advert is equally likely to be aimed at 'saving the children', a self-defeating policy diametrically opposed to conservation efforts. Saving children is #2, near the top of our ethotypic priority list, but bottom of our intellectual moral priority list. The emphasis needs to work further back on the issue, to family planning. How do you sit with these two examples? Perhaps you would like to have your cake and eat it, supporting both? Sadly, we have reached the point on our little planet where that is not an option. Obviously nobody wants to go around killing babies, so the only humane way to turn the tide on our impact on Earth's natural resources is to reduce our reproductive rate. We have the technology – contraception – but our cultures and religions tend to stand in the way.

And so we struggle to tackle the problems we are creating and many people deny them rather than face them. The issues will not go away; they will get worse. We ourselves will go away, but our progeny will inherit the mess we are leaving them. Thus, while our instincts tell us to put the individual first and the planet last, if we follow those instincts and simply address individual welfare issues while ignoring the wider issues, we are dooming ourselves to extinction. Theoretically our intelligence should enable us to use logic to overcome our instincts, but our instincts are much stronger than we realise, and our intelligence is fragmentary at best. Stephen Pinker in his *Enlightenment Now* does a great job of statistically demonstrating how our world has improved in the last two million years, with all measurable parameters improving almost exponentially in the last hundred years. We are a lucky generation! But even Stephen Pinker focusses his attention on just one species – humans. Most of the parameters he assesses are on my lowest priority level, level 5, individual welfare. If you are a human living in a city this, no doubt, is what concerns you most. But it is a collision course for the planet we rely on for our existence. If Pinker re-wrote his book from the perspective of a rhino, or of a frog, he would come to very different conclusions. Many species, in small, isolated populations, face an inexorable process of being extinguished one by one, and it's our fault.

Throughout this book I have tried to avoid using the words 'good' or 'bad'; perhaps now you can see why. While many moralists have pondered how to define these terms, surely it depends first on your assumed priorities? If you take the ethotypic approach, which almost everyone does, then 'good' can be measured against those priorities. And, being human, you inevitably end up with an anthropocentric philosophy, even if a liberal one. But if you take an intellectual approach, all the parameters have changed and some things once deemed 'good' now appear 'bad'. Nor can moral goodness be quantified in units; it can only be comparative.

Taking it a step further, theoretical philosophy questions often hinge on the ethics of saving lives. In a given situation do you sacrifice one life to save many? That sort of thing; the Trolley Problem. It is in all the basic philosophy books. The underlying ethical assumption is always that saving human lives is a 'good' thing. And why not? It always has been so far. But as we increase in numbers and approach the limits of the Earth's finite resources, and are damaging the ecosystems beyond repair, then this basic premise no longer holds good. Philosophers may adopt the ethotypic premise but, as biologists, we see many, many examples of animal populations out-stripping their resources. The results are totally predictable, and not nice. They involve a catastrophic crash, which may or may not be survivable for the species, or for others caught in co-lateral damage. The most obvious of these are the large mammals and apex predators that require large contiguous areas of habitat to maintain minimum viable populations. Lions, tigers, wolves and elephants, all have their habitats eroded month by month by increasing human competition. The atmosphere, climate and the seas are all increasingly polluted and destroyed, by us. With these top welfare priorities deteriorating, all the lower priorities will fail too. Although we have massive computer power that can unlock nature's codes and clearly show the trends and predict what will happen, we are stuck in an evolutionary trap set by our own instinctive behaviour, our 'feelings', our primitive ethotype. So sadly, most of our British wildlife legislation is based on emotion, with scant regard for science. (An interesting point to ponder, if you look in Further Reading at the end of this book, most of the science-based papers are written by multiple authors working in teams, whereas most of the philosophy ones are single-authored, producing individual approaches.)

The Animal Rights movement is based on #2 on the ethotypic list – the individual animal. But this is #5, at the bottom of the intellectual list, emphasising the conflict between the two approaches. One is not sustainable, the other is.

For sure, nature does have its own homeostatic mechanisms that tend to smooth out the worst extremes of population cycles. Predator numbers increase as prey increase until the tide turns and numbers ease back. But this requires intact functioning ecosystems with multiple trophic levels.

Man has done his best to remove all factors limiting human population growth. Our predators have all been eliminated, although we still have extremist reactions about the occasional shark or tiger attack. Disease has been tackled by modern medicine so that infant mortality is down and life span has increased. The result is that births far outweigh deaths and the overall human population is increasing exponentially. Although international travel has increased disease transmission, most pandemics fizzle out with medical treatment and movement restrictions. Undeveloped nations simply starve. Developed nations fight one another. The prognosis for humans thus seems to be war, starvation and mass migration, with massive co-lateral damage to all the other species on the planet.

During the Second World War, Alan Turing and his team at Bletchley Park decoded the German Enigma machine. They developed an early form of computer that could run rapidly through all the possible combinations and thus break the codes that the Nazis were using and which were changed at every midnight. Their code-breaking machine was a major achievement and a breakthrough in the war effort. The ethical difficulties only began once the machine was working. The initial, instinctive approach, was to put individuals first. A convoy in the Atlantic was about to be targeted by German U-boats. Surely these ships should be tipped off and saved? But to have done that would immediately have alerted the Germans that we had somehow accessed their communications system. They would have quickly changed it, rendering the decoding machine useless. Its value lay in not being detected. But how to make use of this information without the Germans realising that their codes had been broken? This was the ethical and statistical difficulty. Basically, calculations had to be made to provide the maximum strategic benefit from the information, but randomised in such a way that the Germans could not easily detect a statistical connection between what the British were doing and their own coded messages. In other words, the good of the many had to be put before the good of the few, even though those few who were being deliberately allowed to be killed by the Germans were husbands, fathers and sons, known individuals.

The key to this ethical decision making, which enabled it to work, was that the decision makers were operating in total secrecy. They could play 'God', if only for a limited time until the war was resolved. If the decisions had been in the public arena, there would have been howls of protests from people wanting to save their relatives and friends. This would have made the whole situation untenable, alerted the Germans, and resulted in much higher casualty rates and perhaps the war being lost. In peace time, politicians face 'transparency', they have elections to win in a short time span, or even if they are dictators, they have somehow to maintain a modicum of support or risk being overthrown. Thus leaders are seldom omnipotent enough to make this type of group benefit decision, and groups will always take the instinctive approach that has served them so well throughout the course of evolution.

You will also notice the inverse relationship between the list of priorities and the time/thinking graph in 2.14. Most of people's thoughts aggregate around the 24 hour to one week period both into the future and into the past. The time spent thinking beyond this period, in both directions, tapers off rapidly. That's what we are like. But the priority list works inversely to this. Whereas at the individual level, an injured animal or person can usually be fixed up in a month or two, going up the priority list, we find that a species restoration programme is usually in the order of 10-30 years or so. Going further up the priority list, restoring whole habitats can take many years, even centuries. When we are establishing new 'ancient' woodlands, we are scheduling for a period of 200-300 years. Restoring coral reefs or deserts are similarly long-term undertakings. To try to remove all the plastic from the oceans may take longer still, and as for climate change, the geographic scale of the problem, the distances and the time-scale involved are so huge, that we struggle even to get our heads around it. So we gravitate towards the here and now, fixing up individual issues but ignoring the big ones.

Thus not only do we have our evolutionary instincts working against us, we have our own time perception limiting us too. Even our perceptions of space work against us; we are concerned about things in our own back yards much more than we are concerned about massive losses of rain forest, or of melting glaciers and ice caps. We are in a trap, and I'm not convinced that technology can wave a magic wand and fix it, when the problem is buried so deep within our own nature.

In this chapter I will review our intellectual priorities in reverse order. Books and theories are all very well, but I shall do it by detailing some of the projects we have done over the last 55 years. Some have had a degree of success, some a degree of failure, but real life brings up all sorts of twists and turns that don't appear in nice, neat academic books.

11.1 Individual welfare

The welfare of the individual is the ethotype's second priority, after the genes. But the intellect's last (fifth) priority.

Most of this book so far, and especially Chapter 5, has been based on the welfare of individuals. When we talk about animal welfare, this is what we mean. Animal hospitals, re-habilitation centres, cat, dog and donkey homes and sanctuaries are all about caring for individual animals, especially cute ones. While this is very worthy, the subject of tear-jerking appeals and endowments, in the wider scheme of things it would make little difference if all of these animals died

A young Red Kite in our kite recovery programme.

tomorrow. That sounds callous but it's true. Mullineaux and Pawson give a useful analysis of what and why animals come into rehabilitation, and what happens to them. About 42% survive to be released back to the wild, but their post-release survival is unknown and a big proportion of the species are ones that are being killed in huge numbers anyway. Thousands of wood-pigeons, feral pigeons and herring gulls are killed as pests every year, so there seems little point in rehabbing them.

11.2 Welfare at species level.

Moving on from individual animal welfare to species management (level 4); this is where many organisations focus their efforts. It is often criticized because management of a species in isolation is often tackling the symptoms rather than the cause, which is at level 3, habitat, or higher. But there is inter-play between the two levels, and they are by no means mutually exclusive. For example, horses became extinct in North America about 11,000 years ago when the ice sheet spread to low latitudes. Reintroduced again by Western colonisers, populations became established in the wild again. In one area of the US west, the official carrying capacity for wild horses is 27,000, but numbers have now risen to 70,000, causing habitat damage and impacting other species. There has been a public outcry against killing the surplus horses and, without natural predators, the situation is becoming untenable. A contraceptive protein called PZP is being attempted but it is impracticable in the badlands. So public revulsion at killing horses leads to destruction of habitats and ultimately the horses will starve and suffer too. It is a lesson we need to learn for the biology of our own species.

One of the common pitfalls at this level is 'iconisation'. A protectionist organisation creates a public image of a species as an 'icon' or 'totem'. This sets it upon a pedestal immune from management. The species has to be totally protected and no targets are set defining when conservation success has been achieved, or when the conservation resources spent on the species, and the level of protection afforded to it, will be eased. Iconising a species means that NGOs can raise money from it; it is part of their PR strategy.

An example is the Peregrine, the raptor with the largest geographical distribution of all. Originally heavily protected by medieval falconers, this species in Britain was hammered badly by Victorian and Edwardian gamekeepers. It was regarded as vermin and featured on every gibbet. It recovered somewhat between the World Wars but then in the Second World War was extirpated all along the south coast to prevent it catching messenger pigeons. The skins of many of them are now in the Natural History Museum at Tring. Pesticides in the 1950s and 1960s caused massive crashes in raptor populations resulting in the '*Silent Spring*' of Rachel Carson. I recorded shell-thinning in raptors in New

Zealand due to DDT and its residues, even in the 1970s. Pesticides went global and 'the average American was unfit for human consumption'. As a result, the plight of the peregrine was – rightly – flagged up and the species was heavily protected, although the pesticide companies were never prosecuted. The American *anatum* Peregrine was virtually exterminated by over-enthusiastic use of chemicals, so Tom Cade in USA and Richard Fyffe in Canada had to build teams of falconers and breeders to re-establish that population. In the UK the situation was not so dire and the peregrine recovered of its own accord, back to around 1500 pairs by the turn of this century. This is approaching the limit of carrying capacity, and the population has remained around the 1800 level ever since. But the species is still touted as rare and endangered with maximum protection. Recently an article explained that the peregrine was so persecuted in the countryside that it was coming into cities to breed. The reality is that cities offer new opportunities for prospective pairs to nest when all the natural cliffs are already taken. At a recent Convention on International Trade of Endangered Species of Wild Fauna and Flora (CITES) Conference of the Parties, Canada proposed that the peregrine be down-listed from Appendix 1 to Appendix 2. It fulfilled all the scientific criteria for down-listing. But a group of countries, mainly the EU, blocked it for political reasons. This of course down-grades CITES itself, from a body with scientific integrity, to one that is just a political pawn subject to the whims of pressure groups.

The peregrine, with 19 sub-species, is the most cosmopolitan of falcon species. At about 1800 pairs, in the UK (the highest since records began) and with a productivity of about 1.5 chicks per year, about 2,700 chicks are produced a year. In a stable sedentary population, this means 2,700 peregrines die each year – over fifty a week. Two years ago, a gamekeeper married to a policewoman stole 15 wild peregrine eggs or chicks in Scotland and sold them. This led to a massive furore of DNA testing and raids by the Wildlife Crime Unit. Last week, one falcon breeder who was suspected of buying one of these peregrines, was raided by six police cars, 22 policemen, two Wildlife Inspectors and someone from the RSPB, to capture all his birds on their nests, with their chicks, and take DNA from them. What crime would one normally need to commit to be raided by 22 policemen? Next time, the gamekeepers on the grouse moors, instead of removing eggs and putting them in incubators, will quietly dispose of them.

The other form of iconisation uses level 5, individual animal welfare. In Britain, the badger is a vector of bovine tuberculosis which cost 46,103 cattle slaughtered in 2017. Many farmers have been put out of business or committed suicide. 'Animal Rights' organisations have pressured to maintain strict protection for the badger. The badger had originally been protected, not because it was rare, but because people had cruelly used them for baiting with dogs. As a result the species has increased in numbers by 88% since 1980. They in turn impact the trophic level below, such as hedgehogs and hares. So now we have hedgehog protection groups. Meanwhile close relatives of the badger, other mustelids such as stoats and weasels, have no protection at all and people show little interest in them. Government attempts to cull badgers in bTb areas have met with hostility from badger groups so that the cost to humanely trap and vaccinate one badger is now around £800. And of course, every change of government leads to a change of policy, when the one thing that wildlife management needs is long-term consistency. The reaction of the farmers, frustrated by lack of consistency is simply to kill the badgers illegally, and often this is the only way that keeps everyone happy. The minister doesn't have to make an unpleasant decision, the Animal Rightist doesn't know it is happening and has won a paper victory, and the people on the ground just get on with it, albeit by less than humane methods, but at no cost to the taxpayer.

While individuals are the building blocks of species, species are the building blocks of functioning ecosystems. Single species conservation programmes are often criticised for their limitations, but they can be rewarding and the results are often measurable. This makes them easier to get funding for, although it also means that some people claim that certain species are in more dire straits than they really are, in order to attract sponsors. There seems to be a spate of sob stories, gloom and doom. Most have a germ of truth, but it can be quite depressing. Everything seems to be on some sort of Red List.

11.2.1 The morality of re-introducing species

"We are committed to reintroducing formerly native species, such as beavers, where there are clear environmental and socio-economic benefits."
   UK Department of Environment, Food and Rural Affairs spokesman February 2020.

The questions people ask are: why re-introduce a species that has become extinct? Aren't we getting along OK without them? Won't they just cause trouble?

This is where the land ethic comes in. One anthropocentric view, common with farmers, and it seems, UK government policy, is that every species should earn its right to exist. It should have some socio-economic or utilitarian value for our own human species. That's a slippery slope! What use are most of the species in nature? What use are the disabled or terminally ill? Why should our species take priority? The utilitarian argument is deeply flawed.

Another, perhaps more enlightened view, is that diversity is good, it makes ecological communities stronger and more stable. Another view is that species diversity has an intrinsic value of its own, regardless of the presence of humans. My own view extends beyond that. Having worked in many far-flung places, I appreciate that the planet is just a small globe, and all we have got. You cannot fly for more than 24 hours in any direction without finding yourself heading back to where you started. I believe that, as far as is feasible, each country or land mass should accommodate its fair share of representative species, at least those that have domiciled there since the last Ice Age. It's all very well saying 'Oh, we don't want those animals here, let them live in Siberia!'. Should we expect other nations to pick up the tab for us? How can we Brits have the sheer nerve to pontificate to the African nations on how to manage elephants if we cannot even manage to host beavers in Britain? The world is a small place. We are reaching the point where there isn't a 'somewhere else' for species that can be challenging to live with.

I was at a CITES conference in Harare in 1997. A few Western nations were trying to pressurise African nations on their trade in elephant ivory. Four of the nations: Botswana, Namibia, Zambia and Zimbabwe currently had problems with elephants outstripping their food supply. They had a surplus of 10,000 elephants. The Brits, skilled at politicking behind the scenes, had got votes backing them from countries who had no elephants or immediate interest in the issue. After the session, one of the African delegates – Botswana I think it was – came up to me in frustration. "It's all very well" he said, "but would you take them?" I had visions of 10,000 elephants being offloaded from cargo planes at Heathrow and wandering down Slough High Street. Funnily enough, this year with a debate going on over trophy hunting, they have made the same offer again, but upped the stakes to 20,000!

The truth of the matter is, not one British farmer or village could accommodate a single elephant on the loose. We are a nation of NIMBYs. (Not In My Back Yard!)

What will happen to the larger African species? How much longer will there be sufficient habitat for them to maintain their populations and ecosystems? We 'Save the Children' in Africa, and curb AIDS, we expect cash crops for our own market needs, year on year our pressure increases. And civil wars mean that troops and poachers with AK47s shoot what they like in reserves. Too many of our efforts are just palliative. We need systemic solutions, and where better to start than on our own front door step?

There is a huge literature on re-introductions, too much for this book. But shooters in the UK currently release about 53 million non-native pheasants and partridges each year, hatched from farmed eggs. These are not 're-introductions' as such because, the birds are non-native and by the following spring, virtually all of them will be dead. So the emphasis has shifted from managing habitat so as to create a sustainable harvestable surplus, to pretty much a 'put and take' scenario. At one level, is this so different from me farming sheep, putting the youngstock out to grass and then killing them? For myself, if I am shooting or hunting game, then I prefer not to kill any more than the habitat can sustain naturally, even if it means I end up giving up game shooting to devote myself to habitat management.

Conservation has become big business, with charities turning over many millions of pounds, busy virtue signalling, doom-mongering and preying on people's guilt feelings. The farming business model has been destroyed under pressure for cheap food and from shambolic government fiscal policy. Journalists rely on creating polarised views and conflict between sectors. Can we bring back, re-introduce 'wildness' or are we doomed to a purged, tamed, canned, urban, selfish future?

The IUCN has guidelines on species re-introductions aimed at deliberate, planned re-introductions of previously indigenous species. Ecologically and ethically re-introducing species that were here previously usually has positives, whereas introducing new species tends to be a risky business. Intentional or non-intentional introductions of non-native species can be devastating. The effects of Japanese Knotweed *Reynoutria japonica*, Signal Crayfish *Pacifastacus leniusculus* in the UK or Cane Toads *Rhinella marina* in Australia are obvious and intransigent. Some, such as fungal and viral diseases, are even more insidious. A high proportion of species living in Britain now are non-native, and we rely on many of them for our needs. How many of the items of food that you have eaten today are indigenous?

11.2.2 Bats conservation

There are thousands of conservation projects all over the world, but because this is a personal journey, I will outline some of the projects I have been involved with; some small, some large. There are plenty of idealists out there telling us what we should do. Talking is easy. When you come round to actually doing something, you are faced with the yawning gap between the talking shops, the theories, and reality with all its unexpected twists and turns.

When I was a teenager in the 60s we lived on the edge of the Quantock Hills in Somerset. Our old stone vicarage was in

On the pheasant farm next to us, the ex-laying pheasants are released after laying. Most are desperately feather-plucked and unable to fly. The buzzards and foxes kill them all within a few days.

a valley called Paradise. Up in the woods behind the house was a cave, called Blacky Topper's Hole. Legend had it that Blacky was a freed slave who took up residence in the cave in the 1800s. When I last visited, the site had been bull-dozed and the cave was filled in. It used to contain bats, Pipistrelles (*Pippistrellus pippistrellus*) I suppose, hanging in crevices in the roof amongst the little stalactites. Sometimes I would collect some of these bats and take them down to our house. Once there I carefully brushed little patches of paint on their elbow joints so that I could tell them apart. Then I left them hanging on the rack of antlers by my bedroom window. I could lie in bed hooting with the tawny owls: 'Ewick Ewick'….. 'Whooo…whoo-oo'. The bats would start to wriggle and wake up, and do a few circuits of the room before heading out into the woods to forage. Some days I would find them roosting back up at Blacky Topper's; other days they would be back on the antlers. We rubbed along comfortably, the bats and me.

Those days are over now. Bats are strictly protected and you need a licence just to handle one. My step-daughter, wanting to make house alterations, had to have bat surveys done (only £3,500), and there is a growing industry of bat surveyors. While this is all commendable in one way, it is soul-destroying in another. It is preservation rather than conservation, and erects barriers between us and them. Rather, we should be proactive and create bat roost and nest sites, and encourage our children to gently handle them. When we built our house here on the farm we included crevices in the soffits, and lap-boarding, which the bats love. So now we have new places for the bats and they are quick to move in. The bats take over the night shift and we have to leave windows open for them. Last year two babies were left cold on the kitchen floor. I don't know what drama had led to them being abandoned. The smaller one was tiny and soon died, but the larger one survived. First it had milk from a dropper every two hours, and as it weaned, it took meal worms, and eventually learned to fly. In real terms it was a total waste of time, but lots of people got to handle that little bat and hang him on their coat fronts. Engagement is surely better than estrangement, and I wonder how many bat boxes one could build for £3,500?

11.2.3 Northern Goshawks

When I was a zoology student at St Andrews there was an oil spill and hundreds of seabirds were washed up on the beach. There were Guillemots (*Uria aalge*), Brunnich's guillemots (*U. lomvia*), Little Auks (*Alle alle*), some divers and some Eider Ducks (*Somateria mollisima*). I rescued about 80 and cleaned them up, but only a handful survived well enough to be released. A lot of messy work and probably a waste of time, but I learned a lot, such as not many people want to help with stinky jobs, and Great Northern Divers (*Gavia immer*) can peck deep holes in your cheek. But I also flew my hawks, one of which was a young goshawk called 'Nipper', destined to join the re-introduction programme.

The Northern Goshawk, along with several other raptor species, had been exterminated in Britain by Victorian shooters. Once Nipper was hunting well I took him over to Doug Weir on Speyside for ringing and release. We hacked out young birds in Argyll (in ornithology this is called a 'soft release'), we also hard released some passage birds. These were sub-adults, trapped in Sweden. Already skilled hunters, they could be released straight out of the travelling boxes. Organised by Robert Kenward and the British Falconers' Club, it was a low-key project and very successful. Now goshawks are back all over Britain and fully protected, and despite still being killed by shooters, they are holding their own and we see them on the farm quite often, doing courtship displays in April. Now and then I think of Aldo Leopold's wolves. Goshawks are the avian wolves, shadows in the woods.

A yearling goshawk hunting at one of our beaver ponds. 2017. David Woodfall.

Sometimes I see them riding high, mobbed by an indignant crow. Occasionally I have surprised one in the act of plucking a pheasant, glaring at me for interrupting, and once a woodcock (*Scolopax rusticola*) in the willows down by the river. I collected a few primaries from the ring of feathers to use as book marks.

11.2.4 New Zealand Falcons – a gene bank

In 1974 I went to New Zealand to do a PhD on the biology of the indigenous falcon there. It is a very unusual falcon; it has short, rounded wings, a long tail and long legs. This enables it to play a dual ecological role of both a falcon and an accipiter, and because it is so sexually dimorphic (males are about 60% of the weight of females), effectively the male plays the role of a merlin and of a sparrowhawk, and the female the role of a peregrine and of a goshawk or Coopers Hawk (*Accipiter cooperii*). It nests both in the forests and in open terrain.

During my time in New Zealand we managed a farm in North Canterbury and I kept one pair of falcons there in an aviary, and another pair living free on the farm, nesting in a barrel in the trees behind the haybarn. Breeding birds of prey in captivity was then in its infancy and I had to build incubators and try out many things, corresponding with Tom Cade at Cornell who was establishing the Peregrine Fund to restore peregrines in North America. Over the next three or four decades we pioneered and developed various techniques for inseminating, incubating and rearing, until we had got the processes down pat. When I left New Zealand in 1978 I donated my breeding falcons to a couple of places in North Island and later managed to get a permit to export one of their progeny and five others from New Zealand to Britain. These six founder birds became the nucleus of our breeding colony which continues to this day on the farm in Wales.

Nowadays we keep about a dozen pairs; some are about 15th generation. We have had a number of students doing under-graduate and post-grad studies on them, and trained quite a few Kiwi students who have returned home with expertise in managing the species. Since then bureaucracy has moved into the Department of Conservation (DOC) in New Zealand. I remember, when it was the Wildlife Service, rangers would release harriers with firecrackers tied to their legs, to 'teach them a lesson'. Now the pendulum has swung full circle and doing anything with wildlife is hedged about with restrictions. (Although the DOC took protection off the harrier so that it could kill them to protect other native birds, and we argued, successfully, that if you are allowed to kill harriers you should be allowed to save them alive and train them.) So our colony of New Zealand Falcons in the UK has raised the profile of the species and had many uses. Numbers of people have been able to train them and fly them and learn about them each year. Some have done under-grad or post-grad studies on them. Managing the colony is a question of managing and documenting a gene bank, to retain genes and maximise genetic diversity. We have records on every egg, chick and parent since 1975. As Oscar Wilde said '*There is only one thing in the world worse than being talked about, and that is not being talked about'*. For wildlife, obscurity can be fatal.

11.2.5 Big falcons - offset conservation

Our other falcons on the farm are gyrfalcons, peregrines and sakers and most of the progeny are sold to the Middle East, raising enough money to keep all the non-paying wildlife work going. We also do field research on them in Asia, and there has been concern that sakers and peregrines are decreasing. Our surveys of *calidus* Peregrines in the high Arctic have shown that their populations are sustaining well, and we even saw a couple of falcons still wearing Arab string jesses nesting in the Taimyr peninsula. Numbers of wild peregrines and sakers are trapped illegally or quasi-legally in Asia to supply the Arab falconry market. Although this does not seem to be the proximal factor in the reduced range of the saker, efforts have been made to control the international trade in these species. But it is no use trying to ban something that is already illegal.

By 1985, we were breeding these species on a regular basis and started to sell them into the Middle East market in direct competition with the wild bird trade. We've bred about 6,000 falcons here, trained about 300 interns or staff and made ten 90-minute instructional films and a book. Now many breeders have set up and the UK is the biggest producer of falcons in the world, saturating the market. Of course, a farmed falcon is naive and has no idea how to hunt. It took about 15 years for the Arabs to learn how to train farmed falcons. Once trained, the domestic falcons are superior; they are usually disease-free, well adapted to captivity, of good shape and colour and moult well. Gradually they took over the market until by about 2005, 95% of the falcons in the UAE were farmed birds produced on a sustainable basis. The CMS (Convention on Migratory Species) formally accepted that breeding these falcons on farms was a sustainable form of offset conservation that could reduce the market for wild-taken birds. Kuwait, Bahrain, Qatar and the Kingdom of Saudi Arabia, are still importing significant numbers of wild birds, but they too are slowly learning how to train farmed birds, and the populations in the wild, in most places, are now holding their own.

11.2.6 Red Kites

When the kite builds, look to lesser linen.
                              The Winter's Tale.

Kites were common scavengers in Shakespeare's time and they line their nests with wool and old cloth, sometimes snatched off the washing line. But in Victorian times kites were decimated by gamekeepers and died out in England and Scotland. In 1985, the British population was down to about 25 breeding pairs in mid-Wales. Their productivity was seldom more than one chick each, and many nests were robbed by egg-collectors, despite intensive wardening, even by the Ghurkhas. We were breeding various raptors at our farm in Wales at that time, so I approached the Kite Committee and suggested that the Nature Conservation Council (as it was then) took eggs from threatened nests and replaced them with dummies, bringing the real eggs to us for

We produced a book for Russian and Kazakh customs officials to identify smuggled raptors, but most of the officials prefer to accept bribes.

Chapter 11 – THE EVOLUTIONARY TRAP   227

Baby kites and falcons.

hatching. In 1986 they visited our facility and we showed them what was possible with artificial incubation and rearing. They agreed, and in the 1987 season the first kite eggs were delivered by field-workers Tony Cross, Iolo Williams and Dee Doody. Some of the eggs were pretty filthy!

Over the next seven years we hatched or reared 53 Red Kites and all were released to the wild. The project was so successful that soon we ran out of foster nests in Wales and that led to the next stage, which was to establish them back in England and Scotland.

Various incidents occurred along the way. One year the field team, using a car wing mirror on a telescopic pole, spotted a very strange egg in the nest of a new pair. The pattern looked familiar. Tony Cross climbed up and retrieved – a tennis ball! The young female, presumably not laying herself, had brought it to the nest and started to incubate it. So Tony replaced it with a buzzard egg, which eventually hatched. Then we swapped

Peter Walters Davies MBE collects kite chicks ready to place in foster nests.

the buzzard chick with a red kite chick from us, so eventually the pair succeeded in fledging a kite chick of their own!

The general plan had been to take one egg from a clutch of two, replacing it with a dummy, so that the kites could hatch their remaining egg, then place a second chick in the nest from the egg that had been artificially incubated. We had a foster-buzzard to rear the chicks. She was an imprint called 'Beast-that-lurks'. For some reason BTL was nice to me but horrid to anyone else who so much as approached her door. She would wait on the floor to grab them if they opened it. BTL could rear twelve kite chicks a season on a roll-on roll-off basis. There were no Cain and Abel squabbles. BTL would feed all the chicks to repletion and then sit on them until next feed time. The result of this was that our chicks were fed well and grew rapidly. But when we came to return a chick to its natural parents at 3-4 weeks old, we found that the original chick was barely half the size. Our chick would have killed it. So we had to do 'musical chairs' with the chicks to get them into matching pairs.

The buzzard 'BTL' rears some kite chicks.

It was clear from this that the kites in mid-Wales were under food stress. That is why they could only rear one, poor quality chick. Often they were reduced to feeding rotten lambs' tails that had fallen off the lambs, complete with the rubber ring. Of course this would impact in the gizzard and kill the chick. Although the kites had hung on in mid-Wales, where there were no gamekeepers to kill them, the habitat was far from ideal. So it seemed better to increase their range, either from the edges, or to start again in a new area where there was more food available.

As the project became more successful, more organisations became interested. The RSPB made a film in 1990 and we hatched chicks for the film in replica nests in our lab. Did we get a free copy of the film? No, we had to buy our own for £14!

There was a bit of politics going on around this time. The iconic Red Kite had become very emblematic of Wales. The Welsh were not keen to supply kites to the English. Also, as the Welsh kites had been through a genetic bottleneck and were very in-bred, fresh blood was needed. So we cast around to see if any neighbouring countries would donate kites and as a result, a plan was made to import kites from Spain for the English releases, and from Sweden for the Scottish releases, starting in the Black Isle. Chicks bought in from the continent still had to be quarantined before release and I designed a hack (soft release) pen which could serve both purposes. When the first pen was ready on an estate near Stokenchurch I took two Welsh Kite chicks which were ready for release but had no foster nest available, in our old Cortina and put them into the release pen. So they were the first kites to fly again in England since extermination in Victorian times.

Feeding stations were set up in Wales to help kites through the winter months. At this time there was a clamp-down on dead farm stock and farmers had to remove all dead animals and incinerate them. This drastically reduced food availability for scavengers during the hard months. Nowadays the feeding stations have to use butchers' meat, which is not a balanced diet for kites and has further implications. But the kites are compensating by attending rubbish dumps!

Of course the releases in England and Scotland were spectacularly successful. With more food around, they often reared three chicks per nest. Soon these chicks were moved on to new release areas. We had kites flying all over the place and the new populations started to link up. By then there were plenty of people and organisations jumping on the band wagon, so I retired from the UK Kite Committee. The project is a success and the work was done. The kites became a multi-million pound jobs gravy train for tourism and conservationists and grads computer modelling populations. Now I can look out of my office window across the valley and sometimes see a dozen kites, not to mention buzzards, and occasionally a goshawk as well!

11.2.7 Red Squirrels

Some years ago, through our local MP, Simon Hart, we were contacted by the Cistercian monks who own 600 acre Caldey Island off the Welsh coast. Once farmed, it was now falling into desuetude and the few monks still there were getting elderly. We first arranged to rid the island of Brown Rats (*Rattus norvegicus*) by systematic poisoning over two winters. Then, through the kind offices of David Mills, we introduced captive-bred Red Squirrels (*Sciurus vulgaris*). This native British species has been decimated by competition with the introduced Grey Squirrel (*S. carolinensis*), and by disease. By putting the red squirrels onto an island, the whole population is essentially in perpetual quarantine and away from grey squirrels. Because the island is privately owned, we hadn't released the squirrels out into 'the wild'. So we didn't need all sorts of permits, which would have stymied the whole operation and kicked it into the long grass.

There are only about 60 acres of mature woodland on the island but the squirrels use the feeders and act as ambassadors to teach visitors about the dire straits of the species. Our initial introduction of ten squirrels by their second season reached about thirty and now the population is too big to monitor. Meanwhile, with rats gone, the seabirds, once confined to the precarious massive cliffs, are beginning to nest on the open grazed areas above the cliffs. A handful of Atlantic Puffins (*Fratercula arctica*) have returned and maybe one day Manx

Captive-bred red squirrel.

Making release pens for the squirrels.

Shearwaters (*Puffinus puffinus*) will take up residence again. The old fields are probably the best place for Skylarks (*Alauda arvensis*) in the whole of Pembrokeshire.

The disastrous effects of introduced mammals on island fauna, and thus flora, are well-known. But eradication of rats, rabbits, cats and so on have created some encouraging turn-arounds, such as at Round Island, off Mauritius.

11.2.8 Brown Hairstreak Butterflies

Often conservation is not about re-introductions, but about looking after what you have already got. Part of the farm when we took it on was becoming over-run with self-sown blackthorn, the food plant of the Brown Hairstreak Butterfly (*Thecla betulae*), which is in decline. The Butterfly Study Group counted the eggs every year and marked each egg branch with a coloured clothes peg. They wanted us to retain the blackthorn below two metres, because that is the preferred height for egg-laying and we fenced off areas as reserves. But later, another expert told us the butterflies lay eggs all over blackthorns and that two metres is just the height of the people searching for them! After some years the group stopped coming; they said they were unable to recruit young people to come and do the work.

We manage the blackthorn to keep it regenerating. It looks a mess, but we are the best farm in Wales for Brown Hairstreaks. They are just a small brown innocuous looking little butterfly that you would hardly notice if you saw one. Does it matter if they go, or is this death by a thousand cuts? I have to admit that I'm not sure if I have ever seen one. They are all little brown fluttery things to me…

Brown Hairstreak. Mike Clarke.

11.2.9 Water Voles

In reaction to the rather nasty trapping methods for wild American Mink (*Neovison vison*) for fur coats, people started farming them. Then Animal Rights activists raided the farms and let the mink out. They were never prosecuted and mink rapidly spread and are now endemic in the UK.

The mink partially filled the niche left by Otters (*Lutra lutra*). Otters were once common and I remember going out with the Otterhounds in Somerset as a teenager. Stalwart ladies in blue serge skirts waded with their notched otter poles. But, as a top predator, the otter crashed along with many raptors owing to ecosystemic poisoning by pesticides in Rachel Carson's *Silent Spring*. Suddenly the otter, once hunted as a pest, became rare, was protected and became an icon. In *The Wind in the Willows*, Otter and his son Portly were good friends of the hero Ratty, the water vole. In a rapid switch of public image, the otter suddenly became The Good Guy. Practically nobody ever saw otters so Henry Williamson's portrayal of Tarka captured the public imagination, just as anything invisible does.

The mink, being smaller than otters, could catch water voles in their tunnels. So, as the mink spread, the water voles became locally extinct. We trapped or shot as many mink as we could, or called out the mink hounds, but it was an uphill battle. They move around so much and pop up unexpectedly.

When we thought we had got our thumb in the eye of the mink we tried releasing water voles on our lake. Derek Gow brought us about 90 and we slowly released them from cages in the reed beds. All went well for about three years until our neighbour who had a pheasant and duck shoot, released about two thousand mallard. They soon quit his shot-over flight ponds and took up residence on our lake. Over the winter they denuded most of the banks almost to mud, leaving the water voles completely exposed and without food. It was the beginning of the end for them and they failed to maintain a minimum viable population and faded away.

Meanwhile otters recovered and the mink seemed to disappear in the face of bigger competition. I tried stocking the lake with trout, but you are not allowed to stock with native brown trout. Your licence is for triploid sterile rainbow trout. So you cannot create a self-sustaining fish population. Once the otters returned, with the help of a local lad poaching with night-lines, the fish were stripped out completely. No broods of wild ducks survived long enough to fly.

But Greylag geese numbers were recovering in the UK, and some started to colonise the lake. Invasive alien Canada Geese had the same idea and every spring the lake is a cacophony of geese battling it out for nest sites. If we are lucky, the otters may not come. In those years we are faced with a plethora of young 'Cannies' all set to take over the world. I don't like to shoot them so sometimes I ask someone else to do it. But if a mother otter with a couple of young ones shows up, everything on the lake is decimated. They hunt assiduously through the reeds and the open water. Once, at silage time, some herring gulls were on the lake having a wash and brush up. An otter came up underneath like a shark and pulled one under, re-surfacing at the shoreline and heading away into the bushes. No more skinny-dipping for me! Definitely a swim suit! Even adult geese were not immune and we caught them on camera dragging away greylags caught on their nests at night. Otters travel widely. I caught two at once in a beaver box trap, and we have picked up several killed on the roads.

While there are lots of laws protecting wildlife, few people realise that one can breed wildlife for re-introduction and

A Water Vole ready for release. Jo Oliver.

An otter takes a greylag off the lake.

It can't drag the goose through the fence so buzzards and scavengers eat the rest.

The otters are quite curious.

restoration programmes. In 2014, 8km of a river in Somerset, England needed dredging and the Environment Agency decided that the water voles had to be removed and translocated first. It cost £135,000 to trap and translocate 55 water voles. That's £2,454 per vole! Yet we can breed them in pens on the farm for a few pounds each. This is a silly misuse of funds. By moving the emphasis from extreme protection to production we could have produced about 13,500 water

Cars are probably the biggest cause of death in British otters. This dog otter was hit at the top of our track.

A cut-bank of our river with old water vole tunnels revealed.

voles on this budget, enough to re-stock dozens of waterways.

But doing a single species project is not as simple as it sounds if you can't get the habitat right. All that are left here of the original population are the old vole tunnels in the riverbanks, mute messages from the past, revealed as the river chisels away at the banksides.

11.2.10 Houbara

I'm including this example of how conservation doesn't necessarily entail working with real animals on the ground. It can equally be about moving the goal posts. The Asian or MacQueen's bustard or Houbara (*Chlamydotis macqueenii*) breeds on the steppes of Kazakhstan, Mongolia, China and Iran and migrates each autumn south, around the Himalayas, through the Arabian Peninsula to Africa. Traditionally the Arabs hunted it with falcons in the winter. There is also the North African houbara (*Chlamydotis undulata undulata*) which is non-migratory, and a small population in the Canaries (*C. u. fuertaventurae*).

When oil was discovered in the Arabian Gulf, Western nations bought the Arab oil for their own energy needs, which meant that the impoverished Arabs suddenly went from rags to riches. With new water bowser trucks they could now access the deep deserts with their flocks and herds and hammer the vegetation. Thus the habitat that wintering and nesting houbara relied on was grazed out and could no longer sustain them. So the Arabs were forced to hunt elsewhere and now could afford to. They rented hunting areas in Pakistan, Kazakhstan, Uzbekistan, Morocco, Libya, Algeria and others from local rulers, tribal leaders and politicians. Those who couldn't afford it went to Azerbaijan to hunt Little Bustards (*Tetrax tetrax*). Local Pakistanis, seeing how much the Arabs would pay to hunt houbara, started trapping resident and migrating houbara and smuggling them into the Gulf to sell to the Arabs for training their falcons. Huddled in boxes in dhows meant that often 90% died in each consignment.

Meanwhile, political unrest and increased human pressure meant that huge areas of nesting and wintering habitat were

Smuggled houbara that have died in transit. Tom Bailey.

We produced a book in English and Arabic covering conservation for sustainable hunting.

being lost. So it was a perfect storm for the houbara and the outlook was grim. In 1989 Mohammed Al Bowardi and Crown Prince Mohammed Bin Zayed established the National Avian Research Centre in Abu Dhabi with two main goals: to create sustainable supplies of falcons and houbara. My role was to lead the falcon work and within twenty years we reached the point where 98% of the falcons used in the UAE were captive bred. But for houbara the road was not so easy. With persistence, progress was made bit by bit and by 2018 about 53,000 houbara were bred in captivity in various projects. These were used to supplement or restore local populations and to produce a surplus for hunting. On paper, a success story. But to put captive-bred houbara back out into the wild requires first suitable areas of habitat, second the young houbara had to learn to survive in the wild and to migrate, and they had to learn to fly strongly to escape predators. Third, the Arabs had to learn to regulate their own hunting behaviour to a sustainable level; a significant cultural shift.

Why not just ban the hunting? And stop buying oil from the Arabs? And stop using our cars and planes? Hmm. Funny that. Westerners still want to import oil! And if you banned hunting, what incentive would there be for Arabs to pour resources into reviving desert habitats? And how would you enforce such a ban when you don't rule their countries? Conservation is a tangled web.

I was on the Houbara Committee from the start and followed developments for many years. It was a complicated ecological, sociological, avicultural, economic and political scenario. Facile quick-fixes were doomed to failure. Slowly – painfully – the houbara situation improved and there was

Helen feeds mealworms to an imprinted male houbara.

Hunting desert hares.

a gradual cultural change on the part of the Arabs. But effectively, for most Arab falconers, what they regarded as their cultural birth-right – houbara hawking – was no longer available. Hunting is now theoretically illegal over most of the Arabian peninsula. Falconers turned to competing their falcons in timed races to the lure. But they still dreamed of hawking houbara and they would pay large sums for farmed houbara to train their falcons, even though they might only go on a short hunting trip once a year.

So we developed robotic prey birds that could be caught by falcons and also used for competitions as a substitute for real houbara. Using these required developing more skills to pilot the plane, and this is where we are now. Each year more people are using the robotic prey and we have recently developed a flying ground near Swindon, UK where we hold 'Hunt Races' each year, with falcons flying artificial prey. The next step is to establish Hunt Racing in the Middle East as a divergence from hunting real houbara. We are making some progress but it is a big cultural shift for them and entails developing new skills. In 2022 we took the top five British teams to race in Saudi. So bit by bit we address conservation and welfare issues, not necessarily by direct confrontation and polarisation, but by seeking viable alternatives and gently steering things towards sustainability. One of the problems is that the young people now spend more time on social media and have less interest in falcons, the desert and their cultural heritage. Who cares if the desert becomes a total wasteland, raped of vegetation, with fossil water all gone? Complicated.

We built a factory and warehouse for making robotic birds.

Painting heads and wings.

A happy customer.

We organise annual Hunt Racing competitions at Vowley in Wiltshire, forming the British Falcon Racing Association.

11.3 Habitats and a land ethic

Young men cut down trees.
Old men plant them.

11.3.1 Deciding a baseline

Going up a level, from species conservation to habitats, when we look at the land, what baseline should we take for our conservation efforts? Should we try to restore the land to how it was when we were children? Or a century ago? Or just after the last Ice Age? Is it actually practicable, given all the pressures on land nowadays? Do we somehow envisage a Garden of Eden where everything was perfect and wonderful? What species were there then? As the ice sheets melted back, Britain had a long period of slow colonisation. Plants arrived and soil built up creating habitats for other trophic levels. The land bridge to Europe was still open so mammals could walk across. Then, about 8,500 years ago, the sea submerged the land bridge and the ecological front door was closed. Beavers had made it across in time, but they didn't make it to Ireland, which was already separated. Fresh birds could still colonise, and some plant seeds, but otherwise that was it. That was the whole cast of our little ecological play, and we call these actors 'natives' or 'indigenous'. Is this what we should aim for, that little cast of actors?

Over the next eight millennia birds accidentally brought in more plant seeds, and more bird species flew in. Humans killed off some of the larger mammals, but introduced new species from Europe. Soon you couldn't easily tell what was indigenous, what was self-introduced, and what was introduced by humans. Does it really matter? In the last millennium or two, humans selectively bred some plants and animals for food and created domesticated strains.

Large areas of fertile land were modified for agriculture and creatures that relied on wild habitats were pushed back. The Victorians exterminated several predator species to preserve game and at the same time, adventuring botanists brought back plants from all corners of the globe.

11.3.2 Shared resources

In earlier days, the family or tribe had to go and hunt for live animals, or search for and forage plant material. There are energy constraints to consider: how far would you go to eat an apple? Are you prepared to go into the kitchen and fetch one? Are you prepared to climb an apple tree in the garden? Are you prepared to steal one from somebody else's orchard? Would you walk a mile to a shop to buy one? How hungry are you? Are there alternative foods available? What are the chances that you would not find an apple after all the effort you have made to get one? Would you be prepared to defend the apple tree in the garden against intruders trying to steal your apples? Would you defend all the apple trees in a five mile radius? Who would you share your apples with? Animals, including humans, are making these decisions all the time.

If you are prepared to defend the apple tree in your garden, then you regard the tree as part of your territory. A territory is by definition a defended space or resource. Maybe you have an apple farm and defend the whole farm against intruders. But there is a limit to how much you can defend. If you tried to defend every apple tree within a five mile radius, you would spend your whole time patrolling until you were exhausted, and you would not have the time or energy for anything else. So most animals have a relatively small territory, and then a much larger area in which they often go and forage, called a 'home range'. Some animals don't have a territory at all, they just have a personal space.

Your territory can be selective in that you might defend it against one type of intruder but not another. You might chase away a parakeet from the apple tree in your garden because it might eat the budding apples. But you might welcome a hawk in the tree because it might deter the parakeets. Or you could side-step the hawk and defend the tree with a plastic owl.

When you go outside your territory into your home range, or even beyond your normally frequented areas, hunting for food or water, you may come across others doing the same thing. You may have a temporary argument over some particularly juicy apples you've both discovered. But at the end of the day you are both sharing the same resource and there is no senior person to share it out fairly. Might is right and you get what you can. These shared resources are called 'the commons'.

It's 1984. I'm sitting in a green womb, a tent hung in a tree in the Black River Gorges of Mauritius. It's pouring with rain and I huddle on a branch that seems to get harder and knobblier with every hour that passes. Only my arm extends outside the nylon canopy, holding a yaggi antenna with which I'm scanning for radio transmissions. I'm tracking and doing time budgets for some of the last wild Mauritius kestrels which live in these forest remnants. Above the silence of the headphones I begin to hear a cacophony of shrieks and yells. Is it the ganja growers? The noise gets louder; there must be dozens of them! Timidly I peer out through a slit in the tent. Then I see them. Twenty or thirty macaque monkeys have arrived at a nearby wild mango tree. Belligerently they set about the tree which is festooned with green mangos. Like vandals they rip off each fruit, take a bite and, finding it sour, fling it to the ground in disgust. After twenty minutes the tree has been thoroughly pillaged yet none of the monkeys has swallowed a bite to eat. The ground below is littered with mangos that now will never ripen. The troupe start to lose interest in the tree and begin to wander away back into the forest, leaving me to my faint bleep-bleeps and contemplating the competitive use of resources shared in common.

Resources held in common are particularly difficult to manage. It may be difficult to find out who has 'commoners' rights', and indeed if humans are the only species sharing the resource or whether other animals also use it. The core problem is, that because all users have unfettered use, then the resource may be exploited to the point of exhaustion. In the case of fisheries, the fishermen with the biggest, most efficient, far-ranging factory ships will scoop up the majority of the fish. Smaller local fishermen go out of business, and competing predator species such as sharks, or whales, become endangered. Without constraints, the resource is harvested beyond its sustainable capacity and it goes into a decline. The resource species may go extinct. Or the harvest may become uneconomical and the fishermen go bust, enabling stocks to recover in a painful cycle of boom and bust.

In the case of a river, users upstream get first chance to use it. They may over-harvest fish stocks or spawning grounds, they may extract too much water, or they may pollute the river. Users downstream must be content with what they get. A similar situation pertains to migratory animals as a resource. Arguments can flare into wars between neighbours.

Similar scenarios are played out all over the world, on the steppes of Mongolia, the desertification of the Middle East and Africa, and the slash and burn farming of the tropical belt. Unless the management of the common resources is taken under a single control (albeit of groups, farm clusters or syndicates of people or nations) so that they can be managed sustainably, then they are doomed. Ethotypic values start to fade out above the tribal level so when a resource is accessed by groups larger than the tribe then there is no ethical controlling mechanism. Formalised legal structures are the only hope then to control human use of common resources.

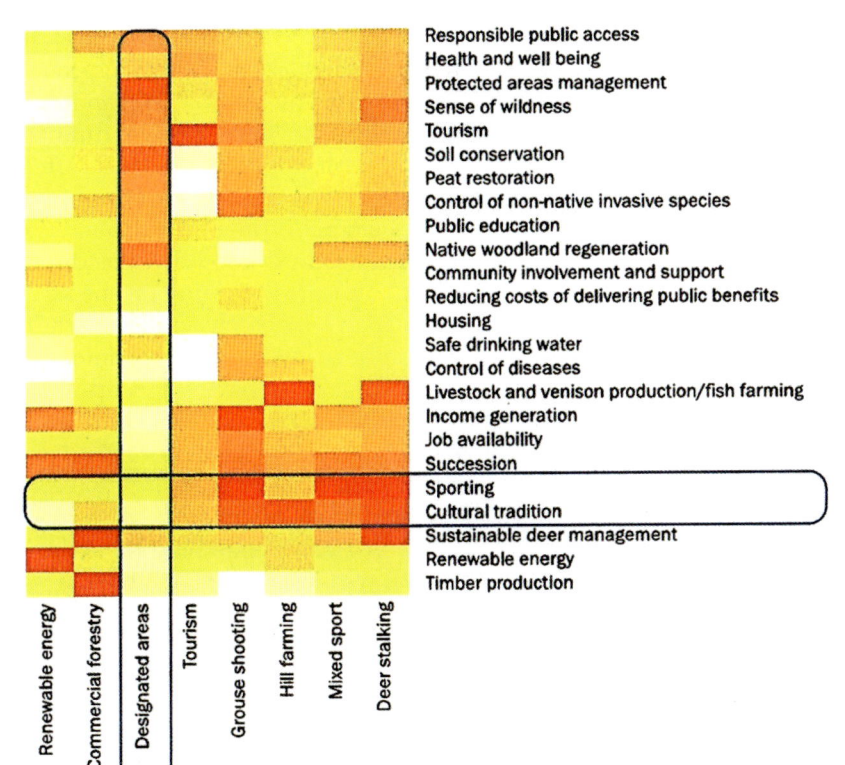

A typical example is the Wildlife Management and Muirburn (Scotland) Bill currently being debated in the Scottish Parliament. It is based on the Independent Review of Grouse Moor Management 2019, widely known as the 'Werritty Report'. The Scottish National Party formed a coalition with the Green Party which motivated this Bill. Persecution of raptors by grouse moor keepers and the creation of patchy habitat by heather burning and regeneration led the Greens to this opinion. But of course it is all much more nuanced than these often simplistic political debates. Ros Bryce, Althea Davies and Steve Redpath from the James Hutton Institute undertook a survey of land managers from the Central Highlands and did a cluster analysis relating the various forms of land management such as commercial forestry, grouse moors, hill farming and so on, with priorities such as public access, protected areas, income generation and sporting interests. Their results show how landscape scale use is complex and there is no 'one size fits all'. The white cells indicate little or no relevance whereas the red cells show a strong correlation.

11.3.3 Managing resources

Shared resources are difficult, but there are some commons that we all use, and we could each of us do something to ameliorate the situation. We all use water. We all use energy. We all breathe air.

When I lived in New Zealand, we collected our water from the roof. Our average annual rainfall is 1200mm and our water tanks hold 10,000 litres. This is enough for all our needs including washing, showers and a flushing toilet. Similar amounts of rain fall in many temperate countries, including Britain. Why then cannot all houses collect their rainwater and at least use it for their grey water needs?

This effectively is like having thousands of beaver dams all over the country, holding back water during heavy rainfall and releasing it gradually, reducing peak flows and reducing downstream flooding. Storm water does not have to be a run-off problem, instead it can be an asset, reducing our demand for mains water and preventing depletion of rivers. As it is, in Britain we use drinking water to flush the toilet and then wonder why we are running out!

Renewable energy has been headlining in recent years, and we have investigated how best to approach this for our farm in Wales. Although we have plenty of wood, burning it emits carbon into the atmosphere creating a greenhouse effect and polluting the air. It is also very labour intensive, even with biomass boilers. Therefore we just keep a small wood burner in the house for top up winter heat. The effects of wood smoke on health are indisputably bad and in densely inhabited areas causes respiratory illnesses, not to mention the release of carbon dioxide and other gases into the atmosphere. But what are the alternatives? Fossil fuels such as coal, oil and gas also create pollution, while being unsustainable. Looking at our carbon budget on the farm: firewood is recycling carbon and is carbon neutral whereas fossil fuels release carbon from locked stores in the ground. They also require mining, transporting and processing whereas our firewood stays here on the farm. We use only hardwood and season it in the shed for two years or more so that we get a clean burn. Our chimneys were clean even after 20 years without sweeping.

Our main heating is geothermal, either with underfloor heating when we have put in new floors, or using the old system of radiators. Together with effective insulation, the energy demand and supply is quite low, but it still takes electricity to pump the water round; more than we expected.

For electricity, we avoid wind turbines because they kill a lot of birds (we have had raptors killed in them), they have a lot of mechanical parts that wear out, and they are noisy and unsightly. We looked at hydroelectricity from the lake where we have a head of about 12 metres, but the potential power output was disappointing, so we opted for solar panels. We have a 30 kw unit, a 15 kw and a 12 kw, on three buildings, two of which are agricultural buildings with big south facing roofs. Surely the time will come when solar panels are integral roof cladding structures, and when architects will design buildings with sun-facing roofs and walls that generate electricity? We also use passive solar in some of the houses. In the old farmhouse, which suffered from damp for years, we tried everything. We removed chimneys, improved damp-proof courses and windows. Nothing really worked. Eventually, in despair, I covered the offending south facing wall with black plastic. Onto this I placed wooden battens in chevron patterns pointing to 10cm holes drilled through the thick stone walls. Onto these battens I attached panels of triple skinned clear polycarbonate with a gap along the bottom. When the sun shines it heats up the air in the 2.5 cm gap between the polycarbonate and the black plastic. Cold air is sucked in at the bottom, heats up and is guided through the holes into the rooms. I admit it is not my aesthetic dream, but as a passive heating system it works splendidly, and surely more elegant commercial cladding designs could be incorporated into new builds?

Well-seasoned hardwood.

For transport, we still use petrol and diesel. Sadly, the days when I could ride a horse into college are now over. But designs for electric vehicles and quad bikes are improving and I think the day is drawing close when at least some of our vehicles can be plugged into the solar panels. Some people seem to be under the impression that by switching from petrol to electric cars, they are somehow avoiding carbon emissions. But where is the electricity coming from? We need to push on to the point that most householders generate their own electricity needs by both creating electricity and reducing their demand, by using more efficient equipment.

For me, travel has been the most difficult issue because I have had to fly all over the world running conservation projects. We now use online meetings to reduce the need of physically transporting bodies around the planet and this is working better, but you still have to meet face to face now and then.

The ethic we are trying to reach is that, as far as possible, each family measures and understands its own resource needs, such as water, energy and electricity, and is responsible for being self-sufficient. Just by being aware of your own usage, you begin to appreciate the load that we are collectively putting on the planet. Instead of trying to foist it onto some anonymous body – the 'Council' or the 'State' – we take responsibility for it ourselves. This doesn't need to be totally fanatical; but it does need to be systemic, mainstream and fully researched and commercially designed. A level 2 priority needs to be addressed by level 5, individuals. By doing this, our ethotypic morality is able to function, even though the problem is beyond the tribal level.

Many people, such as Donald Broom, maintain that because plants or habitats are not sentient and cannot feel pain, then they are not on our moral radar. Again, I think differently. If you confine welfare to unpleasant experiences such as suffering pain or stress, you've missed the point of what welfare is all about. Plants and habitats, whole ecosystems can be in a poor welfare status. They may not be sentient, but they are alive and can be in bad condition. Even life itself need not be a criterion for welfare. If you pollute or poison a body of water, you have reduced its well-being and possibly denied some life forms the opportunity to live there as natural habitat. While non-sentient or even non-living systems cannot themselves have an intrinsic system of morals, this does not lessen or remove our own moral responsibility towards them. If you've ever created a wood, or dug a lake, as I have, you quickly feel a moral responsibility towards it, and by extension all lakes and woods around the world, and all ecosystems. What is an individual anyway, other than a grammatical construct? You can think of a whole lake with all its inhabitants as an individual, just as I can think of you as an individual whereas in reality, you exist commensally with millions of other creatures, your biome.

This level of moral responsibility is not ethotypic, it is learned at an intellectual level. The 'noble savages' did not necessarily cherish habitats. Rather they exploited them for all they were worth, but their impact was not too devastating because their numbers were low. Because of this, many people do not feel this moral burden and certainly do not prioritise it over more immediate concerns.

Conservation should be about maintaining high levels of biodiversity, which is the sign of a healthy habitat. Biodiversity is not just about species diversity, but the structural diversity of habitats and the range of trophic levels. It's not about encouraging the biggest population of any one species but ensuring that each is in balance with the habitat and the resources.

The concept of reserves is a great idea. Everyone should have one. But there can never be enough reserves to maintain all species. Reserves and protected areas are fragile and at the mercy of political whim and expediency. Some are just maintained as an excuse for massacring everywhere else, an offset arrangement, a carbon trade-off. Often they are unable to connect with one another so that populations become genetically isolated. And it is not just big iconic species. In Britain the landscape has been sliced into compartments by motorways, railways and canals. The landscape has been turned over to arable, leaving only small woods and copses as isolated pockets of habitat. Reptiles and small mammals hang on there but drop below their minimum viable population (MVP) levels. Traffic kills the unwary. Cats, uncontrolled by natural constraints, predate the last few individuals. One by one each pocket becomes barren, like lights going off at night. This is how extinction works, insidiously, barely noticed. The baseline has shifted. Before you know it, the species is declared endangered and all sorts of controls are slapped on it. It becomes illegal to attempt any management. But the controls fail to address the actual roots of the problem and the declines continue. We've lost 75% of our insect biomass in the last 30 years and nobody even has a clue how it has happened, let alone what to do about it. How can we reconcile farming with maintaining wildlife habitats?

Land ownership, or lack of it, is part of the problem. Probably the best option is large scale benign private ownership, followed by benign and enlightened state ownership. The worst situation is the 'commons'. The 'commons' consist of two main types: areas of land or water that contain a shared resource, and resources that are shared, but move, such as migratory birds, mammals, fish or rivers. And of course there are 'commons' that include both elements. First described as the 'tragedy of the commons' by Garrett Hardin, shared resources only work when they are not under pressure. Once the resources approach exhaustion the whole system, tragically, collapses. If a resource is controlled by an individual or a limited group of individuals, perhaps a type of syndicate, then its use can be regulated in order to maintain sustainability. This is described by Elinor Ostrom in her eight 'core design principles' in *Governing the Commons*. These principles can overcome the tragedy of the commons when applied by group-acting humans who prefer a bottom-up administration run by themselves rather than a top-down control. In Britain we are developing 'Farm Clusters'. Such groups may put the productivity of the resource ahead of their own immediate interests, or even create a new resource altogether. On the other hand, as we find in the extensive common grazing lands in Wales, the communal management may be sufficient to prevent user arguments by providing 'grazing rights', but does nothing to improve the capacity of the resource itself, so that it gradually deteriorates. Wales still has significant areas of common grazing. It tends to be all take and no give. Little or no fertiliser is applied to common land. Instead, each adjacent farm has a fixed legal quota of stock allowed to graze. These may have been sustainable in times gone by, but gradually the land has been depleted, so that the original stocking rates are no longer sustainable, and the land has become exhausted. Heather and natural grasses are burned off to create a short burst of fertility and a grassy sward, until in the end the land becomes a green desert with a few uneconomic hardy mountain sheep. The fertility and organic matter built up over thousands of years has gone in a few hundred. This has been propped up by a farm subsidy system that has exacerbated the situation and dragged it on for longer. Locally we have moors that sixty years ago had good numbers of grouse and hares, now destitute and home only to foxes and crows.

When the resource is open to all comers, then the ethos is 'first come, first served'. This is what a 'commons' is: a resource open to all comers, and this is how most non-humans treat it too, sometimes resulting in a 'boom and bust' scenario. Territorial

Using only camels there is a limit on how much ground we can hunt in a day.

behaviour is a way of overcoming the commons tragedy and works usually at the small group level. Packs of African Wild Dogs *Lycaon pictus* will defend extensive group hunting territories. Others, especial herbivores, overcome this by becoming nomadic. Herds of American bison and elk, and African ungulates on the savannah, are constantly on the move to fresh pastures. They themselves then become a common resource for their predators.

Predators that rely on nomadic prey are often themselves nomadic. Bedouin in the Arabian peninsula are ardent nomadic hunters. They will hunt all day long and totally ruthlessly. Their ethic is: 'If we don't kill it today it will be gone tomorrow and someone else will get it'. So strong is their hunting drive that it is firmly embedded in their ethotype. It is hugely difficult to get them to take on board the principle of sustainable use, and can you blame them? Unless every last Arab follows the principle, then none will. That is the tragedy of the commons.

We've tried ways around this problem. At the International Festival of Falconry in Abu Dhabi in 2011 I persuaded the government to let us use a fenced off area as a 'managed hunting area'. It was only small, about 8 x 4 km, but had been fenced against camels for about 15 years and some desert plants were re-colonising. They put out some captive-bred houbara and hares. I insisted that no cars or guns should be allowed and that hawking should only be done on foot, horse or camel. This gave a natural limit on the amount of ground that could be covered each day. It worked, everybody had some hawking and there was game left behind. In 2014, at the next festival, I was offered a larger patch, about 25 x 20 km, and we did the same, hunting with 80 camels. But, once the festival was over, the Arabs didn't want to use camels, they wanted to use their 4x4s. With cars you can clean out such a small area in a morning. So then they hired out the ground to hunters and released captive-bred houbaras immediately before the hunting commenced. Of course, with no experience of living in the wild, these naive houbara were totally bewildered with the whole thing and many were mopped up without even attempting to fly away. The reserve organisers had reduced the activity to the level of individual animals, level 5. They made little attempt to manage at level 4, with species management, (the houbara itself is a migratory resource), let alone at level 3, by managing the habitat. And they were worried about poaching because even their own people would not follow the rules. And so a system that could have resulted in improved habitat benefitting many species, is reduced to hunting animals out of cardboard boxes, because the hunters could not use their intellect to overcome their ethotype, and because of the tragedy of the commons.

It is easy for us Westerners to say 'Do this, do that, and do the other, and bingo, everything will be marvellous', but in reality, when we are faced with our own human nature, it can be so hard to change.

Shared commons was the original form of land use by humans when our ancestors relied on hunting. Some cultures moved from place to place to exploit seasonally abundant food sources, often returning to shore-lines to eat seafood as a reliable back up. At low densities, this worked for thousands of years. There were no doubt territorial disputes and tribal warfare, and in some cases, such as the Polynesians in New Zealand, some flightless species were driven to extinction. Problems mainly arose when people settled down and started farming. There was no point in growing a crop if anyone could just come along and eat it. So such crop lands became controlled territories in private or feudal ownership.

Although we often profess to revere primitive and indigenous minority peoples and their cultures, possibly from a liberal sense of caring for the vulnerable, we are only comfortable as long as they remain weak. I wondered why the USA, Canada, the UK, Australia and New Zealand haven't signed the UNESCO Intangible Cultural Heritage Convention and wrote to the UK and NZ Ministers for Culture. Neither gave me a convincing reason for not signing. Could it be that these countries which all have indigenous peoples did not want to give prominence to their cultures over and above their own ethnocentric white Western predominancy? This year, the UK has just signed up to the Convention. Amongst the ICH it wants to support are things such as the Notting Hill Carnival, an event started in my lifetime and celebrating multi-cultural and recent gender-based issues.

Richard White in *Are you an environmentalist or do you work for a living?* contrasted the attitudes of some environmentalists who come across as arrogant, idealistic and disconnected with those of 'peasant' farmers who, although working and living on the land, are seen as environmental desecrators. Being myself both a farmer and an environmentalist I see both sides of this coin. I am Farmer Jekyll and Conservationist Hyde. For sure, there are many farmers whose firm priorities are making income from the land rather than understanding or caring for the environment. In Wales, 86% of farms are loss-making and only survive on state grants so there is little scope for the luxury that is conservation. Having invested their time and money in the land, perhaps for generations, they naturally resent environmentalists telling them what to do. As an environmentalist it is easy to be simplistic and idealistic, after all, the answers are so obvious… or are they?

In the Western world it has recently become fashionable to demonise farmers for pumping out methane and carbon, for being horrid to animals, or if these are not enough, for being rich land-owners. Environmentalists such as Guy Shrubsole and Nick Hayes advocate for public ownership of land, and a common Right to Roam as a panacea. Having worked on conservation projects in some communist countries, and seen the devastation, waste and stupidity, I can't support that one. As Wendell Berry in *The World-Ending Fire* (p 51) points out, public administrators cannot manage land with the care and skills that local owners with a stake in it can.

Perhaps farms should all be abolished and planted in trees! We have entered Richard Bulliet's (*Hunters, herders, and hamburgers*) 'post-domestication' era and are pledging ourselves to the quasi-religion of veganism! We should switch from dairy products to monocultures of soya and almond milk until biotechnology saves us all and creates abundant food in the labs from algae.

It reminds me of when we were promised that nuclear power would solve all our energy needs. I pondered all this as I walked past Hyde Park in London, the crawling jammed traffic, heedless walkers, mindless displays of wealth, churning out noise, filth and noxious gases yet unable to go without food from farmers for more than a day. Is this what we should aspire to? A report, *Consumption-based GHG emissions of C40 cities*, examined the greenhouse gas emissions associated with goods and services consumed by residents of 79 cities, including food, clothing, electronic equipment, air travel, delivery trucks, and construction industries and concluded that cities produce at least 70% of the world's carbon dioxide emissions. Attempts are being made to 'green' cities and farm locally and so on, they are brave efforts but tiny in the broader scheme of things. It needs much more radical thinking, such as heavily taxing commuting, to encourage people to work near home and communicate electronically rather than having this tidal flow of human bodies every day.

11.3.4 Managing a habitat

This talk about baselines and resources is all very well, but a bit theoretical. To achieve anything in real life at habitat level, first you need to own it or at least be able to control it long term. Having been born into this world with no money, the first thing I had to do was make some. Then, whenever I had any spare, I bought land. I started with seven acres and a massive mortgage, but gradually bought three neighbouring farms and built it up to about 280 acres.

Many of our neighbours in Wales regard anything that is not good farmland as 'trash'. One neighbour, who owns a five acre wood, has only been in it twice, despite now being in his fifties. The bramble beds (*Rubus sp*) on the banks, and willows (*Salix sp*) and alders (*Alnus glutinosa*) along the river – all 'trash'. Even the standard trees in the hedgerows need to go; they impede the work of the hedge-trimmer. For these farmers, the only land worth considering is productive farmland, usually grass fields. Leopold on the other hand, went to the other extreme and took an abandoned farm and nursed it through successions back towards climax woodlands. Charlie Burrell is experimenting with a similar approach on a larger scale at Knepp in England.

To my neighbours in Wales, I say 'What about the wildlife?' and to Leopold and Charlie Burrell I say: 'Where is the human food to be grown?' Both approaches have validity but I don't think I'm prepared to devote everything to wildlife and expect other lands to bear the brunt of feeding me. So our challenge is: how to both host wildlife and grow food all on the same farm? It can lead to some uneasy conflicts of interest. And you can't just do what you want; there are plenty of officials with their clipboards, aerial photos and lists of 'compliances' queuing up to tell you all the things you are not allowed to do, and accountants who delight in telling you grim financial news.

One approach is to partition the land. Keep certain bits just for agriculture and other bits just for wildlife. We are doing this on some parts of the farm. Another approach is to have some low-pressure type farming which allows room for wildlife. We do some of this too, by maintaining rough grasslands that support a good variety of flora and fauna while being grazed by sheep or horses in the autumn and winter when many species are dormant.

Old grassland is not easy to manage. Bracken or brambles quickly encroach.

So our first step is to sit down with a map of the farm, walk the land, look at the soil, note the aspect, the drainage, the prevailing winds, and of course the existing land use. Can we create woodland strips that run north-south, acting as windbreaks against the westerlies but not obstructing the sun from the south? Could they link up to form wildlife corridors? How wide do they need to be to provide a good height against the wind, but not hollow and cold underneath? A good shelterbelt can ease the wind for five times its height out in the field, and with the sun on it too, the increased growth from the microclimate can almost compensate for the production from the lost land area.

How are we going to keep the livestock out? We will need a good stock fence. Because of the restrictions on timber treatments the local fence posts will rot out in a dozen years. Should we use pressure-treated imported Baltic pine that will last twice as long? If we cleave our own oak, how will they compare to bought posts, and what will our labour costs be?

What mixture of trees and shrubs should we plant? Can we choose species that will provide food and cover for wildlife all the year round and not be as bald as a coot in winter? Should we buy in trees or grow our own from seeds we have collected? How many changes of pot will each tree need before we are ready to plant it out? If we buy in trees, will they be of local provenance and suitable for these growing conditions? How tall should the seedlings be to out-grow competition? Should we spray around them for the first couple of years to stop them being smothered? What chemical should we use, or not? What about rabbits? Can we keep on top of them just by shooting and hunting them, or do we need to put a guard round each tree? Planting grants demand rabbit guards, even when there are no rabbits. Can we afford biodegradable guards or will we use plastic ones? How to stop the squirrels decimating the trees? What time of year should we plant and will the ground be frozen solid then?

While the commercial foresters want same age softwoods planted in rows to encourage straight timber and allow clear-felling, if we are creating new permanent mixed deciduous woodland, our aims are different. Take a look at some of the new woods in Britain. The species mix comes from a catalogue and even when 'indigenous' (whatever that means), they don't match the self-sown local woods. The trees are of the same age. The ground flora and soil are poorly developed, and worst of all, they are planted in rows. This may be economical for getting young trees established, but it destroys all sense of wildness or spirituality of the wood. For ever after, it is condemned to appear artificial.

Oh dear! So many decisions, and that's just for a simple shelterbelt.

While we are pondering over some of those decisions, let's step back for a moment and take a wider perspective. When we are working at level 3, we need to consider the three basic approaches. These are:
1. Creating new habitat.
2. Restoring habitat.
3. Re-wilding.

Creating new habitat means starting with a clean sheet, from zero. So we need a clear vision of what the new habitat will be like, and how it fits in with and utilises existing natural features such as climate and soil type. For example, you might be designing a garden, and contemplating a theme possibly around a certain ecotype full of suitable exotic plants. The Victorians went through an era of plant-collecting around the world and left many spectacular gardens full of hitherto strange species, some of which, such as rhododendrons and Himalayan Balsam, became feral, and are now designated 'Invasive Alien Species'.

The Invasive Alien Species thing has become mainstream in recent years. It ticks all the boxes for virtue ethics. Many people don't even bother to distinguish between 'Invasive' and 'Alien' or non-indigenous; they are all tarred with the same brush. There is no space to go into detail on this here, other than to note that it is a totally anthropocentric approach (fortunately for us or we might not be here!).

A habitat does not have to be large. Even a window box can provide host plants for butterflies. But moving up the scale a little, what if you want to create a pond for example? A pond is a hole in the ground full of water. Sounds pretty obvious doesn't it? But what type of ground – does it have

Wild cherries are planted in the catalogue woods although I have never seen them here in old woods. They soon get blight.

This endangered indigenous Takahe (Porphyrio hochstetteri) *has been introduced to Maud Island in New Zealand, where introduced non-indigenous mammalian predators have been exterminated.*

enough clay in it to make it water-tight? What size and shape of hole and how to dig it? Where will the water come from, and where will it go to? What licences will you need?

There are dewponds, off-line ponds and on-line ponds and all manner of combinations. I've made about thirty, the largest being 350 metres long. The quickest and easiest way to make a pond is to get beavers; they've made another dozen or so ponds without us lifting a finger. But remember, if you are digging your own pond, to eschew straight lines. Nature is like a beautiful woman, full of curves and never revealing all her charms at the same time. There should always be an unexpected surprise round the next corner! Once you've created your basic habitat, your hole full of water, you can either walk away and see what colonises naturally, or you can seed plant it with some starter plants. Basically, whatever habitat you are creating, you must always start with the lowest trophic levels and work upwards. That can take years. We've found, if you wait for natural colonisation, you can be in for some nasty surprises. And having got there first, your Nasty Surprises can quickly colonise and dominate the habitat for many years to come, and they may be Invasive Aliens. Therefore we usually transplant some plants, and particularly buckets full of mud containing invertebrate larvae and seeds, to get the habitat started and avoid monodominance. Mother Nature and Doctor Time can be great healers of ravaged landscapes, but equally, if you try to fight them, they can bite back with a vengeance. This book is not supposed to be a text book on habitats, so I will not go into detail. But whatever habitat you envisage, you need to gradually establish a wide spectrum of flora and fauna, and a lot of the fauna, to start with will be tiny, often invisible. The first five years for a pond and the first fifteen years for a wood are the most formative years. You can steadily enrich them with a new species here and there as they develop. We have had wetland experts visit some of our five-year-old ponds and not realise that they were not ancient ponds. Re-wilding a field into 'ancient woodland' is not just a question of planting trees and then waiting for a few years. Peterken found that about 40% of the vascular plant species in ancient woods have been unable to colonise new woodland even after 400 years, with no sign that they will do so eventually.

From the hunting point of view, most of it will be pest control in one form or another, and not all of it will be of vertebrates. The 'hunting' may be more about controlling plants. Is managing a hunting resource really 'conservation'? If your project is to create a wild bird shoot or a wild fish water, so that you only cream off a harvestable surplus, if there is one, then yes, I suppose it is a type of conservation with ancillary benefits for other species sharing the resource. If it entails heavily modifying the resource by virtually eliminating all predators of your game, then you are not so much conserving as skewing the resource so that you can take the place of those predators. If you are stocking the ground annually with farmed game, although you may be temporarily enhancing the habitat with game strips and so on to host the released birds, this is not conservation in any meaningful sense. Conversely, if your aim is to create a wildlife reserve rather than a hunting resource, then <u>reserve</u> it for wildlife. Don't go putting in paths and visitor centres and letting in dog walkers. To do that does not prioritise wildlife or the resource; basically you are creating a social amenity for humans, a park, an anthropocentrism.

11.3.5 Designing habitats

If you have a clear ecological vision of what you are aiming for, this is great. But what if you haven't got a clue what you are doing? The settlers to New Zealand in the 1850s wanted to create farmland out of native bush and swamp, in order to feed themselves. New Zealand at that point was already badly screwed up by the impact of Polynesian settlement. All the moas had gone, and many other species. The settlers systematically logged out all the best timber and burnt the rest, creating new areas of open country. This they planted with mixtures of European grasses and clovers, to see what would flourish. Then they found that there were no bees to pollinate the clover. Eventually they managed to find, import and establish some bees, including *Bombus ruderatus* which has a tongue long enough to reach inside the flower head. Then they introduced songbirds to remind them of home, and trout and salmon for the rivers, and pigs, goats, deer and possums, and Chamois (*Rupicapra rupicapra*) and Himalayan Thar (*Hemitragus jemiahicus*) for the high country. Then they found the rabbits and hares were proliferating and eating out the pastures so they introduced cats, ferrets, stoats and weasels. And of course black and brown rats, and mice came along for the ride. What a complete cock-up! It sounds more like the old woman who swallowed a fly.

But hang on a minute; most New Zealand terrestrial indigenous flora and fauna are based in the woodland, the 'bush'. Very few native species colonise open farm land. If the settlers had not brought any species, the farmland would be very impoverished. Indeed 98% of the prey species of the native falcons I studied hunting in open country are introduced.

The pity of course is that the settlers had little understanding of ecology, so now we have a very fragmentary and unbalanced farmland fauna. Should we leave it as it is now? Or should we introduce some more species, this time on a much more considered, scientific basis to gradually create a brand new balanced designer-ecosystem for open farmland? Tricky stuff!

Some of the introduced species, such as possums, cats and mustelids are seriously bad news for native wildlife and the government has an ambitious plan to eradicate them by 2050. How that would be achieved I don't know, bearing in mind that there are 30 million possums at the moment in huge areas of dense mountainous bush. One route is to fence off isolated peninsulas or islands and clear them of all pest species. I am a patron of Picton Dawn Chorus that systematically traps pest species in a buffer zone around a core pest-free zone called Kaipupu Point. Our house is on an adjacent peninsula called The Snout. We catch the possums when we can, as well as feral cats. But trapping is labour intensive, poisoning hits non-target species, and we need better selective self-setting traps or some kind of contraceptives. Such technology could then be used on other species, such as grey squirrels in Britain.

You really need to know what you are doing when creating a vision for new habitat. It takes knowledge, and multidisciplinary practical skills. Oliver Rackham's *Woodlands* is an excellent primer. I tried drawing an Eltonian Food Pyramid once; you should try it. School books show this as a schematic isosceles triangle. It is nothing like that; it is mind-blowing. Start doing it on a numbers basis, and allocate one square or pixel on a graph for each individual organism. Keep it as a simple chain as you can. Start at the top with a single species of apex predator, say for example, a Golden Eagle. How many pairs of breeding eagles do you need to make a minimum viable population? Twenty pairs? Thirty? How many sub-adults will there need to be in support of these pairs? Another 30 birds? So to have a sustainable population, you are probably looking at about a hundred eagles. Now google eagle diet, and eagle food consumption. Knowing the weights of the rabbits, hares, deer, grouse and foxes that the eagles eat, and allowing for wastage of at least 30%, you can calculate numbers of each species that make up the next trophic level for a year, bearing in mind that the eagles can only consume a sustainable harvestable surplus from each species. They must not touch the capital in the bank account, only the interest. For the herbivores, you can skip a trophic level or two and go on to plants. For the foxes, that eat mammals, birds, reptiles, berries and so on, you are opening a can of worms almost literally. Keep going down the food chain to the lowest trophic level you can work with, probably a variety of plants. By now you will have so many pixels that the paper could be kilometres wide. And when you translate this into land area, you end up with maybe more than 10% of the whole of Scotland. This gives you an idea of the scope involved. So if you come up with the bright idea of creating a new population of Golden Eagles, it is not just the eagles, you have to consider; they are just the visible tip of a huge ecological iceberg. Think of all the other animals and plants needed to sustain them, and the huge areas of habitat they need. Then think of the land-owners who manage that habitat, and the political and legal frameworks they have to operate within. It's like a giant ecological Pyramid Scheme.

In order to do these theoretical Eltonian Pyramid calculations you might start at the top and work down through the trophic layers. But when it comes to creating habitat in real life, it is the opposite; you must start at the bottom, get the lowest trophic levels established and then, like building a house, build it up level by level. This is why it is called ecology, because it is like a house. Idealists dream of apex predators such as lynx, bears and wolves, without understanding that you need very big contiguous areas to sustain such species; a few thousand acres is nothing. And although trophic cascades with wolves in the Yellowstone are all the fashion, nothing will cascade unless you have all the trophic levels well represented. Even then it is more of a belly dance than a cascade. When one trophic level expands, the one below diminishes and the one below that expands, then it goes into reverse.

When creating new habitat, scientists and civil servants take the cautious route. They want feasibility studies, demographic modelling and of course, the Precautionary Principle. Too often these are code for wanting to do research and obtain grant funding, combined with a desire to avoid decision making, (the Procrastination Principle). However experienced or clever you are, nature will always have surprises,

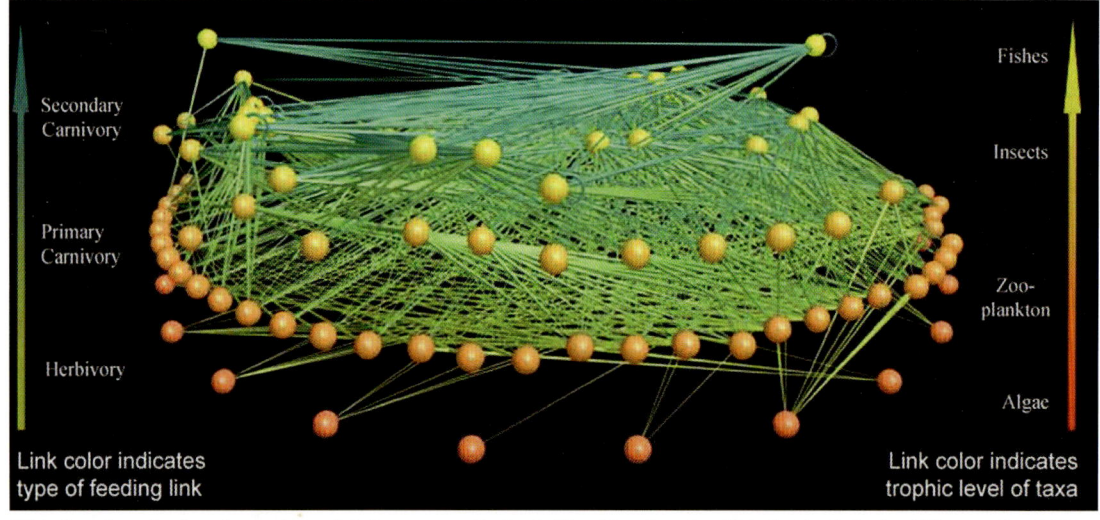

This is what food webs and trophic layers really look like. Food web of Little Rock Lake, Wisconsin. 997 feeding links among 92 trophic species are shown. Image produced with Food-Web3D, written by R. J. Williams, available at the Pacific Ecoinformatics and Computational Ecology Lab (www.foodwebs.org)

small things, a matter of a few metres, can have unforeseen effects. I have very little faith in predictive ecological modelling. When I am creating new habitat, I approach it more like an artist than a scientist. I start with a broad brush and fill in the main elements as best I can. I introduce 'starter packs' of soil, seeds, residual dormant seed beds and invertebrates to colonise as they wish. Gradually, haphazardly, they will establish themselves, forming unique and diverse patchy habitats.

In this way it is possible to recreate 'ancient woodland'. It takes time, and obviously you cannot plant a gnarly 300 year old oak. But you can establish most of the ingredients in the cake and let them get on with it. From the ethical point of view, you have to decide if you are creating woodland, if so, of what type, or a grassland or savannah structure, a wetland, or even a lake bed. The soil, acidity, minerals, rainfall, landscape and hydrology will dictate the key decisions. But are you trying to recreate a baseline habitat that may have been here say 2,000 years ago or before humans unduly influenced the landscape? Do you have some additional considerations such as the potential for commercial forestry, in which case how would you plant it, log it and extract it?

Turning the clock back is all very well but if it takes 300 years to establish some new 'ancient' woodland, perhaps by then it will be out of date? Maybe climate change will mean that the old woodland is no longer best suited to the new warmer climate. Up on the farm in Northumberland is a ridge of limestone rocks and sinkholes. Sitting quietly on the rocks, feeding up a falcon, I can see tracks on the rocks as if someone has ridden a farm bike with knobbly tyres across wet concrete. Looking at the marks more closely, I can see that the tracks are the fossilised imprints of some kinds of tree ferns or cycads about 280 million years old. It's hard to imagine what it must have been like then, with forests of ferns and dinosaurs roaming the area. If the land warms again, perhaps I should be prepared for it? So I have grown some tree ferns from New Zealand from spores. Would I be naughty to put out some of my tree ferns into our woods in Wales, to prepare pro-actively for global warming?

Fossilised tree trunks in Northumberland.

Surely this is introducing a non-native species, a heinous ecological crime!

11.3.6 Creating habitat

Time to get real. If I was to make any difference at this level, I needed to roll up my sleeves and get stuck in. But first I needed all sorts of licences and a plump cheque book, preferably a route to offset some of my costs against tax. Twenty years previously I had already dug an on-line pond at the bottom of our home meadow. I bought the neighbouring farm which had a field full of springs and ditches. It was too wet to farm; three sets of land drains had failed. The old medieval stone drains made of carefully criss-crossed slabs of stone, were clogged up. Later period clay pipe drains were also disjointed and blocked. Recent plastic land drains had also failed. I decided to take the hint and not fight it any more. I dug some test holes and in places there were beds of grey clay from the last Ice Age, two metres deep; just what I needed to make a waterproof lake. In the winters it was too wet to get a digger and tractors down there, and in the summer everything was needed periodically for doing the silage. So it took three years to get the 300 metre dam built, layer on layer rollered 15 cm at a time, 30 metres wide at the base.

Above the lake were springs and above them, the farmyard with cattle sheds and a slurry pit. Bovine Tb was now rampant (and still is) so I gave up with cattle. But I put in three smaller ponds full of reeds to take any runoff from the yards, to ensure the water entering the lake was clean. By about 1998 the lake was full and I planted it with a variety of fringe plants, aquatic plants, invertebrates and trees.

The field before we started.

Chapter 11 – THE EVOLUTIONARY TRAP

Removing top layers to key the dam base.

Digging down through the inter-glacial period into metamorphic shale rock.

Fitting outlet pipes at the lowest points to keep the site drained while excavating.

Creating the dam in layers.

New habitat.

Around the lake I planted ten acres of deciduous woodland. Every autumn I would collect acorns and seeds and grow on local native trees ready to plant out. The edges of the lake had plenty of willow and brown birch. I gave it fifteen years to settle down and then it was ready for the next stage – beavers.

We got a pair of beavers from Derek Gow and built some enclosures for them, swapping yearlings periodically for fresh blood. We put up 700 metres of beaver-proof fence on the down-hill side of the lake and left the rest to them. They built themselves a huge lodge and established a multi-generational family. We let groups of people come and watch them and see how beavers make dams and ponds. Soon we had all sorts

Chapter 11 – THE EVOLUTIONARY TRAP   255

of waterfowl, water rails, kingfishers and lots of dragonflies. The beavers, as a keystone species, had made the whole area blossom with life.

The Eurasian Beaver was last recorded in west Wales in the 17th century, being hunted to extinction for its fur and for its castoreum. I had found mysterious channels in a bog on the farm which appear to be ancient beaver canals. I believe beavers had been here not too long ago, maybe three or four hundred years. The old canals have not changed in the forty years I've known them. I'd love to do a dig and look for beaver-chewed sticks preserved in the anaerobic mud, a message from the past and an inspiration for the future.

We erected pens on the farm following some water courses. Soon we had three families breeding and we applied for a licence to re-introduce them to a river that runs through our farm. Scotland had just completed a five year Trial Release at a cost

When I'm out and about I collect acorns for planting.

Students watching the beavers.

Left: *Part of a network of old canals in wooded-over bog land on the farm.*
Right: *An active beaver canal in one of our beaver pens.*

of £2.2m. It took place at Knapdale in Argyll at a place where, 40 years before, we had reintroduced goshawks. When I visited the beaver site there a female gos flew over me, and I smiled. Some other escaped beavers had started to breed in the catchment of the River Tay and now number two or three hundred. Another family escaped to a river in Devon and Natural England wanted to remove them because of the potential risk of Echinococcus, but the public were up in arms and eventually they were trapped, given the all clear on health and released again for another five year Trial.

After considering our application for almost three years and trying everything to procrastinate, Natural Resources Wales demanded that we did before and after water quality surveys for the whole river system at our own expense. I finally lost patience and withdrew the application. While this is all going on, although everyone is clear that the beaver is back in Britain for good, there is still no legal recognition for the species in Wales, although Scotland and England have now protected it. Declarations of intent in international conventions are one thing. Actually doing it is something else. Apart from the small pilot 'trial' in Argyll, all the populations of beavers in the UK have arisen from unlicensed releases. While at one level governments express well-meaning sentiments towards wildlife management, the civil servants responsible for licensing do not want to put their names to a decision. The farmers, worked up by their unions, worry that the beaver would become an icon, like the badger, and become a management problem. I wonder how much of this real-life stuff finds its way into academic curricula?

There is a whole industry now in making surveys and feasibility studies. Journalists peddle outrage and create polarisation. People scream at each other on social media.

Two of the first Welsh beavers for 400 years, on our farm. 2017. Jo Oliver.

The do-gooders wring their hands and say things like "We need to do this… We need to do that" when they mean someone else should because, apart from virtue signalling, many will not lift a finger without grant money. Many have chips on their shoulders about class and about land-owning. Unlike many countries, Britain is a free country; anyone can buy land but most prefer to spend their money on flash cars, fancy holidays and the latest technology. It is easy to pontificate if you don't have skin in the game. Millions of pounds are wasted on surveys and administrative prevaricating. For example, this latest survey on beavers in Wales was created by the University of Exeter and submitted to Natural Resources Wales, on behalf of the North Wales Wildlife Trusts, with funding received through the Welsh Government Rural Communities – Rural Development Programme 2014-2020, which is funded by the European Agricultural Fund for Rural Development and the Welsh Government in fulfilment of Section 5.2 of the International Union for the Conservation of Nature Guidelines for Reintroductions and Other Conservation Translocations (pause for breath…). The survey found:

Groups statistically *more* likely to support beavers living wild in Wales than oppose, relative to the remaining respondent pool, included:
- female respondents;
- respondents aged 25-34;
- respondents who were resident in Cardiff / Caerdydd;
- respondents whose occupational background was in 'Community & Social Service', 'Education', 'Environment, Nature & Wildlife', or 'Office & Administrative Support';
- and respondents who heard about the survey from a 'Social Media Post' or from a 'Wildlife or Nature Organisation'.

Groups statistically less likely to support beavers living wild in Wales than oppose, relative to the remaining respondent pool, included:
- male respondents;
- respondents aged 65-74;
- respondents who were resident in Denbighshire / Sir Ddinbych, resident in Powys, or resident in Wrexham / Wrecsam;
- respondents whose occupational background was in 'Farming & Agriculture' or 'Fisheries & Aquaculture';
- and respondents who heard about the survey from a 'Farming Organisation' or from a 'Fishing Organisation'.
- (Additionally, respondents who were not identified as resident in Wales were found to be statistically less likely to support beavers living wild in Wales).

So the very structure of the survey creates polarisation. But what all of these organisations and groups ignore is that their human concepts of political boundaries don't apply to other species. Beavers have their own concepts of their territories and what other beavers they will allow in. Wales has no barrier to beavers moving in from England, where they are now well on the way to recovery. The river Wye weaves its way back and forth between England and Wales. There is no need to spend time and money discussing re-introducing beavers; they will come whether anyone likes it or not. Just give it a decade or two. The solution

Beaver ponds amongst the willows.

is to have a Management Plan (which has already been developed for England and Scotland). But even this is just a sop. There is no means to enforce it other than to provide grants to people managing beavers on their own lands. Since the Hunting Act 2004, respect for the law has faded away and people manage badgers, otters, corvids, foxes, raptors etc pretty much as it suits them. The trick is – not to get caught. By and large, local killing is insufficient to impact the wider populations. The surveyed 25-34 year old social worker ladies in Cardiff will feel warm and fuzzy and the farmer who thinks that a beaver's home is called a 'dam' (!) can bump a few off now and then until he gets used to them being around.

People come from the towns to watch the beavers. We show them the dams and canals, the cut trees and the underwater food stores. They marvel at the necklaces of ponds the beavers have made, and all the wildlife that has started to colonise them. The beaver is a keystone species; when you manage them at level 4, as a species, they go straight up

A male Broad-bodied Chaser Libellula depressa, *a new coloniser on our beaver ponds.* Jo Oliver.

the priority scale to level 3, creating habitats. You have to admire their energy and quiet persistence.

11.3.7 Habitats and farming

Sometimes when I am working on conservation projects in faraway countries, such as China, I see the devastating effects humans are having on habitats. Huge areas are denuded and turned into desert. Forests logged out. Lakes and woods devoid of life. Every last little frog, eaten. Within twenty minutes of arriving at the airport I have a hacking cough from the city air pollution. People are hustling all over one another, each desperate to make a living. I come home deeply depressed.

Then I remember the gardener who wrote "No matter how small your garden, you should always keep back an acre or two for trees." I admire both the sentiment and the humour. The thing is, we all struggle with the big concepts. What you really need is to come right back down to earth and take responsibility for a little bit of our planet, even if it is only a window box. Rather than talk in abstracts and generalities, get involved with some specifics and realities.

I'm ashamed to say that I did not read Aldo Leopold's *A Sand County Almanac* until I was researching for this book twenty years ago. I think I must have been influenced by Leopold because I used

We design our houses so that even a wall has built in homes for birds.

to correspond with Fran and Hammie Hamerstrom and went to visit them in the 1970s. They were students of Leopold's and, like him, lived on a farm in Wisconsin. Fran pioneered collecting semen from her imprint male eagle and used to have her 'copulating coat' that her eagle was used to copulating on. The writings of Paul Errington, and of John and Frank Craighead, especially '*Hawks, Owls and Wildlife*' were also influential, and John Craighead kindly let me use some of his photos of falconry in pre-partition India for one of my books. Their PhD studies on predation in Michigan and Wyoming, for all their limitations, gave an insight into predator/prey systems with a breadth and detail that you seldom see.

Aldo Leopold bought a 160 acre farm in Wisconsin, with a dilapidated shed on it that the Leopold family patched up and lived in at weekends. In New Zealand we would call his 'Shack' a 'bach'. The farm itself had been abandoned as the soil was not economically viable for farming. It was gradually returning to woodland and the Leopolds encouraged that process and documented the recolonising of the wildlife. It was there that he developed his 'Land Ethic' that has developed almost a cult following in America and been developed further by people like Callicott and Rolston.

I too always had an interest in farms. My old in-laws had a 35 acre small-holding in the hills of west Wales, then, when I did my PhD in New Zealand we managed a 240 acre farm in North Canterbury, tucked under the foot hills, the 'front country' of the Southern Alps. I worked on over a hundred High Country farms, shepherding, mustering and studying falcons. In 1982 we bought the nucleus of our farm in Wales, an old house with seven acres. Gradually we built it up to 280 acres. We also took on a contrasting 200 acre upland farm in the Northumberland National Park, where we train our falcons in the open landscape. At the same time we had a 16 acre holding in the Waihopai Valley in New Zealand for a decade while we did our falcon work there, before selling it and moving out into the Marlborough Sounds. Recently we've also taken on a 110 acre grass farm in Wiltshire. So I've had a chance to farm in a variety of places and communities, and of course have worked on many others. It enabled me to see some of the diverse issues faced in farming, and some of the common denominators.

Whereas Thoreau could contemplate the natural beauty of Walden Pond from his hut, and Leopold could document the recolonization of his abandoned farm, we set ourselves a somewhat more challenging task. Our farm in Wales is second-hand, very much so. It is an agricultural 'brown field' site. The original building had been a poorly built, modest one storey farmworker's cottage made from stone dug out of the hill. But the location was well chosen, high enough from the valley floor to avoid ground frosts, low enough to avoid the westerly winds, built on solid rock and on a south facing slope, it has all the basic ingredients. Just outside the door is a deep well. The oldest part of the house is only about 300 years old but the land itself has been farmed for several hundred years, cleared from deciduous woodland that clothed the landscape after the last Ice Age, 10,000 years ago. Think of the generations of people struggling to make a living from that land, in all weathers! Occasionally I find traces of them; a carefully laid stone land drain, a length of clay pipe stem, a rusting cart horse shoe, a huge tree with a tell-tale z-bend that had been 'laid' as a sapling in the hedge…Sometimes when the sun is low and casts long shadows, we can just discern long-abandoned tracks angling their ways across the slopes.

In the 1840s, with the agricultural depression, things got so bad that the farmers rose up in arms. They marched past our gate disguised as women and led by 'Rebecca'. The Rebecca Riots spread across the country, destroying the toll gates in protest at the state of the roads, mere muddy tracks, impassable in winter.

The Rebecca Rioters at the toll gates.

Helen's family farm, where she hunted with her hawk thirty years ago, was originally part of the Talley Abbey estate. In the fifteenth century the Abbot wrote to Huw Lewys of Prysaddfed on Anglesy, offering him a horse in exchange for his fine male goshawk.

> *I, fair Tal-y-llychau's Abbot,*
> *Dwelling where the lake lies placid*
> *Hear the ducks of Caio calling*
> *Send request to Huw the Hawker*
> *Who has skill in training tiercels,*
> *For his Goshawk without rival;*
> *I, the Abbot, would possess it.*

Wherever we tread in the fields and woods, we are conscious of those who have gone before us, and mindful of those who would come after us.

So our dual task was first to make a living from the farm, and second to make it prosper for wildlife. Turning a place over to wildlife is one thing. Making a living is something else. To start with I had a job lecturing in wildlife at a nearby college, but in 1989 I resigned from this to live from the farm.

Almost all the farms in Wales are technically bankrupt. Lowland cattle and sheep farms like ours in Wales averaged an income of only £17,000 in 2023, and 86% would be in the red were it not for government subsidies. This is changing at the moment, with emphasis for subsidies going more towards environmental benefits, so difficult times lie ahead for Welsh farmers.

When was this oak laid to make a hedge? A hundred years ago? Two?

Most of the farms were small family units of 90-120 acres, a bit of dairying, some beef or sucklers, and sheep. Until a hundred years ago, the expectations were modest. No electricity, no cars or tractors, no mains water, no paved roads, and of course no TVs, telephones or supermarkets. Families had to grow their own food all the year round, without freezers, and barter the rest, with only a modest cash economy. Living was hard but families scraped by. Now people expect a much higher standard of living and minimum wage, far more than these family farms can support. One by one, old farmers are dying off and young ones can neither afford nor want to take on such a tough lifestyle. The average age of farmer in Wales is 62 and this is by no means unusual. A Welsh government programme aimed at getting young farmers into farming has 23,000 acres on its books but few people want to farm them.

Our farm is currently made up of four original family farms. We bought it in stages over the years and one forgets just how bare everywhere was 45 years ago. The farm map shows very little woodland, just some scrub on the steep banks. A legacy from the war was that every square inch had been worked to produce food. Year by year I planted trees on a little corner here, or dug a pond there.

Of our land, about 40% is good enough to grow silage, up to three cuts a year. We don't grow hay anymore; the weather is too unpredictable, you can easily lose your whole crop. Another 30% is permanent grassland, mainly too steep for machinery. The remaining 30% we have taken out of agriculture to grow woodlands and ponds for wildlife. For the last three decades I've tried to average planting two trees a day every day of my life. Recently, with a grant, we've had contractors plant another 18,000 broadleaved trees on a steep north-facing bank. I think it would be a useful exercise if every school child had to grow a tree from seed each year, and plant it; *The Man Who Planted Trees*, even though it is fictional, is inspirational. It is easy to complain that the government or some other faceless body should be doing something. The real question is – what are <u>you</u> doing?

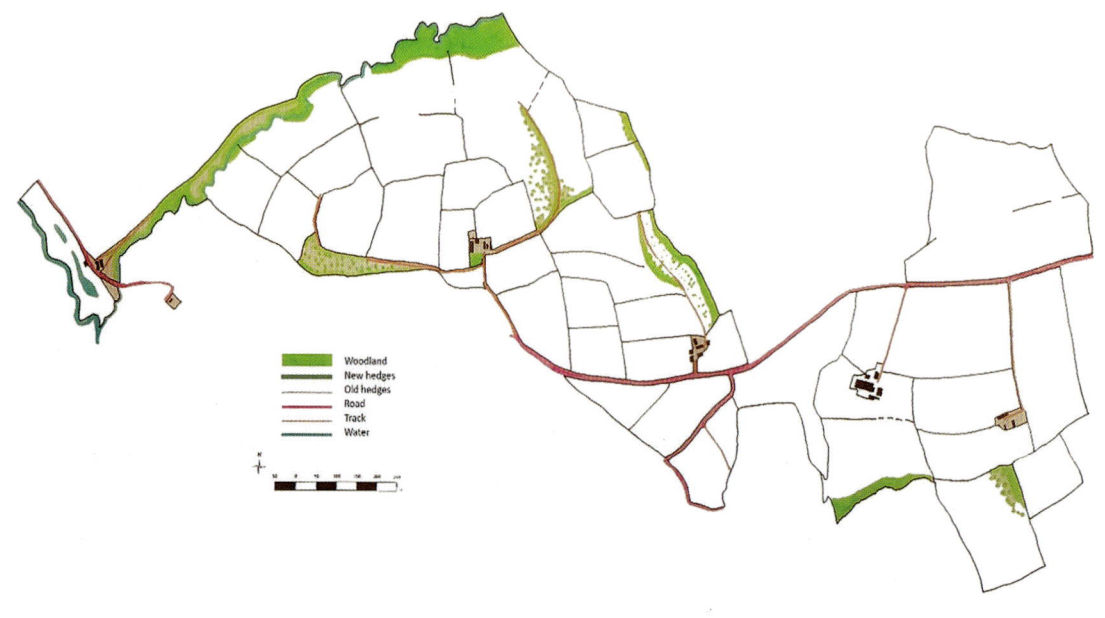

The farm in 1982.

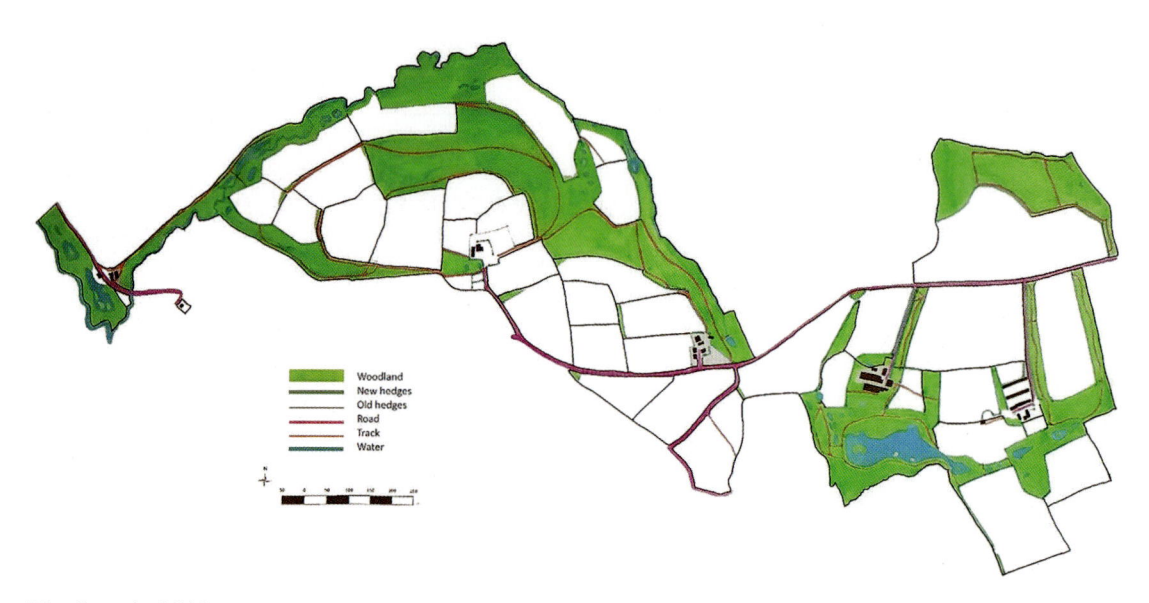

The farm in 2019.

Most of our wooded land is odd corners, boggy bits and steep banks, no good for farming. One of the current conditions for obtaining any subsidy on the land is that it should be in 'good agricultural condition'. This means that any land we take out of farming to plant trees automatically loses income support, so we have lost a third by trying to help wildlife. Two years ago, some impecunious civil servant decided that the area under the drip line of a tree should be deducted from the total farmed field area for subsidy purposes. So people started cutting down any trees scattered within the fields. The calculations got impossibly complicated and in the end they abandoned it when it dawned on them that it was counter-productive for conservation.

The silage fields are in ecological terms, sacrificial. Some have been ploughed and they are laid to short-term rye grass leys which have a high sugar content and grow quickly for silage but are poor for grazing and soil structure.

We used to have skylarks and brown hares in the old days of hay-making, but these species, that have their nests or young out in the grassland, cannot cope with their entire habitat being razed to the ground every six weeks in summer. This is the dilemma – how to integrate profitable farming with wildlife? Whereas to some

Sadly bluebells do not make a good fodder crop, so the field has been sacrificed to rye grass.

First the grass is cut, then the ground is plastered with slurry.

extent we can integrate grazing with grasslands and open woodlands, anything involving mowing or cropping is deadly. Underground, in the soil, changes are going on that we don't fully understand, organic content is being lost and many of the chemicals that are applied are endocrine disruptors. Farm margins are tight; supermarkets sell milk as a loss-leader for less than the price of bottled water.

Another time the whizz scheme was to preserve wildflower meadows by not fertilising the grassland and not cutting hay before 15th July when it had all seeded. Of course wild flowers do not just magically appear in old grasslands; usually we just get one or two species such as buttercups, which are unpalatable to stock. The whole point of making hay is to trap as much nutrition in it as possible for winter feed. It should always be cut when the seed is formed but not dropped, to maximise protein levels. If you leave it until mid-July, all that is left is stalks, fit only for making rope. So of course we stopped making hay in those fields; we just grazed livestock in them instead. And when the subsidy period finished, we went back to applying slurry and mowing for silage. Ten years of delayed hay-making had had no noticeable effect on flowers; instead we have developed a grazing system whereby those fields are kept shut up through spring and summer to allow the flowers, and more importantly the invertebrates, to flourish, and then grazing in the winter so that the vegetation does not become too matted and rank. But at the end of the day, if the residual seed-bed has been destroyed by long monoculture, do not expect wild species to magically appear. A few will, but without intervention some take hundreds of years to re-colonise.

When managing the land, we have to take a long-term view. Some of the land on arable farms is subsidised for use as 'set-aside' in which marginal strips are allowed to lie fallow for a year. Some strips might be planted up with a game crop mix to feed birds in the winter. This is good as far as it goes. But that is only as far as it does go. In reality you need to dedicate an area of land specifically to a set land use for a long period of time to establish the soil flora and fauna. What goes on underground is even more important than what goes on above ground.

During the World War II, farmers were exhorted to 'Dig for Victory' and cultivate every square yard of land. The poor devils who had to work some of our banks and gullies must have suffered, and for such pathetic returns. After that we were told to rip out hedges. Then we were told, no, keep the hedges, they are heritage wildlife corridors and anyone removing them would be prosecuted. But our average field size is only about 5 acres; totally uneconomic for modern farming. Years ago, we moved a couple of old hedges. First we cut them all down very closely, then we dug them up and loaded them on to tipper trailers, then we spread them out along the new ergonomic hedge route lines and banked them tidily. This enabled them to stretch to twice their original length. After a couple of years the residual seed bed had sprouted and to all intents and purposes we now have twice the length of 'ancient hedgerows'. Currently we have 14.4 km of old hedgerows on the farm, and 6.44 km of new hedgerows that we have planted. They cost £2,500 plus 20% VAT each year just to trim them. The new ones are a mixture of species and every area of woodland has a hedge around it to keep it warm. Wind should not be allowed to howl through a wood. We can't move old hedgerows any more. With aerial photography the Council would catch us and prosecute us. They don't understand that hedgerows can be moved and 'grown', while at the same time we are exhorted to farm more efficiently.

The 200 acre upland farm in Northumberland that we've run since 1992 is another ball game altogether. Mostly rushy 'fell' land, with some in-bye hay or silage fields, it produces 'light' lambs for export and cross-bred beef cattle. Soils are poor and water-logged and the economics hinge on subsidy payments. Previously this was based on headage payments, the numbers of animals on the farm. That encouraged farmers to over-stock and push the land, but now it is based on area payments and the vegetation is thicker. Soon it will change to environmental payments, but nobody knows how that would work or be calculated. Current Stewardship Schemes are an administrative nightmare. Upland farmers are a tough and resilient breed, working long hours in conditions that would break most people. But they have no training in conservation. And the young civil servants who come with their clipboards have their university training but little practical or financial experience. Ecologically, much of our British uplands are a disaster and we cannot go on farming it this way. But how can rural communities continue; can people adapt and adjust to new priorities after lifetimes spent in livestock farming?

The reason we have this farm is to train and fly our young falcons and this depends on an open landscape. Many consider this landscape beautiful and coming up from the over-populated and claustrophobic South I always breathe a deep breath when I come over Hadrian's Wall, and my spirits lift. Even the horses smell freedom and start to whinny in the lorry. So there are mixed emotions. We back up against Kielder Forest, the largest man-made forest in western Europe. It is thick with foxes which can no longer be legally hunted with hounds (the only way to find them in forest), and they, together with the crows, hammer the wildlife. The curlews are hanging on by a thread, the lapwings are struggling and our wild hill partridges have gone altogether, as have the red grouse and black grouse. You only see them now in the keepered areas along the grouse moors, where predators are controlled and these vulnerable open country species have a chance. We don't manage to catch with our falcons anything like the number of crows that the RSPB do, but the ones we do catch are the ones that do the damage, and we kill them in the most humane way possible. While I am unenthusiastic about large-bag driven grouse shooting, what other economic mechanism is there to pay gamekeepers to control predators? The public want a 'right to roam', they don't want to pay for it, they want to see wildlife, yet they don't want to see the management that is needed to enable it to survive. It's a sort of group self-delusion.

In a *Guardian* interview, Isabella Tree described her struggle at the Knepp wilding project *'to find the balance between "engaging people with nature, getting young people into it" and visitors overwhelming the wildlife. She worries about professional dog-walkers who bring six dogs each, given that a spaniel's nose is precisely the height of a nesting nightingale. Dog-walkers post delightedly on social media about Knepp's ponds being perfect for doggy wild swimming. But this is less perfect for aquatic wildlife, as anti-flea treatments spread from dogs to the wider environment.*

"It's become people management now," says Tree. *"I have an issue with Guy Shrubsole,"* she says, referring to the co-founder of the Right to Roam campaign group. *"Who wouldn't want their child to be able to swim in every pond? But we haven't yet got enough countryside with recovered wildlife in it to let loose the population – we've got to protect areas for wildlife too."* She hopes a balance can be struck: one riverbank for a path, say, the opposite one kept for wildlife.'

In some countries the state strictly controls the sale of land, but in many countries you can buy land. All you've got to do is make some money first! From the financial point of view, buying farmland in Wales is madness. Land may cost £8,000 an acre and yet only return £100 an acre per year. That's an ROI of 1.25%; hardly a dream investment. It doesn't even keep up with inflation.

But be warned, if you plan to do anything of lasting value for the land, especially at level 3 which entails habitat management, then you need to be thinking long-term. We are not just talking decades, we are talking in perpetuity. Involvement with planting and habitat succession is the exciting stuff. But what happens if, when you die, the land is sold for housing development? Legal succession planning is as important as biological succession planning, if not more so.

In some countries the tradition for land succession is of primogeniture, often, but less so nowadays, through the male line. A farm is passed on to the oldest child, while the others make their own way in life. An alternative is to pass the farm on equally to all the heirs, but that usually entails selling the farm in order for each to receive his or her share.

In traditional Māori society, leadership, land and resource rights can be inherited. Ancestral land was passed down on the basis of continuous occupation (called *ahi kā roa*, a long-burning fire). Today, Māori land can only be left to people who are related through biological kinship, partnership or adoption. This can mean that land, or a resource such as fishing rights, can be jointly owned by hundreds of relatives, some of whom may not even live in New Zealand. This gets more and more complicated and makes any kind of change a slow and legally tortuous affair. The concept is a good one, but perhaps it should revert back to only those tribal members who still live or depend on the land. The Māori tradition parallels that of many cultures owning tribal lands, and of the European Salic Patrimony which held that land could not be sold but must be passed on to all the male heirs. In Britain this was known as gavelkind which in its extreme form of partible inheritance resulted in farms getting smaller and smaller. If you had a 100 acres and four sons, each son inherited 25 acres which is not enough land to make a living. In Wales it was known as *cyfran* and resulted in the weakening of the farms and often, in family feuds. It was formally abolished in 1925. A similar system in Ireland, inflicted by the Catholic Church on its followers, resulted in farms becoming so small that the only crop they could grow was potatoes. When the Potato Blight came in 1845, families starved and many fled to America. Many of the landless children became Catholic priests and nuns, so in a backward kind of a way, for the Church at least, it worked.

For us, having worked on the farm for four decades, we had a moral decision to make. What is more important: the land, or people? Our old 240 acre farm that we lived on in New Zealand in the 1970s has been sub-divided into 18 'lifestyle blocks'. Could we plan succession of the Welsh farm in some way so that instead of it being a level 5 decision, benefitting just a few individuals, we could elevate it to at least a level 3 decision, securing the future of some habitats, and even, in a small way contributing to priority levels 2 and 1, supporting wider systems of resources and ultimately our entire planet? The knock-on effect at this level trickles right down to supporting the future for our own children and grand-children, as well as the future for all living things on the planet.

But how could we do that? As our accountants and lawyers waste no time in telling us: there are also many legal and tax considerations to factor in. And what would our children think? My eldest son already farms on his own account in New Zealand. None of the other children have an interest in farming. So the route we are planning is to establish a farm Trust, called the Bevis Trust. It is named after the book by Richard Jefferies, titled *Bevis: the Story of a Boy*, written in 1882. Jefferies portrayed the rapidly changing rural life at the start of the great agricultural depression of the late 19th century. He had an affection for the traditional practices and customs of the communities he knew but wrote without sentimentality and saw that 'the new' could often exist harmoniously alongside 'the old'. His books contain many fine and vivid sketches of the countryside and show a remarkably keen eye for observing the activities of living creatures and the subtle workings of nature. For him, *The sun was stronger than science; the hills more than philosophy.* He wrote of the area where I was born, and although I was there sixty years later, many things were still the same.

But creating a Trust is not a panacea. Finding Trustees who share the same vision is a challenge, as is providing tax-efficient funding to achieve its objectives. So, at the time of writing, this is a work in progress. Committees and organisations don't always have the same energy as committed individuals on the ground.

For others, conservation is a luxury that somehow has to pay its way. If agriculture cannot balance the books, farms have to diversify into other income streams which are aligned with conservation goals. Access is a two-edged sword. On the one hand people need to get out into the countryside and reconnect with nature. On the other hand, nature doesn't necessarily want to connect with humans, in fact the last thing that wildlife needs, especially in the breeding season, is disturbance from humans and dogs or cats. Some countries, such as Scotland and Sweden, have long had a right to roam but their human population densities are much lower. What can work at low densities does not work beyond a certain tipping point and in the end wildlife cannot cope with constant disturbance. On top of this, while providing a resource to the public, the farmer reaps no benefit and the public regard it as a 'right' rather than a 'responsibility'. This was an opportunity lost both to provide local income and for developing a responsible approach from the visitors rather than a consumptive one. On our farm in Wales we have made 8.4 km of new tracks through the woods so that we can get around and see what is going on without disturbing wildlife.

11.4 International habitat projects

11.4.1 Saker Falcons in Mongolia

If you fly over Mongolia and look down on the steppe grasslands you will occasionally see blotches of bare earth, like amoebae. These are colonies of Brandt's Voles which breed up, then crash, on a cyclical basis. There is nothing left there for the herders' livestock. We had been researching Saker Falcons (*Falco cherrug*) there since the early nineties when the Soviet Union broke up and Mongolia became open to foreigners. We also worked west of the Altai in Kazakhstan and south into Kyrgyzstan, north into Siberia and south and east into China and Tibet.

Some conservationists claimed that the saker was decreasing in both numbers and range and indeed our surveys in Asia, western Russia, the Crimea and Bulgaria found this was so, depending on the status of the steppe grasslands. If people moved to the cities the grasses grew too long and obscured the small mammals such as susliks (*Spermophilus* spp.) so that the sakers could not catch them.

But the sakers themselves were in demand as a resource for Arab falconry and were being heavily trapped in Kazakhstan, Afghanistan, Kirghystan and Pakistan. Our Head of Research in Kazakhstan, Dr Anatoli Levin, found most of the nests raided by

A netted nest. When the adult comes in to incubate, the net is pulled up.

A nesting saker caught by nooses but not found in time.

trappers who netted the nest ledges or set nooses to trap the adults.

So I decided to ask the sakers what to do. First we put out some different designs of artificial nests on the steppe. We knew that in these huge open areas the raptors were nest site limited – there were no cliffs or trees. We suspected that there was a big population of falcons unable to find nests. After three years we came up with a design that ticked all the boxes and then we put out 5,000 of them at 2 km intervals in several study areas. Very quickly most of the nests were occupied; not just by sakers but by European Kestrels, ravens, Upland Buzzards (*Buteo hemilasius*) and even the occasional Steppe Eagle (*Aquila nipalensis*). Within four years our nests were producing 2,500 saker chicks per year and our Mongolian biologists checked them three times during each breeding cycle, microchipping the youngsters.

These raptors were able to prey on the Brandt's voles, smoothing out their

In Pakistan we held workshops for the falcon trappers, teaching them humane management. We gave them medical kits, but of course with no human health service, they used them on their families rather than the falcons.

After three years of trial designs, the sakers told us they preferred cavity nests, safely off the ground and facing away from the sun and wind.

boom and bust cycles and reducing the plagues. We showed the Minister who was duly impressed, as were the herders. We set up a Schools Link programme to tell the children (and thence their parents) about the project and linked them up to schools in other countries.

Biologically the project was a success. We had shown that there was a surplus of sakers and that they could be managed to produce more. The plan had been then for the government to sell licences to the Arabs to harvest some of the young for falconry, with some of the funds going to the local communities to incentivise looking after the nests rather than taking them for scrap metal. But Ministers in Mongolia come and go very quickly and the temptation is for them to make a fast buck for themselves while in office. Deals were struck under the table so we never got proper feedback on harvest rates and CITES controls were of no use. So politically it was a disappointment and in 2016 the UAE pulled the funding because we had not managed to establish a sustainable system. The nests still continue, but at a lower level.

While were were doing this project, we found a lot of raptors were being

Dr Andrew Dixon explains the artificial nest programme to local children.

Electrocuted falcons in Mongolia. Andrew Dixon.

electrocuted. Mongolia was in the process of being electrified and Chinese companies were setting up lines of poles across the steppes. Workers raided all birds' nests within 10 km of the lines for their eggs for food. These poles were the only perches for raptors and they killed everything that landed on them. We had two staff patrolling the lines daily and found that on average one falcon was killed per 10 km of line per week. So this meant our Head of Research, Dr Andrew Dixon, spent several years negotiating with Ministers and power companies to either retro-fit or redesign the poles.

11.4.2 Falcons in vineyards

Another project on a habitat scale was to control pest birds in the vineyards of Marlborough, New Zealand. Vineyards were plagued by introduced European birds such as Blackbirds (*Turdus merula*), Song Thrushes (*Turdus philomelos*) and Starlings (*Sturnus vulgaris*). As the grapes ripened and got sweet, the birds came, ruining each bunch of grapes. So the owners would shoot the birds all day long using men on quad bikes, or they would net whole vineyards at huge expense. The plan was to establish native New Zealand falcons to nest in the vineyards to prey on the birds and reduce their activity levels. The plan worked well and we got

Our Manager, Colin, finds another electrocuted falcon in the vineyards.

Another juvenile female electrocuted.

several pairs established and breeding. A PhD study proved their effectiveness. To hold the falcons there we used staff from the vineyards to provide supplementary feeding. We put up barrels in the trees for nest sites to reduce predation from cats.

Again, the Minister for Conservation came and was impressed. But again the project failed in that vineyard owners with small vineyards didn't want to put in the effort that benefitted his neighbour over the fence, an inverse tragedy of the commons. Instead they cut down all the hedges and trees that they could, to leave no place for the birds to hide. All that were left for hunting perches were unsafe power poles. The falcons were radio-tagged and of those we found dead, 47% were electrocuted. So the project became a campaign to make New Zealand's power poles safe for birds. It was a benefit, but not what we had planned.

11.5 Ecosystems at level two

11.5.1 Arctic peregrines

Another study did not involve modifying habitats, but it brought home to me the importance of habitats on a larger scale. We spent some years fitting satellite tags to calidus Peregrines which nest in northern Siberia. They come north in the spring and nest during the short arctic summer.

Before the autumn gales set in, they, and all the wader species that they prey on, head back south for warmer climes. The first barrier they come to is the vast northern taiga forest. They cannot hunt in the forest so they tend to cross it in one hop, about 700 km per day. From there they visit various lakes and wetlands to feed on ducks and other water birds. They use these places like motorway filling stations, stopping for a while to rest and recover their fat reserves. And just like cars on a motorway, they rely on these stop-over points which stretch like a bead necklace along their route south. Finally they reach destinations with sufficient food for them to live over the winter and moult their feathers. One hung around a mosque in Baghdad all winter, feeding on feral pigeons, another at an irrigated farm in Saudi Arabia. By tracking the falcons we could see where these key stop-over places were for them;

A Siberian peregrine broods her young chicks tightly.

272 HUNTING ETHICS

Migration routes of some of our Siberian Peregrines. Andrew Dixon.

knock out a few and the journey would get difficult because the distances between stop-off points become too great for their energy reserves. Suddenly we begin to realise that these bits of habitat form part of a bigger picture spanning a major part of the land surface of the planet. They are resources held in common. A similar picture emerges in the Americas where the *tundrius* Peregrine migrates from northern Canada down through Mexico into South America. Loss of habitat, loss of prey, poisoning or persecution along the way can be critical to the life cycle of the species.

These migration routes are like invisible aerial rivers. There are similar problems conserving real rivers. What happens upstream affects everything downstream.

11.6 A global 'eco-ethic'

Architects cover their mistakes with creepers.
Cooks cover their mistakes with sauce.
Doctors cover their mistakes with earth.
Mankind covers the Earth with mistakes.

This is where it starts to get gloomy. We are talking now about the big stuff, our top level priority, issues that affect the whole planet. Although people fret about global warming, climate change, carbon emissions and pollution, the biggest issue is the human population explosion. The other issues are consequences of this central issue.

There are 195 nations in the world of which 193 are members of the United Nations. The UN lists 17 Sustainable Development Goals to be achieved by 2030, all of them very worthy aspirations:

GOAL 1: No Poverty
GOAL 2: Zero Hunger
GOAL 3: Good Health and Well-being
GOAL 4: Quality Education
GOAL 5: Gender Equality
GOAL 6: Clean Water and Sanitation
GOAL 7: Affordable and Clean Energy

GOAL 8: Decent Work and Economic Growth
GOAL 9: Industry, Innovation and Infrastructure
GOAL 10: Reduced Inequality
GOAL 11: Sustainable Cities and Communities
GOAL 12: Responsible Consumption and Production
GOAL 13: Climate Action
GOAL 14: Life Below Water
GOAL 15: Life on Land
GOAL 16: Peace and Justice Strong Institutions
GOAL 17: Partnerships to achieve the Goal

Let me re-structure this list for you according to my own list of intellectual priorities:

1. **Earth and sustainable global systems.**
   GOAL 13: Climate Action
2. **Shared regional resources, such as water, and fisheries, the 'commons'.**
   GOAL 14: Life Below Water
   GOAL 15: Life on Land
3. **Habitats for full biodiversity for at least minimal viable populations of all species.**
4. **Single species management programmes.**
   GOAL 6: Clean Water and Sanitation
   GOAL 7: Affordable and Clean Energy
   GOAL 9: Industry, Innovation and Infrastructure
   GOAL 11: Sustainable Cities and Communities
   GOAL 12: Responsible Consumption and Production
   GOAL 16: Peace and Justice Strong Institutions
   GOAL 17: Partnerships to achieve the Goal
5. **Individual animal welfare.**
   GOAL 1: No Poverty
   GOAL 2: Zero Hunger
   GOAL 3: Good Health and Well-being
   GOAL 4: Quality Education
   GOAL 5: Gender Equality
   GOAL 8: Decent Work and Economic Growth
   GOAL 10: Reduced Inequality

All the 14 goals under priorities 4 and 5 benefit only one species – humans. None address the real issue: human demographics, on the contrary, most of the goals listed promote human population growth. The clue is in the title: 'Sustainable Development'. No developments can be sustainable indefinitely on a planet of finite size. The human demand on the planet is already 2.5 times what it can provide. We are living on resource capital. All of these goals are just sticking plaster on a fatal wound of climate change and global extinction of species. Nobody dares to address human population growth.

Do you think nobody realises that? Of course, everyone does! But it is the elephant in the room; nobody dares mention it. Why not? Because nobody knows how to tackle it. Each government relies on support from its citizens, either by democratic votes or various other systems of governing. Nobody wants to return home from a UN meeting with the message 'We've got to estimate the carrying capacity of our country and then reduce our human population to this level'. That, actually, would be 'sustainable'.

So, the message is totally unpalatable, and the political system at international level struggles to function effectively. I am no politician, but I have attended many international conferences of UNESCO and CITES, and negotiated MOUs with and between quite a number of disparate governments. Many of the Ministers I have dealt with have no training or background in the subject they are supposed to administer, and most are in office no more than a year or two, less time than it takes me to wear out a pair of wellies. Most are corrupt, short-termist, and egotistical and each assumes the others are too. Put them all together in a massive conference hall with simultaneous translation and they could easily spend an entire day debating a single sentence, then do cosy deals over dinner.

The leaders of these nations are a dysfunctional bunch. Mainly old men, they range from American presidents (who have to be millionaires), to fragile democracies stumbling along on coalitions, to faceless, inscrutable states and manic despots. None of them are going to propose, let alone do, anything drastic other than perhaps, war. Their one trump card is Time. 'Not our problem; we will be dead by the time it hits the fan.'

So if nothing significant is done internationally, our course remains unsustainable. Only two questions remain:
- When will it hit the fan?
- What form will it take?

Will we keep breeding until it is standing room only? Will we become increasingly dysfunctional so that our social groups disintegrate, so that we fail to make proper pair bonds, so that our breeding rate goes down? Would that happen evenly across the nations or would some nations continue to outbreed others and swamp them? Will wars over resources increase to the point that our human population decreases? But would each war zone totally devastate the landscape in the process? How long can a Western nation survive without electricity or internet?

Would wildlife be impacted before humans? Harari postulates a new Data Age, with artificial intelligence, transhumanism. That might happen for some, but you will not wipe away old ideologies from human cultures in just a few decades. The timescale is too short; conventional prejudices and climate change will influence affairs internationally for a long time to come. Will nuclear war wipe out all or almost all of the humans? Will the Earth regress a few million years in evolutionary terms?

To catch a hare by hand, you approach it at a spiralling tangent so that there is never a clear 'break' point. This is what is happening to us right now. We are crouched, aware of the danger and hoping it will go away, but, because its approach (although inevitable) is insidious, we never feel a break point. The danger of our exponential population growth and the damage we are doing to the climate is huge. It is totally devastating.

But unlike nuclear 'deterrents' which have a sense of urgency, of here and now, these bigger threats are spiralling in and we do not have the courage to make any big decisions. Governments talk vaguely about emissions targets but then squabble about who goes first, or last. Too little too late. Few have the guts to make significant sacrificial changes that could make their country uncompetitive in a world scrabbling for resources, a global tragedy of the commons. Young people, such as Greta Thunberg, who will be affected most, do what they can to make politicians listen, but the politicians are too busy holding on to power to make any uncomfortable decisions.

During a war, the population tends to pull together as a more cohesive social group. Tribulations are tolerated in the common need to fight the war. But our new 'enemies' are too elusive and nebulous for individuals to fight. There are a few things we could do, for example to make everyone self-sufficient for energy needs with house modifications for solar roofing and walling, and reduction in power consumption through technology. By collecting rainwater for grey water use instead of flushing potable water down the toilet. By replacing gyms with food-growing activities. By working on the genome to delete certain genes causing huge suffering and misery. By forcing manufacturers to provide 20 year warranties for their goods instead of built-in obsolescence. By nailing the whole packaging thing to the wall to minimise re-cycling efforts. By totally re-thinking transport systems. By pushing battery technology to provide energy storage and smooth out peaks and troughs. And so on…

But few politicians and democracies have the courage to implement significant or rapid change. Britain has prevaricated over its air and rail transport decisions for years, but we've made great progress in banning single-use shopping bags! Benign dictators at least are able to create changes rapidly. The British politicians argued over Brexit ineffectively right up until the deadline and beyond, and yet this is a simple issue in comparison to population growth and climate change. Neither they, nor the system, will do anything much until it is too late. Artificial Intelligence is amazing and scary, but can it over-come our ethotype? Climate change will not grant us an extension, it is already past the deadline and we don't even recognise it. And so our self-made threats spiral closer and closer, all of us crouched like timid hares.

11.6.1 What can we do?

Our ethotypic morality, together with our learned morality, has served us well throughout our evolutionary history, but now it is leading us into a trap and our population is burgeoning out of control and exhausting the resources of our planet. Realistically, we cannot change our ethotype in the timescale needed. We are approaching crisis point right now with climate change and population expansion. If we continue on the course we are currently on, I think we will be lucky if we survive without a major environmental crisis that could imperil the futures of all the species on this planet, not just our own. That's the bad news.

The good news? Is there any? Let's break it down into manageable chunks. If we cannot change our ethotype, then our only option is to change our learned behaviour, which includes how we imprint our offspring. Also our approach has to be at the level of each individual, each one of us. Instead of claiming our 'rights', we must start to think about our responsibilities. We must also set targets, so that we know what we are aiming for. And to set targets, we need a coherent vision.

My vision is for a world in a state of stasis, in balance with itself so that it can continue indefinitely. The buzzword is sustainability, but this has been hijacked by the marketing industry and politicians. Balance means that things stay 'in balance'. It doesn't mean that nothing changes; it means that if one side of the balance changes, then the other side does too, so that both sides continue to balance one another out. So the concept does not preclude 'progress' as long as it is counter-balanced in other ways. At the moment, governments just shout 'Growth' as an economic panacea.

Within my vision, I would like to see a world in which almost all species are represented, with more than minimal viable populations, and with a support plan such as gene banks of frozen seeds, semen and embryos. Although gene banks are hugely important, a species is not just a collection of genes; memetic material cannot be stored in a gene bank. Culture that is passed on from one generation to the next cannot be bottled. The ancestral knowledge held by the matriarch elephant about migration routes and water sources depends on an unbroken chain of inheritance. Making a species extinct is for me an 'ultimate crime'. To maintain those species entails retaining functioning habitats and ecosystems in which our own species may have a place, but our presence or impact is below a level that destabilises the balance. When I said 'almost all species', I think we should eliminate some diseases, such as smallpox virus, including any stocks held in stores.

To care for all our species in our global Noah's Ark, we need first a thorough audit of numbers and distribution. Some of these audits have been done, especially for iconic endangered vertebrates and plants, but many potentially critical species, such as soil bacteria and fungi, are as yet still undocumented. Leading on from the initial audit, we need to define what remedial action is needed, and this may entail approaches that set aside areas as natural habitat, as well as combined approaches where non-human species are encouraged to share space with humans. That may entail modifying our man-made environments to make them more friendly to non-humans.

All of this will start to define what space is left available for our own species and what standard of living this allows. Perhaps just a few million people on the planet with an American standard of consumptive living, or maybe a hundred times that number living in poverty? Can modern science and technology raise the standard of living while reducing ecological impacts such as climate change and pollution? We know that our population is currently living off global capital; we are unsustainable. We need to define the current carrying capacity of Earth for populations of all species, especially our own. This is a very painful exercise which so far we have studiously avoided. We are running our global business without ever doing the accounts.

Having defined a figure for carrying capacity, we have to work out ways of reaching it, and a time line. If our timeline is too long, we will be overtaken by events and the outcomes will be catastrophic. A shorter timeline to reach carrying capacity will be extremely painful and I have to say my prediction at the moment, for a number of reasons, is that we will fail to achieve it and we will fall victim to the normal biological model which is a boom and bust scenario.

But if we try to reach it, we would wish to do it as painlessly as possible. Population size is controlled by two parameters: births and deaths. Killing groups of people (eugenics), killing certain age groups (maybe everyone over 70 years old), or warfare (haphazard killing primarily of young men) are all approaches we don't even want to think about. So we are left with reducing the birth rate. Even if births are reduced in some areas, which is happening in parts of the developed world, migration is swamping these benefits and just moving the problem around the planet, de-stabilising regional cultures.

There are all sorts of cultural influences going on here and I'm sure you don't need me to explain them all to you. But we have reached the point where doing nothing is not an option. If we fail to take the least painful route, by reducing the birth rate, then we will be faced by more painful options such as warfare or ecological collapse. Let's call a spade a spade. That's the situation we are in. We are biological animals and our planet is limited in size. For sure we could send some people to Mars, but any biologist will quickly disillusion you about that. The only way to colonise Mars is to infect it with the toughest viruses and bacteria from our most hostile Earth environments, and if any of them manage to survive, give them a couple of billion years to evolve into higher life forms. Mars is not a get-out clause for our current human species.

While some Western nations are moving towards a balance between birth and death rates, albeit at levels still above carrying capacity, some other nations are breeding uncontrollably and modern medicine is improving infant survival and thus exacerbating the process. Some of these nations, for example parts of Africa, have land that has conditions to support more but it is badly managed. Look at the collapse of Zimbabwe, the bread basket of Africa. Others are more marginal and subject to increasing desertification, and others are low lying and hostage to increasing sea levels. With our big data systems and artificial intelligence, together with satellite surveillance systems, we can and have documented all of this, and we can predict what will happen next. It really isn't rocket science; what is holding us back are our own ideologies and politics. We have the whole Middle East embroiled in self-destruction because people interpret the Koran differently. We have Third World countries rejecting contraceptives because of Christian preachings. Really? In this day and age?

So we come back to education, especially imprinted learning. This is the toughy. If children are raised with certain values and prejudices, they are pretty much stuck with them for life, which means about 70 years. In that time they will breed more, and imprint them too. No amount of intellectual challenge will change them. I'm sure that what I have written in this book will attract a huge hostile response from people imprinted into religions and not just the dogma, but of wider values too, such as attitudes towards non-human animals, and even 'sub-human animals' such as slaves, and low-caste humans. They have been brought up and imprinted into these views. For them these views are normal and beyond any questioning. So while our ethotype cannot change in the next century or two, I don't think our imprinted values will change within that time frame either.

That only leaves our intellect, open-minded learning and critical thinking. Even countries like America are under siege by religions, be they Creationists or the gun lobby. We cling pathetically to a hope that science will bail us out, but at the moment it is simply making the situation worse. We have become obese on junk food and a labour-saving lifestyle, and intellectually emasculated by addiction to social media. Drugs reduce us to zombies.

I like to think that small is beautiful, that every little bit helps. We can all do our bit to help the environment. But so often our efforts backfire. There is increasing momentum on animal welfare issues, but these focus on my priority level #5, the lowest priority, individuals. Thus many of these efforts are counter-productive because they prevent efforts at higher priority levels such as caring for entire species, caring for entire habitats, caring for entire ecosystems and caring for the whole planet. It is easy to feel warm about caring for a furry animal; you don't really have to face the wider perspective. Once you go up a few levels, you find that to create balance you have to cut things down or kill things in order to conserve habitats and species in the face of increasing demands by humans for food and space. More and more well-intended bits of legislation promoted by animal welfarists are tying the hands of wildlife managers. Young people must connect more with nature, but on a realistic level which faces the facts of life for what they really are. We need to stop being bunny-huggers and become at least habitat-huggers, ecocentric instead of anthropocentric.

Near us in Pembrokeshire is a small community of mainly young people trying to live sustainably. It is a noble effort and a useful social exercise. They build hobbit houses and plant their own food, maybe raise a few chickens. But they are in a constant state of tension between the natural world and modern technology. Should they use electricity, if so, off-grid using solar panels made in China? Should they use chemicals to treat timber to stop their house rotting to the ground in five years, or to save their crops from pests? How much should they use modern medical care or transport? Do they really want to live like medieval peasants so that when February comes there is nothing left in the larder but a few turnips? Now they have businesses running online courses and visits; they are back with the cash economy.

I remember farming in Pembrokeshire in the 1960s. Some of the farms still lived off-grid, with paraffin lamps. Horses had virtually disappeared and neighbours shared some of their new farm machinery and did communal hay-making and shearing. Getting the old Fergie tractor going on a winter's morning could be an ordeal involving a lot of old-fashioned language and spraying 'hippie juice' (ethanol) into the air intake to give it a bit of a kick start. The early machinery gave way to new machines that could make silage much more reliably than hay, but the forage harvesters and combines were too expensive for individual farmers to afford. So contractors set up, going round the farms making silage and so on. We changed our gates from 10 foot, to 12 foot, then to 14 foot, and still the machines would knock the gate posts out and crush the land drains. The social structure changed to more isolationist approaches. The suicide rate for lonely farmers went up. Young people left the countryside because the lifestyle was too

Part of the Lammas Village 2023.

tough and there were more opportunities in the cities. The cities got bigger and bigger. The city people lost their understanding of where their food came from, and their ultimate reliance on the natural world. All of this has happened in the last hundred years, or less.

For myself, I have only a few more years left to live, if I am lucky. I want to do my best towards moving to a sustainable approach and looking after even a small part of the planet at least to level #3, habitat management. Maybe through this book I can reach more people at an intellectual level, and through the farm, physically show people some of the things I am talking about. For you as a reader, having struggled through to the end of this book, perhaps you can reflect on what you can do, especially in the way you rear children. They are the ones facing this mess we are leaving them. Don't raise them with values from thousands of years ago. Raise them with values that will equip them to face the future. There are plenty of projects going on. Try Jane Goodall's *'Roots & Shoots'* initiative for starters.

And what about the future of religions? Many people need a religion; some probably even have one or more genes for spirituality. Does this hard scientific view of the future deny the possibility of existing religions? I would say it does; the two approaches are incompatible. But maybe this is a start of a new religion, a religion that puts caring for the planet at its core? A religion that somehow acknowledges that we have so far been cared for and nurtured by Mother Nature and now, as we have grown up and matured, and as she has grown frail, it is time for us to become responsible children and care for her in our turn. To me, that is a noble 'religion' that I would subscribe to.

Turning the power of religion towards caring for the future of our planet may be the closest we will ever get to Eternal Life. That caring need not be spiritual; it doesn't need to be some kind of mystical Gaia. Pragmatically we are already seeing the impact of plastics on Earth's ecosystems. Recently I saw more plastic on 10 metres of a Bali beach than I have seen in my entire time in New Zealand. Devoting your life towards developing biodegradable materials to replace oil-based plastics seems to me to be a worthy moral goal. If we cannot turn the clock back, then perhaps as it turns forwards we can ensure that we do not repeat the mistakes of the past. For example, extending human life spans may appear to be a worthy cause, but do the maths, look at the re-configured demographic picture that this entails. Search for moral values that prioritise the planet, not the individual. Instead of fearing death, accept it and even welcome it. Without it the whole cycle of life comes to a grinding halt.

11.6.2 Genes and brains

Currently the human genome has been recorded, and our own projects have done the same now for the peregrine, gyrfalcon and saker falcon. But just identifying and recording the base pairings is only the first step. We also have to work out what each gene does, and it is not all that straightforward because they often interact with one another, or work in groups. Few aspects of an organism are controlled by one single gene. But as we find out more, we are making progress with genome editing, the first efforts have been to remove deleterious genes that cause various nasty illnesses and conditions. Genome editing tweaks existing DNA *in situ* by adding, subtracting or substituting a piece that may be as small as a single genetic "letter" (or nucleotide). That not only makes the technique precise, it also resembles the natural process of mutation.

Techniques such as CRISPR/Cas9 and RTDS (Rapid Trait Development Systems) allow changes to single nucleotides leading to fast and accurate genome editing, with massive potential benefits and moral implications. Crop strains created this way are already coming to market. Yet in many countries there is stiff resistance even against the use of genetically modified plants. People have only a hazy concept of genetics and even think that they could assimilate this modified genetic material by eating it. (Cauliflower ear anyone?) Actually you are more likely to assimilate another organism's genetic material by, for example, blood or bone marrow transplants. About 60% of mothers carry genetic material from their foetuses in their organs for the rest of their lives. A few people are even chimeras, carrying the genome of a twin that died and was absorbed early in gestation.

Of course there are many moral aspects to modifying genomes by whatever process, including traditional breeding techniques. Some of these aspects relate to the Precautionary Principle, but others relate to the potential to feed more people with less impact on the earth's resources, leaving more space for other species to live. If on the other hand it is used simply to further expand the human population or create patents for rich companies, then perhaps the moral benefits are neutralised.

How long before some of these techniques show results for humans? What if, as we learn more, we start to correlate certain genes with behavioural traits? We could start to alter our ethotypic behaviour! Could this be a way out of our evolutionary trap? Instead of always thinking 'me first', could we create humans who think 'planet first'? It may seem a bit blue sky thinking, but the component building blocks are almost there technically, right now. The first genetically modified human baby has already been born in China. And if we managed to gene edit some humans who put planet before selves, would we then have destroyed their ethotypic morality that holds social groups together? Would we have thrown the baby out with the bathwater? Would the genetically modified humans be unable to survive in the face of hostility from unmodified humans still operating on primitive instinctive templates? Or alternatively perhaps some tyrant nation would use the technique to produce super aggressive people, the human equivalent of killer bees, or subordinate ones, genetic slaves. China may be doing it already.

Artificial intelligence too is now with us and set to change the world. Amongst other things it brings into question concepts of 'personhood' and 'sentience'. In a way we are creating some kind of mycelial, amorphous super humans. But it won't be really human if it doesn't include elements such as our ethotype. On the other hand, we humans are handicapped by our ethotype, that is why we are caught in the evolutionary trap. Artificial intelligence, without our ethotypic handicap, has the potential to escape the trap into the world of intellect. But can it pull us with it? Only time will tell.

A classic example of the damage we are doing at level three is the perturbation of the soil microbiome. When I was a boy in the 1950s I used to delight in examining all the weird insects stuck on the car radiator, which was about my height. Even though cars did not go very far or fast in those days, there were always plenty of insects splattered on the windscreen. In 2014 I drove all around southern and mid-Britain at the end of June, for three days before crossing north Wales and driving down the length of Wales, a hilly livestock area with no arable farming. My windscreen remained totally clean. Recent reports from Germany show that insect biomass there has declined by over 75% since 1991 and it is likely that the same has happened in UK, but we have no proper long-term monitoring system. These studies are only of flying adult insects caught in Malaise traps; who knows what is happening in the soil and vegetation where the larval forms live?

Why has this happened? Is it the result of damage at the trophic level below, the soil bacteria and micro-organisms? Or has there been a direct effect at this trophic level only? And of course, if the insects are impacted, it has a knock-on effect at the trophic levels above them, such as all the insectivorous species, and their predators. What changes have occurred in the last half a century that could affect huge swathes of countryside, arable and livestock areas alike? For sure, cocktails of pesticides and insecticides have been used in arable farming in this time. Pressures on farming have led to increasingly 'pure' monocultures in which few weeds or insects are tolerated and in which chemicals are applied with accuracy both in terms of geography (guided by GPS systems) and timing. Such crops produce more and sell better. But soil quality is deteriorating and is being exhausted, the proportion of organic matter is decreasing and the balance of soil organisms is upset. Just as your gut microbiome is upset when you take antibiotics, so the soil microbiome can be upset by chemicals that target certain species or groups selectively, allowing others to flourish, and upsetting the balance.

We see this happening in arable farming, but how could I travel through Wales which is pastoral livestock farming, and still find few insects? In this landscape, very few chemicals are applied to the land. For sure in the spring many farmers apply chemical fertilisers to boost the silage fields, but much of the fertiliser is in the form of farm slurry, in other words, cow manure. This is organic material that should be good for soil structure. In the sheep districts, some fields get lime to stop them becoming too acid, but many hill areas get nothing because tractors cannot go there. The only fertiliser they get are sheep droppings, and gradually soil fertility itself is falling.

Confining animals to fields means that gut parasites such as nematodes, cestodes and flukes can build up and affect fertility, growth rates or even be fatal. Therefore the animals are dosed periodically with wormers, some of which, such as Ivermectin, are very persistent. They travel through the gut and kill the worms and then are excreted in the dung where they persist and enter the soil ecosystem. Ivermectin is partly degraded by sunlight, but within the soil it can persist for years and residues can accumulate year on year, which seems to be the point we are reaching now. This is bad news for the dung beetles and insects that colonise the droppings and break them down, and it is bad news for the soil microbiome. It is also bad news for birds that feed on the bugs in the dung. In the past 15 years we have lost our two rookeries on the farm and seldom see rooks at all anymore. So chemicals introduced to affect a handful of species of economic concern can affect others both up and down the food chain. These chemicals have been promoted by vets and the pharmaceutical industry, focussing on levels 5 (individual animals) and 4 (species), with little comprehension or research done at level 3 (ecosystems and habitats). They have been a quick fix, but an ecosystemic disaster.

Another example is *diclofenac*. This is an anti-inflammatory drug sold for use on both humans and farm animals. If an animal being treated with diclofenac subsequently dies, scavengers eating the body pick it up and it causes kidney failure in vultures resulting in die offs of around 99% in the Indian sub-continent. This was flagged up at a conference in Nepal in 2004 which I attended. Subsequently I chaired a meeting between Pakistani government officials and Abu Dhabi officials from what is now the Environment Agency. Although we did succeed in persuading Abu Dhabi to donate $50k to Pakistan, it was a heated meeting and I had to call a break at one point for a cooling off period. The layers of officialdom in Pakistan are so complicated and corruption is so rife that following this meeting I resolved not to raise funds for governments any more, but to ensure that funding went exactly to costs and salaries of fieldworkers themselves. Since then there have been attempts to ban diclofenac in favour of alternatives such as *Meloxicam*. India banned it in 2006 but Pakistan has yet to do so, and it is still available for human use and used illegally on cattle. There are efforts to breed vultures in captivity, and we have done so in the UK, but it is a very slow and costly business and is a waste of time unless the ecosystems are cleaned up.

The use of chemicals, such as contraceptives, antibiotics, insecticides, wormers and anti-inflammatories, intended for one job but then entering and persisting in wider ecosystems is an ecological disaster. They are big business for the pharmaceutical industry, and the life blood of the medical and veterinary professions that have little expertise at level 3 (ecosystems), yet claim authority. The public want cheap food, be it chicken, beef or cereals, and to produce it farmers and the pharmaceutical industry will take short cuts, both on welfare and more importantly on ecosystemic issues. Switching to a vegan diet doesn't make much difference; the ecosystemic issues are still there. Going organic is an ideal solution but realistically it is unaffordable.

Nowadays well-off people in developed countries spend less than 10% of income on food, but in poorer countries it is closer to 40%. In my lifetime, the proportion of income spent on food has halved, partly because wages generally have increased, but also because of these short cuts in food production techniques. Low earners will buy food on price; that is the way of the world. Politicians will bow to pressure from voters and the pharmaceutical industry. With humans increasing in number the outlook looks bleak for the natural world, especially at levels 1-3 which are almost impossible to influence.

Let me take you down a few real-life highways and bye ways of where this kind of decision-making leads. We had a Wiltshire Horn ewe with twin lambs the other day. We had put her to a Texel ram because the market wants carcasses with more meat on them. The first lamb was born OK, but the second was large and she had difficulty delivering it. Andrew assisted and got it out alive but the ewe wouldn't take it. He put them in a small pen on straw but still she kept butting it away. We thus had two choices: to bottle feed the lamb which is uneconomic in terms of bought milk powder and time, or to cut our losses and shoot the lamb. The girls offered to bottle feed the lamb and we kept the ewe in for three days but she still wouldn't properly take it. We thus had a synchronous dual imprint lamb; it would follow its mother but look to the girls for milk. Eventually we had to let the ewe out and the spring grass was growing, but the next day she collapsed and had fits. She was discovered at eight o'clock at night after the vets had gone off-duty. The call out fee for a vet plus the cost of treatment, is more than the value of the ewe. Therefore nobody can afford to call a vet for a sheep; a cow maybe, but not a sheep. Vets prefer small animal practice where the hours are more sociable, there are less travel costs, and the profit margins are better. If we shot the sheep we would either have to shoot the lambs too, or bottle rear them, and of course although one was used to the bottle, the other would refuse it. If we called out the vet and the treatment was unsuccessful we would be left with both a bill and a dead ewe. If we shot the sheep we would have to dispose of the carcase. It is now illegal in the UK to bury animals on the farm unless they are pets such as horses or dogs, or to use an offal pit as we do in New Zealand. You can shoot a deer and let it lie, but not a sheep. We have to ring up Goddards in Haverfordwest, 40 km away. They come in a lorry, take the sheep away and incinerate it, which is polluting and costs £37.50. With no dead animals on the farms, the scavengers such as foxes and kites have lost a major food source, especially during the hard winter months. So kites have been at a low point, and kite feeding stations have been established across Wales. Similar 'vulture restaurants' have been set up in southern EU countries such as Spain. But regulations only allow butcher's meat scraps to be fed to the kites. These are not a balanced diet for producing hatchable eggs. On such a diet the chicks develop rickets. Complete madness!

Farmers, of course, are well aware of all this and often keep a few extra sheep to allow for losses. If a sheep dies, they cut the ear tags off and throw the carcase over the fence into the bushes in the woods. There the foxes quickly dispose of them, but the kites cannot reach them. It's illegal, but more environmentally friendly.

So back to our little moral dilemma. It was getting dark and we were all tired after a long day. I had seen this happen before; a change of diet being kept indoors then let out, plus the demands of producing milk, can cause blood calcium levels to plunge, leading to fits and death. But an injection of calcium borogluconate can make a dramatic recovery. Given that it was not just the ewe's life at stake, but the lambs too, Andrew rang the vets in town and they left a bottle on their door step. Although already worn out, he went into town, collected it and injected the ewe. The next morning she was on her feet, feeling rough and not feeding, but tottering about and in her right mind. By evening she was feeding a little, and the next day she was back to normal with the lambs bouncing around. I wish I could report that all such dilemmas have such a happy ending, but they don't.

Andrew made a note of the ewe's tag number and she will be sold in the autumn, together with the Texel tup. So decisions made at individual level cascade to flock level, and can impact other species as well as having environmental effects. With Brexit, sheep farming in the UK may become uneconomical, opening the market to imports from countries that do not have such legal constraints. Without sheep to rotate the grazing on the fields, the worm cycles will not be broken. If worm eggs from a cow or a horse are on the pasture and a sheep eats them, they cannot develop, so effectively the sheep are naturally 'cleaning' the pasture, and vice versa. If you just keep a single species, worm counts build up, animals, fade, abort or die. But hey, let's just give them all a good dose of Ivermectin….

12 Epilogue

It's one thing to write a book about hunting; plenty of people before me have pondered, theorised and pontificated on the subject. But over the past seven decades, living cheek by jowl with other animals, farming, hunting, hawking, digging ponds and planting trees, and running conservation programmes from the Arctic to New Zealand, I have had many experiences which have shaped this book. Ostensibly about hunting and ethics, you can see how hunting is intertwined with our evolution and history, with our very nature, with our dependence on maintaining habitats and ecosystems and ultimately, with our survival, together with every other animal and living thing on this little planet. So a book about the ethics of hunting of necessity ramifies into all these interdependent elements.

As I sit here at the kitchen table, one of the dogs is lying across my feet so that I cannot move. The dog who lay on my feet 30 years ago when I started this book is long gone. This one is Bonny, a young Munsterlander. Helen has just brought in a cold lamb, a rejected twin. She's fed him some colostrum and Lamlac, milk substitute. It's been a long, wet winter and the land is sodden. The sheep lamb outside and they are earlier than planned this year. The bats are venturing out now from our bedroom roof. Soon the swallows and house martins will be back from Africa. There are still a few woodcock about: Bonny points them as I do my rounds of the farm. They will be heading off home to the Baltic and Siberia soon.

We're pretty international here. We may seem like a little introverted farm in Wales, but we are the world in a microcosm. The greylags are back on the lake from their northern wintering grounds and the dabchicks are trilling. The beavers have been busy all winter and have made a new pond with a 50 metre dam. The frogs and toads have finished their hazardous annual pilgrimages and some of the spawn is hatching now. A kingfisher flits about busily and the wagtails and wrens are preparing their nests around the farmyard. We've got a couple of beaver kits in the stable which we trapped in the autumn. They will go out as soon as we can get some unrelated partners for them. The falcons are laying and every few hours I go to check the eggs in the incubators. When I turn off the light and candle them I can see the blood vessels and the embryos swooping about. In two months' time they will have feathers and be flying. The goshawks and ravens have been displaying and the kites follow me on the quad bike hoping for some left-overs. A young buzzard who frequents a pole on our track has made it through the winter feeding on earthworms. That field is a ryegrass ley; it doesn't tiller well and there is always some bare earth for a sharp eye to spot a worm. The pest control lad with his poison certificate has killed all the moles in the mowing fields so that the mole hills don't contaminate the silage, but in the old grass fields the moles have chains of earthen mounds, each mole's chosen hunting ground. Soon spring will be in full swing. We will take the covers off the horses and they can roll and shed their winter coats. The jackdaws will make off with tufts of hair to line their nests in the quad shed roof.

Once you've managed to get hold of a bit of land, what are you going to do with it in the few short years you might live for? Looking at our farm, how do we measure up against our list of priorities?

Starting at the lowest priority, #5 Individual animal welfare, we have done a number of things. For the sheep, we have installed concrete handling facilities so that we can get them all in, check their feet, dose them, worm them and so on. With wool prices staying lower than the cost of shearing, we have switched to Wiltshire

Horns, a breed that sheds its own wool and doesn't need shearing. This reduces the risk of summer fly strike on wet fleeces. We have given up keeping cattle because of the risk of bovine tuberculosis which is rife in the area, with badgers as wild vectors. We have two old setts of badgers and it seems unlikely that we will be able to keep cattle again any time soon.

In 2001 there was an outbreak of foot and mouth disease in Britain. It came from a pig farm at Heddon on the Wall, not far from our farm in Northumberland. The pig farmer had collected swill from restaurants and not cooked it well enough before feeding it to the pigs. How did the disease come to be in meat served in restaurants in the first place? Nobody got to the bottom of this. Now we have to double tag our sheep and keep records of which field they are in and when we move them. But there was no effort to prevent the disease reaching Britain. At British airports health controls are desultory or non-existent. I have seen boxes of bushmeat fresh in from Africa brought straight through customs, blood making the cardboard soggy. But in New Zealand I have had customs officers take my shoes and clean the last traces of mud off them.

We were not culled but all stock and human movement was stopped during foot and mouth. We still use the *hendre* system, whereby sheep are kept on a high ground farm (*hafod*) in the summer and moved to us on the low ground (*hendre*) in winter. We had about 150 tack ewes wintering and by March almost all the feed had gone and it was time for them to be moved to the hafod. They were heavily in lamb. But they had to stay in the same field which they had eaten out. We were not even allowed to take them across the tarmac public lane. Well, you can imagine the mess! Ewes dropping dead and dying lambs all over the place, the bleating and the hollering. In the end I moved them across the road regardless, into the fields shut up for silage. Then I bulldozed a new gateway through a hedge so that they could reach fresh fields without crossing the road. We had to have foot baths and pressure wash our farm vehicles, and not leave the farm. But the government decided that footpaths could be open so that the public could walk where they wanted. Nothing made any sense. I wonder what the government would have done if foot and mouth was capable of infecting horses? Or dogs, or cats? Or humans? Would they have had the temerity to extend the killings to members of our own moral communities?

That was a bad summer and we couldn't fly the falcons. So I built a log cabin down by the lake and covered it with a turf roof. Silver birches are growing on the roof and wagtails sneak into their nest inside a tussock. The swallows nest inside it, and the wrens commandeer their old nests. And when I hang up a towel after swimming, the bats crawl inside it and use it as a cosy roost. You can wake up in the morning to hear the plop of a water vole or the churring of a dabchick with striped chicks on her back. I needed somewhere quiet, to let new life seep in.

Although we breed healthy falcons, we don't undertake rehabilitation of wild raptors on any scale; most of the time rehabilitation is more for the sake of the rehabbers themselves than for the animals. But if one comes along we will do our best. Last year a neighbour brought in a weak barn owl that was floundering in his slurry pit. After thorough washing and a couple of weeks feeding up, it was clear to go back out. Recently I picked up a buzzard from the side of the road. He was only bruised and after three weeks in a big flight pen he was strong again and we returned him to the same area. But generally, rehabilitating individuals from common species has little benefit to the wild population.

We were driving through the Forest of Dean recently, just on dusk, when we came across a few cars pulled up on the steep verge. There'd been an accident and the victim was lying by the roadside covered in a blanket. It turned out that an old lady had hit a fallow buck and broken two of its legs. She was in tears and meanwhile a vegetarian couple were kindly trying to give the deer some water. What to do? If they called the police, they would just say call a vet. A vet would charge to come out on call after hours – who would pay the bill? How long would it take for the vet to arrive? With two broken legs there was no way the vet could realistically rehab the deer, euthanasia was the only option. The vet would inject it with chemicals making it unfit for the human or wild food chain. So someone would have to take the carcase the next day to be incinerated. Who would do it, and pay that bill? Is incineration really the most ecologically friendly way to dispose of a carcase? How else could one kill it? Back a car over its head? By now the deer, despite its broken legs, was getting a bit frisky. Helen gave the old lady a hug and tried to make her look the other way. I got out my hawking knife and slit its throat. Blood flooded down the road, diluted by the pouring rain. Once the bleeding had stopped we quickly heaved the body into our car and drove to the nearest field gate. There we gralloched the deer and left the steaming guts for scavengers. The next morning we jointed it and put it in the freezer. Given that we had not killed the deer for food, but because of unavoidable welfare reasons, would a vegetarian have been prepared to eat the venison? Or would the moral high ground be to waste it, or maybe feed it to the foxes? I mulled over these questions as I poured on the gravy.

Moving up the priority scale from individuals to species; goshawks, kites and beavers have returned to the farm, along with many plant species. Woodland and wetland habitats have become restored and we are finding a balance for wildlife and farming. Nowadays people talk about 're-wilding' and so on, but there is no special magic to it, just a question of making some space and giving a bit of a helping hand now and then. Above the habitat level, it has been harder to make a difference, but maybe this book will ripple out and you, the reader, will have the opportunity to make a difference in your own way.

This book hasn't been just an academic exercise for me. I've tried to analyse things, and understand why I have done some things, but not others. All of the earnest and heated debates on the philosophy of morality, the books, the lectures, the learned papers, all somehow drop away and become almost irrelevant when faced with real life. That is the acid test. My decisions and actions weren't 'right', they weren't 'correct', they weren't 'true'; they were just me doing the best I could in the circumstances.

Farmers and hunters learned long ago about politicians and administrators. We had a Council Enforcement lady out here a few years ago to inspect the beavers. She wore a body cam to interview me. But she had no wellies and wouldn't walk more than 100 metres down the field before turning back… Why is it that politicians and administrators consider themselves qualified to make ethical decisions for me, over-riding my own sense of responsibility? Surely we should be encouraging people to take responsibility for their own actions, rather than fostering a sense of dependency, of helplessness, of compliance? Freedom means taking responsibility, not abrogating it or ignoring it. I know that what I have done on the farm, and in various conservation projects, has been pitifully small. But equally I've found that politicians and administrators understand even less than I do and that it is folly to rely on them. Their terms of office, their salaries, their grants, are all ephemeral. They define themselves as Head of this, Director of that. Their official positions, like the Emperor's Clothes, define them more than their contributions or abilities.

12.1 Conclusions

If a cockroach or rat walked across your kitchen floor, what would you do? Would you kill it? Are you more 'necessary' than they are? The element of 'necessity' is an anthropocentric indulgence. You have no more claim to be necessary than any other organism on this planet, in fact, given the ecological disasters created by humans, all the other species on the planet would be a lot better off without us. There is no ethical validity in claiming human primacy, but we are so obsessed with ourselves that we take it for granted. Many other species make the same assumption for themselves no doubt. But it is an illusion, a sham; there is no morality in it. We all of us like to think that we are important, but we're not.

The process of writing this book has forced me to confront various issues, to investigate them, and it has clarified my mind to some extent. I've tried to peer through the murk of my pragmatism, and in just doing what I think best, decipher underlying principles and themes. I don't expect you to reach the same conclusions as me – wouldn't it be boring if we were all the same! But maybe you find yourself in a different position now to where you were before you started reading it.

So where does it leave me?

- I don't accept Cartesian dualism, that somehow humans are separate from other mammals. I can see no point during our evolution to warrant it, and no criteria intrinsically separating us. Our claimed differences are clinal and consequential, that is all.
- I believe that all vertebrate behaviour, including human behaviour, shares common roots and that the ethotype of all vertebrates is a core source of behaviour, overlaid by learned behaviour.
- I see no ultimate 'good' or 'bad' in morality; rather its function is the survival of each individual until it has passed on its genes.
- I believe that morality is not just a human construct; it is a mechanism shared by all vertebrates and perhaps some invertebrates too.
- I see no evidence for the existence of any 'Gods' and thus no validity in any statements about morality made by the prescribed religions.
- I believe that considerations at the population level should ultimately trump those at the level of the individual, unpleasant as that may be.
- I believe that, as an animal, a predator and a male, it is in my ethotype to hunt.
- I don't accept that those who disagree with me should prevent me from hunting other than by persuading me to change through force of evidence. Nor have I any wish to impose my views on others.
- I don't believe in Animal Rights or Human Rights as useful concepts.
- I don't accept that there can be a world without suffering and therefore I take as my benchmark of 'acceptability', the kinds and levels of suffering of animals in the absence of humans. While suffering can be deplored as a negative, one should also consider the positives: pleasure and quality of life.
- I do not accept that killing or death are 'bad'; rather they are essential elements in the natural cycle of life.

Translating these into my hunting activities:
- I don't particularly want to go fishing.
- I will eat fish if caught on a sustainable basis.
- I don't at the moment see a more humane way of fishing than with nets.
- I don't support fishing that damages the sea bed or non-target species.
- I don't particularly want to shoot animals recreationally, especially not with a shotgun.
- I do not support large-scale driven game shooting, although I acknowledge the collateral benefits of pest control.
- I will shoot animals for pest control, wildlife management or to kill them humanely.

Chapter 12 – EPILOGUE

Hawking pest crows along Hadrian's Wall before the sycamore tree was cut down.

Pippa Scott-Harden.

- I support hunting with dogs above ground.
- I'm not keen on the use of terriers below ground.
- I don't support allowing domestic cats outside to hunt freely.
- I will trap a mouse in the house.
- I won't eat soya-based products including meat reared on them.
- I support falconry – hunting with raptors.
- I don't support snares other than a means of last resort.
- I'm not keen on intensive livestock farming.
- I support eating meat from humanely killed extensively grazed farm animals.
- I believe that, as far as feasible, the UK should be self-reliant for food.
- I will eat imported fruit when my home-grown fruits are finished.
- I regret the use of monocultures and pesticides.
- I support riding and working horses.
- I do not think cities represent 'civilisation' or the moral high ground.

A Horse in the City

"You can keep your buses and cars,
I'll take a horse."
    "A horse?"
"Yes."
    "Don't be mad; what would you do with a horse?"
"Ride it of course.
You know where I'd ride? I'd ride to the park
And beyond, by the beach, to the hills
And along through the scrub to a place I know
Where a thin little rivulet spills;
And I'd sit in the saddle and dream some dreams,
And after a while I'd take
To a winding trail that I rode as a boy
To the edge of the moonlit lake…
I'd ride to the end of the moonlit trees
And the horse could set the pace
As long as I had the sky and the stars
And the night-wind in my face."
    "If you had a horse. Why, you can't ride."
"I can."
But the fellow laughed,
    "And where in the city would you keep a horse
If you had a horse? You're daft."

Sid Delany

Acknowledgements

Parts of this book have been written over the past thirty years and been published or presented at conferences or government consultations. Many people from various walks of life have participated. Helen Macdonald assisted me when we were working on animal welfare and sustainable hunting issues. Dr Robert Kenward was instrumental in organising the re-introduction programme for the Northern Goshawks and work on sakers in Kazakhstan. My former Heads of Research, Dr Eugene Potapov helped with the statistical treatment of the fox wounding study while Dr Andrew Dixon developed a lot of the work on falcon population management, migration studies and genetics. Drew Love-Jones and Jo Oliver have been involved in the development of the Bevis Trust and the work with beavers, with Derek Gow, Dr Róisín Campbell-Palmer, Charlie Burrell and Gerhard Schwab providing insights into their experiences in the practical and political elements of wildlife management. The Red Kite team – Peter Davis MBE and Peter Walters Davies MBE, Iolo Williams and Dee Doody enthusiastically worked together to create the Kite Restoration programme. Jim Chick, Andrew Knowles-Brown, Nick Kester, Martin Jones, Mark Upton and I spent many years handling the politics of bird of prey management in the UK. Jevgeni Shergalin has been a stalwart at the office for 14 years, always ready with contacts all over the world. Drs Jamie Samour, Tom Bailey and Nigel Barton have helped with veterinary aspects, with editing Falco, and with making educational films. Drs Tom Richter and Adrian Lombard engaged in useful discussions on international bird of prey welfare issues. Drs Fred Launay and Mohammed Saleh have helped with discussions during our work together on wildlife issues in Asia and the Middle East. HE Mohammed Al Bowardi supported much of our work in Asia and the Middle East and gave me a perspective on evolution in Islam. Dr Awadh Ali Saleh, Dr Bohumil Straka and Professor Suleyman Khalaf were my team-mates on the UNESCO work and gave me insights into international politics and culture. I've worked together with Colin Wynn, our falcon manager in New Zealand, and Noel Hyde MNZOM and Debbie Stewart-Badger MNZOM for many decades on falcon and conservation issues in New Zealand. Simon Hart MP and David Mills were instrumental in establishing Red Squirrels on Caldey Island. Over the years, many people on our staff and in our field teams have made me think hard and explain the theoretical aspects that under-pin our applied management techniques, and go back to square one and seek more evidence to clarify the theories.

Jim Barrington took the trouble to go through the book and comment in detail. Jim had at one time been CEO of the League Against Cruel Sports but left it in disgust. We have worked together on animal welfare issues and politics for many years, coming at it from opposite poles and colliding in the middle, always with humour and good grace. It has been a pleasure working with him.

Anja Claus from the Humans and Nature organisation in Chicago also gave me some of her precious time and commented on a draft, giving me useful comments from a different perspective and inviting me to look at things from a modern American standpoint. Thank you Anja for taking so much trouble when you have never even met me.

My wife, Helen, has provided a foil for me in discussions within this book, much of which, by its very nature, is contentious, often with several 'sides' to a debate.

Finally I would like to thank my seven peer reviewers, each one specialist in his or her own field. I will not name them and of course they do not necessarily agree with all I have written. But they have given me welcome advice and made me check and re-check statements I have written.

Further Reading

Chapter 2 The Roots of Behaviour

Aaen-Stockdale, C. 2012. Neuroscience for the Soul. Psychologist. 25(7):520–523.

Ackerman, C. 2017. *Big Five Personality Traits: The OCEAN Model Explained*. PositivePsychology.com.

Adams-Hunt, M. M. and L. F. Jacobs. 2007. Cognition for foraging. In *Foraging: Behaviour and Ecology*. D.W. Stephens, J.S. Brown and R.C. Ydenberg (Eds) pp 105-138. University of Chicago Press.

Ainsworth, M. D. S. 1978. The Bowlby-Ainsworth attachment theory. Behavioral and Brain Sciences (3): 436-438.

Anderson, S. R. 2004. *Doctor Doolittle's Delusion: Animals and the Uniqueness of Human Language*. Yale University Press.

Baldwin, J. M. 1896. A New Factor in Evolution. The American Naturalist 30 (354): 441–451.

Bates, L.A. and R.W. Byrne. 2007. Creative or created: Using anecdotes to investigate animal cognition. Methods 42: 12-21.

Bekoff, M. 2000. Animal emotions: Exploring passionate natures: Current interdisciplinary research provides compelling evidence that many animals experience such emotions as joy, fear, love, despair, and grief—We are not alone. BioScience 50(10): 861–870.

Bekoff, M. 2007. *The emotional lives of animals: A leading scientist explores animal joy, sorrow, and empathy and why they matter*. Novato, CA: New World Library.

Bekoff, M. 2011. Do wild animals suffer from PTSD and other psychological disorders? Psychology Today.

Berger, J. 2007. Fear, human shields and the re-distribution of prey and predators in protected areas. Biol. Letters 22, 3(6): 620-623.

Birch, J., C. Burn, A. Schnell, H. Browning, and A. Crump. 2021. Review of the evidence of sentience in cephalopod molluscs and decapod crustaceans. London School of Economics.

Bitterman, M. E. 1965. The evolution of intelligence. Sci. Am. 212:92–100.

Bitterman, M. E. 1975. The comparative analysis of learning. Science 188:699–709.

Bonanni, R., E. Natoli, S. Cafazzo and P. Valsecci. 2011. Free-ranging dogs assess the quantity of opponents in intergroup conflicts. Anim. Cogn. 14:103–115.

Bowlby, J. 1969. Attachment. Attachment and loss: Vol. 1. Loss. New York: Basic Books.

Bowlby, J. 1973. Attachment and loss. Volume II. Separation, anxiety and anger. In Attachment and loss. volume II. Separation, anxiety and anger. New York: Basic Books.

Bowlby, J. 1980. *Loss: Sadness & depression. Attachment and loss (vol. 3)*; (International psycho-analytical library no. 109). London: Hogarth Press.

Brown, C. 2015. Fish intelligence, sentience and ethics. Animal cognition, 18(1): 1-17.

Brown, C. and K. Laland. 2011. Social learning in fishes. In: Brown C, Krause J, Laland K (eds) *Fish cognition and behavior*. Wiley, Oxford, pp 240–257.

Brown, C., K. Laland and J. Krause. 2011. Fish cognition and behavior. In: Brown C, Krause J, Laland, K (Eds). *Fish cognition and behaviour*. Blackwell Publishing Ltd., pp 1–9.

Bshary, R. 2011. Machiavellian intelligence in fishes. In: Brown C, Krause J, Laland K (Eds). *Fish cognition and behavior*. Blackwell Publishing Ltd., pp 277–297.

Bshary, R., A. Hohner, K. Ait-el-Djoudi and H. Fricke. 2006. Interspecific communicative and coordinated hunting between groupers and giant moray eels in the Red Sea. PLoS Biol 4:e431.

Bshary, R., W. Wickler and H. Fricke. 2002. Fish cognition: a primate's eye view. Anim. Cogn. 5:1–13

Byrne, R., and A. Whiten. 1989. *Machiavellian intelligence II: Extensions and evaluations*. Cambridge University Press .

Costa, P., A, Terracciano and R. McCrae, R. 2001. Gender Differences in Personality Traits Across Cultures: Robust and Surprising Findings. Journal of Personality and Social Psychology, 81 (2): 322-331.

Damasio, A. 1999. *The feeling of what happens*. Heinemann, London.

Dawkins, M. S. 1985. *Unravelling animal behaviour*. Longman.

Dawkins, M. S. 1998. Evolution and animal welfare. Q. Rev. Biol. 73:305–328.

Dawkins, M. S. 2001. Who needs consciousness? Anim. Welf. 10 (Suppl 1):19–29.

De Waal, Frans. 2016. *Are we smart enough to know how smart animals are?* Granta Publications.

Despret, V. 2015. Who made clever Hans stupid? *Angelaki* 20 (2):77-85.

Díaz, A., J. García and L. Pérez. 2023. Gender Differences in the Propensity to Start Gambling. J. Gambl. Stud. 39: 1799–1814.

Douglas, R., and C. Hawryshyn. 1990. Behavioural studies of fish vision: an analysis of visual capabilities. In: Douglas, R, Djamgoz, M. (eds) *The visual system of fish*. Springer, Collett TS.

Dummett, M, 1993. *The Seas of Language*. Oxford University Press.

Duncan, I. J. H. and J.C. Petherick. 1991. The implications of cognitive processes for animal welfare. J. Anim. Sci. 69: 5017–5022.

Emery, N. and N. Clayton. 2004. The mentality of crows: Convergent evolution of intelligence in corvids and apes. Science, 306(5703): 1903-1907.

Fagan, J. F., and L.T. Singer. 1983. Infant recognition memory as a measure of intelligence. Adv. Infancy. Res. 2: 31–78.

Fernö, A., G. Huse, P. J. Jakobsen and T. S. Kristiansen. 2011. The role of fish learning skills in fisheries and aquaculture. In: Brown, C., Krause, J., Laland, K.N. (eds) *Fish cognition and behaviour*. Blackwell, Oxford, pp 278–310.

Ferreira, D. F. 1616. *Arte de Caça de Altaneria*. English translation by Anthony Jack 1996. ISBN 0952690616.

Fisher, J., and R. A. Hinde. 1949. The opening of milk bottles by birds. Br. Birds 42: 347–358.

Fox, N.C. 2022. Understanding the Bird of Prey: New Advanced Edition. Hancock House.

Frank, S, G. F. Jolly and M. H. Woodford. 1956. A Common Gull brought up in the eyrie by a pair

of Peregrines together with their own young. The Falconer 3(30)96-99.
Ganguly, A. and U. Candolin. 2023. Impact of light pollution on aquatic invertebrates: Behavioral responses and ecological consequences. Behav. Ecol. Sociobiol. 77: 104.
Gerlach. G., A. Hodgins-Davis, C. Avolio and C. Schunter. 2008. Kin recognition in zebrafish: a 24-hour window for olfactory imprinting. Proc. R. Soc. Lond. B 275: 2165–2170.
Godfrey-Smith, P. 2016. *Other Minds*. Harper Collins.
Graham, P. 2004. Animal navigation: path integration, visual landmarks and cognitive maps. Curr. Biol. 14: R475–R477.
Grant, P.R. and B.R. Grant. 1997. Hybridisation, sexual imprinting and mate choice. American Naturalist 149:1-18.
Griffin, D. R. 2001. *Animal minds: Beyond cognition to consciousness*. Chicago: University of Chicago Press.
Gurven, M., C. von Rueden, M. Massenkoff, H. Kaplan and M. Lero Vie. 2013. How universal is the Big Five? Testing the five-factor model of personality variation among forager-farmers in the Bolivian Amazon. Journal of personality and social psychology, 104 (2): 354–370.
Haidt, J. 2013. *The Righteous Mind: Why Good People are Divided by Politics and Religion*. Penguin Books.
Halliday, T. R. and P. J. B. Slater. 1983. *Animal*. Blackwells Scientific Publications, Oxford.
Hammermeister, J., M. Flint, A. El-Alayli, H. Ridnour and M. Peterson. 2005. Gender differences in spiritual well-being: are females more spiritually-well than males? Am. J. Health Stud, 20.
Hammond, N. and B. Pearson. 1988. *Birds of Prey Behaviour Guide*. Hamlyn.
Hansell, M. and G. D. Ruxton. 2008. Setting tool use within the context of animal construction behaviour. Trends Ecol. Evol. 23: 73–78.
Harari, Y. N. 2015. *Sapiens: A Brief History of Humankind*. Vintage.
Hare, B. 2005. Human-like social skills in dogs? Trends in Cognitive Sciences. 9 (9): 439–44.
Hare, B. 2013. *The Genius of Dogs*. Penguin Publishing Group. p. 60.
Harlow, H. F. and R. R. Zimmermann. 1958. The development of affective responsiveness in infant monkeys. Proceedings of the American Philosophical Society 102: 501 -509.
Harlow, H. F., Dodsworth, R. O., & Harlow, M. K. 1965. Total social isolation in monkeys. Proceedings of the National Academy of Sciences of the United States of America 54 (1): 90.
Harris, C. R. and M. Jenkins. 2006. Gender differences in risk assessment: Why do women take fewer risks than men? Judgment and Decision making, 1(1): 48–63.
Hess, E. H. 1973. *Imprinting*. D. Van Nostrand Co.
Heyes, C.M. 1993. Imitation, culture and cognition. Anim. Behav. 46: 999–1010.
Heyes, C.M. 1994. Social learning in animals: categories and mechanisms. Biological Review 69: 207-231.
Hogue, M.E., J. P. Beaugrand and P. C. Laguë. 1996. Coherent use of information by hens observing their former dominant defeating or being defeated by a stranger. Behav. Process. 38: 241–252.
Horn, G. 1981. Neural mechanisms of learning: an analysis of imprinting in the domestic chick. Proceedings of the Royal Society of London B213: 101-137.
Immelmann, K. 1972. Sexual and other long term aspects of imprinting in birds and other species. Adv. Study 4: 147-174.
Irwin, D.E. and T. Price. 1999. Sexual imprinting, learning and speciation. Heredity 82: 347-354.
Jang, K. L., W. J. Livesley and P. A. Vemon. 1996. Heritability of the Big Five Personality Dimensions and Their Facets: A Twin Study. Journal of Personality 64 (3): 577–592.
Jastrzebski, A. K. 2018. The neuroscience of spirituality. *Pastoral Psychol*. 67:515–524.
Jefferies, R. 1880. *The Gamekeeper at Home*. Jonathan Cape.
John, O. P. and S. Srivastava. 1999. The Big-Five trait taxonomy: History, measurement, and theoretical perspectives. In L. A. Pervin and O. P. John (Eds.), *Handbook of personality: Theory and research* (Vol. 2, pp. 102–138). New York: Guilford Press.
Kaplan, G. 2016. *Bird Minds*. CSIRO Publishing.
Kelley, J. L., and A. E. Magurran. 2003. Learned predator recognition and anti-predator responses in fishes. Fish 4: 216–226.
Kleppesto, H. T. et al. 2024. The genetic underpinnings of right-wing authoritarianism and social dominance orientation explain political attitudes beyond Big Five personality. Journal of Personality https://doi.org/10.1111/jopy.1292
Kirkwood, J. K. and R. Hubrecht. 2001. Animal consciousness, cognition and welfare. Anim. Welf. 10 (Supplement 1): 5–17.
Kohlberg, L. 1984. *The Psychology of Moral Development: The Nature and Validity of Moral Stages (Essays on Moral Development, Volume 2)*. Harper & Row.
Krebs, J. R. and N. B. Davies. 2009. *Behavioural ecology*. Blackwell Scientific Publications, Oxford.
Lakatos, G. 2009. A comparative approach to dogs' (*Canis familiaris*) and human infants' comprehension of various forms of pointing gestures. Animal Cognition. 12 (4): 621–31.
Lefebvre, L., N. Nicolakakis and D. Boire. 2002. Tools and brains in birds. Behavior 139: 939–973.
Loehlin, J. C., R. R. McCrae, P. T. Costa and O. P. John. 1998. Heritabilities of Common and Measure-Specific Components of the Big Five Personality Factors. Journal of Research in Personality 32 (4): 431–453.
Lorenz, K. 1965. *Evolution and modification of behavior*. University of Chicago Press.
Marzluff, J. and T. Angel. 2013. *Gifts of the Crow*. Atria Paperback.
McFarland, D. 1981. *The Oxford Companion to Animal Behaviour*. Oxford University Press.
McNamara, P. and W. Wildman. 2008. Challenges facing the neurological study of religious behavior, belief, and experience. Method Theory Study Relig. 20(3):212–242.
Mohandas, E. 2008. Neurobiology of Spirituality. In: Singh, A. R and Singh, S. A. (Eds.) *Medicine, Mental Health, Science, Religion, and Well-being*, MSM, 6, Jan–Dec 2008: 63–80.

Morgan, C. J. 1979. Eskimo hunting group, social kinship, and the possibility of kin selection in humans. Ethology and Sociobiology. 1(1): 83-86.

Muller, C. 2015. Dogs can discriminate the emotional expressions of human faces. Current Biology 25 (5): 601–5.

Nair, K, S. Mundkur and A. Tushyan. 2022. Difference in Consumer Shopping Behaviour of Men and Women. International Research Journal of Engineering and Technology 9 (12):91.

Newberg, A. B. 2014. The neuroscientific study of spiritual practices. Front. Psychol. 5:215.

North, S. 2018. Umamimi robotic horse ears – using configurable code profiles to replicate individuality in equine animatronics. https://dl.acm.org/doi/10.1145/3295598.3295606

Pascal, B. 1670. *Pensées de M. Pascal sur la religion et sur quelques autres sujets.*

Pavlov, I.P. 1927. *Conditioned reflexes.* Oxford University Press, Oxford.

Pepperberg, I. M. 1999. *The Alex Studies: Cognitive and Communicative Abilities of Grey Parrots.* Cambridge, MA: Harvard University Press.

Pfungst, O. 1911. *Clever Hans (the horse of Mr Van Osten), Volume 40, The History of Psychology.* Thoemmes Continuum.

Piaget, J. 1932. *The moral judgment of the child.* London: Routledge & Kegan Paul.

Piaget, J. 1936. *Origins of intelligence in the child.* London: Routledge & Kegan Paul.

Piaget, J. 1945. *Play, dreams and imitation in childhood.* London: Heinemann.

Piaget, J. 1957. *Construction of reality in the child.* London: Routledge & Kegan Paul.

Piaget, J., and M. T. Cook. 1952. *The origins of intelligence in children.* New York, NY: International University Press.

Piedmont, R. L. 1999. Does spirituality represent the sixth factor of personality? Spiritual transcendence and the five-factor model. J. Pers. 67(6):985–1013.

Pitt, F. 1948. Hounds, Horses and Hunting. Country Life.

Premack, D. 1986. *Gavagai! or the Future History of the Animal Language Controversy.* Cambridge, MA: MIT Press.

Prior, K. 1995. *On Behavior.* Sunshine Books.

Prior, K. 1999. *Don't Shoot the Dog!* Ringpress Books.

Premack, D. and A. J. Premack. 1984. *The Mind of an Ape,* New York: W W Norton & Co Inc.

Rendell, L. and H. Whitehead. 2001. Culture in Whales and Dolphins. Behavioral and Brian Sciences, 24(2): 309–324.

Rest, J. R. 1979. *Development in judging moral issues.* University of Minnesota Press.

Riemann, R., A. Angleitner and J. Strelau. 1997. Genetic and Environmental Influences on Personality: A Study of Twins Reared Together Using the Self– and Peer Report NEO–FFI Scales. Journal of Personality 65 (3): 449-475.

Roberts, W.A., 1998. *Principles of Animal Cognition.* Boston: McGraw-Hill.

Rosen, B. 1980. Moral dilemmas and their treatment. In, *Moral development, moral education, and Kohlberg.* B. Munsey (Ed) pp. 232-263. Birmingham, Alabama: Religious Education Press.

Rowlands, M. 2012. *Can Animals be Moral?* Oxford University Press.

Rumbaugh, D. M. and S. Savage-Rumbaugh. 1999. Primate Language in Robert A. Wilson & Frank Keil (eds.) *The MIT Encyclopedia of the Cognitive Sciences,* Cambridge, MA: MIT Press.

Safina, C. 2016. *Beyond words: What animals think and feel.* Picador.

Sanders, D. *et al.* 2021. A meta-analysis of biological impacts of artificial light at night. Nat. Ecol. Evol. 5: 74–81.

Sapolsky, R. 2018. *Behave: The Biology of Humans at our best and worst.* Vintage.

Schaffer, H. R., & P. E. Emerson, 1964. The development of social attachments in infancy. Monographs of the society for research in child development, 1-77.

Schjødt, U. and M. van Elk. 2019. The neuroscience of religion. Oxford Handbook of the Cognitive Science of Religion.

Shah, N. 2022. Gender differences in betting behaviour. Online.

Skinner, B. F. 1938. *The behavior of organisms: an experimental analysis.* Appleton-Century-Crofts, New York.

Skutch, A. F. 1976. *Parent birds and their young.* University of Texas Press.

Slagsvold, T. and B.T. Hansen. 2001. Sexual imprinting and the origin of obligate brood parasitism in birds. American Naturalist 158: 355-367.

Slagsvold, T., B.T. Hansen, L.E. Johannessen and J.T. Lifjeld. 2002. Mate choice and imprinting in birds studied by cross-fostering in the wild. Proceedings of the Royal Society of London 269: 1449-1455.

Solomon, R. L. and L. C. Wynne. 1954. Traumatic avoidance learning: the principles of anxiety conservation and partial irreversibility. Psychol. Rev. 61: 353–385.

Soto, C. J. and O. P. John. 2012. Development of Big Five Domains and Facets in Adulthood: Mean-Level Age Trends and Broadly Versus Narrowly Acting Mechanism. Journal of Personality, 80 (4): 881–914.

Spitz, R. 1945. Hospitalism: An inquiry into the genesis of psychiatric conditions in early childhood. Psychoanalytic Study of the Child 1(1): 53-74.

Stevens, J. R., F. A. Cushman and M. D. Hauser. 2005. Evolving the psychological mechanisms for cooperation. Ann. Rev. Ecol. Evol. Syst. 36: 499–518.

Tebbich, S., R. Bshary and A. Grutter. 2002. Cleaner fish *Labroides dimidiatus* recognise familiar clients. Anim. Cogn. 5: 139–145.

Thagard, P. 2024. *Bots and Beasts: What makes Machines, Animals and People smart?* MIT Press.

Thorup, K. *et al.* 2007. Evidence for a navigational map stretching across the continental U.S. in a migratory songbird. https://www.pnas.org/doi/10.1073/pnas.0704734104

Tinbergen, N. 1951. *The Study of Instinct.* Oxford University Press.

Tomasello, M. and J. Call, 1997, *Primate Cognition,* Oxford: Oxford University Press.

Visalberghi, E. 1997. Success and Understanding in Cognitive Tasks: A Comparison Between *Cebus apella* and *Pan troglodytes.* International Journal of Primatology18(5): 811–830.

Walker, L. J., R. C. Pitts, K. H. Hennig and M. K.

Matsuba. 1995. *Reasoning about morality and real-life moral problems.* In M. Killen & D. Hart (Eds.), *Morality in everyday life: Developmental perspectives* (pp. 371–407). Cambridge University Press.
Weir, A.S., J. Chappell and A. Kacelnik. 2002. Shaping of Hooks in New Caledonian Crows. Science, 297(5583): 981.
Weiskrantz, L. (ed.) 1988. *Thought without Language.* Clarendon Press, Oxford.
Westermarck, E. 1891. *The History of Human Marriage.* Macmillan.
Whiten, A. and R. W. Byrne (Eds.). 1997. *Machiavellian Intelligence II: Extensions and Evaluations.* Cambridge University Press.
Winston, R. 2002. *Human Instinct.* Bantam Press.
Wong, G., N. Zane, A. Saw and A. K. K. Chan. 2013. Examining gender differences for gambling engagement and gambling problems among emerging adults. Journal of Gambling Studies 29: 171–189.
Yamagata, S. *et al.* 2006. Is the Genetic Structure of Human Personality Universal? A Cross-Cultural Twin Study From North America, Europe, and Asia. Journal of Personality and Social Psychology 90 (6): 987-998.

Chapter 3 What is 'Hunting'?
Acton, C. R. 1953. *The Foxhound of the Future.* Baylis & Sons.
Adams, C. E., A. L. Jason and J. S. C. Herron. 1997. Understanding Wildlife Constituents: Birders and Waterfowl Hunters. Wildlife Society Bulletin, 25, 653-660.
Adams, W. M. (Ed) 2009. *Recreational Hunting, Conservation and Rural Livelihoods.* Oxford. Blackwell: 59–72.
Ahmad, A. 2016. The Trophy Hunting Debate: A Case for Ethics. Economics and Political Weekly 51:26–27.
Al Mansur. 2001. *On Hunting (Al-Mansur's book).* Compiled by T. Clark and M. Derhalli. Aris & Phillips Ltd.
Allsen, T. 2006. *The Royal Hunt in Eurasian History.* Philadelphia. University of Pennsylvania Press.
Almond, R. 2003. *Medieval Hunting.* Sutton.
Alvard, M.S., J. G. Robinson, K. H. Redford and H. Kaplan. The Sustainability of Subsistence Hunting in the Neo-tropics. Conservation Biology 11(4): 977–982.
Alves, R. R. N., L. E. T. Mendonça, M. V. A. Confessor, W. L. S. Vieira and L. C. S. Lopez. 2009. Hunting Strategies Used in the Semi-arid Region of Northeastern Brazil. Journal of Ethnobiology and Ethnomedicine 5(12).
Appleton, D. H. 1960. *The Bloodhound Handbook.* Nicholson & Watson.
Arkwright, W. 1906. *The Pointer and his Predecessors.* Arthur L. Humphreys.
Backyard chicken project. 2021. The best way to get rid of rats in your chicken coop. https://backyardchickenproject.com/how-to-get-rid-of-rats-in-the-chicken-coop-the-definitive-guide/.
Baillie-Grohman, W.A. (Ed.) 1909. *The Master of Game* by Edward, Duke of York, Chatto & Windus.
Baker, P. J. and S. Harris. 2006. Does culling reduce fox (*Vulpes vulpes*) numbers in commercial forests in Wales, UK. Eur. J. Wildl. Res. 52: 99-108.
Baker, S.E., and D. W. Macdonald. 2012. Not so humane mole tube traps. Animal Welfare, 21: 613-15.
Baker, S.E., S.A. Ellwood, V.L. Tagarielli and D.W. Macdonald. 2012. Mechanical Performance of Rat, Mouse and Mole Spring Traps, and Possible Implications for Welfare Performance. PLOS ONE, 7: e39334.
Baker, S.E., R.F. Shaw, R.P.D. Atkinson, P. West, and D.W. Macdonald. 2015. Potential welfare impacts of kill-trapping European moles (*Talpa europaea*) using scissor traps and Duffus traps: a post-mortem examination study. Animal Welfare, 24: 1-14.
Baker, S.E., S.A. Ellwood, P.J. Johnson and D. W. Macdonald. 2016. Moles and mole control on British farms, amenities and gardens after strychnine withdrawal, Animals 6: 39. Special edition on: Ethical and Welfare Dimensions of the Management of Unwanted Wildlife.
Baker, S.E. 2017. A Voluntary Trap Approval scheme to end trap welfare inequality in the UK. Animal Welfare 26: 131-33.
Baker, S.E., M. Ayers, N.J. Beausoleil, S.R. Belmain, M. Berdoy, A.P. Buckle, C. Cagienard, D. Cowan, J. Fearn-Daglish, P. Goddard, H.D.R. Golledge, E. Mullineaux, T. Sharp, A. Simmons and E. Schmolz. 2022. An assessment of animal welfare impacts in wild Norway rat (*Rattus norvegicus*) management. Animal Welfare 31: 51-68.
BASC and Natural Resources Wales. 2016. Grey squirrel control with live capture traps; guidance from the BASC. BASC and NRW, UK.
Bateson, P. and E. L. Bradshaw. 1997. Physiological effects of hunting red deer (*Cervus elaphus*). Proc. R. Soc. Lond. Biol. Sci. 264, 1707-1714.
Beausoleil, N.J., and D.J. Mellor. 2015. Introducing breathlessness as a significant animal welfare issue. New Zealand Veterinary Journal 63: 44-51.
Beckford, P. 1781. *Thoughts on Hunting.* Hodder and Stoughton.
Bell, S. 2005. Virtual Hunting: Click, Click, You're Dead. Yahoo! Voices 6 August http://voices.yahoo.com/virtual-
Bergström, A. *et al.* 2020. Origins and genetic legacy of prehistoric dogs. Science. 370 (6516): 557–564.
Beukemaj, J. J. 1970. Acquired hook-avoidance in the pike *Esox lucius* L. fished with artificial and natural baits. J. Fish Biol. 2:155–160.
Biben, M. 1979. Predation and predatory play behaviour of domestic cats. Animal Behaviour 27 (1): 81-94.
Bichel, N. 2021. *Comprehending Trophy Hunting: Hunting, Hunters, Trophies and Antis.* Unpublished doctoral dissertation, University of Hong Kong.
Billett, M. 1994. *A History of English Country Sports.* Hale.
Bisazza, A and C. Brown. 2011. Lateralization of cognitive functions in fish. In: Brown C, Krause J, Laland K. N. (eds) *Fish cognition and behavior.* Wiley, Oxford, pp 298–324.
Blaine, D. B. 1870. *The Encyclopaedia of Rural Sports.* Longmans.
Blüchel, K.G. 1997. *Game and Hunting.* Könemann.
Booth, V. R. and D. M. H. Cumming. 2009. The Development of a Recreational Hunting Industry and its Relationship with Conservation in Southern Africa. In Dickson, B., Hutton, J. and Adams, W. M. (Eds), *Recreational Hunting, Conservation and Rural Livelihoods.* (pp. 282-295). Oxford, Wiley-Blackwell.
Botigué, L, *et al.* 2017. Ancient European dog genomes

reveal continuity since the Early Neolithic. Nature Communications. 8: 16082.
BPCA. 2020. The use of air guns in pest control; code of best practice, vsn 2. British Pest Control Association, UK.
Bradley, C. 1912. *Fox-Hunting from Shire to Shire*. Routledge.
Braithwaite, V. A. B and F.A. Huntingford. 2004. Fish and welfare: do fish have the capacity for pain perception and suffering? Anim. Welf. 13:87–92.
Brambell, B. and B. Fisher. 2015. *The Moral Complexity of Eating Meat*, New York: Oxford University Press.
Brander, M. 1964. *The Hunting Instinct*. Oliver & Boyd.
Brander, M. 1971. *Hunting and Shooting from earliest times to the present day*. Weidenfeld & Nicolson.
Brewer, D., T. Clark and A. A. Phillips. 2001. *Dogs in Antiquity, Anubis to Cerberus. On Hunting with Hounds, Xenophon & Arrian*, edited by A, A, Phillips & M. M. Willcock.
British Pest Control Association. 2024. *Pest advice for controlling pigeons, gulls and other birds*. Online.
Broglio, C., A. Gómez, E. Durán, C. Salas and F. Rodríguez. 2011. Brain and cognition in teleost fish. In: Brown C, Krause J, Laland K (eds) *Fish cognition and behavior*. Wiley, Oxford, pp 325–358.
Brottveit, A. and O. Aagedal (Eds) 1999. *Hunting for the Hunting Culture*. Oslo, Abstraktforlag.
Bryden, H. A. 1903. *Hare Hunting and Harriers*. Grant Richards.
Bucknell, B. 2001. *Foxing with Lamp and Rifle*. Foxearth Publishing.
Bucknell, B. 2010. *Going Foxing*. Foxearth Publishing.
Burns, L., V. Edwards, J. Marsh, L. Soulsby and M. Winter. 2000. *Final Report of the Committee of Inquiry into Hunting with Dogs in England and Wales*. London, Stationery Office.
Butler, D. 2006. *Rough Shooting in Ireland*. Merlin Unwin Books.
Buxton, M. 1987. *Ladies of the Chase*. London: The Sportsman's Press.
Caro, J. 2017. Exploring the views on hunting of Spanish hunters: Effect of age and public vs. anonymous opinions. *European Journal of Wildlife Research* 63(6): 1–88.
Carpaneto, G. M. and A. Fusan. 2000. Subsistence Hunting and Bushmeat Exploitation in Central-western Tanzania. Biodiversity and Conservation 9(11): 1571–1585.
Carr, R. 1976. *English Fox Hunting – A History*. Weidenfeld & Nicolson.
Cartmill, M. 1993. *A view to a death in the morning: Hunting and nature through history*. Harvard University Press.
Cassinello, J. 2017. The human hunter. An anthropological, sociological and ecological view. Science, Thought and Culture, 193(786):411.
Chalmers, P. 1936. *The History of Hunting*. Seeley, Service & Co.
Chartered Institute of Environmental Health. 2014. Code of practice for the use of vertebrate traps. Chartered Institute of Environmental Health: London, UK.
Chignell, A., T. Cuneo and M. C. Halteman (Eds). 2016. *Philosophy Comes to Dinner: Arguments about the Ethics of Eating*. New York: Routledge.

Chimay de, J. 1960. *Plaisirs de la Chasse*. Librairie Hachette.
Choquenot, D. and J. Parkes. 2001. Setting thresholds for pest control: how does pest density affect resource viability? *Biological Conservation* 99: 29–46.
Clapham, R. 1928. *Foxes, Foxhounds and Fox-hunting*. Heath Cranton Ltd.
Cloke, P. 1993. The Countryside as Commodity: New Spaces for Rural Leisure. In Glyptis, S. (Ed.) *Leisure and the Environment*. London, Belhaven Press.
Cobham Resource Consultants. 1997. *Countryside Sports: Their Economic, Social and Conservation Significance*. The Standing Conference on Countryside Sports. The College of Estate Management, Whiteknights, Reading.
Cognisense. 2024. *The Value of Shooting: The economic, environmental and social impact of shooting in the UK*. British Association for Shooting and Conservation.
Cohen, J. A. 2003. Is hunting a sport? International Journal of Applied Philosophy, 17(2), 291–326.
Cohen, J. A. 2014. Recreational Hunting. Tourism Recreation Research Vol. 39, No. 1, 15.
Coillte. 2005. *Recreational Hunting, Recreation Policy – Healthy Forestry, Healthy Nation*. Newtownmountkennedy, Co. Wicklow.
Condon, R. G., P. Collings and G. Wenzel. 1995. The Best Part of Life: Subsistence Hunting, Ethnicity and Economic Adaptation among Young Inuit Males. Arctic 48(1): 31–48.
Cone, C. B., (Ed) 1981. *Hounds in the Morning*. Univ Press of Kentucky.
Cooper, C., L. Larson, A. Dayer, R. Stedmanand D. Decker. 2015. Are wildlife recreationists conservationists? Linking hunting, birdwatching, and pro-environmental behavior. The Journal of Wildlife Management, 79(3): 446-457.
Coppinger, R. and R. Schneider. 2017. Evolution of working dogs. In: J. Serpell (Ed.), *The domestic dog: its evolution, behavior and interactions with people*. Cambridge: Cambridge University Press. 21-47.
Corkran, C. 2015. 'An extension of me': handlers describe their experiences of working with bird dogs. Society & Animals, 23: 231-249.
Cote, I. M., and W. J. Sutherland. 1997. The effectiveness of removing predators to protect bird populations. *Conservation Biology* 11: 395–405.
Coughlan, J. 1980. *Hound Trailing, A History of the Sport in Cumbria*. Coughlan.
Cox, G. and M. Winter. 1997. The Beleagured 'Other': Hunt Followers in the Countryside. In Milbourne, P. (Ed.) *Revealing Rural 'Others': Representation, Power and Identity in the British Countryside*. Cassell.
CRRU UK. 2021. CRRU UK Code of Best Practice; Best Practice Guidance for Rodent Control and the Safe Use of Rodenticides. Revision August 2021. 36 pp. Campaign for Responsible Rodenticide Use UK.
Cruzada, S. M. 2019. *Life and death encounters: trans-species anthropology and extended worlds between hunters and animals in southwestern Extremadura*. PhD thesis, Universidad Pablo de Olavide.
Cruzada, S. M., P. P. Chamorro and H. P. Gamuz. 2021. *Hare hunting with greyhounds in Andalusia. Report for registration in the Atlas del Patrimonio Inmaterial de Andalucía*. Andalusian Greyhound Federation and Andalusian Institute of Historical Heritage.

Cummins, J. 1988. *The Hawk and the Hound, The Art of Medieval Hunting*. Weidenfeld & Nicolson,

Cunliffe, J. 2006. *Sighthounds – Their History, Management and Care*. Swan Hill Press.

Cutchins, D., and Eliason. E. A. (Eds.) 2009. *Wild Games: Hunting and Fishing Traditions in North America*. The University of Tennessee Press.

Dabezies, J. M. 2019. Discourses and tensions between hunting, conservation and animal rights in Uruguay. Revista Etnobiología, 17(2): 11.

Dahles, H. 1993. Game Killing and Killing Games: An Anthropologist Looking at Hunting in a Modern Society. Society and Animals, 1(2) 169-184.

Damm, G. R. 2008. Recreational Trophy Hunting: What do we know and what should we do? – In: Baldus, R. D.; Damm, G. R. & Wollscheid, K. (Eds.): *Best Practices in Sustainable Hunting – A Guide to Best Practices from Around the World*, pp. 5–11.

Davis, S. L. 2003. The least harm principle may require that humans consume a diet containing large herbivores, not a vegan diet. Journal of Agricultural and Environmental Ethics 16 (4):387-394.

DEFRA. 2011. *The Control of Rats with Rodenticides: A Complete Guide to best Practice*. http://adlib.everysite.co.uk/adlib/DEFRA/content.aspx?id=000HK277ZX.0B4B1SS7I8E46R.

DEFRA. 2021. *Our action plan for animal welfare*. DEFRA, UK. https://www.gov.uk/government/publications/action-plan-for-animal-welfare.

Delme Radcliffe, E.P. *The Noble Science – A Few General Ideas on Fox-Hunting*. Routledge.

Derr, M. 2012. *How the dog became the dog: From wolves to our best friends*. London: Duckworth.

Di Minin, E, *et al*. 2021. Consequences of Recreational Hunting for Biodiversity Conservation and Livelihoods. One Earth 4.2: 238–53.

Di Minin, E., N. Leader-Williams and C. J. A. Bradshaw. 2016. Banning Trophy Hunting Will Exacerbate Biodiversity Loss. *Trends in Ecology & Evolution*, 31(2): 99-102.

Dickson, B., J. Hutton and W. M. Adams, (Eds). 2009. *Recreational Hunting, Conservation and Rural Livelihoods: Science and Practice*. UK: Wiley-Blackwell.

Dixon, W. S. 1912. *Hunting in the Olden Days*. Constable.

Dizard, J. 2003. *Moral Stakes: Hunters and Hunting in North America*. USA, University of Massachusetts Press.

Dizney, L., P.D. Jones and L.A. Ruedas. 2008. Efficacy of three types of live traps used for surveying small mammals in the Pacific Northwest. Northwestern Naturalist. 89: 171-80.

Dolman, P. M., K. M. Scotland, R. J. Burnside, and N. J. Collar. 2021. Sustainable hunting and the conservation of the threatened houbara bustards. Journal for Nature Conservation, 61, [126000]

Dolman, P. M., N. J. Collar and R. J. Burnside. 2018. Captive breeding cannot sustain migratory Asian houbara *Chlamydotis macqueenii* without hunting controls. Biological Conservation, 228: 357-366.

Dowsley, M. 2009. Inuit-organized Polar Bear Sport Hunting in Nunavut Territory, Canada. Journal of Ecotourism 8(2): 161–175.

Dubois, S., N. Fenwick, E.A. Ryan, L. Baker, S.E. Baker, N.J. Beausoleil, S. Carter, B. Cartwright, F. Costa, C. Draper, J. Griffin, A. Grogan, G. Howald, B. Jones, K.E. Littin, A.T. Lombard, D.J. Mellor, D. Ramp, C.A. Schuppli and D. Fraser. 2017. Consensus principles for ethical wildlife control, Conservation Biology, 31: 753-60.

Ellicot, C. 2010. Hauled to court, forced to pay £1,500 and branded a criminal...for drowning a grey squirrel. Mail Online, 20th July 2010.

Eutermoser, A. 1961. Erläuterungen zur krähenstatistik. Deutscher Falkenorden Jahrbuch 49-50.

Evans, M. 2019. *On Eating Meat: The truth about its production and the ethics of eating it*. Murdoch.

Ewald, J., S. Callegari, N. Kingdon and N. Graham. 2006. Fox-hunting in England and Wales: Its Contribution to the Management of Woodland and Other Habitats. Biodiversity and Conservation 15: 4309-4334.

Fanaro, L. A. 2021. Notes on the relationships between sled dogs and mushers in Tierra del Fuego, Argentina. Tabula Rasa 40: 75-98.

Fine, L. M. 2000. Rights of Men, Rites of Passage: Hunting and Masculinity at Reo Motors of Lansing, Michigan, 1945-1975. Journal of Social History 33(4): 805-823.

Fiorenza, L. et al. 2015. To meat or not to meat? New perspectives on Neanderthal ecology. American Journal of Physical Anthropology 156(S59): 43–71.

Fox, N. C. and H. Macdonald. 1995. *Welfare aspects of killing or capturing wild vertebrates in Britain*. The Hawk Board.

Frain, S. 2005. Rat Hunting : With Ferret, Dog, Hawk and Gun. Crowood Press.

Franklin, A. 1996. Australian Hunting and Angling Sports and the Changing Nature of Human-animal Relations in Australia. Australian and New Zealand Journal of Sociology 32.

Franklin, A. 2001. Neo-Darwinian leisures, the body and nature: hunting and angling in modernity. Body & Society, 7(4), 57–76.

Franklin, A. 2007. The "Animal Question" and the "Consumption" of Wildlife. In Lovelock, B. (Ed.) Tourism and the Consumption of Wildlife: Hunting, Shooting and Sport Fishing. Abingdon, Oxon. Routledge: 31–44.

Frantz, L. A., V. E. Mullin, M. Pionnier-Capitan, O. Lebrasseur and M. Ollivier *et al*. 2016. Genomic and archaeological evidence suggests a dual origin of domestic dogs. Science 352(6290): 1228-1231.

Frantz, S.C. and C.M. Padula. 1983. A laboratory test method for evaluating the efficacy of glueboards for trapping house mice. *In Vertebrate Pest Control and Management Materials:* 4th Symposium, edited by D. E. Kaukeinen, 209–25. American Society for Testing and Materials: Philadelphia, PA.

Fukuda, K. 1997. Different Views of Animals and Cruelty to Animals: Cases in Foxes and Pet-keeping in Britain. Anthropology Today 13(5), 226-228.

Gamuz, H. P. and P. Palenzuela 2021. Hare hunting with greyhounds in Andalucia: from conflict to patrimonialization. Revista Andaluza De Antropología 21: 8 - 44.

Gilbey, W, 1913. *Hounds in Old Days*. (SPC reprint 1979).

Gorman, M. and A. Lamb. 1994. An investigation into the efficacy of mechanical mole scarers. Animal Welfare, 3: 3-12.

Govoroff, N. C. 2006. The Hunter and his gun in Haute-Provence. *Technological choices: transformation in material culture since the Neolithic* (P. Lemonnier, Ed.) Routledge. 227-237.

Grandy, J. W., E. Stallman and D. W. Macdonald. 2003. The Science and Sociology of Hunting: Shifting Practices and Perceptions in the United States and Great Britain. In Salem, D. J. and Rowan, A. N. (Eds.) *The State of the Animals II.* (pp. 107-130). Washington D.C., Humane Society Press.

Grasseni, C. 2005. Disciplining vision in animal biotechnology. Anthropology in Action, 12(2): 44-55.

Greenebaum, J. 2010. Training dogs and training humans: symbolic interaction and dog training. Anthrozoös, 23(2): 129-141.

Griffin, E. 2007. *Blood Sport, Hunting in Britain since 1066.* Yale University Press.

Guagnin, M., A. R. Perri and M. D. Petraglia. 2018. Pre-Neolithic evidence for dog-assisted hunting strategies in Arabia. Journal of Anthropological Archaeology. 49: 225–236.

Gunn, A. S. 2001. Environmental Ethics and Trophy Hunting. Ethics and the Environment 6.1: 68–95.

Hadidian, J., L. J. Simon, and M. R. Childs. 2002. The "nuisance" wildlife control industry: animal welfare concerns. Pages 378–382 in R. M. Timm and R. H. Schmidt, editors. *Proceeding of the 20th Vertebrate Pest Conference.* University of California, Davis, USA.

Harris, R. C., T. R. Helliwell, W. Shingleton, N. Stickland and J. R. J. Naylor. 1999. The physiological response of red deer (*Cervus elaphus*) to prolonged exercise undertaken during hunting. Newmarket: R & W Publications.

Harrison, C. 1991. *Countryside Recreation in a Changing Society.* Bristol, TMS Partnership Limited.

Hartley, O. 1909. *Hunting Dogs.* Harding, Ohio.

Health and Safety Executive. 2003. *Assessment of an Experimental Permit: T3327 as a Vertebrate Control Agent against Foxes.* Health and Safety Executive, Biocides and Pesticides Unit.

Health and Safety Executive. 2013. *Gassing of rabbits and vertebrate pests.* HSE: UK.

Heberlein, T. A. 1987. Stalking the Predator: A Profile of the American Hunter. Environment, 29, 7: 6-11.

Hemingway, E. 1952. *The Old Man and the Sea.* Charles Scribner's Sons.

Heydon, M. J. and J. C. Reynolds. 2000. Fox (*Vulpes vulpes*) management in three contrasting regions of Britain, in relation to agricultural and sporting interests. J. Zool. Lond. 251: 237-252.

Higginson, A. H. 1948. *Foxhunting – Theory and Practice.* Collins.

Hobson, D. 2000. Hunting with Dogs: Conservation and Environment. Submission to the Committee of Inquiry into Hunting with Dogs in England and Wales.

Howe, J. 1981. Fox hunting as ritual. American Ethnologist, 8(2): 278–300.

Hribal, J. 2003. Animals are part of the working class: a challenge to labor history. Labor History, 44(4): 435-453.

Hudson, D. 2004. *Working Pointers and Setters.* Swan Hill Press.

Humane Slaughter Association. 2024. The humane harvesting of fish. Online Guide. https://www.hsa.org.uk/downloads/publications/harvestingfishdownload-updated-with-2016-logo.pdf

Hussain, Sh. 2010. Sport-hunting, Fairness and Colonial Identity: Collaboration and Subversion in the Northwestern Frontier Region of the British Indian Empire. Conservation and Society 8(2): 112–126.

Ingold, T. 1988. *What is an Animal?* London, Unwin Hyman.

Ingold, T. 2000. Hunting and gathering as a way of perceiving the environment" in *Perception of the Environment: Essays in Livelihood, Dwelling and Skill.* London, Routledge.

Itzkowitz, D. 1977. *Peculiar Privilege: A Social History of English Foxhunting 1753-1885.* Sussex, Harvester Press.

Jackson, T. 1989. *Hunter-Pointer-Retriever, The Continental Gundog.* Ashford.

Javenaud, K., C. Linzey and A. Linzey. 2023. *Killing to Kill: An Ethical Assessment of 'Predator Control' on Scottish Grouse Moors.* A report of the Oxford Centre for Animal Ethics.

Jisheng, Y. 2013. *Tombstone: The Great Chinese Famine 1958-1962.* Farrar, Straus and Giroux.

Kaldewaij, F. 2008. Animals and the Harm of Death. in *The Animal Ethics Reader,* S. J. Armstrong and R. G. Botzler, (Eds.) 2nd edition (Abingdon: Routledge, 2008).

Kalof, L. and A. Fitzgerald. 2003. Reading the Trophy: Exploring the Display of Dead Animals in Hunting Magazines. Visual Studies 18(2): 112–122.

Kalof, L., A. Fitzgerald and L. Baralt. 2004. Animals, women, and weapons: Blurred sexual boundaries in the discourse of sport hunting. Society and Animals, 12(3): 237–251.

Kellert, S. R. 2012. *Birthright: People and nature in the modern world.* New Haven: Yale University Press.

Kerasote, T. 1994. *Bloodties: Nature, culture, and the hunt.* Kodansha International.

Keya, K. 1994. Hunting with dogs among the San in the Central Kalahari. African Study Monographs 15:119–34.

King, R. J. H. 2010. Hunting: A return to nature? In N. Kowalski (Ed.), *Hunting - philosophy for everyone: In search of the wild life,* 149-160. Wiley-Blackwell.

Kluger, J. 2002. Hunting Made Easy. Time (11 March).

Knoll, M. 2004. Hunting in the Eighteenth Century. An Environmental History Perspective. *Historical Social Research*, 29(3): 9-36.

Koch, C. (Ed.). 2012. Francis Crick Memorial Conference on Consciousness in Human and Non-Human Animals, Churchill College, University of Cambridge, England. July 7.

Koster, J. 2008. Hunting with dogs without an optimal foraging approach. Current Anthropology, 49(5): 935-944.

Koster, J. 2009. Hunting dogs in the Lowland Neotropics. Journal of Anthropological Research, 65(4): 575-610.

Kwasny, M. 2019. *Putting on the Dog: The Animal Origins of What We Wear.* Trinity University Press.

Labonté, G. S., G. Sanchez, R. E. C. Batista and F. Vander Velden. 2021. "Taming, familiarizing, animalizing: techniques for making hunting dogs in the Amazonia. Tabula Rasa, 40: 25-50.

Le Noël, C. 1999. *On Target: History and Hunting in Central Africa.* Huntington Beach CA: Trophy Room Books.

Leader-Williams, N., J. A. Kayera and G. L. Overton, G.L. (Eds.). 1996. *Tourist Hunting in Tanzania.* Norwich, UK: International Union for the Conservation of Nature and Natural Resources, Pages Brothers.

Lee, R. 2009. Guns, Sheep, and Genes: When and Why Trophy Hunting May Be a Selective Pressure. In B. Dickson, J. Hutton, and W. M. Adams (Eds.), *Recreational Hunting, Conservation and Rural Livelihoods Science and Practice*, pp. 94-107. Wiley-Blackwell.

Lee, R.B. and I. DeVore. 1968. *Man the Hunter. The First Intensive Survey of a Single, Crucial Stage of Human Development - Man's Once Universal Hunting Way of Life*. New York: Routledge.

Lepczyk, C.A., J. E. Fantle-Lepczyk, K. D. Dunham et al. 2023. A global synthesis and assessment of free-ranging domestic cat diet. Nat. Commun. 14, 7809.

Lewis, C. A. (Ed.) 1979. *Horses, Hounds and Hunting Horns*. London, Allen.

Liebenberg, L. 2006. Persistence Hunting by Modern Hunter Gatherers. Current Anthropology 47(6): 1017–1025.

Lien, M. E. and J. Law. 2011. 'Emergent Aliens': On Salmon, Nature, and Their Enactment. Ethnos, 76(1): 65-87.

Lindsey, P., P. A. Roulet and S. S. Romanache. 2007. Economic and conservation significance of trophy hunting industry in sub-Saharan Africa. Biological Conservation, 134, 455-469.

Lindsey, P., R. Alexander, L. Frank, A. Mathieson and S. Romañach. 2006. Potential of trophy hunting to create incentives for wildlife conservation in Africa where alternative wildlife-based land uses may not be viable. Animal Conservation, 9(3): 283-291.

Lindsey, P., R. Alexander, L. Frank, A. Mathieson and S. Romañach. 2007. Trophy Hunting and Conservation in Africa: Problems and One Potential Solution. Conservation Biology 21(3): 880–883.

Littin, S. 2012. Ancient Domesticated Dog Skull Found in Siberian Cave. NASA Space Grant intern, University Communications.

Ljung, P. 2014. *Traditional use of wildlife in modern society: Public attitudes and hunters' motivations*. Swedish University of Agricultural Sciences.

Lombard, M. and L. Phillipson. 2010. Indications of Bow and Stone-tipped Arrow Use 64,000 Years Ago in KwaZulu-Natal, South Africa, Antiquity 84.325 (2010): 635–48.

Longrigg, R. 1974. *The English Squire and His Sport*. Michael Joseph.

Lonsdale, Earl of (Ed) 1936. *Deer, Hare & Otter Hunting*. Seeley, Service & Co.

Loog, L. *et al*. 2019. Ancient DNA suggests modern wolves trace their origin to a late Pleistocene expansion from Beringia. Molecular Ecology. 29 (9): 1596–1610.

Lovelock, B. 2008. *Tourism and the consumption of wildlife: Hunting, shooting and sport fishing*. Routledge.

Loveridge, A. J., C. Packer and A. Dutton. 2009. Science and the Recreational Hunting of Lions. In Dickson, B., Hutton, J. and Adams, W. M. (Eds). *Recreational Hunting, Conservation and Rural Livelihoods*. Oxford. Blackwell: 108–124.

Loveridge, A. J., J. C. Reynolds and E. J. Milner–Gulland. 2007. Does Sport Tourism Benefit Conservation? In Macdonald, D. W. and Service, K. (Eds.) *Key Topics in Conservation Biology*. Oxford. Blackwell: 224–240.

Low, P. 2012. The Cambridge Declaration on Consciousness. Proceedings of the Francis Crick Memorial Conference, Churchill College, Cambridge University, July 7 2012, pp 1-2.

Luke, B. 1997. A Critical Analysis of Hunters' Ethics. Environmental Ethics 19(1): 25–44.

Macdonald, D. W., Tattersall, F.H., Johnson, P.J., Carbone, C., Reynolds, J.C., Langbein, J., Rushton, S.P. and Shirley, M.D. (2000). *Management and Control of Populations of Foxes, Deer, Hares, and Mink in England and Wales, and the Impact of Hunting with Dogs*. London: The Stationery Office.

MacKenzie, J. M. 2017. *The Empire of Nature: Hunting, Conservation and British Imperialism*. Manchester University Press.

Marvin, G. 2001. Cultured Killers: Creating and Representing Foxhounds. Society and Animals, 9, 273-292.

Marvin, G. 2002. Unspeakability, Inedibility, and the Structures of Pursuit in the English Foxhunt. In Rothfels, N. (Ed.) *Representing Animals*. Bloomington and Indianapolis, Indiana University.

Marvin, G. 2005. Sensing nature: encountering the world in hunting. Etnofoor, 18(1): 15-26.

Marvin, G. 2006. Wild killing: contesting the animal in hunting. In *Killing Animals* (The Animal Studies Group, Eds.). University of Illinois Press. 10-29.

Marvin, G. 2010. Challenging animals: project and process in hunting. In Sarah Pilgrim and Jules Pretty (Eds.) Nature and Culture. Earthscan, pp. 163-178.

Marvin, G. and J. M. Dabezies. 2021. Anthropological perspectives on the study of recreational hunting: general and introductory considerations. Revista Andalusian Review of Anthropology, 21:1-7.

Mason, G. and K. Littin. 2003. The humaneness of rodent pest control, Animal Welfare 12: 1-37.

Mason, J. 2005. *The Eskdale and Ennerdale Foxhounds, The History of a Lakeland Pack*, Merlin Unwin.

May, A. N. 2013. *The Fox-Hunting Controversy, 1781–2004: Class and Cruelty*. London: Routledge.

McCorquodale, S. M. 1997. Cultural Contexts of Recreational Hunting and Native Subsistence and Ceremonial Hunting: Their Significance for Wildlife Management. Wildlife Society Bulletin (1973-2006), 25(2), 568-573.

Macdonald, D. W. and P. J. Johnson. 1996. The impact of sport hunting: a case study. In *The exploitation of mammal populations*, by N. and Taylor, V. J. (Eds) Dunstone, 160-207. London: Chapman and Hall.

Meehan, A.P. 1984. *Rats and Mice: Their Biology and Control*. Rentokil Ltd.: Felcourt, East Grinstead, UK.

Milbourne, P. 2003a. Hunting Ruralities: Nature, Society and Culture in Hunt Countries of England and Wales. Journal of Rural Studies, 19:157-171.

Milbourne, P. 2003b. The Complexities of Hunting in Rural England and Wales. Sociologia Ruralis, 43: 289-308.

Mitchell, E. 1991. Shooting Leopards in a Barrel. Time (10 June).

Morris, S. P. 2010. *On hunting: A philosophical case study in animal sports*. Ohio State University.

Moxon, P. R. A. 1998. *Gundogs – Training and Field Trials*. Swan Hill.

Munkwitz, E. 2017. 'The Master is the Mistress': women and fox hunting as sports coaching in Britain, Sport in History, 37:4, 395-422.

Murray, J. K., W. J. Browne, M. A. Roberts and A. Whitmarsh. 2010. Number and ownership profiles of cats and dogs in the UK. Veterinary record 166(6):163-8.

Nadasdy, P. 2007. The gift in the animal: the ontology of hunting and human-animal sociality. American Ethnologist, 34(1): 25-43.

Natural England. 2010a. The Animal Welfare Act 2006: what it means for wildlife; Technical Information Note TIN072. Natural England, Sheffield, UK.

Natural England. 2010b. Moles: options for management and control. Technical Information Note TIN033. Natural England, UK.

Natural England. 2012a. House mice: options for management and control. Technical Information Note TIN034. Natural England, UK.

Natural England. 2012b. Rats: options for controlling infestations. Technical Information Note TIN057. Natural England.

Newall, V. 1983. The Unspeakable in Pursuit of the Uneatable: Some Comments on Fox-Hunting, Folklore, 94/1: 86-90.

Nicholls, J. 2010. *Mole Catching; A Practical Guide*. Crowood: Marlborough, UK.

Noakes, J. 1957. *Horses, Hounds, and Humans: Being the Dramatized Story of R.S. Surtees*. London: Oldbourne.

Noon, C. 2000. *Parson Jack Russell, The Hunting Legend 1795-1883*. Halsgrove.

Norton, A. 1999. *The Place of Hunting in Country Life*. Unpublished Ph.D. Thesis. Department of Geography, University of Bristol.

Ortega y Gasset, J. 1972. *Meditations on hunting*. Charles Scribner's Sons.

Paget, J. O. 1900. *Hunting*. J. M. Dent & Co.

Panksepp, J. *et al.* 2001. The Virtues of Hunting, Philosophy in the Contemporary World 8.2: 113–24.

Parrott, D., R. Quy, K. Van Driel, P. Lurz, S. Rushton, J. Gurnell, N. Aebischer and J. Reynolds. 2009. *Review of red squirrel conservation activity in northern England*. A Report by Fera to Natural England (NECR019). Natural England: Sheffield, UK.

Perri, A. *et al.* 2021. Dog domestication and the dual dispersal of people and dogs into the Americas. Proceedings of the National Academy of Sciences. 118 (6):

Perri, A. R. 2016. Hunting dogs as environmental adaptations in Jōmon Japan. Antiquity. 90 (353): 1166–1180.

Pest Management Alliance. 2017. Code of Best Practice: Humane use of Rodent Glue Boards. Pest Management Alliance, UK.

Pesticides Safety Directorate. 1997. Assessment of humaneness of vertebrate control agents. Evaluation of fully approved or provisionally approved products, no. 171. A report by DEFRA and the PSD. York: UK.

Petersen, D. 2000. *Heartsblood: Hunting, spirituality and wildness in America*. Island Press/Shearwater Books.

Phillips, A. A. and M. M. Willcock. 1999. On *Hunting with Hounds, Xenophon & Arrian*. Aris & Phillips Ltd.

Pierotti, R. and B. Fogg. 2017. *The First Domestication: How Wolves and Humans Coevolved*. Yale University Press.

Plato. *Laws Book VII* : p 824.

Plummer, B. 1986. *Hunters All*. Huddlesford.

Plummer, B. 1991. *The Complete Book of Sight Hounds, Long Dogs and Lurchers*. Robinson.

Porteus, T., J. Reynolds and M. McAllister. 2019. Population dynamics of foxes during restricted-area culling in Britain: Advancing understanding through state-space modelling of culling records. PLoS ONE 14(11).

Posewitz, J. 1994. *Beyond Fair Chase: The Ethics and Tradition of Hunting*. Guilford. Falconguides.

Presser, L. and W.V. Taylor. 2011. An autoethnography of hunting. Crime Law and Social Change 55(5):483-494.

Proctor, H. S., G. Carder and A. R. Cornish. 2013. Searching for animal sentience: A systematic review of the scientific literature. Animals (Basel) 3(3): 882-906.

Recum von, A. F. 2002. *Hunting with Hounds in North America*. Pelican.

Regan, T. 1997. The rights of humans and other animals. Ethics & Behavior 7: 103–111.

Reid, N., C. N. Magee and W. I. Montgomery. 2010. Integrating field sports, hare population management and conservation. Acta Theriologica, 55: 61-71.

Restrepo, S. (Ed.). Bushmeat and food security, technical bases for an integrated management in Colombia (pp. 88-104). Alexander von Humboldt Biological Resources Research Institute.

Rice, M. 2006. *Swifter than the Arrow, the Golden Hunting Hounds of Ancient Egypt*. Tauris.

Ridley, J. 1990. *Fox Hunting*. London: Collins.

Ridley, J. 1998. Animals in the Countryside. In Barnett, A. and Scruton, R. (Eds.) *Town and Country*. (pp. 142-152). London, Cape.

Ritvo, H. 1987. *The animal estate: The English and other creatures in the Victorian Age*. Cambridge, Massachusetts: Harvard University Press.

Rodenticide Resistance Action Group. 2021. Anticoagulant resistance in the Norway rat and guidelines for the management of resistant rat infestations in the UK. RRAG, UK.

Rosser, A. 2009. Regulation and Recreational Hunting. In B. Dickson, J. Hutton, and W. M. Adams (Eds.), *Recreational Hunting, Conservation and Rural Livelihoods: Science and Practice*, pp. 319-340. Wiley-Blackwell.

Ruffer, J. G. 1978. *The Big Shots, Edwardian Shooting Parties*. Viking.

Russell, N. 2002. The Wild Side of Animal Domestication. Society & Animals 10(3): 285-302.

Ryan, E. A. 2021. Non-target interactions and humane evaluation of a captive bolt trap on commensal rodents. MSc thesis, University of British Columbia.

Rycroft, N. 2001. *Rycroft on Hounds, Hunting and Country*, edited by J. F. Scharnberg. The Derrydale Press, USA.

Sandlos, J. 2007. *Hunters at the Margin: Native People and Wildlife Conservation in the Northwest Territories*. Vancouver, British Columbia, Canada: UBC Press.

Sapontzis, S. F. (Ed.) 2004. *Food for Thought: The Debate Over Eating Meat*, NY: Prometheus Press.

Saß, M. (Ed.) 2017. *Hunting without Weapons. On the Pursuit of Images*. Berlin, Boston: De Gruyter.

Savalois, N., N. Lescureux and F. Brunois. 2013. Teaching the dog and learning from the dog: interactivity in herding dog training and use. Anthrozoös, 26(1): 77-91.

Scallan, D. 2012. The Place of Hunting in Rural Ireland. PhD Thesis. National University of Ireland Galway.

Schleidtl, W. M, and M. Shalter. 2018. Dogs and

mankind: Coevolution on the move - an update. Human Ethology Bulletin 33 (2018)1: 15-38.

Schlötelburg, A., A. Geduhn, E. Schmolz, A. Friesen, S. Baker, N. Martenson, G. Le Laidier, M. Urzinger, O. Klute, D. Schröer, A. Brigham and M. Puschmann. 2021. *NoCheRo-Guidance for the Evaluation of Rodent Traps. Part A Break back/Snap traps*. German Environment Agency, Dessau, Germany.

Schwartz, M. 1997. *A history of dogs in the early Americas*. Yale University Press.

Sharp, R. and K. Wollscheid. 2009. An Overview of Recreational Hunting in North America, Europe and Australia. In Dickson, B., Hutton, J., Adams, W. and Wiley, W. (Eds.) *Recreational Hunting, Conservation and Rural Livelihoods*. (pp. 25-38). Oxford, Blackwell.

Sheardown, F. 1999. *The Working Longdog*. Swan Hill.

Shipman, P. 2015. *The Invaders: How humans and their dogs drove Neanderthals to extinction*. Harvard University Press.

Simon, A. 2019. The competitive consumption and fetishism of wildlife trophies. Journal of Consumer Culture, 19(2): 151–168.

Singer, P. and J. Mason. 2006. *The Way We Eat: Why Our Food Choices Matter/The Ethics of What We Eat*. New York: Rodale Press.

Singer, P. 1997. Neither human nor natural: ethics and feral animals. Reproduction, Fertility and Development 9: 157–162.

Stange, M. Z. 1997. *Woman the hunter*. Boston, MA: Beacon Press.

Swanson, H. A., M. E. Lien and G. B. Ween (Eds.). 2018. *Domestication gone wild: politics and practices of multispecies relations*. Durham: Duke University Press, 72-93.

Tan, S., M. L, Stellato, A.C. and L. Neil. 2020. Uncontrolled Outdoor Access for Cats: An Assessment of Risks and Benefits. Animals 10: 258.

Tapper, S. 1992. *Game Heritage: An Ecological Review from Shooting and Gamekeeping Records*. The Game Conservancy.

Tichelar, M. 2017. *The History of Opposition to Blood Sports in Twentieth Century England: Hunting at Bay*. London: Routledge.

Tsing, A. L. 2018. Nine provocations for the study of domestication. In H. Swanson, M. E. Lien, and G. B. Ween (Eds.), *Domestication gone wild: politics and practices of multispecies relations*. Duke University Press. pp. 231-251.

UK Government. 2015. Wild birds: protection and licences. UK Government, UK.

Vitali, T. 1990. Sport hunting: Moral or immoral. Environmental Ethics 12(1): 69-82.

Vollset, K. W., I. Dohoo and R. J. Lennox. 2023. The paradox of predation studies. Biology Letters, 10.1098.

Von Essen, E. 2018. The impact of modernization on hunting ethics: Emerging taboos among contemporary Swedish hunters. Human Dimensions of Wildlife. 23(1): 21-38.

Von Essen, E., E. van Heijgen and T. Gieser. 2019. Hunting communities of practice: Factors behind the social differentiation of hunters in modernity. Journal of Rural Studies. 68: 13-21.

Vorhies, D. 2022. *The Good, the Bad, and the Beautiful: Ethics and Hunting*. MA Thesis. University of Buckingham.

Wallace, R. 2003. *A Manual of Foxhunting*, edited by Michael Clayton. Swan Hill Press.

Warburton, B. and B. G. Norton. 2009. Towards a knowledge-based ethic for lethal control of nuisance wildlife. Journal of Wildlife Management 73: 158–164.

Warburton, B. 1998. The "humane" trap saga: a tale of competing ethical ideologies. Pages 131–137 in D. J. Mellor, M. Fisher, and G. Sutherland, editors. *Ethical approaches to animal-based science*. Proceedings of the conference held in Auckland, September 1997. Australian and New Zealand Council for the Care of Animals in Research and Teaching, Wellington, New Zealand.

Warburton, B., D. M. Tompkins, D. Choquenot and P. Cowan. 2012. Minimising number killed in long-term vertebrate pest management programmes, and associated economic incentives. Animal Welfare 21: 141–149.

Ward, N. 1999. Foxing the Nation: The Economic (In) Significance of Hunting with Hounds in Britain. Journal of Rural Studies, 15: 389-403.

Washburn, S. L. and C. S. Lancaster. 1968. The Evolution of Hunting. In *Man the Hunter*. R. B. Lee and I. DeVore (Eds). Harvard University Press.

Williams, K., I. Parer, B. Coman, J. Burley and M. Braysher. 1995. *Managing Vertebrate Pests: Rabbits*. Australian Government Publishing Service: Canberra, Australia.

Winkler, R. and K, Warnke. 2012. The future of hunting: an age-period-cohort analysis of deer hunter decline. Population and Environment 33(4).

Winter, M., J. Hallett, J. Nixon, C. Watkins, G. Cox and P. Glanfield, P. 1993. *Economic and Social Aspects of Deer Hunting on Exmoor and the Quantocks*. Centre for Rural Studies, Royal Agricultural College, Cirencester, UK.

Woods, A. and G. N. Kerr. 2010. Recreational Game Hunting: Motivations, Satisfactions and Participation. Lincoln University, Canterbury, New Zealand. Land Environment and People Research Report 18.

Woods, M. 1998a. Mad Cows and Hounded Deer: Political Representations of Animals in the British Countryside. Environment and Planning A, 30(7): 1141- 1330.

Woods, M. 1998b. Researching Rural Conflicts: Hunting, Local Politics and Actor Networks. Journal of Rural Studies, 14: 321-340.

Woods, M. 2000. Fantastic Mr Fox? Representing Animals in the Hunting Debate. In Philo, C. and Wilbert, C. (Eds.) *Animals Places, Beastly Places: New Geographies of Human-Animal Relations*. (pp. 182-202). Routledge.

Wrangham, R. 2009. *Catching Fire: How cooking made us human*. Profile Books.

Chapter 4 Predation and Aggression

Anderson, M. and R. A. Norberg. 1981. Evolution of reversed sexual dimorphism and role partitioning among predatory birds, with a size scaling of flight performance. Biological Journal of the Linnean Society 15: 105-130.

Bentson, S. A. 1971. Hunting methods and choice of prey of Gyrfalcons (*Falco rusticolus*) at Myvatn in Iceland. Ibis 113: 468-476.

Buchanan, J. B. 1996. A comparison of behaviour and

success rates of Merlins and Peregrine Falcons when hunting Dunlins during winter. Raptor Research 20:130-131.

Carvalho, M., J. M. Palmeirim, F. C. Rego, N. Sole, A. Santana and J. E. Fa. 2015. What motivates hunters to target exotic or endemic species on the island of São Tomé, Gulf of Guinea?. Oryx, 49(2): 278-286.

Cliff, D. and G. F. Miller. 1996. Co-evolution of pursuit and evasion II: simulation methods and results. In *From Animals to Animats* 4: Proceedings of the Fourth International Conference on Simulation of Adaptive Behaviour (Eds. P. Maes, M. Mataric, J.-A. Meyer and J. Pollack). Cambridge, MA: MIT Press.

Cruzada, S. M. 2019. *Life and death encounters: trans-species anthropology and extended worlds between hunters and animals in southwestern Extremadura.* PhD thesis, Universidad Pablo de Olavide. Olavide Institutional.

Cureo, E. 1976. *The Ethology of Predation*. Springer Verlag, New York.

Dekker, D. 1980. Hunting success rates, foraging habits, and prey selection of peregrine falcons migrating through central Alberta. Can. Field Nat. 94, 371-382.

Dekker, D. 2009. *Hunting tactics of Peregrines and other falcons*. Hancock House.

Dekker, D. and J. Lange, J. 2001. Hunting methods and success rates of gyrfalcons, *Falco rusticolus*, and prairie falcons, *Falco mexicanus*, preying on feral pigeons (rock doves), *Columba livia*, in Edmonton, Alberta. Can. Field Nat. 115: 395-401.

Domenici, P., J. M. Blagburn and J. P. Bacon. 2011. Animal escapology II: escape trajectory case studies. J. Exp. Biol. 214: 2474-2494.

Fitzgerald, A. 2005. The Emergence of the Figure of "Woman-The-Hunter:" Equality or Complicity in Oppression? Women's Studies Quarterly, 33(1/2): 86-104.

Fox, N. C. 1981. Hunting behaviour of trained Northern Goshawks (*Accipiter gentilis*). P121-133 In R. E. Kenward and I. M. Lindsay (Eds) *Understanding the Goshawk*. Proceedings of the IAF 29 September-1 October 1981, Oxford, UK.

Fox, N. C., B. I. M. Fox and T. Bailey. 1993. The hunting behaviour and predatory efficiency of the Mauritius kestrel (*Falco punctatus*). pp. 136-143 In M. K. Nicholls and R. Clarke [Eds.]. *Biology and conservation of small falcons*: Proceedings of the 1991 Hawk and Owl Trust Conference. The Hawk and Owl Trust, London, England.

Giacomelli, S. and M. Gibbert. 2018. He likes to play the hero - I let her have fun shooting. Gender games in the Italian forest during the hunting season. Journal of Rural Studies 62: 164-173.

Hedenstrom, A. and M. Rosen. 2001. Predator versus prey: on aerial hunting and escape strategies in birds. Behav. Ecol. 12: 150-156.

Howland, H. C. 1974. Optimal strategies for predator avoidance: the relative importance of speed and manoeuvrability. J. Theor. Biol. 47: 333-350.

Ingold T. 1980. *Hunters, pastoralists and ranchers: reindeer economies and their transformations*. Cambridge: Cambridge University Press.

Jenkins, A. R. 2000. Hunting mode and success of African Peregrine Falcons: Does nesting habitat quality affect foraging efficiency? Ibis142: 225-246.

Kerasote, T. 1993. *Bloodties: Nature, Culture, and the Hunt.* New York: Kodansha.

Knight, J. (Ed.) 2005. *Animals in Person: Cultural Perspectives on Human-Animal Intimacies*. Oxford, England.

Knight, J. 2006. *Waiting for Wolves in Japan: An Anthropological Study of People-Wildlife Relations*. University of Hawaii Press.

Knight, J. 2012. The Anonymity of the Hunt: a Critique of Hunting as Sharing. Current Anthropology 53 (3): 334-355.

Kruuk, H. 2002. Hunter and hunted: relationships between carnivores and people, Cambridge University Press 5(4): 379-393.

Lee, S. H., H. K. Pak and T. S. Chon. 2006. Dynamics of prey-flock escaping behaviour in response to predator's attack. J. Theor. Biol. 240: 250-259.

List, C. J. 1998. On the Moral Significance of a Hunting Ethic. Ethics and the Environment 3(20: 157-175.

Littlefield, J. 2010. Men on the hunt: Ecofeminist insights into masculinity. Marketing Theory, 10(1): 97-117.

Lopes-Fernandes, M., C. Espírito-Santo and A. Frazão-Moreira. 2022. 'Among predators': the place of humans, Iberian lynx and other wild carnivores. Etnográfica. Revista do Centro em Rede de Investigação em Antropologia.

Luke, B. 1997. A Critical Analysis of Hunters' Ethics. Environmental Ethics 19: 25.

Luke, B. 2007. *Brutal: Manhood and the Exploitation of Animals*. University of Illinois Press.

Nahin, P. J. 2012. *Chases and Escapes*. Princeton, NJ: Princeton University Press.

Pooley, S., M. Barua, W. Beinart, A. Dickman, G. Holmes, J. Lorimer, A. J. Loveridge, D. W. Macdonald, G. Marvin, S. Redpath, C. Sillero–Zubiri, A. Zimmermann and E. J. Milner–Gulland. 2017. An interdisciplinary review of current and future approaches to improving human–predator relations. Conservation biology 31(3): 513-523.

Marlow, F. W. 2007. Hunting and Gathering: The Human Sexual Division of Foraging Labor. Cross-Cultural Research 41:170-196.

Panter-Brick, C., R. H. Layton and P. Rowely-Conwy (Eds). 2001. *Hunter-Gatherers: An Interdisciplinary Perspective*. Cambridge University Press.

Quinn, J. L. and W. Cresswell. 2004. Predator hunting and prey vulnerability. Journal of Animal Ecology 73:143-154.

Rosenfeld, D. L. 2020. Gender differences in vegetarian identity: How men and women construe meatless dieting. Food Quality and Preference (81):103859.

Stanford, C. B. 1999. *The Hunting Apes: Meat-eating and the Origins of Human Behavior*. Princeton University Press.

Chapter 5 Animal welfare issues

Aebischer, N.J., C. J. Wheatley and H. R. Rose. 2014. Factors Associated with Shooting Accuracy and Wounding Rate of Four Managed Wild Deer Species in the UK, Based on Anonymous Field Records from Deer Stalkers. PLoS ONE 9(10): e109698.

Aegerter, J., D. Fouracre and G. C. Smith. 2017. A first estimate of the structure and density of the populations of pet cats and dogs across Great Britain. PLoS ONE 12:e0174709.

AIHTS. 1997. Agreement on international humane trapping standards between the European Community, Canada and the Russian Federation. Retrieved from: https://fur.ca/wp-content/uploads/2015/09/AIHTS-Copy-of-Agreement.pdf

Aitken, G. 2008. Animal Suffering: An Evolutionary Approach. Environmental Values 17: 165–180.

Alaska Outdoors Supersite Methods for dispatching trapped animals. Available online: http://forums.outdoorsdirectory.com/showthread.php/136907-Methods-for-Dispatching-Trapped-Animals

Anderson, D. R. 2001. The need to get the basics right in wildlife field studies. Wildlife Society Bulletin 29: 1294–1297.

Anderson, W. L. and G. C. Sanderson. 1979. Effectiveness of steel shot in 3-inch, 12-gauge shells for hunting Canada geese. Wildlife Society Bulletin 7: 213–220.

Andrews, K. and S. Monsó. 2020. *Rats are Us*. Aeon. March 2020.

Ankney, C. D. 1975. Incidence and size of lead shot in lesser snow goose. Wildlife Society Bulletin 3: 25–26.

Anon. 2011. Gamekeepers and wildlife – the full survey report 2011. https://www.nationalgamekeepers.org.uk/media/178/gamekeepers-and-wildlife-full report.pdf.

Anon. 2012a. *The code of good shooting practice*. Rossett, Wrexham: British Association for Shooting & Conservation.

Anon. 2012b. *Determining the extent of use and humaneness of snares in England and Wales*. Report to DEFRA on contract WM0315.

Anon. 2012c *Snaring in Scotland – a practitioners' guide*. Fourth edition. https://www2.gov.scot/Topics/Environment/Wildlife-Habitats/paw-Scotland/Resources/Goodpracticeadvice/Snaringguide.

Anon. 2016. *Cruel and indiscriminate: why Scotland must become snare-free*. Edinburgh: OneKind.

Anon. 2017. Training Manual for Deer Stalkers. British Deer Society.

Anon. 2019a. *Untold suffering – how thousands of animals are trapped, snared and killed to protect grouse shooting for sport*. Edinburgh: OneKind.

Anon. 2019b. *Gamekeepers: conservation and wildlife* – a new survey. https://www.nationalgamekeepers.org.uk/articles/gamekeepers-and-wildlife-new-report.

Anon. 2019c. Understanding the hunting behaviour of pet cats: an introduction. 15th January 2019. Intelligent Cat Care Blog.

Appleby, M. C., and P. Sandøe. 2002. Philosophical debate on the nature of well-being: implications for animal welfare. Anim. Welf. 11: 283–294.

Armstrong, H. 2019. *A better way – how an alternative to grouse moors could help tackle climate change, increase biodiversity and benefit Scotland's people*. Edinburgh: The Revive Coalition.

Baker, P. and S. Harris. 1997. *How will a ban on hunting affect the British fox population?* Electra Publishing.

Baker P, Thompson R, Grogan A. Survival rates of cat-attacked birds admitted to RSPCA wildlife centres in the UK: implications for cat owners and wildlife rehabilitators. *Animal Welfare*. 2018;27(4):305-318.

Baker, P. J. and S. Harris. 2005. Does culling reduce fox (*Vulpes vulpes*) density in commercial forests in Wales, UK? European Journal of Wildlife Research 52: 99-108.

Baker, P.J., A. J. Bentley, R. J. Ansell and S. Harris. 2005. Impact of predation by domestic cats Felis catus in an urban area. Mammal Review 35: 302-312.

Baker, P.J., S. E. Molony, E. Stone, I. C. Cuthill and S. Harris. 2008. Cats about town: is predation by free-ranging pet cats Felis catus likely to affect urban bird populations? Ibis 150: 86-99.

Baker, S. E. 2017. A voluntary trap approval scheme to end trap welfare inequality in the UK. Anim. Welf. 26:131–133.

Baker, S. E. and D. W. Macdonald. 2000. Foxes and foxhunting on farms in Wiltshire: a case study. Journal of Rural Studies 16, 185–201.

Baker, S. E. and T. M. Sharp. 2015. Welfare in commensal rodent trapping: One step forward, two steps back. Anim. Welf. 24: 369–371.

Baker, S. E., and D. W. Macdonald. 2012. Not so humane mole tube traps. Anim. Welf. 21:613–615.

Baker, S. E., D. W. Macdonald and S. A. Ellwood. 2017. In: *Double Standards in Spring Trap Welfare: Ending Inequality for Rats (Rodentia: Muridae), Mice (Rodentia: Muridae) and Moles (Insectivora: Talpidae) in the United Kingdom*, Proceedings of the Ninth International Conference on Urban Pests, Birmingham, UK, 9–12 July 2017. Davies M. P., Pfeiffer C., Robinson W. H., Editors. Pureprint Group; Uckfield, UK: 2017.

Baker, S. E., S. A. Ellwood, V. L. Tagarielli, and D. W. Macdonald. 2012. Mechanical performance of rat, mouse and mole spring traps, and possible implications for welfare performance. PLoS One 7(6):e39334.

Baker, S.E., T. M. Sharp and D. W. Macdonald. 2016. Assessing Animal Welfare Impacts in the Management of European Rabbits (*Oryctolagus cuniculus*), European Moles (*Talpa europaea*) and Carrion Crows (*Corvus corone*). PLoS One. Jan 4;11(1):

Baldus, R. D., G. R. Damm and K. Wollscheid (Eds.). 2008. *Best Practices in Sustainable Hunting - A Guide to Best Practices from Around the World*. Sustainable Hunting Tourism - Position Paper of the CIC Tropical Game Commission.

Barratt, D. G. 1997. Predation by house cats, Felis catus (L), in Canberra, Australia .1. Prey composition and preference. Wildlife Research 24: 263-277.

Barratt, D. G. 1998. Predation by house cats, *Felis catus* (L.), in Canberra, Australia. II. Factors affecting the amount of prey caught and estimates of the impact on wildlife. Wildlife Research 25: 475-487.

BASC. 2013. *Trapping pest mammals – a code of practice*. Rossett, Wrexham: British Association for Shooting & Conservation.

Bateman, J. A. 1971. *Animal traps and trapping*. Newton Abbot: David & Charles.

Bateman, J. A. 1979. *Trapping: a practical guide*. Newton Abbot: David & Charles.

Bateson, P. 2004. Do animals suffer like us? – the assessment of animal welfare. Vet. J. 168(2):110-111.

Bateson, P. and R. Harris. 2000. *The effects of hunting with dogs in England and Wales on the welfare of deer, foxes, mink and hare*. Report to the Committee of Inquiry into Hunting with Dogs in England and Wales.

Bateson, P. and E. L. Bradshaw. 1997. Physiological effects of hunting red deer (*Cervus elaphus*). Proceedings of the Royal Society of London Series B 264: 1707–1714.

Beale, C. M. and P. Monaghan. 2004. Human disturbance: people as predation-free predators? Journal of Applied Ecology, 41: 335-343.

Beausoleil, N. J. and D. J. Mellor. 2014. Advantages and limitations of the Five Domains model for assessing welfare impacts associated with vertebrate pest control. N Z Vet. J. Jan. 63(1):37-43.

Beausoleil, N.J., S. E. Baker and T. Sharp. 2022. Scientific Assessment of the Welfare of Trapped Mammals-Key Considerations for the Use of the Sharp and Saunders Humaneness Assessment Model. Animals (Basel). Feb 8;12(3): 402.

Bekoff, M. 2007. *The Emotional Lives of Animals: A Leading Scientist Explores Animal Joy, Sorrow, and Empathy and Why They Matter*. Novato, CA: New World Library.

Bentham, J. 1780. "Of The Principle of Utility". pp. 1–6 in *An Introduction to the Principles of Morals and Legislation*. London: T. Payne and Sons.

Beringer, J., L. P. Hansen, W. Wilding, J. Fischer and S. L. Sheriff. 1996. Factors affecting capture myopathy in white-tailed deer. Journal of Wildlife Management 60: 373-380.

Bertsden, J. (Ed) 1999. *Shooting of game/crippling/wounding*. The Ministry of Environment and Energy, Denmark.

Birch, J. et al. 2022. Review of the evidence of sentience in cephalopod molluscs and cephalopod crustaceans. Report to UK Department of Environment, Food and Rural Affairs. https://www.lse.ac.uk/business/consulting/reports/review-of-the-evidence-of-sentiences-in-cephalopod-molluscs-and-decapod-crustaceans.

Blue Angel—The German Ecolabel Non-Toxic Pest Control and Prevention DE-UZ 34 Basic Award Criteria, Edition January 2017, Version 2. 2017 Available online: https://produktinfo.blauer-engel.de/uploads/criteriafile/en/DE-UZ%20034-201701-en%20Criteria.pdf

Bonnington, C., K. J. Gaston and K. L. Evans. 2013. Fearing the feline: domestic cats reduce avian fecundity through trait-mediated indirect effects that increase nest predation by other species. Journal of Applied Ecology 50: 15-24.

Bradshaw, E. L. and P. Bateson. 2000. Welfare implications of culling red deer (*Cervus elaphus*). *Animal Welfare* 9 (1): 3-24.

Bradshaw, R. H. and D. M. Broom. 2000. The welfare of deer, foxes, mink and hares subjected to hunting by humans: a review. CUAWIC Report, (Commissioned by the International Fund for Animal Welfare).

Brakes, P. and M. Donoghue. 2006. *Comprehensive and standardised data on whale killing: welfare considerations*. Proceedings of the Workshop on Whale Killing Methods and Associated Welfare Issues pp 1–4. 11–13 June 2006, St Kitts and Nevis. International Whaling Commission: Cambridge, UK.

Broom, D. M. 1991. Animal welfare: concepts and measurement. Journal of Animal Science 69: 4167-4175.

Broom, D. M. 1999. The welfare of vertebrate pests in relation to their management. In: P.D. Cowan and C.J. Feare (Editors) *Advances in Vertebrate Pest Management*, pp 309-329. Fürth: Filander Verlag.

Broom, D. M. 2001. Evolution of pain. R. Soc. Med. Int. Congr. Symp. Ser. 246:17–25.

Broom, D. M. 2002. Welfare in wildlife management and zoos. Advances in Ethology 37: 4-6.

Broom, D. M. 2006. The evolution of morality. Applied Animal Behaviour Science 100: 20-28.

Broom, D. M. 2022. Some thoughts on the impacts of trapping on mammal welfare with emphasis on snares. In G. Proulx (Ed.), *Mammal trapping: Wildlife management, animal welfare & international standards* (pp. 121–128). Alpha Wildlife Publications.

Broom, D. M. and K. G. Johnson 1993/2000. *Stress and animal welfare*. Dordrecht: Kluwer.

Brown, C. 2015. Fish intelligence, sentience and ethics. Animal Cognition, 18(1): 1-17.

Bryan, H. M., J. E. G. Smits, L. Koren, P. C. Paquet, K. E. Wynne-Edwards and M. Musiani. 2015. Heavily hunted wolves have higher stress and reproductive steroids than wolves with lower hunting pressure. Functional Ecology 29(3): 347–356.

Burgess, R. 2020. How Long Does It Take For Rat Poison To Work? Dalton Engineering. Retrieved from: https://www.daltonengineering.co.uk/blogs/news/how-long-does-it-take-for-rat-poison-to-work

Buss, M. E., R. Gollat and H. R. Timmerman. 1989. Moose Hunter Shooting proficiency in Ontario. Alces 25:98-103.

Butterworth, A. and M. Richardson. 2013. A review of animal welfare implications of the Canadian commercial seal hunt. Marine Policy 38: 457–469.

Callicott, J. B. 1980. Animal liberation: a triangular affair. Environmental Ethics 2: 311–328.

Calver, M., S. Thomas, S. Bradley and H. McCutcheon. 2007. Reducing the rate of predation on wildlife by pet cats: the efficacy and practicability of collar-mounted pounce protectors. Biological Conservation 137: 341-348.

Calver, M.C., J. Grayson, M. Lilith and C. R. Dickman. 2011. Applying the precautionary principle to the issue of impacts by pet cats on urban wildlife. Biological Conservation 144: 1895- 1901.

Campbell, S. T., F. G. Hartley and Z. Fang. 2016. Assessing the nature and use of corvid cage traps in Scotland: Part 3 of 4 – trap operation and welfare. Inverness: Scottish Natural Heritage Commissioned Report No. 933.

Canadian General Standards Board. 1996. *Animal (Mammal) Traps—Mechanically Powered, Trigger-Activated Killing Traps for Use on Land*. National Standards of Canada; Ottawa, ON, Canada.

Catia, F., and P. Eze. 2015. Animals in need: The problem of wild animal suffering and intervention in nature. Relations 3(1): 7–13.

Cattet, M. R. L. 2013. Falling through the cracks: Shortcomings in the collaboration between biologists and veterinarians and their consequences for wildlife. *ILAR J*. 2013;54.

Caudell, J. N. 2013. Review of wound ballistic research and its applicability to wildlife management. Wildlife Society Bulletin 37: 824–831.

Caudell, J. N., B. C. West, B. Griffin and K. Davis. 2009. Fostering greater professionalism with firearms in the wildlife arena. In: Boulanger, J. (Ed) Proceedings of the Thirteenth Wildlife Damage Management Conference pp 95–99. 4-7 May 2009, Saratoga Springs, New York, USA. The Wildlife Society: Bethesda, USA.

Chandroo, K. P., S. Yue and R. D. Moccia. 2004. An

evaluation of current perspectives on consciousness and pain in fishes. Fish 5:281–295.
Clausen, K.K., T.E. Holm, L. Haugaard and J. Madsen. 2017. Crippling ratio: A novel approach to assess hunting-induced wounding of wild animals, Ecological Indicators, 10.1016/j.ecolind.2017.05.044, 80: 242-246.
Colvile, K. 2007. *The natural chase*. Report commissioned by the All Party Parliamentary Middle Way Group and the Veterinary Association for Wildlife Management.
Conner, M. C., E. C. Soutiere and R. A. Lancia. 1987. Drop-netting deer: costs and incidence of capture myopathy. Wildlife Society Bulletin 15: 434-438.
Coupland, R. M., B. P. Kneubuehl, D. I. Rowley and G. W. Bowyer. 2000. Wound Ballistics, Surgery and the Law of War. Trauma 2:1-10.
Crooks, K. R. and M. E. Soulé. 1999. Mesopredator release and avifaunal extinctions in a fragmented system. Nature 400: 563-566.
Crowley, S. L., M. Cecchetti and R. A. McDonald. 2019. Hunting behaviour in domestic cats: An exploratory study of risk and responsibility among cat owners. People and Nature 1(1): 18-30.
CRRU. 2017. CRRU UK: *Rat Control & Game Management*. CRRU-Gamekeepers-Booklet.
Daoust, P. Y., M. Hammill, G. Stenson and C. Caraguel. 2014. A review of animal welfare implications of the Canadian commercial seal hunt: a critique. Marine Policy 43: 367–371.
DEFRA. 1997. Assessment of Humaneness of Vertebrate Control Agents. Evaluation of Fully Approved or Provisionally Approved Products under the Control of Pesticide Regulations 1986, Food and Environment Protection Act, 1985, Part III. Department of Environment, Food and Rural Affairs
DEFRA. 2005. Report of the independent working group on snares. http://archive.DEFRA.gov.uk/wildlife-pets/ wildlife/management/documents/snares-iwgs-report.pdf.
DEFRA. 2013. Monitoring the Humaneness Of Badger Population Reduction by Controlled Shooting. Department for Environment, Food and Rural Affairs: London, UK.
DEFRA. 2015. Guidance: Red meat slaughterhouses: Restraining, stunning and killing animals. Retrieved from: https://www.gov.uk/guidance/red-meat-slaughterhousesrestraining-stunning-killing-animals#animal-stunning-and-killing
Dickman, A. *et al.* 2019. Trophy hunting bans imperil biodiversity. Science 35(64456):874.
Drickamer, L. C., and D.G. Mikesi. 1993. Differences in trapping and killing efficiency of Sherman, Victor and Museum Special traps for house mice. Am. Midl. Nat. 1993;130:397–401.
ECGCGRF (European Community, Government of Canada, and Government of the Russian Federation). 1997. Agreement on international humane trapping standards. Off. J. Eur. Communities 42: 43–57.
Ellis, M. B. and C. A. Miller. 2022. The effect of a ban on the use of lead ammunition for waterfowl hunting on duck and goose crippling rates in Illinois, Wildlife Biology, 10.1002/wlb3.01001, 2022, 2.
Elmeros, M., T.E. Holm, L. Haugaard and A. B. Madsen. 2012.Prevalence of embedded shotgun pellets in protected and in legally hunted medium-sized carnivores in Denmark, European Journal of Wildlife Research, 10.1007/s10344-012-0621-7, 58, 4, (715-719).
Ericsson, G. and H. von Essen. 1998. Moose shot at and not retrieved in Sweden. Swedish Association for Hunting and Wildlife Management.
Etheridge, B, R. W. Summers and R. E. Green. 1997. The effects of illegal killing and destruction of nests by humans on the population dynamics of the hen harrier *Circus cyaneus* in Scotland. Journal of Applied Ecology, 34: 1081-1105.
Falk, K., F. Merkel, K. Kampp and S. E. Jamieson. 2006. Embedded lead shot and infliction rates in common eiders *Somateria mollissima* and king eiders *S. spectabilis* wintering in Southwest Greenland. Wildlife Biology 12: 257– 265.
Fardell, L.L., C. E. M. Nano, C. R. Pavey and C. R. Dickman. 2022. *Small Prey Animal hunting Behaviors in Landscapes of Fear: Effects of Predator Presence and Human Activity Along an Urban Disturbance Gradient*. Frontiers in Ecology and Evolution.
Finley, M. T. and M. P. Dieter. 1978. Toxicity of Experimental Lead-Iron Shot versus Commercial Lead Shot in Mallards. The Journal of Wildlife Management, 42(1): 32–39.
Fishcount (online) http://fishcount.org.uk/uk-strategy#2wild Towards a strategy for humane fishing in the UK.
Fitzgerald, B. M and D. C. Turner. 2000. Hunting behaviour of domestic cats and their impact on prey populations. In: Turner D. C. and P. Bateson (Eds) *The Domestic Cat*. 2nd Edition pp 151-175. Cambridge University Press: Cambridge,
Fox, C. H. and C. M. Papouchis. 2004. *Cull of the Wild—A Contemporary Analysis of Wildlife Trapping in the United States*. Animal Protection Institute; Sacramento, CA, USA.
Fox, N. C. 2022. Understanding the Bird of Prey: New Advanced Edition. Hancock House.
Fox, N. C., N. Blay, A. G. Greenwood, D. Wise and E. Potapov. 2005. Wounding rates in shooting foxes (*Vulpes vulpes*). Journal of Animal Welfare 14: 93-102.
Frauke, E. *et al.* 2017. Sublethal Lead Exposure Alters Movement Behavior in Free-Ranging Golden Eagles. Environmental Science & Technology 51 (10): 5729-5736.
Fur Institute of Canada (FIC) Certified Traps—AIHTS Implementation in Canada. [(accessed on 26 March 2020)];2019 Available online: https://fur.ca/certified-traps/
Gales, N., R. Leaper and V. Papastavrou. 2008. Is Japan's whaling humane? Marine Policy 32: 408–412.
Game and Wildlife Conservation Trust Agreement on International Humane Trapping Standards (AIHTS) 2020 Available online: https://www.gwct.org.uk/advisory/faqs/aihts/
Gentsch, R. P., P. Kjellander and B. O. Röken. 2018. Cortisol response of wild ungulates to trauma situations: hunting is not necessarily the worst stressor. European Journal of Wildlife Research, 10.1007.
George, A. 2003. Standing Committee F, 21 January 2003, Hunting Bill. Hansard.
Gese, E. M., P. A. Terletzky, J. D. Erb, K. C. Fuller, J. P. Grabarkewitz, J. P. Hart, C. Humpal, B. A.

Sampson and J. K. Young. Injury scores and spatial responses of wolves following capture: Cable restraints versus foothold traps. Wildl. Soc. Bull. 2019;43:42–52.

Gladfelter, H. L. 1985. *Deer in Iowa*. Iowa Wildlife Research Bulletin No 38, Iowa Dept of Natural Resources.

Godfray, C. 2018. A review of the government's 25-year Bovine TB Strategy. DEFRA.

Gordon, J. K., C. Matthaei and Y. van Heezik. 2010. Belled collars reduce catch of domestic cats in New Zealand by half. Wildlife Research 37: 372-378.

Græsli, A. R., et al. 2020. Physiological and behavioural responses of moose to hunting with dogs. Conservation Physiology 8(1): 122.

Grandin, T. 2010. Auditing animal welfare at slaughter plants. Meat Science 86: 65–65.

Grant, M. C., J. Mallord, L. Stephen and P. S. Thompson. 2012. *The costs and benefits of grouse moor management to biodiversity and aspects of the wider environment: a review*. Sandy, Bedfordshire: RSPB.

Grayson, J. 2016. Reducing wildlife predation by domestic cats: An approach based on the precautionary principle. oai:researchrepository.murdoch.edu.au:32298.

Green, P. 1992. Killing Deer. Stalking Magazine (November 1992): 21-23.

Gregory, N. G. 2005. Bowhunting deer. Animal Welfare 14: 111–116.

Gregory, N.G., L. M. Milne, A. T. Rhodes, K. E. Littin, M. Wickstrom and C. T. Eason. 1998. Effect of potassium cyanide on behaviour and time to death in possums. New Zealand Veterinary Journal 46: 60–64.

Griffin, D. R. and G. B. Speck. 2004. New evidence of animal consciousness. Animal Cognition 7, 5-18.

GWCT (n.d.). Recommendations on fox snares. Retrieved from: https://www.gwct.org.uk/policy/position-statements/recommendations-on-fox-snares/

GWCT. (b). (n.d.). Larsen trap use in England, Scotland, and Wales. Retrieved from: https://www.gwct.org.uk/advisory/guides/larsen-traps-england-scotland/#dispatch

GWCT. (n.d.). DOC traps. Retrieved from: https://www.gwct.org.uk/game/research/predation-control/tunnel-traps/doctraps/

GWCT. (n.d.). Predation control and conservation. Retrieved from: https://www.gwct.org.uk/policy/position-statements/predation-control-and-conservation/

GWCT. (n.d.). Tunnel traps. Retrieved from: https://www.gwct.org.uk/game/research/predation-control/tunnel-traps/

GWCT. 2019. *The moorland balance – the science behind grouse shooting and moorland management*, second edition. Fordingbridge, Hampshire: Game & Wildlife Conservation Trust.

Hall, C. M., et al. 2017. Community attitudes and practices of urban residents regarding predation by pet cats on wildlife: an international comparison. PloS ONE 12:e0174709.

Hall, C. M., J. B. Fontaine, K. A. Bryant and C. M. Calver. 2015. Assessing the effectiveness of the Birdsbesafe® anti-predation collar in reducing predation on wildlife by pet cats in Western Australia. Applied Animal Behaviour Science 173: 40-51.

Hall, C.M., K. A. Bryant, K. Haskard, T. Major, S, Bruce and M. C. Calver. 2016. Factors determining the home ranges of pet cats: A meta-analysis. Biological Conservation 203: 313-320.

Hamilton, G. D. and H. P. Weeks, Jr. 1985. Cortisol and aldosterone comparisons of cottontail rabbits collected by shooting, trapping, and falconry. Journal of Wildlife Diseases 21: 40–42.

Hammond, T. T. et al. 2019. Physiological and behavioral responses to anthropogenic stressors in a human-tolerant mammal. Journal of Mammalogy 10:1093.

Hampton J. O., P. M. Fisher and B. Warburton. 2020. Reconsidering humaneness. Conserv. Biol. 34(5):1107-1113.

Hampton, J. O. and T. H. Hyndman. 2019. Under-addressed animal welfare issues in conservation. Conservation Biology 33(4):803-811.

Hampton, J. O., B. D. Cowled, A. L. Perry, C. J. Miller, B. Jones, and Q. Hart. 2014. A quantitative analysis of animal welfare out-comes in helicopter shooting: a case study with feral dromedary camels (*Camelus dromedarius*). Wildlife Research 41: 127–145.

Hampton, J. O., D. M. Forsyth, D. I. Mackenzie and I. G. Stuart. 2023. A simple quantitative method for assessing animal welfare outcomes in terrestrial wildlife shooting: the European rabbit as a case study. Animal Welfare 10 (3): 307-317.

Hanley, N., M. Czajkowski, R. Hanley Nickolls and S. Redpath. 2010. Economic values of species management options in human–wildlife conflicts: Hen Harriers in Scotland. Ecological Economics, Volume 70, (1): 107–113.

Harris, R. C., T. R. Helliwell, W. Shingleton, N. Stickland and J. R. J. Naylor. 1999. *The physiological response of red deer (Cervus elaphus) to prolonged exercise undertaken during hunting*. R & W Publications (Newmarket) Ltd.

Harris, S. and B. Thain. 2020. *Hanged by the feet until dead: An analysis of snaring and trapping on Scottish Grouse moors*. A report commissioned by the Director of the League Against Cruel Sports Scotland.

Harrison, A., S. Newey, L. Gilbert, D. T. Haydon and S. Thirgood. 2010. Culling wildlife hosts to control disease: mountain hares, red grouse and louping ill virus. Journal of Applied Ecology 47: 926-930.

Harrop, S. R. 1998. The agreements on international humane trapping standards—Background, critique and the texts. J. Int. Wildl. Law Policy. 1998;1:387–394.

Health and Safety Executive. 2003. *Assessment of an Experimental Permit: T3327 as a vertebrate control agent against foxes*. Biocides and Pesticides Unit, Magdalen House, Bootle, Merseyside.

Henderson, R. J., C. M. Frampton, D. R. Morgan and G. J. Hickling. 1999. The efficacy of baits containing 1080 for control of brushtail possums. Journal of Wildlife Management 63: 1138–1151.

Hicklin, P. W. and W. R. Barrow. 2004. The incidence of embedded shot in waterfowl in Atlantic Canada and Hudson strait. Waterbirds 27: 41–45.

Hiltz, M. and L. D. Roy. 2001. Use of anaesthetized animals to test humaneness of killing traps. Wildl. Soc. Bull. 29: 606–611.

Hiltz, M., L. D. Roy. 2000. In: *Rating Killing Traps Against Humane Trapping Standards Using Computer Simulations. Proceedings of the 19th Vertebrate Pest Conference, San Diego, California*. Salmon L. P. and A. C. Crabb, Editors. University of California; Davis, CA, USA pp. 197–201.

Hollerman, J. J., M. L. Fackler, D. M. Coldwell and Y. Ben-Menachem. 1990. Gunshot wounds: 1. Bullets, ballistics, and mechanisms of injury. American Journal of Roentgenology 155: 685–690.

Holm, T. E. and J. Madsen. 2012. Incidence of embedded shotgun pellets and inferred hunting kill amongst Russian/Baltic barnacle geese *Branta leucopsis*, European Journal of Wildlife Research, 59, 1: 77-80.

Holm, T. E. and L. Haugaard. 2013. Effects of a Danish action plan on reducing shotgun wounding of Common Eider *Somateria mollissima*, Bird Study, 60, 1: 131-134.

Homburg, D. D., S. L. Sheriff, P. H. Geissler and T. Roster. 1982. Shotshell and shooter effectiveness. Lead vs. steel shot for duck hunting. Wildlife Society Bulletin 10: 121– 126.

Horta, O. 2010. Debunking the idyllic view of natural processes. Population dynamics and suffering in the wild. Telos, 17: 73–88.

Hulme, P. E. 2020. One Biosecurity: a unified concept to integrate human, animal, plant, and environmental health. Emerg. Top. Life Sci. Dec 15, 4(5): 539-549.

Huntingford, F.A. *et al*. 2006. Current issues in fish welfare. J. Fish Biol. 68: 332–372.

Iossa, G, C. D. Soulsbury and S. Harris. 2007. Mammal trapping: a review of animal welfare standards of killing and restraining traps. Animal Welfare 16: 335-353.

Irvine, J. 2006. Hunting for sustainability – can hunting be a force for good? A summary of research findings from the Scottish case study. James Hutton Institute.

ISO 1999. 10990-5. *Animal (Mammal) Traps*. International Organization for Standardization; Geneva, Switzerland: 1999. Part 5: Methods for testing restraining traps.

ISO. 1995. *Animal (Mammal Traps)* ISO; Geneva, Switzerland: 1995. Part 4: Non-mechanically powered killing snares. ISO/TC 191/N 99.

ISO. 1999. 10990-4 . *Animal (Mammal) Traps*. International Organization for Standardization; Geneva, Switzerland: 1999. Part 4: Methods for testing killing trap systems used on land and underwater.

Jacobson, H. A., R. L. Kirkpatrick, H. E. Burkhart and J. W. Davis. 1978. Hematologic comparisons of shot and live trapped cotton-tail rabbits. Journal of Wildlife Diseases 14: 82–88.

Johannsen, K. 2021. *Wild animal ethics: The moral and political problem of wild animal suffering*. Routledge.

Johnson, J. 2015. Humanely killed? Journal of Animal Ethics 5(2): 123-125.

Jönsson, B., J. Karlsson and S. Svensson. 1985. Incidence of lead shot in tissues of the bean goose (*Anser fabalis*) wintering in South Sweden. Swedish Wildlife Research 13: 259– 271.

Kasperbauer, T. J. and P. Sandøe. 2015. *Killing as a welfare issue*. Oxford University Press.

Kays, R. W. and A. A. De Wan. 2004. Ecological impact of inside/outside house cats around a suburban nature preserve. Animal Conservation 7: 273-283.

Kays, R., R. R. Dunn *et al*. 2020. The small home ranges and large local ecological impacts of pet cats. Animal Conservation 23 (5): 516-523.

Kestin, S. C. 1995. Welfare aspects of the commercial slaughter of whales. Animal Welfare 4: 11–27.

Kirkwood, J. K. *et al*. (Eds) 2001. Proceedings of the UFAW Symposium: Consciousness, Cognition and Animal Welfare. Volume 10 (Supplement).

Kirkwood, J. K. *et al*. (Eds) 2007. Proceedings of the UFAW/BVA Symposium: Quality of life: the heart of the matter. Volume 16 (Supplement).

Knight, M. 2014. Bring out your dead. Keeping the Balance. Spring 2014: 46-47. https://www.nationalgamekeepers.org.uk/media/91/Carcass%20Disposal.pdf.

Kreeger, T. J. *et al*. 1989. Monitoring heart rate and body temperature in red foxes. Canadian Journal of Zoology 67: 2455-2458.

Kreeger, T. J., P. J. White, U. S. Seal and J. R. Tester. 1990. The pathological responses of red foxes to foothold traps. Journal of Wildlife Management 54: 147-160.

Kuentzel, W. F. and T. A. Heberlein. 1998. Why do hunters skybust? Personal disposition or social influence. Human Dimensions of Wildlife 3(1): 1–15.

Larkin, R. P., T. R. VanDeelen, R. M. Sabick, T. E. Gosselink and R. E. Warner. 2003. Electronic signalling for prompt removal of an animal from a trap. Wildl. Soc. Bull. 31: 392–398.

Lepczyk, C. A., A. G. Mertig and J. G. Liu. 2004. Landowners and cat predation across rural-to-urban landscapes. Biological Conservation 115: 191-201.

Leyhausen, P. 1979. *Cat behavior: the predatory and social behavior of domestic and wild cats*. Garland STM Press: New York, USA.

Liljebäck, N. *et al*. 2023. Prevalence of imbedded and ingested shot gun pellets in breeding sea ducks in the Baltic Sea—possible implications for future conservation efforts, European Journal of Wildlife Research, 10.1007.

Linzey, A. 2009. *Why animal suffering matters: Philosophy, theology, and practical ethics*. Oxford, England: Oxford University Press.

Littin, K. E. 2010. Animal welfare and pest control: meeting both conservation and animal welfare goals. Animal Welfare 19: 171–176.

Littin, K., P. Fisher, N. J. Beausoleil and T. Sharp. 2014. Welfare aspects of vertebrate pest control and culling: ranking control techniques for humaneness. Revue Scientifique et Technique (International Office of Epizootics) 33: 281–289.

Lloyd, H. G. 1963. Spring traps and their development. Annals of Applied Biology 51: 329-333.

Logan, K.A., L. L. Sweanor, J. F. Smith and M. G. Hornocker. 1999. Capturing pumas with foot-hold snares. Wildlife Society Bulletin 27: 201-208.

Loss, S. R., T. Will and P. P. Marra. 2013. The impact of free-ranging domestic cats on wildlife of the United States. Nature Communications 4:1396.

Loss, S. R., T. Will, T. Longcore and P. P. Marra. 2018. Responding to misinformation and criticisms regarding United States cat predation estimates. Biological Invasions 20(12): 3385-3396.

Loyd, K. A. T, S. M. Hernandez, J. P. Carroll, K. J. Abernathy and G. K. Marshall. 2013. Quantifying free-roaming domestic cat predation using animal-borne video cameras. Biological Conservation 160: 183-189.

Loyd, K. A. T., S. M. Hernandez and D. L. McRuer. 2017. The role of domestic cats in the admission of injured wildlife at rehabilitation and rescue centers. Wildlife Society Bulletin 41: 55-61.

Ludders, J. W., R. H. Schmidt, F. J. Dein and P. N. Klein. 1999. Drowning is not euthanasia. Wildl. Soc. Bull. 27: 666–670.

Macdonald, D. W. 2023. Mitigating Human Impacts on Wild Animal Welfare. Animals (Basel). 13(18): 2906.

Macdonald, D. W. and P. J. Johnson. 1996. The impact of sport hunting. In: *The exploitation of mammal populations* (Eds V. J. Taylor & N. Dunstone) pp.160-207. Chapman & Hall, London.

Macdonald, D. W. and S. E. Baker. 2004. Non-lethal control of fox predation: the potential of generalised aversion. Animal Welfare 13: 77-85.

Macdonald, D. W., F. Tattersall, P. Johnson, C. Carbone, J. Reynolds, J. Langbein, S. Rushton and M. Shirley. 2000. *Managing British Mammals: Case studies from the Hunting Debate*. Wildlife Conservation Research Unit.

Macdonald, D. W., F. Tattersall, P. Johnson, C. Carbone, J. Reynolds, J. Langbein, S. Rushton and M. Shirley. 2000. Management and control of populations of foxes, deer, hares and mink in England and Wales, and the impact of hunting with dogs. Report to the Committee of Inquiry into Hunting with Dogs in England and Wales.

Maclean, M. 2007. *Impact of domestic cat predation on bird and small mammal populations*. PhD thesis: University of Exeter, UK.

Madsen, J. and F. Riget. 2007. Do embedded shotgun pellets have a chronic effect on body condition of pink-footed geese? Journal of Wildlife Management 71 (5): 1427-1430.

Mankad, A., U. Kennedy and L. J. Carter. 2019. Biological control of pests and a social model of animal welfare. Environ. Manage. Oct 1;247:313-322.

Marion, S. *et al*. 2020. A systematic review of methods for studying the impacts of outdoor recreation on terrestrial wildlife, Global Ecology and Conservation, 10.1016.

Marks, C. A. 2010. Haematological and biochemical responses of red foxes (*Vulpes vulpes*) to different capture methods and shooting. Animal Welfare 19: 223–234.

Marks, C. A., F. Gigliotti, F. Busana, M. Johnston and M. Lindeman. 2004. Fox control using a para-aminopropriophenone formulation with the M-44 ejector. Animal Welfare 13: 401–407.

Marra, P. P. and C. Santella. 2016. *Cat wars: the devastating consequences of a cuddly killer*. Princeton University Press.

Mason, G. and K. Littin. 2003. The humaneness of rodent pest control. Anim. Welf. 2003: 12:1–37.

Mason, G. and M. Mendl. 1993. Why is there no simple way of measuring animal welfare? Anim. Welf. 2:301–319.

Matthews, K., D. Miller, V. Mell and I. Aalders. 2018. Socio-economic and biodiversity impacts of driven grouse moors in Scotland: Part 3. Use of GIS/remote sensing to identify areas of grouse moors, and to assess potential for alternative land uses. https://sefari.scot/research/socioeconomic-and-biodiversity-impacts-of-driven-grouse-moors-in-scotland.

McDonald, J. L., M. Maclean, M. R. Evans and D. J. Hodgson. 2015. Reconciling actual and perceived rates of predation by domestic cats. Ecol. Evol. 5: 27452753.

McLeod, S. J., G. R. Saunders and A. Miners. 2011. Can shooting be an effective management tool for foxes? Preliminary insights from a management programme. Ecological Management and Restoration 12: 224–226.

McLeod, S. R. and T. M. Sharp. 2014. *Improving the humaneness of commercial kangaroo harvesting*. Rural Industries Research and Development Corporation: Canberra, Australia.

Mcruer, D. L. *et al*. 2017. Free roaming cat interactions with wildlife admitted to a wildlife hospital. Journal of Wildlife Management 81 (1): 163-173.

Medina, F. M., E. Bonnaud, E. Vidal and M. Nogales. 2014. Underlying impacts of invasive cats on islands: not only a question of predation. Biodiversity & Conservation 23: 327-342.

Medina, F.M., E. Bonnaud, E. Vidal, B. R. Tershy, E. S. Zavaleta, C. J. Donlan, B. S. Keitt, M. Le Corre, S. V. Horwarth and M. Nogales. 2011. A global review of the impacts of invasive cats on island endangered vertebrates. Global Change Biology 17: 199-219.

Mellor, D. J , N. J. Beausoleil, K. E. Littlewood, A. N. McLean, P. D. McGreevy, B. Jones and B. Wilkins. 2020. The 2020 Five Domains Model: Including Human-Animal Interactions in Assessments of Animal Welfare. C. Animals (Basel). Oct 14;10(10):1870.

Mellor, D. J. and C. S. W. Reid. 1994. Concepts of animal well-being and predicting the impact of procedures on experimental animals. In: Baker R.M., Jenkin G., Mellor D.J., editors. *Improving the Well-Being of Animals in the Research Environment*. Australian and New Zealand Council for the Care of Animals in Research and Teaching (ANZCCART); Glen Osmond, Australia: pp. 3–18.

Mellor, D. J. and K. E. Littin. 2004. Using science to support ethical decisions promoting humane livestock slaughter and vertebrate pest control. Animal Welfare 13: 127–132.

Mendl, M., O. H. P. Burman and E. S. Paul. 2010. *An integrative and functional framework for the study of animal emotion and mood*. Royal Society: Biological Sciences.

Metsers, E. M., P. J. Seddon and Y. M. van Heezik. 2010. Cat-exclusion zones in rural and urban fringe landscapes: how large would they have to be? Wildl. Res. 37: 47-56.

Meyer, S. 1991. *Being Kind to Animal Pests. A No-Nonsense Guide to Humane Animal Control with Cage Traps*. Meyer Pub. Co; Garrison, IA, USA.

Møller, A. P., J. Erritzøe and J. T. Nielsen. 2010. Causes of interspecific variation in susceptibility to cat predation on birds. Chinese Birds 1: 97-111.

Molony, S.E., P. J. Baker, L. Garland, I. C. Cuthill and S. Harris. 2007. Factors that can be used to predict release rates for wildlife casualties. Animal Welfare 16: 361-367.

Montané, J., I. Marco, X. Manteca, L. López and S. Lavin. 2002. Delayed acute capture myopathy in three roe deer. Journal of Veterinary Medicine 49: 93-98.

Moreno-Zarate, L. et al. 2023. Age ratio, crippling losses and factors affecting daily hunting bags of European Turtle-dove in Spain: Implications for sustainable harvest management of a declining migratory species, Science of The Total Environment, 10.1016/j.scitotenv. 2022.161192, 868, (161192).

Morrison, K. 1979. Bullet Placement and the Behaviour of Shot Deer. Journal of the British Deer Society 4 (8).

Mullineaux, E., D. Best and J. E. Cooper. (Eds). 2003. *British Small Animal Veterinary Association Manual of Wildlife Casualties*. BSAVA.

Munõz-Igualada, J., J. A. Shivik, F. G. Domínguez, L. M. González, A. Aranda-Moreno, M. F. Olalla and C. A. García. 2010. Traditional and new cable restraint systems to capture fox in central Spain. J. Wildl. Manag. 74: 181–187.

Murray, J. K., W. J. Browne, M. A. Roberts, A. Whitmarsh and T. J. Gruffydd-Jones. 2010. Number and ownership profiles of cats and dogs in the UK. Veterinary Record 166: 163-168.

Mustin, K., B. Arroyo, P. Beja, S. Newey, R. J. Irvine, J. Kestler and S. M. Redpath. 2018. Consequences of game bird management for non-game species in Europe. Journal of Applied Ecology, 55: 2285-2295.

National Animal Welfare Advisory Committee. 2005. *NAWAC guideline 09: assessing the welfare performance of restraining and kill traps*. Wellington, New Zealand: Ministry of Agriculture and Forestry.

Nell, V. 1988. *The Psychology of Reading for Pleasure*. Yale University Press.

Nell, V. 2006. Cruelty's Rewards: The Gratifications of Perpetrators and Spectators. Behavioral and Brain Sciences 29(3):211-24.

Nelson, S.H., A. D. Evans and R. B. Bradbury. 2005. The efficacy of collar-mounted devices in reducing the rate of predation of wildlife by domestic cats. Applied Animal Behavioural Science 94: 273-285.

Newth, J. L., R. L. Cromie, M. J. Brown, et al. 2013. Poisoning from lead gunshot: still a threat to wild waterbirds in Britain. *Eur. J. Wildl. Res.* 59: 195–204.

Newth, J. L., M. J. Brown and E. C. Rees. 2011. Incidence of embedded shotgun pellets in Bewick's swans *Cygnus columbianus bewickii* and whooper swans *Cygnus cygnus* wintering in the UK, Biological Conservation 144 (5): 1630-1637.

Newton, I. 2010. *The Sparrowhawk*. Poyser Monographs.

Noer, H. and J. Madsen. 1996. Shotgun pellet loads and infliction rates in pink-footed goose. *Anser brachyrhynchus*. Wildlife Biology 2: 65– 73.

Noer, H., J. Madsen and P. Hartmann. 2007. Reducing wounding of game by shotgun hunting: effects of a Danish action plan on pink-footed geese. Journal of Applied Ecology 44(3):653-662.

Noer, H., J. Madsen, H. Strandgaard and P. Hartmann. 1996. Anskydning Af Vildt (Wounding of game). NERI Thematic Report no. 8. National Environmental Research Institute, Rønde, Denmark.

Norman, F. I. and D. G. M. Powell. 1981. Rates of recovery of bands, harvest patterns and estimates for black duck, chestnut teal, grey teal and mountain duck shot during Victorian open seasons, 1953-77. Australian Wildlife Research 8:659-664.

Norman. F. I. 1976. The incidence of lead shotgun pellets in waterfowl (Anatidae and Rallidae) examined in south-eastern Australia between 1957 and 1973. Australian Wildlife Research 3: 61-71.

Noss, A. J. 1998. The impacts of cable snare hunting on wildlife populations in the forests of the Central African Republic. Conserv. Biol. 12: 390–98.

Nuffield Council on Bioethics. 2021. Genome Editing and Farmed Animal Breeding: Social and Ethical Issues. https://www.nuffieldbioethics.org/publications.

Onderka, D. K. 1999. Pathological examination as an aid for trap selection guidelines: Usefulness and limitations. In: Proulx G., editor. *Mammal Trapping*. Alpha Wildlife Publications; Sherwood Park, AB, Canada: pp. 47–51.

Pain, D. J, I. Carter, A. W. Sainsbury, R. F. Shore, P. Eden, M. A. Taggart, S. Konstantinos, L. A. Walker, A. A. Meharg and A. Raab. 2007. Lead contamination and associated disease in captive and reintroduced red kites *Milvus milvus* in England. Sci. Total Environ. Apr 15;376(1-3):116-27.

Pain, D. J., R. E. Green, M. A. Taggart and N. Kanstrup. 2022. How contaminated with ammunition-derived lead is meat from European small game animals? Assessing and reducing risks to human health, Ambio, 10.1007.

Paquet, P. C., and C. T. Darimont. 2010. Wildlife conservation and animal welfare: Two sides of the same coin? Anim. Welf. 19:177–190.

Pardo, I. and G. B. Prato. 2005. The Fox-hunting Debate in the United Kingdom: A Puritan Legacy? Human Ecology Review 12: 143-155.

Parker, H., F. Rosell and J. Danielsen. 2006. Efficacy of cartridge type and projectile design in the harvest of beaver. Wildlife Society Bulletin 34: 127–130.

Pawlina, I. and G. Proulx. 1999. Factors affecting trap efficiency: A review. In: Proulx G., Editor. *Mammal Trapping*. Alpha Wildlife Publications; Sherwood Park, AB, Canada: pp. 95–115.

Policansky, D. 2008. Trends and Developments in Catch and Release, Global Challenges in Recreational Fisheries 10: 202-236.

Porteus, T. A., J. C. Reynolds and M. K. McAllister. 2019. Population dynamics of foxes during restricted-area culling in Britain: advancing understanding through state-space modelling of culling records. PLoS One, 14(11), e0225201.

Potts, G. R. 2005. Incidence of ingested lead gunshot in wild grey partridges (*Perdix perdix*) from the UK. European Journal of Wildlife Research, 51: 31-34.

Powell, R. A., and G. Proulx. 2003. Trapping and marking terrestrial mammals for research: Integrating ethics, standards, techniques, and common sense. Inst. Lab. Anim. Res. J. 44:259–276.

Proulx, G. 2017. Animal welfare concerns in wildlife research and management. Can. Wildl. Biol. Manag. 6:1–3.

Proulx, G. 2022. *Mammal trapping: Wildlife management, animal welfare & international standards*. Alpha Wildlife Publications.

Proulx, G. 2018. *Intolerable Cruelty—The Truth behind Killing Neck Snares and Strychnine*. Alpha Wildlife Publications; Sherwood Park, AB, Canada.

Proulx, G., and D. Rodtka. 2017. Steel-jawed leghold traps and killing neck snares: Similar injuries command a change to agreement on international humane trapping standards. J. Appl. Anim. Welf. Sci. 20:198–203.

Proulx, G., and D. Rodtka. 2019. Killing traps and snares in North America: The need for stricter checking time periods. Animals. 9:570.

Proulx, G., and M. W. Barrett. 1989. Animal welfare concerns and wildlife trapping: Ethics, standards and commitments. *Trans. West. Sect. Wildl. Soc.* 25:1–6.

Proulx, G., D. K. Onderka, A. J. Kolenosky, P.J. Cole, R. K. Drescher and M. J. Badry. 1993. Injuries and behavior of raccoons (*Procyon lotor*) captured in the Soft Catch™ and the EGG™ traps in simulated natural environments. J. Wildl. Dis. 29:447–452.

Proulx, G., D. Rodtka, M. W. Barrett, M. Cattet, D. Dekker, E. Moffatt and R. A. Powell. 2015. Humaneness and selectivity of killing neck snares used to capture canids in Canada: A review. Can. Wildl. Biol. Manag. 4: 55–65.

Proulx, G., M. Cattet, T. L. Serfass and S. E. Baker. 2020. Updating the AIHTS Trapping Standards to Improve Animal Welfare and Capture Efficiency and Selectivity. Animals (Basel). Jul 24;10(8):1262.

Proulx, G., M. R. L. Cattet and R. A. Powell. 2012. Humane and efficient capture and handling methods for carnivores. In: Boitani L., Powell R.A., Editors. *Carnivore Ecology and Conservation: A Handbook of Techniques.* Oxford University Press; London, UK pp. 70–129.

Reddiex, B., D. M. Forsyth *et al.* 2006. Control of pest mammals for biodiversity protection in Australia I. Patterns of control and monitoring. Wildlife Research 33: 691–709.

Rehnus, M., M. Wehrle and R. Palme. 2013. Mountain hares *Lepus timidus* and tourism: stress events and reactions. Journal of Applied Ecology 51 (1): 6-12.

Reid, N., R. A. McDonald and W. I. Montgomery. 2007. Factors associated with hare mortality during coursing. Animal Welfare 16: 427-434.

Rendle, M. 2006. *Stress and capture myopathy in hares*. Irish hare initiative.

Reynolds, J. 1995. Winter lamping for foxes. The Game Conservancy Review of 1994, 26: 111-113.

Rochlitz, I., D. M. Broom and R. H. Bradshaw. 2008. The review on the welfare of deer, foxes, mink and hares subjected to hunting by humans. (Update). International Fund for Animal Welfare.

Rollin, B. E. 1989. *The unheeded cry: animal consciousness animal pain and science*. Oxford University Press, Oxford, UK.

Rose, J. D., R. Arlinghaus *et al.* 2014. Can fish really feel pain? Fish and Fisheries 15: 97–133.

Russell, G. 1994. Shotgun wounding characteristics. *Maple Tech: Maple in Mathematics and the Sciences (Special Issue)*. Boston: Birkhauser, pp 17-20.

Russell, W. M. S., and R. L. Burch. 1959. *The Principles of Humane Experimental Technique*. Methuen; London, UK.

Ruxton, G. D., S. Thomas and J. W. Wright. 2002. Bells reduce predation of wildlife by domestic cats (*Felis catus*). Journal of Zoology 256: 81-83.

Ryan, T. 2013. Understanding animal abuse: a sociological analysis. Journal of Animal Ethics 3 (2).

Sainsbury, A. W., P. M. Bennett and J. K. Kirkwood. 1995. The welfare of free-living wild animals in Europe: harm caused by human activities. Animal Welfare 43:183-206.

Scott Henderson, J. 1951. Report of the committee on cruelty to wild animals. London: HMSO.

Serfass, T.L., L. Wright, K. Pearce and N. Duplaix. 2017. Animal welfare issues pertaining to the trapping of otters for research, conservation, and fur. In: Butterworth A., editor. *Marine Mammal Welfare*. Springer Nature; Cham, Switzerland, pp. 543–571.

Seymour, C.L., *et al.* 2020.. Caught on camera: The impacts of urban domestic cats on wild prey in an African city and neighbouring protected areas. Global Ecology and Conservation Volume 23, September 2020, e01198.

Sharp, T. 2011. Standard Operating Procedure HOR002: Aerial shooting of horses. Invasive Animals CRC: Canberra, Australia.

Sharp, T. and G. Saunders. 2011. A Model for Assessing the Relative Humaneness of Pest Animal Control Methods, Second Edition. Australian Government Department of Agriculture, Fisheries and Forestry: Canberra, Australia.

Shettleworth, S. J. 2010. *Cognition, evolution, and behaviour, 2nd edn*. Kindle Edition. Oxford University Press, Oxford.

Simmonds, A. 2023. *Treated like Animals: Improving the Lives of Creatures we Own, Eat and Use*. Pelagic Publishing.

Smith-Jones, C. 2012. Head shooting Deer. Journal of the British Deer Society 16: 23–25.

Sneddon, L. U. 2003. The evidence for pain in fish: the use of morphine as an analgesic. Appl. Anim. Behav. Sci. 83:153–162.

Sneddon, L. U. 2011. Pain perception in fish: evidence and implications for the use of fish. J. Conscious Stud. 18: 209–229.

Sneddon, L. U. 2013. Cognition and welfare. In: Brown C, Krause J, Laland K (Eds) *Fish cognition and behaviour*. Wiley, Cambridge, pp 405–434.

Solomon, R. L. and L. C. Wynne. 1954. Traumatic avoidance learning: the principles of anxiety conservation and partial irreversibility. Psychol. Rev. 61: 353–385.

Stocker, L. 2005. *Practical wildlife care, second edition*. Oxford: Blackwell.

Stormer, F.A., C.M. Kirkpatrick and T. W. Hoekstra. 1979. Hunter-inflicted wounding of white-tailed deer. Wildl. Soc. Bull. 7: 10–16.

Swann, W. J. 2000. Wounding rates from shooting in foxes. Submission to the Inquiry into Hunting with Dogs: The Burns Report.

Taggart, M. A. *et al.* 2020. Concentration and origin of lead (Pb) in liver and bone of Eurasian buzzards (*Buteo buteo*) in the United Kingdom. Environmental Pollution Volume 267, 115629.

Tapper, S. 1999. *A question of balance*. Fordingbridge, Hampshire: The Game Conservancy Trust.

The Animal Welfare Act 2006: What it means for wildlife. WML-GU02, England. Available online: https://assets.publishing.service.gov.uk/government/uploads/system/uploads/attachment_data/file/798010/wml-gu02-animal-welfare-act-wildlife-managment.pdf

The Spring Traps Approval (England) Order. 2018. [(accessed on 9 December 2019)]; Available online: http://www.legislation.gov

Thomas, L. H. and W. R. Allen. 2002. *A Veterinary Opinion on Hunting with Hounds.* ABC Print Group

Thomas, R. L., M. D. E. Fellowes and P. J. Baker. 2012. Spatio-temporal variation in predation by urban domestic cats (*Felis catus*) and the acceptability of possible management actions in the UK. PLoS ONE 7(11): e49369.

Thompson, P. S., D. J. T. Douglas, D. G. Hoccom, J. Knott, S. Roos and J. D. Wilson. 2016. Environmental impacts of high-output driven shooting of red grouse *Lagopus lagopus scotica*. Ibis 158: 446-452.

Thomson, L. 2024. Keir Starmer's cat meets Larry: How to introduce another cat into a household. Country Living 8 July 2024.

Tingay, R. and A. Wightman. 2018. *The case for reforming Scotland's driven grouse moors.* Edinburgh: The Revive Coalition. https://revive.scot/publication/the-case-for-reforming-scotlands-driven-grouse-moors/.

Tomasik, B. 2015. The importance of wild-animal suffering. Relations 3(2): 133–152.

Tschanz, B., D. Hegglin, S. Gloor and F. Bontadina. 2011. Hunters and non-hunters: skewed predation rate by domestic cats in a rural village. European Journal of Wildlife Research 57: 597-602.

Turner, D. C. and O. Meister. 1988. Hunting behaviour of the domestic cat. In: Turner DC and Bateson P (Eds) *The Domestic Cat* pp 111-121. Cambridge University Press: Cambridge, UK.

Universities Federation for Animal Welfare. *Humane Management of Mice, Rats and Moles:* Detailed Advice, online.

Urquhart, K. A. and I. J. McKendrick. 2003. Survey of permanent wound tracts in the carcasses of culled wild red deer in Scotland Veterinary Record 152: 497-501.

Urquhart, K. A. and I. J. McKendrick. 2006. Prevalence of 'head shooting' and the characteristics of the wounds in culled wild Scottish red deer. Veterinary Record 159: 75–79.

Van Dyke, F. 1981. Mortality in crippled Mallards. Journal of Wildlife Management 45: 444-453.

van Gerwen, M., J. Nieuwland, H. A. van Lith and F.L. Meijboom. 2020. Dilemmas in the Management of Liminal Rodents-Attitudes of Dutch Pest Controllers.

van Heezik, Y. 2010. Pussyfooting around the issue of cat predation in urban areas. Oryx 44: 153-154.

van Heezik, Y., A. Smyth, A. Adams and J. Gordon. 2010. Do domestic cats impose an unsustainable harvest on urban bird populations? Biological Conservation 143: 121-130.

Vilela, S., A. A. da Silva, R. Palme, K. E. Ruckstuhl, J. P. Sousa and J. Alves. 2020. Physiological stress reactions in red deer induced by hunting activities. Animals, 10(6): 1003.

Virgós, E. et al. 2016. A poor international standard for trap selectivity threatens global carnivore and biodiversity conservation. Biodivers. Conserv. 2016 doi: 10.1007/s10531-016-1117-7.

Warburton B. 2015. *Leghold Traps. A Guideline for Capturing Possums, Ferrets and Feral Cats Using Leghold Traps*. National Pest Control Agencies; Wellington, New Zealand.

Warburton, B. and C. O'Connor. 2004. Research on vertebrate pesticides and traps: do wild animals benefit? Altern. Lab. Anim. Jun;32 Suppl 1A:229-34.

Warburton, B. and J. V. Hall. 1995. Impact momentum and clamping force thresholds for developing standards for possum kill traps. New Zealand Journal of Zoology 22: 39-44.

Warburton, B., N. Poutu, D. Peters and P. Waddington. 2008. Traps for killing stoats (*Mustela erminea*): improving welfare performance. Animal Welfare, 17, 111-116.

Warburton, B. and B. G. Norton. 2009. Towards a knowledge-based ethic for lethal control of nuisance wildlife. Journal of Wildlife Management 73: 158–64.

Watson, A. and J. D. Wilson. 2018. Seven decades of mountain hare counts show severe declines where high-yield recreational game bird hunting is practised. Journal of Applied Ecology 55: 2663-2672.

Webster, J. (Ed). 2006. Sentience in Animals. Applied Animal Behaviour Science. Volume 100, Issues 1-2.

Werritty, A. 2019. Grouse moor management review group: report to the Scottish Government. https://www.gov.scot/publications/grouse-moor-management-group-report-scottish-government/.

White, P.J., T. J. Kreeger, U. S. Seal and J. R. Tester. 1991. Pathological responses of red foxes to capture in box traps. Journal of Wildlife Management 55: 75-80.

Whitfield, D. P., D. R. A. McLeod, J. Watson, A. H. Fielding and P. F. Haworth. 2003. The association of grouse moor in Scotland with the illegal use of poisons to control predators. Biological Conservation, 114: 157-163.

Williamson, M. J., D. J. Curnick, D. M. P. Jacoby, S. M. Durant and H. M. K. O'Neill. 2022. Ethical considerations in natural history film production and the need for industry-wide best practice. Global Ecology and Conservation Volume 34 e01981,ISSN 2351-9894.

Willson, S.K., I. A. Okunlola and J. A. Novak. 2015. Birds be safe: Can a novel cat collar reduce avian mortality by domestic cats (*Felis catus*)? Global Ecology & Conservation 3: 359- 366.

Wilson, J. 2019. *Plant Paradigm*. Yourbooks, New Zealand.

Woinarski, J. C. Z. et al. 2017. How many birds are killed by cats in Australia? Biological Conservation 214: 76-87.

Woodroffe, R., et al. 2005. Welfare of badgers (*Meles meles*) subjected to culling: patterns of trap-related injury. Animal Welfare 14: 11-17.

Woods, M., R. A. McDonald and S. Harris. 2003. Predation of wildlife by domestic cats *Felis catus* in Great Britain. Mammal Review 33: 174-188.

Chapter 6 The Morality of Hunting

Aaltola, E. 2013. Empathy, Intersubjectivity and Animal Ethics. *Environmental Philosophy* 10(2): 75–96.

Anderson, E. 2004. Animal Rights and the Values of Nonhuman Life, in *Animal Rights: Current Debates and New Directions*, C. R. Sunstein and M. C. Nussbaum (Eds.). Oxford: Oxford University Press, chapter 13.

Beauchamp, T. L. and R. G. Frey (Eds.) 2011, *The Oxford Handbook of Animal Ethics*, New York: Oxford.

Bekoff, M. 2000. *The Smile of a Dolphin: Remarkable Accounts of Animal Emotion.* New York: Discovery Books.
Bekoff, M. 2006. *Animal passions and beastly virtues: reflections on redecorating nature.* Temple University Press, Philadelphia.
Bekoff, M. 2007. *The Emotional Lives of Animals: A Leading Scientist Explores Animal Joy, Sorrow, and Empathy — and Why They Matter,* Novato, California: New World Library.
Bekoff, M. and J. A. Byers (Eds.). 1998. *Animal Play: Evolutionary, Comparative, and Ecological Perspectives.* Cambridge: Cambridge University Press.
Bekoff, M. and J. Pierce. 2009. *Wild Justice: The Moral Lives of Animals,* Chicago: University of Chicago Press.
Bekoff, M. and P.W. Sherman. 2004. Reflections on animal selves. Trends Ecol. Evol. 19:176–180.
Bekoff, M., C. Allen, and G. M. Burghardt (Eds.). 2002, *The Cognitive Animal,* Cambridge, MA: MIT Press.
Bentham, J. [1780/1789] 1982, *An Introduction to the Principles of Morals and Legislation,* edited by J. H. Burns and H. L. A. Hart, London: Methuen (Athlone Press 1970).
Boehm, C. 2012. *Moral Origins: The Evolution of Virtue, Altruism and Shame.* Basic Books.
Brown, D. E. 1991. *Human Universals.* McGraw-Hill Education.
Byrne, R., W. Byrne and A. Whiten (Eds.). 1988. *Machiavellian Intelligence: Social Expertise and the Evolution of Intellect in Monkeys, Apes, and Humans.* Oxford: Clarendon Press.
Cahoone, L. 2009. Hunting as a moral Good. Environmental Values 18(1): 67.
Callicot, J. B. 1989. Animal Liberation: A Triangular Affair. In *Defense of the Land Ethic: Essays in Environmental Philosophy.* Albany: State University of New York.
Cartmel, M. 1993. 'The Bambi Syndrome', in *A View to a death in the Morning: Hunting and Nature through History.* Harvard University Press.
Catia, F., and P. Eze. 2015. Animals in need: The problem of wild animal suffering and intervention in nature. Relations 3(1): 7–13.
Causey, A. S. 1989. On the Morality of Hunting. Environmental Ethics 11:327-343.
Cheney, D. L. and R. M. Seyfarth. 1990. *How Monkeys See the World: Inside the Mind of Another Species,* University of Chicago Press.
Chevalier-Skolnikoff, S. 1989. Spontaneous Tool Use and Sensorimotor Intelligence in Cebus Compared with other Monkeys and Apes. Behavioral and Brain Sciences 12(3): 561–588.
Churchill, L. R. 2020. *Ethics for Everyone: A Skills-based Approach.* Oxford University Press.
Clark, S. R. L. 1977. *The moral status of animals.* Oxford, England: Oxford University Press.
Clement, G. 2003. The ethic of care and the problem of wild animals. Between the Species 13(3).
Crary, A. 2016. *Inside Ethics: On the Demands of Moral Thought,* Cambridge, MA: Harvard University Press.
Dahles, H. 1993. Game killing and killing games: an anthropologist looking at hunting in a modern society. Society & Animals 1(2): 169-184.
Darwin, C. 1871. *The Descent of Man* (2 volumes). London: John Murray.

Davis, S. L. 2003. The Least Harm Principle May Require that Humans Consume a Diet Containing Large Herbivores, Not a Vegan Diet. Journal of Agricultural and Environmental Ethics 16. 4:387-94.
Dawkins, R. 1976. *The Selfish Gene.* Oxford University Press.
de Waal, F. B. M. 1989. *Peacemaking Among Primates.* Cambridge, MA: Harvard University Press.
de Waal, F. B. M. 2006. *Primates and Philosophers: How Morality Evolved.* Princeton University Press.
de Waal, F. B. M. and F. Lanting. 1997. *Bonobo: The Forgotten Ape.* Berkeley: University of California Press.
DeGrazia, D. 1996. *Taking Animals Seriously: Mental Life and Moral Status.* Cambridge: Cambridge University Press.
DeMello, M. (Ed.). 2012. *Animals and Society: An Introduction to Human–Animal Studies.* New York: Columbia University Press.
Descola, P. 2013. *Beyond Nature and Culture.* Chicago/London: Univ. Chicago Press.
Digard, J. P. 1994. Relationships between Humans and Domesticated Animals. Interdisciplinary Science Reviews 19(3): 231-236.
Dinets, V. 2016. Spontaneous Development of Hunting-like Behavior in a Juvenile Human: A Case Study. Humanimalia 8:1.
Dizard, J. 1994. *Going Wild: Hunting, Animal Rights and the Contested Meaning of Nature.* Amherst, MA: University of Massachusetts.
Faggella, D. 2018. *Moral Singularity.* Online.
Fox, C. 2002. The Case Against Sport Hunting. Animal Issues 33:2.
Galdikas, B. M. F. 1995. *Reflections of Eden: My Years with the Orangutans of Borneo,* Boston: Little, Brown and Company.
Godfrey-Smith, P. 2016. *Other Minds: The Octopus and the Evolution of Intelligent Life.* Harper Collins.
Godlovich, S., R. Godlovich and J. Harris (Eds.) 1970. *Animals, Men and Morals: An Enquiry into the Maltreatment of the Non-human.* London: Gollancz.
Goodall, J. 1986, *The Chimpanzees of Gombe: Patterns of Behavior,* Cambridge, MA: Harvard University Press.
Goodall, J. 2000, *In the Shadow of Man.* Revised edition New York: Houghton Mifflin Co.
Gray, J. 1992. *Men are from Mars, Women are from Venus.* Thorsens.
Griffin, D. R. 1992. *Animal Minds.* Chicago: University of Chicago Press.
Gruen, L. 2011. *Ethics and Animals: An Introduction.* Cambridge: Cambridge University Press.
Gruen, L. 2015. *Entangled Empathy: An Alternative Ethic for Our Relationship with Animals.* Brooklyn: Lantern Books.
Gruen, L. 2016. Conscious Animals and the Value of Experience" in Stephen Gardiner and Allen Thompson (eds.) *The Oxford Handbook of Environmental Ethics,* New York: Oxford University Press, chapter 8.
Gruen, L. 2021. *The Moral Status of Animals.* Standford Encyclopedia of Philosophy. E. N. Zalta (Ed).
Gunn, A. S. 2001. Environmental Ethics and Trophy Hunting. Ethics and the Environment 6 (1):68-95.
Haraway, D. 2003. *The Companion Species Manifesto: Dogs, People and Significant Otherness,* Chicago, IL: Prickly Paradigm Press.

Haraway, D. 2008. *When species meet*. Minneapolis: University of Minnesota.

Harrisonburg, V. A. and B. Rollin. 1981. *Animal Rights & Human Morality*. Prometheus Books.

Hauser, M. and S. Carey. 1997. Building a Cognitive Creature from a Set of Primitives: Evolutionary and Developmental Insights", in D. D. Cummins and C. Allen (Eds.), *The Evolution of Mind*, Oxford: Oxford University Press, chapter 3.

Hettinger, N. 1994. Valuing Predation in Rolston's Environmental Ethics: Bambi Lovers versus Tree Huggers. Environmental Ethics. Spring. 16:3-20.

Hursthouse, R. 2000. *Ethics, Humans and Other Animals*, London: Routledge.

Jamieson, D. 2003. *Morality's Progress: Essays on Humans, Other Animals, and the Rest of Nature*. Oxford: Oxford University Press.

Jones, R. C. 2013. Science, Sentience, and Animal Welfare. Biology and Philosophy 28(1): 1–30.

Kagan, J. 2010. *The temperamental thread: How genes, culture, time, and luck make us who we are*. Dana Press.

Kant, I. [1785] 1998, *Groundwork of the Metaphysics of Morals (Grundlegung zur Metaphysik der Sitten)*, M. J. Gregor (trans.) Cambridge University Press.

Kellert, S. 1976. *Attitudes and Characteristics of Hunters and Anti-Hunters and Related Policy Suggestions*. PhD thesis. Yale university Behavioral Sciences Study Center. Fish and Wildlife Servicers of US Dept. of the Interior.

Kerasote, T. 1993. *Bloodties: Nature, Culture and the Hunt*. New York: Kodansha International.

Kheel, M. 1995. License to Kill: An Ecofeminist Critique of Hunters' Discourse. In *Animals and Women: Feminist Theoretical Explorations*. C. J. Adams and J. Donovan (Eds). Duke University Press.

Kheel, M. 2008. *Nature Ethics: An Ecofeminist Perspective*. Lanham, MD: Rowman and Littlefield Publishers.

Kim, C. J. 2015, *Dangerous Crossings: Race, Species and Nature in a Multicultural Age*. Cambridge University Press.

King, B. J. 2013. *How Animals Grieve*. University of Chicago Press.

King, R. J .H. 1991. Environmental Ethics and the Case of Hunting. Environmental Ethics 13(1): 59–85.

Knight, J. (Ed.) 2000. *Natural Enemies - People Wildlife Conflicts in Anthropological Perspective*. London: Routledge.

Korsgaard, C. M. 1996. *The Sources of Normativity*. Cambridge: Cambridge University Press.

Korsgaard, C. 2004. Fellow Creatures: Kantian Ethics and Our Duties to Animals, in *The Tanner Lectures on Human Values*, Grethe B. Peterson (Ed.), Volume 25/26, Salt Lake City: University of Utah Press.

Korsgaard. C. 2007. Facing the Animal You See in the Mirror. Harvard Review of Philosophy 16(1): 4–9.

Korsgaard, C. M. 2013. Getting Animals in View. The Point, 6.

Kowalsky, N. (Ed.) 2010. *Hunting-Philosophy for Everyone: In Search of the Wildlife*. Wiley-Blackwell: Chichester.

Kropotkin, P. 1924. *Ethics: Origin and Development*. George Harrap and Co.

Lang, S. 2022. *Hunting as Assemblage: Heritage, History and Practices of the Alsace Hunt*. Uppsala, Department of Archaeology and Ancient History.

List, C. 1997. Is Hunting a Right Thing? Environmental Ethics Winter 19: 405-16.

List, C. 2004. On the Moral Distinctiveness of Sport Hunting. Environmental Ethics. Summer. 26: 155-69.

Loftin, R. W. 1984. The Morality of Hunting. Environmental Ethics. Fall. 6: 241-50.

Lovering, R. 2006. The Virtues of Hunting: A Reply to Jensen, Philosophy in the Contemporary World 13.1: 68–76.

Luke, B. 1997. A Critical Analysis of Hunters' Ethics. Environmental Ethics. Spring. 19: 25-44.

Marcz, L., G. Marvin and M. Gibbert. 2024. Until death do they part: Loving and killing in Swiss on-farm slaughter. Journal of Rural Studies 109: July 2024. 103337.

Marvin, G. 2006. Wild Killing: Contesting the Animal in Hunting, in The Animal Studies Group: *Killing Animals*. Urbana and Chicago: University of Illinois Press (pp. 10 – 29).

Mason, J. and P. Singer. 1990. *Animal Factories*, revised edition, New York: Harmony Books.

McMahan, J. 2005. Our Fellow Creatures. The Journal of Ethics 9(3–4): 353–80.

McMahan, J. 2008. Eating Animals the Nice Way. Daedalus 127(1): 66–76.

Midgley, M. 1983. *Animals and Why They Matter*. Athens, GA: University of Georgia Press.

Nadasdy, P. 2003. *Hunters and Bureaucrats: Power, Knowledge, and Aboriginal-state Relations in the Southwest Yukon*. UBC Press.

Nussbaum, M. C. 2006. *Frontiers of Justice: Disability, Nationality, and Species Membership*. Cambridge: The Belknap Press.

Pauley, J. A. 2003. The Value of Hunting. Journal of Value Inquiry. 27:233-244.

Peterson, D. 2000. *Heartsblood: Hunting, Spirituality and Wildness in America*. Boulder, CO: Johnson Books.

Posewitz, J. 1994. *Beyond Fair Chase: The Ethic and Tradition of Hunting*. Helena and Billings, MT: Falcon Press.

Rachels, J. 1990. *Created from Animals: The Moral Implications of Darwinism*, Oxford: Oxford University Press.

Regan, T. 1983. *The Case for Animal Rights*. Berkeley: University of California.

Rowlands, M. 2012. *Can Animals Be Moral?* New York: Oxford University Press.

Ryder, R. D. 1989. *Animal Revolution: Changing Attitudes Toward Speciesism*. Oxford: Basil Blackwell.

Singer, P. 1993. *Practical Ethics*, second edition, Cambridge: Cambridge University Press.

Singer, P. 1975. *Animal liberation: a new ethics for the treatment of animals*. New York, NY: Random House.

Sorabji, R. 1993. *Animal Minds and Human Morals: The Origins of the Western Debate*. London: Duckworth.

Sözmen, B. 2015. Relations and moral obligations towards other animals. Relations 3(2), 179–193.

Swan, J. 1995. *In defense of hunting*. Harper Collins.

Taylor, P. W. 1981. The Ethics of Respect for Nature. Environmental Ethics 3(3):197–218.

Tickle, L. 2018. The practice of hunting as a way to transcend alienation from nature. The Journal of Transdisciplinary Environmental Studies 17:22–37.

Van de Pitte, M. 2003. The moral basis for public

policy encouraging sport hunting. Journal of Social Philosophy 34(2): 256–266.
Van DeVeer, D. 1979. Interspecific Justice. Inquiry 22(1–4): 55–79.
Varner, G. E. 1998. *In Nature's Interests*. New York: Oxford University Press.
Varner, G. E. 2012. *Personhood, Ethics, and Animal Cognition: Situating Animals in Hare's Two Level Utilitarianism*. New York: Oxford University Press.
Vitali, T. 1990. Sport Hunting: Moral or Immoral? Environmental Ethics. Spring.12: 69-82.
von Essen, E. 2017. The Impact of modernization on hunting ethics: Emerging taboos among contemporary Swedish hunters. Human Dimensions of Wildlife 23(1), 21–38.
von Essen, E. 2018. "We need to talk … " evolving conversations about wildlife ethics in hunting media. Humanimalia 10(1): 157–182.
von Essen, E. and H. P. Hansen. 2018. Policing peers between law and morality: A socio-legal perspective on managing misconduct in hunting. International Journal of Rural Criminology 1(4).
Vorhies, D. 2022. *The Good, the Bad, and the Beautiful: Ethics and Hunting*. MA Thesis. University of Buckingham.
Wade, M. 1990. Animal Liberationalism, Ecocentrism, and the Morality of Sport Hunting. Journal of the Philosophy of Sport 17 :15–27.
Walker, R. L. 2007. Animal Flourishing: What Virtue Requires of Human Animals, in *Working Virtue: Virtue Ethics and Contemporary Moral Problems*, R. Walker and P. J. Ivanhoe (Eds.) Oxford: Oxford University Press.
Wendy, J. 1995. *Aspects of Wounding of White-tailed Deer by Bowhunters*. Thesis. West Virginia University, Morgantown, West Virginia.
Whiten, A., J. Goodall, W.C. McGew, T. Nishida, V. Reynolds, Y. Sugiyama, C.E.G. Tutin, R.W. Wrangham and C. Boesch. 1999. Cultures in chimpanzees. Nature, 399(6737): 682–685.
Williams, J. 1995. The Killing Game. In P. Houston, Ed. *Women on Hunting*. Hopewell, N.J. Ecco Press. 248-6.
Wilson, E. O. 1981. *Genes, Mind and Culture: The Coevolutionary Process*. Harvard University Press,
Wood, A. W. 1998. Kant on Duties Regarding Nonrational Nature. Proceedings of the Aristotelian Society Supplement, LXXII: 189–210.
Wood, F, Jr. 1997. *The Delights and Dilemmas of Hunting*. Lanham, MD: University Press of America.
Young, G. C. 2013. Doing My Part. Peterson's Hunting, March :56-61.

Chapter 7 The Mechanism of Morality
Adams, C. J. and J. Donovan (Eds.). 1995. *Animals and Women: Feminist Theoretical Explorations*. Durham, NC: Duke University Press.
Adams, C. J. and L. Gruen (Eds.). 2014. *Ecofeminism: Feminist Intersections with Other Animals and the Earth*. New York: Bloomsbury Press.
Adams, W. M. 2009. Sportsman's Shot, Poacher's Pot: Hunting, Local People and the History of Conservation. In B. Dickson, J. Hutton, and W. M. Adams (Eds.), *Recreational Hunting, Conservation and Rural Livelihoods: Science and Practice*, pp. 127-140. Wiley-Blackwell.
Antunes, A.P. *et al*. 2019. A conspiracy of silence: Subsistence hunting rights in the Brazilian Amazon. Land Use Policy, 84: 1-11.
Barceló, A., M. Grimalt and J. Binimelis. 2015. Territorial, social and environmental implications of local hunting societies in Mallorca. In: Antoni Barceló *et al*. (Eds.) XXIV Congress of the Spanish Association of Geographers. Spatial analysis and geo-graphic representation: innovation and application, pp 1543-1552.
Blackmore, S. 1999. *The Meme Machine*. Oxford University Press.
Clayton, M. 2004. Endangered Species: Foxhunting – the history, the passion and the fight for survival. London: Swan Hill Press.
Delgado, M. L., J. L. Rengifo Gallego and J. M. Sánchez Martín. 2019. The social hunting model: evolution and characterization in Extremadura. Boletín de la Asociación de Geógrafos Españoles, 82,2793: 1-37.
Dennett, D. 1991. *Consciousness Explained*. Penguin Scientific.
Fox, N.C. 1977. The Shape of the Nesting Territory in the New Zealand Falcon, Journal of Raptor Research: Vol. 11(4):100-103.
Frederick II of Hohenstaufen. 1250. *The Art of Falconry*. Translated by C.A. Wood and F.M. Fyfe. (1943) Stanford Press.
Gutiérrez, J. E. 2013. The potential of hunting societies as a conservation- tool in Spain. Ecosystems 22(2):104-106.
Herman, D. J. 2014. Hunting and American Identity: The Rise, Fall, Rise and Fall of an American Pastime. The International Journal of the History of Sport. 31(1-2): 55-71.
Kellert, S. R. 1978. Attitudes and Characteristics of Hunters and Antihunters. In Transactions of the Forty-Third North American Wildlife and Natural Resources Conference, March 18–22 Phoenix, Arizona, Kenneth Sabol (Ed). Washington, D.C.: Wildlife Management Institute, pp. 412–23.
Kerasote, T. 1993. *Bloodties – nature, culture, and the hunt*. New York, NY: Random House.
Kheel, M. 1996. The Killing Game: An Ecofeminist Critique of Hunting. Journal of the Philosophy of Sport 23: 30–44.
Korsgaard, C. M. 2012. A Kantian Case for Animal Rights. In *Animal Law: Developments and Perspectives in the 21st Century*. M. Michel, D. Kühne, and J. Hänni (Eds). Zürich: DIKE.
Kurzweil, R. 2024. *The Singularity is Nearer*. Penguin Books.
Lopez, B. H. 1978. *Of Wolves and Men*. Charles Scribner's Sons.
Lorenz, K. 1954. *Man Meets Dog*. Methuen, London.
Lund, V., C. M. Mejdell, H. Rocklingsberg, R. Anthony and T. Hastein. 2007. Expanding the moral circle: farmed fish as objects of moral concern. Dis. Aquat. Org. 75:109–118.
Maccoby, H. 1982. *The Sacred Executioner*. Thames & Hudson, London.
Macdonald, D. W. *et al*. 2016. Cecil: A Moment or a Movement? Analysis of Media Coverage of the Death of a Lion, *Panthera leo*. Animals 6: 26.
Macdonald, D. W. *et al*. 2016. Conservation or the Moral High Ground: Siding with Bentham or Kant.

Conservation Letters 9(4): 307–08.
Macphail, E. M. 1998. *The evolution of consciousness.* Oxford University Press, Oxford
May, A. N. 2013. *The Fox-hunting Controversy, 1781-2004. Class and Cruelty.* Ashgate.
Midgley, M. 1983. *Animals and Why They Matter.* Penguin Books.
Miklósi, Á., J. Topál and V. Csányi. 2004. Comparative social cognition: what can dogs teach us? Anim. Behav. 67:995–1004.
Nicol, C. J. 1996. Farm animal cognition. Anim. Sci. 62:375–391.
Panksepp, J. 2005. Affective consciousness: core emotional feelings in animals and humans. Conscious Cogn. 14:30–80.
Parker, S.T., R. W. Mitchell and M. L. Boccia. 1994. *Self-awareness in animals and humans: developmental perspectives.* Cambridge University Press, New York.
Proops, L. and K. McComb. 2012. Cross-modal individual recognition in domestic horses (*Equus caballus*) extends to familiar humans. Proc. R. Soc. Lond. B 279:3131–3138.
Serpell, J. 1986. *In the Company of Animals.* Basil Blackwell Ltd.
Strathern, M. 2005. *Kinship, Law and the Unexpected: relatives are always a surprise.* New York: Cambridge University Press.
Surtees, R.S. 1847. *The Analysis of the Hunting Field.* London.
Tichelar, M. 2006. Putting Animals into Politics: The Labour Party and Hunting in the First Half of the Twentieth Century. Rural History 17:213-34.
von Essen, E., E. Van Heijgen and T. Gieser. 2019. Hunting communities of practice: Factors behind the social differentiation of hunters in modernity. Journal of Rural Studies 68: 13-21.

Chapter 8 Shared Ethical Values
Anon. 2023. Cats Protection submission of 3 March 2023 PE1938/J: Scottish Parliament.
Apostolou, M. and M. Shialos. 2017. Why Men Hunt and Women Gather for Recreation? An Evolutionary Perspective. Evolutionary Psychological Science 4(1): 8-16.
Bye, L. M. 2003. Masculinity and rurality at play in stories about hunting. Norsk Geografisk Tidsskrift - Norwegian Journal of Geography 57(3): 145-153.
Byrd, E., J. Lee and N. Widmar. 2017. Perceptions of Hunting and Hunters by U.S. Respondents. Animals 7(12): 83.
Cahoone, L. 2009. Hunting as a moral good. Environmental Values 18(1): 67–89.
Causey, A. S. 1989. On the morality of hunting. Environmental Ethics 11(4): 327–343.
Dubos, R. 1968. *So Human an Animal: How We Are Shaped by Surroundings and Events,* Scribner's Sons, New York.
Fardell, L.L., C.R. Pavey and C.R. Dickman. 2023. Influences of roaming domestic cats on wildlife activity in patchy urban environments. Frontiers in Ecology and Evolution, 10.3389/fevo.2023.1123355, 11.
Fitzgerald, A. 2005. The Emergence of the Figure of "Woman-The-Hunter:" Equality or Complicity in Oppression? Women's Studies Quarterly 33(1/2): 86-104.
Greenberg, D. 2020. First They Came for the Hunts – Lessons from an Insider's View of the Hunting Act for the Role of Tolerance in the Rule of Law. Speech to the R.S. Surtees Society 5 November 2020.
Herzog, H. A. 2007. Gender differences in human-animal interactions: A review. Anthrozoos 20: 7-21.
Hyde, W. W. 1916. The prosecution of animals and lifeless things in the Middle Ages and modern times. University of Pennsylvania Law Review 64: 693-730.
Kellert, S. R. and J. K. Berry. 1987. Attitudes, knowledge, and behaviors toward wildlife as affected by gender. Wildlife Society Bulletin 15(3): 363-371.
Kheel, M. 1995. License of Kill: An Ecofeminist Critique of Hunters' Discourse. In *Animals and Women: Feminist Theoretical Explorations.* C. J. Adams and J. Donovan (Eds.). Durham, NC: Duke University Press.
List, C. 1997. Is Hunting a Right Thing? Environmental Ethics. Winter 19: 405-16.
List, C. 2004. On the Moral Distinctiveness of Sport Hunting. Environmental Ethics. Summer. 26: 155-69.
List, C. J. 2013. *Hunting, fishing, and environmental virtue: Reconnecting sportsmanship and conservation.* Oregon State University Press.
Littlebird, L. 2001. *Hunting Sacred, Everything Listens.* Santa Fe, NM. Western Edge Press.
Loftin, R. W. 1984. The Morality of Hunting. Environmental Ethics. Fall. 6: 241-50.
Loss, S., T. Will and P. Marra. 2013. The impact of free-ranging domestic cats on wildlife of the United States. Nat. Commun. 4: 1396.
Lovelock, B. (Ed.) 2008. *Tourism and the consumption of wildlife hunting, shooting and sport fishing.* New York: Routledge.
Luke, B. 1997. A critical analysis of hunters' ethics. *Environmental Ethics* 19(1): 25–44.
Marvin, G. 2006. Wild Killing: Contesting the Animal in Hunting. The Animal Studies Group Killing Animals. Urbana and Chicago: University of Illinois Press pp. 10 – 29.
Munsche, P. B. 1981. *Gentlemen and Poachers: The English Game Laws 1671-1831.* Cambridge University Press.
Murray, J. K., W. J. Browne, M.A. Roberts and A. Whitmarsh. 2010. Number and ownership profiles of cats and dogs in the UK. Veterinary record 166(6): 163-8.
Parkes, C. and J. Thornley. 1994. *Fair Game: The Law of Country Sport and the Protection of Wildlife.* Pelham Books.
Pauley, J. A. 2003. The Value of Hunting. Journal of Value Inquiry 27: 233-244.
Peterson, M. N. 2004. An approach for demonstrating the social legitimacy of hunting. Wildlife Society Bulletin, 32(2): 310–321.
Piazza, J. *et al.* 2015. Rationalizing meat consumption. The 4Ns. Appetite 91: 114–128.
Plous, S. 1991. An attitude survey of animal rights activists. Psychological Science 2: 194-196.
Posewitz, J. 1994. *Beyond Fair Chase: The Ethics and Tradition of Hunting.* Guilford: Falconguides.
Putnam, R. 2011. A review of the various legal and administrative systems governing management of large herbivores in Europe. In R. Putnam, M. Apollonio, and R. Andersen (Eds.), *Ungulate management in Europe: Problems and practices* (pp. 54–79). Cambridge University Press.

Putnam, R. M. Apollonio, and R. Andersen (Eds.), *Ungulate management in Europe: Problems and practices*. Cambridge University Press.

Pye-Smith, C. 2006. *Rural Rites: Hunting and the Politics of Prejudice*. London: All Party Parliamentary Middle Way Group.

Pye-Smith, C. 2023. *Rural Wrongs: Hunting and the Unintended Consequences of Bad Law*. R.S. Surtees Society.

Rolston, H. 1988. *Environmental Ethics: Duties and Values in the Natural World*. Philadelphia. Temple University Press.

Russ, T. and J. Foster. 2010. *Law of Fieldsports*. Wildy, Simmons and Hill Publishing.

Stange, M. Z. 1997. *Woman the hunter*. Place of publication not identified: Diane Pub.

Swan, J. A. 1999. *The Sacred Art of Hunting: Myths, Legends and Modern Mythos*. Willow Creek Press, Wisconsin.

Sykes, B. 2018. *The Wolf Within – The Astonishing Evolution of the Wolf into Man's Best Friend*. William Collins.

Tan, S.M.L., A.C. Stellato and L. Niel. 2020. Uncontrolled Outdoor Access for Cats: An Assessment of Risks and Benefits. Animals 10: 258;

Taylor, P. 1986. *Respect for Nature: A Theory of Environmental Ethics*. Princeton: Princeton University.

Trouwborst, A. and H. Somsen. 2020. Domestic Cats (Felis catus) and European Nature Conservation Law—Applying the EU Birds and Habitats Directives to a Significant but Neglected Threat to Wildlife, Journal of Environmental Law, Volume 32 (3): 391-415.

Vitali, T. 1990. Sport Hunting: Moral or Immoral? Environmental Ethics. 12: 69-82.

Wall, W. A. 2005. A Framework Proposal for Conservation-hunting Best Practices. In Freeman, M. M. R., Hudson, R. J. and Foote, L. (Eds.) *Conservation Hunting: People and Wildlife in Canada's North*. (pp. 11-17). Occasional Publication No. 56. Canadian Circumpolar Institute, Edmonton, Alberta.

Williams, J. 1995. The Killing Game. In P. Houston, Ed. *Women on Hunting*. Hopewell, N.J. Ecco Press. 248-6.

Williams, V. 2019. *Hunting And Fishing Attitudes, Behaviors And Ethics Related To Gender And Aggression*. MA Thesis, University of North Dakota.

Wood, F, Jr. 1997. *The Delights and Dilemmas of Hunting*. Lanham, MD: University Press of America.

Chapter 9 Morality: the judges

Alpha, R. 2015. *What Is Sport: A Controversial Essay About Why Humans Play Sports*. Bookbaby.

Boddice, R. 1977. Manliness and the Morality of Field Sports. In E.A. Freeman and D. C. Itzkowitz, *Peculiar Privilege: A Social History of Foxhunting, 1753-1885*. Hassocks, Sussex: Harvester Press.

Colling, S. 2013. *Animals without Borders: Farmed animal resistance in New York*. Faculty of Social Sciences, Brock University St. Catharines.

Curnutt, J. 1996. How to argue for and against sport hunting. Journal of Social Philosophy 27(2): 65–89.

Donovan, J. 1996. Attention to suffering: A feminist caring ethic for the treatment of animals. Journal of Social Philosophy 27(1): 81–102.

Donovan, J. 2006. Feminism and the treatment of animals: From care to dialogue. Signs 31(2): 305–329.

Engster, D. 2006. Care Ethics and Animal Welfare. Journal of Social Philosophy 37(4): 521–536.

Fischer, A., et al. 2013. (De)legitimising hunting – Discourses over the morality of hunting in Europe and eastern Africa. Land use policy 32: 261-270.

Gaard, G. 2002. Vegetarian ecofeminism: A review essay. Frontiers: A Journal of Women Studies, 23(3): 117–146.

George, J. 1999. *A Rural Uprising: The battle to save hunting with hounds*. J.A. Allen, London.

Gibson, K. 2014. More than murder: Ethics and hunting in New Zealand. Sociology of Sport Journal, 31(4): 455–474.

Heberlein, T. A. and G. Ericsson. 2005. Ties to the Countryside: Accounting for Urbanites Attitudes Toward hunting, Wolves, and Wildlife. Human Dimensions of Wildlife 10: 213-227.

Hettinger, N. 1994. Valuing predation in Rolston's environmental ethics: Bambi lovers versus tree huggers. Environmental Ethics 16(1): 3–20.

Hobbes, T. 1651. *Leviathan*. 1994. Edwin Curley, (Ed). Hackett, Indianapolis.

Hodges, C. 2008. *The Link: Cruelty to animals and violence towards people*. Animal Legal & Historical Center. Michigan State University College of Law.

Hoyle, R. W. (Ed.) 2007. *Our Hunting Fathers: Field sports in England after 1850*. Carnegie Publishing, Lancaster.

Irish Council Against Blood Sports. 2011. The Facts About Carted Deer Hunting. Available at: http://www.banbloodsports.com/leaf-stag.htm.

Irish Council Against Blood Sports. 2013. Campaigns: Ban Hare Coursing. Available at: http://www.banbloodsports.com/.

Javenaud, K., C. Linzey and A. Linzey. 2023. *Killing to Kill: An Ethical Assessment of 'Predator Control' on Scottish Grouse Moors*. A report of the Oxford Centre for Animal Ethics.

Jegatheesan, B., M. J. Slegers, E. Ormerod and P. Boyden. 2020. Understanding the link between animal cruelty and family violence: The bioecological systems model. International Journal of Environmental Research and Public Health, 17(9): 3116.

Kellert, S. R. 1978. Attitudes and Characteristics of Hunters and Anti-hunters. Transactions of the Forty-third North American Wildlife and Natural Resources Conference 43: 412-423.

Leader Williams, N. 2009. Conservation and Hunting: Friends or Foes? In Dickson, B., Hutton, J. and Adams, W. J. (Eds.) *Recreational Hunting Conservation and Rural Livelihoods*. pp. 9-24. UK, Wiley-Blackwell.

Ljung, P. E., S. J. Riley, T. A. Heberlein and G. Ericsson. 2012. Eat prey and love: Game-meat consumption and attitudes toward hunting. Wildlife Society Bulletin, 36(4): 669–675.

Luke, B. 1998. Violent Love: Hunting, Heterosexuality and the Erotics of Men's Predation. Feminist Studies 24(3): 627.

Malcolmson, R. W. 1973. *Popular Recreations in English Society, 1700-1850*. Cambridge: Cambridge University Press.

Matheny, G. 2003. Least Harm: A Defense of Vegetarianism from Steven Davis's Omnivorous Proposal. Journal of Agricultural and Environmental Ethics 16, 505–511.

McGowen, R. 2007. Cruel Inflictions and the Claims of Humanity in Nineteenth-Century England. In

K. Watson (Ed.), *Assaulting the Past*. Cambridge: Cambridge Scholars' Press, pp 38-57.

McLeod, C. 2007. Dreadful/Delightful killing: The contested nature of duck hunting. Society & Animals, 15(2): 151–167.

Moss, A. 1961. *Valiant Crusade: The History of the RSPCA*. London: Cassell.

Munkwitz, E. 2018. Angels and Amazons: Fox-hunting and Sporting Emancipation for Women. The International Journal of the History of Sport 35:6, 511-529,

Munro, L. 1998. Framing Cruelty: The Construction of Duck Shooting as a Social Problem. Society and Animals, 52.

Nell, V. 2006. Cruelty's rewards: the gratifications of perpetrators and spectators. Behav. Brain Sci. 29(3): 211-24.

RISE (Rural Ireland Says Enough). 2012. Campaign to Protect Rural Sports. Available at: http://risecampaign1.wordpress.com/

Rollin, B. 1981. *Animal Rights and Human Morality*. Prometheus Books.

Scallan, D. 2012. The Place of Hunting in Rural Ireland. PhD Thesis. Department of Geography School of Geography and Archaeology College of Arts, Social Sciences and Celtic Studies National University of Ireland Galway.

Scully, M. 2002. Dominion: *The Power of Man, the Suffering of Animals and the Call to Mercy*. New York: St. Martin's Griffin.

Shaw, W. W. 1977. A Survey of Hunting Opponents. Wildlife Society Bulletin 5: 19-24.

Sheppard, V. 1979. *My Head against the Wall: A decade in the fight against bloodsports*. Moonraker Press.

Stange, M. Z. 1997. *Woman the hunter*. Boston, MA: Beacon Press.

Thomas, R. H. 1983. The Politics of Hunting. Aldershot: Gower Publishing Co,

Tichelar, M. 2017. *The History of Opposition to Blood Sports in Twentieth Century England: Hunting at Bay*. Routledge, London.

von Essen, E. and M. Allen. 2021. Killing with kindness: when hunters want to let you know they care, Human Dimensions of Wildlife 26, 2: 179-195.

Wood, W. and A. H. Eagly. 2002. A cross-cultural analysis of the behavior of women and men: Implications for the origins of sex differences. Psychological Bulletin 128(5): 699–727.

Woods, F. 1997. *The Delights and Dilemmas of Hunting: The Hunting versus Anti-hunting Debate*. Lanham: United Press of America.

Woods, M. 2003. Deconstructing Rural Protest: The Emergence of a New Social Movement. Journal of Rural Studies 19: 309-325.

Woods, M. 2004. Politics and Protest in the Contemporary Countryside. In Holloway, L. and Kneafsey, M. (Eds.) *Geographies of Rural Cultures and Societies*. pp. 103-125. Ashgate.

Chapter 10 Morality: Enforcement Systems

Aaltola, E. 2012. *Animal suffering: Philosophy and culture*. Palgrave Macmillan.

Aarnio, J. and E. Aaltola. 2024. "Has an Ugly Caw": The Moral Implications of How Hunting Organizations Depict Nonhuman Animals, Anthrozoös, 37:1: 37-54.

Adams, C. J. 2014. *Sexual politics of meat: A feminist-vegetarian critical theory* (20th anniversary ed.). Bloomsbury.

Allen, C. and M. Bekoff. 1997. *Species of mind: The philosophy and biology of cognitive ethology*. MIT Press.

Al-Otaibi, D. 1996. Falconry in Arabia. Al-Rimayah. Dec 1996: 50-51.

Anon, A. 1990. Animal Welfare Committee looks at animal rights. J. Amer. Vet. Med. Assoc. 196(1).

Anon. 2015. The Economics of Poaching, Trophy and Canned Hunting. International Wildlife Bond. Ethnobiology, 17(2): 11-24.

Armstrong, S. J. and R. G. Botzler, (Eds.) 2008. *The Animal Ethics Reader*. 2nd ed. London: Routledge.

Baquedano, S. 2017. Speciesist hierarchies in Western thought. Review of Philosophy, Universidad del Norte, pp. 251-271.

Barona, E. 2016. *Introduction to the study of Human-Animal interactions (HAS)*. MA thesis. Universidad Nacional de Educación a distancia (Spain).

Bastian, B., S. Loughnan, N. Haslam and H. R. M. Radke. 2012. Don't mind meat? The denial of mind to animals used for human consumption. Personality and Social Psychology Bulletin, 38(2): 247–256.

Bekoff, M. 2007. *The emotional lives of animals*. New World Library.

Bentham, J. 1789. *An introduction to the principles of morals and legislation*. Clarendon.

Blattner, C. E. 2019. The recognition of animal sentience by the law. Journal of Animal Ethics, 9(2): 121–136.

Boone and Crockett Club. 2021. Position Statement - Fair Chase. Available at: https://www.boone-crockett.org/bc-position-statement-fair-chase.

Brightman, R. 1993. *Grateful Prey: Rock Cree Human-Animal Relationships*, University of California Press, Berkeley, Los Angeles, Oxford.

Bronner, S. 2007. Hare coursing and the ethics of tradition. Folk Life 47(1): 3-38.

Bulliet, R. 2005. *Hunters, Herders and Hamburgers: The Past and Future of Human-Animal Relationships*. New York. Columbia University Press.

Burns, L., V. Edwards, J. Marsh, L. Soulsby and M. Winter. 2000. *Report of the Committee of Inquiry into hunting with dogs in England and Wales*. London: Stationery Office.

Cahoone, L. 2009. Hunting as a moral good. Environmental Values 18(1): 67–89.

Calarco, M. 2008. *Zoographies: The Question of the Animal from Heidegger to Derrida*. New York. Columbia University Press.

Callicutt, J. B. 1980. Animal Liberation: A Triangular Affair. Environmental Ethics 2(4): 311–338.

Carman, M. 2017. Protectionist activism, or the dissimilar imputations of dignity to animals and humans. Contemporary Ethnographies 3(4): 128-155.

Cartmill, M. 1993. *A View to a Death in the Morning: Hunting in Nature and Culture Through History*. Harvard University Press, Cambridge MA and London.

Cherry, C. 2010. Shifting Symbolic Boundaries: Cultural Strategies of the Animal Rights Movement. Sociological Forum, Vol. 25, No. 3, September 191.

Cirelli, M. 2002. *Legislative trends in wildlife management*. FAO.

Cohen, E. 2014. Recreational hunting: Ethics, experiences

and commoditization. Tourism Recreation Research, 39(1): 3–17.

Cohen, J. A. 2003. Is hunting a sport? International Journal of Applied Philosophy. 17(2): 291-326.

Connell, J. 1901. The Confessions of a Poacher. Reprinted as *The King of the Poachers* by Tideline, 1983.

Cruzada, S. M. 2017. We are indigenous too: the vulnerability of naturalism in Western contexts of interspecies coexistence. Ethnographic Journal 21(1).

Dabezies, J. M. 2019. Discourses and tensions between hunting, conservation and animal rights in Uruguay. Ethnobiology, 17(2): 11-24.

Degrazia, D. 1996. *Taking animals seriously: Mental life and moral status*. Cambridge University Press.

Degrazia, D. 2002. *Animal Rights: A Very Short Introduction*. Oxford: Oxford University Press.

Descola, P. 2004. Indigenous cosmologies of the Amazon. Tierra adentro. Indigenous Territory and Perception of the Environment. 39: 25-36.

Descola, P. 2009. Human Natures. Social Anthropology, Vol. 17, (2): 145-157.

Dickson, B., J. Hutton and W. M. Adams. 2009. *Recreational Hunting, Conservation and Rural Livelihoods*. John Wiley, Oxford.

Dizard, J. 1999. *Going Wild: Hunting, Animal Rights, and the Contested Meaning of Nature*. Amherst, University of Massachusetts Press.

Dizard, J. E. 2003. *Mortal Stakes: Hunters and Hunting in Contemporary America*. University of Massachusetts Press, Amhurst and Boston.

Donaldson, S. and W. Kymlicka. 2011. *Zoopolis: A Political Theory of Animal Rights*. New York: Oxford University Press.

Donovan, J. and C. J. Adams (Eds.). 2007. *The Feminist Care Tradition in Animal Ethics*. New York: Columbia University Press.

Dooley, M. (Ed) 2022. *Against the tide: the best of Roger Scruton's columns, commentaries and criticism*. Bloomsbury.

Dunne, P. 1996. 'Before the Echo' in D. Petersen, *The Hunter's Heart: Honest Essays on Blood Sports*, Owl Books, New York pp. 30-34.

European Commission. 2004. Guidance Document on Hunting under Council Directive 79/409/EEC on the conservation of wild birds 'The Birds Directive'.

Evans, A. B., and M. Miele. 2019. Enacting public understandings: The case of farm animal welfare. Geoforum 99: 1–10.

Falzon, M. A. 2008. Flights of passion: Hunting, ecology and politics in Malta and the Mediterranean. Anthropology Today 24(1): 15–20.

Frelund, F-X. 2009. *Capturing the Intangible: Perspectives on the Living Heritage*. UNESCO.

Garner, R. 2016. 'Welfare, Rights, and Non-ideal Theory,' in *The Ethics of Killing Animals*, T. Višak and R. Garner (Eds). Oxford: Oxford University Press pp. 215–28.

Garrido, F. E., F. Castro and R. Villafuerte. 2017. Control hunting of wild animals: Health, money, or pleasure? European Journal of Wildlife Research 63(6): 1–4.

Geiser, T. 2017. The Experience of "Being a Hunter": Towards a Phenomenological Anthropology of Hunting, Hunter Gatherer Research 3(2): 229-251.

Giono, J. 1953. *The Man Who Planted Trees*. Harvill Press.

Gold, M. 1995. *Animal Rights: Extending the Circle of Compassion*. Oxford, Jon Carpenter.

González A. and I. Ávila Gaitán. 2019. Animal resistance: ethics, perspectivism and politics of subversion. Tabula Rasa Journal. N. 31.

González, M. et al. 2008. *Reasoning and acting in defense of animals*. Madrid: Catarata.

Graham, L., N. Stephens-Griffin and T. Wyatt. 2022. "It's just totally lawless out here": A rural green criminological exploration of foxhunting, policing, and 'regulatory capture'. Criminological Encounters Vol 5(1): 52-69.

Griffin, D. R. 2001. *Animal minds: Beyond cognition to consciousness*. The University of Chicago Press.

Gutiérrez, C. 2009. *The animal movement: analysis from the new social movements*. PhD thesis in Anthropology of Iberoamerica, Universities of Salamanca, Valladolid and León.

Haggard, L. R. (Ed.) 1935. *I Walked By Night*. Nicholson & Watson, 1935.

Hanna, E. 2006. Fair chase: To where does it lead? In J. Manore & D. G. Miner (Eds.), *The culture of hunting in Canada*, pp 239-260. University of British Columbia Press.

Haraway, D. 2016. *Companion species manifesto: Dogs, people and significant otherness*. Prickly Paradigm Press.

Harrop, S. 1998. The agreement on international humane trapping standards – Background, critique and the texts. Journal of International Wildlife Law & Policy 1(3): 387-394.

Henriksen, G. 2009. *I Dreamed the Animals: Kaniuekutat: The Life of an Innu Hunter*. Berghahn Books, New York and Oxford.

Hidalgo de Trucios, S. J. and J. I. Rengifo Gallego (Eds.) 2020. *Responsible hunting on the horizon of the 21st century*. Publications University of Extremadura.

Higbee, D. and D. Bruzina (Eds.) 2018. *Hunting and the Ivory Tower. Essays by Scholars Who Hunt*. University of South Carolina Press.

Hills, A. 2005. *Do animals have rights?* Cambridge, England: Icon Books.

Huizinga, J. 2002. *Homo ludens*. Madrid: Alianza/Emecé.

Hussain, S. 2010. Sports-hunting, Fairness and Colonial Identity. Collaboration and Subversion in the Northwestern Frontier Region of the British Indian Empire. Conservation and Society 8(2): 112-126.

Jones, A. 1997. *A Quiet Place of Violence: Hunting and Ethics in the Missouri River Breaks*. Bangtail Press, Bozeman, MT.

Kellert, S. 1978. Attitudes and Characteristics of Hunters and Antihunters. Transactions of the North American Wildlife Resources vol 43: 412-423.

King, R. 1991. Environmental Ethics and the Case for Hunting. Environmental Ethics vol 13: 59-85.

Linnard, W. 1984. *The Nine Huntings: A Re-examination of Y Naw Helwriaeth'*. Bulletin of the Board of Celtic Studies, 31: 119-32.

List, C. T. 1998. On the Moral Significance of a Hunting Ethic. Ethics and the Environment 3.(2): 157–75.

Loughnan, S., N. Haslam and B. Bastian. 2010. The role of meat consumption in the denial of moral status and mind to meat animals. Appetite, 55(1): 156–159.

Luke, B. 1997. A critical analysis of hunters' ethics. Environmental Ethics, 19(1): 25-44.

Makoto, S. N. and E. Cheon. 2017. Reconsidering nature: The dialectics of fair chase in the practices of American Midwest hunters. Proceedings of the 2017 CHI conference on human factors in computing systems. Denver, Colorado, USA, ACM.

Manning, R. B. 1993. *Hunters and Poachers: A Social and Cultural History of Unlawful Hunting in England. 1485-1640*. Clarendon Press, Oxford.

Marvin, G. 1986. Honour, Integrity, and the Problem of Violence in the Spanish Bullfight. In D. Riches (Ed.) *The Anthropology of Violence*. Basil Blackwell, Oxford.

Marvin, G. 2010. Challenging Animals: Project and Process in Hunting. In S. Pilgrim and J. Pretty (Eds) *Nature and Culture: Rebuilding Lost Connections*, Earthcan, London and Washington, D.C.

McHenry, T. 1993. Policy and legal tools for the management of wildlife resources. Unasylva. Policy and Legislation, 44(1).

Mcintyre, T. 1996. *The way of the hunter: The art and the spirit of modern hunting*. E.P. Dutton.

Méndez A. 2020. Latin America: animal movement and struggles against speciesism. Nueva Sociedad, Nº 288. ISSN: 0251-3552.

Midgley, M. 1983. *Animals and why they matter*. University of Georgia Press.

Milton, K. 2002. *Loving Nature. Towards an Ecology of Emotion*. London: Routledge.

Murphy, A. 2019. No wonder fox hunting is still prevalent: The ban is designed to fail British Wildlife. The Conversation. 30th January. https://theconversation.com/no-wonder-fox-huntingis-still-prevalent-the-ban-is-designed-to-fail-british-wildlife-110454

Murphy, A. J. 2006. *Values, Rights and Foxes: A Sociological Study of the Moral Discourse of Fox Hunting*. Unpublished PhD Thesis. Department of Social Sciences and Law, Brunel University

Nelson, R. 1983. *Make Prayers to the Raven: A Koyukon View of the Northern Forest*, The University of Chicago Press, Chicago and London.

Newark, T. 2018. *Protest Vote: Britain's Maverick Politicians: How Politicians Lost the Plot*. Gibson Square Books Ltd,

Ortega y Gasset, J. 1968. *La Caza y Los Toros*, Revista de Occidente S.A. Madrid.

Palmer, C. 2010. *Animal ethics in context*. Columbia University Press.

Petersen, D. 2000. *Heartsblood: Hunting, Spirituality, and Wildness in America*, Island Press/Shearwater Books, Washington D.C. and Covelo CA.

Peterson, M. N., T. Chesonis, K. T. Stevenson and H. D. Bondell. 2017. Evaluating relationships between hunting and biodiversity knowledge among children. Wildlife Society Bulletin 41(3): 530-536.

Pinker, S. 2018. *Enlightenment Now*. Allen Lane.

Poliak, L. 2021. (Dis)interspecies encounters: tensions around wild boar hunting in Uruguay. Revista Andaluza de Antropología, (21): 45-61.

Poliak, L. and J. M. Dabezies. 2021. Doggy entanglements: the big game dog in Uruguay from different social collectives. Tabula Rasa 40(1): 90-122.

Posewitz, J. 1994. *Beyond Fair Chase: The Ethic and Tradition of Hunting*, Falcon Publishing, Helena, MT.

Puri, R. 2005. *Deadly Dances in the Bornean Rainforest*, KITLV Press, Leiden.

Ramp, D. and M. Bekoff. 2015. Compassion as a practical and evolved ethic for conservation. Bioscience 65(3): 323–327.

Regan, T. 1983. *The case for animal rights*. University of California Press.

Rollin, B. E. 1992. *Animals rights and human morality* (3rd ed.). Prometheus.

Rothgerber, H. 2014. Efforts to overcome vegetarian-induced cognitive dissonance among meat eaters. Appetite 79: 32–41.

Ryder, R. 1971. Experiments on Animals. In Godlovitch S., Godlovitch R. and Harris J. (Eds.), *Animals, Men and Morals* (pp. 41-82). London: Victor Gollancz.

Scruton, R. 1996. *Animal Rights and Wrongs*. London: Demos.

Singer, P. 1974. All animals are equal. Philosophical Exchange, 5(1): 103–116.

Singer, P. 1975. *Animal liberation: A new ethics for our treatment of animals*. Harper Collins.

Singer, P. 1977. *Animal liberation: Towards an end to man's inhumanity to animals*. St Albans, England: Granada Publishing,

Singer, P. 2016. 'Afterword,' in *The Ethics of Killing Animals*, T. Višak and R. Garner (Eds.) Oxford: Oxford University Press, pp. 229–36.

Taylor, A. 1996. Animal Rights and Human Needs. Environmental Ethics 18: 249 - 60.

von Essen, E. 2018. The impact of modernization on hunting ethics: Emerging taboos among contemporary Swedish hunters. Human Dimensions of Wildlife 23(1): 21-38.

von Essen, E. 2020. The changing wildlife tableau of hunting magazine covers. Society & Animals, 30(4): 363-385.

von Essen, E., and M. Allen. 2021. Killing with kindness: When hunters want to let you know they care. Human Dimensions of Wildlife 26(2): 179-195.

von Essen, E., H. P. Hansen, H. N. Källstrom, M. N. Peterson and T. R. Peterson. 2015. The radicalisation of rural resistance: how hunting counter publics in the Nordic countries contribute to illegal hunting. Journal of Rural Studies 39: 199-209.

Chapter 11 The Evolutionary Trap

Ancillotto, L., M. T. Serangeli and D. Russo. 2013. Curiosity killed the bat: Domestic cats as bat predators. *Mamm. Biol.* 78:369–373.

Andueza, A., M. Lambarri, V. Urda, I. Prieto, L. F. Villanueva and C. Sánchez-García. 2018. *Evaluation of the economic and social impact of hunting in Spain*. Ciudad Real, Fundación Artemisam.

Asgarzadeh, M., A. Lusk, T. Koga and K. Hirate. 2012. Measuring oppressiveness of streetscapes. Landsc. Urban Plan. 107(1):1–11.

Auster, R. E., A. Puttock, S.W. Barr and R. E. Brazier. 2023. Learning to live with reintroduced species: Beaver Management Groups are an adaptive process. *Restoration Ecology* 31, e13899.

Auster, R. E., K. Frith, S. W. Barr and R. E. Brazier. 2023. *Perceptions of Eurasian Beavers Living Wild in Wales: Results of an Online Public Survey*. University of Exeter.

Baker, P., R. Thompson and A. Grogan. 2018. Survival rates of cat-attacked birds admitted to RSPCA wildlife centres in the UK: Implications for cat owners and wildlife rehabilitators. Anim. Welf. 27:305–318.

Baldus, R. D, and A. E. Cauldwell. 2004. Tourist hunting and its role in development of wildlife management areas in Tanzania. Paper presented to the Sixth International Game Ranching Symposium, Paris, France, July 6–9, 2004.

Barkham, P. 2024. We sold everything off, even the semen flasks': the film about the farming couple who struck gold by rewilding. The *Guardian* 6 June 2024.

Barnes, J. I. and J. L. V de Jagr. 1995. Economic and financial incentives for wildlife use on private land in Namibia and the implications for policy. Research Discussion Paper No 8. Windhoek, Namibia: Directorate of Environmental Affairs, Ministry of Environment and Tourism.

Berry, W. 2018. *The World-Ending Fire*. Penguin.

Brazier, R. E. et al. 2020. Beaver: Nature's ecosystem engineers. WIREs Water 8, e1494.

Bubeník, A. B. 1989. Sport hunting in continental Europe. In R. J. Hudson, K. R. Drew, and L. M. Baskin (Eds.), *Wildlife production systems: economic utilisation of wild ungulates*. Cambridge, UK: Cambridge University Press.

Buller, H. 2008. Safe from the wolf: biosecurity, biodiversity, and competing philosophies of nature. Environment and Planning A, 40(7): 1583-1597.

Bulliet, R.W. 2007. *Hunters, Herders and Hamburgers*. Columbia University Press.

Callicott, J. B. 2014a. Environmental ethics: I. overview. In S. G. Post (Ed.), *Encyclopedia of bioethics*, 994-1006. Macmillan Reference USA.

Callicott, J. B. 2014b. *Thinking like a Planet: the Land Ethic and the Earth Ethic*. Oxford University Press.

Campbell-Palmer, R. et al. 2016. *The Eurasian Beaver Handbook: Ecology and Management of Castor fiber*. Pelagic Publishing Ltd.

Carson, R. 1962. *Silent Spring*. Penguin Books.

Child, B. 2005. Principles, practice, and results of CBNRM in Southern Africa. In: Child, B. and Lyman, M. (Eds). *Natural resources as community assets: lessons from two continents*. Madison, WI: Sand County Foundation, and Washington, DC: The Aspen Institute.

Coelho, M. 2009. *Roman Legal Tradition and the Mismanagement of Hunting Resources*. WP 29/2009/DE/SOCIUS. ISEG, Lisbon.

Coles, B. 2019. *Avanke, Bever, Castor: the story of Beavers in Wales*. WARP.

Convention on Biological Diversity. 2004. *Addis Ababa principles and guidelines for the sustainable use of biodiversity*.

Craighead, J. J. and F. C. Craighead. 1969. *Hawks, Owls and Wildlife*. Dover Publications.

Danzberger, J. 2009. Hunting: an essential element in rural development. Mediterráneo Económico, 15, 183-203.

Dauphiné, N. and R. J. Cooper. 2008. Impacts of free-ranging domestic cats (*Felis catus*) on birds in the United States: A review of recent research with conservation and management recommendations; Proceedings of the fourth international partners in flight conference: Tundra to tropics; McAllen, TX, USA. 13–16 February 2008; pp. 205–219.

Deakin, R. 2007. *Wildwood: A Journey through Trees*. Penguin.

Decker, D. J. et al. 2016. Governance Principles for Wildlife Conservation in the 21st Century. Conservation Letters 9: 290–295.

Delgado, L. M. M. et al. 2021. Consequences of recreational hunting for biodiversity conservation and livelihoods. OneEarth, 4 (2): 238-253.

Demezas, K.G. and W. D. Robinson. 2021. Characterizing the Influence of Domestic Cats on Birds with Wildlife Rehabilitation Center Data. Diversity. 2021;13:322.

Dennis, R. 2021. *Restoring the Wild*. William Collins.

Dixon, A. et al. 2020. Variation in Electrocution Rate and Demographic Composition of Saker Falcons Electrocuted at Power Lines in Mongolia. Journal of Raptor Research 54(2): 136-146,

Ericsson, G. and T. A. Heberlein. 2003. Attitudes of hunters, locals and the general public in Sweden, now that the wolves are back. Biological Conservation 111: 149-159.

European Commission. 2004. *Guidance document on hunting in accordance with Council Directive 79/409/EEC on the conservation of wild birds*. Wild Birds Directive.

Feinnes, J. 2022. *Land Healer*. Witness Books.

Fox, N. C. and J. W. Lock. 1978. Organochlorine residues in New Zealand birds of prey. Journal of Ecology 1:118-125.

Fox, N. C. 2000. *A Global Strategy for the Conservation of Falcons and Houbara*. The Environmental Research and Wildlife Development Agency, Abu Dhabi.

Fox, N. C. and C. Wynn. 2010. The impact of electrocution on the New Zealand falcon (*Falco novaeseelandiae*) Notornis Vol. 57: 71-74.

Freeman, M., R. Hudson and L. Foote. (Eds.) 2005. *Conservation Hunting: People and Wildlife in Canada's North*. CCI Press.

Gilbert, J. M. 1979. *Hunting and Hunting Reserves in Medieval Scotland*. John Donald.

Gow, D. 2020. *Bringing Back the Beaver*. Chelsea Green Publishing.

Gross, M. 2019. Hunting wildlife to extinction. Current Biology 29(12), R551-R554.

Hardin, G. 1968. *The Tragedy of the Commons*. American Association for the Advancement of Science.

Hayes, N. 2020. *The Book of Trespass*. Bloomsbury Circus.

Hill, C. M. 2015. Perspectives of "Conflict" at the Wildlife–Agriculture Boundary: 10 Years On. Human Dimensions of Wildlife 20, 296–301.

Holsman, R. 2000. Goodwill hunting? Exploring the role of hunters as ecosystem stewards. Wildlife Society Bulletin, 28(4): 808–816.

Hwang, T., N. Yoshizawa, J. Munakata and K. Hirate. 2007. A study on the oppressive feeling caused by the buildings in urban space: Focused on the physical factors corresponding with oppressive feeling. J. Environ. Eng. 616: 25–30.

IUCN & SSC. 2013. *Guidelines for Reintroductions and Other Conservation Translocations, Version 1.0*. https://portals.iucn.org/library/efiles/documents/2013-009.pdf.

Jefferies, R. 1884. *The Life of the Fields*. Oxford University Press.

Jepson, P. and C. Blythe. 2020. *Re-Wilding: The Radical New Science of Ecological Recovery*. Icon Books.

Jorgensen, D. 2015. Rethinking rewilding. Geoforum, 65: 482-488.

Kellert, S. R. 1996. *The Value of Life: Biological Diversity and Human Society*. Washington, D.C.: Island Press.

Kenward, R. and R, Sharp. 2008. Use Nationally of Wildlife Resources Across Europe", in Manos, P. and Papathanasiou, J. [Eds.] GEM-CON-BIO: *Governance & Ecosystems Management for the Conservation of Biodiversity*. Thessaloniki, pp 117-132.

Knezevic, I. 2009. Hunting and Environmentalism: Conflict or Misperceptions, Human dimensions of wildlife, 14(1): 12-20.

Knight, R. L. and S. Riedel, (Eds). 2002. *Aldo Leopold and the Ecological Conscience*. Oxford University Press, New York.

Larson, D. 2018. *Ethics and the Future of the Hunt*. Independently printed.

Legge, S., J. C. Z. Woinarski, C. R. Dickman, B. P. Murphy, L. A. Woolley and M. C. Calver. 2020. We need to worry about Bella and Charlie: The impacts of pet cats on Australian wildlife. Wildl. Res. 47:523–539.

Long, S. A. 2004. *Livelihoods and CBNRM in Namibia: the findings of the WILD Project*. Final Technical Report of the Wildlife Integration for Livelihood Diversification Project.

Lopes-Fernandes, M. and A. Frazão-Moreira. 2017. Relating to the wild: key actors' values and concerns about lynx reintroduction. Land Use Policy 66: 278-287.

Loss, S., T. Will and P. Marra. 2013. The impact of free-ranging domestic cats on wildlife of the United States. Nat. Commun. 2013;4:1396.

Loyd, K., S. Hernandez and D. Mcruer. The role of domestic cats in the admission of injured wildlife at rehabilitation and rescue centers. Wildl. Soc. Bull. 2017;41:55–56.

Maby, R. 2007. *Beechcombings: The Narratives of Trees*. Vintage Books, London.

Mahoney, S. 2004. The Seven Sisters: pillars of the North American wildlife conservation model. Bugle: The Journal of the Rocky Mountain Elk Foundation Sept/Oct: 144.

Martínez, E. 2009. Territorial visions of the Spanish Hunting Boom, 1970-1989. Boletín de la A.G.E, 51, 325-351.

Mcruer, D. L., L. C. Gray, L. A. Horne and E. E. Clark. 2017. Free-roaming cat interactions with wildlife admitted to a wildlife hospital. J. Wildl. Manag. 81:163–173.

Monbiot, G. 2013. *Feral: Searching for Enchantment on the Frontiers of Rewilding*. Allen Lane.

Mullineaux, E. and C. Pawson. 2024. Trends in Admissions and Outcomes at a British Wildlife Rehabilitation Centre over a Ten-Year Period (2012–2022). Animals (Basel) Jan. 14(1):86.

Neumann, R. P. 1998. *Imposing wilderness: Struggles over livelihood and nature preservation in Africa*. Berkeley: University of California.

Onyejekwe, E. 2022. Improving the welfare of both wildlife and domestic cats. Vet. Nurs. J. 2022;37:20–25.

Ostrom, E. 2002. Reformulating the commons. Environment and Society 5-25.

Ostrom, E. et al. 2012. *The Future of the Commons*. Institute of Economic Affairs Monographs.

Peterken, G. F. 1993. Long term floristic development of woodland on former agricultural land in Lincolnshire. In Watkins, C. (Ed) *Ecological Effects of Afforestation*. Wallingford: CABI.

Peterken, G. F.1996. *Natural woodland: ecology and conservation in northern temperate regions*. Cambridge University Press.

Potapov, E., N. C. Fox et al. 2000. Nest site selection in Mongolian Sakers. Proceedings of the Second International Conference on Saker Falcons and Houbara Bustard. Ulanbaatar.

Quirós-Fernández, F., J. Marcos, P. Acevedo and C. Gortázar. 2017. Hunters serving the ecosystem: the contribution of recreational hunting to wild boar population control. European Journal of Wildlife Research 63(3): a57.

Ramadori, D. 2006. Sustainable use of wildlife. In: Bolkovic, M. L, and Ramadori D. (Eds.). *Wildlife Management in Argentina. Sustainable use programs* (pp.9-14). Dirección de Fauna Silvestre, Secretaría de Ambiente y Desarrollo Sustentable.

Rebanks, J. 2020. *English Pastoral: An Inheritance*. Penguin.

Redford, K. H . 1990. The ecologically noble savage. *Orion* 9: 24–29.

Redpath, S. M., S. Bhatia and J. Young. 2015. Tilting at wildlife: reconsidering human–wildlife conflict. Oryx 49:222–225.

Reid, N., C. Magee and W. I. Montgomery. 2010. Integrating fieldsports, hare population management and conservation. Acta Theriologica 55(1): 61-67.

REIS, A. C. 2009. More than the Kill: Hunters' Relationships with Landscape and Prey. Current Issues in Tourism 12(5&6): 573–587.

Robinson, J. G. and E. L Bennett. 2000. *Hunting for sustainability in tropical forests*. New York, NY: Columbia University Press.

Schmidt, J. J. and M. Dowsley. 2010. Hunting with polar bears: problems with the passive properties of the commons. Human Ecology, 38(3): 377- 387.

Scruton, R. 1998. *On Hunting*. London: Yellow Jersey Press.

Scruton, R. 2012. *Green Philosophy: How to Think Seriously About the Planet*. London: Atlantic Books.

Scruton, R. 2014. 'Parfit the Perfectionist.' Philosophy 89(4): 621–34.

Shrubsole, G. 2019. *Who Owns England?: How We Lost Our Green and Pleasant Land, and How to Take It Back*. William Collins.

Simberloff, D,. I. M. Parker and P. N. Windle. 2005. Introduced species policy, management and future research needs. Frontiers in Ecology and the Environment 3 (1): 12-20.

Stépanoff, C. and J. Vigne (Eds.). 2018. *Hybrid communities: biosocial approaches to domestication and other trans-species relationships*. New York: Routledge.

Swanson, H. A., M. E. Lien and G. B. Ween. 2018. *Domestication Gone Wild: Politics and Practices of Multispecies Relations*. Durham, NC: Duke University.

Tapper, S. 1992. *Game Heritage: An Ecological Review from Shooting and Gamekeeping Records*. The Game Conservancy.

Tree, I. 2019. *Wilding: The Return of Nature to a British Farm*. Picador.

Van Vliet, N. 2018. 'Bushmeat Crisis' and 'Cultural

Imperialism' in Wildlife Management? Taking value orientations into account for a more sustainable and culturally acceptable wildmeat sector. Frontiers in Ecology and Evolution 6: 112.

Vitali, T. R. 1992. The Dialectical Foundation of the Land Ethic. In Proceedings, Governor's Symposium on North America's Hunting Heritage, Montana State University, Bozeman, US, 16–18 July (1992), 203–14.

Waggoner, P. E. 1994. *How Much Land Can Ten Billion People Spare for Nature*. Ames, IA. Council for Agricultural Sciences and Technology, No. 121.

Wall, B. and B. Child. 2009. When Does Hunting Contribute to Conservation and Rural Development?. In B. Dickson, J. Hutton, and W. M. Adams (Eds.), *Recreational Hunting, Conservation and Rural Livelihoods: Science and Practice*, pp. 255-265. Wiley-Blackwell.

Warwick, H. 2024. *Cull of the Wild: Killing in the Name of Conservation*. Bloomsbury Wildlife.

Webster, J. 2008. *Limping towards Eden: A practical approach to redressing the problem of our dominion over the animals*. John Wiley & Sons.

White, R. 1997. Are you an environmentalist or do you work for a living?. In W. Cronon (Ed.) *Uncommon Ground: Rethinking the Human Place in Nature*. W.W. Norton & Co, New York.

Williams, I. (Ed.) 1909. *Casgliad o Waith Ieuan Deulwyn (Collected works of Ieuan Deulwyn)*. Bangor MS Society.

Woods, M., R. A. McDonald and S. Harris. 2003. Predation of wildlife by domestic cats Felis catus in Great Britain. Mammal Rev. 2003;33:174.

Yoon, I. *et al*. 2005. Interactive 3D visualisation of highly connected ecological networks on the WWW. Conference: Proceedings of the 2005 ACM Symposium on Applied Computing (SAC), Santa Fe, New Mexico, USA, March 13-17, 2005.

Zhang, Y., Z. Gu, B. Bold *et al*. 2024. Environmental effects on reproduction in a managed population of the harvested and Endangered Saker Falcon *Falco cherrug*. Bird Conservation International: 34.

Zimmermann, A., B. McQuinn and D. W. Macdonald. 2020. Levels of conflict over wildlife: Understanding and addressing the right problem. Conservation Science and Practice 2, e259.

Index

acceptance period, 18
acorns, 50, 254, 255
adrenal glands, 43
Africa, 10, 11, 65, 136, 142, 166, 189, 191, 223, 233, 238, 276, 283, 284
aggression, 12, 97, 206
Ainsworth, 21
algorithms, 15, 176
Altricial species, 18, 19, 24, 27
amygdala, 43
animal welfare, 12, 76, 90, 94, 95, 106, 113, 117, 118, 131, 135, 136, 137, 140, 159, 185, 188, 189, 193, 198, 205, 215, 216, 219, 220, 221, 273, 277, 283, 289
anthropocentric, 11, 35, 98, 135, 136, 144, 177, 194, 212, 213, 217, 222, 247, 277, 286
anthropoid apes, 33, 144, 201
anthropoids, 21
anthropologist(s), 12, 71, 73, 105, 161, 179, 180, 201
anthropology, 10
anthropomorphic, 42
anti-hunters, 13, 56, 95, 116, 129, 206, 213
Aplomados, 10
Arabia, 39, 114, 161, 184, 191, 211, 226, 233, 235, 243, 271
art, 17, 39, 40, 71, 153, 177
arthropods, 11
Artificial intelligence, 11, 38, 152, 176, 177, 185, 207, 274, 275, 276, 280
Ashmore, 9
asynchronous dual imprinting, 20
attachment, 18, 21, 29, 31
Australia, 10, 117, 130, 141, 189, 223, 244
Australopithecus, 48
Autism, 16
balance, 12, 35, 45, 53, 69, 74, 75, 76, 77, 78, 79, 80, 84, 89, 105, 108, 114, 115, 142, 185, 193, 211, 212, 216, 241, 265, 267, 275, 276, 277, 280, 285
Baldwin Effect, 39, 40
bantams, 23
beagles, 10, 57, 62
beavers, 10, 76, 97, 132, 141, 162, 222, 237, 248, 254, 255, 256, 257, 258, 263, 285, 289
Bekoff, 41, 145
beliefs, 11, 28, 48, 67, 92, 143, 161, 166, 187
Berger, 43
berries, 45, 64, 65, 71, 94, 101, 104, 105, 162, 202, 250
Blackmore, 30, 167
Bobby, 8, 18
Boehm, 40, 71, 144, 201, 202
Bonding, 18, 19, 21, 22, 154, 167
bonding period, 18
Born Again egg, 23, 24
Bowlby, 21, 29
Breeding behaviour, 31, 33, 109
Bumblebee, 25, 26
cage traps, 10, 127
Cambrian, 17
Canada, 10, 94, 221, 231, 244, 272
canceleer, 38
cat, 10, 12, 16, 22, 23, 30, 52, 53, 59, 60, 61, 62, 69, 71, 81, 89, 98, 99, 102, 104, 107, 113, 116, 117, 127, 131, 133, 134, 135, 136, 137, 138, 140, 141, 162, 170, 180, 181, 190, 195, 197, 198, 199, 200, 205, 219, 230, 242, 249, 267, 270, 284, 287
cat-owner, 12, 59, 69, 113, 117, 137, 140, 198, 200, 206
cattle, 10, 11, 53, 71, 90, 92, 94, 136, 168, 221, 252, 260, 265, 281, 284
cephalopods, 11, 13
Changeable Hawk-Eagle, 38
chickens, 10, 19, 88, 90, 95, 141, 203, 277
Chimpanzees, 17, 40, 64, 71, 97, 140, 164, 194, 201
China, 10, 82, 94, 142, 156, 160, 191, 233, 259, 267, 277, 279, 280
chordates, 41
Christianity, 183, 215
civilisation, 12, 38, 56, 75, 101, 153, 179, 184, 185, 287
Clever Hans, 35, 36, 38
clicker training, 29
conditioned reflexes, 29
conditioning, 19, 23, 30, 77, 147, 172, 209
conscience, 12, 22, 27, 28, 115, 147, 149, 153, 173, 201, 202, 203, 204, 212
consciousness, 38, 39, 41, 42, 87, 96, 131
copulate, 16, 23, 29, 102
Core ethotype, 17, 19, 21, 25, 31, 33, 109, 113, 169, 179
Creationism, 28, 188
Creativity, 31, 177
critical period, 19, 86, 209
crow, 25, 37, 38, 50, 67, 68, 69, 70, 73, 75, 78, 79, 81, 83, 84, 85, 88, 112, 115, 195, 197, 225, 242, 265, 287
cruelty, 12, 106, 137, 138, 139, 140, 198, 204, 205, 215
cuckoos, 28
culture, 17, 33, 40, 41, 43, 48, 86, 89, 92, 108, 131, 136, 137, 140, 151, 154, 155, 156, 157, 158, 160, 161, 163, 169, 177, 180, 183, 187, 189, 190, 191, 192, 203, 210, 213, 214, 217, 244, 266, 274, 275, 276, 289
curiosity, 31, 40, 101, 102
Czech Republic, 10
Dartmoor, 37
deception flight, 38
deer, 13, 18, 21, 52, 53, 60, 62, 81, 97, 107, 113, 114, 118, 123, 127, 129, 130, 131, 132, 135, 159, 163, 172, 181, 189, 201, 211, 249, 282, 285
demographics, 12, 28, 59, 60, 65, 158, 273
Denmark, 10, 124, 130
developmental period, 17, 18, 33, 64, 104, 151
Díaz, 45
diet, 12, 17, 25, 31, 53, 64, 65, 69, 89, 90, 92, 94, 95, 98, 99, 100, 110, 113, 142, 228, 249, 281, 282
Direct Flying Attack, 37, 38
dogs, 9, 10, 11, 13, 16, 18, 20, 22, 23, 27, 29, 30, 37, 42, 43, 44, 47, 51, 52, 53, 54, 55, 57, 58, 60, 62, 63, 67, 69, 70, 71, 74, 76, 77, 80, 81, 83, 84, 85, 94, 97, 98, 100, 102, 104, 106, 107, 108, 114, 115, 116, 120, 123, 126, 127, 129, 130, 131, 132, 134, 135, 137, 138, 140, 141, 145, 147, 163, 166, 167, 168, 170, 171, 172, 173, 184, 187, 190, 194, 195, 196, 197, 198, 199, 200, 201, 202, 205, 209, 213, 215, 219, 221, 243, 265, 267, 282, 283, 284, 287
domestication, 11, 71, 141, 245
dominance hierarchies, 28, 30, 31, 97, 183, 209
Don't shoot the Dog, 29
dorsal ventricular ridge, 19
dual imprinting, 20
ducks, 9, 10, 70, 125, 126, 132, 224, 231, 260, 271
Dummett, 38
education, 30, 136, 193, 209, 211, 257, 272, 273, 276
eggs, 9, 16, 23, 25, 28, 53, 60, 67, 83, 111, 181, 196, 203, 215, 221, 223, 226, 227, 230, 270, 282, 283
elephant, 17, 47, 59, 66, 163, 217, 218, 222, 273, 275
Emerson, 21
emotional contagion, 36

emotional intelligence, 35, 36, 38
emotions, 41, 42, 53, 112, 185, 265
empathy, 17, 31, 32, 36, 37, 38, 99, 101, 135, 138
endocrine system, 16
Eosimiidae, 33
epigenetic, 14
ethic, 10, 11, 12, 16, 39, 40, 52, 60, 68, 78, 83, 88, 89, 115, 116, 130, 140, 144, 145, 169, 174, 180, 183, 185, 187, 189, 191, 193, 211, 212, 215, 217, 222, 237, 241, 243, 247, 283
Ethics Committees, 39, 180, 211
ethologist, 38, 201
ethology, 19, 173
ethotypic templates, 14, 16, 102, 105, 150, 173, 182, 183
evolution, 9, 16, 17, 18, 33, 40, 42, 54, 56, 70, 71, 77, 108, 145, 146, 148, 149, 152, 156, 161, 167, 178, 185, 189, 202, 216, 219, 283, 286, 289
evolutionary trap, 12, 41, 152, 183, 185, 188, 216, 218, 279, 280
Evolutionists, 28
extroversion, 17
eyesight, 18
falconry, 9, 10, 30, 66, 77, 78, 102, 159, 160, 162, 181, 187, 192, 212, 226, 243, 259, 267, 269, 287
falcons, 9, 10, 13, 19, 20, 23, 25, 28, 29, 30, 37, 38, 43, 44, 48, 50, 52, 66, 67, 69, 75, 78, 85, 88, 96, 98, 99, 102, 103, 104, 105, 115, 141, 148, 151, 160, 167, 173, 181, 182, 183, 186, 197, 209, 225, 226, 227, 233, 234, 235, 249, 259, 265, 267, 268, 270, 271, 283, 284
family, 16, 22, 27, 31, 40, 57, 65, 66, 80, 90, 149, 151, 153, 155, 156, 162, 166, 167, 168, 170, 175, 179, 181, 183, 185, 186, 188, 190, 192, 204, 206, 216, 217, 237, 241, 254, 256, 259, 260, 261, 266
farming, 9, 11, 17, 19, 28, 59, 68, 82, 88, 89, 90, 91, 92, 94, 95, 96, 98, 110, 112, 137, 140, 161, 223, 230, 238, 239, 242, 244, 245, 257, 259, 260, 261, 263, 264, 265, 266, 280, 282, 283, 285, 287
fear, 19, 20, 22, 25, 27, 32, 43, 44, 67, 109, 127, 151, 197, 198, 209
fear response, 19, 20, 22, 25, 27, 32, 43, 44, 109, 209
ferreting, 12
ferrets, 10, 61, 62, 81, 107, 133, 196, 249
filial imprinting, 18, 19, 20
Finland, 10
fisherman, 12, 44, 54, 55, 77, 78, 79, 116
fishing, 12, 44, 45, 53, 54, 55, 58, 60, 63, 70, 77, 78, 79, 82, 88, 89, 107, 108, 115, 133, 159, 162, 198, 257, 266, 286
flicker fusion frequency, 23
flicker fusion threshold, 48
food-caching, 35
forager, 9, 17, 42, 44, 45, 50, 64, 68, 79, 89, 99, 101, 113, 162
fox, 10, 52, 56, 57, 58, 61, 62, 73, 78, 79, 80, 81, 83, 84, 85, 86, 89, 93, 95, 98, 107, 111, 115, 117, 118, 119, 120, 123, 124, 125, 126, 127, 128, 129, 130, 132, 134, 135, 137, 159, 161, 167, 171, 179, 184, 195, 196, 197, 198, 199, 204, 205, 223, 242, 249, 250, 258, 265, 282, 285, 289
fox hounds, 10
France, 10
fungi, 10, 71, 89, 104, 105, 154, 275
futurians, 46
Game Books, 9, 78
gamebirds, 18, 114
gassing, 61, 62, 86, 107, 127, 133
gazehounds, 10, 61, 62, 107, 133
geese, 9, 10, 130, 231
gender, 17, 31, 33, 34, 45, 57, 64, 65, 86, 89, 99, 100, 101, 154, 183, 204, 244, 272, 273
Gender roles, 31, 65, 100

genes, 13, 14, 15, 16, 40, 43, 65, 66, 67, 70, 100, 101, 102, 108, 109, 112, 144, 145, 146, 147, 148, 151, 152, 153, 154, 155, 156, 167, 182, 183, 185, 189, 191, 192, 216, 219, 225, 274, 275, 278, 279, 286
genotype, 13, 14, 15, 17, 146, 147, 148, 149, 152, 154, 167, 179
Germany, 10, 69, 110, 280
goats, 11, 249
Gods, 11, 83, 207, 208, 286
goose, 23, 60, 232
gorilla, 39, 63, 64, 201
goshawk, 10, 15, 19, 43, 65, 75, 78, 79, 80, 111, 160, 224, 225, 229, 256, 260, 263, 285, 289
Gulf States, 10
gyrs, 10
habitat, 19, 25, 44, 53, 59, 66, 67, 80, 87, 92, 94, 98, 99, 108, 110, 114, 115, 116, 139, 142, 152, 169, 173, 186, 188, 213, 214, 215, 216, 217, 218, 219, 220, 223, 228, 233, 234, 237, 239, 241, 242, 244, 245, 247, 248, 249, 250, 251, 252, 254, 259, 263, 266, 267, 270, 271, 272, 273, 275, 277, 278, 281, 283, 285
habituated behaviour, 14
habituation, 19, 25, 41, 43, 209
Haidt, 43
Hand in Hand, 28, 71, 149, 151
Harari, 15, 176, 274
hare, 21, 37, 38, 57, 62, 68, 81, 135, 159, 172, 195, 197, 199, 200, 205, 221, 235, 242, 243, 249, 263, 274, 275
Harlow, 21, 29
harriers, 10, 45, 57, 62, 74, 181, 225
Harris, 124, 125, 129
Harris Hawks, 10, 67
Hawk-eagles, 10, 38
hawking, 10, 15, 36, 37, 49, 65, 72, 73, 76, 77, 79, 88, 105, 114, 155, 166, 202, 207, 235, 243, 283, 285, 287
hearing, 18, 37, 48, 51, 80, 198, 205
Heaven, 44, 79
Heinroth, 18
Helen, 51, 52, 171, 234, 260, 283, 285, 289
Hell, 44, 55, 79
heron, 25, 77
herring gull, 60, 220, 231
Hess, 18
historians, 46
homing, 19
Homo sapiens, 11, 77
hormones, 9, 14, 15, 16, 23, 24, 41, 42, 147, 148, 151, 152, 181, 203
horses, 10, 13, 15, 18, 30, 36, 37, 44, 51, 52, 57, 58, 69, 71, 73, 77, 78, 95, 140, 161, 165, 168, 170, 172, 194, 202, 203, 204, 209, 220, 245, 265, 277, 282, 283, 284, 287
humanities, 11
humour, 17, 31, 259, 289
Hungary, 10
Huntaway, 44
hunter, 9, 10, 11, 13, 14, 17, 33, 37, 42, 44, 45, 50, 53, 54, 56, 57, 58, 59, 64, 68, 69, 71, 76, 77, 79, 81, 85, 89, 95, 97, 99, 100, 101, 103, 104, 106, 113, 114, 115, 116, 129, 137, 138, 159, 161, 162, 179, 182, 183, 184, 187, 190, 202, 205, 206, 211, 212, 213, 224, 243, 244, 245, 285
hunting behaviour, 33, 69, 99, 102, 103, 104, 234
hunting with dogs, 9, 58, 60, 63, 69, 77, 106, 127, 131, 132, 134, 135, 197, 198, 199, 205, 287
hybrids, 10
hyperstriatum, 19
identical twins, 15
Imagination, 31, 47, 158, 189, 231

imitation, 30, 41, 42, 125, 212, 222, 259
imprinting, 15, 18, 19, 20, 21, 22, 23, 24, 25, 27, 28, 29, 30, 32, 33, 34, 42, 43, 44, 65, 109, 150, 170, 183, 201, 209
incest, 24, 25
incest taboo, 24
incubator, 23, 114, 221, 225, 283
infant mortality, 32, 34, 218
insects, 13, 49, 53, 64, 97, 110, 280, 281
insight, 30, 41, 77, 105, 149, 259, 289
instinct, 10, 13, 14, 15, 16, 17, 18, 19, 21, 23, 24, 29, 31, 35, 39, 42, 47, 50, 56, 64, 67, 68, 71, 77, 80, 99, 100, 101, 102, 104, 113, 116, 134, 137, 139, 145, 146, 151, 152, 153, 154, 155, 171, 172, 179, 183, 184, 185, 188, 192, 216, 217, 219
intellect, 18, 39, 42, 144, 145, 151, 152, 153, 169, 175, 185, 188, 212, 216, 217, 219, 244, 277, 280
intelligence, 11, 31, 34, 35, 36, 38, 39, 40, 41, 47, 48, 101, 135, 152, 176, 177, 185, 207, 209, 210, 216, 217, 274, 275, 276, 280
internet, 40, 53, 116, 167, 174, 175, 176, 180, 185, 190, 201, 207, 274
introversion, 17
intuition, 31, 42, 149
invertebrates, 41, 53, 63, 95, 110, 251, 252, 264, 286
Ireland, 10, 237, 266
jays, 17, 50
Jefferies, 35, 78, 266
Jesuits, 18
Jews, 28, 166
kestrels, 10, 163, 186, 238, 268
Kingdom Animalia, 11
Kohlberg, 22
Koko, 39, 193
Kyrghyzstan, 10, 161
Lamarck, 40
lamb, 18, 21, 22, 23, 44, 84, 102, 112, 126, 139, 147, 172, 173, 228, 265, 281, 282, 283, 284
Language, 27, 32, 37, 38, 39, 40, 41, 47, 48, 50, 148, 158, 161, 170, 176, 180, 185, 191, 277
lanners, 10
leaf, 11, 12
learned behaviour, 15, 17, 18, 19, 30, 32, 34, 35, 41, 64, 65, 100, 145, 147, 150, 151, 152, 172, 173, 185, 188, 189, 209, 275, 286
life expectancy, 32, 34
linguistics, 38, 40
lion, 15, 52, 64, 96, 97, 98, 101, 116, 164, 217, 218
Lorenz, 18
luggers, 10
lurchers, 10, 57, 62, 107, 125, 126
Lyre-bird, 14
Macaque, 13, 193, 238
Machiavellian, 38
malimprinting, 20
mammals, 10, 18, 19, 23, 35, 37, 62, 63, 81, 82, 87, 105, 109, 110, 125, 135, 137, 144, 154, 162, 178, 181, 196, 197, 199, 200, 218, 230, 237, 242, 250, 267, 286
Manchuria, 39, 178
Manuka, 51
marshmallow test, 47, 147, 202, 209
Maslow, 14
Mauritius, 13, 163, 186, 230, 238
mechanistic, 18, 42, 147, 201
meme, 30, 39, 41, 84, 100, 139, 148, 156, 157, 158, 159, 160, 163, 167, 186
memories, 38, 46, 47, 67, 167
memory, 14, 19, 31, 35, 112, 146, 165, 173, 177, 181
mentor, 18, 30, 41

Menura novaehollandiae, 14
merlin, 10, 25, 50, 225
Mexico, 10, 272
mice, 10, 12, 50, 53, 60, 62, 63, 81, 85, 86, 87, 107, 110, 135, 198, 249
Middle East, 11, 105, 136, 176, 189, 211, 226, 235, 238, 276, 289
mind-reading, 37
mink hounds, 10, 57, 231
Miocene, 17
Molesworth, 25
Mongolia, 10, 11, 39, 66, 95, 136, 149, 150, 151, 161, 179, 187, 191, 233, 238, 267, 268, 269, 270
mood-matching, 37
moral community, 16, 37, 91, 99, 134, 142, 154, 157, 163, 165, 168, 169, 170, 172, 173, 190, 194, 206
moral consideration, 31, 144, 163
moral values, 12, 22, 67, 69, 97, 99, 102, 144, 147, 149, 152, 157, 169, 175, 186, 187, 188, 194, 201, 213, 279
Morocco, 10, 233
Moses, 16
mouse, 47, 53, 62, 85, 86, 87, 98, 103, 110, 127, 133, 134, 138, 287
music, 17, 40, 41, 177
Musical ability, 31
Muslim, 28, 65, 180
Mutations, 16, 39, 112, 144
navigation, 19
nest, 9, 14, 15, 16, 17, 19, 20, 21, 22, 23, 24, 25, 69, 88, 110, 126, 139, 141, 149, 150, 151, 155, 161, 181, 182, 199, 200, 215, 221, 224, 225, 226, 227, 228, 229, 231, 263, 267, 268, 269, 270, 271, 283, 284
Netherlands, 10
Neurotheology, 11
New Zealand falcons, 9, 10, 38, 98, 182, 225, 270
non-human animal, 11, 38, 39, 92, 99, 164, 186, 213, 214, 277
nurture, 15, 147, 278
nuts, 10, 17, 45, 64, 65, 71, 94, 104, 142, 162, 202, 214
obligate, 33, 64, 83, 99, 104, 169, 183
octopuses, 41, 105
oikophilia, 19, 22
optimism, 17
orcas, 30, 102, 116, 151, 189
otter hounds, 10
Pakistan, 10, 65, 191, 233, 267, 268, 281
parenting, 17, 31, 32, 114
Pascal, 42
pencil, 40, 67
penguins, 30, 103, 116
Peregrine, 10, 20, 23, 25, 29, 45, 88, 99, 150, 220, 221, 225, 226, 271, 272, 279
personality, 15, 17, 32, 151, 167, 183, 193, 209
pessimism, 17
Pfungst, 35
pheasants, 10, 13, 39, 79, 80, 114, 130, 165, 223,
phenotype, 13, 14, 15, 16, 17, 29, 33, 64, 69, 71, 99, 102, 103, 146, 147, 148, 149, 151, 154, 156, 158, 167, 170, 183, 185, 203
philopatry, 19, 27
philosophers, 39, 105, 145, 146, 148, 152, 153, 163, 169, 185, 188, 189, 218
philosophy, 10, 53, 152, 173, 180, 189, 217, 218, 267, 285
phobias, 32, 43
Piaget, 22, 30, 47
pig dogs, 10
pigeons, 10, 60, 83, 88, 113, 114, 115, 130, 194, 197, 220, 271

pigs, 10, 86, 90, 136, 141, 194, 249, 284
Pinker, 15, 147, 217
pipit, 50
Pliocene, 17
pointers, 10, 57, 71, 79, 80, 114, 116
poisons, 10, 61, 62, 70, 81, 87, 107, 109, 127, 133, 196
politicians, 13, 17, 98, 145, 158, 159, 174, 180, 191, 193, 194, 203, 204, 205, 210, 211, 219, 233, 274, 275, 281, 285
post-traumatic stress disorder, 23
precocial, 18, 19, 20, 27, 44
primate, 21, 22, 135, 145
prior, 63, 159
PTSD, 23, 52, 138
punishment, 30, 47, 112, 172, 191, 194, 209, 210, 211
rabbit, 9, 10, 16, 21, 37, 62, 69, 75, 80, 81, 95, 98, 107, 110, 113, 132, 137, 140, 141, 165, 168, 170, 171, 187, 195, 197, 205, 230, 246, 247, 249
Raptors, 30, 38, 45, 62, 67, 69, 77, 81, 88, 107, 130, 132, 133, 149, 150, 172, 196, 197, 220, 226, 230, 239, 240, 258, 268, 269, 270, 284, 287
rats, 10, 13, 23, 53, 60, 62, 81, 86, 87, 93, 95, 98, 107, 110, 127, 135, 137, 140, 141, 165, 197, 205, 206, 213, 229, 230, 249
rearing systems, 21, 90
Reciprocity, 40, 69, 104, 202
recreational hunting, 45, 59, 67, 78, 79, 89, 95, 104, 113, 115
Red-tails, 10
reinforcement, 25, 27, 28, 41, 147, 209, 210
religion, 11, 16, 17, 27, 28, 31, 32, 41, 47, 48, 67, 71, 91, 113, 136, 140, 143, 145, 148, 158, 164, 166, 169, 175, 177, 183, 184, 185, 187, 207, 217, 245, 277, 278, 286
reproduction, 102, 188
reptiles, 19, 105, 185, 196, 197, 242, 250
re-wilding, 44, 247, 248
rifles, 10, 60, 70, 83, 114, 119, 120, 123, 125, 126, 127, 130, 132, 137
Roberts, 36
robotic prey, 30, 48, 50, 104, 235
role partitioning, 11, 33, 34, 65, 99, 100
Safina, 37, 41
sakers, 10, 226, 267, 268, 269, 289
Schaffer, 21
sciences, 11, 145
seals, 30, 57, 103, 116, 188
selection pressure, 38, 64, 101, 148, 154, 156, 184
sense of smell, 18, 23, 51
sensitive period, 18, 23, 24, 44
sentience, 18, 41, 53, 91, 105, 110, 112, 195, 212, 280
setters, 10
sexual maturity, 19, 24
sexual partner, 28, 29
sheep, 10, 11, 16, 18, 19, 21, 22, 28, 44, 48, 53, 63, 69, 71, 78, 85, 90, 92, 93, 94, 95, 104, 110, 114, 126, 136, 140, 141, 143, 153, 157, 168, 171, 172, 173, 181, 186, 188, 214, 223, 242, 245, 260, 261, 280, 282, 283, 284
sheepdogs, 10
shellfish, 10, 45, 63, 64, 65, 89, 101
shikras, 10
shooting, 9, 53, 58, 59, 60, 66, 71, 73, 76, 77, 78, 79, 80, 83, 84, 85, 88, 114, 115, 116, 117, 118, 119, 123, 124, 125, 126, 127, 128, 129, 130, 131, 134, 137, 138, 143, 159, 162, 197, 198, 205, 212, 223, 246, 265, 286
shotguns, 10, 70, 71, 80, 85, 119, 120, 123, 125, 126, 130, 137
Siberian Arctic, 10
Siberian peregrines, 25, 272
siblings, 19, 22, 23, 24, 25, 32, 67, 142, 148, 168, 183

Skinner, 28
Smokey, 42
snakes, 43, 67
social group, 15, 19, 38, 39, 65, 89, 97, 135, 140, 145, 149, 152, 153, 154, 155, 157, 158, 159, 162, 163, 164, 167, 169, 173, 174, 175, 176, 177, 178, 180, 188, 189, 190, 192, 201, 203, 204, 210, 211, 274, 279
socialisation, 18
sociality, 17, 167, 183
soldiers, 17, 109, 112, 143, 156, 167, 169, 178
sound, 40, 50, 51, 54, 63, 67, 79, 97, 109, 111, 113, 140, 142, 143, 171, 173, 180, 190, 202, 205, 220, 233, 247, 249, 260
South Africa, 10
spandrel, 40
spaniels, 10, 57, 71, 79
sparrowhawks, 10, 72, 111
Species specific instincts, 31
speech, 39, 193
spiders, 43, 67
spirituality, 11, 17, 28, 183, 184, 247, 278
Spitz, 29
spring traps, 10, 62, 128
squirrels, 17, 50, 62, 75, 86, 165, 196, 206, 229, 230, 247, 249, 289
St James, 25
stag hounds, 10
stimulus, 13, 15, 23, 29
Sweden, 10, 124, 224, 228, 267
sympathy, 36, 37, 139
synchronous dual imprint, 20, 282
taxonomy, 11, 13, 158, 179, 195
temperament, 15, 17, 25, 31, 109, 151, 187
Temporal resolution, 49
territorial behaviour, 12, 15, 40, 157, 162, 175, 178, 188
territory, 16, 31, 40, 42, 86, 97, 98, 158, 159, 162, 163, 167, 171, 173, 181, 186, 237, 238
Time, 11, 45, 47, 77, 83, 186, 248, 274
tractor, 20, 25, 43, 90, 91, 211, 252, 261, 277, 280
trauma learning, 23, 44, 209
treme, 39, 167
tribalism, 17, 32, 166, 191
Tribe, 11, 31, 34, 156, 157, 158, 159, 161, 167, 179, 185, 186, 188, 189, 204, 216, 237, 239
Troglodytes troglodytes, 14, 64
universal traits, 31
USA, 10, 45, 115, 197, 199, 221, 244
Utilitarianism, 42, 180, 186
values, 12, 22, 27, 28, 64, 67, 69, 78, 84, 97, 99, 102, 106, 144, 145, 147, 149, 152, 154, 157, 158, 169, 174, 175, 180, 185, 186, 187, 188, 189, 191, 192, 193, 194, 201, 204, 211, 213, 215, 216, 239, 276, 277, 278, 279
variable ratio reward, 44, 203
vertebrates, 11, 13, 17, 18, 30, 34, 41, 42, 44, 62, 63, 65, 103, 104, 105, 110, 145, 146, 154, 157, 178, 185, 188, 192, 217, 248, 251, 275, 286
Virtual Reality, 40, 208
voles, 50, 141, 230, 231, 232, 233, 267, 268
waterfowl, 18, 110, 116, 130, 255
Westermarck effect, 24
wildlife management, 55, 59, 61, 67, 86, 88, 89, 91, 113, 189, 196, 205, 221, 239, 256, 286, 289
wildness, 43, 44, 141, 223, 247
Wong, 45
Wren, 14, 64
Yunnan, 39, 155, 160
Zimbabwe, 10, 30, 222, 276
zoologist, 9, 10, 12